Global Legal Insights
International Arbitration

2018, Fourth Edition
Contributing Editor: Joe Tirado
Published by Global Legal Group

GLOBAL LEGAL INSIGHTS - INTERNATIONAL ARBITRATION

2018, FOURTH EDITION

Contributing Editor
Joe Tirado, Garrigues UK LLP

Production Editor
Andrew Schofield

Senior Editors
Suzie Levy
Caroline Collingwood

Group Consulting Editor
Alan Falach

Publisher
Rory Smith

We are extremely grateful for all contributions to this edition.
Special thanks are reserved for Joe Tirado for all of his assistance.

Published by Global Legal Group Ltd.
59 Tanner Street, London SE1 3PL, United Kingdom
Tel: +44 207 367 0720 / URL: www.glgroup.co.uk

ISBN 978-1-912509-05-8
ISSN 2056-5364

Printed and bound by CPI Group (UK) Ltd, Croydon, CR0 4YY
May 2018

CONTENTS

PREFACE

Following the success of the third edition, we are pleased to present the fourth edition of *Global Legal Insights – International Arbitration.* The book contains 35 country chapters, and is designed to provide general counsel, government agencies and private practice lawyers with a comprehensive insight into the realities of international arbitration by jurisdiction, highlighting market trends and legal developments as well as practical, policy and strategic issues.

In producing *Global Legal Insights – International Arbitration*, the publishers have collected the views and opinions of a group of leading practitioners from around the world in a unique volume. The authors were asked to offer personal views on the most important recent developments in their own jurisdictions, with a free rein to decide the focus of their own chapter. A key benefit of comparative analyses is the possibility that developments in one jurisdiction may inform understanding in another. I hope that this book will prove insightful and stimulating reading.

Joe Tirado
Garrigues UK LLP

Andorra

Miguel Cases
Cases & Lacambra

Introduction

Law on arbitration

The Andorran Arbitration Act 47/2014 of 18 December 2014 (hereinafter "**AAA**") is not specifically based on the United Nations Commission for the International Trade Law ("**UNCITRAL**") model law, but has been inspired by it, based on the need to foster commercial relationships and have a faster and specialised alternative dispute resolution mechanism.

New York Convention

On 11 February 2015, the Andorran Official Gazette declared the adherence of the Principality of Andorra to the International Convention on the Recognition and Enforcement of Foreign Arbitral Awards (New York, 1958). The Principality of Andorra ratified the New York Convention on the Recognition and Enforcement of Foreign Arbitral Awards on 19 June 2015, and it entered into force on 17 September 2015 without any reservations.

No other conventions concerning the recognition and enforcement of arbitral awards have been signed by the Principality of Andorra.

Domestic and international arbitration

The AAA governs both domestic and international arbitration. International arbitration has a special section (articles 62 to 73) where the main differences with domestic arbitration regulation are set out:

- Domestic form requirements do not apply to international arbitration agreements.
- The validity of the international arbitration agreement will be analysed according to the law selected by the parties, the law applicable to the controversy, or the Andorran law.
- An application for the setting-aside of a domestic award must be made within three months of the date of notification, whereas for international awards, applications must be made within two months of the date of notification.

Overview of arbitration bodies and any foreign arbitration institutions

As of the date of writing, no kind of arbitration body exists in the Principality of Andorra. Nevertheless, a new law to create an Arbitration Court (*Tribunal d'Arbitratge del Principat d'Andorra*) is currently going through parliament (*Consell General*). This law is likely to come into force in the first half of 2018.

As of the date of writing, no special national courts for international arbitration exist in the Principality of Andorra.

Arbitration agreement

Formalities of the arbitration agreement and drafting of arbitration clauses

Requirements needed for the arbitration agreement and the drafting of arbitration clauses are:

- The arbitration agreement must express the parties' willingness to submit to arbitration all or certain disputes arising between them in respect of a given legal relationship, whether contractual or otherwise.
- The arbitration agreement must directly express the procedure for appointing an arbitrator, or arbitrators, or indirectly express the procedure by reference to the appointment procedure contained in an arbitral institution rule.
- The arbitration agreement may adopt the form of a clause in an agreement.
- If the arbitration agreement is contained in an adhesion contract, its validity and interpretation will be governed by the rules applicable to such contracts.
- Whatever form it takes, the arbitration agreement must be in writing, in a document signed by the parties.
- The arbitration agreement will be deemed to exist if, in an exchange of statements of claim and defence, the existence of an agreement is alleged by one party and not denied by the other.
- The arbitration agreement will also be valid if the exchange of letters, telegrams, telexes, faxes or other telecommunication methods ensure a record of the agreement is kept.

What disputes are arbitrable?

The AAA establishes that consumer and labour arbitration are excluded from its scope. At the same time, it is established that arbitration under AAA is allowed for all matters of which the parties are free to dispose.

Joinder/consolidation of third parties

The AAA does not contain any specific provision on joinder or consolidation of a third party and nor does it provide a regulatory framework for consolidation of arbitral proceedings.

Principles of competence-competence and separability

The principle of competence-competence is expressly recognised in the AAA, which clearly states that arbitrators may rule on their own jurisdiction, including any pleas with respect to the existence or validity of the arbitration agreement, or any others the acceptance of which would prevent consideration of the merits of the case. Their decision may only be challenged by means of an application to set aside the final or a separate award on jurisdiction.

Under the AAA, the principle of competence-competence includes the separability principle in the sense that the validity of the arbitral agreement established as a clause of a contract, does not depend on the validity of the contract itself, the arbitrator having competence to judge and declare the validity of the arbitral agreement even if the contract is declared null.

Arbitration procedure

Commencing proceedings

Unless otherwise agreed by the parties, arbitration will commence on the date on which a request to submit the dispute to arbitration is received by the respondent, as stated in the AAA, meeting the requirements established in the arbitration agreement.

Place of arbitration

The parties may freely determine the place of the arbitration. Failing such agreement, it will be determined by the arbitrators, taking into consideration the circumstances of the case and the convenience of the parties. Arbitrators may, unless otherwise agreed by the parties and only after notifying them, meet at any place they deem appropriate for hearing witnesses, experts or the parties, inspecting goods or documents, or examining persons.

Rules on evidence

At the beginning, the parties are free to choose the applicable rules on evidence, subject in any case to the requirements of the institution at which the arbitration will take place as well as observing the principles of equality, review and rebuttal. The AAA briefly regulates this matter in articles 44 and 45 by which, subject to any contrary agreement by the parties, the arbitrators will decide whether to hold oral hearings for the presentation of statements or evidence and the issuance of conclusions, or whether the proceedings will be conducted in writing only. Unless the parties have agreed that no hearings will be held, they will be announced by the arbitrators at an appropriate stage of the proceedings, if so requested by a party.

Rules on privilege and disclosure

There are no rules or laws providing for an arbitrator's privilege or immunity. Nevertheless, the AAA establishes the arbitrator's liability for damages in case of improper performance of their duties based on bad faith, temerity or wilful misconduct.

With regard to disclosure rules, according to articles 5.2.c and 39.2 of the AAA, the arbitrators, the parties, the experts and the arbitral institutions are bound to honour the confidentiality of the information received on the occasion of arbitration according to the confidentiality principle, unless the parties agree otherwise. This principle is one of the main advantages of the arbitration system and one of the reasons for its success, since it allows the parties to protect their public reputation. However, in case of international arbitration, parties must expressly stipulate the confidentiality of the arbitration in the arbitration agreement (article 67.2).

IBA Rules on the taking of evidence

IBA Rules are not positive law in the Principality of Andorra. Consequently they are merely indicative, not binding; arbitrators are not obliged to follow the IBA provisions. As of today there is no case law of the Andorran courts on this issue; it can only be supposed that the IBA Rules may be taken into account in the same way they are considered in neighbouring jurisdictions.

Rules regarding expert evidence

The AAA establishes that, unless otherwise agreed by the parties, arbitrators may, at their own initiative or at the request of either party, appoint experts to advise them on specific matters, as well as request any of the parties to provide documents or goods to the expert for inspection. Parties may also provide reports of experts appointed by them. Unless otherwise agreed by the parties, if one party requires or the arbitrators deem it necessary, the expert, after presenting the report either orally or in writing, may participate in the proceeding and answer the questions of the parties.

New LCIA and IBA guidelines

Currently, there are no guidelines to take into consideration the new LCI and IBA guidelines beyond the consideration of their principles as mere inspirations for international arbitrations held in the Principality of Andorra. These rules are not considered as positive law in the jurisdiction.

Confidentiality of proceedings

The arbitrators, the parties, the experts and the arbitral institutions are bound to honour the confidentiality of the information received on the occasion of arbitration, unless the parties agree otherwise. However, in the case of international arbitration, the parties must expressly stipulate the confidentiality of the arbitration in the arbitration agreement.

Arbitrators

Appointment of arbitrators

According to the AAA, in arbitration not to be decided *ex aequo et bono* and conducted by a single arbitrator, such person will be required to be an attorney if acting as such, unless otherwise agreed by the parties. When arbitration is conducted by three or more arbitrators, at least one must be an attorney.

Additionally, the parties are free to agree on a procedure for appointing the arbitrator or arbitrators, providing the principle of equality is honoured. Failing such agreement, the AAA establishes some rules for the appointment of an arbitrator:

- In an arbitration with a sole arbitrator, he will be appointed by the court (*Secció Civil de la Batllia*) at the request of a party.
- In an arbitration with three (3) arbitrators, each party may appoint one arbitrator, and the two (2) arbitrators thus appointed may appoint the third arbitrator, who may preside the proceedings. If a party fails to appoint the arbitrator within thirty (30) days of receipt of a request to do so from the other party, or if the two arbitrators fail to agree on the third arbitrator within thirty (30) days of the latest acceptance, the appointment will be made by the court at the request of a party.

Where more than one claimant or respondent is involved, the arbitration must consist of three arbitrators: the respondent may appoint one arbitrator, and the former another, and the two (2) arbitrators thus appointed may appoint the third arbitrator, who may preside the proceedings. The system of appointment is the same as explained above.

If a party does not comply with the established proceeding, the parties or arbitrators do not reach an agreement in accordance with the established proceeding, or a third party does not perform its functions, any party may apply to the competent court to appoint the arbitrators or, as appropriate, to adopt the necessary measures therefor. When arbitrators have to be appointed by the court, it will draw up a list of three names for each arbitrator to be appointed, and appoint them by lot.

Challenge of arbitrators

Arbitrators may be challenged only in the event that justifiable doubts affecting their impartiality or independence arise, or if they do not meet the qualifications agreed to by the parties. A party may challenge an arbitrator appointed by him, or in whose appointment he has participated, only for reasons of which he/she becomes aware after the appointment was made.

The procedure under which the challenge of an arbitrator shall take place is established in the AAA. The parties may agree on a procedure for challenging arbitrators but, in the absence of such agreement, a party who intends to challenge an arbitrator must state in writing the grounds for the challenge within fifteen (15) days after becoming aware of the acceptance, or of any circumstances that may give rise to justified doubts about the arbitrator's impartiality or independence.

Unless the challenged arbitrator withdraws from his office or the other party agrees to the challenge, the arbitrators – excluding the challenged arbitrator – shall decide on the challenge. If a challenge under any of the precedent procedures is not successful, the challenging party may submit the challenge as grounds for objecting to the award.

IBA Guidelines on conflict of interest

As happens with respect to the IBA Rules on evidence, the IBA Guidelines on conflict of interest are not positive law in the Principality of Andorra. Consequently, they are merely indicative, not binding; arbitrators are not obliged to follow the IBA Guidelines. As of today there is no case law of the Andorran courts on this issue; it only can be supposed that the IBA Rules may be taken into account in the same way they are considered in neighbouring jurisdictions.

Terminating an arbitrator's mandate

An arbitrator's mandate is terminated when the arbitral proceedings terminate, either if it is with a final award or if: i) the claimant withdraws his claim, unless the respondent takes exception thereto and the arbitrators acknowledge a legitimate interest on his part in obtaining a final settlement of the dispute; ii) the parties mutually agree on the termination of the proceedings; or iii) the arbitrators find that continuation of the proceedings is unnecessary or impossible.

Immunity of arbitrators

As previously indicated, arbitrators are not afforded immunity from suit. They are subject to a very high standard of liability, which means they could be responsible for damages and prejudices caused when acting in bad faith, temerity or wilful misconduct, as determined in article 25.1 of the AAA. Arbitrators or arbitral institutions acting on their behalf will be bound to take liability insurance or equivalent security for the amount established in the specific arbitral institution rules.

Secretaries to the Arbitral Tribunal

The AAA establishes that the arbitrators, under the parties' agreement, may appoint one secretary and fix his/her administrative functions and remuneration. The draft of creation of the Arbitration Court establishes that the bylaws of the entity shall fix the requirements and the proceeding to become General Secretary.

Interim relief

Types of interim relief available

Article 28 of the AAA establishes that, unless otherwise agreed by the parties, arbitrators are allowed to grant any interim measures deemed necessary in connection with the object of the dispute, at the request of any party. In such cases, the arbitrators may order any party:

- to maintain or restore the *status quo* until the dispute is resolved;
- to adopt measures to avoid any current or imminent damage in the arbitration proceeding or refrain from carrying out certain acts that may cause damages or interference in the arbitration proceeding;
- to provide some means to preserve the necessary goods to allow the execution of the final award; or
- to keep evidence that may be relevant to resolve the dispute.

Applying for interim relief

Parties may apply to both courts and arbitral tribunals in order to be granted any interim measure.

With regard to the interim reliefs adopted by arbitral tribunals, the AAA provides that those interim measures must be connected to the subject matter of the dispute, being enforceable before any court. Regardless of the form adopted by arbitral decisions on interim measures, the rules on setting-aside and enforcement of the awards will apply to them.

In addition, the arbitration agreement does not prevent the parties, prior to or during the arbitral proceedings, from applying to a court for interim relief, or the court from granting such measures.

Can and do national courts order anti-suit injunctions in aid of international arbitration?

The Andorran law does not provide for the granting of any form of anti-suit injunctions and, as of today, no court has granted an anti-suit injunction in support of an agreement to arbitrate.

Can and do national courts order anti-arbitration injunctions in aid of domestic litigation?

The Andorran law does not provide for the granting of any form of anti-arbitration injunction and, as of today, no court has granted an anti-arbitration injunction in support of an agreement to arbitrate.

Security of costs

The AAA establishes that arbitrators may, at the request of the parties, adopt any interim measures deemed necessary in connection with the object of the dispute, requiring the claimant to furnish sufficient security.

Arbitration award

Formal requirements

An arbitration award must fulfil the following formal requirements in order to be valid and enforceable:

- It must be issued within six (6) months (extendable for a further two (2) months by reasoned resolution of the arbitrators) of the date of submission of the statement of defence or of the expiration of the deadline therefor, unless otherwise agreed by the parties.
- It must be issued in writing and signed by the arbitrators. Arbitrators may specify the sense of their votes.
- It must explain the grounds upon which it is based unless the award is issued as a way of termination by mutual agreement of the parties.
- It must contain the date, the name, address of the parties, their attorneys and the arbitrators, the place of arbitration, a concise summary of the claims of the parties, and the evidences and the decision.
- It must contain a decision regarding the costs of the arbitration, subject to the agreement of the parties.
- It must be expressly notified to the parties on arbitration, according to the form and within the time frame agreed by them or, failing that, by delivering a signed copy of the award to each party.

Time frame

Subject to any contrary agreement of the parties, the arbitrators must deliver the award within six months of the date of submission of the statement of defence or, failing that, the deadline for its submission. Unless otherwise agreed by the parties, this term may be extended by the arbitrators for a period of no longer than two (2) months under a duly justified ground. Additionally, the failure to deliver the award on time will not affect its validity, unless otherwise agreed by the parties.

Costs for the parties

An arbitral tribunal may order costs for the parties. The AAA establishes that the award shall express, subject to agreement by the parties: the arbitrators' decision on arbitration costs, to include the arbitrator's fees and expenses and, as appropriate, the fees and expenses of the parties' defence or representatives; the cost of the service rendered by the institution conducting the arbitration; and all other expenses incurred in the arbitral proceedings.

Interest

The AAA does not expressly regulate the possibility of claiming interest on arbitration costs. However, there is no legal impediment to including interest in the final award but only regarding the principal amount claimed in the proceedings.

Challenge of the arbitration award

Appeal of an arbitration award

As a general rule, an arbitration award cannot be appealed before the ordinary courts in the Principality of Andorra. An arbitration award constitutes *res judicata*, which means that there are no other actions against it except for those seeking to set it aside or, as appropriate, the object of a request of review under provisions on final sentences established in our Procedural Law (Article 30 *bis* of the Transitory Act on Judicial Proceedings of 21 December 1993).

Grounds for challenge

The AAA provides a restricted list of grounds under which an award can be challenged before the Supreme Court of Justice (*Tribunal Superior de Justicia*). All of such reasons must be demonstrated, in any case, by the applicant party:

- The arbitration agreement did not exist or was not valid.
- The applicant party did not properly receive notice of the appointment of an arbitrator and/or of the arbitration proceedings, or otherwise was not able to present their case.
- The arbitrators decided on questions not subject to their jurisdiction.
- The arbitrators did not observe the agreement of the parties regarding their appointment and/or the arbitral proceeding, unless such agreement does not respect any imperative provision of the AAA or, failing such agreement, the arbitrators have proceeded against the AAA.

On the other hand, the Supreme Court, at its own initiative or at the request of the Public Prosecutor, may challenge the arbitration award if it verifies that the award decided on non-arbitrable matters or violated public policy.

Modifying the arbitration award

The AAA establishes that the parties are entitled to apply for the correction, rectification and clarification of the award and/or the issuance of an additional award within thirty (30) days after its notification, unless another time is agreed by the parties. A party may apply for this modification of the arbitration award when some of the following circumstances apply:

- miscalculation or clerical, typographical or similar errors in the arbitration award;
- need of clarification of a specific point or part of the award;

- need of an additional award to resolve the claims made and not resolved in the award; or
- overreach of the award to non-arbitrable matters or matters not submitted to arbitration.

Once the application is made, the arbitrators shall make the correction or rectification, clarify the interpretation or issue an additional award within sixty (60) days.

Recent examples of successful and unsuccessful challenges of arbitral awards

Due to the recent coming into force of the AAA and the fact that as of today an arbitration institution does not exist in the Principality of Andorra, case law on challenges of arbitral awards remains unexplored.

Enforcement of the arbitration award

International conventions

The enforcement of international awards is regulated in article 61 of the AAA, which refers to the application of the Convention on Recognition and Enforcement of Arbitral Awards made in New York on 29 April 1977.

In order to enforce an international arbitration award, the formal requirements needed in the Principality of Andorra are established in our Procedural Law (article 19 of the Qualified Act on Justice of 3 September 1993, and articles 47 and subsequent of the Transitory Act on Judicial Proceedings of 21 December 1993), by reference to the Andorran legal system on the recognition and enforcement of international judicial sentences.

Can an arbitration award be enforced if it has been set aside at the courts of the seat of arbitration?

No, it cannot be enforced. In accordance with the article V.1.E of the Convention of New York and article 61 of the AAA, recognition and enforcement of the award may be refused if the party against whom it is invoked proves that the award has been set aside at the courts of the seat of arbitration. Articles 47 and subsequent of the Transitory Act on Judicial Proceedings of 21 December 1993 regulate the proceeding on the recognition and enforcement of international judicial sentences and arbitral awards. Once the Supreme Court of Justice receives the demand of exequatur, it will notify the party against whom execution is sought and this party will have thirty (30) days to oppose the enforcement and prove that the award has been set aside.

Investment arbitration

The Principality of Andorra signed one bilateral investment treaty (“**BIT**”) with the United Arab Emirates in 2017. It has not yet signed any multilateral investment treaties (“**MITs**”).

To the best of our knowledge, there have not been any investment arbitration cases against the Principality of Andorra. Nor does the Principality have any experience in investment arbitration.

Miguel Cases
Tel: +376 728 001 / Email: Miguel.Cases@caseslacambra.com
Miguel Cases is the managing partner of Cases & Lacambra. He leads the Corporate and Banking & Finance practice and is qualified to practise both in Spain and the Principality of Andorra, where he is the resident partner.
He has extensive experience as an arbitrator and in arbitration proceedings, being regularly appointed as a specialised arbitrator in financial instruments.
He is a regular lecturer in international business schools in its specialty areas and in particular financial instruments which simulate or replicate cash flows.

Cases & Lacambra

C/ Manel Cerqueda i Escaler 3-5, AD700 Escaldes d'Engordany, Principality of Andorra
Tel: +376 728 001 / URL: www.caseslacambra.com

Angola

Nuno Albuquerque, Conceição Manita Ferreira & Luísa Castro Ferreira
N-Advogados & CM Advogados

Introduction

Angola has become one of the fastest-growing economies in the world, and therefore is positioned to become an active member of the global economic community, since it has a privileged geographic location on the coast of the Atlantic Ocean, and abundant natural and human resources. Its economic development policies are focused on private investment, so Angola is perfectly placed to provide interested investors with financial incentives that increase potential for return on capital.

In recent years, Angola has been undertaking deep legal reforms in order to modernise its legal system so it can foster investment projects in the country.

Given that growing process of political and economic opening-up of Angola, it is becoming necessary to give more security, certainty and juridical predictability in regard to the resolution of eventual conflicts arising from internal and external relations.

Therefore, since Angola is experiencing exponential economic growth and an increase in the international transactions and foreign direct investments involving Angola and/or Angolan parties, the practice of international arbitration in Angola is also growing. Nevertheless, as things stand there have only been a small number of domestic arbitration cases. However, given the reforms of the last few years, it is expected that the use of arbitration for domestic cases with a foreign element (i.e., where a party has foreign shareholders) will increase. Also, there are an increasing number of arbitrations relating to Angolan parties where recognition and enforcement in Angola are important issues to consider, and an increasing number of investment arbitration cases relating to Angola or Angolan parties can be seen as well.

Currently, Arbitration in Angola is regulated by Law no. 16/03, of 25 July 2003, the "Voluntary Arbitration Law" (VAL).

The VAL was, for the most part, inspired by the Portuguese Arbitration Law from 1986. This law does not strictly follow the UNCITRAL Model Law; however, it includes many solutions that are common to the ones found in that Model Law. In contrast to the Model Law, we can point out the following aspects:

- the VAL contains no provision on definitions;
- it does not provide for rules on interpretation;
- it adopts the disposable rights criterion in regard to arbitrability;
- it does not address the issue of preliminary decisions;
- it does not distinguish between different types of awards; and

- it permits appeal on the merits in domestic arbitrations, unless the parties have agreed otherwise.

Also regarding this matter, Decree no. 4/06, of 27 February 2006, has the purpose of promoting institutional arbitration in Angola, and deals with the licensing procedures for the incorporation of arbitration centres. The Ministry of Justice is the entity empowered to authorise the incorporation of arbitration centres in Angola.

Until this date, the Ministry of Justice has authorised the creation of five arbitration centres:

- Harmonia – Integrated Center for Studies and Conflict Resolution;
- Arbitral Juris;
- CAAL – Angolan Center of Arbitration of Conflicts;
- Center of Mediation and Arbitration of Angola;
- CEFA's Arbitration Center; and
- CREL – Extrajudicial Resolution of Conflicts Center.

Arbitration is also foreseen in other legislation, namely the following:

- Private Investment Law (Law no. 14/15, of 11 August 2015);
- the Mobile Values Law (Law no. 22/15, of 31 August 2015);
- the Petroleum Activities Law (Law no. 10/04, of 12 November 2004); and
- the Public Procurement Law (Law no. 20/10, of 7 September 2010).

However, the majority of arbitration cases conducted in Angola continue to be *ad hoc*.

Normally, the Angolan state and companies in the public sector accept, without any complaints, the use of arbitration to resolve disputes with foreign investors.

Also, in 2016, Angola took another major step on international arbitration, as Angola signed the New York Convention on the Recognition of Foreign Arbitral Awards. On 6 March 2017, Angola deposited its instrument of accession to the Convention with the UN Secretary General. Under article XII(2), the Convention will enter into force in Angola on 4 June 2017, 90 days after the deposit of its instrument of accession.

Arbitration agreement

According to article 1 of the VAL, the parties may opt to use arbitration for disputes regarding disposable rights (i.e., those rights that the parties can construct and extinguish by act of will, and those which parties can renounce).

Only disputes reserved by law to the State Courts or to some other type of proceedings cannot be submitted to arbitration. Therefore, all commercial disputes are due to be subject to arbitration.

First of all, in order to resort to arbitration and while celebrating a contract, the parties must establish an arbitration clause (in the contract or in the form of a separate agreement for future disputes arising from a defined legal relationship) or an arbitration agreement (signed by the parties to resolve an immediate dispute), which states that any dispute must be resolved using arbitration, instead of seeking judicial courts.

In order to be valid and effective, the arbitration agreement must comply with several requirements. The arbitration agreement must be in written form (article 3 of the VAL) and will be void if:

- it is not made in writing;
- it goes against the provisions stated in article 1 of the Law; or
- the object of the arbitration is not specified and there is no other way to specify it.

The VAL only includes rules on the expiration of the arbitration agreement, and does not include rules on the modification and revocation of the arbitration agreement. Thus, the Arbitration Agreement and the Arbitration Clause expire when:

- any of the arbitrators dies, is excused, becomes disabled for the exercise of the arbitration and is not replaced;
- a majority cannot be reached in the deliberations (in cases where the arbitration is collective); and
- the award is not rendered by the established deadlines.

However, according to section 4 of article 2 of the Law, the arbitral clause or convention is not automatically void when the contract where it is inserted is void, if it is clear that the will of the parties is to have an arbitral clause or convention regardless of the validity of the contract.

Regarding the competence of the arbitral tribunal, article 31 states that the arbitral tribunal may decide on its own jurisdiction (the principle of competence-competence). This decision can only be syndicated in impugnation or opposition to the execution of the Arbitral Award.

This means that the award of the arbitral tribunal by which it rules on its own jurisdiction, including any objections with respect to the existence or validity of the arbitration agreement, can only be appreciated by the judicial court after the arbitral tribunal has rendered the award.

This legal provision gives a letter of law to the fundamental principle of arbitration, the principle of competence-competence: that the arbitral tribunal has full competence to resolve all questions raised in the arbitral proceedings relating to it, whether of a substantive nature relating to the merits of the case, or of a procedural nature. The principle of competence-competence preserves the autonomy of the arbitral tribunal in relation to the jurisdiction of the state courts.

Arbitration procedure

In line with the Model Law, the parties are free to agree on the procedural rules (directly or by reference to an institution). In the absence of that agreement, the tribunal will have the power to determine the rules (as stated in article 16). The same reasoning applies to the place of arbitration (as stated in article 17).

The arbitration begins when the request for submission of the dispute to arbitration is received by the Respondent – if nothing otherwise is stipulated by Agreement of the parties. This request for submission of the dispute to arbitration is generally named "notice to arbitration". The notification can be made by any means, as long as it is possible to prove its receipt by the other party.

The notification must contain:

- the identification of the parties;
- the indication that they wish to submit the conflict to arbitration;
- the indication of the Arbitration Agreement; and
- the subject of the conflict, if that is not already stated in the Arbitration Agreement.

Also, if the parties are due to nominate the arbitrators, the claimant party must indicate the arbitrator chosen by them in the notice to arbitration, and must also invite the other party to indicate their arbitrator. If the arbitration procedure is to be commanded by a single arbitrator, the notifying party must suggest an arbitrator, and invite the other party to accept that suggestion. However, the nomination can also be made by a third party. If that happens, the notifying party must also notify that third party to appoint and communicate the appointment of the arbitrator to both parties.

As article 16 of the Law states, the parties can agree about the rules of the arbitration. However, if those rules aren't defined until the acceptance of the first arbitrator, the arbitrators must define the rules of the arbitration.

The seat of the arbitration is also determined by agreement of the parties in the Arbitration Agreement or later. Regarding the seat of the arbitration, as happens on the rules of arbitration, if the parties do not agree until the acceptance of the first arbitrator, the seat of arbitration must also be chosen by the arbitrators.

The arbitration procedure must respect the following principles and rules:

- the principle of equal treatment of the parties;
- the right to response must be granted in all phases of the procedure; and
- both parties must be heard, orally or by writing, before the rendering of the award.

These are the fundamental principles and rules that must be respected in any procedure. Breach of these principles and rules may lead to the setting-aside of the award.

Also, the parties must be represented by a constituted lawyer – meaning one that is allowed to practise in Angola (i.e. an Angolan lawyer). In effect, the National Council of the Angolan Bar Association decided on 31 March 2014 that only lawyers with a valid registration can intervene as a lawyer in arbitration proceedings.

According to article 24 of the Law, in national arbitration, the arbitral court must decide in accordance with the national law, unless the parties establish that the conflict is to be solved by referring to equity. However, if the parties agree on the decision by the rules of equity, they automatically renounce the right to appeal the award.

On the other hand, in international arbitration, the parties are free to designate the applicable law, and may do so by referring to a specific national law or state legal system. If the parties do not agree in this matter, the arbitral court must decide what substantive law to apply, resorting to the conflict rule which it considers applicable to the dispute.

Regarding the production of proof, in arbitration all means of proof allowed by law are accepted. There is no specific rule in Angolan law establishing limits to the permissible scope of disclosure or discovery. If the proof depends on a third party and that third party refuses to collaborate, the parties or the Arbitral Court can request the Judicial Court to carry out the procedure so that proof is produced.

The procedure ends when the award is deposited or after the award becomes definitive, if a withdrawal happens, since the withdrawal is free at any time of the procedure.

If the arbitral award is not rendered within the applicable time limit or if for some reason the tribunal becomes incomplete and a new arbitrator is not appointed, the proceedings will not be dismissed, but the arbitral agreement itself will be deemed to have lost its validity (for that specific dispute) (article 5 of the Law).

The law allows the parties to agree on a time limit to render the award, but if nothing is said until the acceptance of the first arbitrator, the said time limit will be of six months, and will only be extended by agreement of the parties (article 25 of the Law). Instead of agreeing on a specific limit, the parties may refer the dispute to institutional arbitration (providing that the rules of the institution contemplate the extension of the time limit to render the award).

After all the diligences on the process are made, the arbitrators must decide and render an award, which is to be notified to the parties and deposited in the secretariat of the Provincial Court of the place of arbitration.

Arbitrators

The arbitral tribunal may be composed of a single arbitrator or several, but there must always be an odd number of arbitrators (article 6, paragraph 1 of the Law).

<u>Appointment</u>

The arbitrators are appointed by the parties in the Arbitration Agreement or in *posterior* writing. However, the VAL establishes supplementary criteria to be used in cases where the parties have not established the means of designating a single or several arbitrators. Indeed, if the parties do not agree on the designation of the arbitrators, or on the way they are to appoint the arbitrators, each of the parties appoints one arbitrator, and the arbitrators appoint the third arbitrator, which completes the composition of the arbitral court (article 8, paragraph 1 of the Law).

The VAL is silent as to the means of constituting the arbitral tribunal in the case of multiple parties.

<u>Requirements of the arbitrators</u>

The arbitrators can be singular persons who are in the full enjoyment and exercise of their civil capacity (article 9, paragraph 3 of the Law). Arbitrators must be independent and impartial.

The arbitrators are free to accept the designation but, once accepted, the excuse of functions is only admissible if it is justified by supervening cause that makes it impossible for the arbitrator to exercise their functions.

Any person invited to exercise the functions of an arbitrator has to reveal immediately all circumstances that may cause doubts about their impartiality and independence. If any circumstance causes a founded doubt of the impartiality and independence of the arbitrator, they may be refused the right to arbitrate. However, the party that appoints the arbitrator can only refuse the designation if the motive is subsequent to the appointment.

In case of failure to appoint one arbitrator, and unless the parties have agreed on another appointing authority, the missing arbitrator will be nominated by the president of the local State Court (article 14 of the Law).

<u>Replacement</u>

An arbitrator can be replaced in cases of death, refusal, permanent disability for performance of their duties, or if the appointment becomes void.

The motives for the refusal are very similar to the ones established by the UNCITRAL Model Law. They are contemplated in article 10 of the VAL.

The VAL addresses the matter of challenging the arbitrator when there is reasonable doubt about his or her impartiality or independence, or when he or she manifestly does not possess the qualifications that were previously agreed upon by the parties (article 10, paragraph 2 of the Law).

If the arbitrators do not step down, the decision on this is made by the Tribunal, with appeal to the State Courts (article 10 of the Law).

Interim relief

Interim relief may be granted in arbitration, unless otherwise stated by the parties. Any of the parties may require that the court orders interim measures, related to the object of the conflict, namely the provision of guarantees that it considers necessary. Interim relief is stated in article 22 of the Law, which is inspired by article 17 of the UNCITRAL Model Law. However, it does not specify what kind of measures are admitted.

This does not, however, prevent the parties from requesting from the Judicial Court, in terms of the Civil Procedure rules, any procedure they deem necessary to prevent or protect the injury of rights.

It is essential that the petitioner alleges and proves two requirements: the *periculum in mora* and the *fumus bonus iuris*.

Arbitration award

The law contains a number of provisions regarding the award and its preparation (articles 24 to 33 of the Law).

Unless the parties agree otherwise, under article 25 of the Law, the Arbitration Award must be rendered in the timeline of six months after the acceptance of the last arbitrator. Any extension to that timeline must be agreed by the parties and cannot be decided unilaterally by the arbitrators. There is also the possibility for the parties to agree that, if any instruction measure is necessary, the timeline is suspended during that period of time for which the instruction is in course. The decision must be rendered with the presence of all of the arbitrators, by simple majority, except if the parties have stipulated a larger majority. The parties can also establish that, if the arbitrators cannot reach an agreement, the decision can be made by the president of the court.

Under article 27 of the Law, the Arbitration Award must be made in writing and must contain the following information:

- identification of the parties;
- reference to the Arbitration Agreement;
- object of the conflict;
- seat of arbitration;
- location and date on which the award was rendered;
- decision and justification for the decision;
- signature of the arbitrators; and
- indication of the expenses associated with the process and their distribution between the parties.

However, the statement of a decision given in accordance with the rules of equity is sufficient with a statement of the facts that are considered proved.

If any arbitrator disagrees with the decision, the reasons for the disagreement must also be stated in the decision.

Also, under article 23 of the Law, the fees and costs of the process and their division between the parties must be agreed by the parties, unless this decision results from regulations of arbitration chosen under article 16 of the Law.

The decision is to be notified to the parties, who can ask for the correction of material errors, obscurities or clarification of doubts, within 10 days. The court has 30 days to respond to such requests.

Throughout the process, the parties can also reach an agreement regarding the subject of the conflict. Under article 28 of the Law, the agreement must be submitted to the court for homologation.

The withdrawal is also admitted, as long as the other party agrees with it, according to paragraph 4 of article 20 of the Law. The withdrawal must also be homologated by the court.

Challenge of the arbitration award

For domestic arbitrations, the Arbitration Award can be challenged in two ways:

- annulment of the award; or
- appeal of the award.

Appeal can be waived by the parties, but not their right to request the award to be set aside.

The **annulment** of the award can happen in the following cases:

- when the conflict is not sought to be solved through arbitration;
- when the court that rendered the award is incompetent;
- when the arbitral agreement has expired;
- when the arbitral court has been irregularly constituted;
- when the decision doesn't contain the justification;
- when the decision has violated the principles of equality of response and that fact has influenced the resolution of the conflict;
- when the court has decided on questions that were not to be decided or when it did not decide on questions that it should decide; or
- when the arbitral court, in cases where it decides through equity and custom, did not comply with public order or with the Angolan legal order.

The arguments of incompetence of the court and irregularity of the constitution of the court can only be invoked if, during the process, the exception of incompetence of the court or irregularity of its constitution have been also invoked and the court declared itself competent to resolve the conflict, or if the irregularity had influence on the final decision.

Omitting to pronounce can only be admitted if it is demonstrated that the lack of decision on a certain question or issue was determinant to the final decision.

The annulment must be addressed to the Supreme Court and the deadline to submit the annulment is 20 days from the date of notification of the Arbitral Award. The right to require the annulment of the award cannot be waived.

On the other hand, the award can also be **appealed** in the same way that a judicial award can be appealed.

The appeal is to be addressed to the Supreme Court and the deadline to submit the appeal is 15 days from the date of notification of the Arbitral Award.

However, there is a slight difference in the law when it comes to international and domestic arbitration.

When we come across **international arbitration**, the principle is of non-appeal (as stated in article 44 of the Law), except when the possibility of appeal is expressly agreed by the parties.

On the other hand, when it comes to **domestic arbitration**, the principle is of the admissibility of the appeal, except if the parties expressly renounce that right (as stated in article 36 of the Law).

Enforcement of the arbitration award

National awards

Article 33 of the Law states that the award has to be fulfilled in 30 days. If this does not happen, the non-lacking party can coercively execute/enforce the award.

Awards rendered in Angola (i.e., awards rendered within domestic arbitrations and awards rendered in Angola, within international arbitrations) are enforceable exactly as if they were decisions rendered by the State Court (article 37 of the VAL).

If the deadline given by the court to voluntarily accomplish the award is over, or if such deadline isn't fixed by the court, the interested party has 30 days after the notification of the award to enforce it before the Provincial Court, in the terms stated in the Civil Process Law.

The requirement for the enforcement must be accompanied by the arbitral award, its rectification or clarification, and the proof of notification and deposit of the award.

The summoned party has the right to give opposition to the enforcement, with grounding on the motives stated in articles 813 and 814 of the Angolan Civil Procedure Code:

- unenforceability of the award;
- falseness of the process or transfer or infidelity of the latter, when one or the other influences in terms of the enforcement;
- illegality of the claimant;
- illegality of the defendant;
- undue accumulation of executions;
- unlawful coalition of claimants;
- fault or nullity of the first summons to the action, when the defendant has not intervened in the proceedings;
- uncertainty, illiquidity or unenforceability of the obligation;
- *res judicata* prior to the sentence that is to be enforced;
- any fact that extinguishes or modifies the obligation, provided that it is after the close of the discussion in the declaration process, and is proved by a document. The prescription of the right or obligation can be proven by any means; or
- any fundament that is sufficient to annul the award.

The opposition must be filed within eight days from the date the defendant is notified of the enforcement process. The decision on opposition to the enforcement is not appealable.

International awards

Angola has ratified the Convention on the Recognition and Enforcement of Foreign Arbitral Awards (New York 1958) via Resolution no. 38/2016, which was published in the Official Gazette of the State on 12 August 2016. Following its ratification, on 6 March 2017 Angola deposited its instrument of accession to the New York Convention with the Secretary General of the United Nations. In light of Article XII (2), the New York Convention entered into force on 4 June 2017, 90 days after the instrument had been deposited with the UN Secretary General.

Angola made a reservation pursuant to which the Convention will only apply to the recognition and enforcement of awards issued in the territory of another contracting state.

Among the main differences that are anticipated in relation to the old regime (in which all foreign arbitral awards had to be subject to a process of foreign decision recognition before the judicial courts), we underline the future inapplicability of article 1096 of the Angolan Civil Procedure Code regarding the requirements for foreign award confirmation, which will be replaced by articles IV and V of the New York Convention.

To provide certainty that foreign arbitral awards are practically enforceable in the country, Angola may need to harmonise both the provisions of the Voluntary Arbitration Law and the Angolan Civil Procedure Code with its Convention obligations.

Investment arbitration

Investment arbitration is not specifically regulated under Angolan law. Therefore, unless more favourable rules have been adopted in international instruments, the Voluntary Arbitration Law applies to investment arbitration.

The New Private Investment Law of Angola prescribes, under paragraph 3 of article 46, that conflicts and their interpretation can be resolved by arbitration. However, paragraph 4 of the same article states that that arbitration must take place in Angola, and the governing law applicable must be Angolan law.

This Law also has the aim to foresee the main guarantees granted to foreign investors in the scope of public international law or established by the international jurisprudence of the various arbitration institutions, namely:

- the Angolan State shall ensure, irrespective of the origin of capital, fair, non-arbitrarily discriminatory and equitable treatment of incorporated companies and companies and the foreign investor's assets (article 15);
- payment of a fair compensation, prompt and effective in the case of expropriation or requisition for weighty and justified reasons (article 16, paragraph 3);
- protection of intellectual and industrial property rights;
- protection of acquired rights over possession;
- non-interference in the management of private companies, except in cases expressly provided for by law; and
- non-cancellation of licences without judicial or administrative proceedings.

Also, as stated above, Angola became a signatory country of the New York Convention in 2016.

Additionally, the Bilateral Investment Treaties provide for the authorisation or consent of the Angolan State to arbitration in terms that allow the foreign investor immediate recourse to international arbitration, without the need to enter into any subsequent arbitration agreement.

In these cases, the arbitral tribunal shall consist of three arbitrators, each party being responsible for choosing one arbitrator and the third arbitrator being the arbitrator-president chosen by agreement between the other two. In the absence of an agreement for the choice of the third arbitrator, the latter, under the most diverse investment contracts, shall be appointed by one of the following entities:

(i) the General Secretariat of the Paris International Chamber of Commerce (ICC);

(ii) a designation authority appointed by the Secretary General of the Permanent Court of Arbitration of The Hague, under the UNCITRAL Regulation; and

(iii) the President of the Provincial Court of Luanda, at the request of either party.

Angola has the following bilateral treaties with other States:

- the United Kingdom of Great Britain and Northern Ireland (2000);
- Germany (2003);
- Namibia (2005);
- South Africa (2005);
- Italy (2006);
- Portugal (2009);
- Switzerland (2009); and
- Russia (2009).

They all refer to the arbitration of disputes for the International Centre for the Settlement of Investment Disputes (ICSID) and the Complementary Mechanism for the Administration of Conciliation, Arbitration and Inquiry Procedures (CIRDI), as well as for the Arbitral Tribunal of the International Chamber of Commerce (ICC), or even for an international arbitrator or tribunal to be designated by special agreement or established in accordance with the UNCITRAL Rules of Arbitration.

In summary, it can be said that Angola does indeed protect foreign investments through arbitration, namely in the private investment sector, and has taken steps to reduce bureaucracy and facilitate international arbitration and investment arbitration, namely and most importantly, by ratifying one of the most important arbitration conventions that was missing from the Angolan legal system, the New York Convention of 1958.

Third-party funding

No regulation on third-party funding of arbitration exists in Angola. Given the fact that there is no regulation on third-party funding, it would seem prudent for arbitration agreements to include certain provisions to ensure less uncertainty in potential claims, and in particular: (1) the obligation to disclose the existence of funding agreements in the event of disputes, and the content to be disclosed; and (2) acknowledgment by the parties that, as a security measure to avoid a potential annulment of the award or refusal of its recognition and enforcement under the 1958 New York Convention, the funder's eventual uplift should not comprise any recovery of costs or indemnity due to the prevailing party in the arbitration or litigation.

Nuno Albuquerque
Tel: +244 926 227 178 / 928 391 751 / Email: nunoalbuquerque@nadv.pt
Born on 19 July 1964, in Angola. Nuno has a law degree, University of Coimbra (1988). Nuno is inscribed in Portugal's bar association, as a lawyer, since 1990; in Angola's bar association, since 2008; in Paris' bar association, since 2014. He is an insolvency administrator, inscribed in the official list since 1995. Nuno is the executive director of CAAL – Angolan arbitration centre for litigation, since 2012. He is a certified mediator – public and private mediation ICFML, Catholic University, Oporto, 2014. Arbitrator for CAAD – Administrative Arbitration Centre; for TAD – Sports Arbitral Court (where he is also Vice-President) since 2015; for the Arbitration Centre for Property and Real Estate, since 2016. Nuno was the founding partner of "N-ADVOGADOS – Nuno Albuquerque, Deolinda Ribas, Sociedade de Advogados, RL" (now N-Advogados & CM Advogados).

Conceição Manita Ferreira
Tel: +244 222 735 332 / Email: mdcmanita@gmail.com
Born on 16 February 1959. Conceição is member no. 559 of the Angolan Bar Association. Conceição is graduated in Law by Agostinho Neto University (2005), and has a Masters Degree in Legal and Economic Sciences, by the same University. She has also taken courses in Social Research and Economic Analysis; Emergency and Disaster Management; and Basic Financial Management and Control for Managers. From 1983 to 1999 she was in the UNHCR; from 1995 to 1999 as Representative for Middle and Lower Juba Regions in Somalia. From 2005 to 2011 she worked at RGT Law Firm, Luanda, as Executive Director/Head of Labour/Family Law Departments. In 2007 she worked in the UNHCR, Luanda, as National Protection Officer. She is currently a Consultant, Mediator and Lawyer, Head and main partner of N-Advogados & CM Advogados.

Luísa Castro Ferreira
Tel: +244 926 227 178 / +351 253 609 330/310
Email: luisacastroferreira@nadv.pt
Born on 23 September 1989. Luísa has a law degree, University of Minho (2011), and a Masters in Administrative Law, University of Minho, 2014. Luísa is legally qualified to give professional training, 2017. Luísa has been inscribed in Portugal's bar association, as a lawyer, since 2014, and has worked at N-Advogados & CM Advogados since 2015. She was a speaker at the Study Session on European Public Procurement Law, University of Minho, March 2013, and at the 1st Public Procurement Congress of Cape Verde, November 2014. She is co-author of the article, "e-Procurement and Public e-Procurement", in "The New Code of Administrative Procedure – for Professor Cândido de Oliveira" and author of the article "The Electronic Public Procurement", in "Minutes of the First Congress of Public Purchases of Cape Verde", 2015.

N-Advogados & CM Advogados

Rua Domingos do Ó, N.º 61, 1º Andar, escritório N.º 13, Edifício Acácias Place, Benguela, Angola
Tel: +244 926 227 178 / +351 253 609 330/310 / Fax: +351 253 609 311 / URL: www.nadv.pt

Austria

Dr. Christian W. Konrad & Dr. Heidrun Halbartschlager
Konrad & Partners

Introduction

Austria has a long-standing tradition of fostering arbitration as a method of dispute resolution between commercial parties that goes back to the codification of arbitration law in 1895. Over the years, the consistency of a well-established legal framework, together with the arbitration-friendly case law of the local courts, have served Austria well in establishing itself as a major arbitration hub in Europe, particularly for disputes involving parties from CEE and SEE.

The Austrian arbitration law is governed by Sections 577–618 of the Austrian Code of Civil Procedure (**ACCP**) which does not distinguish between national and international arbitration proceedings. With the 2006 revision, Austrian arbitration law was aligned with international developments and the requirements and standards of more recent international arbitral practices. The ACCP's provisions were brought in line with the widely recognised UNCITRAL Model Law on International Commercial Arbitration (**UNCITRAL Model Law**).

With the 2013 revision of the ACCP, the Austrian Supreme Court became the first and final instance for the majority of arbitration-related matters. As a result, challenges of arbitral awards are now dealt with directly by a special division of the Austrian Supreme Court. This reform aimed at shortening the proceedings before state courts in annulment matters and ensures high-quality decisions by specialised Supreme Court judges.

The Vienna International Arbitral Centre (**VIAC**), which is attached to the Austrian Federal Economic Chamber, was established in 1975 and has since maintained its position as one of the leading arbitration institutions in Europe. As of today, more than 1,600 arbitral proceedings have been administered under its rules. VIAC's recent statistical reports show that disputes relating to financial services and banking, manufacturing, business ownership as well as aerospace and defence currently account for the largest share of its caseload.

VIAC has been cautious to preserve its traditions while also keeping pace with recent trends in international arbitration. In 2013, it amended its arbitration rules by introducing, among others, new provisions on multi-party arbitration, expedited proceedings and advance on costs in order to meet the demands of the international arbitration community.

An updated version of the Vienna Rules entered into force on 1 January 2018 applying to proceedings that are commenced after 31 December 2017. *Inter alia*, VIAC will now also administer purely domestic cases and has introduced an electronic case management system. Moreover, it is now explicitly provided that arbitrators and parties as well as their representatives shall conduct the proceedings in a cost-effective and efficient manner, which may also be taken into consideration when determining the arbitrators' fees and costs. In addition, a respondent may now request security for costs if it shows cause that the recoverability of a potential claim for costs is, with a sufficient degree of probability, at risk. Furthermore, the registration fees and administrative fees for low amounts in dispute have been reduced and at the same time the administrative fees for very high amounts have been slightly increased.

In line with recent trends to increase transparency regarding the appointment of arbitrators, VIAC has introduced a list indicating the names of arbitrators acting in VIAC proceedings which were pending on or filed after 1 January 2017. The list called *"VIAC Arbitral Tribunals 2017"* is available on the institution's website and provides information *inter alia* with regard to the role of the arbitrator (sole arbitrator, chairman, co-arbitrator), the mode of appointment (by the parties, the co-arbitrators or the VIAC-Board), the date of the transfer of the file to the arbitrator, and whether or not the arbitration is still pending.

Apart from VIAC, ICC Austria contributes to promoting arbitration in Austria by, *inter alia*, organising seminars, nominating arbitrators and advising on arbitration and mediation clauses.

Austria is also a party to the New York Convention on the Recognition and Enforcement of Foreign Arbitral Awards 1958 (**New York Convention**), to which it no longer maintains reservations, and the European Convention on International Commercial Arbitration 1961 (**European Convention**). In addition, Austria has signed and ratified the ICSID Convention and the Energy Charter Treaty.

Arbitration agreement

The definition of an arbitration agreement contained in Section 581(1) ACCP follows Article 7(1) UNCITRAL Model Law. For an arbitration agreement to be valid, certain minimum requirements have to be met. First, the parties thereto must be definable. In principle, these are the parties to the main contract. It has to be noted, however, that under certain circumstances third parties may also be bound by an arbitration agreement. Second, the arbitration agreement has to indicate the parties' will to have their dispute finally resolved in arbitration proceedings, and third, the arbitration agreement has to make reference to a "specified legal relationship". The parties may choose to refer only a specific dispute to arbitration or, generally, any potential dispute arising from a specified legal relationship. However, an agreement in general terms that "all disputes that may arise between two parties for any reason shall be submitted to arbitration" would be invalid due to insufficient specificity.

Parties may agree to submit their dispute to arbitration before or after it has arisen. The arbitration agreement may be concluded in the form of a separate contract, as well as in a contractual clause.

The form that an arbitration agreement must comply with can be fulfilled in two ways. First, it can be met by the signature of the parties on the document containing the arbitration agreement. This arguably includes every adequate form of electronic signature. The second means to conclude an arbitration agreement is by exchange of letters, faxes, emails or other forms of communication exchanged by the parties that provide "proof of the existence of the agreement". In other words, the parties must choose a mode of transmitting the information that evidences the text of the agreement. It is not sufficient for a letter, fax or email to be accepted orally; on the contrary, the acceptance must also be in writing. Electronic storage, such as on a CD-ROM or computer hard disc should, however, suffice.

Section 583(2) ACCP addresses separate arbitration agreements (as opposed to arbitration clauses included in a contract). When an agreement which fulfils the form requirements set forth above refers to a document which contains an arbitration agreement, it shall constitute an arbitration agreement if the reference is such that it makes the arbitration agreement part of the contract. This provision clarifies that the arbitration agreement does not have to be attached physically to the signed document. This is particularly relevant for arbitration clauses contained in general terms and conditions.

The consequences of a formally invalid arbitration agreement are severe, as they are considered to have no legal effect and as a result the arbitral tribunal lacks jurisdiction.

Any formal defect of the arbitration agreement, however, shall be cured in the arbitration proceedings by entering an appearance in the case, if no objection is raised at the latest with the respective first submission on the merits. If a party fails to raise a timely objection, it is generally barred from raising this defence at a later stage. This facilitates legal certainty and helps to reduce dilatory tactics.

Special form requirements apply to arbitration agreements between entrepreneurs and consumers and to certain employment matters. Such agreements with consumers are only valid if concluded after the specific dispute has arisen. In addition, both the consumer and the employee have to receive written legal advice on the differences between arbitration and court proceedings. Furthermore, the arbitration agreement must be contained in a separate document signed by the consumer or employee and such a document must only comprise agreements relating to the arbitral proceedings. Importantly, if the arbitration agreement provides for a seat of arbitration in a state that is different from the state of the consumer's or employee's domicile, residence or place of work at the time the contract was concluded or at the time of commencement of the arbitral proceedings, such an agreement is only binding if it is invoked by the consumer or employee. However, these special requirements do not apply to members of the boards of stock corporations and managing directors of limited liability companies.

Unlike the UNCITRAL Model Law, the ACCP expressly governs objective arbitrability in its Section 582 and provides that all pecuniary disputes may be the subject of an arbitration agreement. Such disputes include, among others, corporate disputes, disputes over anti-trust claims and competition law claims that are generally arbitrable. Non-pecuniary claims are arbitrable if the law allows the parties to conclude a settlement on the subject matter. Claims involving family law, as well as all claims arising out of contracts that are even only partially subject to the Landlord and Tenant Act or the Limited Profit Housing Act, are expressly excluded and may not be validly referred to arbitration.

The principle of competence-competence – the arbitral tribunal's power to decide on its own jurisdiction – is widely acknowledged and provided for under Section 592 ACCP. Austrian arbitration law expressly stipulates that the decision on jurisdiction can be made either jointly with the ruling on the merits or by a separate arbitral award (an arbitral tribunal may not render its decision on jurisdiction in the form of a procedural order). If the jurisdictional question is factually and legally detached from any decision on the merits, this often results in a bifurcation of the proceedings and hence leads to a separate award that may be challenged before the Supreme Court like any other award.

Unlike Article 16 UNCITRAL Model Law, the separability doctrine is not expressly enshrined in the ACCP. This doctrine refers to the principle that an arbitration agreement is at the outset treated as separate from the underlying contract in which it is contained, or to which it refers. The doctrine of separability is widely accepted by Austrian scholars, although it has only been applied on a case-by-case basis by the state courts. In most cases, the Austrian Supreme Court has confirmed that the invalidity or voidness of the main contract does not automatically result in the invalidity or voidness of the arbitration agreement. Austrian law approaches the issue of separability as a matter of contract interpretation. Which disputes are covered by an arbitration agreement must be determined on the basis of the scope of the arbitration agreement and interpreted in accordance with the intention of the parties.

Joinder of third parties and consolidation of proceedings are not expressly governed by statutory provisions of the Austrian arbitration law. However, where parties have agreed to apply the Vienna Rules, Articles 14 and 15 provide a clear and comprehensive framework in relation to these aspects. A joinder may be requested at any stage of the proceedings by either party or by the third party to be joined. The decision on whether the request is granted, and to what extent it is within the discretion of the arbitral tribunal, whereby the tribunal has to hear the parties to the arbitration and the third party to be joined, unless the latter submitted the request itself. Consolidation of two or more proceedings may be granted, provided that the place of arbitration is the same for all proceedings. Moreover, unless the same arbitrators have been appointed to serve in all relevant proceedings, all parties must consent to the consolidation. The request for consolidation is decided upon by the VIAC Board. The Board has to hear – by way of written submissions – all parties to the proceedings to be consolidated as well as the arbitrators that have already been appointed, considering all relevant circumstances, as for instance, the stage of the respective proceedings and the compatibility of the respective arbitration agreements.

Arbitration procedure

The ACCP does not contain a list of mandatory provisions and allows the parties to deviate from most of its provisions by agreement, for example, by reference to institutional arbitration rules. The statute uses wording such as "unless otherwise agreed", or "if nothing else has been agreed upon", and thereby clarifies that these provisions are within the disposition of the parties, and are therefore non-mandatory. Mandatory provisions comprise, for example: the right to be heard; the right to fair and equal treatment; the competence-competence of the arbitral tribunal; the parties' right to notification of the proceedings and of representation; the uneven number of arbitrators and a party's right to challenge an arbitrator; and provisions on actions for setting aside the award.

Apart from such mandatory provisions, parties are allowed to freely agree on the rules of the procedure. Where the parties have failed to determine the applicable procedural rules, the arbitral tribunal has wide discretion in the conduct of the proceedings. Where the parties have not agreed upon a specific substantive law, the arbitral tribunal has to apply such rules as it considers to be appropriate.

The same interplay between the principle of party autonomy and the arbitral tribunal's wide discretionary powers characterises the evidentiary procedure. Parties are free to agree on the applicability of the IBA Rules on the Taking of Evidence in International Arbitration. However, the parties' freedom to determine the rules of the proceedings is restricted by mandatory law authorising the arbitral tribunal to carry out the taking of evidence, to rule upon the admissibility of evidence and to freely evaluate its results.

Arbitral tribunals do not have any coercive powers. Where such coercive powers are necessary, an arbitral tribunal may request judicial assistance. Notably, a request for judicial assistance is not limited to the measures of enforcement existing under Austrian law. Rather, an arbitral tribunal may request the enforcement of any measure which does not violate Austrian public policy.

Thus, in principle, a court will enforce a tribunal's order against a third party to produce a document if the third party is under a civil law obligation to do so. An arbitral tribunal's request for court assistance regarding document production on the part of a party to the arbitration is, however, less likely to be granted, since it could lead to the party in question adversely affecting its own position in the proceedings.

As there is no express statutory regulation in the ACCP, in principle the parties are free to agree whether and to what extent an obligation exists to keep the proceedings themselves, and the documents pertaining to it, confidential. However, party autonomy in this regard is limited by the parties' rights to protect and/or pursue their rights and claims. Hence, a confidentiality agreement cannot restrict a party in relation to the initiation of enforcement proceedings, or to commence setting-aside proceedings even if these proceedings are public, as is the case in Austria. If the parties have not concluded an express agreement concerning the duty to keep the proceedings confidential, it is questionable whether the conclusion of an arbitration agreement implies such a duty. Austrian scholars are mainly of the opinion that such an implied duty of confidentiality has no basis in Austrian law. Hence, parties are well advised to include an explicit confidentiality agreement in their arbitration clause.

Arbitrators

In principle, parties are free to appoint whichever arbitrators they choose, and are not necessarily restricted to selecting lawyers. Whilst there are no statutory requirements regarding the qualification of an arbitrator, parties may agree on specific prerequisites, skills and qualifications which the arbitrator must meet. In principle, active Austrian state court judges are excluded from acting as arbitrators. Violation of this prohibition, however, has only disciplinary consequences and does not lead to the invalidity of the arbitration or the arbitral award. The ACCP does not comprise any rules on the use of administrative secretaries to arbitral tribunals. They are, however, frequently used to support the arbitral tribunal with administrative tasks; of course, no decision-making power may be delegated to the administrative secretary.

Naturally, arbitrators must be independent and impartial. Whether an arbitrator meets these criteria is decided by applying an objective third-party test. Prior to their appointment and throughout the proceedings, arbitrators are under the obligation to disclose any circumstance which may give rise to doubts as to their impartiality or independence (Section 588(1) ACCP). Although the IBA Guidelines on Conflict of Interest in International Arbitration do not have the force of law in Austria (or elsewhere), they are also taken into account in arbitration proceedings conducted in Austria.

If a party has doubts as to the arbitrator's impartiality or independence, it may challenge the arbitrator. In the absence of an alternative agreement, the deadline for challenging an arbitrator is four weeks from the constitution of the arbitral tribunal or the moment the challenging party became aware of the circumstances giving rise to doubts as to the arbitrator's impartiality or independence. (Section 589(2) ACCP.) Unless the arbitrator resigns from office or the other party agrees to the challenge, the arbitral tribunal including the challenged arbitrator is required to decide upon the challenge. If the challenge is unsuccessful, the challenging party may, within four weeks upon receiving the decision refusing the challenge, refer the case to the Austrian Supreme Court for its review. Only in disputes involving consumers, and in labour law disputes, are courts on the Regional Court level deemed competent. Whilst the challenge is pending with the Austrian Supreme Court, the arbitral tribunal, including the challenged arbitrator, may continue the proceedings and render an award (Section 589 (3) ACCP).

Under Austrian law, an arbitral tribunal must consist of an uneven number of arbitrators. Thus, where the office of a member of an arbitral tribunal is terminated before the proceedings end, a new arbitrator must be appointed. An arbitrator's office ends upon: (i) his or her death; (ii) a successful challenge; (iii) a voluntary resignation; (iv) whenever the parties jointly agree on the termination of his or her mandate; and (v) a decision of the Austrian Supreme Court that the arbitrator is unable to fulfil his or her duties, or to do so within a reasonable period of time (Section 590 ACCP).

Interim relief

Interim measures may only be ordered against a party to the arbitral proceedings and shall not interfere with the rights of third parties. For a request for interim or protective measures to be granted, such a measure must be necessary to avoid the frustration or considerable impediment of future enforcement proceedings, or the risk of irreparable harm. Further, the party against which the measures are directed must be heard.

The ACCP follows the UNCITRAL Model Law allowing parties to arbitral proceedings to request a state court to issue interim measures, even where the arbitral tribunal has already been constituted. This also applies if the seat of the arbitration is not within Austria. As this is a matter of mandatory law, parties may not validly waive their right to turn to a state court with a request for interim measures. As statutory provisions grant such powers also to the arbitral tribunal, parties to arbitral proceedings are free to choose the forum for their application.

However, since arbitral tribunals have no coercive powers, once granted but not complied with, interim measures may only be enforced by the competent district courts. Thus, even though arbitral tribunals have the authority to grant interim or protective measures of types which are unknown under Austrian law, at the enforcement stage, state courts may have to adapt the interim relief granted to enforcement measures known under Austrian law which closest reflect the measures ordered by the tribunal.

Arbitral award

Since the ACCP does not set time limits for rendering the final award, parties are free to agree on a maximum duration. The parties may, for example, agree on an expedited procedure under the Vienna Rules. This provides that a final award shall be rendered within six months starting from the transfer of the file to the arbitral tribunal.

The arbitral award must be in writing and signed by the arbitral tribunal. Where an arbitrator is prevented from signing the award, it is sufficient if the award is signed by the majority of the members of the arbitral tribunal (a note written on the award itself must explain the reasons for any missing signature). The award must indicate the seat of the arbitration and the date on which it was issued. Until recently, it was the prevailing opinion among Austrian scholars that an award that is not reasoned, although unlawful, does not permit the challenging of the award. In a fairly recent decision of the Austrian Supreme Court it was held, however, that an award may be challenged if its reasoning is incomprehensible from an objective viewpoint, or if it contains phrases which are meaningless within their respective context.

Remedies possibly granted by the arbitral tribunal depend on the parties' agreement. As a result, arbitrators are not limited by Austrian arbitration law when choosing remedies. In principle, arbitrators are vested with wide-reaching powers to grant any form of relief. However, an arbitral tribunal seated in Austria arguably may not grant any form of punitive damages, as such an award may possibly violate public policy.

The decision on costs must be made in the form of a separate award or together with the final award. Besides the outcome of the arbitral proceedings, the arbitrators may take into account other circumstances which had an impact on the course of the proceedings. Thus, while generally the principle "costs follow the event" applies, tribunals are free to exercise discretion in determining to what extent either party shall bear the costs.

Although the ACCP is silent on issues regarding interest on the principal claim, it is recognised that arbitral tribunals have the power to award interest. Under Austrian law, this aspect is a question of substantive, not procedural law. As a result, the parties' right to, and the amount of, interest is governed by the law applicable to the substance of the dispute.

Challenge of the arbitral award

Section 611 ACCP allows for a very narrow scope of judicial control of arbitral awards where the seat of arbitration is in Austria. Such control is limited to an exhaustive list of grounds. Austrian courts are not allowed to conduct a *révision au fond* of an arbitral award, meaning that courts cannot revise the legal and factual basis of the arbitral tribunal's decision. Parties may not validly agree to waive grounds for setting aside or to expand the scope of grounds. The ACCP limits the extent to which an award may be challenged even further than the UNCITRAL Model Law, by excluding mere violations of the arbitral procedure as agreed by the parties.

The following types of grounds require party action to set aside the award:

- grounds concerning the right to be heard;
- grounds concerning the scope of the arbitration agreement;
- grounds concerning the arbitral tribunal;
- procedural *ordre public*; and
- certain grounds which, in state court proceedings, are required for a revision of a court judgment to re-open the court proceedings.

Grounds based on the substantive *ordre public* and grounds concerning objective arbitrability may be invoked by the parties as well as *ex officio* by the courts.

Since January 2014, the Austrian Supreme Court is the first and final instance to hear and decide upon challenges of arbitral awards. Generally, an action to set aside an arbitral award may be filed within three months starting from the day on which the award is served upon the party acting as claimant in the annulment proceedings. A different time period must be observed where the ground invoked for setting aside an award is based on Section 611(2) No. 6 ACCP. This provision refers to provisions where an appeal for resumption against a judgment of a state court can be filed. In this case, the time period within which the action for setting aside the award must be brought has to be determined in accordance with the respective provisions on the action for resumption. Thus, in such cases, the time period requirements as set out by the respective provisions governing the re-opening of state court proceedings apply to challenges based on Section 611(2) No. 6 ACCP, and not the general time period requirement of three months.

In case an award is successfully challenged, it is set aside *ex tunc*. According to Section 584(4) ACCP, if an award is set aside due to the arbitral tribunal's lack of jurisdiction, the statute of limitations remains interrupted provided the claim is immediately brought before the competent forum. The party challenging the award may request the postponement of the enforcement of the award. If the setting-aside procedure is successful, the enforcement must be discontinued.

In addition to the grounds listed above, Articles 617 and 618 ACCP provide for grounds to set aside an arbitral award which apply only to consumer arbitration and to certain employment disputes. Such grounds concern violations of mandatory law, lack of written advice on the differences between arbitration and litigation before consenting to arbitration on the part of the consumer/employee, and further grounds which would justify re-opening state court proceedings.

Enforcement of the arbitral award

If the seat of arbitration is in Austria, the award is "domestic" and may be enforced like any other judgment by a state court. If the seat of arbitration is outside Austria, the arbitral award is "foreign" and subject to recognition and enforcement under the New York Convention. The applicant for enforcement of a foreign award must seek a declaration of enforcement (*exequatur*) and an authorisation for enforcement.

The party seeking a declaration and an authorisation for enforcement must provide the court with the arbitral award and – if so requested by the competent court – the arbitration agreement and certified translations thereof. The court that grants the enforcement authorisation will not review any legal matters relating to the arbitration proceedings, but will only examine certain form requirements, with the exception that the grounds for setting aside an award due to the lack of objective arbitrability and the violation of Austrian substantive public policy have to be examined *ex officio* and might ultimately lead to the denial of enforcement.

The competence to issue a declaration of enforceability and an enforcement authorisation rests with the district court in whose territorial jurisdiction the opposing party has its seat or domicile, or where immovable or movable assets against which enforcement is sought are located. The first instance district court decision is an *ex parte* court order, i.e. made without holding a hearing or hearing the opposing party. In principle, the decision may be appealed by both parties within four weeks.

It is important to note that even where a foreign arbitral award has been set aside at the seat of the arbitration on grounds of public policy, Austrian courts would not automatically refuse enforcement but would examine the grounds on their own.

Investment arbitration

Austria is a party to more than 60 bilateral investment treaties (**BITs**): 2015 saw the first and, to date, only investment treaty claim brought against the Republic of Austria. In this case, the majority shareholder of an Austrian bank sought redress for damages allegedly caused through state court proceedings and investigations involving the bank and some of its executives. The claim was rejected by the ICSID tribunal on the basis that it lacked jurisdiction to hear the dispute.

Austrian companies, on the other hand, have made more frequent use of the country's BITs. In total, 20 investor-state arbitrations have been initiated by Austrian investors, 11 of which are still pending. Notably, the finance sector accounts for approximately one quarter of these claims. In fact, all four ICSID cases introduced by Austrian investors in 2017 concern the finance sector. Twelve of the Austrian BITs are intra-EU BITs, i.e. investment agreements with other Member States of the European Union. The status of these BITs is subject to considerable debate: the European Commission has, on multiple occasions, expressed its view that such treaties are in conflict with the EU single market, as they afford special protection to citizens of the respective BIT signatories, excluding investors from all other EU Member States. On this basis, the Commission has initiated infringement proceedings against five Member States, including Austria, over the termination of their respective intra-EU BITs. These proceedings remain pending.

In parallel, the European Court of Justice has been requested to issue a preliminary ruling on investor-state dispute settlement provisions in intra-EU BITs and their compatibility with EU law. In its landmark decision of 6 March 2018, the Court declared the investor-state arbitration clause in a BIT between the Netherlands and Slovakia to be incompatible with EU law on the basis of its "adverse effect on the autonomy of EU law". Although the full implications of the Court's judgment are yet to be seen, it is expected to have wide repercussions on intra-EU BITs and investor-state dispute settlement in general.

In April 2016, Austria, Germany, Finland, France and the Netherlands submitted a so-called "non-paper" to the Council of the European Union, suggesting a compromise solution in the form of a single agreement between all EU Member States. The proposal foresees a phasing-out of existing intra-EU BITs, followed by appropriate investment protection through other means. Such means to protect intra-EU investment could either involve conferring jurisdiction to hear investment disputes to the European Court of Justice or, alternatively, establishing an entirely new system for investment protection, modelled after the Unified Patent System. As a third alternative, the "non-paper" suggests relying on the Permanent Court of Arbitration to administer intra-EU investor-state disputes, based on a special agreement concluded between all EU Member States. Whether any of these proposed solutions will become reality remains to be seen.

Dr. Christian W. Konrad
Tel: +43 1 512 95 00 / Email: c.konrad@konrad-partners.com
Dr. Christian W. Konrad is the Founding Partner of Konrad & Partners, an international law firm offering comprehensive legal services in the area of dispute resolution, with a particular focus on international commercial and investment arbitration. He has represented international organisations and businesses in a broad range of arbitration and litigation disputes. The disputes involved long-term energy contracts, complex construction contracts, concession agreements, entitlement to natural resources, immunity from jurisdiction, infrastructure projects, as well as mergers and acquisitions. He regularly advises clients on the protection of their investments and on the enforcement of arbitral awards and court judgments. Dr. Konrad frequently acts as arbitrator, is a fellow of the Chartered Institute of Arbitrators and a member of the panels of various arbitration institutions worldwide. Dr. Konrad serves as Vice-President of the Kosovo Permanent Tribunal of Arbitration.

Dr. Heidrun Halbartschlager
Tel: +43 1 512 95 00 / Email: h.halbartschlager@konrad-partners.com
Dr. Heidrun Halbartschlager is a Senior Associate at Konrad & Partners, an international law firm offering comprehensive legal services in the area of dispute resolution with a particular focus on international commercial arbitration. She has represented clients in disputes governed by various substantive and procedural laws and has acted as counsel in *ad hoc*, as well as institutional arbitrations including under the ICC, LCIA and VIAC Rules and has also represented clients in contentious proceedings before national courts. She has advised companies across a broad range of commercial and industrial sectors including energy, construction and telecommunications. Dr. Halbartschlager has additionally advised clients on the recognition, enforcement and setting aside of arbitral awards in a variety of jurisdictions.

Konrad & Partners

Rotenturmstrasse 13, 1010 Vienna, Austria
Tel: +43 1 512 95 00 / Fax: +43 1 512 95 00 95 / URL: www.konrad-partners.com

Belgium

Vanessa Foncke & Sébastien Champagne
Jones Day

Introduction

Due to the early adoption of industrialisation, its central location and highly skilled work force, Belgium has always been an attractive nation to trade with. Its economy today is mostly service-based, but many industries are still active in Belgium, such as steel, textile, chemicals, pharmaceuticals, automobiles, electronics and IT. Those industries rely heavily on imports of raw materials. In turn, exports account for over two-thirds of Belgian GNP.

It is, therefore, not surprising that Belgium has a strong tradition of implementing measures to reinforce its position as a reliable trade partner and to stimulate international trade. Most notably, Brussels is the capital of the EU and home to many international institutions. Over time, this has allowed Belgium and Brussels to develop into the international business hubs they are today.

The Belgian legislation and customs in relation to arbitration reflect this tendency. Belgium has had modern arbitration legislation in place since 1972 and parties generally face few problems when enforcing arbitration agreements and arbitral awards through the Belgian courts.

As a result, arbitration in Belgium and/or involving Belgian parties has flourished and has become the most common method of dispute resolution in M&A and other large international business transactions and projects.

The Belgian arbitration community has evolved along with the market, with a growing number of Brussels-based law firms having dedicated and sophisticated arbitration teams. Belgium is also home to a vast base of experienced, multilingual and internationally acclaimed arbitrators.

To consolidate the growth of recent years, the Belgian arbitration legislation was entirely replaced by a new Arbitration Act in 2013 (inserted in Part VI of the Belgian Civil Procedure Code), which is based on the UNCITRAL Model Law and is entirely in line with modern international practice.

Legislative framework

The Belgian Arbitration Act in Part VI of the Civil Procedure Code ("BAA") is applicable to all arbitration proceedings initiated on or after 1 September 2013, where the seat of arbitration is located in Belgium. Parties to foreign arbitrations may also expressly choose to apply the BAA, regardless of the seat of arbitration. Some of the provisions of the BAA, most notably the provisions on the *exceptio arbitri*, interim relief by the state courts and recognition and enforcement of arbitral awards, are applicable whenever such issues are brought before a Belgian court.

The key objectives of the reform were to:

- make arbitration more efficient;
- provide more flexibility to the parties;
- limit court intervention; and
- centralise arbitration-related litigation before a limited number of courts, mostly deciding on expedited proceedings.

The BAA is a close rendition of the UNCITRAL Model Law on International Commercial Arbitration, and as such does not make a distinction between domestic and international arbitrations.

The structure of the BAA mirrors the structure of the Model Law and adds one chapter on time limitations:

- general provisions (Art. 1676-1680);
- arbitration agreement (Art. 1681-1683);
- composition of the arbitral tribunal (Art. 1684-1689);
- jurisdiction of the arbitral tribunal (Art. 1690-1698);
- conduct of the arbitration (Art. 1699-1709);
- the arbitral award and closing of the proceedings (Art. 1710-1715);
- challenge of the arbitration award (Art. 1716-1718);
- recognition and enforcement of arbitral awards (Art. 1719-1721); and
- statute of limitations (Art. 1722).

An English translation of the BAA is available on the website of CEPANI at http://www.cepani.be/en/arbitration/belgian-judicial-code-provisions.

In addition, arbitration in Belgium may be governed by a number of multilateral and bilateral treaties. If and when a treaty is applicable, its provisions supersede the BAA. Most notably, it concerns:

- the Geneva Convention of 26 September 1927 on the Execution of Foreign Awards;
- the New York Convention of 10 June 1958 on the Recognition and Enforcement of Foreign Arbitral Awards (but application in Belgium subject to reciprocity);
- the European Convention of 21 April 1961 on International Commercial Arbitration; and
- bilateral enforcement and recognition treaties with France, Germany, Switzerland, the Netherlands and Austria.

Arbitration institutions and *ad hoc* arbitration

While *ad hoc* arbitration still occurs frequently, the majority of arbitrations in Belgium are administered by arbitral institutions.

There are a number of arbitral institutions in Belgium, the leading institution being CEPANI, the Belgian Centre for Arbitration and Mediation. CEPANI was founded in 1969 by the Federation of Belgian Enterprises and the Belgian National Committee of the International Chamber of Commerce and currently is the most widely used and most sophisticated arbitral institution in the country. The CEPANI Arbitration Rules have been redrafted in 2013 at the inception of the new BAA and remain largely inspired by the ICC Arbitration Rules.

Belgian parties regularly also opt for arbitration under the ICC Arbitration Rules. A choice of other arbitral institutions, such as NAI, DIS, LCIA and VIAC, is less common but not unheard of.

Finally, there are a number of other, typically sectoral or regional, arbitration institutions (e.g., for rental disputes, in the diamond industry and in the grains and seeds industry).

Arbitration agreement

Definition

An arbitration agreement within the meaning of the BAA is "*an agreement by the parties to submit to arbitration all or certain disputes which have arisen or which may arise between them in respect of a defined legal relationship, whether contractual or not*". That is a verbatim adoption of Art. 7 of the Model Law.

Formalities in relation to the arbitration agreement

Like all agreements under Belgian law, arbitration agreements require: (i) a valid object; (ii) a valid cause; (iii) parties that are capable to contract; and (iv) valid consent. There are no further requirements or formalities in relation to arbitration agreements. In particular, it is no longer required that an arbitration agreement is evidenced in writing. That approach deviates from Art. II of the New York Convention, but is permissible under the more favourable law provision of Art. VII of that Convention.

Arbitrability

An arbitration agreement can only be enforced if the subject matter thereof is arbitrable. In that respect, the new BAA has put in place a two-step test for arbitrability:

(i) Does the dispute involve a monetary claim?

(ii) If not, could the dispute be validly settled by the parties?

Only disputes that fall under neither of these two criteria are not arbitrable.

Exceptions to this step may still derive from specific legislation. For instance, the following disputes are in principle not arbitrable under Belgian law, or only under certain limitations: most employment claims; disputes concerning exclusive distributorship contracts; consumer rights disputes; and most insurance disputes. For most of those exceptions, the arbitrability issue only applies where the arbitration agreement was entered into prior to the emergence of the dispute, and parties are usually free to refer a dispute to arbitration once the dispute has arisen.

Public entities can, in principle, take recourse to arbitration, but only under certain circumstances.

Kompetenz-Kompetenz and severability

When a claim is governed by a valid arbitration agreement, the Belgian courts must decline jurisdiction. However, the courts cannot raise the existence of an arbitration agreement *ex officio*. The fact that a dispute is pending before the courts despite the existence of an arbitration agreement, does not prevent ongoing arbitration proceedings from moving forward and does not limit the right to initiate new arbitration proceedings.

In accordance with the principle of '*Kompetenz-Kompetenz*', the arbitral tribunal shall decide on challenges to its jurisdiction. Such challenges must, at the latest, be raised in the first written submission of the objecting party. The arbitral tribunal's decision that it has jurisdiction may only be contested together with the award on the merits.

The principle of severability of the arbitration clause is also enshrined in the BAA. Hence, the invalidity or nullity of the agreement in which the arbitration clause is embedded shall not affect the validity of the arbitration clause.

Joinder of third parties and consolidation of proceedings

Under the BAA, third parties may join or may be joined to an existing arbitration, provided that all parties and the arbitral tribunal agree on the joinder.

The point of departure is different in relation to consolidation. As there are no provisions in the BAA pertaining to consolidation, a tribunal will not have the power to so order unless the parties agree to that effect. Such agreement may follow from the institutional rules that the parties have chosen.

Arbitration procedure

Procedural rules in the BAA

The BAA provides a set of procedural rules which apply in cases where the parties have not made other arrangements. These statutory procedural rules do not apply if and to the extent the parties have opted for the rules of an arbitral institution.

However, the BAA provisions on impartiality and independence of the tribunal, equality of the parties and the right to be heard are mandatory in all cases.

Seat of arbitration

If the parties did not agree on a seat of arbitration, it is for the arbitral tribunal to determine the place of arbitration, taking into account all the facts and circumstances of the case before them. If the tribunal does not determine the seat of arbitration, the place in which the award is rendered is deemed to be the seat of the arbitration.

The seat of arbitration is merely a legal concept and does not prevent the tribunal from conducting hearings or other procedural activities elsewhere. The main purpose of the seat is to determine the applicable *lex arbitri*. As mentioned above, the BAA is applicable when the seat of arbitration is located in Belgium.

Applicable law

The parties have wide discretion as to the applicable law on the merits. They may select the laws of a particular country or another body of law (e.g., the UNIDROIT principles). They may also allow the tribunal to decide as an *amiable compositeur* or *ex aequo et bono*. The choice for a specific national law does not include the private international law of that jurisdiction.

In the absence of choice by the parties, the tribunal may apply the law it considers most appropriate.

In any event, the arbitral tribunal must decide in accordance with the terms of the agreement in contractual disputes, and with any trade usages when the parties involved are commercial entities.

Commencement of arbitration

The commencement date of the arbitration is the date on which the request for arbitration is communicated, in accordance with Art. 1678 of the Civil Procedure Code. The commencement of the arbitration interrupts the statute of limitations for the underlying claims. The arbitration rules selected by the parties may add requirements for the valid commencement of the arbitration (e.g., payment of a filing fee).

Evidence

The parties and/or the tribunal have wide discretion as to the rules of evidence they wish to apply. Most commonly, the IBA Rules on the taking of evidence in international arbitration are applied.

(a) *Document production*

Belgium is a civil law jurisdiction and there is no common law style (pre-trial) discovery, disclosure or other far-reaching document production before the Belgian courts. The production of specific documents before the Belgian courts can only be obtained in accordance with the conditions set out in Art. 877 of the Civil Procedure Code and this usually excludes requests for categories of documents.

In arbitration, the BAA allows a tribunal to order the production of documents without further qualifications. Arbitral tribunals can and regularly do order the production of (categories of) documents which, in the same circumstances, probably could not be obtained through the courts. Usually, such orders are based on the aforementioned IBA Rules.

Contrary to arbitral tribunals, Belgian courts also have the power to order third parties to produce certain documents on the basis of Art. 877 of the Civil Procedure Code.

(b) *Witness evidence*

While written witness statements are frequently encountered, oral witness evidence remains highly exceptional before the Belgian civil courts, notably because the Civil Procedure Code puts forward onerous procedural requirements in that regard.

This is in stark contrast with the practice that has developed in arbitration in Belgium and that has left questions of witness evidence largely to party autonomy and/or the tribunal's discretion. The new BAA reaffirmed the existing practice and included a few additional provisions aimed at further enhancing the parties' and tribunal's discretion in this respect. For instance, the BAA now specifically provides that "any person" may be heard by the tribunal, whereas the previous arbitration act still distinguished between parties (and their representatives) and witnesses *sensu stricto*.

The new BAA also abolished the requirement that unwilling witnesses be deposed by the courts only: a witness can now still only be compelled to give testimony by court order, but the courts may order the witness in question to appear directly before the tribunal.

(c) *Expert evidence*

The arbitral tribunal may appoint (*ex officio* or upon party request) experts to report on specific issues of a technical or factual nature. The tribunal cannot delegate legal questions to an expert and, in any event, the expert's opinion shall only serve as a non-binding advice to the tribunal. The parties may exclude the tribunal's power to order an expert appraisal.

The parties may request or the tribunal may order *ex officio* that the expert witness(es) attend the hearing and be subjected to questioning.

Experts can be challenged in much the same way as arbitrators (see below).

Language

Contrary to the courts, arbitral tribunals are not bound by Belgium's strict language laws. The parties can freely agree on the language(s) of the proceedings and evidence submitted in another language is not automatically considered inadmissible. However, the tribunal may require the parties to provide a translation with each piece of evidence that is not in the language(s) of the proceedings.

Confidentiality

There is no express provision in the BAA on the confidentiality of arbitration proceedings. Parties, however, often include confidentiality obligations in the underlying agreement or in the terms of reference. Some institutional arbitration rules (such as Art. 25 of the CEPANI Rules) also provide for confidentiality obligations in the absence of an agreement between the parties.

Arbitrators

Appointment

Parties are free to determine the number of arbitrators, provided that the tribunal is composed of an odd number of arbitrators. In the absence of an agreement between the parties, a tribunal will be composed of three arbitrators.

Parties are also free to agree upon the procedure for the appointment of arbitrators, provided that the independence and impartiality of the arbitrators is guaranteed. Absent agreement, the parties can each appoint one arbitrator, and both party-appointed arbitrators elect the president of the tribunal.

If the parties cannot agree on a sole arbitrator, a party fails to appoint an arbitrator, or the party-appointed arbitrators cannot agree on a presiding arbitrator, the court may appoint such arbitrator(s) at the request of one the parties.

Arbitrator challenges

Once an arbitrator is nominated, he or she must communicate all circumstances which give rise to justifiable doubts as to his or her independence and impartiality. An arbitrator can only be challenged if such justifiable doubts exist, or when he or she does not fulfil the contractual requirements the parties have agreed upon (e.g., nationality, profession, experience, etc.). A party cannot challenge the appointment of the arbitrator it nominated on grounds which that party was aware of at the time of appointment.

The BAA does not provide guidance on what constitutes justifiable doubts that could give rise to an arbitrator challenge. In practice, most parties resort to the IBA Guidelines on conflicts of interest.

The parties are free to agree upon a procedure for arbitrator challenges, but usually opt for the mechanism provided by the applicable institutional arbitration rules. Absent such agreement or applicable rules, the BAA provides that the party wishing to bring a challenge must do so within 15 calendar days from the arbitrator's appointment, or from the moment that party became aware of the circumstances giving rise to justifiable doubt concerning the arbitrator's independence and/or impartiality. The arbitrator in question is then given the opportunity to step down within 10 days. If he or she refuses to step down, the challenging party has 10 days to submit its challenge to the court, which will decide in summary proceedings. The court's decision is not open to appeal.

Arbitrator challenges cannot be used as a dilatory tactic, because the BAA explicitly provides that the arbitral proceedings continue (and an award can be rendered) pending a decision by the court on the challenge.

Termination of the arbitrator's mandate

The arbitrator's mandate comes to an end upon termination of the arbitral proceedings, i.e.

signature and notification of the final award either exhausting the tribunal's jurisdiction or ordering the closing of the proceedings, in case of claimant's withdrawal of the claim or the parties' agreement to close the proceedings. However, the tribunal may be requested to resume its mandate in order to correct or interpret the award or to remedy an annulment ground in the award.

The arbitrator's mandate will also automatically terminate upon expiry of the deadline (agreed between the parties, set by the arbitration institution or imposed by the court) to render the arbitral award.

Arbitrator immunity

Arbitrators may be held liable under Belgian law. They cannot, however, be held liable for errors in law. In addition, most institutional rules provide for some form of immunity.

Tribunal secretaries

The BAA does not contain any particular provisions in relation to tribunal secretaries. When a secretary to the tribunal is appointed, typically either the guidelines provided by the chosen arbitration institution or the internationally established best practices are applied.

Interim relief

Absent contrary agreement between the parties, interim relief can be obtained both before the state courts and before the tribunal (i.e. either the tribunal deciding on the merits or an emergency arbitrator if no tribunal has yet been constituted and the institutional rules provide for emergency arbitration). Seeking interim relief before the state courts does not amount to a violation, nor a waiver of the arbitration agreement.

An arbitral tribunal may order any interim or conservatory measure it considers appropriate. There are, however, three limitations; a tribunal may not order: (i) *ex parte* interim relief; (ii) attachment or freezing orders; and (iii) measures binding upon third parties. Aside from those three exceptions, there are no limitations on the type of interim relief a tribunal may order or the timing thereof. The tribunal may also amend, suspend or terminate an interim or conservatory measure, even if such measure was initially ordered by the state courts.

Interim measures may include (but are not limited to) security for costs, the payment of a preliminary sum of money, the continued performance of a contract pending the proceedings, the preservation of property or evidence, injunctions, etc. A tribunal also has the power to reinforce its interim decisions by ordering accessory penalty payments in case of non-compliance.

Awards granting interim relief are declared immediately enforceable upon application to the courts by the enforcing party. The courts do not have the power to review the merits of the interim relief which has been granted by the tribunal.

Arbitral award

Formal requirements

Arbitral awards must be made in writing and must be signed by the members of the tribunal. The BAA has made explicit provisions to accommodate truncated tribunals where necessary. In principle, awards must be signed by all arbitrators, but a signature from the majority of the arbitrators suffices if the reason for the omitted signature is stated.

At least the following elements must be mentioned: names and domiciles of all parties and arbitrators; the place of arbitration; the date the award is rendered; and the subject matter of the dispute.

Substantively, all awards must be reasoned. The parties cannot discharge the tribunal from its obligation to state the reasons on which its decision is based.

Awards must be notified to the parties as soon as they have been rendered. The deadline for initiating annulment proceedings starts running as of the date of notification of the award. The requirement that an award must be deposited with the competent court of first instance of the place of arbitration has been abolished.

Arbitration costs

In principle, costs can be recovered by the prevailing party, in full or in part, as the tribunal considers appropriate. The tribunal has the widest possible discretion. Usually, a costs-follow-the-event approach is taken, also taking into account the conduct of the parties. The parties may agree in advance on the allocation and/or distribution of arbitration costs.

No costs are *a priori* non-recoverable. Unless agreed otherwise, the costs typically include arbitrator fees and expenses, counsel and representative fees and expenses, costs relating to evidence, institution fees and costs, etc.

Correction, interpretation and additional award

The BAA provides for a possibility to rectify calculation, typographical or other material mistakes in an award.

In addition, if the parties agree to make such a request, a tribunal which has rendered a final award may be requested to reconvene in order to clarify or interpret certain aspects of the award which the parties consider ambiguous.

Finally, the rendering of an additional award may be requested if the tribunal omitted certain claims from its award.

All three of these requests must be made within one month after the notification of the award.

Challenge of the arbitral award

Grounds for annulment

The annulment grounds in the BAA are subdivided into grounds which the court can raise *ex officio* and grounds that must be invoked by the party wishing to obtain annulment.

Annulment can be obtained if, and only if:

(i) the party making the application demonstrates that:
- the arbitration agreement is invalid;
- the rights of defence were violated;
- the award deals with a dispute not provided for in, or not falling within, the terms of the arbitration agreement;
- the award is not reasoned;
- irregularities occurred in the composition of the arbitral tribunal;
- the arbitral tribunal has exceeded its powers; or

(ii) the Court of First Instance finds that:
- the subject-matter of the dispute is not capable of settlement by arbitration;

- the award violates public policy; or
- the award was obtained fraudulently.

Additional hurdles to annulment

An important limitation on annulment claims is that parties may not file for annulment if they were aware of the annulment ground during the arbitration yet did not raise it at that point in time.

Furthermore, where irregularities can still be remedied by reconvening the arbitral tribunal, the court may suspend the annulment proceedings to allow the arbitral tribunal to resume the arbitral proceedings or to take such other action as, in the latter's opinion, will eliminate the annulment grounds.

Annulment procedure

The parties may file for annulment before the competent court of first instance of the place of arbitration, within three months after the notification of the award and provided that no other form of recourse before the tribunal (e.g., correction, interpretation, contractual appeal mechanism) is possible. There is no appeal against the decision of the court of first instance on the annulment application. Only a Supreme Court recourse may be possible.

To avoid delaying ongoing arbitration proceedings, tribunal decisions affirming jurisdiction can only be challenged together with the award on the merits.

The interplay between full annulment claims and opposition against an enforcement order has recently also been regulated. If a party challenges an enforcement order (rendered *ex parte* at the request of the enforcing party – see below), yet also wishes to have the award annulled, the annulment action must be brought together with the opposition against the enforcement order. This is to avoid the defendant having two chances to avoid an unfavourable award, potentially even before different judges. Annulment proceedings on the occasion of an enforcement order will only be possible if the three-month period for an annulment claim has not yet lapsed.

Exclusion of annulment possible for non-Belgian parties

Non-Belgian parties may exclude annulment proceedings by way of an express agreement.

Third party annulment

A recent decision by the Belgian Constitutional Court has granted third parties the right to also initiate third party annulment proceedings, provided that they have an interest in the outcome of the arbitration. Third parties have such a right in relation to Belgian court judgments and the Constitutional Court ruled that the absence of the same right in relation to arbitral awards constituted discrimination.

Enforcement of the arbitral award

Ex parte proceedings to obtain an enforcement order

Enforcement of arbitral awards in Belgium is subject to exequatur proceedings before the Belgian courts. Such proceedings are conducted *ex parte*, at the request of the party wishing to enforce an award. The court must declare an award enforceable unless it determines that one of the three abovementioned *ex officio* grounds for annulment is applicable.

The competent court will be the court of first instance of the place of the arbitration if the award was rendered in Belgium. Only the courts of first instance where there is also a court of appeal are competent in arbitration matters, i.e. the courts of Ghent, Antwerp, Brussels, Mons and Liège. If the award was rendered abroad, the competent court will be determined by the domicile or place of business of the defendant. In the absence of such a domicile or place of business in Belgium, the courts of the effective place of enforcement will be competent.

Once the award is declared enforceable, the decision must be served upon the defendant. As from that moment onward, enforcement measures can be taken in accordance with Belgian procedural law, as if the award were a judgment rendered by a Belgian court. Merely conservatory measures, however, can be taken on the basis of an award which has not yet been declared enforceable.

Adversarial proceedings to challenge an enforcement order

Service of the enforcement decision upon the defendant starts the clock for opposition proceedings, which must be brought within one month. Those proceedings will, in contrast to the initial *ex parte* proceedings, be entirely adversarial. The decision of the court of first instance can only be challenged directly before the Belgian Supreme Court. The intermediary step of appeal before the courts of appeal has been abolished.

Grounds for refusal of enforcement

The grounds on which the defendant can oppose the enforceability decision are, broadly speaking, the same as the abovementioned annulment grounds. An additional ground for refusal exists when the arbitral award has, for some reason, not yet become binding upon the parties or has been annulled or suspended elsewhere.

The Belgian courts take a very pro-arbitration approach in enforcement matters. The grounds for annulment or enforceability are interpreted restrictively and annulments or refusals to enforce will usually only occur when serious procedural irregularities have taken place.

No distinction between domestic and foreign awards (subject to treaty application)

The enforcement regime is the same, whether the award was rendered abroad or in Belgium. However, where a (bilateral or multilateral) treaty applies between Belgium and the country in which the award was rendered, the treaty provisions will prevail over the general provisions of the BAA. Aside from the multilateral New York and Geneva Conventions, bilateral treaties exist with Germany, France, Switzerland, the Netherlands and Austria.

Investment arbitration

Belgium is a contracting state to the ICSID Convention and has signed over 60 BITs within the framework of the 'Belgo-Luxembourg Economic Union' (BLEU). Belgium is also a party to the Energy Charter Treaty. There is a specific regime applicable to the recognition and enforcement of ICSID awards, which deviates significantly from the general regime.

Only one investment arbitration has been initiated against Belgium so far. The claim for €871 million was brought in September 2012 by the Chinese insurance group Ping An, under the BLEU-China BITs of 1984 and 2005. Ping An had invested in the Belgian Fortis group and sought compensation over the Belgian government's bailout, nationalisation and sale of the Fortis group to BNP Paribas. The ICSID tribunal decided in 2015 that it lacked jurisdiction.

It should be noted that as a result of recent anti-vulture fund legislation, sovereign assets located in Belgium are generally not eligible for attachment measures unless: (i) the foreign state expressly and specifically agrees that the property in question is eligible for attachment; (ii) the property was earmarked by the sovereign state specifically for the satisfaction of the claim for which attachment is being pursued; or (iii) it is established that the property is specifically in use or intended by the foreign power for commercial purposes and the property in question is located in Belgium, and provided that the property in question relates to the entity against whom the underlying claim is directed.

The anti-vulture fund legislation most notably affects enforcement efforts in Belgium relating to the Yukos bankruptcy. The former Yukos shareholders had attempted to enforce the 2014 Yukos award against Russian assets located in Belgium and had obtained a number of attachment orders in June 2015. However, after the annulment of the underlying arbitral award by the Dutch courts in April 2016, the Belgian attachment orders against those assets were lifted in June 2017 (despite pending appeal against the Dutch annulment decision). Whereas the 2015 attachment orders escaped the anti-vulture fund legislation's temporal scope, any new attachment request will be subject to the new regime.

The constitutionality of the anti-vulture fund legislation was also challenged by the former Yukos shareholders, but the legislation was upheld by the Belgian Constitutional Court in its decision of 27 April 2017. In November 2017, the former Yukos shareholders announced that they would not seek further enforcement in Belgium.

Vanessa Foncke
Tel: +32 645 15 58 / Email: vfoncke@jonesday.com

Vanessa Foncke is a partner in the Global Dispute practice of Jones Day. She practises in all aspects of dispute resolution and contract negotiations. Her experience covers the representation of Belgian and foreign clients in a broad range of contractual and commercial disputes in all stages of court and administrative proceedings, and she also conducts internal compliance investigations.

Ms. Foncke also has extensive experience in domestic and international commercial arbitration both as counsel and arbitrator. She is a member of the board of administration and of the executive committee of CEPANI, the Belgian institution for arbitration and mediation. She is ranked in *Chambers Global* (Arbitration), *Chambers Europe* (Arbitration), *The Legal 500 EMEA* (Dispute Resolution) and *Who's Who Legal* (Arbitration).

Vanessa is a graduate of Ghent University (J.D. *magna cum laude*) and Columbia University (LL.M. James Kent Scholar; Fulbright Scholar). She is a member of the Flemish section of the Brussels Bar.

Sébastien Champagne
Tel: +32 645 15 20 / Email: schampagne@jonesday.com

Sébastien Champagne is a partner in the Global Dispute practice of Jones Day. He focuses on domestic and cross-border litigation, representing clients in complex commercial disputes, such as contractual, regulatory and competition disputes.

He represents major national and international corporations in pretrial negotiations and in litigation before judicial and administrative courts. His clients are active in various sectors, including the telecom, industrial equipment, transportation, and IT industries. He is also experienced in the drafting and negotiation of commercial and telecom-related agreements.

Sébastien is regularly active in arbitration as counsel or arbitrator. He is also a deputy judge at the French speaking Commercial Court of Brussels.

Sébastien is a graduate of the Catholic University of Louvain, Belgium (J.D. 1993) and New York University (M.C.J. 1994). He is a member of the French-speaking section of the Brussels Bar. He is annually endorsed for dispute resolution in *Chambers* and *The Legal 500*.

Jones Day

Regentschapsstraat 4, 1000 Brussels, Belgium
Tel: +32 2 645 14 11 / Fax: +32 2 645 14 45 / URL: www.jonesday.com

Brazil

Eduardo Maccari Telles, Gustavo Fernandes de Andrade & Daniel Becker
Tauil & Chequer Advogados in association with Mayer Brown

Introduction

Institutionalisation

Having been noted in a number of Brazilian legal compilations as far back as Article 160 (3) of the Constitution of 1824, arbitration has been a part of the country's justice system for almost 200 years. However, it was only as recently as 1996, through Law No. 9.307/96, the Brazilian Arbitration Act, that Brazil institutionalised arbitration. Furthermore, it was not until 2001 that the act was fully applied by a court; in a historic appeal of a foreign award of the Kingdom of Spain, No. 5206-8/247.5, the Brazilian Supreme Court ("STF") ruled that arbitration conformed to Article 5, item XXXV, of Brazil's Constitution of 1988 as an alternative dispute resolution method.

Jurisdiction

Brazil, a federative republic composed of 26 states and a federal district that is home to its capital, has only one federal law – the aforementioned act – dedicated to regulating arbitration throughout the territory.

Notably, the Brazilian Arbitration Law has been influenced by but not yet incorporated the UNCITRAL Model Law.

Recent changes

The Brazilian legal system entered into a new era of dispute resolution with legislation regarding alternative dispute resolution ("ADR") coming into force in 2015 with the enactment of the Mediation Act (Law No. 13.140/2015) and an amendment to the Arbitration Act (Law No. 13.129/2015) with several provisions that strengthen arbitration. The 2015 revisions:

- Introduced a very important concept: the arbitration letter. Its purpose is to facilitate the communications between arbitrators and judges by creating a standard method for the exchange of procedural orders and decisions between courts and arbitral tribunals.
- Set forth regulation of judicial assistance for arbitration, codifying the proceedings that used to be regulated solely by case law. For instance, the arbitrator is now legally authorised to revoke provisional measures granted by the courts before the arbitral tribunal is constituted.
- Introduced a provision that lawsuits related to arbitration proceedings may be processed under court secrecy in case it is proved that confidentiality has been provided in the arbitration clause.
- Outlined the public institution Brazilian National Council of Justice's ("CNJ") target that every capital city of the 26 Brazilian states establishes at least two lower courts specialising in arbitration-related disputes.

- Clarified certain aspects of the former Brazilian Arbitration Law, such as express authorisation of arbitration involving public entities. The only conditions imposed by the new legislation are that the proceedings are publicly conducted and in accordance with rules of Brazilian Law.
- Included a provision in Act No. 6.404/76, which regulates companies' activities, that allows the withdrawal of a shareholder who does not agree with the inclusion of the arbitration clause in the company bylaws.

Local bodies

There are a number of local arbitration bodies with headquarters in Brazil, such as the Business Chamber of Arbitration ("CAMARB"), the Brazilian Center of Mediation and Arbitration ("CBMA"), the International Chamber of Commerce ("ICC"), and the Chamber of Commerce Brazil-Canada ("CCBC"). Each of these institutions has its own set of procedural rules.

Going forward

During the past few decades, in large part due to the success of arbitration as an effective fast-track procedure, ADR methods have grown increasingly popular and significant in Brazil.

Now, with the aforementioned legal innovations and organisational structures helping to reduce transactional costs, speed up processes and resolve transnational disputes more effectively, Brazil has certainly started to attract more and more international arbitrations, consolidating its position as a safe and reliable neutral forum.

Arbitration agreement

Formalities

In Brazil, the arbitration agreement may be entered into either before (arbitration clause) or after the dispute arises (arbitration commitment). Whichever route the parties may take, the Brazilian Arbitration Act does not identify the elements of the arbitration agreement that will, one way or the other, put aside the state courts' jurisdiction on the matter and render it to the arbitral tribunal. It is important to highlight, however, that generally the arbitration agreement is set out in the contract that establishes the relationship between the parties.

The Brazilian legislation requires an arbitration clause to be in writing, and it may be inserted into the contract itself or into a separate document to which it refers. Furthermore, in subscription contracts, the clause will only be valid if the adhering party takes the initiative to initiate the arbitration proceeding or it expressly agrees with its initiation. Moreover, the clause must be included in an attached written document to contract or in boldface type, with a signature or special approval for that clause.

Additionally, arbitration agreements in general must contain: (i) the name, profession, marital status and domicile of the parties; (ii) the name, profession and domicile of the arbitrator or arbitrators, or, if applicable, the identification of the institution to which the parties have entrusted the appointment of the arbitrators; (iii) the subject matter of the arbitration; and (iv) the place where the award shall be rendered. In case any of the requirements are missing, the agreement will be deemed null and void.

Finally, the arbitration agreement may contain, if the parties wish: (i) the place or places where the arbitration will be held; (ii) if the parties agree, the provision authorising the arbitrators or arbitrators to decide on equity; (iii) the time limit for making of the arbitral award; (iv) an indication of national law or institutional rules applicable to the arbitration, if agreed upon by the parties; (v) a statement regarding responsibility for the fees and costs of the arbitral proceedings; and (vi) the fees of the arbitrator or arbitrators. These elements, however, are not requirements, and, in case they are missing from the arbitration agreement, it will still be valid and the arbitration procedure may still commence.

Scope and arbitrability

As in France and Portugal, the Brazilian Arbitration Law sets forth the transferability of property rights as the criteria for arbitrability. Therefore, those who are capable of entering into contracts may make use of arbitration to resolve conflicts regarding freely transferable property rights; that is, rights that can be freely disposed or traded, as the proprietor has full legal capacity to do so.

In this regard, it is important to note that the legislation provides that Public Bodies may also make use of arbitration in order to resolve their conflicts, just as long as they are related to transferable public property rights.

Generally speaking, if the matter does not pervasively involve public rights or infringes public policy, arbitrability rests assured. Hence, by way of example, family and succession law, as well as criminal law, are not subject to arbitration.

Consolidation or joinder of parties or claims

The Brazilian Arbitration law does not provide for consolidation of arbitration proceedings. Nonetheless, nothing prevents interested parties from presenting a request before the court that may order the consolidation of the proceedings, if all parties unequivocally consent.

From another point of view, no arbitral tribunal or state court has the jurisdiction to compel a third party who is not subject to the arbitration agreement to join a specific arbitral proceeding. Equally, the consolidation of arbitral proceedings can only be granted in cases in which all the parties expressly consent or if the possibility was provided for in the arbitration agreement entered into by the parties.

We only have notice of one single case related to the consolidation of arbitral proceedings in Brazil. In this case, the 19th Civil Chamber of Rio de Janeiro State Court of Justice ruled on the appeal filed by Consórcio Construtor Centro-Oeste – CCCO, Eit Empresa Industrial Técnica S/A – EIT, Energ Power S/A – ENERG and Themag Engenharia EW Gerenciamento Ltda. – THEMAG, that three arbitral proceedings must be consolidated as one. The consolidation was granted through a precautionary measure in which one of the interested parties requested an interim measure to suspend the three ongoing arbitral proceedings until a final decision was made on the consolidation issue, as the three arbitral proceedings had linked claims and if they were submitted to different arbitral tribunals, they could have conflicting awards.

On its ruling, the reporting judge emphasised the existence of a valid arbitral clause which transfers to the arbitrators the entire jurisdiction to decide the issues related to the disputed contracts. However, he pointed out that until the arbitral tribunal is set up, the parties are allowed to ask the courts to ensure a useful result of the arbitration, since the courts have a monopoly on the coercive power to determine measures such as the consolidation of linked arbitral claims. Moreover, the judge highlighted that the court had to intervene due to loopholes in the arbitral rules of the Fundação Getulio Vargas Conciliation and Arbitration Chamber – CCAFGV concerning consolidation before the arbitral tribunals are constituted, in order to ensure legal certainty and effectiveness of decisions. The one downside of seeking relief from a state court is that confidentiality of the matter was compromised at some level.

Separability and the tribunal's competence to determine its own jurisdiction

The principle of *kompetenz-kompetenz* is fully recognised in Brazil. As provided for in the Brazilian Arbitration Act in its Article 8, sole paragraph, the arbitral tribunal has jurisdiction to determine its own jurisdiction and to decide issues concerning the existence, validity and effectiveness of the arbitration agreement, as well as the contract containing the arbitration clause.

Coequally, the principle of separability is also applied in Brazil, as the Arbitration Act establishes in its Article 8 that the arbitration clause which forms part of a contract shall be treated as an agreement independent and separable of the other terms of the contract. Thus, a decision declaring that a contract is null and void does not necessarily mean that the arbitration clause is invalid.

Arbitration procedure

Commencement of the proceedings

The arbitration commences when the appointment is accepted by the sole arbitrator or by the last arbitrator of the tribunal. The Brazilian Arbitration Law does not impose any particular requirements with respect to the form of the arbitrators' acceptance of their appointments, it being incumbent on the parties to demonstrate the arbitrators' recognition of their assignment.

In this sense, it should be noted that the Brazilian Arbitration Law, incorporating the provision of Article 18 of the International Chamber of Commerce, determines that an addendum (Terms of Reference) can be drafted together with the parties, becoming an integral part of the arbitration agreement, in case the arbitration has already been commenced and the arbitrator or arbitration tribunal concludes there is a need to clarify a matter set forth in the arbitration agreement. The Business Chamber of Arbitration (or, as we will call it, "CAMARB") is an example of arbitral institution that incorporated this provision in its own regulation (item 6.1 of CAMARB's regulation), as it only allows the commencement of the arbitral proceedings after the signature, by the parties, of the terms of reference.

Place of arbitration and hearings

The seat of arbitration is the location selected as the place of arbitration and sets the procedural law governing the arbitration, that, as is well-known, may be different from the substantive law ruling the dispute. The choice of the seat of arbitration can be made in the arbitration agreement or selected on the parties' behalf by the arbitrators or arbitral institution.

Usually, the arbitrators will determine that the hearing will be held in the seat of the arbitration. Nevertheless, Brazilian Arbitration Act does not forbid that it takes place elsewhere, as it only states that the testimony of the parties and witnesses shall be taken at places, dates and hours previously communicated in writing to the parties, and that a written record of such testimony shall be signed by the party or witness, or at his request, also by the arbitrators.

Therefore, although we cannot say that it is common practice in Brazil, it is fair to admit, for example, the possibility of realising the hearing outside of the seat of arbitration, if the parties negotiate it in the arbitration agreement or an arbitration institution has its own set of rules for the matter.

Procedural rules regarding evidence

The Brazilian Arbitration Law determines that arbitrators must comply with the procedure agreed upon by the parties in the arbitration agreement, which may refer to the rules of an arbitral institution or specialised entity.

It is also possible for the parties to empower the sole arbitrator or the arbitral tribunal to regulate the procedure. In this case, the arbitral tribunal ought to conduct the arbitration however it considers appropriate, provided that it respects the principles of due process of law, equal treatment of the parties, impartiality of the arbitrator and freedom of decision.

Considering the possibility that the arbitration agreement is silent on the question, the internal regulations of the arbitral institutions often defer the choice of procedures to the arbitral tribunal.

In any event, the Brazilian Arbitration Law levels the arbitrators' powers with those conferred to the judges, meaning that the arbitral tribunal may rule on the production of any evidence it deems relevant, including expert evidence and hearing the parties' and witnesses' testimony. Therefore, in case the arbitrator dismisses the request for the production of specific evidence, it cannot be considered as an offence to contradictory or due process of law, as the sole arbitrator or the arbitral tribunal has the jurisdiction to freely decide on which evidence it considers important for the judgment of the claim.

In this sense, if an arbitrator is replaced during the arbitral procedure, the national arbitration law determines that the alternate, at his discretion, may even determine what evidence will be repeated.

In case a hearing date is established by the arbitral tribunal, if a party fails, without good cause, to comply with a request to render personal testimony, the arbitral tribunal has the competence to give due consideration to such behaviour when issuing the award; and if a witness, under the same conditions, is absent, the arbitrator or the chairman of the arbitral tribunal may request the state court to compel the appearance of the defaulting witness, upon evidence of the existence of an arbitration agreement.

Finally, in regard to expert evidences, even though its production is rather common in domestic and international proceedings in Brazil, there are no specific rules regarding the matter in the Arbitration Law. However, the parties are free to regulate its production on the arbitration agreement, taking into consideration any set of procedural rules they may see fit, such as the *IBA Rules on the Taking of Evidence in International Arbitration* or any other regulations from domestic and international arbitration institutions and courts. Most frequently, though, the party requesting the production of the expert evidence bears all of its costs.

<u>Privacy and confidentiality</u>

Although the Brazilian Arbitration Act is silent on confidentiality, the parties can address it expressly in the arbitration agreement, deciding its reach and applicable exceptions. Moreover, as previously mentioned, the relatively recent innovations in the Brazilian arbitration legislation included the provision that the lawsuits related to arbitration proceedings may be processed under judicial secrecy in case it be proved that confidentiality has been provided in the arbitration convention.

While our legislation does not address confidentiality directly, the inclusion of a privacy and confidentiality clause in the arbitration agreement is almost unanimous in Brazil.

Arbitrators

<u>Appointment of arbitrators</u>

In Brazil, any individual with legal capacity who is trusted by the parties may act as their arbitrator. Bearing this in mind, the parties, when elaborating the arbitration agreement, should choose the number of arbitrators that will compose the tribunal, and may mutually agree to set up a specific procedure for the appointment of arbitrators, or they may choose the rules of an arbitral institution or specialised entity.

By mutual agreement, the parties can choose not to be bound by the provision of the rules of an arbitral institution or specialised entity that requires the appointment of sole arbitrator, co-arbitrator, or chairman of the tribunal from the respective roaster of arbitrators. However, the arbitral institution's control over the appointment of arbitrators is preserved and in the event of impasse and with multiparty arbitration, the respective applicable institutional rules shall be observed.

Under the Brazilian Arbitration Act, an arbitrator may only be challenged if circumstances exist that give rise to justifiable doubts as to his or her impartiality, independence or discretion or if the person does not possess the qualifications agreed to by the parties. For this reason, prior to accepting the service, an individual appointed to serve as arbitrator has to disclose any circumstances likely to give rise to justifiable doubts as to his or her impartiality or independence.

The party wishing to raise issues related to the jurisdiction, suspicion or impediment of an arbitrator or arbitrators, must do so at the first opportunity, after the commencement of the arbitration by presenting a motion either directly to the arbitrator or to the chairman of the arbitral tribunal, setting forth their reasons with the pertinent evidence, and when the challenge of suspicion or impediment is accepted, the alternate indicated in the arbitration agreement will assume their position. In case no substitute has been appointed, the rules of the arbitral institution or specialised entity shall apply.

It is common practice in Brazilian courts to refer to the *IBA Guidelines for Conflict of Interest* as an authoritative source for defining the limits of the arbitrator's conduct before entering into impartiality territory. For example, like in the *IBA Guidelines*, the Brazilian Arbitration Law establishes that individuals somehow linked to the parties or to the submitted dispute, by any of the relationships that characterise the impediment or suspicion of judges, are prevented from serving as arbitrators.

As for the arbitrator's immunity, the Brazilian Arbitration Law establishes that by performing their service, the arbitrators are considered comparable to public officials for the purpose of criminal law. On the other hand, the legislation is silent on the arbitral tribunal's civil liability for when the arbitrator acts in fraud or bad faith.

The arbitrator's mandate terminates by the tribunal's final award, along with the arbitral proceeding itself.

Interim relief

Prior to the commencement of the arbitration, the parties may only seek provisional measures of protection and urgent relief from a judicial court. In case the provisional measure is granted, its efficacy is conditioned to the filling, by the interested party, of the request for arbitration within 30 (thirty) days from the date the respective decision takes effect, according to the Brazilian Arbitration Act.

Once the arbitration has commenced, the arbitrators will have the sole jurisdiction for maintaining, modifying or revoking the provisional or urgent measures granted previously by a court, as well as granting other injunctive and urgent reliefs.

In order to facilitate the communication between the arbitral tribunal and the state court, the Brazilian Arbitration Act and Civil Procedure Code established the arbitration letter, in which case the arbitral tribunal may issue an arbitration letter so that the judicial court offers assistance or imposes compliance, in the area of their territorial jurisdiction, of an act requested by the arbitrator. In this respect, if the arbitration is confidential, the respective court proceedings in compliance with the arbitration letter will also be carried out privately.

Arbitral award

The Brazilian Arbitration Act requires that the award be in writing and signed by the arbitrators. If there are several arbitrators, the decision shall be made by majority vote and, in case majority determination fails, the opinion of the chairman of the arbitral tribunal shall prevail. Any eventual dissenting arbitrator may, if he so wishes, render a separate decision from the award.

In addition, the award must contain: (i) the date and place where the award is rendered; (ii) a report including the names of the parties and a summary of the dispute; (iii) the grounds of the decision with due analysis of factual and legal issues, including, if need may be, a statement that the award is rendered in equity; and (iv) the dispositive by which the arbitrators shall resolve the questions presented before them, establishing a time limit for the compliance with the decision. The absence of any of these requirements makes the award null and void (Article 26 of the Brazilian Arbitration Act).

If the parties reach a settlement during the course of the arbitral proceedings, the arbitrator or arbitral tribunal may render an arbitral award declaring such fact at the parties' request. This award must contain the same requirements provided for in Article 26.

The arbitral award shall also decide on the parties' duties regarding costs and expenses for the arbitration, as well as on any amount resulting from bad faith conduct, if applicable, complying with the provisions of the arbitration agreement. In relation to the costs that should be shouldered by the parties, the expenses may include fees and expenses of the arbitrators, expert witnesses, legal fee and any other expenses incurred due to the arbitral proceeding. The Brazilian Arbitration Law is silent with respect to the arbitral tribunal's ability to include interest on costs, so the tribunal's jurisdiction shall be determined by the arbitration agreement or by the procedural rules adopted by the arbitrators.

Once the award is signed, the sole arbitrator or the chairman of the arbitral tribunal must send a copy of the decision to the parties by mail or by other means of communication, with confirmation receipt, or through direct delivery to the parties, with return receipt. There is no legal imposition regarding a time limit for the delivery of the award, but it is certain that its receipt sets the timeliness for any challenge to the arbitral award, as will be explained later.

Challenging the arbitral award

Pursuant to Article 18 of the Brazilian Arbitration Law, the parties do not have a right to appeal on the merits of an award.[1] In this sense, the parties cannot agree on the possibility of submitting the award to a second tier of judicial authority, under the penalty of incurring an offence against public policy.

However, it is discussed among the scholar's doctrine that there is nothing to prevent the parties from negotiating a private and internal path for revision of the arbitral award, without the intervention of the judiciary. In other words, it is possible that the parties establish, within the scope of the arbitral procedure itself, the appeal they may find necessary, as long as its judgment is completed by another private board, with different arbitrators. Still, experience clearly shows that this type of provision is not usual among domestic or international arbitrations, as it increases the costs and the duration of the procedure.

From another point of view, not to say that there is no means of modifying an arbitral award, a party may seek to have the arbitral tribunal clarify any omission, obscurity, contradiction or clerical and typographic error in an award. The presentation of said motion for clarification must be made within five days from the receipt of notification of the respective award.

In case a motion for clarification is presented, the arbitrator or the arbitral tribunal must decide within 10 days, or within the timeframe agreed to by the parties, the amendment of the arbitral award, which shall be communicated to the parties.

Finally, even though the arbitral award is unappealable, in accordance with Article 33 of the Brazilian Arbitration Law, an interested party may file an annulment action before one of the state courts to set aside the award, by declaring its nullity, in the cases set forth in Article 32:

Article 32. An arbitral award is null and void if:

I. The arbitration agreement is null.

II. It is made by an individual who could not serve as an arbitrator.

III. It does not comply with the requirements of Article 26 of this Law.

IV. It has exceeded the limits of the arbitration agreement.

V. It does not resolve the entire dispute submitted to arbitration. (REVOKED)

VI. It has been duly proved that it was made through unfaithfulness, extortion or corruption.

VII. It is rendered after the time limit has expired, in compliance with Article 12, item III of this Law.

VIII. It violates the principles set forth by Article 21, Paragraph 2 of this Law.

The request for the declaratory nullity of the arbitral award, whether partial or final, must be filed within 90 days from the receipt of notification of the respective award, or of the decision on a motion for clarification. Nevertheless, as in other jurisdictions across the globe, vacating an arbitration award is usually an uphill battle, since the courts tend to respect the arbitrators' decisions.

Enforcement of the arbitral award

Since July 2002, Brazil has been a member state of the New York Convention, a treaty for the recognition and enforcement of foreign arbitral awards. In order to be recognised or enforced in Brazil, a foreign arbitral award is only subject to homologation by the Superior Court of Justice ("STJ"),[2,3] which must render an *exequatur*, exercising limited control over the foreign award and, in similar fashion, to most of the assessment systems tied to the Italian tradition, analyse its formal aspects, without reviewing the merits of the award.

According to the provisions of the New York Convention, the requirements for the recognition of foreign awards are the following: (a) compliance with Brazilian public policy, sovereignty and good moral principles; (b) rendered by an authority with jurisdiction; (c) rendered in a proceeding where the parties have been given the opportunity to be heard and fully present their cases; (d) final and binding; and (e) certified by the Brazilian consul residing in the country where it was rendered together with a sworn translation of the award into Portuguese.

There are certain limited grounds upon which the court may refuse to enforce a foreign arbitral award. These grounds, which are adamant, are set out in Articles 38 and 39 of the Brazilian Arbitration Act, which were based on the New York Convention, as it follows:

Article 38. Recognition or enforcement of the foreign arbitral award may be refused if the party against which it is invoked, furnishes proof that:

I. The parties to the arbitration agreement were under some incapacity.

II. The arbitration agreement was not valid under the law to which the parties have subjected it or, failing any indication thereon, under the law of the country where the award was made.

III. It was not given proper notice of the appointment of an arbitrator or the arbitral proceedings, or was otherwise unable to present his case.

IV. The arbitral award was issued beyond the scope of the arbitration agreement and it was not possible to separate the exceeding portion from what was submitted to arbitration.

V. The commencement of the arbitration proceedings was not in accordance with the submission agreement or the arbitration clause.

VI. The arbitral award has not yet become binding on the parties or has been set aside or suspended by a court in the country where the arbitral award was made.

Article 39. Recognition or enforcement of a foreign arbitral award will also be refused if the Superior Court of Justice finds that:

I. According to Brazilian law, the object of the dispute cannot be settled by arbitration.

II. The decision violates national public policy.

Foreign awards that have been set aside at the courts of the seat of arbitration cannot be enforced in Brazil, as expressively established on the Brazilian Arbitration Law.

Investment arbitration

In the 1960s, Brazil refused to sign the Washington Convention of 1965, which created the International Centre for the Settlement of Investment Disputes ("ICSID"), on the basis that the convention's provisions conferred the investors a privileged position in relation to the host country, as only the investor would have the possibility of instituting the arbitral proceeding.

On the other hand, following worldwide trends, Brazil signed 14 bilateral investment treaties ("BITs") in the 1990s, having also entered into the Agreement for the Promotion and Reciprocal Protection of Investments in MERCOSUL, which encompassed investments in South America. Concurrently, Brazil signed the Buenos Aires' Agreement for the Promotion and Reciprocal Protection of Investments with countries that were not part of MERCOSUL.

However, Brazil did not ratify the 14 BITs, nor the agreements for promotion and protection of investments, and, therefore, they are not in force. The main reason for the non-ratification for the treaties is the idea that the existence of an arbitration agreement between an investor and a host country will always favour the investor unreasonably.

Still in regard to the agreements and the BITs, it is important to highlight that considering that Brazil was not part of the Washington Convention, the clauses related to arbitration between investors and the countries only regulated, as a general rule, the application of procedural rules.

Our understanding is that Brazil is unlikely to participate in the Washington Convention, as investment arbitration is still very incipient in the country and considering that the negative experiences of several countries have exposed the limitations of this type of agreement, in particular, its inadequacy as a method to resolve an investor-state dispute.

In this context, Brazil has elaborated a new model of investment agreements, the Investment Cooperation and Facilitation Agreement ("ACIF"), which seeks to encourage reciprocal investment through the establishment of an intergovernmental mechanism for the disclosure of opportunities, the exchange of information and the projection of business facilitation initiatives. Brazil has already signed ACIFs with Angola, Chile, Colombia, Malawi, Mexico, Mozambique and Peru.

The approach adopted in the ACIFs is based, to some extent, on the standard rules of treatment found in most BITs. For example, the ACIFs forbid direct expropriation; with some exceptions, ACIFs state that the parties should allow investment-related transfers and they also impose transparency obligations, such as the publication of laws and regulations and the best efforts to provide opportunities for stakeholders to give their opinion on the proposed measures.

For now, it is still hard to predict the future of investment arbitration in Brazil, but one thing is sure: when it comes to promotion and protection of investments, the new agreements entered into by Brazil set the country on a fairly different path from the one adopted by the countries that signed your traditional investments treaties, such as the Washington Convention.

* * *

Endnotes

1. Article 18. An arbitrator is the judge in fact and in law, and his award is not subject to appeal or recognition by judicial court.
2. Article 34. A foreign arbitral award shall be recognised or enforced in Brazil in accordance with international treaties effective in the internal legal system, or, in its absence, in strict accordance with the terms of this Law.

   Article 35. In order to be recognised or enforced in Brazil, a foreign arbitral award is only subject to homologation by the Superior Court of Justice.
3. Ruling No. 9 of the Superior Court of Justice.

Eduardo Maccari Telles
Tel: +55 21 2127 4229 / Email: etelles@mayerbrown.com
Eduardo Maccari Telles is a partner in the Rio de Janeiro office of Tauil & Chequer Advogados. Eduardo concentrates his practice in trial, litigation and arbitration, tax and administrative law. He represents national and foreign companies as well as governmental institutions, and he assists them in all types of dispute resolution for tax, civil, labor, intellectual property and environmental cases as well with tax and labor consulting. Eduardo has experience in energy and insurance litigation as well, being responsible for coordinating the firm's Brazil litigation practice. Since 2000 he has also served as a state attorney in the Attorney's Office of the State of Rio de Janeiro. His other professional assignments have included work as a tax attorney with the National Institute of Social Security (1998-2000), as a legal counselor with Rangel, Penna da Rocha & Daiha Associated Attorneys (2000-2006), as external counsel for the Brazilian Institute of Municipal Administration (2000-2004) and as Treasury representative on the Taxpayer Council of the State of Rio de Janeiro (2004).

Gustavo Fernandes de Andrade
Tel: +55 21 2127 4271 / Email: gfernandes@mayerbrown.com
Gustavo Fernandes de Andrade is a partner of the Litigation and Arbitration practices in the Rio de Janeiro office. With more than 20 years of experience, Gustavo customarily represents companies in complex litigation and arbitration procedures, in disputes arising of engineering and construction projects, energy, telecommunications, mergers and acquisitions, commercial contracts and financial transactions, with a focus on all areas of civil, commercial and constitutional law. Gustavo has acted as counsel before the major international and national arbitration institutions such as the ICC, LCIA, FGV, CAMARB, CBMA, CAM-CCBC, ABDM and CIESP/FIESP. He has acted before the Superior Court of Justice in cases of recognition of foreign arbitral awards.
Gustavo holds an LL.M. degree, focused on Arbitration, International Law and European Law, from the University of Cambridge (2005), and an LL.M. degree, focused on Constitutional Law, International Law and Comparative Law, from the University of Pennsylvania (1999). He is admitted to the Brazilian Bar Association for the Rio de Janeiro and Distrito Federal sections. Gustavo publishes extensively in his practice areas, especially on the subject of arbitration involving the public administration. He is also constantly invited to give lectures. Gustavo has been with Tauil & Chequer in association with Mayer Brown since 2014. Previously, he was a partner at Sergio Bermudes Advogados. He is also a state attorney for the state of Rio de Janeiro.

Daniel Becker
Tel: +55 21 2127 1640 / Email: dbecker2@mayerbrown.com
Daniel Becker is an associate in the Rio de Janeiro office of Tauil & Chequer Advogados in association with Mayer Brown. He is a member of the Litigation & Dispute Resolution and International Arbitration practices. His work involves representing clients in arbitration and judicial proceedings in Brazil and abroad, in complex matters related to diverse industry sectors.

Tauil & Chequer Advogados in association with Mayer Brown

Rua Teixeira de Freitas, 31 - 9º Andar, Rio de Janeiro / Av. Presidente Juscelino Kubitscheck, 1.455 - 5 e 6º Andares, São Paulo, Brazil. Tel: +55 21 2127 4229 / +55 11 2504 4696 / Fax: + 55 21 2127 4211 / + 55 11 2504 4211

British Virgin Islands

Mo Haque QC & Charlotte Walker
Campbells

Introduction

The British Virgin Islands, or more affectionately the BVI, requires no introduction to those who have either visited its shores or been involved in offshore commerce. It sits on the eastern borders of the Caribbean Sea, and enjoys political sovereignty and economic stability. As a British Overseas Territory, its citizens are British citizens and, by extension, citizens of the European Union.[1]

The BVI has long been the world's leading destination for company incorporation. The Registry now houses the titles of approaching one million companies. It offers investors highly developed corporate legislation which provides a greater degree of operational flexibility than would usually be found in their domiciliary states. The BVI Courts are naturally well-versed in corporate litigation.

The BVI's legal system descends from, and follows, the English common law.[2] Litigants in the BVI have the comfort and security of knowing that the ultimate appeal lies to the Judicial Committee of the Privy Council of the United Kingdom – the members of which are Justices of the United Kingdom's Supreme Court. It is quite usual for Judges from England to preside over cases in the BVI Commercial Court.

Arbitration is a relative newcomer to the arena of dispute resolution. Although there has been an Arbitration Act on the statute books for over 40 years,[3] it was not readily suited to international work, not least because the BVI was not a party to the New York Convention ("the Convention").[4] However the *status quo* was altered after the BVI became subject to the Convention on 25 May 2014[5] and, on 1 October of the same year, passed the Virgin Islands Arbitration Act 2013 ("the Act"). This adopts many of the provisions of the UNCITRAL Model Law ("Model Law").[6,7]

It is not an understatement to say that there has been a sea-change in attitude towards arbitration. The British Virgin Islands International Arbitration Centre ("BVIIAC") is a statutory body created pursuant to the Act.[8] Its purposes include the facilitation and promotion of the BVI as an arbitral hub. The Government has invested heavily in arbitration, commissioning a purpose-built home with state-of-the art amenities in Road Town, Tortola. This opened in November 2016 and is the only such facility in the Caribbean.

The stated aim of the BVIIAC is to become the regional centre of choice for the resolution of disputes arising out of business activity, investments and projects worldwide. Nearly 2,000 of the world's leading arbitration practitioners are members of BVIIAC's panel of arbitrators. The BVIIAC has its own set of rules ("the Rules"),[9] based on the 2010 UNCITRAL Arbitration Rules, and which will apply to any arbitration administered by the BVIIAC.

Parallel to this, in the interest of promoting the BVI as an arbitral hub, the Government has eased immigration formalities for parties and their representatives who travel to the BVI for arbitrations. The hope is that the BVI will soon become the preferred regional venue for international arbitration.

The BVI Commercial Court is widely known to be arbitration-friendly. As stated by Leon J in ***Hualon Corporation (M) SDN BHD (in receivership) v Marty Limited***:[10]

> *It is clear in the Act, in the extension of the New York Convention to this jurisdiction, in the arbitration jurisprudence of this jurisdiction (including before the Act), and in the public commitment of the Territory to arbitration as part of its strategic plan, that the Territory of the Virgin Islands as a matter of public policy strongly supports the use of arbitration to resolve international commercial and other disputes.*

The Act contains express stipulations that the Court should not interfere with an arbitration unless the Act permits it to do so[11] and, if it does, should give due regard to the wishes of the parties and the provisions of the arbitration agreement.[12] In ***Vendort v Evrostroy***[13] it was held that an applicant could rely on an arbitration award alone to obtain a statutory demand (and to present a winding-up petition), without the need to first enforce the award or for any further order of the Court.

As the Rules came into force only in November 2016, it is too soon to say whether they will be adopted in future agreements involving BVI entities. However, we anticipate that they will prove to be popular. Accordingly this chapter will consider, in tandem, arbitrations carried out without and within the auspices of the BVIIAC. We believe that the BVIIAC will become an appealing venue for arbitrations, as it conveniently lies between North and South America, and will be regarded as an excellent neutral jurisdiction in which to resolve disputes.

The arbitration agreement

<u>Formalities</u>

The formalities required by the Act for any arbitration agreement follow those set out in Article 7 of the Model Law.[14] Thus, arbitration agreements must be in writing, and may be contained in arbitration clauses in broader agreements or in separate agreements. Being "*in writing*" is widely defined, and includes electronic communications such as email.[15]

The Rules operate at the election of the parties, wherever the arbitration is conducted. The BVIIAC has drafted a model arbitration clause, which may be used if the parties agree to come within the procedure of the BVIIAC.[16]

<u>Arbitrability</u>

There is nothing within the Act that limits the scope of any arbitration. The procedure is clearly tailored towards commercial disputes, and the remedies available to arbitral tribunals would not be suitable for other types of claim (such as non-financial family disputes). Where there is dispute, the BVI Court will follow English common law by limiting the scope of any arbitration to prohibit arbitrators considering matters that might trespass on to the territory of public policy.[17]

<u>Joinder</u>

There is no express mechanism within the Act that permits joinder of another party to an arbitration. By contrast, Article 17(5) of the Rules permits the tribunal to allow any other party to the arbitration agreement to be joined into the arbitration. If a respondent to a claim wishes to join another party, it may do so when putting in its Response to the claim.[18] The Rules do not permit a third party that is not a party to the arbitration agreement to apply to be joined.

The Act does contain a procedure permitting competing arbitrations to be consolidated.[19] It allows a Court, on application, to consolidate two or more arbitral proceedings where there are commonalities of law, fact, relief or for other good reason. The Court may also stay arbitrations pending conclusion of other arbitrations dealing with the same factual matrix. This part of the Act only applies automatically to agreements entered into before the Act came into force[20] (i.e. before 1 October 2014) or within six years after coming into force[21] (i.e. any agreements until 30 September 2020) which provide for domestic arbitrations.[22] The parties may agree that this section does not apply.[23]

Competence-competence and separability

Section 32(1) of the Act preserves the doctrine of *competence-competence* found at Article 16 of the Model Law, namely that the arbitral tribunal has the power to rule on all matters connected to the arbitration, including its own jurisdiction and the validity of any arbitration agreement. The same section enshrines the doctrine of separability, meaning that for the purposes of considering its jurisdiction, the tribunal treats the arbitration clause as standing independently of the balance of the agreement. A ruling that the arbitral tribunal does not have jurisdiction is not open to appeal.[24]

Arbitration procedure

The object of the Act is "*to facilitate the fair and speedy resolution of disputes by arbitration without unnecessary delay or expense*".[25] Article 17 of the Rules carries a similar sentiment.

Commencement

Arbitral disputes commence on the date at which the Respondent receives a request that the dispute be referred to arbitration, unless otherwise agreed.[26] The form of the request is not prescribed. Where any limitation period refers to the bringing of an action, it is deemed to mean the commencement of arbitral proceedings.[27]

For an arbitration conducted through the BVIIAC, the party wishing to commence arbitration should communicate the same to the other parties, and send a notice of arbitration to the Secretariat of the BVIIAC.[28] Arbitral proceedings are deemed to commence on the date of receipt of that notice, subject to the payment of the correct fee. The Respondent then only has 30 days within which to communicate and send a response.[29]

Any challenges to the jurisdiction of the tribunal must be made no later than the submission of the statement of defence.[30]

Place of arbitration

The Act contains no geographical constraint upon the place of arbitration, but in default of agreement it is left to the tribunal to decide.[31] For BVIIAC arbitrations, the parties are also free to agree the place of arbitration but, if no agreement is reached, then the venue will default to Road Town, Tortola, the capital of the BVI. The tribunal still has the power to decide that another venue is more appropriate.[32]

Procedural requirements

Parties may adopt their own agreed procedure,[33] failing which the tribunal can conduct the arbitration in any manner that it considers appropriate.[34] The initial step is usually the selection and appointment of the arbitral tribunal (which we deal with below). The tribunal can then consider any challenges to jurisdiction and scope and move on to look at specific procedural requirements relevant to the case being considered, such as the timings of Statements of Claim and Defences,[35] and whether oral hearings are necessary.[36]

The Rules are slightly more restrictive in that they require the tribunal to set out a provisional timetable after receiving representations.[37]

Evidential rules

An arbitral tribunal is not bound by the rules of evidence, but may receive relevant evidence and give it appropriate weight.[38] The Rules mirror precisely Article 19(2) of the Model law which gives the tribunal the power to determine admissibility, relevance, materiality and weight. In this author's view, there is no significant difference. In practice, this evidential rule makes appeals against the substance of arbitration awards extremely difficult.

If the parties agree, the arbitral tribunal may make reference to the IBA Rules on the Taking of Evidence in International Arbitration 2010 ("the IBA Rules"), though there is no statutory compulsion to do so.

Expert evidence

It is, of course, for the parties to agree whether or not expert evidence is necessary. The tribunal also has the power to appoint an expert to consider specific issues, and may order a party to produce documents, goods or property for inspection by the expert.[39]

It is sometimes the case that a party will be reluctant to co-operate with the court-appointed expert. If that should occur, the tribunal has the ability to request assistance from the competent Court in the BVI, which can order the attendance of any person and the production of any evidence.[40] However, this power to order documents to be produced is limited by Section 54(9) of the Act, which provides that a person is not required to produce in arbitral proceedings any document or other evidence that he would not be required to produce in civil proceedings before a court.

The Rules allow the tribunal to appoint an expert after consulting with the parties.[41] There is no veto available to a disgruntled Claimant or Respondent, though they may object to the appointment on the grounds of qualification, impartiality or independence.[42]

The tribunal may also appoint assessors to assist in the assessment of costs.[43] The parties are unable to object to such an appointment.

Confidentiality

It is normal in most arbitrations that proceedings remain confidential arising, as they will, from commercial contracts which contain confidentiality clauses. The BVI Courts follow the English common law in implying a term that the arbitral proceedings and documents are confidential.[44] The Act places this on a statutory footing by providing that no party is to publish, disclose or communicate any information relating to the arbitral proceedings or the award unless either agreed,[45] required to protect a legal right or enforce or challenge the award,[46] as required by law,[47] or to any professional or other adviser of any party.[48]

Article 17(6) of the Rules states that the arbitral proceedings are confidential to the parties and tribunal, save where disclosure of an award is required pursuant to a legal duty or to protect or pursue a legal right.[49] This confidentiality extends to the existence of proceedings and any pleadings, evidence, documents and other materials save ones that are already in the public domain.[50]

Arbitrators

Appointment

The parties are free to choose the number of arbitrators[51] and the procedure for selection.[52] A procedure is set out in the Act of what should occur if the parties are not in agreement as to the choice of tribunal. These include making applications to the Court.[53]

The Rules provide a parallel system. If the parties cannot agree the number of persons on the tribunal, then three will be appointed.[54] Each party may nominate an arbitrator in the respective notice of arbitration[55] and Response.[56] The appointment is made by the appointing authority, who is the CEO of BVIIAC.[57] The arbitrators are not required to be drawn from the list of panel of arbitrators that is maintained by the BVIIAC.[58]

Any arbitrator appointed has a duty to declare matters that might give rise to doubts about his or her independence or impartiality.[59]

Challenge

A challenge to the appointment of an arbitrator can only be on the narrow ground of there being doubts about their independence, impartiality or qualifications.[60] The Rules only allow challenges for doubts about impartiality and independence,[61] presumably because the CEO of the BVIIAC will no doubt initially check the qualifications of the arbitrator to assess his or her suitability for the case.

The Act incorporates the timings for challenges to be made, as set out at Article 13 of the Model Law, namely that a party has 15 days to send to the tribunal written reasons for the challenge.[62] The tribunal will then decide and, if so determined, may continue the arbitration (notwithstanding any further request to the Court, which must be made within 30 days of the tribunal's decision).[63] If the Court ultimately upholds the challenge, it may set aside any award that has been made.[64]

The Rules contain slightly different timings.[65] It provides that in the event of a challenge, a committee formed of three arbitrators from the BVIIAC panel will decide the matter.[66] The decision that is made is final and no further appeal lies to the Court.[67]

Immunity

Judicial immunity from suit is a well-established principle of English common law. However, it was not clear that arbitrators shared the same protection.[68] Any remaining doubt is removed by Section 101(1) of the Act, which gives the tribunal and any of its employees or agents, immunity for actions carried out in their capacity as a tribunal, unless they have acted in bad faith. There is a similar statutory immunity for the BVIIAC or its members.[69]

The Rules provide similar protection for arbitrators, any person appointed by the arbitrator, the BVIIAC and any of its employees.[70] The exception is if there has been "*intentional wrongdoing*".[71] This is probably more narrow than the 'bad faith' exception within the Act.

Interim relief

The arbitral tribunal has broad powers to grant interim measures which: (a) preserve the *status quo*; (b) prevent any action that may harm the arbitral process; (c) preserve assets; and/or (d) preserve evidence.[72,73] The preconditions for the grant of an interim measure require the party requesting the measure to satisfy the tribunal that: (i) if any harm caused is not remediable by damages, then the harm caused by not granting the measure substantially outweighs harm that would be caused by granting it; and (ii) that there is a reasonable possibility that the requesting party will succeed on the merits of the claim.[74]

Section 33(2) of the Act specifically excludes from the definition of the above interim measures those procedures set out at Section 54 of the Act. These are: the power of the arbitral tribunal to make orders giving security for costs; directing the discovery of documents or delivery of interrogatories; and directing evidence be given by affidavit and in relation to the preservation of evidence or the testing of properties. The tribunal can exercise those powers without needing to balance the relative harm caused, or to consider the wider merits of the case. Should a party not comply with an order made under Section 54, the tribunal may dismiss or stay the claim.[75] There is no obvious reason why the Act does not expressly allow a Response to be dismissed should a Respondent be in default. This is likely to be a slip of the draftsman's pen rather than a statutory choice to deliberately create an inequality of arms.

The tribunal may ask the requesting party to provide appropriate security[76] and to disclose any material change in circumstances.[77] If it transpires later that the interim measure should not have been granted, the requesting party may be liable for costs and damages.[78] The arbitral tribunal's decisions will be reinforced by orders of the Court.[79]

The Rules provide a tribunal with very similar powers in relation to a BVIIAC arbitration.[80]

The arbitration award

Formalities

The formalities of the award required by Article 31 of the Model Law are brought into BVI law by Section 65 of the Act. Thus the award must be in writing, signed by all or the majority of arbitrators,[81] and should provide reasons for the decision unless otherwise agreed.[82] For BVIIAC arbitrations, as well as the formalities, the Award is also submitted to the Secretariat for any suggestions. Only after that can the Award be rendered.[83]

Within 30 days of the Award being received, a party may ask that it be corrected or specific points be interpreted.[84] The Act allows the tribunal 30 days to respond;[85] the Rules allow 30 days for corrections,[86] but 45 days for interpretations.[87]

The parties may also ask for an additional award in respect of claims presented in the arbitration, but not decided in the Award. The tribunal is initially permitted 60 days within which to respond.[88]

Remedies available to the tribunal

The arbitral tribunal is able to grant any relief that a Court could have granted had the matter been litigated.[89] However, unless the parties agree, it does not have the power to order specific performance in relation to a contract relating to land or interests in land.[90]

Costs

The Act provides that costs are in the complete discretion of the arbitral tribunal.[91] When it comes to taxation, it is not bound to follow the scales and practices adopted by the Court.[92] Indeed, it contains a provision that actually renders void any agreement by the parties that each party should bear its own costs[93] unless the agreement to arbitrate was made after the dispute arose.[94] This is an unusual intervention, given the freedom of parties to otherwise choose nearly every other aspect of how their disputes should be resolved.

The costs regime in the Rules uses as a starting point that the unsuccessful party ought to carry the costs of the arbitration. However, the tribunal can apportion costs taking into account the circumstances of the case.[95] This follows traditional litigation.

As yet, the issue of the costs of third party litigation funding has not yet arisen in the BVI. The Courts would not allow this, but the English High Court in the landmark case of

Essar Oilfields Services Limited v Norscot Rig Management PVT Limited[96] held that it is permissible to recover those costs in arbitral proceedings.

Challenge to the award

Seasoned practitioners will appreciate that it is not straightforward to challenge the decision of an arbitral tribunal.

Section 79(1) of the Act incorporates Article 34 of the Model Law and allows for challenges to the Court to be made as set out below. By contrast, the Rules do not include any explicit mechanism whereby the Award can be challenged. It is to be noted that Article 34(2) of the Rules provides that awards shall be "*final and binding on the parties*". It is open to argument whether these words alone are sufficient to displace any further recourse to the Court. Parties are certainly advised to consider the potential effects of this section before agreeing that the BVIIAC Rules are to apply to any arbitration that may arise in the future.

Under the Act, any potential applicant to the Court must first ensure it has exhausted all avenues in the arbitration itself.[97] Having done so, any application to set aside the Award must only be made on one or more of the following grounds:

(i) incapacity of a party;

(ii) invalidity of the arbitration agreement;

(iii) lack of proper notice of the appointment of the arbitrator or proceedings;

(iv) inability to present the case;

(v) the Award oversteps its jurisdiction in dealing with irrelevant matters;

(vi) the tribunal or procedure was not in accordance with the agreement of the parties (unless the agreement itself would not have been lawful);

(vii) the subject matter of the dispute is not capable of being arbitrated; or

(viii) the Award is contrary to public policy.

Challenges may also be made on the grounds that there has been a serious irregularity affecting the tribunal, the proceedings or the award.[98] The Act defines "*serious irregularity*" as one or more of the following which has or may cause substantial injustice:[99]

(i) A failure by the tribunal to comply with Section 44 of the Act. That section imports Article 18 of the Model Law requiring the arbitrator to act with equality, fairly, impartially and with independence.

(ii) The tribunal exceeding its powers (otherwise than exceeding its jurisdiction).

(iii) A failure to conduct proceedings in accordance with the parties' agreement.

(iv) A failure to deal with the issues.

(v) A failure by the tribunal to correct and/or interpret the Award if so requested by the parties.

(vi) The Award being obtained by fraud or being in any way contrary to public policy.

(vii) A failure to comply with the form of Award.

(viii) Irregularity in the conduct of the proceedings.

Right to appeal

Finally, parties have a limited right to appeal to the Court on a point of law.[100] Unless the counter-party consents, leave of the Court will be required.[101] The parties thus will have to consider whether an agreement should contain an automatic appeal on a question of law. If leave is required, it will only be given if the question of law: was one that was before the tribunal; is one that would substantially affect the rights of one or more of the parties; and the tribunal's decision was obviously wrong or, where the point is of general importance, is at least open to serious doubt.[102] Any further applications to appeal require leave of the Court.[103]

Enforcement of the award

The BVI is a contracting state to which the (New York) Convention applies. The Convention is widely regarded as one of the most successful international treaties, with 150 countries falling under its umbrella.

The Convention is set out in Part X of the Act. Section 84 of the Act provides that Convention awards are enforceable in the territory in the same manner as they would be in any other Convention country. The preconditions are merely that originals, or certified copies, of the Arbitration Agreement and Award are provided (suitably translated if necessary).[104] The Courts will recognise the Award, and enforcement can only be challenged on grounds similar to those in which a domestic award could be challenged, namely:[105]

(i) the parties to the agreement were under some incapacity or the arbitration agreement was not valid under the law of the agreement or under the law of the country where the award was made;

(ii) the losing party was not given proper notice of the appointment of the arbitrator or of the arbitration proceedings or was otherwise unable to present his or her case;

(iii) the Award deals with matters falling outside the terms of the submission to arbitration, or contains decisions on matters beyond the scope of the submission – provided that if the decisions on matters submitted to arbitration can be separated from those not submitted, then that part of the award may be recognised and/or enforced;

(iv) the composition of the arbitral authority or the arbitral procedure was not in accordance with the agreement of the parties, or, failing such agreement, was not in accordance with the law of the country where the arbitration took place;

(v) the Award has not yet become binding on the parties, or has been set aside or suspended by a competent authority of the country in which, or under the law of which, that award was made;

(vi) the subject matter of the difference is not capable of settlement by arbitration under the law of that country; or

(vii) the recognition or enforcement of the Award would be contrary to the public policy of that country.

If necessary, the Convention will be interpreted in accordance with the principles of international law, as set out in Articles 31 and 32 of the Vienna Convention on the Law of Treaties.

Non-convention awards are similarly enforceable in the BVI.[106] The grounds for not enforcing are identical save for an important additional provision that the Court may refuse to enforce an award for any other reason, if it considers it just to do so.[107] There is no such discretion in relation to Convention awards.

* * *

Endnotes

1. Although under Council Regulation No. 1932/2006 citizens of British Overseas Territories "without the right of abode in the UK" were classified as non-EU nationals, the conferring of British citizenship in 2002 means most such citizens acquired the right of abode in the United Kingdom along with British citizenship, and hence are not considered by the EU as third-country nationals.
2. Section 72 of the Common Law (Declaration of Application) Act (Cap 13) of 1705 provides that English common law is extended to the BVI. Sections 13 to 21 of the Eastern Caribbean Supreme Court (Virgin Islands) Act incorporate the rules of common law and equity from time to time in force in England. *Veda Doyle v Agnes Deane HCVAP 2011/020* confirmed that where there is no local statute, the Court will have regard to the English common law.
3. BVI Arbitration Ordnance 1976.
4. Convention on the Recognition and Enforcement of Foreign Arbitral Awards (New York, 1958).
5. On 24 February 2014, the United Kingdom submitted a notification to extend territorial application of the Convention to the British Virgin Islands.
6. United Nations Commission on International Trade Law Model law on International Commercial Arbitration (1985), with amendments as adopted in 2006.
7. Section 4 of the Act gives the UNCITRAL Model Law force of law, save as amended.
8. Section 93(1) of the Act.
9. Pursuant to Section 107 of the Act.
10. BVIHC (Com) 2014/0090.
11. Section 3(2)(b) of the Act.
12. Sections 3(2)(c) of the Act.
13. BVIHCP 2012/0041. (This decision was upheld by the Court of Appeal BVIHCVAP 2012/0041 and the Privy Council [2016] UKPC 15.)
14. Section 17 of the Act.
15. Section 17(3) of the Act.
16. http://bviiac.org/Portals/0/Files/Arbitration%20Documents/2016BVIIACArbitrationClause.pdf.
17. *Fulham FC Ltd v Richards & anr [2011]* EWCA Civ 855.
18. Article 4(2)(a) of the Rules.
19. Schedule 2 Paragraph 1 of the Act.
20. Section 90(1)(a)(i) of the Act.
21. Section 90(1)(b) of the Act.
22. Meaning those which do not provide for any jurisdiction save for the BVI: Section 90(2) of the Act.
23. Section 91 of the Act.
24. Section 32(4) of the Act.
25. Section 3(1) of the Act.
26. Section 47 of the Act, incorporating Article 21 of the Model Law.
27. Section 12(2) of the Act.
28. Article 3(2) of the Rules.
29. Article 4(1) of the Rules.

30. Section 32 of the Act implementing Article 16(2) of the Model Law.
31. Section 46(1) of the Act.
32. Article 18 of the Rules.
33. Section 45(1) of the Act.
34. Section 45(2) substituting Article 19(2) of the Model Law.
35. Section 49(1) of the Act applying Article 23 of the Model Law.
36. Section 50 of the Act applying Article 24 of the Model Law.
37. Article 17(2) of the Rules.
38. Section 45(3) of the Act.
39. Section 52(1) of the Act applying Article 26 of the Model Law.
40. Sections 53(1) and (2) of the Act.
41. Article 29(1) of the Rules.
42. Article 29(2) of the Rules.
43. Section 52(2) of the Act.
44. *Glidepath BV and Ors v John Thompson and Ors [2005]* EWHC 818 (Comm).
45. Section 16(1).
46. Section 16(2)(a) of the Act.
47. Section 16(2)(b) of the Act.
48. Section 16(2)(c). This is a curious addition, because one would expect the other party to have disclosed any relevant information to its own advisers.
49. Article 34(8) of the Rules.
50. Article 17(7) of the Rules.
51. Section 21(3) of the Act.
52. Section 22(2) of the Act.
53. Section 22 of the Act generally.
54. Article 7(1) of the Rules.
55. Article 3(3)(g) and 3(4) of the Rules.
56. Article 4(2)(b) of the Rules.
57. Article 6(1) and 6(3) and Article 7(3) of the Rules.
58. Article 7(4) of the Rules.
59. Section 23 of the Act implementing Article 12(1) of the Model Law.
60. Section 23 of the Act implementing Article 12(2) of the Model Law.
61. Article 12(1) of the Rules.
62. Section 24(1) of the Act.
63. Section 24(1) of the Act.
64. Section 24(5) of the Act.
65. Article 13 of the Rules.
66. Article 13(5) of the Rules.
67. Article 13(5) of the Rules.
68. *Sutcliffe v Thackrah* [1974] AC 727 and *Arenson v Arenson* [1977] AC 405.
69. Section 102 of the Act.
70. Article 16(1) of the Rules: the parties agree to waive any claim.

71. Article 16(1) of the Rules.
72. Section 33 of the Act applying Article 17 of the Model Law.
73. For instance, the worldwide freezing injunction granted in *PT Ventures SGPS SA v Vidatel Ltd BVIHC* (Com) 2015/017.
74. Section 34 of the Act applying Article 17A of the Model Law.
75. Section 54(3) of the Act.
76. Section 38 of the Act incorporating Article 17E of the Model Law.
77. Section 39(1) of the Act incorporating Article 17F(1) of the Model Law.
78. Section 40 of the Act incorporating Article 17G of the Model Law.
79. Section 43 of the Act replacing Article 17J of the Model Law.
80. Article 26 of the Rules.
81. If any arbitrator's signature is missing, a reason should be provided: Section 65(1) of the Act.
82. Section 65 of the Act. The Award should also be dated and have the location set out: Section 65(3) of the Act.
83. Article 34(5) of the Rules.
84. Section 67 of the Act applying Article 33 of the Model Law; Articles 37(1) and 38(1) of the Rules.
85. Section 65(2) of the Act.
86. Article 38(2) of the Rules.
87. Article 37(2) of the Rules.
88. Section 67 of the Act incorporating Article 33(4) of Model Law; Article 39 of the Rules.
89. Section 68(1) of the Act.
90. Section 68(2) of the Act.
91. Section 72(1) and (2) of the Act.
92. Section 72(6) of the Act.
93. Section 72(8) of the Act.
94. Section 72(9) of the Act.
95. Article 43(2) of the Rules.
96. [2016] EWHC 2361.
97. Paragraph 7(1) of Schedule 2 of the Act.
98. Paragraph 4 of Schedule 2 to the Act.
99. Paragraph 4(2) of Schedule 2 to the Act.
100. Paragraph 5(1) of Schedule 2 to the Act.
101. Paragraph 6(1) of Schedule 2 to the Act.
102. Paragraph 6(4) of Schedule 2 to the Act.
103. Paragraph 6(6) of Schedule 2 to the Act.
104. Section 85 of the Act applying Article IV of the Convention.
105. Article 5 of the Convention as set out at Sections 86(2) and (3) of the Act.
106. Section 82(1) of the Act.
107. Section 83(2)(c) of the Act.

Mo Haque QC
Tel: +1 284 494 2423 / Email: mhaque@campbellslegal.com
Mo is a Partner in Campbells' Litigation, Insolvency and Restructuring Group and is based in the British Virgin Islands. He is an English QC and has 20 years of experience at the English Bar in commercial litigation, international arbitration and dispute resolution.
Mo has advised upon a breadth of cases ranging from insolvency and winding-up issues through to the professional liabilities of directors, liquidators and receivers. He has appeared before pretty much every form of tribunal as well as in numerous arbitrations. He has advised clients in the laws of different jurisdictions and under different rules (ICC, LCIA and UNCITRAL).

Charlotte Walker
Tel: +1 284 494 2423 / Email: cwalker@campbellslegal.com
Charlotte is an Associate in Campbells' Litigation, Insolvency & Restructuring Group where she specialises in multi-jurisdictional commercial litigation and contentious corporate liquidations and receiverships. Charlotte joined Campbells in 2018 from a global law firm in the British Virgin Islands. Charlotte trained and qualified as a solicitor at Macfarlanes LLP in London. Charlotte advises and appears before the Courts on behalf of creditors, shareholders, provisional and official liquidators, directors, managers and other professional service providers in relation to the restructuring and liquidation of companies and other entities. Charlotte also has an active general litigation practice involving widely varying commercial contexts and structures, but with a particular emphasis on shareholder and investment fund disputes.

Campbells
Floor 3, Banco Popular Building, PO Box 4467, Road Town, Tortola VG-1110, British Virgin Islands
Tel: +1 284 494 2423 / Fax: +1 284 494 2475 / URL: www.campbellslegal.com

Canada

Julie Rosenthal, Brad Halfin & Tamryn Jacobson
Goodmans LLP

Introduction

Canada is a federal state, made up of 10 provinces and three territories. Under the Canadian Constitution, the administration of justice falls within the jurisdiction of the provinces. Accordingly, each province has enacted its own legislation governing arbitrations. In addition, the federal government has enacted legislation which governs arbitrations involving a department of the federal government, a Crown corporation, or raising issues of maritime or admiralty law.[1]

With one exception, each province has enacted two arbitration statutes: one that governs international commercial arbitrations, and one that governs all other arbitrations.[2] Thus, for example, the province of Ontario has enacted the *Arbitration Act, 1991*, which governs domestic arbitrations,[3] and the *International Commercial Arbitration Act, 2017* governing international commercial arbitrations.[4]

Virtually all of the provinces (except Quebec) have incorporated the UNCITRAL 1985 Model Law into their respective statutes. For example, in British Columbia, the *International Commercial Arbitration Act*[5] largely replicates the provisions of the 1985 Model Law. And recently, Ontario became the first jurisdiction in Canada to amend its international commercial arbitration legislation to reflect the changes made to the Model Law in 2006. The *International Commercial Arbitration Act, 2017* provides that the Model Law "has force of law in Ontario", albeit subject to certain exceptions and modifications as set out in the Act.[6]

For ease of reference, this chapter will focus on the law governing international arbitrations in Ontario and British Columbia. To the extent that arbitration is being considered in other provinces or under the federal statute, the relevant legislation should be consulted.

There are a number of local arbitration bodies, including ADR Chambers International (in Ontario), the ADR Institute of Canada (in Ontario), the British Columbia International Commercial Arbitration Centre and the Canadian Commercial Arbitration Centre (in Quebec). Each of these institutions has its own set of procedural rules.

And, if parties so desire, they can also avail themselves of the services of international arbitral institutions, such as the International Court of Arbitration of the International Chamber of Commerce or the London Court of International Arbitration, for international arbitrations conducted in Canada.

Arbitration agreements

<u>Formalities</u>

Both the Ontario and the British Columbia statutes governing international arbitration expressly require arbitration agreements to be in writing, although the writing requirement can be established by an exchange of letters or emails.[7] This is a departure from the statutes governing domestic arbitrations in most provinces, which do not require an arbitration agreement to be in writing.[8] Because the domestic statutes generally apply to all arbitrations not governed by the international statutes,[9] it may be possible to have an oral agreement to arbitrate an international dispute which would be governed by a domestic statute.

The arbitration agreement may be entered into either before or after the dispute arises. Most commonly, the arbitration agreement is set out in the commercial document which establishes the relationship between the parties (for example, purchase and sale agreement, joint venture agreement, licence agreement, etc.).

Scope and arbitrability

The international arbitration statutes apply only to "commercial" arbitrations.[10] Within the scope of "commercial" activity, the arbitration agreement can be as narrow or broad as the parties wish. The broadest arbitration agreement can provide that all disputes between the parties be resolved by arbitration. More commonly, however, disputes arising out of, or in connection with, the particular agreement in which the arbitration agreement is contained are submitted to arbitration. Alternatively, parties can agree to arbitrate only very specific disputes – for example, purchase price adjustment disputes arising out of a purchase and sale agreement.

The availability of arbitration may be limited by legislation. For example, certain provincial consumer protection statutes have been held to oust the jurisdiction of an arbitrator, at least in connection with that aspect of the parties' dispute that is addressed by the statute.[11]

Separability and the tribunal's competence to determine its own jurisdiction

Both the British Columbia statute and the Ontario statute provide that the arbitral tribunal is competent to determine its own jurisdiction, including determinations as to the existence or validity of the arbitration agreement.[12] That principle has been consistently enforced by Canadian courts.[13] A decision by the arbitral tribunal as to its jurisdiction may be appealed to the court within 30 days.[14] At first instance, a court must limit itself to a *prima facie* analysis of the application of the arbitration clause, and must defer all other jurisdictional issues to the arbitration tribunal.[15]

The statutes also provide that an arbitration clause that forms part of a larger contract shall be treated as independent and separable.[16] Again, the Canadian courts have interpreted and applied those statutory provisions in a consistent and predictable manner.[17]

Consolidation or joinder of parties or claims

The Model Law does not provide for consolidation of arbitration proceedings. However, both the Ontario and the British Columbia statutes provide that the court may order consolidation of proceedings, if all parties consent.[18] (Such a consolidation order can be made upon application of all parties.) These provisions are useful in circumstances where the parties have agreed in the arbitration agreement (or subsequently) to consolidation, but cannot agree on the process to be followed, as it provides a mechanism for the court to grant directions. The statutes also provide that parties can agree to consolidate arbitration proceedings without a court order.[19]

Neither an arbitral tribunal nor a court can compel a third party who is not subject to the arbitration agreement to join in the arbitral proceedings. A court also cannot consolidate or join arbitral proceedings unless all parties consent or unless provided for in the arbitration agreement.[20] For this reason, parties are well-advised to ensure that the arbitration agreement requires all subcontracts or related agreements to contain a consolidated arbitration clause.

Arbitration procedure

Commencement of arbitration

Both the British Columbia and Ontario statutes provide that, unless otherwise agreed by the parties, arbitral proceedings are deemed to commence on the date on which a request for that dispute to be referred to arbitration is received by the respondent.[21]

The statutes do not impose any particular requirements with respect to the form of the request or with respect to the manner of delivery, beyond stating that the request can be delivered personally or to the respondent's place of business, habitual residence or mailing address.[22]

However, if the arbitration agreement provides that the initiating request for arbitration is to take a particular form or is to be delivered in a particular manner, or that certain procedural steps must be completed to commence the arbitration, then those requirements must be satisfied. Thus, the Ontario Court of Appeal found that an arbitration had not been commenced within the required 12-month period specified in the contract because the notice of arbitration, despite having been served on the other party, had not been filed with the relevant institution as required by the arbitration agreement.[23]

Following the requirements set out in the arbitration agreement for commencing the arbitration is particularly important in the context of contractual limitation periods (such as the 12-month period in the above-noted case), as well as statutory limitation periods. Canada generally has fairly short limitation periods for properly initiating claims as compared to other countries. (For example, the general limitation period in Ontario and BC is two years from discovery of the claim.)[24]

Place of arbitration

The seat or place of the arbitration will determine the procedural law (*lex arbitri*) governing the arbitration (which may be different from the substantive law governing the dispute).[25]

Ordinarily, the hearing will be held in the seat of the arbitration, although the parties can agree otherwise. For example, if an arbitration agreement provides for the arbitration to take place in Toronto, Ontario, the parties could agree for the hearings to be held in Vancouver, British Columbia and be deemed to be taking place in Toronto. In such circumstances, the Ontario statute would still govern the procedure of the arbitration and, if the parties were in need of court assistance (for example, in appointing an arbitrator), they would have to apply to the Ontario courts.[26]

Procedural rules and evidence

With certain minor exceptions,[27] the choice of procedural rules is left up to the parties to decide. Thus, for example, an arbitration agreement can provide that the governing rules shall be those of a particular arbitration institution, for example, the rules of the International Chamber of Commerce (ICC), ADR Institute of Canada, Canadian Commercial Arbitration Centre, British Columbia International Commercial Arbitration Centre, or the London Court of International Arbitration (LCIA), among others. Instead of using the rules of an institution, an arbitration agreement can also set out its own ad hoc procedural rules, in as much or as little detail as the parties desire.

If, however, the arbitration agreement is silent on the question of procedure, then the various statutes generally defer the choice of procedure to the arbitral tribunal.[28] This includes the power to determine the admissibility, relevance, materiality and weight of any evidence.[29] In that regard, arbitrators in Canada often refer to the IBA *Rules on the Taking of Evidence in International Arbitration* when making decisions about the production and exchange of documents and the admissibility of evidence.

For those arbitrations that may involve the use of expert evidence, the typical practice in Canada is for the parties to exchange expert reports prior to the hearing. It should also be noted that the statutes governing international arbitrations provide that the arbitral tribunal may appoint its own expert to report to it on specific issues, unless otherwise agreed by the parties,[30] although this is quite rare in Canada.

Privacy and confidentiality

It is recommended that parties address confidentiality obligations expressly in the arbitration agreement (including any applicable exceptions, for example, public company disclosure obligations). Alternatively, the parties can incorporate the rules of an institution that satisfactorily address confidentiality obligations.

Both the Ontario and British Columbia statutes are silent on confidentiality, and the Canadian courts have not consistently determined whether an arbitration will be subject to an implied obligation of confidentiality absent an express confidentiality provision in the arbitration agreement. Therefore, if confidentiality is desired and if it is not addressed in the arbitration agreement, it is important that the parties enter into a confidentiality agreement or have the arbitral tribunal issue a confidentiality order.

Arbitrators

The arbitration agreement can specify the number of arbitrators and the method of appointment or can refer to the rules of an institution which will determine the number of arbitrators. Where the arbitration agreement is silent, the Ontario and British Columbia statutes both provide that the arbitral tribunal shall be composed of three arbitrators (this is contrasted with their respective domestic acts which default to a single arbitrator), with one arbitrator being appointed by each of the parties and the third being appointed by agreement of the two appointees.[31] Where there is a failure to comply with the appointment procedure (either the one agreed to by the parties or the one imposed by statute, as applicable), a party may apply to the court for assistance in appointing the tribunal.[32]

Under both the Ontario and the British Columbia statutes, an arbitrator may be challenged only if circumstances exist that give rise to justifiable doubts as to his or her impartiality or independence, or if he or she does not possess qualifications agreed to by the parties.[33] Any challenge to an arbitrator must be advanced within 15 days of the party becoming aware of the issue,[34] and shall be made initially to the arbitral tribunal (or in accordance with the procedure agreed upon by the parties) and, if not successful, to the court.[35]

In determining whether there are justifiable doubts as to the arbitrator's impartiality or independence, Canadian courts have recently begun referring to the 2014 IBA *Guidelines for Conflict of Interest* as an authoritative source.[36] The *Guidelines* are, to a large degree, consistent with the already-developed jurisprudence.

Both the Ontario and the British Columbia statutes provide that an arbitrator's mandate terminates if he or she becomes *de jure* or *de facto* unable to perform his functions or for other reasons fails to act without undue delay, *and* he or she withdraws from office or the parties agree on the termination.[37] If a dispute remains concerning the arbitrator continuing to act (for example, if only one party alleges that the arbitrator has become unable to act or has unduly delayed), a party may ask the court to decide on the termination of the mandate.[38]

Arbitrators who are acting in a "judicial or quasi-judicial capacity" are generally immune from civil liability in Canada absent fraud or bad faith.[39] The requirement for acting in a judicial or quasi-judicial capacity means that an arbitrator who is performing a valuation function may not enjoy the benefits of immunity.[40] The factors that must be present for immunity are:

1. there must be an existing dispute which the parties have submitted to the arbitrator;
2. the arbitrator must be acting in a judicial or quasi-judicial manner; that is, he or she receives evidence and hears argument in coming to his or her decision; and
3. the arbitrator must be fulfilling his or her function as an independent party, in compliance with the mandatory provisions of the applicable legislation.[41]

Most of the institutional rules also include a provision exempting the institution and arbitrators from liability, absent wilful wrongful acts. In addition, many arbitrators require that parties sign an arbitration engagement agreement which contains various provisions, including immunity.

Interim relief

Depending on the terms of the arbitration agreement and the applicable procedural rules, parties to an international arbitration may have access to a broad range of interim relief in Canada. That interim relief may be sought either from the arbitral tribunal or from the courts.[42]

In British Columbia, section 17 of the *International Commercial Arbitration Act* provides that an arbitral tribunal may order interim relief, unless otherwise agreed by the parties.[43]

In Ontario, the powers to award interim relief have been expanded by the coming into force of the *International Commercial Arbitration Act, 2017*. The jurisdiction to award interim relief is granted by Article 17 of the Model Law, which permits an arbitral tribunal, at the request of a party, and absent an agreement to the contrary, to "grant interim measures" in order to:

(a) maintain or restore the *status quo* pending determination of the dispute;
(b) take action that would prevent, or refrain from taking action that is likely to cause, current or imminent harm or prejudice to the arbitral process;
(c) provide a means of preserving assets out of which a subsequent award may be satisfied; or
(d) preserve evidence that may be relevant and material to the resolution of the dispute.[44]

Such interim relief may be granted only if the moving party proves that:

(a) irreparable harm is likely to result without the interim relief;
(b) the irreparable harm "substantially outweighs" the harm that is likely to be caused by the granting of the interim relief; and
(c) there is a "reasonable possibility" that the moving party will succeed on the merits of the claim.[45]

The party seeking interim relief shall be liable for any costs and/or damages caused thereby, if the arbitral tribunal later determines that the relief should not have been granted. Such costs or damages may be awarded at any point during the proceedings.[46]

An interim order (other than one granted *ex parte*, discussed below) can be enforced upon application to the Superior Court, unless the tribunal provides otherwise.[47] Enforcement may only be refused in limited circumstances (e.g., incapacity of the responding party, lack of notice, contrary to public policy).[48]

The tribunal may grant interim relief without notice to the other party (unless otherwise agreed to by the parties), provided that the tribunal considers that notice would risk frustrating the purpose of the relief sought.[49] A party seeking such an *ex parte* order must make full disclosure to the tribunal of "all circumstances that are likely to be relevant" to the request for relief, with that disclosure obligation continuing until the opposing party has had an opportunity to present its case.[50] If relief is granted on an *ex parte* basis, notice shall be given immediately afterwards to the other party,[51] and an opportunity shall be given "at the earliest practicable time" for that party to present its objection to the interim relief.[52] It should be noted, however, that such an order, made without notice, is not enforceable by the court and does not constitute an award.[53]

If the parties have agreed to arbitrate their dispute through an arbitration institution, that institution's procedures regarding interim relief will govern. The ICC International Court of Arbitration has special emergency procedures whereby the ICC can appoint an arbitrator on an urgent basis, where required.[54] Similarly, Article 6 of the International Centre for Dispute Resolution's *International Dispute Resolution Procedures* provides for the appointment of an emergency arbitrator to grant interim relief.[55]

However, parties may be better off seeking interim measures from the courts rather than arbitral tribunals because, unlike arbitrators, courts can make certain orders binding on third parties (e.g., *Mareva* injunctions). Moreover, seeking relief from the courts may be more practical if the matter is urgent and an *ad hoc* arbitral tribunal is still being established without the benefit of a set of rules from an arbitral institution that specifically provide for a process and timetable to seek and be awarded urgent interim relief.[56]

The arbitral award

Both the Ontario and the British Columbia statutes require that the award be in writing and signed by the arbitrator(s).[57] The award must state the date and place of the arbitration, and must set out the reasons for the decision (unless the parties have agreed that no reasons are to be given).[58] The award, once signed by the tribunal, must be delivered to each party.[59] No time limits are imposed for the delivery of the award.

If the matter settles prior to delivery of the arbitral award, the parties can ask the arbitral tribunal to prepare an award reflecting the settlement.[60] Such an award is binding and is of the same force and effect as an award reflecting the arbitral tribunal's decision on the merits.[61]

The Ontario statute is silent with respect to the arbitral tribunal's ability to award costs and interest. As a result, the tribunal's power to award costs and/or interest is determined by the arbitration agreement or by the procedural rules adopted for the arbitration, which may contain specific provisions as to costs.[62] British Columbia's legislation provides that, unless otherwise agreed to by the parties, costs of the arbitration are at the discretion of the arbitral tribunal. It also provides that the costs of the arbitration may include fees and expenses of arbitrators and expert witnesses, legal fees, administration fees and any other expenses incurred in connection with the arbitral proceedings.[63]

The mandate of the arbitral tribunal, along with the arbitral proceedings themselves, are terminated by the tribunal's final award.[64] Alternatively, the arbitral tribunal may terminate the proceedings before giving a final award, if:

1. the claimant withdraws his claim and the respondent does not object;
2. the parties agree on the termination of proceedings; or
3. the arbitral tribunal determines that the continuation of the proceedings is either unnecessary or impossible.[65]

Challenging the arbitral award

Neither the Ontario statute nor the British Columbia statute provide a right of appeal on the merits of an award.[66] It is not clear whether such a right can be granted by agreement of the parties.[67]

However, a party may apply to the courts to set aside the award.[68] Article 34(2) of the Model Law (adopted as part of the law of Ontario) provides the following grounds upon which an award may be set aside:

34(2) An arbitral award may be set aside by the court specified in Article 6 only if:

(a) the party making the application furnishes proof that:

  (i) a party to the arbitration agreement referred to in Article 7 was under some incapacity, or the said arbitration agreement is not valid under the law to which the parties have subjected it, or failing any indication thereon, under the Law of this State; or

  (ii) the party making the application was not given proper notice of the appointment of an arbitrator or of the arbitral proceedings or was otherwise unable to present his case; or

  (iii) the award deals with a dispute not contemplated by, or not falling within the terms of the submission to arbitration, or contains decisions on matters beyond the scope of the submission to arbitration, provided that, if the decisions on the matter submitted to arbitration can be separated from those not so submitted, only that part of the award which contains a decision on matters not submitted to arbitration may be set aside (which decisions can be separated from matters within the submission to arbitration); or

  (iv) the composition of the arbitral tribunal or the arbitral procedure was not in accordance with the agreement of the parties, unless such agreement was in conflict with a provision of this Law from which the parties cannot derogate, or, failing such agreement, was not in accordance with this Law; or

(b) the court finds that:

  (i) the subject matter of the dispute submitted to arbitration is not capable of settlement by arbitration under the law of this State; or

  (ii) the award is in conflict with the public policy of this State.

Applications to set aside an award must be made within three months of the receipt of the award to the courts of the province constituting the seat of the arbitration.[69] The Court may, when asked to set aside an award, where appropriate and if requested by a party, suspend the proceedings to set aside the award for a period of time to allow the arbitral tribunal an opportunity to resume the arbitral proceedings or take other actions, which, in the tribunal's opinion, will eliminate the grounds to set aside the award.[70]

A party may seek to have the arbitral tribunal correct any clerical, typographic or computation errors in an award, or may request the arbitral tribunal to interpret a specific point in the award. Such a request must be made within 30 days of receiving the award.[71] The arbitral tribunal may also correct any clerical, typographic or computation errors on its own initiative within 30 days of the date of the award.[72] The formalities of the award, as set out above, apply equally to any corrections or interpretations made.[73]

Enforcement of the arbitral award

All Canadian provinces and territories, with the exception of Quebec, have adopted and ratified the *New York Convention* allowing for the recognition and enforcement of arbitral awards from its signatory states. Among the adopting provinces, most have appended the *New York Convention* as schedules to their respective international commercial arbitration statutes, while the remainder have enacted legislation incorporating the *New York Convention*.[74] In Quebec, the *Civil Code of Procedure* provides that foreign arbitral awards will be recognised and enforced, if the matter in dispute is one that may be settled by arbitration in Quebec and if the award is not contrary to public policy. It also provides that the *New York Convention* should be "taken into account" when determining the scope of a party's right to have an award recognised and enforced.[75]

For those provinces that adopted or incorporated the *New York Convention*, it should be noted that in Canada, the *Convention* will apply only to differences arising out of legal relationships, whether contractual or not, which are considered as "commercial" under the laws of Canada,[76] except in the case of the Province of Quebec where the law does not provide for such limitation.[77]

Common to all jurisdictions (other than Quebec) is the requirement that a party seeking to enforce an award must supply an authenticated original award (or a certified copy), and a copy of the arbitration agreement (or a certified copy).[78] If the language of the award is not in English, the party seeking to enforce the award must supply a certified translation of the award.[79]

There are certain limited grounds upon which the court may refuse to enforce an arbitral award. These grounds, as set out in the Model Law,[80] are the same as the grounds noted above for setting aside an award, with the addition that an award may not be enforced if the party against whom the award is invoked furnishes proof that "[T]he award has not yet become binding on the parties or has been set aside or suspended by a court of the country in which or under the law of which the award was made."[81]

The most commonly cited basis for a refusal to enforce a foreign arbitral award is a failure by the arbitral tribunal to adhere to the norms of procedural fairness. Although the courts also have the power to refuse enforcement on the ground of public policy, they have been much more reluctant to invoke that ground for refusing to enforce an award.[82] Thus, for example, in *Corporacion Transnacional de Inversiones S.A. de C.V. v. Stet International S.p.A*, it was held that the court will only refuse to enforce an award in circumstances where the award offends the most basic and explicit principles of justice and fairness, or if it "evidences intolerable ignorance or corruption on the part of the arbitral tribunal".[83] Among the (admittedly rare) situations where the court will refuse enforcement based on public policy are situations where enforcement of the award would result in the plaintiff enjoying double recovery.[84]

The Ontario Court of Appeal in *Popack v. Lipszyc* recently held that reviewing courts have a residual discretion to refuse to set aside an award, or enforce an award, even if the court finds that one of the enumerated grounds in Articles 34 or 36 has been breached. The Court found that this residual discretion is "significantly affected" by the enumerated ground which has been breached.[85] Courts in other Canadian jurisdictions have similarly held that the courts retain a residual discretion to enforce or refuse to set aside an award depending on the effect of the breach.[86]

It should be noted that for most provinces, when a party seeks to enforce a foreign arbitral award, provincial limitation periods apply. For those provinces that have adopted the *New York Convention*, the provincial limitation periods are applicable by virtue of Article III of the *Convention*, which provides that each contracting state must recognise arbitral awards in accordance with the rules of procedure of that territory. The Supreme Court of Canada recently held that "rules of procedure" was broad enough to encompass provincial limitation periods.[87] Accordingly, in most jurisdictions an arbitral award should be subject to the general limitation period applicable to most causes of action, which in most provinces is two years.

In Ontario and Quebec, however, the situation is slightly different. Ontario's legislation incorporates a 10-year limitation period to commence an application to recognise or enforce an arbitral award. This limitation period commences from the date the award was made, or, if proceedings at the place of the arbitration were commenced, the date on which those proceedings concluded.[88] Quebec's statutory provision states that an arbitral award (once recognised by the court) is enforceable in the same manner as a judgment or order of the court.[89] In such circumstances, at least one author has suggested that an argument could be made that the enforcement of arbitral awards should be treated, for limitations purposes, the same as court orders. The limitation period in this respect is 10 years.[90]

Investment arbitration

Investment treaties

In recent years, Canada has emerged as a leading state in international investment arbitration. As of February 28, 2018, Canada has ratified 37 bilateral investment treaties, which are known in Canada as Foreign Investment Promotion and Protection Agreements ("FIPAs"). Notably, Canada has ratified FIPAs with 37 trading partners, including China and Russia.[91] In addition, Canada has concluded negotiations on (but has not ratified) a further six FIPAs[92] and is in the process of negotiating nine more.[93]

Canada has also ratified 13 free trade agreements ("FTAs").[94] Historically, the most prominent among those was the North American Free Trade Agreement ("NAFTA"), between Canada, the United States and Mexico. However, the future of that Agreement is unclear, in light of the ongoing negotiations to "modernize" NAFTA.[95] As a result, other free trade agreements are coming to the fore. Most prominent among them is the Comprehensive Economic and Trade Agreement with the European Union that came into force late in 2017.[96] In addition, in light of the announcement by the United States that it would not be ratifying the previously-signed Trans-Pacific Partnership, Canada and the remaining signatories have recently concluded negotiations in respect of the Comprehensive and Progressive Agreement for Trans-Pacific Partnership. That Agreement is expected to be signed in the spring of 2018.[97]

The FIPAs and FTAs to which Canada is a signatory generally provide that investors may submit a claim to arbitration under:

1. the International Centre for Settlement of Investment Dispute ("ICSID") rules – which are appropriate for matters arbitrated under the ICSID *Convention on the Settlement of Investment Disputes Between States and Nationals of Other States*;
2. the ICSID *Additional Facility Rules* – which are appropriate if one (but not both) of the parties to the dispute is a contracting member state or a national of a contracting member state under the ICSID *Convention*;
3. the UNCITRAL Arbitration Rules; or
4. another body of rules approved by the parties to the agreement (e.g., the London Court of International Arbitration Rules).[98]

In addition, Canada has ratified the ICSID *Convention on the Settlement of Investment Disputes Between States and Nationals of Other States*. Pursuant to the ICSID *Convention*,

Canadians who invest in other ICSID member states[99] and who find themselves in a dispute relating to that investment may rely upon an arbitration under the ICSID *Convention* to resolve their disputes.[100] However, unless the investor has the consent of the other parties to the dispute, it is open to a contracting state to ask the investor first to exhaust local administrative or judicial remedies before having recourse to the ICSID process.[101] Foreign investors who are nationals of ICSID contracting states also have reciprocal rights under the ICSID *Convention* in Canada.[102]

According to the information made public by the Canadian Government, as at February 28, 2018, Canada is a party to seven active investment arbitration disputes. Six of those disputes were brought under Chapter 11 of NAFTA.[103] The remaining dispute, which was commenced in 2016, was brought by Global Telecom Holding S.A.E., an Egyptian-based telecommunications services company, under the Canada-Egypt FIPA and claims damages of "at least $1.32 billion CAD".[104]

<u>Canada's Model FIPA</u>

The Canadian government introduced its "Model FIPA" in 2004.[105] Although the FIPAs that Canada has entered into with major trading partners, such as China and Russia, typically provide for their own customised procedures for arbitration claims, the FIPAs that Canada has entered into with many smaller countries adopt the procedures set out in the Model FIPA. Such agreements provide for, among other things, fair and equitable treatment in accordance with international law, public access to hearings and a procedure to be followed in accordance with the ICSID Rules, the UNCITRAL Arbitration Rules or another body of rules approved by the parties to the agreement (e.g., the London Court of International Arbitration Rules).

<u>Canada's enforcement of investment arbitration awards</u>

Canada is generally an enforcement-friendly jurisdiction. For example, in *United Mexican States v. Cargill Inc.*,[106] Mexico sought to set aside part of a US$77m arbitral award for losses that Cargill and its Mexican subsidiary sustained when Mexico imposed additional duties and permit requirements on the importation of high fructose corn syrup into Mexico. The arbitral tribunal, which was seated in Toronto, determined that Mexico had breached Chapter 11 of NAFTA when it imposed restrictions on the importation of the corn syrup. The tribunal awarded damages for "downstream losses" that Cargill's Mexican subsidiary suffered, as well as for "upstream losses" that the U.S. parent company suffered when it could no longer sell the corn syrup to its Mexican subsidiary.

Mexico applied to the Ontario Superior Court to set aside the US$41m portion of the arbitral award that related to upstream losses, on the basis that these damages were sustained by a U.S. producer and were therefore unrelated to an "investment" in Mexico as defined in Article 1139 of NAFTA. The application judge dismissed Mexico's application on the basis that Mexico's objection went to the merits of the decision, which was beyond the scope of review for the court.[107]

Mexico's subsequent appeal to the Ontario Court of Appeal was dismissed. The Court of Appeal determined that the proper standard of review was "correctness", but held that the arbitral tribunal was correct in holding that it had jurisdiction to decide the scope of damages suffered by Cargill and that NAFTA imposes no territorial limit on those damages.[108] The Supreme Court of Canada subsequently rejected Mexico's application for leave to appeal.[109] The decision in *Cargill* is consistent with the long-standing approach of Canadian courts, which is to proceed on the basis "that an expert international arbitral tribunal acted within its authority", and that judicial interference should be limited to extraordinary cases.[110] As is the case with international arbitration awards generally, the Canadian courts are loathe to interfere with investment treaty arbitration awards, and deference is afforded to the arbitral decision provided that the arbitration has followed the correct procedures and conducted a fair hearing.[111]

* * *

Endnotes

1. *Commercial Arbitration Act*, R.S.C. 1985, c. 17, as amended, s. 5(2).
2. The province of Quebec does not have an international arbitration statute. Instead, all arbitrations that take place in the province are subject to the provisions of the *Civil Code of Quebec*, CQLR c. C-1991, Part XVIII and other sections, including section 2895, 3121, 3133 and 3148.
3. *Arbitration Act*, 1991, S.O. 1991, c. 17, s. 2(1), which states that the act applies to all arbitrations in the province unless its application is excluded by law, or unless the *International Commercial Arbitration Act* applies.
4. *International Commercial Arbitration Act*, 2017, S.O. 2017, c. 2, s. 5(3).
5. *International Commercial Arbitration Act*, R.S.B.C. 1996, chapter 233.
6. *International Commercial Arbitration Act*, 2017, S.O. 2017, c. 2, s. 5(1).
7. *International Commercial Arbitration Act*, 2017, S.O. 2017, c. 2, Model Law, Chapter II, Art. 7(2), see also International Commercial Arbitration Act, R.S.B.C. 1996, c. 233, part 2, s. 7(3).
8. *Arbitration Act*, 1991, S.O. 1991, c. 17, s. 5(3), see also *Arbitration Act*, R.S.B.C. 1996, c. 55, s. 1 definition of "arbitration agreement".
9. *Arbitration Act*, 1991, S.O. 1991, c. 17, s. 2(1), see also *Arbitration Act*, R.S.B.C. 1996, c. 55, s. 1 definition of "arbitration agreement".
10. *International Commercial Arbitration Act*, 2017, S.O. 2017, c. 2, Model Law, Chapter I, Art. 1(1), see also *International Commercial Arbitration Act*, R.S.B.C. 1996, c. 233, part 1, s. 1(1). The British Columbia statute provides a non-exclusive list of when an arbitration will be considered "commercial", for example, disputes relating to a trade transaction for the supply or exchange of goods or services, a joint venture, construction, insurance, licensing, financing, banking, etc. (*International Commercial Arbitration Act*, R.S.B.C. 1996, c. 233, part 1, s. 1(6)). The various domestic arbitration statutes are not limited to "commercial" arbitration.
11. *Seidel v. TELUS Communications*, 2011 SCC 15.
12. *International Commercial Arbitration Act*, 2017, S.O. 2017, c. 2, Model Law, Chapter IV, Art. 16(1), see also *International Commercial Arbitration Act*, R.S.B.C. 1996, c. 233, part 4, s. 16(1).
13. See, for example, the Supreme Court of Canada decision of *Dell Computer Corp v. Union des Consommateurs*, [2007] 2 SCR 801 and the *Ontario Court of Appeal decision of Dancap Productions Inc. v. Key Brand Entertainment Inc.*, 2009 ONCA 135.
14. *International Commercial Arbitration Act*, 2017, S.O. 2017, c. 2, Model Law, Chapter IV, Art. 16(3), see also *International Commercial Arbitration Act*, R.S.B.C. 1996, c. 233, part 4, s. 16(6).
15. *Dell Computer Corp v. Union des Consommateurs*, [2007] 2 S.C.R. 801.
16. *International Commercial Arbitration Act*, 2017, S.O. 2017, c. 2, Model Law, Chapter

IV, Art. 16(1), see also *International Commercial Arbitration Act*, R.S.B.C. 1996, c. 233, part 4, s. 16(1).

17. *DG Jewelry Inc. v. Cyberdiam Canada Ltd* (2002), 21 CPC (5th) 174 (Ont. S.C.J.) para 20, *Krutov v. Vancouver Hockey Club Ltd.* 1991, 30 A.C.W.S. (3d) 164, para 15.
18. *International Commercial Arbitration Act*, 2017, S.O. 2017, c. 2, s. 8(1), see also *International Commercial Arbitration Act*, R.S.B.C. 1996, c. 233, part 5, s. 27(2).
19. *International Commercial Arbitration Act*, 2017, S.O. 2017 c. 2, s. 8(2) and 8(3), see also *International Commercial Arbitration Act*, R.S.B.C. 1996, c. 233, part 5, s. 27(3).
20. *Liberty Reinsurance Canada v QBE Insurance and Reinsurance (Europe) Ltd* (2002), 42 C.C.L.I. (3d) 249 (Ont. S.C.J.) para 22-23.
21. *International Commercial Arbitration Act*, 2017, S.O. 2017, c. 2, Model Law, Chapter V, Art. 21, see also *International Commercial Arbitration Act*, R.S.B.C. 1996, c. 233, part 5, s. 21.
22. *International Commercial Arbitration Act*, 2017, S.O. 2017, c. 2, Model Law, Chapter I, Art. 3, see also *International Commercial Arbitration Act*, R.S.B.C. 1996, c. 233, part 1, s. 3.
23. *Bell Canada v. The Plan Group*, 2009 ONCA 548.
24. *Limitations Act*, 2002, SO 2002, c. 24 schedule B, s. 4; *Limitation Act*, SBC 2012, c. 13, s. 6. Limitation periods vary by province.
25. Brian Casey, *Arbitration Law of Canada: Practice and Procedure*, 2nd ed. (New York: JurisNet, LLC, 2011) at 56; McEwan and Herbst, *Commercial Arbitration in Canada, A Guide to Domestic and International Arbitrations*, (Toronto: Canada Law Book 2014) at 7:10.
26. See, e.g., *United Mexican States v. Karpa* (2005), 136 A.C.W.S. (3d) 200 (ONCA), para 1.
27. For example, the parties cannot contract out of the requirement that the parties be treated with equality and that each party be given a full opportunity of presenting his or her case (*International Commercial Arbitration Act*, 2017, S.O. 2017, c. 2, Model Law, Chapter V, Art. 18, see also *International Commercial Arbitration Act*, R.S.B.C. 1996, c. 233, part 5, s. 18).
28. *International Commercial Arbitration Act*, 2017, S.O. 2017, c. 2, Model Law, Chapter V, Art. 19, see also *International Commercial Arbitration Act*, R.S.B.C. 1996, c. 233, part 5, s. 19.
29. *International Commercial Arbitration Act*, 2017, S.O. 2017, c. 2, Model Law, Chapter V, Art. 19(2), see also *International Commercial Arbitration Act*, R.S.B.C. 1996, c. 233, part 5, s. 19(3).
30. *International Commercial Arbitration Act*, 2017, S.O. 2017, c. 2, Model Law, Chapter V, Art. 26, see also *International Commercial Arbitration Act*, R.S.B.C. 1996, c. 233, part 5, s. 26.
31. *International Commercial Arbitration Act*, 2017, S.O. 2017, c. 2, Model Law, Chapter II, Art. 10 and 11, see also *International Commercial Arbitration Act*, R.S.B.C. 1996, c. 233, part 3, s. 10 and 11.
32. *International Commercial Arbitration Act*, 2017, S.O. 2017, c. 2, Model Law, Chapter II, Art. 11, see also *International Commercial Arbitration Act*, R.S.B.C. 1996, c. 233, part 3, s. 11.
33. *International Commercial Arbitration Act*, 2017, S.O. 2017, c. 2, Model Law, Chapter III, Art. 12(2), see also *International Commercial Arbitration Act*, R.S.B.C. 1996, c. 233, part 3, s. 12(3).

34. *International Commercial Arbitration Act*, 2017, S.O. 2017, c. 2, Model Law, Chapter III, Art. 13(2), see also *International Commercial Arbitration Act*, R.S.B.C. 1996, c. 233, part 3, s. 13(2).
35. *International Commercial Arbitration Act*, 2017, S.O. 2017, c. 2, Model Law, Chapter III, Art. 13, see also *International Commercial Arbitration Act*, R.S.B.C. 1996, c. 233, part 3, s. 13.
36. *Jacob Securities Inc. v Typhoon Capital BV*, 2016, ONSC 604, para 41.
37. *International Commercial Arbitration Act*, 2017, S.O. 2017, c. 2, Model Law, Chapter III, Art. 14(1), see also *International Commercial Arbitration Act*, R.S.B.C. 1996, c. 233, part 3, s. 14(1).
38. *International Commercial Arbitration Act*, 2017, S.O. 2017, c. 2, Model Law, Chapter III, Art. 14(1), see also *International Commercial Arbitration Act*, R.S.B.C. 1996, c. 233, part 3, s. 14(2).
39. See, for example, *Flock v Beattie, 2010 ABQB 193*. Although this case was an Alberta case regarding the Alberta domestic Act, it also canvasses the applicable Canadian and international law.
40. Brian Casey, *Arbitration Law of Canada: Practice and Procedure*, 2nd ed. (New York: JurisNet, LLC, 2011) at 154.
41. Brian Casey, *Arbitration Law of Canada: Practice and Procedure*, 2nd ed. (New York: JurisNet, LLC, 2011) at 154, citing *Sport Maska Inc. v. Zittrer*, [1988] 1 SCR 564 and certain English cases.
42. With respect to the courts' jurisdiction to grant interim relief, see: *African Mixing Technologies (PTY) Ltd. v. Canamix Processing Systems Ltd.*, 2014 BCSC 2130 at para. 55; and see: *TLC Multimedia Inc. v. Core Curriculum Technologies Inc.*, [1998] B.C.J. No. 1656 at para. 35 (S.C.). In addition, in Ontario, the *International Commercial Arbitration Act*, 2017 expressly provides that interim relief can be sought from the courts. S.O. 2017, c. 2, Model Law, Chapter IV A, Art. 17 J.
43. Section 17 of the *International Commercial Arbitration Act* R.S.B.C. 1996, chapter 233.
44. *International Commercial Arbitration Act*, 2017, S.O. 2017, c. 2, Model Law, Chapter IV A, Art. 17.
45. *International Commercial Arbitration Act*, 2017, S.O. 2017, c. 2, Model Law, Chapter IV A, Art. 17 A(1).
46. *International Commercial Arbitration Act*, 2017, S.O. 2017, c. 2, Model Law, Chapter IV A, Art. 17 G.
47. *International Commercial Arbitration Act*, 2017, S.O. 2017, c. 2, Model Law, Chapter IV A, Art. 17 H(1).
48. *International Commercial Arbitration Act*, 2017, S.O. 2017, c. 2, Model Law, Chapter IV A, Art. 17 I.
49. *International Commercial Arbitration Act*, 2017, S.O. 2017, c. 2, Model Law, Chapter IV A, Art. 17 B.
50. *International Commercial Arbitration Act*, 2017, S.O. 2017, c. 2, Model Law, Chapter IV A, Art. 17 F(2).
51. *International Commercial Arbitration Act*, 2017, S.O. 2017, c. 2, Model Law, Chapter IV A, Art. 17 C(1).
52. *International Commercial Arbitration Act*, 2017, S.O. 2017, c. 2, Model Law, Chapter IV A, Art. 17 C(2).
53. *International Commercial Arbitration Act*, 2017, S.O. 2017, c. 2, Model Law, Chapter IV A, Art. 17 C(5).

54. ICC Rules, Art. 29.
55. ICDR Rules, Art. 6.
56. Kenneth J. McEwan, *Commercial Arbitration in Canada: A Guide to Domestic and International Arbitrations* (Toronto: Canada Law Book, 2004+) at 6-31.
57. *International Commercial Arbitration Act*, 2017, S.O. 2017, c. 2, Model Law, Chapter VI A, Art. 31(1). see also *International Commercial Arbitration Act*, R.S.B.C. 1996, c. 233, part 6, Article 31(1). In Ontario, in proceedings with more than one arbitrator, the signatures of the majority of the tribunal is sufficient, so long as the reason for any omitted signature is stated.
58. *International Commercial Arbitration Act*, 2017, S.O. 2017, c. 2, Model Law, Chapter VI A, Art. Art. 31(2) and (3), see also *International Commercial Arbitration Act*, R.S.B.C. 1996, c. 233, part 6, Art. 31(3) and (4).
59. *International Commercial Arbitration Act*, 2017, S.O. 2017, c. 2, Model Law, Chapter VI A, Art. 31(4), see also *International Commercial Arbitration Act*, R.S.B.C. 1996, c. 233, part 6, Art. 31(5).
60. *International Commercial Arbitration Act*, 2017, S.O. 2017, c. 2, Model Law, Chapter VI A, Art. 30(1), see also *International Commercial Arbitration Act*, R.S.B.C. 1996, c. 233, part 6, Art. 30(2).
61. *International Commercial Arbitration Act*, 2017, S.O. 2017, c. 2, Model Law, Chapter VI A, Art. 30(2), see also *International Commercial Arbitration Act*, R.S.B.C. 1996, c. 233, part 6, Art. 30(4).
62. J. Brian Casey, *Arbitration Law of Canada: Practice and Procedure*, 2nd Ed., (New York: JurisNet, LLC, 2011), s.8.6.2, pgs. 362-363; McEwan and Herbst, *Commercial Arbitration in Canada, A Guide to Domestic and International Arbitrations,* (Toronto: Canada Law Book 2014) at 11:20.10.
63. *International Commercial Arbitration Act*, R.S.B.C. 1996, c. 233, part 6, s. 31(7) – (8).
64. *International Commercial Arbitration Act*, 2017, S.O. 2017, c. 2, Model Law, Chapter VI A, Art. 32(1), see also *International Commercial Arbitration Act*, R.S.B.C. 1996, c. 233, part 6, Art. 32(1).
65. *International Commercial Arbitration Act*, 2017, S.O. 2017, c. 2, Model Law, Chapter VI A, Art. 32(2), see also *International Commercial Arbitration Act*, R.S.B.C. 1996, c. 233, part 6, Art. 32(2).
66. Casey, *Arbitration Law of Canada: Practice and Procedure*, 2nd Ed., (New York: JurisNet, LLC, 2011), s. 8.10, p. 372, s. 9.2.2 p. 392.
67. Casey, *Arbitration Law of Canada: Practice and Procedure*, 2nd Ed., (New York: JurisNet, LLC, 2011), s. 8.10, p. 372, s. 9.2.2 p. 393. In *Hall Street Associates L.L.C. v. Mattel Inc. 128 S. Ct. 1396*, the United States Supreme Court concluded that it was not open to the parties to expand the powers of review granted by statute. See also McEwan and Herbst, *Commercial Arbitration in Canada, A Guide to Domestic and International Arbitrations* (Toronto: Canada Law Book 2014) at 10:50.20.
68. International Commercial Arbitration Act, R.S.O. 1990 c. I.9, Model Law, Chapter 2, Art. 6, wherein the Court is defined as the Superior Court of Justice; see also *International Commercial Arbitration Act*, R.S.B.C. 1996, c. 233, part 7, Art. 34(2) wherein the Court is defined as the Supreme Court.
69. Casey, *Arbitration Law of Canada: Practice and Procedure*, 2nd Ed., (New York: JurisNet, LLC, 2011), s. 10.3.2, p. 439-440; *International Commercial Arbitration Act*, 2017, S.O. 2017, c. 2, Model Law, Chapter VII A, Art. 34(3), see also *International Commercial Arbitration Act*, R.S.B.C. 1996, c. 233, part 7, Art. 34(3).
70. *International Commercial Arbitration Act*, 2017, S.O. 2017, c. 2, Model Law, Chapter

VII A, Art. 34(4), see also *International Commercial Arbitration Act*, R.S.B.C. 1996, c. 233, part 7, Art. 34(4).

71. *International Commercial Arbitration Act*, R.S.O. 1990 c. I.9, Model Law, Chapter VI-A, Art. 33(1), see also *International Commercial Arbitration Act*, R.S.B.C. 1996, c. 233, part 6, Art. 33(1) and (2).
72. *International Commercial Arbitration Act*, R.S.O. 1990 c. I.9, Model Law, Chapter VI-A, Art. 33(2), see also *International Commercial Arbitration Act*, R.S.B.C. 1996, c. 233, part 6, Art. 33(3).
73. *International Commercial Arbitration Act*, R.S.O. 1990 c. I.9, Model Law, Chapter VI-A, Art. 33(5), see also *International Commercial Arbitration Act*, R.S.B.C. 1996, c. 233, part 6, Art. 33(7).
74. Casey, *Arbitration Law of Canada: Practice and Procedure*, 2nd Ed., (New York: JurisNet, LLC, 2011), s.10.3.1, p. 437. Ontario's *International Commercial Arbitration Act*, 2017, S.O. 2017, c. 2, most recently incorporated the New York Convention as Schedule 1.
75. *Code of Civil Procedure*, R.S.Q. c. C-25.01, s. 948-949.
76. McEwan and Herbst, *Commercial Arbitration in Canada, A Guide to Domestic and International Arbitrations* (Toronto: Canada Law Book 2014) at 1:40.
77. The term commercial applies broadly to contractual and non-contractual commercial relationships such as leasing, construction, investment, financing, etc., but does not include labour and employment disputes or consumer claims. McEwan and Herbst, *Commercial Arbitration in Canada, A Guide to Domestic and International Arbitrations* (Toronto: Canada Law Book 2014) at 1:80; *Boroski v. Heinrich Fiedler Perforiertechnik GmbH* (1995), 29 C.P.C. (3d) 264 (Alta. Q.B.), see also *Patel v. Kanbay International Inc.* (2008), 93 O.R. (3d) 88 at paras. 12-13 (C.A.).
78. *International Commercial Arbitration Act*, 2017, S.O. 2017, c. 2, Model Law, Chapter VIII A, Art. Art. 35(2), see also *International Commercial Arbitration Act*, R.S.B.C. 1996, c. 233, part 8, Art. 35(2).
79. *International Commercial Arbitration Act*, 2017, S.O. 2017, c. 2, Model Law, Chapter VIII A, Art. 35(2), see also *International Commercial Arbitration Act*, R.S.B.C. 1996, c. 233, part 8, Art. 35(3).
80. *International Commercial Arbitration Act*, 2017, S.O. 2017, c. 2, Model Law, Chapter VIII A, Art. 36(1), see also *International Commercial Arbitration Act*, R.S.B.C. 1996, c. 233, part 8, Art. 36(1).
81. *International Commercial Arbitration Act*, 2017, S.O. 2017, c. 2, Model Law, Chapter VIII A, Art. 36(1)(a)(v), see also *International Commercial Arbitration Act*, R.S.B.C. 1996, c. 233, part 8, Art. 36(1)(a)(vi).
82. See, for example, *Schreter v. Gasmac Inc.,* [1992] O.J. No 257 at paras. 47-52 (Gen. Div.), see also *Beals v. Saldhana* [2001] O.J. No. 2586 at paras. 34-35, 84-86 (C.A.).
83. *Corporacion Transnacional de Inversiones S.A. de C.V. v. Stet International S.p.A* [1999] O.J. No. 3573 at para. 30 (S.C.J.) and see *Quintette Coal Limited v. Nippon Steel Corp. et al.,* [1990] B.C.J. No. 2241 at paras. 27 and 32 (C.A.).
84. *Subway Franchise Systems of Canada Ltd. v. Laich,* 2011 SKQB 249 at para. 40; and see *Lambert Re:*, [2002] O.J. No. 3163 (C.A.), affirming *Lambert Re:*, [2001] O.J. No. 2776 at para. 76 (S.C.J.).
85. *Popack v. Lipsyzc*, 2016 ONCA 135, affirming *Popack v. Lipsyzc*, 2015 ONSC 3460 at para. 28-29.
86. *The United Mexican States v. Metalclad Corporation*, 2001 BCSC 664 at para. 127-129; *Rheaume v. Société d'investissements l'Excellence Inc.*, 2010 QCCA 2269 at para. 61.

87. *Yugraneft Corp. v. Rexx Management Corp.* 2010 SCC 19 at paras. 14-23, see also Casey, *Arbitration Law of Canada: Practice and Procedure*, 2nd Ed., Jurisnet, 2011, at s. 10.4.2, p. 454-455.
88. *International Commercial Arbitration Act*, 2017, S.O. 2017, c. 2, part III, Art. 10.
89. *Code of Civil Procedure*, R.S.Q. c. C-25.01, s. 951.2.
90. Casey, *Arbitration Law of Canada: Practice and Procedure*, 2nd Ed., (New York: JurisNet, LLC, 2011), at s. 10.4.2, p. 455. Given that the Quebec statutory provision appears to presume that the foreign arbitral award has already been recognised by the local courts, it is not clear whether one would succeed in an argument that there is no limitation period for an application to recognise a foreign arbitral award (as opposed to an application to enforce an award that has already been recognised). See also, *Civil Code of Quebec*, CQLR c. C-1991, Art. 2924.
91. Canada also has FIPAs in force with the following countries: Argentina; Armenia; Barbados; Benin; Cameroon; Costa Rica; Côte d'Ivoire; Croatia; Czech Republic; Ecuador; Egypt; Hong Kong; Hungary; Jordan; Kuwait; Latvia; Lebanon; Mali, Panama; Peru; Philippines; Poland; Romania; Senegal; Serbia; Slovak Republic; Tanzania; Thailand; Trinidad and Tobago; Ukraine; Uruguay; and Venezuela. See: Global Affairs Canada, "Trade and Investment Agreements", (6 March 2017) online: http://www.international.gc.ca/trade-agreements-accords-commerciaux/agr-acc/fipa-apie/index.aspx?lang=eng.
92. Canada has signed (but has not yet ratified) FIPAs with Burkina Faso, Guinea, Mongolia and Nigeria. Canada has concluded FIPA negotiations (but has not yet signed FIPAs) with Albania, Bahrain, Madagascar, Moldova and Zambia. See: Global Affairs Canada, "Trade and Investment Agreements", (6 March 2017) online: http://www.international.gc.ca/trade-agreements-accords-commerciaux/agr-acc/fipa-apie/index.aspx?lang=eng.
93. Canada is in the process of negotiating FIPAs with Ghana, India, Kazakhstan, Kenya, Kosovo, Macedonia, Pakistan, Tunisia and the United Arab Emirates. See: Global Affairs Canada, "Trade and Investment Agreements", (6 March 2017) online: https://www.international.gc.ca/trade-commerce/trade-agreements-accords-commerciaux/agr-acc/index.aspx?lang=eng.
94. Canada also has FTAs with the following countries and organisations: Chile; Colombia; Costa Rica; European Free Trade Association (consisting of Norway, Switzerland, Iceland and Liechtenstein); Honduras; Israel; Jordan; Korea; Panama; and Peru. See: Global Affairs Canada, "Trade and Investment Agreements", (6 March 2017) online: http://www.international.gc.ca/trade-agreements-accords-commerciaux/agr-acc/fta-ale.aspx?lang=eng.
95. Global Affairs Canada, "Canada-European Union Comprehensive Economic and Trade Agreement (CETA)", (6 March 2017) online: http://www.international.gc.ca/trade-commerce/trade-agreements-accords-commerciaux/agr-acc/ceta-aecg/chronology-chronologie.aspx?lang=eng.
96. See: Justin Trudeau, Prime Minister of Canada, News, "Next steps for the Canada-EU Comprehensive Economic and Trade Agreement", (30 October 2016), online: http://pm.gc.ca/eng/news/2016/10/30/next-steps-canada-eu-comprehensive-economic-and-trade-agreement.
97. See: Global Affairs Canada, "Trade and Investment Agreements", (6 March 2017) online: https://www.international.gc.ca/trade-commerce/trade-agreements-accords-commerciaux/agr-acc/index.aspx?lang=eng.
98. See, for example, Government of Canada, "Agreement between Canada and [State] for the Promotion and Protection of Investments", (2004), online: http://www.italaw.com/documents/Canadian2004-FIPA-model-en.pdf [Model FIPA] at pages 26-27; see also:

Global Affairs Canada, "Agreement Between Canada and the Hashemite Kingdom of Jordan for the Promotion and Protection of Investments", (signed 30 November 2014) online: http://www.treaty-accord.gc.ca/text-texte.aspx?id=105176&lang=eng at Article 27; see also Global Affairs Canada, "Agreement Between Canada and the Republic of Peru for the Promotion and Protection of Investments", (signed 14 November 2006) online: http://www.treaty-accord.gc.ca/text-texte.aspx?id=105078&lang=eng at Article 27.

99. There are currently 161 ICSID member states. A full list can be found at: International Centre for Settlement of Investment Disputes, "Database of ICSID Member States", online: https://icsid.worldbank.org/en/Pages/about/Database-of-Member-States.aspx.

100. Article 25 of the ICSID Convention.

101. Article 26 of the ICSID Convention.

102. Article 25 of the ICSID Convention.

103. Global Affairs Canada, "Cases Filed Against the Government of Canada", (1 January 2005) online: http://www.international.gc.ca/trade-agreements-accords-commerciaux/topics-domaines/disp-diff/gov.aspx?lang=eng.

104. Global Affairs Canada, "Trade Topics: Dispute Settlement: Global Telecom Holdings S.A.E. v. Government of Canada", (28 June 2016) online: http://www.international.gc.ca/trade-agreements-accords-commerciaux/topics-domaines/disp-diff/gth_sae.aspx?lang=eng.

105. Government of Canada, "Agreement between Canada and [State] for the Promotion and Protection of Investments", (2004), online: http://www.italaw.com/documents/Canadian2004-FIPA-model-en.pdf [Model FIPA] at pages 26-27.

106. *United Mexican States v. Cargill Inc.*, 2011 ONCA 622, leave to appeal to SCC refused, [2011] S.C.C.A. No. 528.

107. *United Mexican States v. Cargill Inc.*, 2010 ONSC 4656.

108. *United Mexican States v. Cargill Inc.*, 2011 ONCA 622 at para. 74.

109. *United Mexican States v. Cargill Inc.*, [2011] S.C.C.A. No. 528.

110. *United Mexican States v. Cargill Inc.*, 2011 ONCA 622 at para. 33; see also *Consolidated Contractors Group S.A.L. (Offshore) v. Ambatovy Minerals S.A.*, 2016 ONSC 7171 at para. 34; and see *Canada (Attorney General) v. Mobil Investments Canada Inc.*, 2016 ONSC 790 at para. 34.

111. Alan Redfern and Martin Hunter, *Law and Practice of International Commercial Arbitration* 3rd ed. (London: Sweet & Maxwell 1999) at p. 433.

Julie Rosenthal
Tel: +1 416 597 4259 / Email: jrosenthal@goodmans.ca

Julie Rosenthal is a partner in the litigation group at Goodmans. She joined the firm in 1998 after clerking for Mr. Justice Frank Iacobucci at the Supreme Court of Canada.

Julie has extensive experience in complex commercial disputes, white-collar crime, internal investigations, domestic and international arbitration, injunctions and competition law, as well as judicial review and patent-related disputes. She has appeared before the Supreme Court of Canada, the Federal Court of Appeal, the Federal Court, and all levels of Court in Ontario. She has been counsel on a number of international arbitrations, including matters conducted under the ICC Rules, LCIA Rules, UNCITRAL Rules and on an *ad hoc* basis.

Brad Halfin
Tel: +1 416 597 4252 / Email: bhalfin@goodmans.ca

Brad Halfin is a partner in the litigation group at Goodmans. He focuses principally on the areas of commercial/construction litigation and arbitrations. His practice involves a broad range of commercial litigation matters including contract disputes, arbitrations involving real estate valuations and insurance defence. Brad has appeared at all levels of civil court in Ontario, including the Commercial Court and the Court of Appeal. He has also been involved in several domestic arbitration proceedings. Brad is also a contributing editor to LexisNexis Practice Advisor's Insolvency and Restructuring section on Construction Liens.

Tamryn Jacobson
Tel: +1 416 597 4293 / Email: tjacobson@goodmans.ca

Tamryn Jacobson is a partner in the litigation group at Goodmans, and has a broad-based civil and commercial litigation practice, with particular interest in arbitration work. She has significant experience with both international (*ad hoc*, ICC and LCIA) and domestic arbitrations, dealing with disputes covering many industries (e.g., technology, banking, mining, construction, retail, hospitality). She has also appeared before all levels of court in Ontario. Tamryn also has an active *pro bono* practice. She is involved with Law Help Ontario, acting as duty counsel for low-income litigants at the Ontario Superior Court of Justice. She also serves as a director and the Secretary of the AIDS Committee of Toronto (ACT), and is the Chair of ACT's Leadership and Governance Committee.

Goodmans LLP

Bay Adelaide Centre, 333 Bay Street, Suite 3400, Toronto, ON M5H 2S7, Canada
Tel: +1 416 979 2211 / Fax: +1 416 979 1234 / URL: www.goodmans.ca

Cayman Islands

Mo Haque QC & Andrew Pullinger
Campbells

Introduction

The Cayman Islands (colloquially known as 'Cayman') lie enviably in the warm waters of the north western Caribbean. Drawn by its exceptional beaches and clement weather, it attracts tourists from the world over. Being only an hour's flight from Miami it is also a natural offshore hub for many North American clients. It is a British Overseas Territory which enjoys political stability and has a well-founded reputation for a strong and impartial judiciary.

The legal system descends from the English common law, so its decisions draw wisdom from influential precedents created in the courts of many Commonwealth states. Any ultimate appeal lies to the Judicial Committee of the Privy Council of the United Kingdom – the members of which are Justices of the United Kingdom's Supreme Court. Judges from England will often preside over cases in the courts of the Cayman Islands.

Cayman is the world's fifth-largest financial centre and home to more than 80% of the world's hedge funds. Cayman's 11,000 funds have combined assets in excess of US$6 trillion. The Court is therefore experienced in considering disputes of the highest magnitude and regularly produces judgments which are relied upon in many jurisdictions. Its laws and legal system are well-developed and extremely well-versed in the financial and corporate arenas.

Arbitration in the Cayman Islands as a viable form of alternative dispute resolution was traditionally not suited to international cases. The old Arbitration Act of 2001 was based on England's Arbitration Act 1950. It contained what would now be considered a weakness relating to the wider powers of the Court to control arbitration proceedings. A prime example was the Court's power to continue court proceedings that had been commenced despite there being a valid arbitration clause. These anachronisms were remedied by the Arbitration Law, 2012 ("the Law"). This was modelled on England's Arbitration Act 1996 and the provisions of the UNCITRAL Model Law ("Model Law").[1,2] It was a complete and effective overhaul of the former arbitration position in the Cayman Islands, and a response to the growing importance of arbitration as a dispute resolution alternative.

In common with many jurisdictions, the Cayman Islands has seen arbitration growing in popularity.[3] Arbitration clauses are increasingly being included in commercial contracts and there is anecdotal evidence of greater recognition among practitioners and clients alike of the potential benefits of arbitration in the jurisdiction. As a result, there are now many reported cases from the Grand Court which relate to arbitrations in the Cayman Islands. No doubt the pro-arbitration legal framework and policies, relative ease of travel to the Cayman Islands and business-friendly immigration rules help to make arbitration a sensible alternative for many potential litigants. Arbitration is firmly on the menu of choices available to clients operating in the Cayman Islands.

The guiding principles

The provisions of the Law are expressly stated to be founded on the following principles:[4]

(i) the object of arbitration is to obtain the fair resolution of disputes by an impartial arbitral tribunal without undue delay or undue expense;

(ii) the parties should be free to agree how their disputes are resolved, subject only to such safeguards as are necessary in the public interest; and

(iii) in matters governed by the Law the court should not intervene except as provided in the Law.

These provide the bedrock for the construction and operation of arbitration clauses in the Cayman Islands.

The arbitration agreement

<u>Formalities</u>

The formalities required by the Law for any arbitration agreement follow those set out in Article 7 of the Model Law. Thus agreements must be in writing, and may be contained in arbitration clauses in wider agreements or in separate agreements. Being "*in writing*" includes electronic communications such as email or anything which provides a record of the agreement.[5] A suggested model clause is included in a Schedule to the Law for the parties to include if they are unable to agree the formulation of the arbitration clause.[6]

The Law includes an opt-out where one of the parties is a consumer in an arbitration agreement entered into in the Cayman Islands. In such a case, after a dispute has arisen, the consumer must certify in writing that he has read and understood the arbitration agreement and agrees to be bound by its terms before it may be enforced.[7] Although the term "consumer" is broadly defined in the Law, the Grand Court has confirmed that the provision applies only to individuals acting for purposes that are wholly or mainly outside their trade, business, craft or profession.[8]

<u>Arbitrability</u>

There is nothing within the Law that limits the scope of any arbitration save where it is contrary to public policy or the dispute is not capable of resolution by arbitration. The issue is determined on a case-by-case basis, with the vast majority of commercial disagreements being considered to be receptive to arbitration.[9] However, that is not always the case. In ***Cybernaut Growth Fund***[10] it was held that a petition to wind up a company and appoint an arbitrator was not arbitrable. However, this decision was doubted, but not overruled, in the appellate court in ***Re SPhinX Group***[11] where it was held that an argument over the distribution of a reserve in a court-supervised liquidation could be determined by arbitration.

In certain instances, statutory remedies and orders pursuant to regulatory laws are only available from the Grand Court.

<u>Joinder</u>

There is no express mechanism within the Law that allows joinder of another party to the arbitration. Parties may agree to consolidate proceedings or hearings, but the arbitral tribunal has no other power enabling it to do so.[12] Confirmation of this came in ***Unilever v ABC International***[13] where the respondent to an arbitration failed in its attempt to commence arbitral proceedings against several previous owners of the Claimant company.

<u>Competence-competence and separability</u>

Section 27 of the Law preserves the doctrine of *competence-competence* (found at Article 16 of the Model Law) that the arbitral tribunal has the power to rule on all matters connected to the arbitration, including its own jurisdiction and the validity of any arbitration agreement. The same section enshrines the doctrine of separability, meaning that for the purposes of considering its jurisdiction the tribunal treats the arbitration clause as standing independently of the balance of the agreement. Any matter concerning the jurisdiction of the arbitral tribunal must be raised in the arbitration itself. The tribunal can then either deal with the matter as a preliminary question or in its award on the merits.[14] This enables the arbitration to continue notwithstanding any such application. A ruling that the arbitral tribunal does not have jurisdiction is open to application to the Court as long as the application is made within 30 days.[15]

Proceedings commenced in breach of an arbitration agreement

Where a party to an arbitration agreement commences proceedings in the courts of the Cayman Islands in breach of an arbitration agreement, the Court is bound to stay such proceedings on the application of a party to the arbitration agreement made at any time after the acknowledgment of service and before taking any step in the proceedings.[16]

The Grand Court's jurisdiction to grant an anti-suit injunction to restrain a party from continuing proceedings instituted in a foreign jurisdiction in breach of a Cayman arbitration agreement was first recognised in ***Origami Partners***.[17] An anti-suit injunction was recently granted by the Grand Court in ***BDO Cayman Ltd v Argyle Funds SPC Inc***[18] to restrain the joint official liquidators of a Cayman company from continuing proceedings commenced in New York in breach of arbitration agreements.

Arbitration procedure

General duties

The general duties of the arbitral tribunal are to: (a) act fairly and impartially; (b) allow each party a reasonable opportunity to present its case; (c) conduct the arbitration without unnecessary delay; and (d) conduct the arbitration without incurring unnecessary expense.[19]

Commencement

Arbitral disputes commence on the date at which one party: (a) gives the other notice of an intention to submit a dispute; (b) serves on the other a notice requiring it to appoint or agree to the appointment of an arbitrator; or (c) serves on the other a notice requiring it to submit the matter to an arbitrator already named in the agreement.[20] The form of the notice is not prescribed.

Seat of arbitration

The Law contains no geographical restriction upon the seat of arbitration, but in default of agreement it is left to the tribunal to decide, having regard to the circumstances of the case and the convenience of the parties.[21] Hearings, and meetings among tribunal members, may be convened at any place the tribunal considers appropriate.[22]

Procedural requirements

The parties are free to agree the rules of the tribunal, failing which it will conduct the arbitration as it sees as appropriate.[23] It is not uncommon for agreements to refer to the rules of international organisations such as the AAA, LCIA and ICC. The tribunal can then deal with any challenges to jurisdiction and scope, and move on to consider specific procedural requirements relevant to the case being considered such as the timings of Statements of Claim and Defences,[24] and whether oral hearings are necessary.

Evidential rules

An arbitral tribunal is not bound by the rules of evidence but may inform itself in relation to any matter as it thinks fit.[25] The Law also follows precisely Article 19(2) of the Model law which gives the tribunal the power to determine admissibility, relevance, materiality and weight.[26] The Grand Court in ***Appalachian Reinsurance (Bermuda) Ltd v Mangino***[27] upheld a decision not to have an oral hearing in a summary judgment application relying in part on the parties' agreement that the tribunal was not obliged to follow "*judicial formalities or rules of evidence*". In practice this evidential rule makes appeals to the substance of arbitration awards difficult though decisions taken irrationally may still be challenged on the grounds that the Award is contrary to natural justice.

Expert evidence

The parties may agree whether or not expert evidence is necessary and, if so, the number of experts. Where there is no agreement the tribunal may appoint experts and require the parties to provide access to, or produce, documents, goods or property for inspection by the expert.[28]

Confidentiality

Arbitral proceedings are generally confidential arising, as they often will, from commercial contracts containing confidentiality clauses. The Caymanian Courts will follow the English common law in implying a term that the arbitral proceedings and documents are confidential.[29] The Law enshrines this by making arbitrations both private and confidential[30] and theoretically making actionable any disclosure of confidential information by a party or the tribunal.[31] There is no record of arbitrations.

Should the arbitration require intervention by the court for any reason, any party may request that applications to the court be heard in private, and that information only be published if the court is satisfied that the information is not of a type that a party would wish to remain confidential. Judgments in court proceedings arising out of arbitrations may be published (as normal) but any party has the right to apply for parts of the judgment to remain undisclosed or undisclosed[32] for a certain period of time.[33]

Arbitrators

Appointment

The parties are free to choose the number of arbitrators on the tribunal[34] (in practice, almost always either one or three) and the procedure for selection.[35] In default, the Law provides there shall be a single arbitrator.[36] The UK Supreme Court held in ***Jivraj v Hashwani***[37] that it was not contrary to equality legislation to include arbitration clauses that stipulated the religion (and, by extension, the race, nationality and gender) of an arbitrator. It is therefore unlikely that the Cayman Courts would strike down similar arbitration clauses.

Any arbitrator appointed has a duty to declare matters that might give rise to doubts about his or her independence or impartiality.[38]

Challenge

A challenge to the appointment of an arbitrator may only be made on the narrow ground of there being justifiable doubts about his or her independence, impartiality or qualification for the role.[39]

The parties may agree on the procedure for challenging an arbitrator.[40] If there is no such agreement, then the Law incorporates the timings of challenge contained at Article 13 of the Model Law, namely that a party has 15 days to send written reasons for the challenge to the tribunal.[41] The tribunal will then decide, and any further challenges must be made to the Court within 30 days of the tribunal's decision.[42] The arbitration may continue in the interim.[43] There is no further appeal from the decision of the Court.[44]

A party may apply to the Court for an arbitrator to be removed who is physically or mentally incapable of conducting proceedings (or where there exist justifiable doubts about the same).[45] Likewise an arbitrator may be removed by the Court where he or she has refused or failed to conduct proceedings properly or with due expedition, and the same has or could lead to substantial injustice to a party.[46]

Immunity

It was not clear whether arbitrators shared the long-established principle of judicial immunity from suit to be found in the English common law.[47] Any doubt in the Cayman Islands is removed by Section 25 of the Law which gives the tribunal and any of its employees or agents immunity for negligent acts or omissions or mistakes of law or procedure. Liability still remains for actions carried out in bad faith.[48]

Interim relief

The Law has a system of 'Interim Measures' and 'Preliminary Orders'[49] mirroring that in the Model Law.

Unless the parties agree otherwise, the arbitral tribunal has broad powers to grant interim measures which: (a) preserve the *status quo*; (b) prevent any action that may harm the arbitral process; (c) preserve assets; and/or (d) preserve evidence.[50] A grant of an interim measure will only be made if the party requesting the measure can satisfy the tribunal that: (i) if any harm caused is not remediable by damages, then the harm caused by the measure substantially outweighs harm that would be caused by not granting it; and (ii) there is a reasonable possibility that the requesting party will succeed on the merits of the claim.[51]

At the same time as requesting a without-notice interim measure, a party may also seek a preliminary order, the purpose of which is to direct the counter-party not to frustrate the purpose of the interim measure requested.[52] This will be granted if the tribunal believes that the counter-party would frustrate the interim measure had it received notice of the application.[53] This is a more serious measure because it carries with it a negative connotation about the rectitude of the counter-party. Immediately after making a preliminary order, the tribunal will give notice to any other parties, and grant them an opportunity to present their case at the earliest practicable time.[54] A preliminary order will expire 20 days after its issue.[55]

The tribunal may ask the requesting party to provide appropriate security in connection with the interim measure.[56] By contrast, the party applying for a preliminary order must provide security unless the tribunal regards it as inappropriate or unnecessary to do so.[57] The tribunal may require any party requesting an interim measure to promptly disclose any material change in circumstances.[58] A party applying for a preliminary order must disclose all circumstances that are relevant to the granting or maintaining of the order.[59] If it later transpires that the interim measure or preliminary order should not have been granted, the requesting party may be liable for costs and damages.[60] These can be awarded at any time during the proceedings.[61]

The arbitration award

Formalities

The formalities of the Award required by Article 31 of the Model Law are brought into the Law by Section 63. The Award must be in writing, signed by all or the majority of arbitrators,[62] and should provide reasons for the decision, unless otherwise agreed or the matter has been settled on agreed terms.[63] The Award must state on its face the date of the Award and the seat of the arbitration.[64] There is no time limit within which an Award must be made following the conclusion of the tribunal proceedings,[65] but (as stated above) the parties may apply for an arbitrator to be removed if he or she has not acted with due expedition. In practice, awards are typically produced promptly. If the time for making an Award is stipulated in the arbitration agreement, the parties may, unless they agree otherwise, apply to the Court for an extension of time.[66]

Within 30 days of an Award being received a party may ask, on notice, that it be corrected for minor mistakes[67] or that specific points be interpreted.[68] The Law allows the tribunal 30 days to respond.[69] The parties may also within 30 days ask for an additional award in respect of claims presented in the arbitration, but not decided in the Award.[70] The tribunal is initially permitted 60 days within which to respond.[71]

Remedies available to the tribunal

The parties are able to agree the powers of the tribunal when it comes to available remedies.[72] Unless the parties otherwise agree, the arbitral tribunal is able to award any relief that a Court could have awarded had the matter been litigated in a civil court.[73] Unlike some other jurisdictions, there is nothing that prevents the tribunal making an award for specific performance in respect of land.

The Law gives the tribunal a discretionary power to award interest on some or all of any Award for any period.[74] The rate of interest after the Award is the same as that for a judgment debt.[75] In the Cayman Islands this rate is to be found in the *Judgment Debts* (*Rates of Interest*) Rules 2012. This will vary depending on the currency in which the award was made. For instance, damages in US dollars gather interest at 2.375%, but in South African Rand the relevant rate is 7.125%.[76]

Costs

The Law provides that unless otherwise expressly stated, costs are at the complete discretion of the arbitral tribunal.[77] There are no provisions which direct the way in which the discretion ought to be exercised. It is likely to be guided the law of the arbitration agreement.

Third party funding

There has been a trend in the Cayman Islands towards the recovery of third party funding. The Grand Court has approved the same where it has been used to fund liquidation estates which could not otherwise have afforded their actions.[78] The English High Court in the landmark case of ***Essar Oilfields Services Limited v Norscot Rig Management PVT Limited***[79] has held that it is permissible to recover those costs in arbitral proceedings. This position was adopted in ***A Company v A Funder***,[80] where such funding was obtained by a party seeking to recognise and enforce a New York arbitration award in the Cayman Islands.[81]

It was said by Segal J that:

> "*Cayman has an important, world-class court system and litigation culture and there is no reason why responsible, properly regulated commercial litigation funding undertaken in accordance with the principles I have set out should not have a place in this jurisdiction. As has been accepted in other leading financial centre common law jurisdictions and as the Chief Justice noted in* ***Quayum****, the law of maintenance and champerty has evolved reflecting the evolution of public policy and that evolution should be reflected in Cayman law.*"

Challenge to the award

Seasoned practitioners know the difficulties in challenging a final decision of an arbitral tribunal. Section 75(1) of the Law broadly follows Article 34 of the Model Law and permits the court to set aside an Award on any of the following grounds:

(i) incapacity of a party;

(ii) invalidity of the arbitration agreement;

(iii) lack of proper notice of the appointment of the arbitrator or proceedings;

(iv) inability to present the case;

(v) the Award oversteps its jurisdiction in dealing with irrelevant matters;

(vi) the panel or procedure was not in accordance with the agreement of the parties (unless the agreement itself would not have been lawful);

(vii) the making of the Award was induced or affected by fraud, corruption or misconduct on the part of the Arbitrator;

(viii) a breach of natural justice occurred in connection with the making of the Award by which the rights of any party has been prejudiced;

(ix) the subject matter of the dispute is not arbitrable; or

(x) the Award is contrary to public policy.

Any application to the court must be made within 30 days of the aggrieved party receiving the Award.[82]

Whilst there is no express provision allowing the Court to set aside an Award on the grounds that a serious irregularity has taken place, this will generally be caught by the power to set aside an award on the ground that there has been a breach of natural justice.

Parties have a limited right to appeal to the Court on a point of law.[83] Leave of the Court will be required.[84] Leave will only be given if the question of law: was one that was before the tribunal; is one that would substantially affect the rights of one or more of the parties, and the tribunal's decision was obviously wrong; or, where the point is of general importance, is at least open to serious doubt.[85] Any further applications to appeal require leave of the Court, and will only be given if the matter is of general importance or there is other special reason.[86]

Any applications to set aside Awards or appeals must be made within 30 days of an Award and only after all arbitral processes have been exhausted.[87]

Enforcement of the award

The Caymans Islands is a signatory to the (New York) Convention. The Convention is widely regarded as one of the most successful international treaties, with about 157 participant nations. The enforcement of awards made in such countries is governed in the Cayman Islands by the Foreign Arbitral Awards Enforcement Law (1997 Revision).

The preconditions set out in the Convention are that originals, or certified copies, of the Arbitration Agreement and Award are provided (suitably translated if necessary).[88] The Courts will recognise the Award, and enforcement can only be challenged on grounds similar to those in which a domestic award could be challenged, namely:[89]

(i) the parties to the agreement were under some incapacity or the arbitration agreement was not valid under the law of the agreement or under the law of the country where the award was made; or

(ii) the losing party was not given proper notice of the appointment of the arbitrator or of the arbitration proceedings or was otherwise unable to present his or her case; or

(iii) the award deals with matters falling outside the terms of the submission to arbitration, or contains decisions on matters beyond the scope of the submission, provided that if the decisions on matters submitted to arbitration can be separated from those not submitted, then that part of the award may be recognised and/or enforced; or

(iv) the composition of the arbitral authority or the arbitral procedure was not in accordance with the agreement of the parties or, failing such agreement, was not in accordance with the law of the country where the arbitration took place; or

(v) the award has not yet become binding on the parties, or has been set aside or suspended by a competent authority of the country in which, or under the law of which, that award was made; or

(vi) the subject matter of the difference is not capable of settlement by arbitration under the law of that country; or

(vii) the recognition or enforcement of the award would be contrary to the public policy of that country.

If necessary, the Convention will be interpreted in accordance with principles of international law as set out in Articles 31 and 32 of the Vienna Convention on the Law of Treaties.

Section 72(5) of the Law provides that any arbitral award, irrespective of the country in which it was made, shall be enforceable.

It is relatively straightforward to enforce an arbitral award in the Cayman Islands, particularly by comparison to the enforcement of foreign judgments, which generally fall to be enforced under the common law. An award will be enforced as if it was a domestic judgment, and all the ordinary enforcement mechanisms are therefore available.

* * *

Endnotes

1. United Nations Commission on International Trade Law Model Law on International Commercial Arbitration (1985), with amendments as adopted in 2006.
2. Section 4 of the Act gives the UNCITRAL Model Law force of law save as amended.
3. https://www.campbellslegal.com/client-advisory/rise-arbitration-cayman-islands-3319/.
4. Section 3(3). See also *Appalachian Reinsurance (Bermuda) Ltd v Greenlight Reinsurance Ltd* [2014] 1 CILR 152.
5. Section 4(3) of the Law.
6. Section 4(2) of the Law.
7. Section 8(1) of the Law.
8. *BDO Cayman Ltd v Argyle Funds SPC Inc (in Official Liquidation)* (FSD No. 163 of 2017). A note produced by Campbells is at: https://www.campbellslegal.com/client-advisory/anti-suit-injunction-granted-grand-court-restrain-cayman-liquidators-continuing-new-york-litigation-3676/.
9. Section 26(1) of the Law.
10. [2014] (2) CILR 4133.
11. *Re.* SphinX Group of Companies (Cause CICA 06/2015).

12. Section 36 of the Law.
13. [2008] CILR 87.
14. Section 27(8) of the Law.
15. Section 27(9) of the Law.
16. Section 9 of the Law.
17. *Origami Partners III LP v Pursuit Capital Partners (Cayman) Limited* [2012] (2) CILR 191.
18. *BDO Cayman Ltd v Argyle Funds SPC Inc (in Official Liquidation)* (FSD No. 163 of 2017).
19. Section 28 of the Law.
20. Section 12(1) of the Law.
21. Section 30(2) of the Law.
22. Section 30(3) of the Law.
23. Section 29 of the Law.
24. Section 32(1) of the Law.
25. Section 33(6) of the Law.
26. Section 29(3) of the Law.
27. *Appalachian Reins (Bermuda) Ltd. v Mangino* [2014] (1) CILR 152.
28. Section 37 of the Law.
29. *Glidepath BV and Ors v John Thompson and Ors* [2005] EWHC 818 (Comm).
30. Section 81(1) of the Law.
31. Section 81(2) of the Law.
32. Section 84(3) of the Law.
33. Section 84(3)(b) of the Law.
34. Section 15(1) of the Law.
35. Section 16(1) of the Law.
36. Section 15(2) of the Law.
37. [2011] UKSC 40.
38. Section 18(1) of the Law.
39. Section 18(3) of the Law.
40. Section 19(1) of the Law.
41. Section 19(2) of the Law.
42. Section 19(4) of the Law.
43. Section 19(6) of the Law.
44. Section 19(5) of the Law.
45. Section 20(1)(a) of the Law.
46. Section 20(b) of the Law.
47. *Sutcliffe v Thackrah* [1974] AC 727 and *Arenson v Arenson* [1977] AC 405.
48. Section 25(4) of the Law.
49. Part VIII of the Law.
50. Section 44 of the Law.
51. Section 45(1) of the Law.

52. Section 46(1) of the Law.
53. Section 45(2) of the Law.
54. Section 47(2) of the Law.
55. Section 47(4) of the Law.
56. Section 49(1) of the Law.
57. Section 49(2) of the Law.
58. Section 50(1) of the Law.
59. Section 50(2) of the Law.
60. Section 51(1) of the Law.
61. Section 51(1) of the Law.
62. If any arbitrator's signature is missing, a reason should be provided: Section 63(1)(b) of the Law.
63. Section 63(2) of the Law.
64. Section 63(3) of the Law.
65. Section 59(2) of the Law.
66. Section 60(1) of the Law.
67. Section 69(1)(a) of the Law.
68. Section 69(1)(b) of the law applying Article 33 of the Model Law.
69. Section 69(2) of the Law.
70. Section 69(4) of the Law.
71. Section 69(5) of the Law, which can be extended by 30 days: Section 69(6).
72. Section 57(1) of the Law.
73. Section 57(2) of the Law.
74. Section 58(1) of the Law.
75. Section 58(3) of the Law.
76. http://www.gov.ky/portal/pls/portal/docs/1/11525535.PDF.
77. Section 64(1) of the Law.
78. *Re.* ICP Strategic Credit Income Fund Ltd [2014] 1 CILR 314.
79. [2016] EWHC 2361.
80. Unreported, 23 November 2017, Segal J.
81. A note produced by Campbells is at: https://www.campbellslegal.com/client-advisory/cayman-court-approves-litigation-funding-agreement-3561/.
82. Section 75(2) of the Law.
83. Section 76(1) of the Law.
84. Section 76(1) of the Law.
85. Section 76(4) of the Law.
86. Section 76(11) of the Law.
87. Section 77(2) and (3) of the Law.
88. Article IV of the Convention.
89. Article V of the Convention.

Mo Haque QC
Tel: +1 284 494 2423 / Email: mhaque@campbellslegal.com
Mo is a Partner in Campbells' Litigation, Insolvency and Restructuring Group and is based in the British Virgin Islands. He is an English QC and has 20 years of experience at the English Bar in commercial litigation, international arbitration and dispute resolution.
Mo has advised upon a breadth of cases ranging from insolvency and winding-up issues through to the professional liabilities of directors, liquidators and receivers. He has appeared before pretty much every form of tribunal as well as in numerous arbitrations. He has advised clients in the laws of different jurisdictions and under different rules (ICC, LCIA and UNCITRAL).

Andrew Pullinger
Tel: +1 345 949 2648 / Email: apullinger@campbellslegal.com
Andrew is a partner in Campbells' Litigation, Insolvency & Restructuring Group and specialises in commercial litigation, international arbitration and dispute resolution. He has extensive experience acting for and advising clients in relation to complex and high value disputes, typically with a cross-border element.
Andrew has experience litigating in jurisdictions throughout the world, as well as conducting institutional and *ad hoc* arbitrations under a variety of different rules (including ICC, LCIA, AAA and UNCITRAL). Prior to joining Campbells in January 2014, Andrew practised at DLA Piper in both Australia and London. In London, Andrew specialised in international dispute resolution with a particular focus on international arbitration. He has extensive experience coordinating and leading teams in major, complex and high value disputes. He has particular expertise advising clients in respect of investment fund and other financial services disputes (especially claims against administrators and custodians), professional negligence claims and a broad range of contractual disputes. His clients have included foreign governments, major banks, leading professional services firms and other multinationals spanning a number of sectors.

Campbells

Floor 4, Willow House, Cricket Square, Grand Cayman KY1-9010, Cayman Islands
Tel: +1 345 949 2648 / Fax: +1 345 949 8613 / URL: www.campbellslegal.com

China

Ning Fei, Shengchang Wang & Jing Liu
Hui Zhong Law Firm

Introduction

Arbitration is on the rise in China. This is largely attributed to the compounded consequences of two critical phenomena: on the one hand, the dynamic growth of China's economy over the last decades has inevitably brought with it a high volume of disputes; and on the other, the implementation of the Arbitration Law of the People's Republic of China (1994) has shaped a pro-arbitration environment, which in turn attracts more and more parties to resolve disputes through arbitration in China.

According to the statistics released by the Law Office of the State Council of the PRC, up to 2017, 235 arbitration commissions have been established in China's major cities. Altogether, these arbitration bodies accepted over 200,000 new arbitration cases in 2016, with a total disputed amount over RMB 469.5 billion Yuan (equivalent to US$ 71 billion). Among the 235 arbitration commissions, China International Economic and Trade Arbitration Commission (CIETAC), Beijing Arbitration Commission (BAC), Shenzhen International Court of Arbitration (SCIA), Shanghai International Economic and Trade Arbitration Commission (SHIAC), and China Maritime Arbitration Commission (CMAC) have gained international reputations and become leading arbitration institutions in the Asia-Pacific regions.

Other well-known arbitration institutions in the world, such as Hong Kong International Arbitration Centre (HKIAC), Singapore International Arbitration Centre (SIAC), and the International Court of Arbitration of the International Chamber of Commerce (ICC Court), have set up their representative offices in Shanghai, China to expand arbitration services to business-people. It is envisaged that the presence of foreign arbitration institutions in mainland China will help improve China's arbitration system and environment as well.

China is not yet a territory of UNCITRAL Model Law, but the Model Law was taken as a guide when the Arbitration Law was drafted. The basic principles of modern arbitration have been introduced into China's arbitration. Nevertheless, there are still some distinctions between the Arbitration Law and Model Law, such as *ad hoc* arbitration, interim protection measures and judicial review of arbitration.

The Arbitration Law applies to both domestic and international arbitration. Within the Arbitration Law, there is a bifurcated treatment of the two types of arbitration. For domestic arbitration, the people's court may examine certain substantive issues of arbitral awards in the process of setting-aside or enforcement, while in international arbitration, the people's court is normally required to abstain from touching on the merits of the arbitral awards. Calls for revision of the Arbitration Law have been soaring in recent years.

China is a contracting state to the New York Convention on the Recognition and Enforcement of Foreign Arbitral Awards (the 1958 New York Convention). China acceded to the 1958 New York Convention on 22 January 1987 and it entered into force in China on 22 April 1987. When acceding to the Convention, China made a reciprocity reservation and commercial reservation pursuant to Article I of the Convention. Upon resumption of sovereignty over Hong Kong and Macao, the government of China extended the territorial application of the Convention to Hong Kong SAR and Macao SAR in 1997 and 2005 respectively.

China has made bilateral arrangements on mutual recognition and enforcement of arbitral awards with Hong Kong SAR (2000) and Macao SAR (2007).

China is a contracting state to the Convention on the Settlement of Investment Disputes between States and Nationals of Other States (the ICSID Convention). China signed the Convention on 9 February 1990, deposited the ratification on 7 January 1993, and the Convention was effective in China from 6 February 1993. Up to the end of 2017, China has concluded 145 bilateral investment treaties (BITs) and 21 other treaties with investment provisions (TIPs). Of the 145 BITs, 16 are signed but not in force, and 14 are terminated.

There are no special national courts for international arbitration. Despite this, the Supreme People's Court has endeavoured to centralise and harmonise the standards for recognition and enforcement of arbitration agreements and arbitral awards as well as for the setting-aside of arbitral awards. The concrete method is to set up a unique, level-by-level report mechanism, which is discussed in detail below.

Arbitration agreement

The Arbitration Law provides that an arbitration agreement shall not be made orally and must be in writing. The Contract Law (1999) stipulates that 'in writing' means a contract, letter or electronic message that is capable of expressing its contents in a tangible form (Article 11). As to the content of an arbitration agreement, Article 16 of the Arbitration Law provides that an arbitration agreement shall include three elements to be valid:

- the expression of the parties' intention to submit to arbitration;
- the subject matters to be arbitrated; and
- the arbitration institution selected by the parties.

In addition, Article 17 of the Arbitration Law provides that an arbitration agreement shall be invalid under any of the following circumstances:

- matters agreed upon for arbitration are not arbitrable;
- an arbitration agreement was concluded by persons without or with limited capacity for civil acts; or
- one party forces the other party to sign an arbitration agreement by means of duress.

It is obvious that the Arbitration Law encourages institutional arbitration, and an agreement for *ad hoc* arbitration under the Arbitration Law is in general invalid. However, the Supreme People's Court has made a breakthrough for *ad hoc* arbitration by issuing a judicial interpretation named the Opinions on Providing Judicial Safeguards for the Construction of Pilot Free Trade Zones (No. 34 [2016]), which recognises the validity of an arbitration agreement providing for *ad hoc* arbitration to be conducted in mainland China between or among the specific entities, i.e., the enterprises that are registered within the Pilot Free Trade Zones.

Article 2 and Article 3 of the Arbitration Law deal with the issue of arbitrability from different angles. According to Article 2, both contractual disputes and tortious disputes are arbitrable if they occur between parties on an equal footing, related to economic interest and covered by the arbitration agreement. Article 3 lists two typical situations where the subject matters are non-arbitrable: disputes over marriage, adoption, guardianship, child maintenance and inheritance; and administrative disputes falling within the jurisdiction of the relevant administrative organs according to law. A Public-Private Partnership (PPP) contract may contain both arbitrable and non-arbitrable disputes, the distinction of which depends on whether they are solely related to the exercise of governmental or administrative power.

The Arbitration Law is silent on joinder/consolidation of third parties. This issue is left for various arbitration rules.

The 2015 CIETAC Rules introduce new provisions allowing the joinder of additional parties under the same arbitration agreement to the existing arbitration proceedings. The admissibility of the joinder will be decided by either the arbitration institution or the arbitral tribunal after it hears from all parties including the additional party (Article 18).

Consolidation of two or more arbitrations with multiple parties is a complicated issue. The core of the issue is that all parties must be bound by an existing arbitration agreement or there is a consensus reached by all parties. The arbitration commission plays a central role in making a decision on consolidation. According to Article 19 of the 2015 CIETAC Rules, CIETAC may consolidate arbitrations if any of the following circumstances exists: (i) all of the claims in the arbitrations are made under the same arbitration agreement; (ii) the claims in the arbitrations are made under multiple arbitration agreements that are identical or compatible and the arbitrations involve the same parties as well as legal relationships of the same nature; (iii) the claims in the arbitrations are made under multiple arbitration agreements that are identical or compatible and the multiple contracts involved are constituted by a principal contract and its ancillary contract(s); or (iv) all the parties to the arbitrations have agreed to consolidation.

The Chinese law recognises the separability of an arbitration agreement. Both Article 19 of the Arbitration Law and Article 57 of the Contract Law stipulate that the validity of an arbitration agreement is independent from the underlying contract. Modification, rescission, termination of the contract or its being declared invalid does not affect the validity of an arbitration agreement.

The Arbitration Law fails to expressly regulate the *competence-competence* of an arbitral tribunal. While Article 20 of the Arbitration Law provides that if the parties object to the validity of the arbitration agreement, they may apply to the arbitration institution for a decision or to a people's court for a ruling, it does not preclude an arbitration institution from authorising an arbitral tribunal to make a decision on the jurisdictional issue if necessary. This is particularly true where the jurisdictional dispute is not merely a *prima facie* issue but also involves factual determination to be carried out by an arbitral tribunal. In fact, many Chinese arbitration rules have a special provision stating that the arbitral tribunal may decide on the jurisdictional issue with authorisation from the arbitration institutions.

Arbitration procedure

According to Article 22 and Article 23 of the Arbitration Law, a party may commence an arbitration by submitting an application for arbitration, which shall specify:

- the name, gender, age, occupation, work unit and address of the party;

- the name, domicile and the name and position of the legal representative or the person in charge of the legal entity;
- the reliefs sought and facts and grounds on which the claim is based; and
- evidence and the source thereof, the name and address of the witness.

Additional requirements for the commencement of an arbitration proceeding may be tailored by the parties or formulated by various arbitration rules. For example, the parties may set conciliation within a specific time period as a condition precedent to arbitration. Under Article 13 of the 2015 CIETAC Rules, failure to complete all formalities (including paying deposit of arbitration fees) by the claimant may result in rejection of the application for arbitration and the arbitration proceeding being deemed not to have commenced.

The Chinese arbitration rules clearly distinguish the place (or seat) of arbitration from the place of hearing. While the place of arbitration must be fixed either by the parties or by the arbitral tribunal to be one specific place, the place of hearing can be more than one place and can be anywhere that the tribunal deems convenient to all participants.

Chinese law has abundant rules of evidence applied to arbitration. Articles 43-46 of the Arbitration Law and Articles 63-81 of the Civil Procedural Law set out various rules of evidence covering most of the imperative issues, including the types of evidence, the burden of proof, the examination and verification of evidence, witness, expert, appraiser, interim protection measure for evidence, and power of collecting evidence by the judge/arbitrator on his/her own initiative. During the process of arbitration, an arbitral tribunal may invite the parties to reach further agreement on rules of evidence or decide appropriate rules of evidence at its own discretion.

Article 68 of the Civil Procedural Law deals with privilege and disclosure issue. It provides that evidence which involves any state secret, trade secret or individual privacy shall be kept confidential, and if it is necessary to present such evidence in hearing, such evidence shall not be presented in hearing open to the public. Attorney-client privilege is generally respected and protected.

In recent years, there has been an increasing tendency for the parties to agree on, and for the arbitral tribunal to apply or seek guidance from, the IBA Rules on the Taking of Evidence in International Arbitration. In many aspects, the CIETAC Guidelines on Evidence (2015) resemble the IBA Rules. The so-called "soft law" such as IBA guidelines and LCIA guidelines are being taken into account by more and more practitioners and arbitrators as useful reference in Chinese arbitration.

In Chinese arbitration, there are two types of expert: expert appointed by the arbitral tribunal; and expert appointed by the parties. Experts can furnish the arbitral tribunal with written statement on facts or law. To ensure the parties are provided with a reasonable opportunity to present their cases, experts may be called upon to be present at the oral hearing, and examined by the parties.

Arbitration in China is normally confidential, unless the parties have agreed otherwise or the arbitral tribunal has decided otherwise. Article 40 of the Arbitration Law stipulates that an arbitration shall not be conducted in public. If the parties agree to a public hearing, the arbitration may proceed in public, except those concerning state secrets.

Arbitration rules adopted by the Chinese arbitration institutions often go further to state that all participants to arbitration shall assume the responsibility of keeping all matters relating to arbitration confidential.

Arbitrators

Arbitration in mainland China is predominantly administered by arbitration commissions, each of which maintains its own panel of arbitrators. Generally, arbitration commissions only allow parties to choose arbitrators from their panel lists. In recent years, a few arbitration commissions like CIETAC and BAC have begun to take a more liberal approach, allowing parties who have reached agreement otherwise to nominate and appoint arbitrators from outside the existing panel lists, but subject to confirmation by the chairman of the arbitration commissions. All arbitrators must meet the qualification requirements laid down by Article 13 (for arbitrators of Chinese nationals) or Article 67 (for arbitrators of foreign nationals) of the Arbitration Law. The arbitration rules promulgated by each arbitration commission contain detailed methods of appointment, including appointment by default in case one party fails to do so.

The Arbitration Law stipulates that the parties shall have the right to challenge an arbitrator on any one of the following grounds (Article 34):

- the arbitrator is a party in the arbitration or a close relative of a party or of a party's counsel in the arbitration;
- the arbitrator has a personal interest in the case;
- the arbitrator has any other relationship with a party, or a party's counsel, in a case that may affect the impartiality of the arbitration; or
- the arbitrator has privately met with a party or a party's counsel, or accepted an invitation to entertainment or a gift from a party or a party's counsel.

The Arbitration Law provides that if a party challenges an arbitrator, it shall submit its challenge statement not later than the closing of the final hearing. The chair of the arbitration commission is empowered to decide whether the challenge should be approved.

Almost every arbitration commission has published its own ethical rules of arbitrators, many of which borrow some experiences enriched by the IBA Guidelines on Conflicts of Interest in International Arbitration. In this case, an arbitrator must abide by the applicable ethical rules in addition to the statutory requirements. According to the principle of party autonomy, the parties may also agree that the IBA Guidelines on Conflicts of Interest in International Arbitration be applied to their specific arbitration. An arbitrator's mandate is usually terminated with dismissal of the case or by rendering of an arbitral award, or on exceptional occasions, by rendering a substitute arbitral award after re-arbitration. Arbitrators are entitled to be reimbursed for their arbitrators' fees and expenses.

There is no immunity provision for arbitrators in the Arbitration Law, nor does it appear in the arbitration rules adopted by the Chinese arbitration commissions. The issue of immunity can be an area left for future regulation. Nevertheless, under Article 38 of the Arbitration Law, an arbitrator may be imposed with sanctions in two situations:

- where the arbitrator has privately met with a party or a party's counsel, or has accepted an invitation to entertainment or a gift from a party or a party's counsel, and the circumstances are serious; or
- while arbitrating the case, the arbitrator has accepted bribes, resorted to deception for personal gain or perverted the law in the ruling.

Under these circumstances, the Arbitration Law provides that the arbitrator concerned shall assume liability "according to the law". The scope of liability of an arbitrator is uncertain as yet and it is to be further observed.

A salient feature of Chinese institutional arbitration is that secretaries to arbitral tribunals are widely used and almost all secretaries are appointed by the arbitration commissions. The primary function performed by the secretaries is to assist the arbitral tribunals to administer arbitration proceedings. An arbitral tribunal may employ its own secretary selected from outside the secretariat, but only with consent from both parties.

Interim relief

According to Article 100 of the Civil Procedural Law (2013), there are three types of interim measures available for a party to seek from the people's court (i.e., preservation of property, preservation of evidence, and order to act or not to act). Article 101 of the Civil Procedure Law permits a party to apply for interim measures prior to initiating arbitration owing to urgent situations and upon providing a guarantee. Articles 28, 46 and 68 of the Arbitration Law provide that the competent people's courts, which have jurisdiction over an application for interim measures, are the courts where the preserved property or evidence, or the domicile of the party against whom the application is sought, is located. It is generally understood that under the current Chinese law, the power to take interim measures in aid of arbitration is exclusively reserved for the people's court, as Article 28 and Article 46 of the Arbitration Law expressly require that an arbitration commission, upon receipt of one party's application for interim measures, must pass on the application to the competent people's court for the said court to examine and make a ruling.

Subject to the restrictive provisions of Chinese law, an arbitral tribunal has very limited power to order interim measures that do not call for compulsory enforcement. For instance, an arbitral tribunal may issue an interlocutory award ordering sale of perishable goods, inspection and test run of equipment in dispute, audit of accounting records, or suspension or prevention of a party from carrying on certain conduct during the process of the arbitration. The arbitral tribunal may draw an adverse conclusion if one party breaches the orders. The Chinese law is silent on the issue of security for costs. Whether an arbitral tribunal may order a party to provide security for costs under the Chinese law is a controversial issue and in practice, no reported case shows that an arbitral tribunal seated in mainland China has ordered security for costs.

Many Chinese arbitration rules, such as those adopted by CIETAC, SHIAC, SCIA and BAC, contain new rules of arbitration to set out special provisions regarding emergency arbitrators who may order interim measures. However, the operation of these rules will largely depend on whether the applicable national law permits exercise of power by an emergency arbitrator. Under the current Chinese law, the answer is negative. There are calls for the Arbitration Law to be revised to catch up with the mainstream in this respect.

It is clear that under Article 100 of the Civil Procedural Law, the people's court has the power to order certain conduct from a party or prohibit the party from certain conduct. Accordingly, at least at a theoretical level, the Chinese court may order anti-suit injunctions in aid of international arbitration, or order anti-arbitration injunctions in aid of domestic litigation. In practice, the Chinese court normally takes an alternative approach to achieve the same goal. For instance, if the parties are bound by a valid arbitration agreement and one party chooses to file a lawsuit before the people's court, under Article 124 (2) of the Civil Procedural Law, the court shall notify the plaintiff to apply to an arbitral institution for arbitration if, in accordance with law, both parties are bound by a written arbitration agreement and they are prohibited from instituting an action in a people's court. The notice can be made either orally or in written form.

Arbitration award

Obviously an arbitral award shall be rendered in written form. An oral award will not be able to meet the requirements set out by Article 54 of the Arbitration Law. As to the content of an award, Article 54 of the Arbitration Law provides that an arbitral award must state the arbitration claims, the matters in dispute, the grounds upon which an award is given, the results of the award, the allocation of the arbitration fees and the date of the award. It further requires that the award must be signed by the arbitrators and sealed by the arbitration commission (for institutional arbitration). A dissenting arbitrator may choose not to sign the arbitral award, but the validity, finality and enforceability of an arbitral award will not be affected if an arbitrator dissents.

If an arbitral award is made in accordance with a settlement agreement reached by the parties through a successful conciliation, either conducted by an arbitrator-turned-mediator or by any other neutrals, the arbitral award is categorised as a consent award. For a consent award, the facts of the dispute and the reasons on which the award is based may not be stated in the award (Article 49 of 2015 CIETAC Rules). If a settlement agreement infringes the right of a third party or is contrary to the public interest, the tribunal has to power to decline recording the settlement agreement as a consent award (Article 46 of the 2016 SCIA Rules).

The Arbitration Law does not set out any time limit within which an arbitral award must be rendered. This issue is normally dealt with by the relevant arbitration rules.

In practice, the time limit for making an award may vary depending upon the types of arbitral procedure. For an ordinary arbitration procedure, the 2015 CIETAC Rules state that an arbitral tribunal shall render an award within six months from the date the arbitral tribunal is formed (Article 48). In summary procedure, the time limit is three months (Article 62), and for domestic arbitration, the time limit is four months (Article 71). The president of the Arbitration Court of CIETAC may, at the request of an arbitral tribunal, extend the time period if the president considers it truly necessary and the reasons for the extension are truly justified.

The Arbitration Law contains no specific guidance for arbitrators on how to allocate arbitration fees. This issue is left for the relevant arbitration rules. In general, the arbitration rules empower arbitrators with the broadest discretion to make decisions on cost allocation. An arbitral tribunal has the power to determine in an arbitral award that the losing party shall compensate the winning party for the expenses reasonably incurred by it in pursuing the case. The test of reasonableness is determined by an arbitral tribunal on a case-by-case basis. When an arbitral tribunal finds it necessary, it may decide that the party who has delayed the arbitration proceedings or acted in bad faith bear all, or a larger proportion, of arbitration costs. The recoverable costs awarded to a prevailing party may include an arbitration body's administrative fees, arbitrators' fees, attorneys' fees, in-house fees and costs, costs of witnesses, appraiser's fees, travel expenses and other reasonable costs. As third party funding for arbitration becomes popular, it is envisaged that under Chinese law an arbitral tribunal is not precluded from awarding arbitration costs in relation to that transaction.

The issue of interest is usually dealt with by the applicable substantive law and an arbitral tribunal may award it at the request of one or both parties. Very often, arbitral tribunals seated in mainland China award simple or compound interest on principal claims, calculated from the date due until the date of actual payment.

Challenge of the arbitration award

The Chinese law generally adopts the principle of finality of an arbitral award. Under Article 57 of the Arbitration Law, an arbitral award shall become legally effective on the date it is made. Article 9 of the Arbitration Law declares that the single ruling system shall be applied in arbitration. The arbitration commission shall not accept any application for arbitration, nor shall a people's court accept any action submitted by the party in respect of the same dispute after an arbitration award has already been given in relation to that matter. In other words, an arbitral award has the effect of *res judicata* regarding the same dispute that has already been adjudicated by an arbitral tribunal.

Adhering to the principle of finality, an arbitral award is not subject to appeal before the people's court. Nor does the court have the power to modify an arbitral award. In the process of setting-aside proceedings, however, the people's court has the power to rule to remit the arbitral award to the original arbitral tribunal to re-arbitrate the dispute if it is satisfied that the previous procedural irregularities in arbitration are remediable. Article 61 of the Arbitration Law provides that if the people's court holds that the case may be re-arbitrated by the arbitral tribunal after receipt of the application for setting-aside of an award, the court shall inform the arbitration tribunal of re-arbitration of the case within a certain period of time, and rule to suspend the setting-aside procedure. If the tribunal accepts to conduct re-arbitration, it may render a new award in substitution of the original award. If the arbitral tribunal refuses to re-arbitrate, the people's court shall rule to resume the setting-aside procedure.

The Arbitration Law provides that a court that has the primary and exclusive jurisdiction over setting aside an arbitral award is the intermediate people's court where the arbitration institution is domiciled (Article 58). Though the Arbitration Law is silent on *ad hoc* arbitration, theoretically the court that has primary and exclusive jurisdiction over the setting-aside of an *ad hoc* arbitral award shall be the intermediate people's court where the *ad hoc* arbitration takes place.

The court may rule to set aside an award on any of the grounds enumerated by law at the request of a party, or rule to nullify an arbitral award if the court finds *ex officio* that the award is contrary to the social public interest (i.e., public policy).

The grounds for setting aside an arbitral award vary depending upon the nature of the award. The Chinese law gives a bifurcated treatment towards pure domestic arbitration and foreign-related arbitration. The main distinction is whether the court may take a judicial review on the merits of the arbitral award that is brought into setting-aside proceedings.

A court may rule to set aside a domestic arbitral award if a party can furnish evidence to prove that there exist any of the following circumstances (Article 58 of the Arbitration Law and Article 237 of the Civil Procedural Law):

- there is no agreement for arbitration;
- the matters awarded are out the scope of the arbitration agreement or are beyond the limits of authority of an arbitration commission;
- the composition of the arbitral tribunal or the conduct of arbitration proceedings violates the procedures prescribed by law;
- the evidence on which the award is based is forged;
- evidence that has sufficient impact on the impartiality of an award has been discovered as having been concealed by the opposite party; or

- arbitrators have accepted bribes, resorted to deception for personal gains or perverted the law in the award.

A court may rule to set aside a foreign-related arbitral award if a party can furnish evidence to prove that there exist any of the following circumstances (Article 70 of the Arbitration Law and Article 274 of the Civil Procedural Law):

- the parties concerned have not stipulated an arbitration clause in the contract or have not subsequently reached a written agreement for arbitration;
- the applicant is not duly notified to appoint the arbitrator or to proceed with the arbitration, or the applicant fails to state its opinions owing to reasons for which the applicant is not held responsible;
- the composition of the arbitral tribunal or the conduct of arbitration proceedings is not in conformity with the rules of arbitration; or
- matters for arbitration are out of the scope of the arbitration agreement or are beyond the limits of authority of the arbitration commission.

The court shall form a collegiate bench to hear the application. Should any of the aforesaid grounds be found, the arbitral award shall be ruled to be set aside. The limitation of action for a party to apply for setting aside an award is six months starting from the date of receipt of the award, otherwise the application is time-barred.

No doubt the setting-aside of an arbitral award will have adverse effect on the finality of an arbitration. For the sake of avoidance of possible misconduct by the local courts or undue influence from local protectionism, the Supreme People's Court has set up a level-by-level report mechanism in respect of the setting-aside of arbitral awards ever since 1998 by virtue of issuing the Notice of Certain Matters Pertaining to Setting Aside of Foreign-related Arbitral Awards (No. 40 [1997]). In the said Notice, the Supreme People's Court decides that a level-by-level report mechanism applies to the setting-aside of Chinese foreign-related arbitral awards, arbitral awards made in foreign countries, and arbitral awards made in Hong Kong, Macao and Taiwan regions. This mechanism is reiterated and reinforced in 2017 by the Provisions of the Supreme People's Court on Report for the Approval of Arbitration Cases that are Subject to Judicial Review (No. 21 [2017]). According to the mechanism, if both the intermediate and high people's courts find that such an arbitral award should be set aside, an intermediate people's court must report its finding and opinion to the competent high people's court, which must report its finding and opinion to the Supreme People's Court. The level-by-level reports are made through the internal channels of the court system and they are not open to the parties or the public. Only after the Supreme People's Court has agreed in a written reply may an intermediate people's court issue its ruling to set aside an arbitral award.

In 2017, the level-by-level report mechanism was reiterated and reinforced by the Provisions of the Supreme People's Court on Report for the Approval of Arbitration Cases that are Subject to Judicial Review (No. 21 [2017]). In addition, the level-by-level report mechanism was extended to the regime of domestic arbitration. Article 3 of the said Provisions provides that the high people's court, if it intends to agree with the intermediate people's court or the special people's court that the setting-aside of a domestic arbitral award is to be granted, it shall report to the Supreme People's Court for approval under the following circumstances, and only after case review by the Supreme People's Court can a ruling be rendered according to the opinion of the Supreme People's Court: (1) the domiciles of the parties to the arbitration case that is subject to judicial review are located in different provinces; or

(2) the ground upon which the setting-aside of a domestic arbitral award is to be refused is violation of social and public interests.

Despite being criticised for lack of transparency, it is widely recognised that the role the Supreme People's Court plays in the level-by-level report mechanism is very helpful for harmonising the criterion of setting-aside, and effective in combating potential local protectionism. According to a statistic released by the Supreme People's Court, amongst the arbitral awards that had been filed to the people's courts for setting aside during the time period 2013-2015, 5.33% of foreign-related arbitral awards were ruled being set aside, and 15.77% of domestic arbitral awards were ruled being set aside. With implementation of the 2017 judicial interpretation on a level-by-level report mechanism, it is expected that the percentage of domestic arbitral awards set aside will decrease in the coming years.

Enforcement of the arbitration award

The PRC Arbitration Law sets out a general obligation on parties to comply with an arbitral award. If a party fails to comply with the award within the time period specified by the award, the successful party is entitled to apply to the competent people's court for compulsory enforcement of the award.

An arbitral award is recognisable and enforceable unless there is a ground for non-enforcement. For the purpose of enforcement, it is imperative to identify what type of an arbitral award it belongs to at the outset, since the grounds for refusal of enforcement of an arbitral award vary depending upon the type of an arbitral award. Generally, there are six types of arbitral awards that may be sought for enforcement in mainland China and the grounds for refusal of enforcement are contained in different sources of law as follows:

- the arbitral award under the 1958 New York Convention (Convention award): Article V of the 1958 New York Convention;
- the arbitral award of a foreign country that is not a contracting state to the 1958 New York Convention (non-Convention award): Article 283 of the Civil Procedure Law which requires that the enforcement shall be pursued under the principle of reciprocity;
- the arbitral award made in Hong Kong SAR or Macao SAR: the Supreme People's Court Interpretations on recognition and enforcement of Hong Kong arbitral awards (2000) or Macao arbitral awards (2007), under which the grounds for refusal basically mirror Article V of the 1958 New York Convention;
- the arbitral award made in Taiwan region: according to the Supreme People's Court Stipulation on Recognition and Enforcement of Arbitral Awards Made in Taiwan Region (2015), under which the grounds for refusal also highly resemble Article V of the 1958 New York Convention;
- the foreign-related arbitral award made in mainland China: identical to those for setting aside a foreign-related arbitral award made in mainland China (Article 71 of the Arbitration Law, Article 274 of the Civil Procedure Law); and
- the pure domestic arbitral award made in mainland China: identical to those for setting aside a domestic arbitral award made in mainland China (Article 237 of the Civil Procedure Law).

The level-by-level report mechanism was first set up by the Supreme People's Court in the regime of enforcement. In 1995, the Notice of the Supreme People's Court on the Disposal of the Relevant Issues concerning Foreign-Related Arbitration and Foreign Arbitral Matters by People's Courts (No. 18 [1995]) was issued by the Supreme People's Court. This Notice applies to non-enforcement of Chinese foreign-related arbitral awards, arbitral awards made in foreign countries, and arbitral awards made in Hong Kong, Macao and Taiwan regions. According to the mechanism, an intermediate people's court must report its finding and opinion to the competent high people's court, which must report its finding and opinion to the Supreme People's Court if both the intermediate and high level people's courts find that such an arbitral award should be denied enforcement. Only after the Supreme People's Court has agreed in a written reply may an intermediate people's court issue its ruling to refuse enforcement.

The level-by-level report mechanism was reiterated and reinforced in 2017 by the Provisions of the Supreme People's Court on Report for the Approval of Arbitration Cases that are Subject to Judicial Review (No. 21 [2017]) issued by the Supreme People's Court, and it was also extended to the regime of domestic arbitration. Similar to setting-aside of arbitral awards, an intermediate people's court may rule to deny enforcement only after an internal level-by-level report process has been completed. The Supreme People's Court has a final say on non-enforcement of two types of domestic arbitral awards: (1) the domiciles of the parties to the arbitration case that is subject to judicial review are located in different provinces; or (2) the ground upon which the enforcement of the domestic arbitral award is to be refused is violation of social and public interests.

The procedural requirements for enforcement of an arbitral award can be summarised as follows:

- application is made to the people's court in the place where the party against whom the enforcement is sought is domiciled or where the property subject to enforcement is located;
- documents to be submitted include a written application for enforcement, original or notarised and authenticated copies of the arbitral award and arbitration agreement, proof of the applicant's identity and valid power of attorney;
- fees and expenses for enforcement are paid in deposit; and
- the time limit for submission of an application for enforcement is two years, commencing from the last date of voluntary compliance prescribed by the arbitral award or, failing that, from the date that the arbitral award becomes binding.

According to a statistic released by the Supreme People's Court, amongst the arbitral awards that had been filed to the people's courts for enforcement during the time period 2013-2015, 0.14% of foreign-related arbitral awards were ruled to deny enforcement, and 4.67% of domestic arbitral awards were ruled non-enforcement.

It is believed that in general, the Chinese courts will not recognise or enforce an arbitral award that has been set aside by the court at the place of arbitration. Article 9 of the PRC Arbitration Law states that in case an arbitral award is set aside, the available remedy for the parties is either to reach a new arbitration agreement between them in respect of the same dispute in order to re-apply for arbitration, or to initiate a lawsuit before the competent court without concluding a new arbitration agreement. Whether the Chinese court will take a liberal approach to allow enforcement of an annulled arbitral award in the future is still open for further observation.

Investment arbitration

China is a contracting state to the ICSID Convention, which became effective in China from 6 February 1993. On 7 January 1993, China notified ICSID pursuant to Article 25(4) of the Convention, that the Chinese Government would only consider submitting to the jurisdiction of the ICSID disputes over compensation resulting from expropriation and nationalisation. This notice may be deemed as a limitation of consent to ICSID arbitration by the Chinese Government. However, the limitation imposed by this notice would be deemed lifted if China agrees to liberalise the scope of disputes submitted to ICSID arbitration by a subsequent BIT or multinational treaty.

Up to 31 December 2017, China has concluded 145 bilateral investment treaties (BITs) and 21 other treaties with investment provisions (TIPs). China is a contracting party to the China-Japan-Korea Agreement for the Promotion, Facilitation and Protection of Investment. This trilateral treaty became effective on 17 May 2014 in China and it provides a wide range of options to resolve investment disputes, which, *inter alia*, includes ICSID arbitration and arbitration under the UNCITRAL Rules. The Free Trade Agreement between China and Australia became effective on 20 December 2015. The China-Hong Kong CEPA Investment Agreement became effective on 28 June 2017.

***Development of investor-State arbitration in Mainland China*:** A notable development in Mainland China is that both SCIA and CIETAC announced in recent years that they would accept and administer investor-State arbitration cases concerning BITs claims and other investment treaty claims. SCIA introduces UNCITRAL Rules to administer investor-State arbitration and CIETAC publishes its own arbitration rules for international investment disputes. While China's One Belt, One Road (OBOR) Initiative will inevitably bring with it numerous investor-State arbitrations, it is anticipated that the Chinese arbitration institutions may play a greater role in resolving OBOR disputes.

ICSID arbitrations where China is a respondent: Over the years there have been three ICSID arbitration cases to which China is a respondent. The Claimants are Malaysian investor Ekran Berhad (ICSID Case No. ARB/11/15), Korean investor Ansung Housing Co., Ltd (ICSID Case No. ARB/14/25), and German investor Hela Schwartz Gmbh (ICSID Case No. 17/19), respectively. The ICSID Case No. ARB/11/15 was settled and the proceedings were discontinued on 16 May 2013. The ICSID Case No. ARB/14/25 was concluded in the form of an arbitral award rendered by the arbitral tribunal on 9 March 2017, ruling that the investor's claim was time-barred by a three-year limitation of prescription embodied in the 2007 China-Korea BIT. The ICSID Case No. ARB/17/19 was registered on 21 June 2017 and it is still pending. There is no case of the kind where China has accepted the ICSID award and paid the investors yet. Nevertheless, it is widely admitted that China will be involved in more and more investor-State arbitration cases, and that the enforcement issue will emerge sooner or later in the coming years.

Enforcement of investor-State arbitral award in Mainland China: By acceding to the 1965 ICSID Convention, China undertakes the treaty obligation to recognise and enforce the ICSID award by virtue of Article 54 (1) of the said Convention which provides that "[e]ach Contracting State shall recognize an award rendered pursuant to this Convention as binding and enforce the pecuniary obligations imposed by that award within its territories as if it were a final judgment of a court in that State." Article 54 (3) further addresses that enforcement of the ICSID award "shall be governed by the laws concerning the execution of judgments in force in the State in whose territories such execution is sought". However, the Chinese law does not offer specified rules of implementation on how to enforce an ICSID Convention. In general, Article 283 of the PRC Civil Procedural Law (2012) allows a winning party to apply directly to the intermediate people's court at the place of domicile of the party against whom enforcement is sought or at the place where the property thereof is located, and the people's court shall process the application in accordance with an international treaty concluded or acceded to by China or under the principle of reciprocity. Assuming that China is a defendant and a losing party to an ICSID award, it would not be easy to identify which court is an appropriate forum for recognising and enforcing the ICSID award, since the plain understanding of the terms "domicile" and "property" under Article 283 of the PRC Civil Procedural Law may arguably be interpreted to the effect that they are directed to any intermediate people's court in Mainland China.

Further, the Supreme People's Court made it clear in 1987 that an investor-State award cannot be recognised and enforced under the 1958 New York Convention. In the Notice of the Supreme People's Court on Implementing the Convention on the Recognition and Enforcement of Foreign Arbitral Awards Acceded to by China (No. 5 [1987]), it is stated that disputes between foreign investors and the host government are not considered to be a "commercial legal relationship", on which China had made a reservation when acceding to the 1958 New York Convention.

It is therefore desirable for the Chinese legislative body or the Supreme People's Court to introduce new rules, or at least clarify what exact procedural rules shall be followed in the future, in order to give clearer guidance on recognition and enforcement of an investor-State arbitral award.

Ning Fei
Tel: +86 10 5639 9688 / Email: feining@huizhonglaw.com

Mr. Ning Fei is an executive partner at Hui Zhong Law Firm and currently practises in the Beijing and Shanghai offices. He specialises in commercial arbitration and litigation. Mr. Fei has represented both Chinese and foreign clients in over 100 commercial arbitration and litigation cases, and appeared before Chinese and international arbitral tribunals, as well as the courts of the PRC at various levels up to the Supreme People's Court. He has experience of CIETAC, HKIAC, SIAC, the Arbitration Institute of SCC and LCIA as an arbitrator, a practitioner and a Chinese law expert. Mr. Fei has been ranked a top-notch litigator and a first band arbitration lawyer by Chambers Asia since 2006. Mr. Fei is the first mainland China lawyer who has been invited to act as a Council member of the Hong Kong International Arbitration Center. He has also been invited by the Singapore International Arbitration Center to act as an advisory member. Before founding Hui Zhong Law Firm, Mr. Fei was a partner at Jun He Law Office, heading the dispute resolution practice team from 2008 to 2013. Before joining the firm of Jun He, he was the managing partner of Haiwen & Partners' Shanghai office. Between 1989 and 1993, he worked at the CIETAC secretariat. He also worked as a foreign associate at a Swiss law firm in Zurich, and a British law firm in London for three years.

Shengchang Wang
Tel: +86 10 5639 9688 / Email: wangshengchang@huizhonglaw.com

Mr. Shengchang Wang is a senior consultant at Hui Zhong Law. He specialises in commercial arbitration and mediation. Mr Wang is the former vice-chairman and former secretary general of CIETAC and has handled more than 200 arbitration cases under the auspices of CIETAC, ICC, SCC Institute, HKIAC, SIAC and *ad hoc* arbitration. Mr Wang is an advisory member of International Council for Commercial Arbitration (ICCA). His key works include *International Arbitration in the People's Republic of China* (Butterworths, Singapore 1995 and 2000, co-author), *Resolving Disputes in the PRC* (*FT*, Hong Kong, 1996), *Theory and Practice of Combining Arbitration with Conciliation* (Law Press, Beijing, 2001), and *Arbitration in China: A Practical Guide* (Sweet & Maxwell, 2004, co-general editor).

Jing Liu
Tel: +86 21 2226 1200 / Email: liujing@huizhonglaw.com

Mr. Jing Liu is a senior consultant of Hui Zhong Law Firm and is based in Hui Zhong's Shanghai office. He specialises in international commercial arbitration, BIT arbitration, international trade law, investment law, financial law, corporate business law and intellectual property law, etc. Mr. Liu is the former Deputy Secretary General of the Hong Kong International Arbitration Centre (HKIAC). He started his professional career at the Secretariat of CIETAC and thereafter he practised for several years with the China and International Arbitration Group of Freshfields Bruckhaus Deringer (Hong Kong). He is admitted at the New York Bar. Mr. Liu is a graduate of Nanjing University and UC Berkeley.

Hui Zhong Law Firm

Suite 2304 One Indigo, No. 20 Jiuxianqiao Road, Chaoyang District, Beijing 100016, China
Tel: +86 10 5639 9688 / URL: www.huizhonglaw.com

Ecuador

Hernán Pérez Loose
Coronel & Pérez

Introduction

In Ecuador, arbitration between private individuals or corporations and governmental entities can take place within different spheres. First, these kinds of arbitration – also known as "private-public" arbitration – may be held under the auspices of bilateral international treaties (BIT) that have been designed to protect and encourage the flow of investments between the signatory nations. This kind of arbitration has expanded dramatically in recent years. Private-public arbitration can also take place at international level but outside the umbrella of any international treaty. In these cases, the arbitration typically takes place under the auspices of private institutions such as the International Chamber of Commerce or the rules of the United Nations Commission on International Trade Law. Finally, private-public arbitration may also be an entirely domestic affair. In this case, the applicable rules are established by the national legislatures.

In recent years, private-public arbitration has been the subject of extensive controversy. Because public policy considerations typically overshadow controversies between public entities and private individuals or entities, some critics have argued that arbitration is not well-suited to settling them. Among other things, they question the fact that arbitrators who sit in private-public arbitral tribunals and who are called to pass judgment on the decisions of public entities, are private attorneys who, unlike ordinary judges, are not socially or politically accountable. A more extreme view sees private-public arbitration as a perverse manifestation of economic globalisation.

As in most Latin American countries, Ecuador has experienced some tensions in the field of private-public arbitration. A period during which the country adopted a friendly approach toward this type of arbitration was followed by a period that reversed that policy drastically. These unfriendly policies toward private-public arbitration were adopted during the last decade under successive governments of socialist ideology. While the new administration has given signals of reversing these policies again, the obstacles are manifold. In the realm of domestic arbitration, matters have been different. Ecuador has maintained a friendly approach to this type of arbitration.

This chapter examines Ecuador's shifting policies toward private-public arbitration during recent years, from a period of openness to a period of rigidity. It also analyses the legal provisions that are applicable to this kind of arbitration when it takes place under the rules of domestic jurisdiction.

The demise of the Calvo paradigm

Ecuador's mistrustful attitude towards foreign jurisdiction is rooted in the doctrines of the

Argentinian jurist and diplomat, Carlos Calvo. Published in the early 20th century, his works on international law were highly influential in Latin America for several decades. Calvo questioned the subjection of states to a minimum international standard in their treatment of foreign nationals, believing that foreigners who settled under one state's jurisdiction were subject to the same treatment from the state authorities as nationals; neither better nor worse. Disputes between foreign nationals and the host state were thus not truly international disputes, and were certainly not subject to international rules. They were essentially domestic issues subject to national law, and should not therefore be resolved by diplomatic means but by the host state's ordinary courts.[1]

As Pedro Roffe points out, the Calvo Doctrine has two components. The first is the principle that foreign nationals who conclude contracts with the state implicitly waive the right to request diplomatic protection should any dispute arise from these contracts. The other is the ban on subjecting contracts between the state and foreign individuals (natural or legal persons) to the jurisdiction of any but domestic courts.[2] Both the diplomatic and jurisdictional component were welcomed by Latin American governments. In view of the coercive means used by some foreign governments to settle their nationals' commercial disputes with the host states, the Calvo Doctrine played a crucial role in constructing a legal discourse in defence of national sovereignty during the 19th century and a good part of the 20th.[3]

However, in 1992, Ecuador began to abandon its position of mistrust towards foreign jurisdiction, a shift that involved taking different steps at both domestic and international level. As part of the process, the regulatory framework of arbitration, including private-public arbitration, was entirely redrafted.

Constitutional reforms

The shift began in 1996 when Congress enacted a group of constitutional reforms. One of these consisted of adding the phrase, "*except for international agreements*", after the Calvo Doctrine-based rule that barred the government from submitting its contractual disputes with foreign entrepreneurs to non-Ecuadorian courts.[4] Although the reform required the state to sign "*international agreements*" beforehand, the fact is that it weakened the Calvo Doctrine. The reform allowed any doubts about the validity of some BITs that Congress had already ratified to be quashed,[5] and allowed others that had already been signed to be ratified. It also enabled Congress to ratify the 1965 Washington Convention.[6]

A further important reform that year was the introduction of a clause into the constitution, recognising arbitration as an "*alternative procedure for resolving disputes*".[7] With this, arbitration achieved constitutional status; the reforms were later accepted by a constituent assembly and introduced with identical wording into the new constitution in 1998.[8] In addition to these changes, this new constitution incorporated some provisions that were in keeping with the prevailing liberal approach, particularly with regard to foreign investment. As the price of oil had dropped substantially in the preceding years, it was becoming increasingly more difficult for the state to bear the cost of public programmes alone.

Privatisations, arbitrations

However, even before the 1996 constitutional reform, Ecuador had already taken certain steps that were favourable to arbitration, especially private-public arbitration. In 1993 Congress enacted the State Modernisation Law, aiming to pave the way for the privatisation of public services.[9] Among other matters, the law recognised arbitration as an option for settling disputes between the state and companies that would participate in the privatisation processes. In the very same year Congress enacted a reform of the Hydrocarbons Law, authorising state oil entity Petroecuador to submit disputes arising from exploration and exploitation contracts to arbitration.[10] In the following year, the government issued the Terms for Participation Contracts for the Exploration and Exploitation of Hydrocarbons, which provided for the possibility of submitting "*disputes of a legal nature originating in the interpretation or enforcement of contracts*" to arbitration.[11] Acknowledging that the state was now willing to submit disputes "of a legal nature" and not exclusively of "a technical nature" to arbitration was a step that clearly revealed the shift that was under way. In October 1996, Congress also passed the Electricity Sector Regime Law, in which private-public arbitration was accepted as a formula for settling disputes between the regulator and concession holders.[12]

Although Congress recognised that private-public arbitration was a valid procedure by means of these laws, the lawmakers failed to regulate how and under what conditions it should be undertaken. As the only regulations in force were the CPC's "arbitration proceedings", it should have been understood that this was the procedure to follow in such cases. However, as the CPC rules suffered from many technical limitations, the use of domestic arbitration by government agencies affected by the legal reforms mentioned above was almost non-existent. Oil contracts were the exception, but these were signed in the framework of the avalanche of BITs that were ratified during that period.

The AML

This ambiguity was overcome in 1997 with the enactment of the Arbitration and Mediation Law (AML).[13] This was the first time that Ecuador had regulated arbitration by means of a special act, as an independent institution and not just as a chapter in civil procedure legislation. More importantly, however, the entire section dealing with CPC "arbitration proceedings" was repealed.

The AML marked a substantial shift for arbitration. The procedure laid down by the new law followed UNCITRAL model guidelines: establishing the "*kompetenz-kompetenz*" principle; protecting party autonomy; recognising the validity of the arbitration clause; limiting judicial review solely to annulment actions against awards on exceptional procedural grounds; authorising the creation of arbitration and mediation centres as institutions responsible for administering arbitration procedures; and facilitating the enforcement of national and foreign arbitral awards. One of the issues regulated under the new law, which will be discussed in the following section, was private-public arbitration.

Besides regulating arbitration, Congress introduced an article into the AML repealing a century-old civil code rule that characterised as against public law any agreement whereby the parties were subjected to a "alien law".[14] The repeal ended a source of uncertainty concerning the law applicable to contracts with international elements, and which in some way also affected arbitration. This change was later reflected in some decisions made by the Supreme Court and other courts which were more in line with modern private international law.[15]

The AML was generally welcomed by various sectors that were particularly linked with chambers of commerce and industry, and commercial lawyers. Arbitration presented itself to many as an opportunity to speed up the settling of legal disputes, and a positive alternative to an increasingly unreliable legal system. The latter was, and still is, one of the factors to have had the greatest influence in arbitration's favour, including private-public arbitration. The Ecuadorian courts' lack of independence and transparency has been one of the country's most serious and enduring problems.[16] Furthermore, the state has displayed an authoritarian streak in recent years, creating a high degree of legal uncertainty, with the result that not only has human rights protection been seriously undermined – fairly serious in itself – but the whole democratic system has been affected.[17]

Enthusiasm for arbitration was such that a law was enacted in 2000 making it obligatory for privatisation contracts to include an arbitration clause. However, this reform was later quashed by the Constitutional Tribunal in response to a petition from trade unions and some political leaders. The Tribunal found that the obligatory arbitration established by the law was in breach of the "alternative" nature that arbitration should have, according to the constitution.[18]

During the first decade that the law was in force, ordinary courts showed a constructive attitude towards arbitrators' work and decisions, and chambers of commerce set up arbitration centres to administer arbitration proceedings. The problems that arbitration, especially private-public arbitration, were to encounter arose from 2008 onwards, partly as a result of the new constitution that was adopted that year, and partly due to a series of decisions taken by the new government.

The return of the Calvo Doctrine?

In 2008, a new constituent assembly was convened. It was largely dominated by various left-wing political and social movements, and particularly by the movement headed by Rafael Correa, who had been elected President of the Republic in late 2006. A key element in this political change was the central part the state would play in the economy and society, after almost a decade in which a more liberal view had prevailed. The new political coalition's aspirations to increase the state's role were underpinned by facts. Starting in 2006, there was an extraordinary increase in the price of crude oil, and this boom meant that over the following decade the Ecuadorian state received more revenue than all the governments in its history put together. The new constitution that was adopted in 2008 reflected the view of the state as the main protagonist in the organisation of the economy and society, just as the 1998 Constitution had reflected the opposite stance.

BITs in the spotlight

One of the main points on these political movements' agenda was their rejection of BITs, and especially international investment arbitrations. At that time, Ecuador had been sued under these treaties by various international companies, and several disputes with oil companies had achieved particular public prominence. In a few short years, Ecuador would be the country with the most international arbitration lawsuits filed against it with the ICSID, second only to Argentina.

Constitutional changes

The main changes affecting private-public arbitration were at constitutional level, as they had been in 1996, though in a different direction. First of all, the assembly stated in article 190 that in government contracts, arbitration "*shall be accepted after a favorable ruling by the Attorney-General's Office, in conformity with conditions provided for by law*". That is to say, three of the conditions the 1997 AML laid down for the validity of private-public arbitration acquired constitutional status: that arbitration should be used for contractual disputes; that it should be carried out in accordance with the law, i.e., not with equity; and that the Attorney-General's Office would issue a prior report.

The second constitutional change was the adoption of a radical response towards investment arbitration. Article 422 of the new constitution included a clause barring the state from concluding "*treaties or international instruments where the Ecuadorian State yields its sovereign jurisdiction to international arbitration entities in disputes of contractual or commercial nature between the State and natural persons or legal entities*". According to the article, however: "*The treaties and international instruments that provide for the settlement of disputes between States and citizens in Latin America by regional arbitration entities or by jurisdictional organizations designated by the signatory countries are exempt from this prohibition. Judges of the States that, as such or their nationals, are part of the dispute cannot intervene in the above*". The article ends by stating that, "*In the case of disputes involving the foreign debt, the Ecuadorian State shall promote arbitration solutions on the basis of the origin of the debt and subject to the principles of transparency, equity, and international justice.*"

The drafters of article 422 clearly had BITs in mind, although the article does not completely reject investment arbitration. What it does is impose certain conditions on the treaties: arbitration must be administered by centres situated in Latin America; these centres should be set up by the states parties, and the arbitrators cannot be either judges or nationals of the states parties in the dispute. The article's final point covers certain political groups' aspiration to submit the developing world's foreign debt to international arbitration.

The third constitutional change entailed a strange paradox which, while almost imperceptible, has had significant consequences. While retaining the diplomatic component of the Calvo Doctrine, the 2008 constituent assembly removed the jurisdictional aspect as it had been accepted for several decades; thus, the constitutional bar preventing the state from signing contracts with foreigners that included clauses submitting the agreement to a non-Ecuadorian jurisdiction was eliminated. It is difficult to reconcile the removal of the Calvo Doctrine with the political discourse that inspired the assembly.[19] As will be seen later, this constitutional change has had important legal implications.

Denouncing BITs

Ecuador took a further step by deciding to denounce both its BITs and the 1965 Washington Convention. In January 2007, when the 1998 Constitution was still in force, the executive announced its intention to denounce BITs concluded by Ecuador during the 1990s, beginning with those signed with developing countries. The legislative assembly, for its part, initiated the procedure for denouncing all the BITs that were in force. Although the 2008 Constitution did not require a statement on a treaty's constitutionality as a condition for denouncing it, and in reality the BITs could have been denounced with or without article 422, the executive and the legislative assembly decided to request the Constitutional Court's opinion as to the BITs' constitutionality or otherwise.[20] It was not difficult for the Court to find that the arbitration clauses in the BITs breached article 422 of the new constitution.

As for the ICSID Convention, once the 2008 Constitution came into force the executive notified the ICSID secretary that Ecuador would be withdrawing from the treaty.[21]

In addition to these decisions, a reform of the AML rules for enforcing foreign arbitral awards should also be mentioned. The new rules are set out in the General Organic Code of Processes (GOCP) enacted by the legislative assembly in May 2015.[22] Unlike those set out in the AML, the new conditions for recognising and enforcing arbitral awards make it extremely difficult to enforce international arbitral awards in Ecuador. Among other things, they establish a double exequatur, and impose on the interested party the burden of proving that "*the right of defence of the parties*" was ensured during the arbitration.[23] Where arbitral awards against the state are concerned, the interested party also has to prove that the award "*is not in conflict with the provisions in the constitution and the law*".[24]

Ban on domestic private-public arbitration

Correa's government had not only international arbitration in its sights. In 2012, the president adopted a radical position with respect to domestic private-public arbitration. By means of a presidential order, the government instructed public entities not to include any more arbitration clauses in public contracts, and from then onwards state disputes with contractors were heard only in the common courts.

The foregoing decisions and steps were adopted in the context of denunciations of the inequities of the international dispute settlement regime for investment developed since the 1980s. The arbitral tribunals were denounced as being intrinsically biased against Ecuador, although the fact that Ecuador had, in many cases, obtained favourable decisions from these tribunals was omitted.

Much ado about nothing?

The hostility of the discourse regarding both international and domestic private-public arbitration contrasts with some of the positions Ecuador adopted. First of all, in spite of the harsh criticism of BITs as instruments that undermined national sovereignty, because of the presence of private-public arbitration, the procedures to denounce these treaties were never concluded. After the Constitutional Tribunal ruled that BITs were unconstitutional, the international denunciation procedure was never completed, and they therefore remain in force.

Secondly, during the last decade the government signed important public contracts in areas such as finance, oil and telecommunications with foreign institutions and investors, in which it has accepted that its contractual disputes will be settled by arbitration in the London International Court of Arbitration (LICA) and other similar centres. Submitting government contracts to non-Ecuadorian jurisdictions has been possible because of the removal of the Calvo Doctrine's jurisdictional component from the 2008 Constitution, as noted above. To this should be added the enactment of a law in October 2010 allowing government agencies to accept that disputes arising from their contracts with foreign governments and public or private entities may be settled by other nations' courts and legislation with the Attorney General's permission.[25] Finally, in several cases Ecuador has also accepted that disputes deriving from public contracts signed with foreign investors may be settled by domestic arbitration centres. This is in contrast to the situation *vis-à-vis* such contracts signed with Ecuadorian nationals, for whom arbitration is not an option, as noted above.

Thirdly, with the aim of encouraging private investment, the government has enacted two special laws – the Organic Code for Production, Trade and Investment[26] and the Organic Law for Public-Private Partnerships and Foreign Investment[27] ("PPP Law") – which enable the state and other public entities to sign investment contracts under which disputes can also be settled via international arbitration in certain conditions. Moreover, the regulations of the PPP Law, which were made public in June 2016, went so far as to acknowledge that the BITs signed by Ecuador are still in force, despite all the criticism they have received.

The mismatch between policies and the discourse challenging the international regime for settling disputes over foreign investment, especially private-public arbitration, can effectively be explained by the fact that, in spite of its enormous income from oil, Ecuador needs foreign financial resources to sustain its development plans. Neither international funders, particularly China, which became Ecuador's chief source of external financial resources, nor foreign investors in general, have been willing to channel their loans and investments through contractual arrangements without a guarantee that international arbitration will be available as a dispute settlement mechanism. In addition, after several years of government vacillation and internal conflicts, Ecuador decided to sign a trade agreement with the European Union. This was at odds with the process of denouncing the BITs, as well as with the general policy of hostility towards arbitration under these treaties. To some, this was the reason why the government virtually halted its denunciation of BITs.[28] Many of the clauses in the agreement with the EU are similar to those in the BITs, a contradiction that was highlighted by Carlos Gaviria, president of the Ecuadorian Citizens' Commission for a Comprehensive Audit of Investment Protection Treaties and of the International Arbitration System on Investments (CAITISA), in his letter of resignation. Mr. Gaviria justified his decision in view of the Ecuadorian government's announcement that it was reopening diplomatic negotiations for a trade agreement with the EU.[29]

While Ecuador was following this somewhat erratic policy with regard to private-public arbitration, at various levels in the public sphere, the investment arbitrations that had begun prior to the 2008 Constitution continued. Meanwhile, new cases were initiated under the BITs, following UNCITRAL rules – once Ecuador had withdrawn from ICSID – or under the rules of arbitration of the ICC.

Private-public arbitration in Ecuador

As outlined above, the 1997 AML introduced certain special rules with regard to private-public arbitration, as a result of which this could be said to have achieved an independent status that it had not previously possessed. As soon as arbitration centres were set up, private-public arbitration under the AML began to develop normally. As the previous section mentions, this was the result of an evolutionary process in which various domestic and international factors converged. Although the process was affected by the President's 2012 decision, it is likely to be resumed by a new government. What follows is an analysis of the main characteristics of Ecuador's private-public arbitration regime.

<u>Requirements</u>

(i) *Legal nature of the dispute*

Ecuador's private-public arbitration is limited to disputes deriving from contractual relationships.[30] In drawing this line, a vast area of disputes that regularly arise between the public administration and private individuals were excluded from arbitration. These include disputes related to administrative acts (licences, permits, etc.); liability for public service deficiencies; civil service conflicts; taxation disputes; and urban development and environmental protection issues. These affairs remain within the aegis of the contentious-administrative jurisdiction.

(ii) *Authorising official*

The arbitration clause or agreement must be signed by the highest authority in the public entity;[31] thus, lower-ranking officials are prevented from signing these clauses or agreements.

(iii) *Prior authorisation from the Attorney General*

An arbitration clause or agreement is only valid if it has been previously approved by the Attorney General. During the first few years that the AML was in force, this was only required when the parties agreed to submit an already existing dispute to arbitration. Distinguishing one case from the other was not easy, and there were certain conflicts over the matter. However, based on the changes in the 2008 Constitution, it is clear that this approval is necessary regardless of whether the dispute between a public entity and a contractor already exists or not.[32]

(iv) *Arbitrators must decide by law, not by equity*

The AML requires the arbitrators in private-public arbitration to decide in accordance with the law, and not according to equity.[33] This rule reversed a tradition that had allowed the arbitrators in arbitrations in which one party was a public entity to decide by equity. The rule has been justified based on the "principle of legality" to which the public administration is bound.[34] As public entities are obliged to act solely within the limits imposed by the law, arbitrators cannot decide according to equity in settling their disputes.

(v) *Choice of arbitrators*

Once the AML-stipulated validity requirements for the arbitration clause or agreement have been met, the parties must try to resolve their disputes by mediation first.[35] Should the disagreements persist, the parties appoint arbitrators as agreed, and if this proves impossible the task falls to the arbitration centre to which the parties have submitted their case. The most commonly used arbitration centres for private-public arbitration are those attached to chambers of commerce or industry.

Arbitrators for public-private arbitration are chosen using the same process used in private arbitration. Neither the AML nor the arbitration centres specify any special requirements or knowledge from the arbitrators, and arbitrators in private-public arbitration can be challenged on the same grounds as ordinary judges. In this type of arbitration, the defence of a public entity generally falls to its legal advisors, although engaging external lawyers is permitted by law. The rule barring judges from meeting one party's lawyers without the other party's being present is also applicable in arbitration.

Another of the private arbitration rules that is also applicable in private-public arbitration stipulates that arbitrators have the power to decide on the validity of the arbitral clause or agreement to settle the dispute.[36] In private-public arbitration, the arbitrators should pay particular attention to fulfilling AML requirements for the validity of the arbitral clause or agreement. Moreover, since the AML requires arbitration procedures to be carried out according to private civil procedural law,[37] private-public arbitration is subject to virtually the same procedural rules as both arbitration and ordinary private actions.

(vi) *Confidentiality*

Under the AML, arbitration procedures are confidential unless the parties expressly agree otherwise.[38] However, this rule is not, or at least should not be applicable to private-public arbitration, as it involves matters of public interest, so there is legislation to ensure that the public has access to such procedures. In practice, however, public entities are very reluctant to disclose documents concerning their actions. As many government contracts are exempt from the preparatory procedures provided for in the Organic Law of the National Public Procurement System (OLNPPS), it is very difficult to find out about their conditions, including the clauses referring to dispute settlement.

<u>Adversarial procedure</u>

Arbitration in Ecuador is adversarial, just like normal court civil proceedings, and consequently the key players in disputes are the parties and not the arbitrators. The only exception to this rule is the authority held by judges - and hence arbitrators - to request certain evidence in addition to that presented by the parties if they consider it necessary to clarify the parties' arguments. However, this power is not generally used by either judges or arbitrators. The new GOCP expanded this authority to order evidence *ex officio* to protect fundamental constitutional rights, and whether judges and arbitrators will use it in practice remains to be seen. The same applies to private-public arbitration. There is no general rule in the AML giving arbitrators in private-public arbitrations special powers to steer the arbitration process in view of the public interest involved. The Attorney General can exercise a certain oversight in private-public arbitration when a state interest is at stake, but only as one of the parties.

(vii) *Annulment of arbitral awards. Enforcement of foreign awards*

The AML rules regulating annulment actions against arbitral awards are equally applicable to both private and private-public arbitration. The grounds for annulling an arbitral award are essentially violations of due process.[39] Ecuadorian law does not cover the fact that a decision is against the public interest as grounds for annulment. Where private-public arbitration is concerned, other grounds for annulling arbitral awards provided for in the AML are violations of the requirements stipulated for public-private arbitration, especially the lack of authorisation from the Attorney General to sign an arbitration clause or agreement.

The way the new GOCP regulates the enforcement of foreign awards against the state is somewhat unusual. As well as establishing difficult conditions for enforcing international arbitral awards, the GOCP requires proof that international awards against Ecuador do not "*contravene the provisions of the constitution and the law*".[40] When arbitral awards against the state are enforced, the state has immunity with respect to funds deposited in the Central Bank.

(viii) *Arbitrator independence and impartiality*

In line with the 1998 constitution, article 75 of the 2008 constitution recognises the right of all individuals to "the effective, impartial and expeditious protection of their rights and interests", and article 168 guarantees the independence of judicial bodies, both with respect to other branches of government (external independence) and other bodies in higher levels of the judicial hierarchy (internal independence). Case law has tended to view arbitration as a legal procedure *per se*, subject more to the law than to the parties' wishes, and arbitrators are therefore considered judges – the main difference being that the former exercise jurisdiction only temporarily. It is for this reason that the constitutional guarantee of independence and impartiality is applicable to both judges and arbitrators, including arbitrators in public-private arbitration. The temporary nature of arbitrators' work should not in principle affect their duty of impartiality, and in this aspect, they are subject to the same control as ordinary judges.

The principle that arbitrators exercise jurisdiction in the same way as ordinary judges, albeit on a temporary basis, and the fact that arbitrators in private-public arbitrations cannot settle in equity but only in law, means that arbitrators in public-private arbitrations must resolve issues by following the principles of law on which the legal rules applicable to the case are based. This means that arbitrators should apply administrative law principles, particularly in disputes involving administrative contracts, in the way case law and doctrine have interpreted them, as ordinary judges are expected to.

(ix) *Powers of review*

Because both the constitution and the AML restrict arbitration to contractual disputes, arbitrators' powers of review over the conduct of public officials differ in intensity and scope to those of administrative courts. However, even with respect to administrative acts undertaken during contract enforcement, arbitral tribunals have been uncertain. Some tribunals felt they had the power to annul administrative acts; although others believed they did not, this did not prevent them from ruling on the financial consequences of such acts.

There is no solution to the possible inconsistencies in private-public arbitration case law; the National Court acts solely as a court of cassation and is forbidden by statute to review the merits of awards.

(x) *Constitutional rights and due process*

Although annulment actions are the only monitoring mechanism there is over arbitral awards, and the grounds for annulment are limited in number and restrictive in their interpretation, the Constitutional Court has indicated that it could still use an extraordinary action of protection to review possible violations of constitutional rights that arbitral tribunals may incur. While the Court has agreed to review arbitral awards in this way in very few cases, and has dismissed the petitions in most of them, any party considering that its right to due process has been breached in an arbitration has this additional control in its favour. In any event, constitutional case law has found arbitration not to be a denial of the right to access to justice but an alternative means to it, in line with the text of the constitution.

Conclusions

The current administration announced recently that it is committed to review the unfriendly policies of the last decade with respect to international investment arbitration. The process will not be an easy one, because of the presence of article 422 of the constitution. Domestic private-public arbitration has not suffered from the changes that have affected international investment law. In this area, the present law in Ecuador follows the pattern of private arbitration. The concerns voiced by some critics of investment arbitration are tempered by the fact that private-public arbitration in Ecuador is limited to contract disputes. It is a field where public policy issues are seldom at stake.

* * *

Endnotes

1. For an early reaction to the Calvo doctrine, see AH Feller, "Some Observations on the Calvo Clause" (1933) 27 AJIL 461-68. For the constitutional and international law implications of the Calvo clause in Latin America, see MR García-Mora, "The Calvo Clause in Latin American Constitutions and International Law" (1950) MarqL Rev 205-19. For the impact of the Calvo doctrine on the international regime for foreign investment, see D. Manning-Cabrol, "The Inminent Death of the Calvo Clause and the Rebirth of the Calvo Principle: Equality of Foreign and National Investors" (1995) 26 *Law and Policy in International Business* 1169-2000; O.M. Garibaldi; "Carlos Calvo Redivivus: The Rediscovery of the Calvo Doctrine in the Era of Investment Treaties" TDM 5 (2006), www.transnational-dispute-management.com.
2. Roffe, Pedro. *Calvo y su vigencia en América Latina*, UNCTAD Reprint Series No. 53 (1984).
3. Lipson, Charles, *Standing Guard: Protecting Foreign Capital in the Nineteenth and Twentieth Century*, University of California Press, 1985.

4. *Official Register* No. 863. January 16, 1996, p.7.
5. By the time of this constitutional amendment was promulgated in the *Official Register*, Ecuador had already signed BITs with Argentina (1994), Bolivia (1995), Chile (1993), China (1994), El Salvador (1994), France (1993), Great Britain and Northern Ireland (1994), Paraguay (1994), United States (1993), and Venezuela (1994). Once the amendment was promulgated in 1996, these BITs were approved by Congress, as well as others that were signed by the President thereafter.
6. See Legislative Resolution No. R-22-053. February 7, 2001.
7. See *Official Register* No. 863. January 16, 1996, p.6.
8. See *Official Register* No. 1. August 11, 1998, pp.1-39.
9. See Law for the modernisation of the State, privatisations, and provision of public services by the private initiative. *Official Register* No. 349. December 31, 1993.
10. See *Official Register* No. 326, November 29, 1993, p. 3.
11. See Excecutive Decree No. 1416, *Official Register* No. 364 of January 21, 1994.
12. See article 21 of the Law of the Electrical Sector. *Official Register*, Supplement, No. 43 of October 10, 1996.
13. See *Official Register* No. 145 of September 4, 1997.
14. From its enactment in 1861, the Ecuadorian Civil Code contained a rule that declared null, "Any promise made in Ecuador to be subject to a jurisdiction not recognised by Ecuadorian laws." According to the code, promises of this type were null and void because they "contravene Ecuadorian public law". Ecuadorian case law interpreted this rule in a way that was highly questionable and much more restrictive than the interpretation it was given in Chile, for example, where the same provision existed. Hence, contracts with international elements, in which it is not unusual for the parties to agree that the agreement will be subject to one of the jurisdictions with which the contract has links, were annulled based on this civil code rule. In one case, the Ecuadorian judges even ignored the 1928 Convention on Private International Law (Bustamante Code), ratified by 14 states in Latin America and which enables the nationals of states parties to choose the applicable law for international contracts.
15. See Supreme Court of Justice. First Chamber on Civil and Mercantile Law, Sentence No. 217, (*Teresa García Franco v. Società Italiana per Condotte d'Acqua Spa*). Official Register No. 109 of June 29, 2000, pp. 22-26; Second Judgeship of Guayaquil. Trial No 470-D-04 (*Andina de Licores S.A. (Andilicor) v. E & J Gallo Winery*), August 8, 2005.
16. See Basabe Serrano, Santiago, *Jueces sin toga. Políticas judiciales y toma de decisiones en el Tribunal Constitucional del Ecuador* (1999-2007). Quito: FLACSO, Sede Ecuador, 2011. Pasara, Luis, *Independencia judicial en la reforma de la justicia ecuatoriana*, Lima. Fundación para el Debido Proceso; Centro de Estudios de Derecho, Justicia y Sociedad; Instituto de Defensa Legal, 2014; *Human Right Watch,* Ecuador Report, https://www.hrw.org/americas/ecuador.
17. Carlos de la Torre and Andres Ortiz Lemos, "Populist Polarization and the Slow Death of Democracy in Ecuador," *Democratization* 23, 2 (2016): 221-241; Enrique Peruzzotti, "Elected Authoritarianism in South America: Argentina, Venezuela and Ecuador," University of Miami Center for Hemispheric Policy, July 2, 2013.
18. Constitutional Tribunal. Resolution No. 193, *Official Register* No. 234, 29 December 2000, p. 23.
19. Political Constitution, 2008, article 307: "Contracts entered into by the State with foreign natural persons and legal entities shall implicitly entail the waiver by these persons of any diplomatic immunity…"

20. For a critical view of the role of the Constitutional Court in ruling on the constitutionality of a treaty as condition for its denounciation, see Christian Masapantas Gallegos, "*Análisis del dictamen No. 023-10-DTI-CC de la Corte Constitucional para el período de transición referente al Tratado entre la República del Ecuador y la República Federal de Alemania sobre foment y recíproca protección de inversiones de capital' (Caso No. 006-10TI)*" in *Revista de Derecho Foro* 17 (1), Universidad Andina Simón Bolívar, 2012 pp. 141-175.
21. See Executive Decree No. 1823 of July 2, 2009, *Official Register* No. 632 of July 13, 2009.
22. General Organic Code of Processes (GOCP). *Official Register* No. 506, Supplement, of May 22, 2015.
23. GOCP, article 104, 4.
24. GOCP, article 104, 5.
25. Organic Planning and Public Finances Code. *Official Register* No. 206 (Supplement Three), 22 October 2010, General Provision Five.
26. Official Register No. 351, 29 December 2012.
27. Official Register No. 652, Supplement, 18 December 2015.
28. According to Manuel Rodríguez, "It seems to be no coincidence that in the case of the BITs signed by Ecuador with EU member countries (Germany, Great Britain, France, Sweden, the Netherlands, Spain and Italy) these denunciation processes **were paralysed after Ecuador asked to participate in the European Trade Agreement**. This is despite the fact that all these BITs have been judged unconstitutional by the Constitutional Tribunal and that in four of these cases the denunciation of the treaty has even been approved in the Ecuadorian legislature." (Original emphasis). See https://lalineadefuego.info/2016/01/26/diagonal-hace-publico-los-resultados-de-la-auditoria-sobre-tratados-de-inversion-en-e, ecuador-por-manuel-rodriguez/, last consulted 24 May 2016, 21:35.
29. http://www.polodemocratico.net/noticias/titulares/7363-carlos-gaviria-renuncia-a-comision-de-auditoria-de-tratados-de-inversion-de-ecuador-por-suscripcion-de-acuerdo-comercial-con-union-europea, last consulted 24 May 2016, 21:23.
30. LAM, article 4, fourth paragraph. See also the Constitution.
31. AML, article 4, fifth paragraph.
32. Constitution, article 190 ("In public contracts will proceed arbitration in law, prior the favourable opinion of the State Attorney General, in accordance to the conditions set in the law.")
33. *Id.*
34. Constitution, article 226.
35. AML article 15.
36. AML article 22.
37. AML article 37.
38. AML article 34.
39. AML article 31.
40. GOCP article 104, second paragraph.

Hernán Pérez Loose
Tel: +593 4 251 9900 / Email: hperez@coronelyperez.com

Mr. Pérez Loose obtained his law degree at the Universidad Católica Santiago de Guayaquil, and later obtained his LL.M. in Comparative Law at NYU and an LL.M. and SJD at the Harvard Law School.

Mr. Pérez Loose is one of the founding partners of Coronel & Pérez. He was the legal counsel to *Empresa Eléctrica del Ecuador Inc.* (Emelec) from 1992 to 1998. Emelec was the largest private distributor of power in Ecuador. Mr. Pérez Loose was involved as counsel to Duke Energy in an ICSID arbitration (ARB 04/19) against Ecuador. He has also acted as expert witness on Ecuadorean law in various investment arbitrations on behalf of such companies as Occidental, Perenco, Burlington and Murphy.

Mr. Pérez Loose has vast experience in public contracts, administrative law, arbitration and foreign investments. He has worked as legal adviser to Sumifru International, a subsidiary of Sumitomo Corp, Shell Corp and some Ecuadorian companies including Grupo Vilaseca and El Universo. He was legal counsel to the President of the Republic of Ecuador from 1982 to 1984, as well as to the Attorney General of Ecuador from 1979 to 1980, and was part of the team of attorneys in the international division of the First National Bank of Boston. He is a life member of the American Society of International Law and American Society of Comparative Law. He is also a member of the International Bar Association.

Mr. Pérez Loose is licensed to practise as a foreign legal consultant in the State of New York.

Coronel & Pérez

Av. 9 de Octubre 100 y Malecón, Quito, Ecuador
Tel: +593 4 251 9900 / URL: www.coronelyperez.com

England & Wales

Joe Tirado
Garrigues UK LLP

Introduction

London continues to be a major hub for the resolution of commercial disputes, particularly by way of arbitration. As a result, the English courts are frequently faced with issues that are both central and ancillary to international arbitral proceedings. In such matters, the English courts have a long tradition of seeking to support arbitration and enforcing arbitral agreements and awards.

Underpinning the courts' approach is the Arbitration Act 1996 (the "**1996 Act**"), which still provides a sound framework for arbitration users and the courts. In addition, the United Kingdom has a suite of legislation in place to assist with the enforcement of arbitral awards.

England (in particular, London) remains one of the leading international arbitration centres of the world and is frequently selected as a seat of arbitration.[1]

The 1996 Act and relevant conventions

While not structurally based upon the UNCITRAL Model Law on International Commercial Arbitration (1985) (the "**1985 Model Law**"), the 1996 Act shares many of the main features of the 1985 Model Law. The 1996 Act is split into three parts:

- Part I (sections 1–84) sets out the structure to support anticipated or ongoing arbitral proceedings, including provisions as to appointment of a tribunal and the powers of the English court to support ongoing arbitral proceedings;
- Part II (sections 85–98) primarily concerns domestic arbitration, including consumer arbitration agreements and statutory arbitrations; and
- Part III (sections 99–104) concerns the recognition and enforcement of foreign arbitral awards.

The United Kingdom (which includes the jurisdiction of England & Wales) signed and ratified the New York Convention in 1975. The United Kingdom has also signed and ratified the Geneva Convention on the Execution of Foreign Arbitral Awards 1927.

With regard to other reciprocal arrangements, the Foreign Judgments (Reciprocal Enforcement) Act 1933 provides for the enforcement of arbitral awards from certain former Commonwealth countries. The Arbitration (International Investment Disputes) Act 1966 makes provision for the recognition and enforcement of ICSID awards. Under section 99 of the 1996 Act, the Arbitration Act 1950 (the predecessor to the 1996 Act) remains in effect with regard to the enforcement of certain awards that do not fall under the New York Convention.

London-based international dispute resolution institutions

London has emerged as a key seat for arbitration, and a number of leading institutions are based in London. The London Court of International Arbitration ("**LCIA**") is a renowned international arbitration institution with an impressive history and, as of 1 October 2014, a newly revised set of arbitration rules. The Chartered Institute of Arbitrators ("**CIArb**") administers arbitrations under its own rules and acts as an appointing authority. The Centre for Effective Dispute Resolution ("**CEDR**") is a London-based mediation and alternative dispute resolution body which administers arbitration under UNCITRAL Rules.

There are also a number of institutions catering for disputes arising in a particular trade area or industry. The London Maritime Arbitrators Association ("**LMAA**") has been the longstanding leading arbitral institution with respect to maritime disputes, with its own set of procedural rules. Commodity disputes are regularly conducted under the rules applicable to that commodity, for example the London Metal Exchange ("**LME**").

Arbitration agreement

The formalities surrounding an arbitration agreement are similar under English law as to other jurisdictions. Section 5 of the 1996 Act requires an arbitration agreement to be in writing or evidenced in writing. This requirement reflects section 7 of the 1985 Model Act (and the 2006 version of the UNCITRAL model act, the "**2006 Model Act**"). Section 5 of the 1996 Act allows for unsigned agreements, an exchange of communications, or an agreement "*evidenced in writing*". The English courts have interpreted "writing" to mean a record kept by any means, including electronic records or communications including email.[2]

Arbitrability

The arbitration agreement is defined in section 6 of the 1996 Act as "*an agreement to submit to arbitration present or future disputes (whether they are contractual or not)*".

The parties may decide to include all disputes arising between them to be decided by arbitration, or they may limit the recourse to arbitration strictly to one type of dispute or to disputes concerning the breach of one contract.

However, some types of dispute cannot be referred to arbitration by reason of mandatory law and/or public policy. The English Court of Appeal observed in the case of *Fulham Football Club Ltd v Richards & Anr*[3] that arbitrability will be determined by considering whether:

> "*…the matters in dispute… engage third party rights or represent an attempt to delegate to the arbitrators what is a matter of public interest which cannot be determined within the limitations of a private contractual process*".[4]

Joinder of third parties and consolidation of proceedings

Section 35 of the 1996 Act provides that arbitral tribunals shall not have the power to consolidate proceedings unless the parties agree to confer such power on the tribunal. Selection of the arbitration rules of an arbitral institution, where such arbitration rules allow for consolidation, can be seen to be an indirect conferral of such powers by the parties on the arbitral tribunal. Powers of consolidation can be found in many arbitration rules maintained by leading arbitral institutions. For example, the updated arbitration rules of the LCIA (which entered into force from 1 October 2014) provide at Article 22 for joinder and consolidation in particular circumstances.

Jurisdiction and competence-competence

The question of whether a tribunal had (or has) jurisdiction is often dependent on an examination of the meaning and scope of the relevant arbitration agreement (valid or otherwise). English courts tend to adopt a commercial pragmatism when it comes to interpreting arbitration agreements, particularly in the context of multi-party and multicontract disputes. For example, the Court of Appeal in *Yegiazaryan v Smagin [2016] EWCA Civ 1290* found that unclear wording in a standalone agreement between the claimant and respondent amounted to an arbitration agreement and entitled the claimant to file an LCIA arbitration against the respondent under two other agreements in which the respondent was not himself named as a party.[5]

Section 30 of the 1996 Act clearly sets out that, unless otherwise agreed by the parties, the arbitral tribunal has the power to rule on its own substantive jurisdiction, including deciding: (a) whether there is a valid arbitration agreement; (b) whether the tribunal is properly constituted; and/or (c) what matters have been submitted to arbitration in accordance with the arbitration agreement. Alternatively, if the arbitral tribunal gives its permission (or if the parties agree), the English court can determine a preliminary issue of jurisdiction. This latter power of the English courts is set out in section 32 of the 1996 Act.

Separability

Separability of the arbitration agreement is preserved by section 7 of the 1996 Act, together with the approach of the English courts in associated case law. Section 7 of the 1996 Act states:

> "*Unless otherwise agreed by the parties, an arbitration agreement which forms or was intended to form part of another agreement (whether or not in writing) shall not be regarded as invalid, non-existent or ineffective because that other agreement is invalid, or did not come into existence or has become ineffective, and it shall for that purpose be treated as a distinct agreement.*"

The English courts have upheld the approach reflected in this wording in cases such as the case of *Beijing Jianlong Heavy Industry Group v Golden Ocean Group Limited & Ors,*[6] where it was held that the arbitration agreement was valid even where the underlying guarantee agreement was illegal as a matter of Chinese law (China being the place of performance of the underlying agreement).

Arbitration procedure

Commencing an arbitration

Section 14 of the 1996 Act provides that arbitral proceedings are commenced by a written notice to the other party/parties or the appointing authority. This is the default procedure unless the parties agree otherwise. Institutional rules can add further requirements as to the content of such notice and payment of any initial institutional fees.

Seat of arbitration

For international arbitrations seated in England & Wales, the typical seat of arbitration selected by the parties or the court is London. There is no requirement under English law that procedural and evidential hearings physically take place at the seat of arbitration.

Applicable law

The arbitral tribunal will apply the substantive law chosen by the parties to the merits of the dispute.[7] Further, if the parties agree, the tribunal may determine the dispute in accordance with other considerations such as rules UNIDROIT, etc. Where the parties have not chosen or agreed to the substantive law, section 46 requires that the tribunal apply the substantive law identified by the conflict of laws which are applicable.

Following the decisions of *Sulamérica Cia Nacional De Seguros S.A. and others v Enesa Engenharia S.A.*[8] and *Arsanovia Ltd v Cruz City 1 Mauritius Holdings,*[9] the English commercial court in *Habas Sinai Ve Tibbi Gazlar Istihsal Andustrisi AS and VSC Steel Company Ltd*[10] held the proper law of the arbitration agreements to be determined by undertaking a three-stage enquiry into: (i) express choice; (ii) implied choice; and (iii) the law with which the arbitration agreement has the closest and most real connection.

Rules on evidence

Section 34 of the 1996 Act sets out the evidential matters over which the tribunal has authority, including: the form of written statements of case and submissions; the location and timing (and form) of hearings; the extent of document production; all issues as to admissibility and weight of evidence; the manner in which evidence shall be tendered or exchanged; and the extent to which the arbitrators should take the initiative in ascertaining the facts and the law.[11]

Arbitration rules chosen by the parties along with procedural guidelines such as the IBA Rules on the Taking of Evidence in International Arbitration (2010) (the "**IBA Rules**") will guide the arbitral tribunal on the rules of procedure and evidence. The arbitral tribunal will set down the procedural timetable along with additional rules on evidence (if any) that would be adopted.

Privilege

English law recognises the existence of legal privilege, a right which enables a person to resist compulsory disclosure of certain categories of information. However, the 1996 Act is silent on the existence and treatment of issues of privilege. Most often, the question as to which rules of privilege to apply to a given set of communications will be determined by the tribunal.[12] If the parties so agree, the tribunal might also be guided by the IBA Rules.

Disclosure

The English Civil Procedural Rules (CPR Rule 31.16) provide that the court may order disclosure by a party prior to the commencement of proceedings, with the aim of encouraging early resolution of the dispute, assisting procedural fairness and saving costs. However, these rules do not apply to arbitration proceedings.[13] As stated above, it is ultimately for the tribunal to decide on the scope of document production.

Generally an arbitral tribunal would take into account that the scope of document production will differ according to the legal and cultural backgrounds of the parties and the seat of arbitration. The approach of tribunals in England is generally conservative and 'fishing expeditions' are not welcome and, indeed, are positively discouraged.[14]

Expert evidence

Section 37 of the 1996 Act gives the power to the tribunal to appoint its own expert(s), but each party shall be given a reasonable opportunity to comment on any information, opinion or advice offered by the expert. Section 37 is not a mandatory section.

As with many other matters of procedure, it is at the tribunal's discretion which rules to follow regarding expert evidence. Arbitral institutional rules such as those of the LCIA or the ICC may guide the tribunal, or similarly other rules agreed by the parties such as the IBA Rules.

There is an increasing trend among arbitrations seated in England & Wales (as with international arbitrations seated elsewhere) towards attempting to get opposing expert witnesses to find common ground. This can lead to methods proposed or imposed by the arbitral tribunal such as "hot tubbing" and expert witness conferencing, under which experts are questioned simultaneously with a view towards identifying any common ground together with, generally, getting results from the two experts which are directly comparable and based on the same set of parameters and assumptions.

Confidentiality

The 1996 Act has no provision relating to confidentiality. Under English common law there is an implied term of the arbitration agreement that the arbitration is private and the evidence, along with the pleadings, are considered to be confidential.[15] There are certain exceptions to the implied term. The details of arbitral proceedings may become public due to a court order for disclosure or if it is necessary for the protection of the legitimate interests of one of the parties, or where there is public interest in disclosure.[16]

In a LCIA arbitration, arbitration proceedings are considered to be private unless the parties consent or the arbitral tribunal directs.[17] Further, Article 30 of the LCIA rules provides that parties as a general rule must undertake to keep all awards, along with materials in the proceeding created for the arbitration, as confidential.

Guidelines for counsel

All English solicitors are bound by ethical rules under English law. However, in international arbitration in any jurisdiction there are difficulties, as lawyers from different jurisdictions operate under different ethical codes and boundaries.

The guidelines under the 2014 LCIA Rules (General Guidelines for the Parties' Legal Representatives, Annex to the LCIA Rules) seek to level this playing field. Those guidelines state that counsel should not: (1) engage in activities intended unfairly to obstruct the arbitration or jeopardise the finality of the award (for example, by repeated challenges which the legal representative knows are unfounded); (2) make false statements; (3) rely upon false evidence; (4) conceal any document ordered to be produced by the tribunal; or (5) make unilateral undisclosed contact with any member of the arbitral tribunal.[18]

The LCIA guidelines are mandatory and apply to any counsel acting in any LCIA arbitration proceedings commenced under the new rules.

In case of misconduct, the LCIA Rules provide at Article 18.6 for the following sanctions: (1) a written reprimand; (2) a written caution as to future conduct; and (3) a reference to the legal representative's regulatory and/or professional body.

The IBA Guidelines on Party Representation 2013 is another set of guidelines which seek to apply a uniform standard to counsel in international arbitrations. However, such guidelines are only applicable if the parties specifically agree to them for a given dispute.

Arbitrators

Appointments in general

Parties to an arbitration in England & Wales are free to agree on the number of arbitrators, the appointment of arbitrators and whether a chairman or umpire is to be appointed to the tribunal. Parties may also impose restrictive qualifications on the appointment of arbitrators.[19] The UK Supreme Court case of *Jivraj v Hashwani*, exemplifies the notion that parties are free to impose (by virtue of agreement) a criteria or necessary qualification on the appointment of arbitrators.[20]

Procedure

Article 16 of the 1996 Act states that the default position is that an arbitral tribunal will generally consist of a sole arbitrator unless the parties to the arbitration request otherwise, or else if it is determined that a three-member tribunal is appropriate for the matter at hand.[21] In case of sole arbitrator, the parties must jointly appoint the arbitrator within 28 days of service and in case of three arbitrators, each party shall appoint one arbitrator within 14 days. The two appointed arbitrators shall appoint a third arbitrator as the chairman of the tribunal.[22]

Challenging an arbitrator

Parties to a proceeding may challenge the appointment of an arbitrator if that arbitrator has not acted fairly and impartially in his treatment of the parties. The Arbitration Act imposes a duty upon arbitrators to treat the parties fairly and equally.[23]

Under the LCIA Rules, prior to appointment, the prospective arbitrator candidate has to sign a declaration that no circumstances known to him are likely to give rise to any justified doubts as to his impartiality or independence, other than those disclosed by him.[24] This duty is a continuing duty as arbitrators appointed to proceedings must also disclose any circumstances that arise after the date of declaration and prior to the arbitration conclusion, which may affect their impartiality.

Section 24 of the 1996 Act allows the party to an arbitral proceedings to apply to the court to remove an arbitrator on the grounds that the arbitrator is not impartial or independent; does not possess the qualifications; has failed to conduct the proceedings in a proper manner; and mental or physical incapacity. The court will not exercise this power if the arbitral tribunal or the institution has the power to remove arbitrators, unless it is satisfied that the parties have exhausted any recourse to that institution or person.

Common law on impartiality and IBA Guidelines on conflicts of interest

The English common law provides for a general test for impartiality. In *R v Gough* it was that there should exist a real danger of bias.[25] The later judgment of *Locabail v Bayfield*[26] serves to provide practical guidance on the timing and level of disclosure.

The IBA Guidelines on Conflicts of Interest in International Arbitration provide a number of provisions which directly address the issue of how and when impartiality may exist and what are the requirements imposed on the arbitrators. The IBA guidelines are considered a reflection of actual practice incorporated into the arbitration by the parties. Usually, arbitral tribunals in England & Wales, especially the LCIA, will on occasion refer to the IBA guidelines to provide clarity, but it is not bound by the guidelines.

LCIA challenges

The Arbitration International Journal in its special 'Challenges' issue,[27] has published digests of reasoned arbitral challenge decisions of the LCIA court. A challenge of an arbitrator is most often resolved by the president or vice president of the LCIA court or by means of a division of the court consisting of three or five members, appointed by the president or the vice president. In practice, challenges are most commonly resolved by a division of the court. The usual practice for submission and resolution of a challenge is for written submissions and supporting documents to be submitted by the challenging party, the challenged arbitrator and the other party or parties. Challenges are usually resolved on paper as oral submissions are a rare alternative taken by the court.[28]

Immunity of arbitrators

Section 29 of the 1996 Act grants immunity to the arbitrator unless bad faith is proven. The LCIA and the ICC Rules similarly exclude liabilities where fraud, misconduct or bad faith have not been proven. This is most often seen as a consequence of the consensual nature of arbitral proceedings and the trust placed in tribunals to resolve disputes. Immunity as such helps to provide a degree of finality to the proceedings by preventing parties from holding the arbitrators liable where they disagree with the result of proceedings.[29]

Secretaries to the arbitral tribunal

There are no rules governing the conduct of the secretaries to the arbitral tribunal. In practice, there are instances of arbitrators appointing arbitral secretaries under the LCIA Rules. The LCIA in the FAQ section of the website lays down the function of administrative secretaries by confining: "*their activities to such matters as organising papers for the Tribunal, highlighting relevant legal authorities, maintaining factual chronologies, keeping the Tribunal's time sheets and so forth*".[30]

A recent survey conducted by White & Case and Queen Mary University,[31] held that the use of tribunal secretaries is most common in arbitrations of Latin American respondents (62%), while least common in arbitrations of respondents from North America (23%) and Asia (26%).[32]

Interim relief

Interim relief is available from both the English courts and London-seated arbitral tribunals.

The English courts have broad powers under section 44 of the 1996 Act as to interim relief in support of arbitral proceedings. These powers are typically invoked on an urgent basis before an arbitral tribunal has been composed and, once an arbitral tribunal is constituted, the court will only act where the tribunal has no power or is unable to act effectively (section 44(5)). The court's powers under section 44 can be exercised in support of foreign-seated arbitrations if the court considers that it is appropriate to do so (section 2(3)),[33] but do not extend to a non-party to an arbitration agreement outside of the jurisdiction.[34]

Similarly, section 38 of the 1996 Act specifies that arbitral tribunals have broad powers as to interim relief (including the power to order security for costs), although such powers can face limitations due to practical considerations, such as the ability to enforce an interim order such as an asset-freezing injunction against third parties which are not party to the arbitral proceedings. An arbitral tribunal might also choose to issue an interim award against one party for the payment of sums, pursuant to section 39 of the 1996 Act.

Broad powers to grant interim relief

The English courts have interpreted their powers under section 44 broadly. For example, section 44(3) states that the court may make orders in cases of urgency for the purposes of preserving "*evidence or assets*". The courts have interpreted "*assets*" to include contractual rights.

English courts also allow an injunction against court proceedings ("anti-suit injunctions") by which the contractual rights of the parties that include the right to have disputes referred to and resolved by arbitration are protected.

Following the ECJ decision in *Allianz SpA and Others v West Tankers Inc,*[35] the English courts may not grant an anti-suit injunction to restrain proceedings commenced in the court of another EU member state. However, anti-suit injunctions remain available in respect of proceedings brought outside the EU.[36] If no arbitration proceedings have commenced and none are intended (thereby precluding an application under section 44 of the 1996 Act), but a party nonetheless seeks to protect its rights under an arbitration agreement, the courts have jurisdiction to award a final anti-suit injunction under section 37 of the Senior Courts Act 1981.[37]

English courts can order anti-arbitration injunctions in aid of domestic litigation, but rarely do so. *Excalibur v Texas Keystone Inc,*[38] is one of the rare examples of the Commercial Court intervening in an arbitration that was subject to oversight by the New York, not English, courts.[39]

The powers of the court do not extend to ICSID arbitrations, where any relief should be sought from the tribunal.[40]

Although the 1996 Act applies mainly to arbitrations seated in England and Wales, there are some provisions which apply even if the seat is elsewhere or has not been determined. These powers mainly relate to applications to stay court proceedings brought in breach of an arbitration agreement (section 9) or in order to exercise the English court's powers to secure the attendance of witnesses (section 43) or to grant injunctive relief in support of the arbitration (section 44).

The rules of a number of arbitral institutions, such as the LCIA and the ICC, now also provide for the appointment of an emergency arbitrator to grant interim relief in situations where the arbitral tribunal has yet to be appointed.

Security for costs

Under section 38(3) of the 1996 Act, the arbitral tribunal can pass an order for security of costs of the arbitration. There are no grounds given under section 38(3), but they usually relate to the claimant's inability to pay, and classic examples include the claimant's insolvency or likely refusal to pay, and the consequent difficulties of enforcement.

Section 68(3) only allows the tribunal to order the claimant to provide the security for costs. The LCIA Rules under Article 25, however, allow the tribunal to ask for security for costs of the arbitration and legal fees, as well as security for all or part of the dispute.

Arbitration award

Formal requirements

The parties are free to agree on the form of the award.[41] In the absence of any agreement, the award must be in writing and signed by all the arbitrators (or all those assenting to it). Further, unless it is an agreed award or the parties have agreed to the contrary, the award must contain reasons and state the seat of the arbitration and the date on which it is made.[42] The award will take effect from the date on which all the above conditions are met.

The tribunal is not subject to a time limit in rendering its award. If the arbitration agreement imposes such a time limit, upon application by the tribunal or by any party to the proceedings, the court may extend such time limit if it is satisfied that a "*substantial injustice*" would otherwise result.[43]

Costs for the parties

Unless otherwise agreed by the parties, the tribunal may make an award allocating the costs of the arbitration between the parties.[44] Under the 1996 Act, costs of the arbitration include the arbitrators' fees and expenses, those of any arbitral institution used during the proceedings, and the legal or other costs of the parties; for example, translators, venue hire, travel expenses.[45]

Unless the parties otherwise agree, the tribunal will award costs of the arbitration on the basis of the general principle that costs should "follow the event", *i.e.* that the unsuccessful party should pay the successful party's recoverable costs.[46]

Interest

The parties are free to agree on the tribunal's power to award interest under section 49 of the 1996 Act. The default position is that the tribunal may award simple or compound interest at such rates and with such rests as it considers appropriate, up to the date of the award and from the date of the award to the date of payment, on: the whole or part of any amount awarded in respect of the principal claim; and any award as to costs.[47] No mandatory or customary rate of interest is applicable.

Challenge of the arbitration award

The English courts have generally followed a policy of non-interference in the arbitral process with respect to challenges to arbitral awards. Such challenges are rarely successful.

There are three grounds on which a party may appeal (or challenge) an award made under the 1996 Act:

- The tribunal lacked substantive jurisdiction under section 67.
- A party may challenge an award on the grounds of serious irregularity under section 68.
- An appeal to the court under section 69 on a question of law arising out of an award made in the proceedings.

Section 67: Substantive jurisdiction

Under section 67 an award can be challenged on the basis that it was made without jurisdiction. The award could be the substantive award on the merits of the claims, or may be a separate preliminary award containing the tribunal's ruling on its own jurisdiction.

Section 67 is mandatory and parties cannot contract out of the right to challenge an award on the basis of substantive jurisdiction.[48] The phrase "*substantive jurisdiction*" is defined in section 30(1) and section 82 of the 1996 Act. Thus challenge can be made on:

- existence or validity of the arbitration agreement;
- constitution of the tribunal; and
- scope of the arbitration agreement.

The validity of the arbitration agreement can be called into question under section 67. It may be argued that the arbitration agreement is invalid due to some flaw with the contract in which it is contained. The principle of separability, however, would generally mean that the invalidity of the contract does not affect the arbitration agreement, unless the basis of invalidity may be such as to render both the contract and the arbitration agreement invalid – for example, lack of capacity.[49]

In *B v A*,[50] the court held that an error by a tribunal in the application of the chosen law does not lead to a lack of substantive jurisdiction. The House of Lords in *Fiona Trust & Holding Corp v Privalov*[51] held that the parties to an arbitration agreement, as rational businessmen, should be assumed to have intended that any dispute arising out of the relationship into which they had entered, or purported to have entered, should be decided by the same tribunal. This assumption can only be departed from in case the arbitration agreement makes it clear that the parties intended to exclude certain questions from the arbitral jurisdiction.

The hearing under section 67 is a full one. Each party has the right to put to the court all arguments and evidence (and evidence not presented to the tribunal). The process is not a judicial review but a complete retrial.[52]

Section 68: Serious irregularity

Section 68 is also a mandatory section and the parties cannot contract out of it. The serious irregularity could be related to the award or proceedings or to the tribunal. The irregularity should cause or would cause "*substantial injustice*". It requires a high threshold for the courts to set aside the award under section 68.

Section 68(2) lists a few of the following kinds of irregularities, which is exhaustive in nature:

- Failure by the tribunal to comply with section 33 of the 1996 Act (which sets out the tribunal's general duties, such as the duty to give each party a reasonable opportunity to put its case).
- The tribunal exceeding its powers (other than in relation to its substantive jurisdiction).
- Failure by the tribunal to deal with all the issues that were put to it.
- The award being obtained by fraud or in a manner contrary to public policy.

In *Fidelity Management SA v Myriad International Holdings BV,*[53] Morrison J held that section 68 was a '*long stop*' to deal with '*extreme cases where ... something ... went seriously wrong with the arbitral process*'.[54]

In a recent case of *Lorand Shipping v Davof Trading (Africa) B.V. (MV "Ocean Glory"),*[55] there was a rare example of a successful application under section 68.

<u>Section 69: Appeal on a point of law</u>

Section 69 of the 1996 Act allows the parties to arbitral proceedings to appeal to the court on a question of law. This is one of the most controversial sections with respect to international arbitration. This section is not mandatory and can be excluded by agreement between the parties. Arbitral rules like the LCIA and the ICC Rules exclude any appeal on a question of law.[56]

The reported decisions under section 69 tend to be in the field of shipping/maritime, commodities, construction and rent review cases.[57] The appeal can be only against English law and not a foreign law. Thus appeal under section 69 is not available if it has been determined according to the law of another jurisdiction or another system.[58] There will also be no appeal on questions of fact.

An appeal under section 69 can be brought with the agreement of all the other parties to the arbitration or with the leave of the court. Pursuant to section 69(3), permission to appeal will only be granted if all of the following requirements are satisfied:

- That the determination of the question will substantially affect the rights of one or more of the parties.
- That the question of law is one which the tribunal was asked to determine.
- The decision of the tribunal is obviously wrong; or the question is one of general public importance and the tribunal's decision is open to serious doubt.
- That, despite the agreement of the parties to resolve the matter by arbitration, it is just and proper for the court to determine the question.

Procedure for challenging awards

Any application to challenge an award or appeal must be brought within 28 days of the date of the award or, if there has been any arbitral process of appeal or review, of the date when the applicant or appellant was notified of the result of that process.[59]

Further, no application or appeal under sections 67, 68 or 69 may be brought unless the applicant or appellant has first exhausted any available arbitration process of appeal or review and any available recourse for correction of the award under section 57.[60]

The court may order, on any application under section 67, 68 or 69, security for costs of the application or appeal. The application may even be dismissed if such an order is made and not complied with.[61]

Section 70(6) provides that on any application under sections 67, 68 or 69, the court may order the applicant or appellant to provide security for the costs of the application or appeal. The application or appeal may be dismissed if such an order is made and then not complied with.

Enforcement of the arbitration award

Most international arbitration awards in the United Kingdom will be enforced under the 1975 New York Convention. Further, as noted above, the UK is also party to the 1927 Geneva Convention on the Execution of Foreign Arbitral Awards. However, very few states are signatories to the Geneva Convention and not to the New York Convention.

Other reciprocal arrangements under which international arbitration awards might be enforced exist, such as the 1933 Foreign Judgments (Reciprocal Enforcement) Act, which provides for the enforcement of arbitral awards from certain former Commonwealth countries.

The enforcement of awards delivered by ICSID Tribunals will be take place pursuant to the 1996 Act.

The 1996 Act incorporates into English law the provisions for the recognition and enforcement of awards which are found in the New York Convention.[62] In particular, pursuant to section 102, a party seeking the recognition or enforcement of a New York Convention award must produce: (i) the duly authenticated original award or a duly certified copy of it; and (ii) the original arbitration agreement or a duly certified copy of it.

Further, if the award or agreement is in a foreign language, the party must also produce a certified translation of it.

As a practical note, assuming the enforcement proceedings are not contested, enforcement should be a matter of weeks and the costs should be relatively minimal. The courts retain the discretion to enforce an award that has been set aside or suspended by the courts in the seat of arbitration,[63] but in practice this is quite rare.

In England & Wales the courts generally adopt a pro-arbitration approach and are in favour of the enforcement of international arbitration awards. The courts very rarely refuse to enforce awards on public policy grounds.[64]

One particular case in which the enforcement of an ICC award was refused is the case *Dallah Estate and Tourism Holding Company v Ministry of Religious Affairs, Government of Pakistan*.[65] In this case the award was refused enforcement on the grounds, *inter alia*, that the Government of Pakistan had not been a party to the operative arbitration agreement. The Supreme Court applied French law as the governing law, concluding that there was no evidence of a common intention on the part of Dallah and the Government of Pakistan to make the Government a party to the arbitration agreement.

The decision in the Supreme Court case of *IPCO v NNPC [2017] UKSC 16* provides, among other matters, clarification regarding the role of security in the enforcement of New York Convention awards in England & Wales, and is likely to be of significant value internationally in respect of interpretation of Article V of the New York Convention. Lord Mance (with whom the other justices agreed) concluded that the court had no power to make an award debtor's properly arguable right to resist enforcement (on the grounds provided by section 103(2) or 103(3) of the 1996 Act conditional on the provision of security). The Supreme Court held that the express power to order security under the 1996 Act, section 103(5) was not applicable in those circumstances – that subsection applied only while the

English court was adjourning its decision pending the outcome of a challenge to the award in the curial court.

On the subject of the role of curial court, in *Maximov v OJSC Novolipetsky Metallurgichesky Kombinat [2017] EWHC 1911 (Comm)*, the English High Court dismissed an attempt to enforce a Russian award that had already been annulled by the seat courts in Moscow, holding, among other matters, that it was not enough to show that the Russian courts' decisions were manifestly wrong or even perverse to succeed under section 103(2)(f) of the 1996 Act.

Further, *Maximov v OJSC Novolipetsky Metallurgichesky Kombinat* demonstrates that award creditors have a very high hurdle to surmount when attempting to enforce awards that have been annulled by the court of the seat of the arbitral proceedings.

Investment arbitration

The United Kingdom drafted its first Model Agreement for the Promotion and Protection of Investments ("IPPA") in 1971, which led to negotiating IPPAs with various developing countries.[66] The first IPPA was with Egypt in 1976.[67] At the moment, UK has signed 110 IPPAs or Bilateral Investment Treaties ("BITs").[68]

The UK government is generally favourable to investment treaty arbitration. It has ratified the ICSID convention on 23 December 1981 and implemented the Washington Convention by the Arbitration (International Investment Disputes) Act 1966.

The only multilateral investment protection treaty to which the United Kingdom is a party is the Energy Charter Treaty ("ECT"), which entered into force in 1998.

<u>Features of the Bilateral Investment Treaties</u>

- *Investor*

As regards companies, most of the UK's BITs define "*Investor*" as a company incorporated or constituted under the laws of a Contracting Party. This even includes companies incorporated or constituted in territories to which the BIT is extended; for example, Jersey, Guernsey, the Isle of Man expressly.

- *Definition of investment*

The Model UK IPPA defines the term '*investments*' broadly:

"*Every kind of asset and in particular, though not exclusively ... (i) movable and immovable property and any other property rights such as mortgages, liens, or pledges; (ii) shares in and stock and debentures of a company and any other form of participation in a company; (iii) claims to money and to any performance under contract having a financial value; (iv) intellectual property rights, goodwill, technical processes and know-how; and (v) business concessions conferred by law or under contract, including concessions to search for, cultivate, extract or exploit natural resources.*"[69]

All UK BITs refer to a non-exhaustive list of eligible assets under the definition, but make no reference to indirectly controlled assets. The ECT, on the other hand, refers to indirectly controlled assets: "*every kind of asset, owned or controlled directly or indirectly*".[70]

- *Fair and equitable treatment*

The majority of the UK's BITs, (and the ECT) provide that each Contracting Party shall accord fair and equitable treatment to investment. Article 2(2) of the UK Model BIT states:

"*Investments of nationals or companies of each Contracting Party shall at all times be accorded fair and equitable treatment ...*"

The fair and equitable treatment standard in the UK BIT is not linked with international law or customary law.

- *Umbrella clause*

Most UK BITs consists of an umbrella clause. Article 2(2) of the UK Model BIT states:

"Each Contracting Party shall observe any obligation it may have entered into with regard to investments of nationals or companies of the other Contracting Party."

- *Expropriation*

Article 5(1) of the UK Model BIT covers expropriation:

"Investments of nationals or companies of either Contracting Party shall not be nationalised, expropriated or subjected to measures having effect equivalent to nationalisation or expropriation (hereinafter referred to as 'expropriation') in the territory of the other Contracting Party except for a public purpose related to the internal needs of that Party on a non-discriminatory basis and against prompt, adequate and effective compensation. Such compensation shall amount to the genuine value of the investment expropriated immediately before the expropriation or before the impending expropriation became public knowledge, whichever is the earlier, shall include interest at a normal commercial rate until the date of payment, shall be made without delay, be effectively realizable and be freely transferable. The national or company affected shall have a right, under the law of the Contracting Party making the expropriation, to prompt review, by a judicial or other independent authority of that Party, of his or its case and of the valuation of his or its investment in accordance with the principles set out in this paragraph."

That expropriation should be for a public purpose related to the internal needs of the Contracting Party is common to UK BITs. Some of the BITs lay down more specific conditions in which expropriations may be carried out; for example, the UK-India BIT permits expropriations "*related to the internal requirements for regulating economic activity*". In the UK-China BIT, the term "*market value*" has not been included to define compensation for expropriation.[71]

Another feature of the expropriation clauses under some UK BITs is that they also protect the minority shareholders.[72]

<u>National treatment and most-favoured nation</u>

All UK BITs include national treatment and most-favoured nation (MFN) clauses.

Article 3(1) of the Model UK BIT is the national treatment clause:

"Neither Contracting Party shall in its territory subject investments or returns of nationals or companies of the other Contracting Party to treatment less favourable than that which it accords to investments or returns of its own nationals or companies or to investments or returns of nationals or companies of any third State."

Article 3(2) of the Model UK BIT provides:

"Neither Contracting Party shall in its territory subject nationals or companies of the other Contracting Party, as regards their management, maintenance, use, enjoyment or disposal of their investments, to treatment less favourable than that which it accords to its own nationals or companies or to nationals or companies of any third State."

These provisions do not extend to the benefits of membership of a customs union, a monetary union or a free trade area, nor to taxation agreements.[73] Further, Article 3(2) clarifies that these provisions will not extend on account of the UK's membership to the European Union.

Procedural rights under the BIT

Article 8 of the Model UK BIT contains two versions. The first provides resolution of disputes under the ICSID Convention where both states have signed the ICSID Convention. The investor shall bring the claim to the ICSID if the claim is not resolved in three months' time.

The second version provides that after three months, the investor can submit to investment arbitration. The parties may agree to any of the three institutions: ICSID, the ICC International Court of Arbitration, or an *ad hoc* tribunal constituted under the UNCITRAL Rules. If parties fail to agree within three months, the investor can refer the dispute to arbitration under the UNCITRAL Rules.

Decisions against UK

There has been no publicly available award against UK. There has been only one case, *Ashok Sancheti v United Kingdom*,[74] where an English court addressed issues relating to a UK BIT where the claimant sought to stay proceedings as he had filed a request for arbitration under the UK-India BIT. The English Court refused to grant the stay on the grounds that the Corporation of London (which was the defendant in the court proceedings) was not a party to the arbitration agreement under section 9 of the BIT.

There have been other instances where an English court has ruled on issues related to investment arbitration but a UK bilateral treaty was not involved.[75]

* * *

Endnotes

1. In the 2015 International Arbitration Survey: Improvements and Innovations in International Arbitration prepared by the School of International Arbitration, Queen Mary, University of London, in partnership with White & Case, London was listed as the most used (45%) and most preferred (47%) seat of arbitration.
2. *Bernuth Lines Ltd v High Seas Shipping Ltd* [2006] 1 Lloyd's Rep 537.
3. [2011] EWCA Civ 855.
4. *Fulham Football Club*, per Patten J. at paragraph 40.
5. The decision in *Yegiazaryan v Smagin* also shows that a dispute arising in relation to a series of agreements is capable of being heard in a single arbitration, even if the parties named in each of the agreements are not identical. Where there is uncertainty, as in that case, regarding the meaning of an arbitration clause, the apparent commercial purpose should prevail over formalistic or technical interpretation. See also, *Autoridad del Canal de Panamá v Sacyr [2017] EWHC 2228 (Comm)* which demonstrates the court's realistic and commercial approach to the interpretation of Section 9 of the 1996 Act when it comes to ensuring respect for the parties' decision to arbitrate rather than litigate.
6. [2013] EWHC 1063 (Comm).
7. Section 46 of the 1996 Act.
8. [2012] EWCA Civ 638.
9. [2013] 2 All ER 1.
10. [2013] EWHC 4071 (Comm).
11. Joseph Tirado, Sherina Petit, *et al.*, Chapter 23: Factual Evidence in Julian D. M. Lew, Harris Bor, *et al.* (eds), *Arbitration in England, with chapters on Scotland and Ireland,* Kluwer Law International 2013 pp. 483–550.

12. *Ibid* at endnote 15.
13. See *EDO Corporation v Ultra Electronics Limited [2009] EWHC 682* (Ch) and subsequently in *Travelers Insurance Company Ltd v. Countrywide Surveyors Ltd* [2010] EWHC 2455 (TCC) (6 September 2010), the courts held that a claim for pre-action disclosure cannot be entertained where the underlying dispute is going to be referred to arbitration. In sum, the power to order pre-action disclosure in accordance with the Senior Courts Act 1981, s. 33(2) can only be invoked by an applicant who appears likely to be a party to subsequent court proceedings.
14. Tirado, Petit, *supra* at fn 15.
15. See *Michael Wilson & Partners Ltd v Emmott* [2008] EWCA Civ 184 and *Ali Shipping Corporation v 'Shipyard Trogir'* [1999] 1 WLR 136.
16. Julian D.M. Lew, Chapter 21: Confidentiality in Arbitrations in England in Julian D. M. Lew, Harris Bor, *et al.* (eds), Arbitration in England, with chapters on Scotland and Ireland, Volume (© Kluwer Law International; Kluwer Law International 2013) pp. 441–454.
17. Article 19 of the LCIA Rules.
18. See Sapna Jhangiani, "How Far Do The New LCIA Guidelines For Parties' Legal Representatives and the IBA Guidelines On Party Representation go?", Kluwer Arb Blog http://kluwerarbitrationblog.com/blog/2014/05/21/how-far-do-the-new-lcia-guidelines-for-parties-legal-representatives-and-the-iba-guidelines-on-party-representation-go/.
19. Article 15 of the 1996 Act.
20. *Jivraj v Hashwani*: Parties to arbitral proceedings had entered into a joint venture agreement which provided for an *ad-hoc* arbitration in London. The agreement stipulated that the arbitral tribunal must belong to a particular religious set (i.e. Ismaili Muslims). The claimant argued that the stipulation was contrary to the Employment Equality (Religion and Beliefs) Regulations Act 2003. The Supreme Court held that arbitrators are not employees and are not therefore covered by the aforesaid Act. Therefore, qualifications concerning religion, beliefs, or otherwise, can be justly imposed upon the arbitral tribunal by agreement of the parties to the proceedings.
21. The default position under the LCIA Rules 2014 is also that unless parties have agreed otherwise, a sole arbitrator will be appointed.
22. Section 16(5) of the 1996 Act.
23. Section 33 of the 1996 Act.
24. Article 5.4 of the LCIA Rules.
25. *R v Gough* [1993] AC 658, House of Lords case – on appeal from the Court of Appeal. The appellant claimed that a member of the jury present at the first instance was biased towards him due to the fact that he and the jury member were neighbours, and that due to a lack of impartiality the judgment should be overturned. The appeal was dismissed under the notion that a "real danger of bias" must exist and that bias should be established on the basis of the possibility (rather than the probability) of bias.
26. [1999] EWCA Civ 3004. The court held that the notion of judge in regards to impartiality is extended to include all judicial decision-makers, including arbiters, jurors, etc. Impartiality will automatically result in disqualification if any pecuniary or proprietary interest is held by the decision maker in the claimant.
27. Volume 27 Number 3, 2011.
28. Oral submissions are very rare – only two so far: LCIA REF NO UN 7949 (3 December 2007) and LCIA ref no 3488 (July 11 2007).

29. Redfern & Hunter, Oxford University Press 2009, para 5.55.
30. See http://www.lcia.org/Frequently_Asked_Questions.aspx#Secretaries.
31. 2012 Current and Preferred Practices in the Arbitral Process: International Arbitration Survey.
32. See also Berwin Leighton Paisner's 2016 International Arbitration Survey which focusses on the role of tribunal secretaries in international commercial arbitration.
33. The judgment in *Company 1 v Company 2 [2017] EWHC 2319 (QB)* illustrates that a party seeking urgent interim relief from the English court in support of arbitration proceedings seated outside England faces a significant challenge trying to persuade the court to grant such relief, even where, as here, the parties have agreed that English law will govern the procedure of the arbitration.
34. See, *DTEK Trading v Morozov* [2017] EWHC 94 (Comm).
35. C-185/07 [2009] AC 1138.
36. See, for example, *Midgulf International Ltd v Groupe Chimique Tunisien* [2010] EWCA Civ 66; *Shashoua and ors v Sharma* [2009] EWHC 957 (Comm).
37. *AES Ust-Kamenogorsk Hydropower Plant LLP v Ust-Kamenogorsk Hydropower Plant JSC* [2011] EWCA Civ 647.
38. [2011] EWHC 1624 *(Comm).*
39. 78 Arbitration, Issue 1 t 2012, Chartered Institute of Arbitrators (2012).
40. *ETI Euro Telecom International NV v Republic of Bolivia & Anor* [2008] EWCA Civ 880.
41. Section 52(1) of the 1996 Act.
42. Sections 52(3)-(5) of the 1996 Act.
43. Section 50 of the 1996 Act.
44. Section 61(1) of the 1996 Act.
45. Section 59 of the 1996 Act.
46. Section 61(2) of the 1996 Act.
47. Sections 49(3) and 49(4) of the 1996 Act.
48. Robert Merkin and Louis Flannery, Arbitration Act 1996, 5th Edition, Informa Law, p.292.
49. David Wolfson and Susanna Charlwood, Chapter 25: Challenges to Arbitration Awards in Julian D. M. Lew , Harris Bor, *et al.* (eds), *Arbitration in England*, with chapters on Scotland and Ireland, (© Kluwer Law International; Kluwer Law International 2013) pp. 527–562.
50. [2010] EWHC 1626 (Comm).
51. 2007] UKHL 40.
52. Robert Merkin and Louis Flannery, Arbitration Act 1996, 5th Edition, Informa Law, p.296.
53. [2005] EWHC 1193 (Comm).
54. David Wolfson and Susanna Charlwood, Chapter 25: Challenges to Arbitration Awards in Julian D. M. Lew , Harris Bor, *et al.* (eds), *Arbitration in England*, with chapters on Scotland and Ireland, (© Kluwer Law International; Kluwer Law International 2013) pp. 527–562.
55. [2014] EWHC 3521 (Comm).
56. See Art. 34(6) of the ICC Rules and Art 26.8 of LCIA Rules.
57. Robert Merkin and Louis Flannery, Arbitration Act 1996, 5th Edition, Informa Law, p.322.
58. David Wolfson and Susanna Charlwood, Chapter 25: Challenges to Arbitration Awards

in Julian D. M. Lew , Harris Bor, *et al.* (eds), Arbitration in England, with chapters on Scotland and Ireland, (© Kluwer Law International; Kluwer Law International 2013) pp. 527–562. See also *Schwebel v. Schwebel* [2010] EWHC 3280 (TCC).
59. Section 70(3) of the 1996 Act.
60. Section 70(2) of the 1996 Act.
61. Section 70(6) of the 1996 Act.
62. Sections 101-103 of the 1996 Act.
63. Section 103(2)(f) of the 1996 Act.
64. See, *Westacre Investments Inc v Jugoimport-SPDR Holding Co Ltd* [1999] 3 WLR 811, where enforcement was ordered despite public policy considerations relating to alleged illegality and *Sinocore v RBRG [2017] EWHC 251 (Comm)*, where attempts were made to set aside an order granting permission to enforce a CIETAC award and for judgment to be entered in the terms of the award on public policy grounds even though the award creditor had participated in fraudulent behaviour. In *Stati v Kazakhstan [2017] EWHC 1348 (Comm)*, the High Court decided that an application to set aside an order granting permission to enforce a SCC award should proceed to trial to determine whether the award had been procured by fraud, even though attempts to set aside the award at the court of the seat had failed. See also *Taurus Petroleum v SOMO [2017] UKSC 64*, for a demonstration of the court's pro-enforcement approach. In this case, the Supreme Court re-emphasised the clear policy of the English courts to ensure the efficient recognition and enforcement of arbitral awards, and agreed that it would be inconsistent to allow an international arbitration award to be turned into an English judgment for the purpose of enforcing the award and then to limit the means available for enforcement on the grounds of an allegedly insufficient connection with the jurisdiction.
65. [2010] UKSC 46.
66. Alejandro Escobar and Kate Hill, Chapter 14: Multilateral and Bilateral Investment Treaties and the United Kingdom in Julian D. M. Lew, Harris Bor, *et al.* (eds), *Arbitration in England,* with chapters on Scotland and Ireland, Kluwer Law International 2013 pp. 267–292.
67. *Ibid.*
68. See http://investmentpolicyhub.unctad.org/IIA/CountryBits/221#iiaInnerMenu.
69. Article 1(a) of Model BIT.
70. Article 1(6) of the ECT.
71. Alejandro Escobar and Kate Hill, Chapter 14: Multilateral and Bilateral Investment Treaties and the United Kingdom in Julian D. M. Lew, Harris Bor, *et al.* (eds), *Arbitration in England*, with chapters on Scotland and Ireland, Kluwer Law International 2013 pp. 267–292.
72. A Contracting Party which expropriates a company incorporated or constituted in accordance with its own laws, and in which nationals of the other Contracting Party own shares, shall ensure that the expropriation provision of the BIT is applied to the extent necessary to guarantee prompt, adequate and effective compensation in respect of such shares.
73. Further See Article 7 of Model UK BIT: "*The provisions of this Agreement relative to the grant of treatment not less favourable than that accorded to the nationals or companies of either Contracting Party or of any third State shall not be construed so as to preclude the adoption or enforcement by a Contracting Party of measures which are necessary to protect national security, public security or public order, nor shall these provisions be construed to oblige one Contracting Party to extend to the nationals or*

companies of the other the benefit of any treatment, preference or privilege resulting from:
(a) any existing or future customs, economic or monetary union, a common market or a free trade area or similar international agreement to which either of the Contracting Parties is or may become a party, and includes the benefit of any treatment, preference or privilege resulting from obligations arising out of an international agreement or reciprocity arrangement of that customs, economic or monetary union, common market or free trade area; or
(b) any international agreement or arrangement relating wholly or mainly to taxation or any domestic legislation relating wholly or mainly to taxation; or
(c) any requirements resulting from the United Kingdom's membership of the European Union including measures prohibiting, restricting or limiting the movement of capital to or from any third country."

74. [2008] EWCA 1283.
75. See *Occidental Exploration & Production Co. v Ecuador* [2005] EWCA Civ. 1116; *Czech Republic v European Media Ventures SA* [2007] EWCA 2851; *ETI Euro Telecom International NV v (1) Bolivia (2) Empresa Nacional de Telecommunicaciones Entel SA* [2008] EWCA Civ 880.

Joe Tirado
Tel: +44 207 796 1940 / Email: joe.tirado@garrigues.com

Joe Tirado is the Co-Head of International Arbitration and ADR at leading Spanish and Latin American firm, Garrigues UK LLP, and is based in London. He has over 25 years of dispute resolution experience and has handled hundreds of cases as counsel, arbitrator, mediator, and expert determiner in both English and Spanish.

Joe is recognised as a ranked individual for international arbitration and ADR in leading legal directories, where he is described as "first class" and "best known for his work on energy-related disputes, but is also recognised for his financial services and public international law expertise" and work in Latin America, the CIS and India.

Joe is a solicitor-advocate with full rights of audience before all civil courts, an accredited mediator, an ICSID conciliator and panel member of a number of leading arbitration and mediation panels. He has extensive experience of both commercial and investment arbitration.

Joe has been involved in a wide variety of contested matters in the UK and over 50 other countries. He has handled high-value cases in a number of sectors, including banking and finance; commodities; construction and engineering; energy (oil & gas, renewable and power generation); food and beverage; information, communication and technology (ICT); mining; petrochemical; pharmaceutical; professional services; sport; transport (automobile and aviation); and travel.

He has also conducted and advised on international commercial and investment arbitrations under all the major international arbitration rules before the leading international arbitration institutions, including the ICC, LCIA, SCC, ICDR/AAA, SIAC, CCIG, DIAC, and VIAC as well as "pure" *ad hoc* and UNCITRAL arbitrations.

Joe regularly sits as an arbitrator, mediator and expert determiner in both English and Spanish.

Garrigues London LLP

100 Cheapside, London EC2V 6DT, United Kingdom
Tel: +44 20 7398 5820 / Fax: +44 20 7398 5839 / URL: www.garrigues.com

Finland

Markus Kokko & Niki J. Welling
Borenius Attorneys Ltd.

Introduction

Arbitration in Finland is governed by the Arbitration Act of 1992 (967/1992 as amended). The Act was 'inspired' by the UNCITRAL Model Law in place at the time, but did not correspond to it word for word. Nevertheless, it did not conflict with the Model Law, nor has its interpretation been considered to conflict with how arbitration practice has evolved since then, either domestically or internationally. The Arbitration Act contains a few sections applicable to foreign arbitral proceedings and awards. Only minor amendments have been made since its enactment. At present, the legal community in Finland involved in arbitration is calling for a revision of the act in order for it to correspond to contemporary standards in terms of content.

The judiciary's attitude towards arbitration is quite positive, and attorneys also tend to recommend arbitration in business-to-business disputes due to the advantages it affords. The fact that state courts often have limited knowledge of industry realities, despite otherwise being competent, also plays a role in attorneys' positive attitude towards arbitration. Finland is party to, and has ratified, the New York Convention on the Recognition and Enforcement of Foreign Arbitral Awards.

The main centre for domestic or international arbitration is the Arbitration Institute of the Finnish Chambers of Commerce (the "Institute"). The present Arbitration Rules of Finnish Chambers of Commerce (the "Arbitration Rules") entered into force as of 1st June 2013. The key objective of the Arbitration Rules was to address issues such as expediency and cost-efficiency, multi-party administration, arbitrator-ordered interim relief and increased confidentiality.

The Arbitration Rules now stipulate a sole arbitrator to be the default number of arbitrators, unless the parties agree otherwise. If the board of the Institute considers it appropriate, the number of arbitrators may nevertheless be three. The challenge and replacement regimes concerning the arbitrators have also been conformed to the UNCITRAL Rules.

The reduction of the time and cost of proceedings has been addressed by stipulating that a preparatory conference shall be held (Art. 29), a procedural timetable shall be set up (Art. 30), a cut-off date prior to the hearing shall be set (Art. 33), the proceedings shall be officially closed, barring additional statements or claims (Art. 39), and the main rule is now that the award shall be given within nine months from the date on which the tribunal received the case file from the Institute (Art. 42).

The Arbitration Rules also contain provisions on arbitrator-ordered interim relief. The arbitral tribunal may grant "any interim measures" it deems appropriate. What standards should be applied to the evaluation of whether an interim relief measure is appropriate have deliberately been left out in order to allow for flexibility in this respect. According to the Arbitration Rules, a party may seek a court-ordered interim measure only in appropriate circumstances.

In addition to the above, the Arbitration Institute has also revised the rules for expedited arbitration, although the expedition procedure is quite seldom used.

Arbitration agreement

As a general rule, if a civil law case may be settled outside of court, the case is arbitrable. The exception is that consumers are not bound by arbitration agreements concluded before the dispute has arisen. Arbitration is not applicable to non-discretionary (indispositive) matters.

For an arbitration agreement to be valid, it must be in writing. Arbitration agreements concluded by way of correspondence are also acceptable. Arbitration clauses in wills, deeds of gift, bills of lading or similar documents, in the bylaws of an association, of a foundation, of a limited liability company or of another type of company or corporate entity, and by which the parties or the person against whom a claim is made are bound, shall have the same effect as separately concluded arbitration agreements.

The wording of the arbitration agreement is obviously subject to the normal rules of contract law, and can be interpreted or dismissed entirely if it is found lacking in clarity or enforceability. It is therefore recommended that due care be taken when drafting an arbitration clause. Consumers are not bound by an arbitration agreement made before a dispute has arisen, but are equally bound to an arbitration agreement concluded once a dispute has actualised.

The separability doctrine is applied in Finland. As a result, arbitrators may rule on the validity of a contract which includes an arbitration clause. The invalidity of the contract will therefore not automatically lead to the invalidity of the arbitration agreement. Arbitrators may also rule on their own competency (*kompetenz-kompetenz*).

Although it has not been stated *expressis verbis* in the Arbitration Act, arbitrators are generally considered to have the power to estimate damages when a party is unable to bear its burden of proof to the full extent (even if these powers haven't been granted to the arbitrator in the arbitration agreement). To this extent, guidance on the powers of the arbitrators may be found in the Code of Judicial Procedure.

The Arbitration Rules include detailed provisions on the constitution of an arbitral tribunal in multi-party cases, joinder of additional parties to pending arbitration proceedings, claims between multiple parties, claims under multiple contracts (including multiple arbitration agreements) and on the consolidation of two or more arbitrations into a single arbitration proceeding.

Arbitration procedure

The Arbitration Act does not contain very many provisions on the procedure of the proceedings. According to the Act, the parties may agree on the procedure to be applied and, in the absence of such an agreement, the arbitrators are empowered to decide on the procedure, taking into account the requirements of impartiality and expediency. The arbitrators may not impose fines or undertake other coercive measures to enforce their procedural orders. The proceedings may physically take place outside the seat of arbitration.

The proceedings are not confidential as such. The arbitrators have a duty of confidentiality, but a corresponding duty concerning the parties must be based on an agreement or applicable arbitration rules.

A party to an arbitration may, if the arbitral tribunal considers it appropriate, petition a court to order the production of documents for the purpose of the arbitration, in which case the court will apply the Code of Judicial Procedure on the matter.

Finland does not have extensive discovery or disclosure proceedings concerning evidence in civil law disputes. The court may nevertheless order a party to present a document or another piece of evidence which may be relevant as evidence in the dispute when petitioned by a party. Refusal may be sanctioned with a fine, and the court may order an executive officer (bailiff) to execute the order.

As the main rule is that a party must be able to present its own evidence in support of its claims, the Code of Judicial Procedure is based on the notion that the requested evidence must be specified and relevant as evidence in the case. Usually the requirement of specificity is quite strictly interpreted. A petition concerning a narrow category of documents may nevertheless be successful, as courts have been somewhat more flexible during the last decade. However, as a rule of thumb it may be stated that the petition, and the subsequent order to produce, should be specific enough for an executive officer to be able to enforce the order by executing it himself. The court may order a third party to produce the evidence as well.

The rules on privilege in the production of documents are for the most part similar to the exemptions of giving testimony in the main hearing. Some information and documentation (such as business and trade secrets) is protected by law and can therefore not be subject to a production order.

A public official, a healthcare professional, an attorney or counsel, a court-appointed mediator or auxiliary mediator may not present a document if it can be assumed that the document contains something on which he or she may not be heard as a witness. In addition, a witness may refuse to give a statement which would reveal a business or professional secret, unless very important reasons require that the witness be heard on the subject matter. Similarly, a party may refuse to provide a document containing this kind of information. The court will examine the grounds for refusal prior to deciding on the issue. Partial production of a document may also be ordered.

There is an exception to the confidentiality obligation and right of an attorney. An attorney might be ordered to testify and produce documents if he has not acted for the client in court proceedings (i.e. only acted in an advisory role) and the testimony relates to investigating an aggravated offence. In-house counsels are considered normal employees of a company and as such, do not enjoy any special confidentiality rights or obligations.

The IBA Rules on the Taking of Evidence in International Arbitration are frequently invoked, especially in disputes involving foreign parties (international arbitration). Even though Finland traditionally has had a rather dismissive stance concerning, for instance, disclosure, the stance on document production has nevertheless loosened up in domestic arbitration as well, and the apprehensive attitude found in the Code of Judicial Procedure no longer corresponds to the attitudes of seasoned arbitrators. An arbitral tribunal is not bound by the Code of Judicial Procedure and is consequently not obligated to apply the principles found in it, even when both parties are domestic.

Adverse inferences may be drawn by the arbitral tribunal if a party refuses to produce the requested evidence (drawing adverse inferences is naturally beset by its own set of problems concerning the conclusions one might be able to draw based on a refusal). Parties are nevertheless quite prone to adhere to orders issued by tribunals, and refusal rarely becomes an issue in proceedings.

The Arbitration Act does not contain provisions on expert witnesses. The Arbitration Rules, on the other hand, allows the arbitral tribunal to appoint one or more experts to report on specific issues after consulting the parties.

Electronic production of documents has not surfaced as a real problem, due to a restrictive view on document production in general. At the moment, no steps are being taken to prepare for possible problems concerning electronic production that might surface in the future.

A party may petition a state court to appoint one or more arbitrators to the tribunal. Correspondingly, a court may relieve an arbitrator when requested to do so by the parties. A court may also enforce the production of evidence (including witness testimony) if it is considered necessary by the arbitral tribunal.

Notwithstanding the *lis pendens* rule applicable to the relationship between the arbitration proceedings and court proceedings, a state court may grant interim relief when petitioned to do so by a party. The Code of Judicial Procedure is applicable to the application for interim relief.

Arbitrators

Unless the parties have agreed otherwise (or applicable institutional arbitration rules provide for rules on the arbitrators), three arbitrators shall be appointed. However, the starting point in the Arbitration Rules, in the absence of agreement between the parties, is that only one arbitrator is appointed unless the board of the Institute considers three arbitrators appropriate, considering the circumstances. Foreign nationals are *expressis verbis* allowed. An arbitrator shall be impartial and independent of the parties. Arbitrators have not been afforded immunity and are, as a starting point, liable for their actions.

The arbitral tribunal may rule on an arbitrator challenge. A challenge shall be presented within 15 days from the time at which a party became aware of the grounds for the challenge. Based on the Arbitration Rules, the Board of the Arbitration Institute may release an arbitrator, if it accepts a challenge made by a party due to, e.g. partiality. Where an arbitrator has been replaced, the reconstituted arbitral tribunal shall, after consulting with the parties, decide if and to what extent prior proceedings will be repeated before the reconstituted arbitral tribunal.

National courts will examine the matter only after an award has been rendered.

The IBA Guidelines on conflict of interest are not binding on tribunals or courts. The guidelines are nevertheless invoked quite frequently in challenge cases, and it can be said that the guidelines are taken into account when deciding on a challenge.

Based on the Arbitration Rules, the arbitral tribunal may, after consulting with the parties, appoint a secretary when deemed appropriate. A secretary shall meet the same requirements of impartiality and independence as any arbitrator. Secretaries for arbitral tribunals are utilised to a certain degree and are more common in complex, high-value disputes involving an abundance of factual issues.

Interim relief

Under the Arbitration Rules of the Arbitration Board of the Finnish Chambers of Commerce, Article 36.5, a party in need of urgent interim measures that cannot await the constitution of an arbitral tribunal may apply for the appointment of an emergency arbitrator in accordance with Appendix III of the Arbitration Rules ("Appendix III"), unless the parties have exercised their right to opt out of the application of the provisions contained in Appendix III, i.e. specifically excluded the possibility of emergency arbitration in the relevant underlying agreement.

If the emergency arbitrator proceedings have not been ruled out, parties normally have the freedom to choose between applying for interim measures from the court from the emergency arbitrator, or even from the arbitral tribunal or arbitrator.

The purpose of emergency arbitrator proceedings is to get access to interim measures where the client's need for interim relief is so urgent that it cannot wait for the constitution of the arbitral tribunal. Where the urgency requirement is not fulfilled, the emergency arbitrator shall dismiss the Applicant's request for interim measures of protection.

The emergency arbitrator shall have the same power to grant any interim measures of protection as the arbitral tribunal. The scope of interim measures available under the Arbitration Rules is wide, since the arbitral tribunal may, at the request of a party, grant any interim measures it deems appropriate.

The practicability of arbitrator-ordered interim measures is limited by the fact that under the Arbitration Rules, the arbitral tribunal, and also the emergency arbitrator, shall give the party against which the request is directed an opportunity to submit comments before deciding whether to grant any interim measure. The right to comment on interim measures before they have been ordered may defeat the element of surprise sometimes needed to make full use of such protective measures.

Even if the provisions of the Appendix concerning emergency arbitrator proceedings are applied, the parties are not prevented from seeking urgent interim measures of protection from a competent judicial authority such as the local courts, at any time prior to making an application for the appointment of an emergency arbitrator, and in appropriate circumstances even thereafter.

Interim measures are regulated under Finnish law in the Code of Judicial Procedure, when measures are applied from general courts. Under the Code of Judicial Procedure, the court may order "precautionary measures" in situations set out in Chapter 7 of the Procedural Code. Usually the party petitioning for interim relief must post security for the potential damage an injunction may cause the other party.

The court may order the seizure of property if the petitioner establishes its receivable to be likely, and there is a danger that the other party hides or otherwise acts in a manner that endangers the receivable.

If the petitioner establishes the likelihood of him having some other enforceable right, and there is a danger that the other party, by doing or neglecting to do something, endangers or otherwise diminishes the right from being realised, the court may: (i) under the threat of a fine, order the other party to refrain from doing something; (ii) under the threat of a fine, order the other party to do something; (iii) entitle the petitioner to do something or have something done; (iv) order the property of the other party to be set into the custody of an agent (trustee); or (v) order any other measure which is necessary to safeguard the right which needs to be protected.

The order must be proportional to the right which is to be safeguarded, and may not cause unreasonable harm to the other party. The system for interim relief is quite flexible in that it recognises different kinds of rights and the need to protect them, and has, for instance, successfully been used to prevent a strike by a labour union and to prevent a party from terminating an agreement.

Arbitration award

The arbitration award must be made in writing and must be signed by the arbitrators. If an arbitrator refuses to sign the award, an explanation as to the refusal shall be provided. Unless the parties explicitly agree that the arbitrators shall base their award on equity (*ex aequo et bono*), the arbitrators must base their award on the law.

The arbitral tribunal's final decision on the merits of the case constitutes the final award rendered by the tribunal. In addition to final awards, the tribunal may issue separate awards during the course of the proceedings. The tribunal may also render consent awards and additional awards if requested by the parties. The tribunal may furthermore order the parties to bear the costs of the arbitration, and also allocate the costs *inter partes*. An award on both the main issues in dispute as well as costs may include interest if the applicable substantial law allows for it.

The arbitral tribunal may, by way of a separate award, decide an independent claim presented to the tribunal. A separate award may also be given concerning a part of a claim which has been admitted by the respondent. A separate award may also be rendered, with the consent of the parties, concerning an issue which determines how the rest of the dispute shall be resolved. The tribunal may, for instance, rule on a time-bar issue or divide a damages case by first ruling on the grounds of liability, and only rule on the amount of damages after that.

Additional awards are also possible if the arbitral tribunal neglects to rule on a claim in its actual award. In addition, the arbitral tribunal may correct clerical errors in the award at the behest of a party. The tribunal may also, on its own initiative, correct the clerical error after having heard the parties on the issue.

Based on the Arbitration Rules, the award shall be rendered within nine months of the tribunal having received the case file from the Arbitration Institute.

Enforcement and challenge of the arbitration award

The enforcement of arbitral awards is decided on by the state courts. As a rule, the state court will apply the *in favorem pro validitate* rule on its deliberation, and the threshold for setting the award aside is quite high. Very many of arbitral proceedings take place in Helsinki, and other district courts may not be as familiar with arbitral law. Thus, it is recommended to seat the arbitration in Helsinki. Finland has ratified the New York Convention on the Recognition and Enforcement of Foreign Arbitral Awards, and foreign arbitral awards are therefore enforceable in Finland. Arbitral awards are challenged every now and then, but challenges are quite seldom accepted by the courts. In principle, an award can be enforced even though it has been successfully challenged in the place of arbitration.

An arbitral award can be set aside by the court on the basis of either invalidity or nullity. The award is considered invalid if: (i) the case was inarbitrable; (ii) the award contradicts the foundations of the judicial system (*ordre public*); (iii) the award is so unclear and incoherent it cannot serve as a basis for enforcement; or (iv) the award has not been signed by the arbitrators (majority suffices, but an explanation must be provided for why the minority has not signed the award). The award is considered null if: (i) the arbitrators have exceeded their powers; (ii) the arbitrators have been appointed in the wrong manner; (iii) an arbitrator has been incompetent due to bias; or (iv) the arbitral tribunal has not afforded a party sufficient opportunity to present its case.

There have recently been a few attempts at challenging arbitration awards in high-value cases. Challenges have nevertheless often been appeals on the merits concealed in claims on the issues described above. The courts have not been convinced, and the *in favorem pro validitate* principle has been upheld.

Enforcement of a foreign arbitral award can be denied by the court if: (i) the arbitration agreement has been invalid (due to certain grounds); (ii) a party has not been informed of the proceedings or has otherwise been inhibited or unable to present its case; (iii) the arbitral tribunal has exceeded its powers; (iv) the composition of the arbitral tribunal or the arbitration itself has significantly deviated from the arbitration agreement; or (v) the arbitral award has not yet become binding in the country in which it was given, or if it has been set aside in that country. The arbitral award may not be enforced to the extent that the arbitral award contradicts the foundations of the Finnish legal system (*ordre public*).

The party enforcing the award or the judgment always bears the risk for the other party's insolvency. If the execution is unsuccessful due to lack of assets, the party enforcing the award will have to pay its own legal costs, in addition to not being able to retrieve the claimed amount.

Investment arbitration

Finland signed the Convention on the Settlement of Investment Disputes between States and National of other States (also known as the ICSID Convention or the Washington Convention) on 14 July 1967 and deposited its instrument of ratification on 9 January 1969. Finland attained status as a Contracting State to the ICSID Convention on 8 February 1969. There is only one case on ICSID record involving parties of Finnish nationality (claimants). The case was largely successful for the claimants.

Finland has signed Bilateral Investment Treaties (BITs) with over 60 countries. Most of these BITs have entered into force and allow recourse to arbitration as a means of dispute resolution.

Finland has also signed the Energy Charter Treaty and ratified it on 16 December 1997.

Markus Kokko
Tel: +358 20 713 3482 / Email: markus.kokko@borenius.com

Markus regularly advises major domestic and international clients on dispute resolution and corporate crime cases.

Markus has in-depth experience of domestic and international corporate and commercial disputes and he has acted as lead counsel in numerous extensive cases. His field of experience encompasses cases related to a wide variety of business sectors, such as the chemicals industry, financial markets, international trade, retail and wholesale, mining, services and consultancy.

Markus also has an exceptional track record in handling a broad range of litigation and arbitration cases, including *ad hoc* proceedings as well as proceedings governed by ICC Rules, SCC Rules and the Arbitration Rules of the Finland Chamber of Commerce.

In addition, Markus frequently advises companies and executives in relation to complex corporate crime cases and criminal investigations regarding, *inter alia*, insider trading, environmental violations, corruption, imports and exports and tax.

Markus' efficient and client-oriented approach has earned him an excellent reputation which has been recognised by rankings in *Chambers Global, Chambers Europe, Legal 500* and *Best Lawyers*. Furthermore, Markus also serves as an arbitrator and he has written many articles on litigation and arbitration.

Markus heads the firm's Litigation & Arbitration and Corporate Crime teams.

Niki J. Welling
Tel: +358 20 713 3483 / Email: niki.welling@borenius.com

Niki is specialised in questions related to dispute resolution. In addition to both domestic and international litigation and arbitration, Niki also advises clients on general corporate and commercial law as well as employment law. Niki frequently represents clients in both arbitration (ICC, SCC, FAI) and court proceedings relating to e.g. sale of goods, construction and real estate, joint venture projects, corporate conflicts and insolvency. Niki has also gained experience in corporate crime-related work and Administrative Court proceedings.

Borenius Attorneys Ltd.
Eteläesplanadi 2, 00130 Helsinki, Finland
Tel: +358 20 713 33 / Fax: +358 20 713 3499 / URL: www.borenius.com

France

Christophe Dugué
Avocat au Barreau de Paris

The purpose of this paper is to briefly set forth the main features of French arbitration law, a modern legislation which, together with a pro-arbitration case law and the presence of the International Chamber of Commerce, explains why Paris remains at the forefront of international arbitration places.

In the introduction we shall examine why Paris is and remains an attractive place as seat of the arbitration and the main features of French arbitration law that aim at increasing the efficiency of arbitration. The following sections shall address the salient points regarding the arbitration agreement, the arbitration procedure, the arbitrators, interim relief, the arbitral award, the challenge and enforcement of the arbitral award and, finally, investment arbitration.

Unless otherwise provided, references made below to "Articles" are references to articles of the French Code of Civil Procedure as modified by the Decree of 13th January 2011. Quotations of articles of this decree are based on the English version that can be accessed at http://parisarbitration.net/wp-content/uploads/2017/02/EN-French-Law-on-Arbitration.pdf.

Introduction

The selection of Paris as the seat of the arbitration

International arbitration is the preferred mechanism for the resolution of commercial or investment international disputes. In order to ensure efficient arbitration proceedings and enforcement of the award, private parties and State entities very often elect for Paris as the seat of their arbitration. Many reasons explain the choice of Paris among all international arbitration places.

1. The drafting of the arbitration clause: the importance of selecting the seat of arbitration

When they opt for arbitration for the resolution of disputes that might occur in connection with their contract, parties are concerned that their case does not end up before a State court that they did not intend to choose in the first place.

This is the reason why they must take particular care when drafting the arbitration clause of their contract. When they opt for institutional arbitration, it is wise to reproduce the standard clause generally proposed by the chosen institution. This will ensure that arbitration will be administered by the proper institution chosen by the parties.

It is also useful to consider supplementing the clause in order to specify the place of arbitration.

This is a point that parties often tend not to address *ab initio*, when they agree on the terms of their contract. In such an event they bear the risk that difficulties arise at the stage of introduction of the arbitration proceedings, at a time when the parties are not likely to agree on anything. Increased costs and additional delays might result from the selection process of the seat by the institution or by the arbitral tribunal, not to mention a possible intervention of State courts, with the risk that the seat so selected ends up being different from the one that the parties would have otherwise chosen. Careful drafting of the arbitration clause could easily have avoided unnecessary debates and uncertainties that disrupt the arbitral proceedings.

2. What is the seat of arbitration? What are the consequences attached to the seat of arbitration?

The seat of arbitration is the place where the award will be deemed to have been made, and not the place where hearings are actually held (whatever the seat of the arbitration, the arbitrators and the parties are at liberty to select any place(s) they deem convenient to hold their meetings).

The legal consequences attached to the place where the seat is located, is that the *lex loci arbitri* will come into play before and after the award is made by the arbitral tribunal.

Before the award is rendered, the choice of the seat carries the determination of the competence of the State courts in the event of difficulties as early as at the stage of the constitution of the arbitral tribunal, or to order provisional or conservatory measures before the arbitral tribunal is in place; the courts of the seat of arbitration may also be requested to resolve any other difficulties in the conduct of the proceedings (as far as these issues cannot be resolved by the arbitral tribunal or the institution administering the proceedings).

Once the award is rendered and the arbitral tribunal is *functus officio*, proceedings for annulment of the award shall be heard before the State courts of the seat and for the grounds determined pursuant to the law of the seat. Depending on the location selected, and resulting applicable law, these reasons may be very limited or instead allow a full review of the merits of the case. It is thus of the utmost importance to select a seat that authorises the annulment of the award for a limited number of reasons only.

The selection of the seat is thus important for several reasons: when opting for arbitration the parties want a flexible, neutral, fast and efficient procedure. It follows that the intervention of State courts should be as limited as possible and with the aim to promote the smooth conduct of the arbitration proceedings, not to hinder them.

In addition, the parties' intent is to have a binding arbitration award that is enforceable in all countries. As a result, a seat that authorises the annulment of the award for a limited and predetermined number of grounds must be given preference.

3. What are the criteria to be considered for the selection of the seat of arbitration? How to choose a seat of arbitration?

In sum, an arbitration seat that meets the needs of the parties must be located in a State:

- that is a signatory to the New York Convention of 10th June 1958 on the Recognition and Enforcement of Foreign Arbitral Awards;
- whose laws are favourable to arbitration; and
- the courts of which intervene positively in support of arbitral proceedings and do not interfere to derail the arbitration proceedings.

While not the only one, Paris meets all these criteria with the benefit of specialised judges, institutions and arbitration professionals that provide a secure legal environment allowing for the smooth conduct of arbitral proceedings, also meeting the objectives of speed and efficiency. In addition, Paris provides all the logistic advantages that are necessary for the conduct of arbitration proceedings.

To choose Paris as the seat of arbitration, it suffices to add to your arbitration clause: "*The seat of the arbitration shall be Paris, France.*"

French arbitration law aims at increasing the efficiency of arbitration

1. The recent modernisation of French arbitration law

French international arbitration legislation (that is not based on the UNCITRAL Model Law) was introduced in the French Code of Civil Procedure by a Decree N°81-500 enacted on 12th May 1981. This was already a very liberal and pro-arbitration regime that was interpreted by the Paris Court of Appeals (which is the competent judicial court for all applications for the recognition and enforcement of international arbitration awards in France) and by the Cour de Cassation in order to favour the recourse to international arbitration.

This regime was recently reformed by Decree N°2011-48 of 13th January 2011 (which entered into force on 1st May 2011) in order to further modernise the legal framework and incorporate the jurisprudence developed by French courts.

As a result, there is no drastic change in the regime applicable to international arbitration but rather a consolidation of recognised principles of case law such as the recognition of arbitration agreements "by reference" to another document that contains the arbitration clause (Article 1443), and the autonomy of the arbitration clause (Article 1447). It also incorporates both positive (Article 1465) and negative (Article 1448) effects of the well-known (and of French origin) principle of "*compétence-compétence*": it is for the arbitrators to rule on their own jurisdiction and national courts must decline jurisdiction when there is an arbitration agreement (with the exception of cases where the arbitration is manifestly void or inapplicable). It is worth noting in this respect that French courts strictly comply with the negative effect of the principle of "*compétence-compétence*".

A number of innovations aiming at increasing efficiency of arbitration proceedings also result from the recent Decree.

2. Some innovations to increase efficiency

The major innovation regarding domestic arbitration is that the appeal of the award is no longer available as of right: it cannot be appealed unless expressly provided otherwise by the parties (Article 1489). This change is in line with the rules of many legal systems and Article 34 of the UNCITRAL Model Law that serves as a basis for arbitration law in many countries.

In international arbitration, the Decree confirms the position of the case law that the "*arbitration agreement shall not be subject to any requirement as to its form*" (Article 1507) and aligns the position of French law to the one of the most modern laws (and competitors in terms of place of arbitration …) such as Swiss law: an application to set aside an award or an appeal against an enforcement order no longer suspends the enforcement of the award (Article 1526), which appears to be the most efficient (and sometimes criticised) measure to achieve greater efficiency of the arbitration process. In the same vein, the Decree provides for the possibility for the parties to an international arbitration to agree at any time to waive their right to set aside an award (Article 1522).

All these provisions contribute to greater efficiency in international arbitration and illustrate the confidence placed by French arbitration law in the arbitral institution.

There is a very clear line of French case-law establishing that the French courts can recognise and enforce awards which have been set aside elsewhere, including by courts of the seat of the arbitration (see, Norsolor, Cour de Cassation, 9th October 1984; Hilmarton, Cour de

Cassation, 23rd March 1994 and 10th June 1997; Chromalloy, Paris Court of Appeals 14th January 1997; and Putrabali, Cour de Cassation, two decisions of 29th June 2007).

The analysis made by French courts is that the law of the seat of the arbitration is not the source of validity of an arbitral award, and that the law of the country where enforcement is sought is applicable to determine if an award must be recognised and enforced.

French law will thus determine the conditions for the recognition of the arbitral award as part of the French legal order, without regard to the grounds for which the award was set aside by other courts in any other jurisdiction. The rule established by French case law is that an international award is not part of any national legal order, but rather a decision of an autonomous arbitral legal order and must be recognised in France even if it was set aside at the seat of the arbitration.

3. When is arbitration international?

Although the regime applicable to domestic and to international arbitration tends to be fairly similar, the distinction between domestic and international arbitration is maintained. The French Code of Civil Procedure remains divided in two sections dealing respectively with domestic arbitration (Articles 1442 to 1503) and international arbitration (Articles 1504 to 1527). It is specifically provided (Article 1506) that a number of provisions set forth under the section governing domestic arbitration also apply to international arbitration; these provisions are mainly general fundamental procedural principles governing any arbitration with a seat in France.

The criterion to characterise international arbitration is of an economic nature: "*an arbitration is international when international trade interests are at stake*" (Article 1504). This is another illustration of the existence of an autonomous legal arbitral order, since it is not for the parties to determine the international character of their arbitration but rather the existence of objective economic criteria resulting from the existence of a flux of services, goods or funds across national frontiers and this irrespective of the nationality of the parties, the law applicable to the merits or to the procedure, or the seat of the arbitration.

In sum, French law appears to offer a regime that is more favourable than the one provided for by the UNCITRAL Model Law as well as the one resulting from the New York Convention on the Recognition and Enforcement of Foreign Arbitral Awards of 10th June 1958, which France signed on 25th November 1958 and ratified on 26th June 1959.

Arbitration agreement

<u>What are the formalities needed for the arbitration agreement and the drafting of the arbitration clause?</u>

A written arbitration agreement is mandatory for domestic arbitration (Article 1443) but not for international arbitration (Article 1507). The same rules apply to the arbitration clause (i.e. the arbitration agreement agreed upon by the parties at the time they enter into a contract and that shall apply to all disputes that might arise in connection with the contract) and the submission agreement (i.e. the agreement of the parties to submit a specific dispute to arbitration, agreed upon by the parties at the time there is a dispute for which no arbitration clause was concluded) (Article 1442).

In any event, the consent to arbitration must be established and, as a result, it is preferable to provide for arbitration in writing (in the contract at stake, or on invoices, or by reference to another document that includes the arbitration agreement) since this is the best evidence that will be available both before courts or arbitrators (if one party challenges the jurisdiction of the arbitral tribunal) and at the time of recognition and enforcement of the award (since the proof of the existence of an arbitration agreement shall be required along with the award).

French courts will determine the existence of the parties' consent to arbitrate their dispute. In doing so, the assessment of the existence, validity and scope of the conventional power to engage a party to the arbitration is conducted without reference to any national law: "*by virtue of a substantive rule of law in international arbitration, the existence and validity of an arbitration clause shall be assessed without reference to national law, but only under the control of the parties to resort to arbitration in terms of the circumstances of the case*" (see, Shackleton, Cour de Cassation, 16th March 2016, confirming the decision of the Paris Court of Appeals of 24th June 2014).

As outlined above (see Introduction) a specific and detailed agreement agreed upon at the outset will allow the parties to avoid uncertainties, waste of time and money at the time a dispute arises. Such an agreement need not be very long but must clearly record the parties' intent to resort to arbitration and, as a minimum, indicate if the arbitration is institutional (with the exact name of the institution) or *ad hoc*, and in both cases the rules that are applicable, the number of arbitrators, the language of the arbitration and the seat of the arbitration. Finally one might consider adding whether or not the arbitration shall be confidential, since this is not to be taken for granted (and some institutions such as the ICC do not provide for confidentiality in their rules).

What disputes are arbitrable?

Pursuant to Article 2059 of the French Civil Code, parties can opt for arbitration for disputes relating to private patrimonial rights (excluded are, for example, family law, criminal law, succession law, for which the rights cannot be freely disposed of by a party; see Article 2060 of the French Civil Code). Arbitration is not available to public entities in connection with domestic disputes (Article 2060 of the French Civil Code); however, such restriction does not apply to international arbitration.

In its earlier version, Article 2061 of the French Civil Code expressly provided for the validity of an arbitration clause inserted in a contract concluded in connection with professional activities. Pursuant to Article 11 of the Law of "Modernization of Justice in the 21st Century" dated 18th November 2016, this Article 2061 was modified, extending the scope of the arbitration clause. As now drafted, this Article 2061 of the French Civil Code provides that: "*The arbitration clause must have been accepted by the party against whom it is opposed, unless the latter has succeeded to the rights and obligations of the party which originally accepted it. When one of the parties has not contracted in the course of his professional activity, the clause cannot be opposed to him.*" The innovation lies in the fact that this article does not refer to the validity of the arbitration clause but rather its effects (the "opposability") and that as now drafted, consumer disputes can be referred to arbitration, and arbitration proceedings can be commenced so long as the party that "has not contracted in the course of its professional activity" does not object (in which case, the dispute shall be referred to competent judicial courts). This very recent change should not affect international arbitration and its exact consequences remain to be determined by case law. (On this modification, see Charles Jarosson and Jean-Baptiste Racine, *Les dispositions relatives à l'arbitrage dans la loi de modernisation de la justice du XXIe siècle*, Rev. Arb. 2016, pp.1007 *et seq.*).

What rules exist for the joinder/consolidation of third parties?

As a matter of principle, the arbitration agreement is binding on parties to the contract that contains the arbitration clause.

This does not mean that non-signatories cannot be parties to arbitration proceedings. French courts take into account the behaviour of the parties from which acceptance to be bound by the arbitration clause can be inferred; for example, the non-signatory's involvement in the negotiation, execution or performance of the contract (See, for example, *État libyen*, Paris Court of Appeals, 28th October 2014).

Do the principles of "*compétence-compétence*" and separability apply?

1. The principle of "compétence-compétence"

As already indicated above (see Introduction), the principle of "*compétence-compétence*" is enshrined in the French Code of Civil Procedure in two articles that relate to the positive and negative aspects of this principle and that apply to both domestic and international arbitration.

Article 1465 relates to the positive aspect, pursuant to which it is for the arbitral tribunal to rule on its own jurisdiction ("*the arbitral tribunal has exclusive jurisdiction to rule on objections to its jurisdiction*") and Article 1448 relates to the negative aspect of the principle, according to which judicial courts shall decline jurisdiction in the presence of an arbitration agreement ("*when a dispute subject to an arbitration agreement is brought before a court, such court shall decline jurisdiction*").

There is very little room left for French courts when parties have provided for arbitration, since the only exception allowing a court to retain its jurisdiction, and only if requested to do so by a party ("*A court may not decline jurisdiction of its own motion*"), is subject to two cumulative conditions: there is no arbitral tribunal seized as yet and the "*arbitration agreement is manifestly void or manifestly not applicable*" (Article 1448).

As a matter of example, the presence of multiple arbitration clauses under various agreements shall not *per se* render the arbitration clause inapplicable.

In a recent decision of 30th March 2016, Inthemix, the Paris Court of Appeals held that the Paris Commercial Court had validly declined its jurisdiction since "*under the terms of Article 1448 of the Code of Civil Procedure, when a dispute subject to an arbitration agreement is brought before a court of the State, it declares itself incompetent unless the arbitral tribunal is not yet seized and if the arbitration agreement is manifestly void or manifestly inapplicable*".

The Court of Appeals held that "*manifest inapplicability of the arbitration clause*" which must be established by the applicant, does not result from "*the interdependence of the three contracts at stake that form a unified economic undertaking according to the will of the parties*" nor from the fact that they are "*signed by different persons, have different objects, relate to different obligations and are subject to distinct disputes*". The Court of Appeals notes that the arbitration clauses at stake "*are not inconsistent with each other to make inapplicable the arbitration clause in the franchise agreement*".

Obviously, the principle of "*compétence-compétence*" is not designed to deprive the parties of the possibility to obtain interim or conservatory measures from judicial courts, although preference is given to the arbitral tribunal, once constituted.

As long as the arbitral tribunal is not in place, Article 1449 expressly provides for the jurisdiction of State courts: "*The existence of an arbitration agreement, insofar as the arbitral tribunal has not yet been constituted, shall not preclude a party from applying to a court for measures relating to the taking of evidence or provisional or conservatory measures. Subject to the provisions governing conservatory attachments and judicial security, application shall be made to the President of the Tribunal de Grande Instance or of the Tribunal de Commerce who shall rule on the measures relating to the taking of evidence in accordance with the provisions of Article 1452 and, where the matter is urgent, on the provisional or conservatory measures requested by the parties to the arbitration agreement.*"

2. The separability of the arbitration agreement: the principle of autonomy

French courts have long established that the validity of the arbitration agreement is not affected by the invalidity of the contract in which it is inserted; the arbitration clause is independent from the contract.

The so-called autonomy of the arbitration agreement is now expressly set forth in Article 1447 (applicable to both domestic and international arbitration): "*The arbitration clause is independent from the contract to which it refers. The validity of the former is not affected by the nullity of the latter.*"

French case law applies this principle of autonomy in a very pro-arbitration fashion, since the arbitration agreement is also considered to be independent from the law governing the contract, and its validity must be assessed "*subject to the prior application of the mandatory rules of French law and public international order, according to the shared will of the parties, without the need to refer to State Law*" (Dalico, Cour de Cassation, 20th December 1993). Recent case law accepts the "survival" of the arbitration agreement even if the contract is inexistent or never existed (see, for example, So Good International Ltd, Cour de Cassation, 28th November 2006).

Arbitration procedure

How are the arbitration proceedings commenced?

There is no specific requirement to start an arbitration procedure, which usually results from the filing of a request for arbitration with the respondent or the institution referred to in the arbitration clause.

Can hearings take place outside the seat of the arbitration?

As already mentioned in the Introduction above, the seat of the arbitration bears no relevance to the determination of the place where the arbitrators and the parties meet, which can be the same place as the one of the seat, but can also be any place that the parties and the arbitrators deem more convenient.

Procedural rules

The parties, the arbitrators and counsels may have to deal with many procedural matters which, if not properly addressed in due course, can lead to numerous procedural incidents that will entail increased costs and delays.

As part of these questions are:

- What are the rules on evidence?
- What rules are applicable regarding privilege and disclosure?
- Are the IBA Rules on the taking of evidence taken into account?
- Are there any rules regarding expert evidence?
- Are there any guidelines for Counsel to take into account any guidelines such as the LCIA or IBA?
- Are arbitration proceedings confidential?
- Can the evidence and pleadings be kept confidential?

1. The procedural rules shall be fixed by the parties and/or the arbitral tribunal

The answer to these questions and any other issue of procedural or organisational nature is that it is for the parties, failing which the arbitral tribunal, to decide what they deem appropriate in the context of their case.

Article 1464, paragraph 1 and 2 applicable to domestic arbitration provide that: "*Unless otherwise agreed by the parties, the arbitral tribunal shall define the procedure to be followed in the arbitration. It is under no obligation to abide by the rules governing court proceedings. However, the fundamental principles governing court proceedings set forth in Articles 4, 10, Article 11, paragraph 1, Article 12, paragraphs 2 and 3, Articles 13 through 21, 23 and 23-1 shall apply.*"

The same principle is in fact applied in international arbitration where, unless the parties have agreed upon specific rules, the arbitral tribunal determines (in consultation with the parties) the procedural rules applicable.

In any event, a few procedural questions are specifically dealt with in the French Code of Civil Procedure: due process, the taking of evidence, confidentiality and the obligation to act diligently and in good faith.

2. Due process

An arbitral tribunal with a seat in France will have to act fairly and ensure that due process is observed, since the award might otherwise not be enforceable.

This requirement states the obvious for every one familiar with international arbitration. It stems from the provisions of Article 1510, which states that: "*Irrespective of the procedure adopted, the arbitral tribunal shall ensure that the parties are treated equally and shall uphold the principle of due process.*"

Should this not be the case, the award might be set aside on two grounds (due process, international public policy) that can be found at Article 1520 pursuant to which, "*An award may only be set aside where: (...) (4) due process was violated; or (5) recognition or enforcement of the award is contrary to international public policy.*"

3. Evidence

The parties and the arbitral tribunal can freely devise the rules that they consider fit for the arbitration proceedings. They can thus decide that the arbitral tribunal shall apply, or be allowed to make reference to, rules such as the IBA Rules on the Taking of Evidence in International Arbitration (which rules, as a practical matter, are often used by arbitral tribunals with a seat in France).

As part of the elements introduced by the Decree of May 2011 is the possibility for a party to request the arbitral tribunal, once it is constituted, to summon a third party to appear before the President of the *Tribunal de Grande Instance* for the purpose of obtaining the evidentiary document that the party to the arbitration intends to rely upon.

Article 1469 paragraph 1 (applicable to both domestic and international arbitration) provides as follows: "*If one of the parties to arbitral proceedings intends to rely on an official [acte authentique] or private [acte sous seing privé] deed to which it was not a party, or on evidence held by a third party, it may, upon leave of the arbitral tribunal, have that third party summoned before the President of the Tribunal de Grande Instance for the purpose of obtaining a copy thereof [expédition] or the production of the deed or item of evidence*)."

This is another illustration of the primacy given to arbitral tribunals and of the support that French courts must provide to facilitate the conduct of arbitration.

4. Confidentiality

With respect to domestic arbitration, Article 1464, the fourth paragraph provides that: "*Subject to legal requirements, and unless otherwise agreed by the parties, arbitral proceedings shall be confidential.*" This applies to both the parties and the arbitral tribunal. This provision is not detailed (Is the existence of the arbitration confidential? Is the award confidential?), and it does not apply to international arbitration. In both types of arbitrations, however, the deliberations of the arbitral tribunal are confidential (Article 1479).

As a result, international arbitration is not confidential as of right under French law.

This does not mean that international arbitration cannot be confidential, but this is an issue that needs to be addressed either before the arbitration is commenced (in the arbitration agreement), or at any point in the course of the proceedings (in the procedural rules discussed at the outset by the parties and the arbitral tribunal, or by means of a specific request made before the arbitral tribunal).

The first place where confidentiality provisions may be found are the rules of arbitration of the institution selected by the parties. However, the rules selected by the parties to govern the arbitration proceedings may contain confidentiality provisions or not. For example, the ICC Rules do not contain confidentiality provisions (other than the confidential character of the work of the International Court of Arbitration, Article 6 of Appendix I); the Swiss Rules contain a detailed provision (Article 44). Even if they exist, the confidentiality provisions of the rules might not be as detailed or specific as might be required by the parties.

Parties should therefore consider drafting specific confidentiality provisions in their arbitration clause (both for domestic and international arbitration) in order to cover, when appropriate, the existence of the arbitration and the documents and materials used in the proceedings (written submissions, exhibits, witness statements, expert reports, procedural orders and other communications with the arbitral tribunal, transcripts of hearings …) as well as oral exchanges made during the arbitration proceedings.

If not found in the applicable rules of arbitration of the institution chosen by the parties or in the arbitration clause, such detailed provisions on confidentiality can also be dealt with at the stage of establishing the terms of reference (which might also prove useful to supplement the procedural rules that result from the set of rules applicable to the dispute).

In any event, Parties can also request the arbitral tribunal to rule by way of procedural orders on certain matters to preserve the confidentiality of the proceedings, or of some pieces of information. This is often the case for the confidentiality of trade secrets or know-how that might need to be disclosed in the course of the arbitration proceedings, and that are not the subject of a patent or a confidentiality agreement (although a partial award would seem preferable, since it would be enforceable as an order is not). The ICC rules, Article 22(3), contemplate such a possibility: "*Upon the request of any party, the arbitral tribunal may make orders concerning the confidentiality of the arbitration proceedings or of any other matters in connection with the arbitration and may take measures for protecting trade secrets and confidential information.*"

5. The obligation of diligence and good faith

One major innovation, applicable to both domestic and international arbitration, lies in the provisions of the third paragraph of Article 1464 which provide that: "*Both parties and arbitrators shall act diligently and in good faith in the conduct of the proceedings.*"

This innovation is in line with recent development in international arbitration in order to tackle with the criticism that arbitration proceedings are exceedingly costly and take too much time.

Arbitral Institutions such as the ICC or the LCIA have recently introduced the same obligation of diligence. (See, ICC Rules 2012, Article 22(1): "*Article 22 Conduct of the Arbitration 1 – The arbitral tribunal and the parties shall make every effort to conduct the arbitration in an expeditious and cost-effective manner, having regard to the complexity and value of the dispute*"; LCIA Rules 2014, Article 14.4 (ii): "*Under the Arbitration Agreement, the Arbitral Tribunal's general duties at all times during the arbitration shall include: (...) (ii) a duty to adopt procedures suitable to the circumstances of the arbitration, avoiding unnecessary delay and expense, so as to provide a fair, efficient and expeditious means for the final resolution of the parties' dispute.*") The 2018 revision of the Rules of Arbitration of the Association For Arbitration that shall be released shortly also contains a provision similar to Article 1464.

In sum, it is for the parties and the arbitral tribunal to design the procedural rules, which is usually done at the time when the terms of reference are signed or in the first procedural order issued simultaneously by the arbitral tribunal (or any subsequent procedural order issued by the arbitral tribunal to rule upon any such issue).

Arbitrators

Appointment of arbitrators

The constitution of the arbitral tribunal is dealt with in great detail by French law (Articles 1450 to 1461).

- An arbitrator must be a natural person and a legal person can only administer the arbitration. This provision of Article 1450 is not applicable to international arbitration. As noted by a commentator (see Thomas Clay, *Code de l'arbitrage commenté*, Lexis Nexis, 2015, p. 57), this entails that French courts will grant exequatur to an international award with a seat outside of France that is "signed" by an institution, and that an arbitration agreement that would designate a legal person as the arbitrator would be deemed valid (in such a case such legal person would be considered as administering the procedure).
- An arbitral tribunal shall comprise a sole arbitrator or an uneven number of arbitrators (Article 1451).
- Each party is granted the right to nominate an arbitrator (Article 1452).
- The agreement of the parties regarding the appointment of the arbitrator(s) must be followed.

Judicial courts play a specific role in the event of difficulties in connection with the constitution of the arbitral tribunal: Articles 1451, 1452, 1453, 1454, 1455, 1456, 1459 and 1460 refer to the "*judge acting in support of the arbitration*" (the "*juge d'appui*") which is the President of the *Tribunal de Grande Instance* (Article 1459) who has exclusive jurisdiction to finalise the constitution of the arbitral tribunal.

Duty of disclosure: Are the IBA guidelines on conflict of interest taken into account?

Pursuant to the second paragraph of Article 1456, before accepting a mandate, arbitrators must disclose "*any circumstance that may affect his or her independence or impartiality*", and this obligation to be independent and impartial is of a permanent nature, since the arbitrator "*shall disclose any such circumstance that may arise after accepting the mandate*".

Notorious facts or participation in arbitration academic or social events need not be disclosed and the IBA Guidelines on Conflicts of Interests in International Arbitration are frequently referred to.

The scope of such disclosure encompasses objective circumstances (such as a flow of business with a party or a counsel involved in the arbitration) as well as subjective circumstances (for example, friendly relationship) that, in the mind of the parties, can cast a reasonable doubt as to the arbitrator's independence or impartiality. There appears to be a significant flow of judicial decisions on this topic, which merely reflects the tendency of parties to challenge awards rather than an actual lack of impartiality or independence of arbitrators.

Removal and challenge of arbitrators

An arbitrator may only be removed by unanimous consent of the parties (Article 1458) or in the event the parties cannot agree, by the person responsible for administering the arbitration (i.e. institutional arbitration or *ad hoc* arbitration with an appointing authority vested with the power to administer the proceedings) or where there is no such person, by the judge acting in support of the arbitration (Article 1456, final paragraph).

Regarding the challenge of arbitrators, the provisions of Article 1466 might serve as a guardrail. Article 1466 imposes on parties a duty to raise "*in a timely manner*" before the arbitral any irregularity in the conduct of the proceedings that such party is aware of, failing which "*without a legitimate reason*" such party "*shall be deemed to have waived its right to avail itself of such irregularity*". The knowledge of any irregularity, which encompasses any element regarding the constitution of the arbitral tribunal, that is not raised in due course by a party, will prevent such party from challenging the arbitrator, and ultimately from challenging the award on such ground.

Immunity of arbitrators?

French law does not provide for the immunity of the arbitrators which can be held liable (including on criminal grounds) as a result of the performance of their mission in the event of wilful misconduct, gross negligence or denial of justice (see, Thomas Clay, *op. cit.* p. 58; Cour de Cassation, 15th January 2014).

Secretary to the arbitral tribunal

It is fairly common that arbitral tribunals with a seat in France are assisted by an administrative secretary. This function is not the subject of specific provisions of the French Decree on arbitration; however, such a person acts under the directives and responsibility of the arbitral tribunal and it is certain that its lack of partiality or independence would taint that of the arbitral tribunal and could give rise to the same consequences as for an arbitrator that did not meet the requirements of Article 1456.

As a practical matter, the presence of a secretary is subject to the agreement of the parties and this person is also required to provide a statement of independence and impartiality. (See, for example, the Note to Parties and Arbitral Tribunals on the Conduct of the Arbitration under the 2012 ICC Rules of Arbitration that contains an entire section devoted to the appointment, duties and remuneration of administrative secretaries, and provides in particular that "*Administrative Secretaries must satisfy the same independence and impartiality requirements as those which apply to arbitrators under the Rules. ICC staff members are not permitted to serve as Administrative Secretaries*.")

Interim relief

What types of interim relief are available to the parties? Can the parties apply to both courts and arbitral tribunals for such interim relief?

As already indicated (see above, 'Arbitration agreement, 1. The principle of *competence-competence*'), Article 1449 expressly provides for the possibility to obtain interim relief from the arbitral tribunal, once constituted, of from judicial courts prior to the constitution of the arbitral tribunal: "*The existence of an arbitration agreement, insofar as the arbitral tribunal has not yet been constituted, shall not preclude a party from applying to a court for measures relating to the taking of evidence or provisional or conservatory measures. Subject to the provisions governing conservatory attachments and judicial security, application shall be made to the President of the Tribunal de Grande Instance or of the Tribunal de Commerce who shall rule on the measures relating to the taking of evidence in accordance with the provisions of Article 1452 and, where the matter is urgent, on the provisional or conservatory measures requested by the parties to the arbitration agreement.*"

This provision is consistently applied by French courts. (See, for example, Paris Court of Appeals, 29th March 2016: "*However, according to Article 1449 of the Code of Civil Procedure, applicable to international arbitration under Article 1506 1 of the code, the existence of an arbitration agreement does not preclude, in case of emergency, the referral to the national judge so long as the arbitral tribunal is not constituted to obtain an interim measure, such request to be brought before the presiding judge of the Tribunal de Grande Instance or the commercial court.*")

Any kind of interim relief can be obtained from an arbitral tribunal, save for attachments and judicial security for which judicial courts retain exclusive jurisdiction.

These powers are vested in arbitral tribunals by virtue of Article 1468: "*The arbitral tribunal may order upon the parties any conservatory or provisional measures that it deems appropriate, set conditions for such measures and, if necessary, attach penalties to such order. However, only courts may order conservatory attachments and judicial security. The arbitral tribunal has the power to amend or add to any provisional or conservatory measure that it has granted.*"

Anti-suit injunctions

1. What are anti-suit injunctions?

Anti-suit injunctions are orders obtained from a judicial court by a party in order to restrain another party from bringing or continuing an arbitration case. The judicial court is requested to protect its own jurisdiction or the jurisdiction of the appropriate forum other than the arbitration that it is requested to order a party to refrain from bringing, or to withdraw or suspend an arbitration.

Anti-suit injunctions raise the issue of which national courts and arbitral tribunals have jurisdiction to decide on the validity, scope and effectiveness of an arbitration agreement and in which order (see on this topic, *Anti-Suit Injunctions in International Arbitration*, 2003, IAI Series on International Arbitration N°2, Emmanuel Gaillard Ed., Juris Publishing, Inc.).

2. Can French courts order anti-arbitration injunctions in aid of domestic litigation?

Such injunctions are, in essence, anti-arbitration measures designed to derail arbitration proceedings or resist enforcement of an award.

As such, they are unlikely to be obtained from French courts, unless – when reviewing an award for recognition or enforcement purposes – French courts disagree on the decision of the arbitrators regarding their own jurisdiction and set aside the award. In such an event it is however doubtful that French courts would issue an anti-arbitration injunction. French courts might retain their jurisdiction, in the event that an action is brought before them and they determine that there is no arbitration clause, or that such clause is invalid and that they are the court of competent jurisdiction as a result of applicable rules of conflict.

3. Can French courts order anti-suit injunctions in aid of international arbitration?

In the event that a French judicial court is seized of a dispute that is either pending before an arbitral tribunal or that is the subject of an arbitration clause, it will have to decline its jurisdiction by virtue of the negative effect of the principle of "*compétence-compétence*" (Article 1448).

French arbitration law contains many provisions regarding the role of the "*juge d'appui*", whose function is to act in support of the arbitration process in connection with difficulties in the constitution of the arbitral tribunal but is not defined in the law so as to encompass the equivalent of anti-suit injunctions. French court would thus not issue pro-arbitration injunctions.

This does not mean that French courts would not give effect to anti-suit injunctions issued by foreign courts.

4. Would French courts give effect to a foreign anti-suit injunction?

There is at least one decision of the French Cour de Cassation giving effect to a foreign anti-suit injunction issued in the context of litigation proceedings (and not arbitration) that can serve as an indication of the rule that would apply should enforcement of an anti-arbitration injunction be sought in France.

In the In Zone Brands International INC decision of 14th October 2009, the Cour de Cassation decided that in its decision of 17th April 2009, the Court of Appeals of Versailles held exactly first, that "*having regard to the jurisdiction clause freely accepted by the parties, no fraud could result from the seizure by the American Company of the courts designated by the jurisdiction clause*"; second that "*there cannot be denial of justice, since the purpose of the decision of the Georgian judge is precisely to rule on its own jurisdiction and to give effect to the agreement on jurisdiction entered into by the parties*"; and finally that "*is not contrary to international public policy the 'anti-suit injunction' the sole purpose of which (...) is, as in the present case, to sanction the violation of a pre-existing contractual obligation*".

In sum, the issuance of an anti-suit injunction against a French company does not contravene French international public policy and should therefore be given effect by French courts.

Arbitral award

Making of the award

The award is the decision reached by the majority of the arbitrators, unless the arbitration agreement provides otherwise, and it must be signed by all the arbitrators (Article 1513, applicable to international arbitration).

In order to ensure efficiency and avoid deadlock situations, French law expressly provides that if there is no majority the chairman of the arbitral shall rule alone and that should an arbitrator refuse to sign, the chairman shall make a mention thereof in the award that it shall sign alone (Article 1513, third paragraph). Finally, the same Article 1513 confirms that an award made in such circumstances shall have the same effect as if signed by all arbitrators or made by majority decision.

As to the content of the award, Article 1481 (applicable to both domestic and international arbitration) lists the elements that an award must contain (name and details of the parties and their counsels, names of the arbitrators, date when and place where the award was made). In addition, an award must state "*succinctly*" the respective claims and arguments of the parties and the reasons upon which it is based (Article 1482).

Pursuant to Article 1483 which is not applicable to international arbitration, an award that does not comply with these requirements is void. As a result, French courts have ruled that an international award cannot be set aside on the ground of a lack of motivation, which is not in itself contrary to French international public policy.

Effects of the award

As soon as made, the arbitral award is *res judicata* with respect to the claims adjudicated in that award (Article 1484), and the powers vested in the arbitrators cease with respect to such claims (Article 1485). As a practical matter, in the event of an interim award the powers vested with the arbitrators remain on all claims, and in the case of a partial award their powers remain to adjudicate the remainder of the dispute not decided by such award.

An interesting feature introduced by the Decree of 13th January 2001 is that "*the award may be declared provisionally enforceable*" (Article 1484, second paragraph, applicable to both domestic and international arbitration).

This provision is to be read in conjunction with Article 1496 (domestic arbitration) pursuant to which, unless declared provisionally enforceable, enforcement of the award shall be stayed until the expiry of the time limit for the appeal or action to set aside or, if such action is filed, until it is decided. In sum it is highly advisable in connection with domestic arbitration to require that the award be declared provisionally enforceable in order to expedite enforcement of the award.

Regarding international arbitration, Article 1526 goes further since it expressly provides that "*neither an action to set aside an award nor an appeal against an enforcement order shall suspend enforcement of an award*". This is perhaps the most important innovation (that is inspired from Swiss law) introduced by the Decree of 13th January 2011 and is a complete upturn of the previous rule.

In the matter of international arbitration, provisional enforcement need not to be requested, it exists as of right.

The only limitation of provisional enforcement might occur when it could "*severely prejudice the rights of one party*" (Article 1526, international arbitration), in which case a stay might be requested from the first president of the Court of Appeals of Paris ruling in expedited proceedings ("*référé*"). The same recourse (although in slightly different terms) is provided for domestic arbitration, when enforcement of the award could "*lead to manifestly excessive consequences*" (Article 1497).

Challenge of the arbitral award

The set of rules to challenge an arbitral award vary for domestic and international arbitration, which is a further demonstration that the determination of the domestic or international character of the arbitration is essential (this was in particular a crucial point in the so-called "Tapie case"). All recourses are centralised before the Court of Appeals of the place where the award was made (domestic arbitration: Article 1494, and international arbitration: Article 1519).

Appeal

An international award cannot be appealed (Article 1518). The principle in domestic arbitration is now that the award cannot be appealed unless the parties have provided otherwise (Article 1489).

It must be noted that an application for revision of the award can be filed in the event of fraud (Article 1502).

Action to set aside

The only recourse against an international award is an action to set aside (Article 1518). The possibility for the parties to waive their right to any recourse against the award in international arbitration was introduced by the Decree of 13th January 2011 (see, Article 1522).

The five grounds to set aside an award are listed, exhaustively, at Article 1520: "*An award may only be set aside where: (1) the arbitral tribunal wrongly upheld or declined jurisdiction; or (2) the arbitral tribunal was not properly constituted; or (3) the arbitral tribunal ruled without complying with the mandate conferred upon it; or (4) due process was violated; or (5) recognition or enforcement of the award is contrary to international public policy.*" With respect to domestic arbitration, there is a sixth ground set forth at Article 1491 that relates to the lack of reasons upon which the award is based, or when one of the elements detailed above (see above, 'Arbitral award – Making of the award') is missing.

These conditions apply both to the recognition and enforcement of arbitral awards made abroad or in international arbitration. There is thus no review on the merits and it must be noted regarding the notion of international public policy that it is construed very narrowly by French courts.

Both the law and French case law are pro-arbitration and as a result it is very rare that an award is successfully challenged in France.

Enforcement of the arbitral award

In the case of awards rendered outside of France, applications for enforcement are centralised and can only be filed before the *Tribunal de Grande Instance* of Paris which enforces the award by rendering an enforcement ("*exequatur*") order. This is an *ex parte* procedure that requires the filing by the requesting party of an original copy of the award together with evidence of the arbitration agreement, which serves as a basis for the jurisdiction of the arbitral tribunal that made the award (Article 1516) together with a translation in French when such documents are in a foreign language (Article 1515).

The order shall be served to the other party, after which an appeal against the order can be filed before the Paris Court of Appeals (Article 1525) on the same grounds as the ones set forth to set aside an award by Article 1520.

As detailed above (Introduction, "Some innovations to increase efficiency"), French courts do enforce arbitral awards that are annulled by courts of the seat of the arbitration. This is consistent with the pro-arbitration stance that prevails in France.

To conclude, the arbitration regime provided by French law is more favourable than the one resulting from Article V(1) of the New York Convention of 10th June 1958 on the Recognition and Enforcement of Foreign Arbitral Awards, which is a possibility contemplated at Article VIII of this convention. Since courts in certain jurisdictions would deny recognition of awards that would have been annulled at the seat of arbitrations, parties willing to secure the enforcement and circulation of their award should not hesitate and opt for Paris as the seat of their (next) arbitration. In so doing they would ensure that their award can hardly be annulled at the seat in France, which will in turn facilitate its recognition elsewhere.

Regarding the New York Convention and its application, UNCITRAL provides very useful and freely accessible tools intended to "*assist judges, arbitrators, practitioners, academics and Government officials to use resources relating to the New York Convention more efficiently*". It has very recently published its Secretariat Guide on the Convention on the Recognition and Enforcement of Foreign Arbitral Awards, 1958 (New York) in order to "*promote the uniform and effective interpretation and application of the New York Convention with a view to limit the risk that State practice might diverge from its spirit*". This Guide is supplemented by an online platform, making available case law implementing the New York Convention from multiple common law and civil law jurisdictions (cases are reported in the form of summaries highlighting the interpretation and application of specific provisions of the New York Convention by States, and the full text of the original language decisions is also available), as well as other useful resources relating to the New York Convention. (See: http://newyorkconvention1958.org/.)

Investment arbitration

Investments made by nationals of certain countries on the territory of another foreign host country are the subject of various multinational or bilateral investment treaties (known as "BITs") concluded to protect investments and enhance international commercial relationship.

France is a party to many such BITs as well as international treaties such as the Energy Charter Treaty (which it signed on 17th December 1994, see https://energycharter.org/who-we-are/members-observers/). France is also one of the Contracting States of the Convention on the Settlement of Investment Disputes between States and Nationals of Other States (submitted to States for signature on 18th March 1965 and which entered into force on 14th October 1966), also known as the ICSID Convention. The ICSID Convention established the International Centre for Settlement of Investment Disputes ("ICSID") which is designed to offer institutional and procedural support to tribunals or parties in arbitrations among investors and states.

There is only one ICSID arbitration case currently pending against France (*Erbil Serter v. French Republic*, ICSID Case No. ARB/13/22) which is the first case ever registered against France before ICSID.

According to (limited) information made publicly available on the ICSID website (see Case Details, available at https://icsid.worldbank.org/en/Pages/cases/casedetail.aspx?CaseNo=ARB/13/22), the case relates to ship hull design and is based on the Turkey–France BIT of 2006. ICSID Convention Arbitration Rules apply and French is the language of the arbitration. The Claimant, Mr. Erbil Serter, is of Turkish nationality and the Respondent is the French Republic. The case was registered on 10th September 2013, the arbitrator appointed by the Claimant accepted his appointment on 3rd February 2014, and the arbitrator appointed by the Respondent accepted his appointment on 14th February 2014. This case is still pending.

Christophe Dugué, ACIArb
Avocat au Barreau de Paris
Tel: +33 6 1525 1425 / Email: christophe.dugue@dbmail.com

Admitted to the Paris Bar (1992) Christophe Dugué serves as arbitrator and also acts as counsel in international arbitration cases.

With over two decades of experience in international arbitration in institutional (especially ICC, AFA, CAIP and Swiss Rules) and *ad hoc* (including UNCITRAL) arbitration cases, Christophe Dugué regularly serves as chairman, sole arbitrator or co-arbitrator in ICC, AFA and *ad hoc* international arbitration proceedings (appointments by the parties, by the ICC and by the AFA).

He also acts as counsel and has been involved as lead counsel in cases with parties from Asia, Africa (North Africa, West and South Africa), Europe, the Middle East and North America and has represented clients ranging from individuals and mid-sized companies to Government-owned entities and major international corporations.

He practises both in English and French, under a variety of applicable laws from both civil law and common law jurisdictions.

Cases involved industries such as banking, chemicals, construction (including FIDIC), defence, electronic components, energy, IT, infrastructures, joint-ventures, M&A transactions, mining, oil & gas, private equity and transport infrastructure industries, amongst others.

Christophe Dugué's former experience includes notably 10 years as a Partner at Shearman & Sterling LLP's international arbitration practice group in Paris and also the creation of an international arbitration boutique firm in Paris.

Christophe Dugué is an associate member of the Chartered Institute of Arbitrators (CIArb), and a member of the International Arbitration Institute (IAI), the *Comité Français de l'Arbitrage* (CFA), the Swiss Arbitration Association (ASA), the *Association Française d'Arbitrage*/Association For Arbitration (AFA). He is on the panel of arbitrators of the Asian International Arbitration Centre, AIAC (formerly known as the Kuala Lumpur Regional Centre for Arbitration) since 2014, and also on the list of neutrals of the Mediation & Conciliation Network (MCN), India.

https://fr.linkedin.com/in/christophe-dugué-24b5233a

Christophe Dugué, Avocat au Barreau de Paris

Tel: +33 6 1525 1425 / Email: christophe.dugue@dbmail.com
https://fr.linkedin.com/in/christophe-dugué-24b5233a

Germany

Catrice Gayer & Thomas Weimann
Herbert Smith Freehills Germany LLP

Introduction

Germany – Arbitration-friendly civil law jurisdiction

The use of arbitration as a dispute-resolution mechanism in Germany has a long-standing tradition. In most areas of business and commerce, institutional and *ad hoc* arbitration is commonly and successfully used.

German arbitration law is part of the German code of civil procedure (*Zivilprozessordnung* ("ZPO")) and is contained in Sections 1025 to 1066[1] thereof.

The ZPO is based on the UNCITRAL Model Law on International Commercial Arbitration of 1985 ("ML"). Therefore, users will find it particularly easy and predictable to apply.

Under the principle of territoriality, the ZPO is applicable to all arbitrations with a place of arbitration in Germany (Section 1025(1)). Further, the ZPO applies to all arbitrations, whether *ad hoc* or institutional. German lawmakers opted for a unified system: the ZPO provides a single set of rules for national and international arbitration.

Currently, a working group of the Federal Ministry of Justice is analysing if the ZPO needs to be revised.

Germany is a signatory state of the United Nations Convention on Recognition and Enforcement of Foreign Arbitral Awards of 1958 (New York Convention or "NYC"). Germany has not declared a commercial or reciprocity reservation (Article I(3) NYC). Pursuant to Section 1061(1), recognition and enforcement of foreign arbitral awards is governed by the NYC. Germany has also ratified, *inter alia*, the European Convention on International Commercial Arbitration of 1961 ("European Convention").

German lawmakers decided to grant the functional competence for arbitration-related matters to the regional higher courts (*Oberlandesgericht* ("OLG") (Section 1062)) (e.g. appointment and challenge of arbitrators; setting aside and enforcement of (foreign) awards and orders for interim measures; declaring arbitration proceedings admissible). This usually ensures consistent, quick and arbitration-friendly decisions. An appeal against orders of the OLG is limited to complaints on a point of law (*Rechtsbeschwerde*) with the German Federal Court of Justice (*Bundesgerichtshof* ("BGH")) (Sections 1065(1), 1062(1) Nos. 2 and 4).

The most well-known arbitration institution in Germany is the German Institution of Arbitration (*Deutsche Institution für Schiedsgerichtsbarkeit* ("DIS")). The DIS administers national and international arbitration proceedings under the DIS arbitration rules which have been revised. The new DIS Rules entered into force on 1 March 2018 ("DIS Rules 2018").

A number of industry-focused arbitration institutions exist in Germany (e.g. German Maritime Arbitration Association ("GMAA"), *Waren-Verein der Hamburger Börse*, arbitration institutions with stock and commodity exchanges). The Chinese European Arbitration Centre ("CEAC") administers international Asia-related arbitration proceedings.

Arbitration agreement

Does the principle of competence-competence apply?

According to the *Kompetenz-Kompetenz* principle, an arbitral tribunal can decide on its own jurisdiction (Section 1040(1) sentence 1). An arbitral tribunal's decision assuming jurisdiction is not binding or final for a court. Any agreement by parties to confer the final and binding decision to an arbitral tribunal is not valid, but in principle, will not invalidate the arbitration agreement as a whole.

Jurisdiction and preliminary rulings of arbitral tribunals

If a party raises objections regarding the jurisdiction of the arbitral tribunal (Section 1040(2)), the arbitral tribunal can assume jurisdiction by way of a preliminary ruling (Section 1040(3)). A preliminary ruling is not an award for the purposes of setting aside proceedings (Section 1059). The ZPO provides a special procedure to have the ruling overturned (Section 1040(3)). The opposing party must file an application with the court within one month after its receipt. Otherwise, the opposing party is precluded from invoking the invalidity of an arbitration agreement in any post-award proceedings. An arbitral tribunal can render an award, although the proceedings under Section 1040(3) are still pending. Reversing its own case law, the BGH recently held that the issuance of an award does not render the application (Section 1040(3)) inadmissible. Further, the three-month deadline for the award debtor to file a setting-aside application against the award will only start to run after the service of the court's decision (Section 1040(3)) denying the jurisdiction of the arbitral tribunal (by way of analogy of Section 1059(3) sentence 2) (BGH, 9.8.2016, NJW 2017, 488).

Does the principle of separability apply?

The arbitration agreement is an agreement independent of the existence, validity or termination of the main contract (Section 1040(1) sentence 2).

What are the substantive mandatory requirements of an arbitration agreement?

According to Section 1029(1), an arbitration agreement is an agreement by the parties to submit to arbitration all or certain disputes which have arisen or which may arise between them in respect of a defined legal relationship, whether contractual or not.

The first requirement of a "defined legal relationship" only precludes the validity of arbitration agreements providing that all future disputes between the parties, without any reference to a specific relationship (e.g. a specific contract or framework agreement) will be resolved by arbitration.

The fulfilment of the second requirement often raises problems: the parties' agreement to submit all or certain disputes to arbitration. It is essential that it can be clearly and unambiguously derived from the arbitration agreement that the parties' intention was to exclude the state courts as a dispute resolution forum and to have any disputes resolved by arbitration. If this requirement is fulfilled, courts enforce arbitration agreements even if the arbitration institution is not unambiguously designated (e.g. KG Berlin, 3.9.2012, SchiedsVZ 2012, 337). Likewise, the parties should clearly use the term *arbitration* and avoid terms such as conciliation, mediation, expert determination, or any other form of alternative dispute resolution. The parties can still agree on multi-tier arbitration agreements.

Non-mandatory requirements

It is highly recommended for parties to agree on non-mandatory issues in the arbitration agreement:

- set of arbitration (institutional or *ad hoc*) rules (e.g. of the DIS, ICC, VIAC, SIAC);
- place of arbitration (e.g. Düsseldorf, Germany);
- number of arbitrators and/or procedure for the constitution of the arbitral tribunal; and
- language of the arbitration.

If the parties wish to apply institutional arbitration rules, it is highly advisable to use the model arbitration clauses of the various arbitration institutions. The latter publish their model clauses on their official websites in various languages.

Emergency arbitrator and expedited proceedings rules – opt in or opt out?

Parties need to carefully check whether emergency arbitrator or expedited proceedings rules apply automatically by agreeing on a set of institutional rules ("opt-out system" (e.g. Article 29(6)b) ICC Rules) or whether they have to explicitly agree to the application of these rules in the arbitration agreement ("opt-in system", e.g. Article 45(1) VIAC Rules). Under the DIS Rules 2018, the arbitral tribunal shall discuss the application of the rules of the expedited proceedings with the parties in the case management conference (Section 27.4 (ii) and Annex 4 DIS Rules 2018). The parties should also agree on the rules of law governing the dispute in their choice-of-law clause (Section 1051).

(International) mandatory rules and arbitration agreements

Counsel and in-house lawyers need to be particularly considerate of (internationally) mandatory rules when drafting an arbitration agreement and a choice-of-law clause in an agency agreement. The rights of an agent to claim indemnity or compensation – after the principal's termination of an agency agreement – is enshrined in the national laws of the member states of the EU based on Articles 17-19 of Council Directive 86/653/EEC. Articles 17-19 are qualified as internationally mandatory rules, if an agent operates its principal activity and has its seat in the EU (ECJ, Ingmar, C-381/98, EuZW 2001, 50). An arbitration agreement providing for a place of arbitration outside of the EU in tandem with a choice-of-law clause for the governing law of a non-EU country was refused enforcement by a court in Germany (OLG München, 17.5.2006, WM 2006, 1556). The court held that this tandem would pose a "reasonable threat" that an arbitral tribunal (e.g. seated in California) would not apply an agent's mandatory claim for compensation.

In 2016, the BGH overturned the highly disputed decision of the OLG München in *causa* Pechstein (OLG München, 15.1.2015, SchiedsVZ 2015, 40). The BGH held that the arbitration agreement between the ice speed skater Claudia Pechstein and the ISU was valid (BGH, 7.6.2016, SchiedsVZ 2016, 268). It ruled, in particular, that the arbitration agreement would not violate: (i) the German antitrust law prohibition on abuse of a market dominant position (Section 19(1) of the German code against restraints of competition (*Gesetz gegen Wettbewerbsbeschränkungen* ("GWB")); (ii) the fundamental right to free exercise of profession (Article 12(1)GG (German constitution)); or (iii) the right to fair proceedings under Article 6 of the European Convention of Human Rights. Claudia Pechstein has filed a constitutional appeal (*Verfassungsbeschwerde*) against the decision of the BGH with the German Constitutional Court (*Bundesverfassungsgericht*). The decision of the German Constitutional Court is still outstanding. It is expected that Claudia Pechstein will initiate proceedings with the ECHR if her constitutional appeal is dismissed.

Form requirements of an arbitration agreement

Section 1031 requires an arbitration agreement to fulfil the "writing" requirement. Only arbitration agreements between businessmen (Section 14 of the German civil code (*Bürgerliches Gesetzbuch* ("BGB"))) not involving consumers, will be addressed herein.

An orally concluded arbitration agreement does not suffice. The writing requirement is fulfilled if the agreement is signed by the parties or if it is contained in an exchange of letters, telefaxes or other means of telecommunication (e.g. emails), which provide a record of the agreement. The list of means of communication in Section 1031(1) is not exhaustive.

Unlike the ML, Section 1031(2) also provides a more lenient writing requirement. An arbitration agreement is deemed to be in writing if it is contained in a document transmitted from one party to the other party. Unless the receiving party raises objections without undue delay, the contents of the document, and thus the arbitration agreement, become part of the contract in accordance with common usage. Thus, an exchange of means of telecommunications containing the arbitration agreement is not required. Section 1031(2) is of high practical importance in business transactions. Often, contracts are concluded orally and one party confirms the content of the agreement by a commercial letter of confirmation (*kaufmännisches Bestätigungsschreiben*). If such a letter reflects the result of the negotiations without significant deviations, the recipient will be deemed to be bound by the contract, unless the recipient objects without undue delay.

A contract, complying with the form requirements of subsections 1 or 2 of Section 1031 (signature, exchange of means of communications, failure to raise objections), can also contain a reference to a separate document containing an arbitration agreement. Often arbitration agreements are included in separate standard terms and conditions ("STC"). As long as the reference is such as to make the arbitration agreement part of the contract, the form requirements are fulfilled (Section 1031(3)).

The assessment of the validity of an arbitration agreement in STC is two-fold:

- *First*: An arbitration agreement will be validly incorporated into the contract, if the reference is unambiguous and the recipient had the opportunity to review the arbitration agreement (actual review is not required). In recent decisions, courts confirmed that the threshold for a valid incorporation is low. It is sufficient to send the STC containing the arbitration agreement to the other party. It is not necessary to send the institutional rules (referred to in the arbitration agreement) to the other party as long as they are publicly available (e.g. on the website of the arbitration institution) (KG Berlin, 13.6.2016, 20 SchH 1/16).
- *Second*: If German law governs this question, the validity of the STC, and thus of the arbitration agreement itself, is subject to the specific validity requirements set out in Sections 305(1), 307(1), (2) BGB (also applicable between businessmen (Section 310(1) BGB)). An arbitration agreement which fulfils the requirements of a just constitution of an arbitral tribunal and a fair treatment of the parties will be usually considered valid.

Full review of the arbitration agreement and special procedure for admissibility of arbitration proceedings

In case a party initiates court proceedings in violation of an arbitration agreement, the opposing party must invoke the existence of the arbitration agreement prior to the beginning of the oral hearing (Section 1032(1)) (*Schiedseinrede*). Otherwise, it will be deemed that the opposing party has waived its right to arbitrate. The party initiating the court proceedings bears the burden of proof for the invalidity of the arbitration agreement.

Further, the ZPO stipulates a special procedure not mirrored in the ML: a party can file an application with the OLG to determine, in particular, whether the arbitration agreement is valid (Sections 1032(2), 1062(1) No. 2). This application is admissible prior to the constitution of an arbitral tribunal.

Both procedures (Sections 1032(1) and (2)) apply also if the place of arbitration is outside of Germany (Section 1025(2)). In principle, the courts will make a full review of the validity of the arbitration agreement at this pre-arbitration stage. In many other jurisdictions, the courts assess the validity of the arbitration agreement only on a *prima facie* basis at such a stage, and make a full review only in post-award proceedings. The German approach ensures that parties do not spend time and costs on arbitration proceedings, resulting in an arbitral award which will be set aside or refused enforcement due to an invalid arbitration agreement.

What disputes are arbitrable?

Any claim involving an economic interest is arbitrable. Thus, any monetary claims, also involving questions of antitrust law, the use of intellectual property rights ("IPR"), etc., are arbitrable. The term "economic interest" is broadly interpreted. Further, even claims not involving an economic interest are arbitrable, if the parties are entitled to conclude a settlement on the issue in dispute (Section 1030(1)).

Disputes on the existence of a lease of residential accommodation within Germany are not arbitrable (Section 1030(2)). Due to the rising importance of disputes arising out of (patent) licence agreements, it has been recently heavily discussed in the German arbitration community whether the validity of patents is arbitrable (at least with *inter partes* effect between the parties of the arbitration).

Scope of an arbitration agreement

In a recent decision, a regional court in Germany decided that follow-on damage claims – based under German law on e.g. Section 33 GWB and to be qualified as tortious claims – fall within the scope of a model arbitration clause ("arising out of" or "in connection with") contained in a supply agreement between a claimant and a respondent/cartelist supplier (LG Dortmund, 13.9.2017, NZKart 2017, 604). The court stressed that the ECJ's interpretation principles as to whether forum selection clauses comprise follow-on damage claims (CDC/Akzo Nobel *et al* (ECJ, C-352/13)) are not applicable to arbitration clauses.

What rules exist for joinder/consolidation of third parties?

The ZPO does not provide any rules for joinder and consolidation of third parties. The parties can agree on institutional rules providing for these cases (e.g. Article 7 ICC Rules or Section 19 DIS Rules 2018). If German law applies to this question, a third party might be bound to an arbitration agreement, if rights and obligations arising out of a main contract containing it, have been validly assigned.

Arbitration procedure

Commencing arbitration proceedings

Pursuant to Section 1044, arbitration proceedings commence on the date on which a request for a dispute is received by the respondent. Many institutional rules, if agreed upon by the parties, deem proceedings to be commenced on the date on which the institution receives the request for arbitration (e.g. Article 4(2) ICC Rules or Section 6.1 DIS Rules 2018).

The request under Section 1044 has only to state the names, the subject-matter of the dispute and contain a reference to the arbitration agreement. If the parties agree on a set of institution rules, the requirements of a request for arbitration (Article 4(3) ICC Rules or

Section 5.2 DIS Rules 2018) are much more elaborate than under Section 1044. A claimant has, e.g., to also state the relief sought, nominate an arbitrator and set out the facts giving rise to the claims.

If German substantive law applies to this question, the statute of limitations period is suspended on the date the arbitration proceedings begin (Section 204(1) No. 11 BGB).

Can hearings take place outside of the place of arbitration?

Yes, according to Section 1043(2), unless the parties agree otherwise.

What are the rules on evidence?

Except for mandatory provisions of the ZPO (in particular, the right to be heard, equal treatment of the parties and representation by counsel (Sections 1042(1) and (2)), the parties are free to determine the procedure themselves or by reference to institutional rules (Section 1043(3)). Failing an agreement of the parties, the arbitral tribunal has wide discretion to conduct the arbitration as it considers appropriate (Section 1043(4)).

The applicable rules on evidence will depend, *inter alia*, on the legal background of the arbitrators and parties, the nature of the dispute and the parties' expectations. Arbitral tribunals and parties can therefore tailor-make the procedure. It is good practice, mostly at the beginning of the proceedings, that an arbitral tribunal will issue special procedural rules and a procedural order no.1 after having heard the parties. The DIS Rules 2018 enhance the German tradition of pro-active arbitrators in order to make proceedings more efficient, quicker and cost-effective, stipulating a mandatory agenda for the case-management conference. Irrespective of whether the arbitration is international or national, the arbitrators need to address during the conference whether the parties confer upon the arbitral tribunal the explicit power to give a preliminary assessment of the merits of the case (Section 27.4 (i) and Annex 3).

Arbitral tribunals lack coercive powers. They cannot compel witnesses or experts to appear. They cannot administer oaths. Further, they cannot order a third party to produce documents. A party, with the approval of the arbitral tribunal, or the arbitral tribunal itself, can request a court to assist in the taking of evidence or to perform other judicial acts (Section 1050).

Taking of evidence in national arbitrations

The continental civil law tradition of Germany, and a limited inquisitorial approach, will prevail. Written witness statements are the exception. During an evidentiary hearing, an arbitral tribunal will examine witnesses first. Counsel to parties will typically ask additional, in particular, follow-up questions to the witness to test the witness' credibility and the probative value of the statement. An arbitral tribunal may give directions, such as which facts it considers (ir)relevant, and give a preliminary assessment on the merits of the case, unless the parties agree otherwise. Document production between the parties is the exception.

Parties can appoint their own experts. Further, the ZPO provides a framework for arbitral tribunal-appointed experts (Section 1049), subject to the parties' agreement. The arbitral tribunal may appoint one or several experts and order a party to give the expert any relevant information or to produce, or grant access, to any relevant documents (Section 1049(1)). Experts have a continuing obligation to be impartial and independent (Sections 1049(3), 1036). Otherwise, a party can challenge the expert. This challenge procedure is a special feature of the ZPO, not provided for in the ML. The deadline is two weeks after becoming aware of the expert's appointment or after becoming aware of the circumstances giving rise to the challenge (Sections 1049(3), 1037(2)).

The arbitral tribunal will decide on the expert's challenge. Recourse to the state courts against an arbitral tribunal's dismissal of such a challenge is excluded (*e.arg.* Section 1049(3)), but an award debtor can later invoke the expert's lack of impartiality and independence in post-award proceedings (Section 1059(2) No. 1(d), Article V(1)(d) NYC). Sometimes the information raising doubts as to the impartiality and independence of an expert only becomes known after the award is issued, because the expert violated its ongoing disclosure obligation. Under the former jurisprudence of the BGH, an award debtor may challenge the award with this new information only in particularly serious and manifest cases of an expert's lack of impartiality and independence. The BGH reversed this case law and applies now a more lenient threshold: the new information must – from an *ex-ante* perspective – raise doubts as to the impartiality and independence sufficient to challenge the expert (BGH, 2.5.2017, SchiedsVZ 2017, 317).

Taking of evidence in international arbitrations

Written witness statements are commonly used. In particular, if a common-law party is involved, the examination of witnesses will follow the common law tradition (direct, cross- and re-examination). Sometimes also a hybrid system between common and civil traditions will be adopted.

As regards document production, arbitral tribunals use the IBA Rules on the Taking of Evidence (of May 2010) (Article 3) ("IBA Rules") as guidelines. Usually they will clarify in the special procedural rules that they are not bound by them and use Redfern schedules. Subject to the circumstances of the case, German arbitration practitioners apply the requirements of document production under Article 3 IBA Rules rather strictly (the law applicable to the merits, the burden of proof, and the involvement of a party from a common law jurisdiction often plays a role). This strict approach minimises costs and increases the efficiency and speed of arbitration proceedings. It is common practice that the parties appoint experts. The IBA Rules (Articles 5 and 6) are often used as guidelines. German arbitration practitioners in international arbitrations also use witness conferencing with experts and witnesses.

What rules are applicable regarding privilege and disclosure?

In civil court proceedings, in principle, discovery or disclosure of documents by an opposing party does not exist. The threshold under the exceptions (e.g. Sections 422, 423, 142) is very high. Accordingly, rules regarding privilege do not exist either in the ZPO. This may change in the future, as a new exception has been transposed to German law from the European Directive on Antitrust Damages Actions in June 2017: in antitrust follow-on damage claims both claimants and respondents may request disclosure of evidence necessary for their case or their defence (Section 33g GWB).

Up to now, however, in international arbitrations in Germany, various approaches to determine the applicable law to the question of privilege, and different concepts of privilege in numerous jurisdictions, often arise under the IBA Rules (Article 9(2)(b)). Therefore, German arbitration practitioners are experienced in finding appropriate solutions, ensuring a level playing field between parties from different jurisdictions.

Are arbitration proceedings confidential? Can the evidence and pleadings be kept confidential?

The ZPO is silent on whether arbitration proceedings are confidential.

The BGH held that an arbitrator has a confidentiality obligation under his/her arbitrator's contract with the parties (BGH, 5.5.1986, NJW 1986, 3077, 3078), unless the contrary is clearly indicated.

As regards the confidentiality obligations of parties, the legal situation is not clear: if the parties have not explicitly agreed in their contract or in their arbitration agreement on the confidentiality of the arbitration proceedings, it is subject to scholarly debate whether an implied obligation can be derived from either of the contracts.

Therefore, in practice, the parties and the arbitral tribunal often conclude a confidentiality agreement at the outset of the arbitration proceedings (e.g. in the terms of reference of ICC proceedings). The wording of such a confidentiality agreement should be broad, so it also encompasses e.g. the parties' pleadings, expert reports and witness statements. Unlike the ICC Rules, Section 44.1 DIS Rules 2018 obliges, *inter alia*, parties, counsel and arbitrators to keep the arbitration confidential.

Experts, witnesses, court reporters, etc. are not bound by such a confidentiality agreement. Therefore, separate agreements should be concluded with them.

Arbitrators

Appointment of arbitrators

Unless the parties agree otherwise, the number of arbitrators shall be three (Section 1034(1)).

Party autonomy also prevails as regards the procedure of the appointment of the arbitral tribunal (Section 1035(1)). Failing an agreement by the parties, the default rules of the ZPO provide a standard procedure: In case of a three-member tribunal, each party appoints its own arbitrator and the two party-appointed arbitrators shall appoint the chairman. Should a party fail to appoint its own arbitrator and subsequently fail to do so within one month of a request by the other party, the other party may request the court to make the appointment. In case the party-appointed arbitrators fail to agree on the chairman within one month of their appointment, or in case the parties fail to agree on a sole arbitrator, the court will make the appointment upon request of a party (Section 1035(3)).

The ZPO stipulates a special procedure, not mirrored in the ML, which safeguards, also between businessmen,[2] an equal treatment of the parties in the constitution of the arbitral tribunal (Section 1034(2)). This procedure allows a court, upon application of one party, to appoint a substitute arbitrator if the arbitration agreement grants preponderant rights to one party (e.g. only one party has the right to nominate the sole arbitrator or the chairman). The disadvantaged party must make the application within two weeks after becoming aware of the constitution of the arbitral tribunal.

Deviating from the ML (Article 11(1)), the ZPO does not prohibit persons from acting as an arbitrator due to their nationality, unless the parties agree otherwise (e.g. Article 13(5) ICC Rules). Depending on the matter in dispute, engineers, accountants, etc. are nominated as arbitrators, particularly in national arbitrations. In contrast to its previous version, the DIS Rules 2018 no longer require a sole arbitrator or the president to be a lawyer.

How can arbitrators be challenged?

Arbitrators must be impartial and independent (Section 1036). Their duty to disclose circumstances that give rise to justifiable doubts as to their impartiality or independence is ongoing from the time of their appointment (Section 1036(1) sentence 2). Otherwise, they can be challenged (Section 1036(2)).

As regards challenges, a two-tier system applies: first, a party has to file a challenge (a "written statement of the reasons of the challenge") with the arbitral tribunal. The deadline is two weeks after the constitution of the arbitral tribunal or after the challenging party becomes aware of the circumstances enumerated in Section 1036(2) (1037(2) sentence 1).

In practice, the challenged arbitrator – even if not obligated to do so by law – often refrains from participating in the tribunal's decision on the challenge.

Second, if the challenge is dismissed, the challenging party may apply to the OLG (within one month) to decide on the challenge (Sections 1037(3) sentence 1, 1062(1) No. 1). Otherwise the challenging party is precluded from invoking in post-award proceedings that the arbitral tribunal was not properly constituted (Section 1059(2) No. 1(d) or Article V(1)(d) NYC) (unless public policy applies). The OLG is not bound by the decision of the arbitral tribunal or a third party (e.g. ICC Court (Article 14 ICC Rules) or DIS Arbitration Council (Section 15.4 DIS Rules 2018)). The parties cannot validly waive recourse to the courts under Section 1037(3). A complaint on a point of law against a decision of the courts with the BGH is not admissible (Section 1065(1)).

The IBA Guidelines on Conflicts of Interest in International Arbitration of 2014 ("IBA Guidelines") are widely known and used by arbitrators in Germany. Courts tend to consider the principles (red, orange and green lists) laid down in the IBA Guidelines, even if not explicitly referring to them.

How is an arbitrator's mandate terminated?

It is terminated, in particular:

- if an award is issued (the arbitral tribunal becomes *functus officio*);
- if an arbitrator withdraws from his/her office;
- by a court's decision in a challenge procedure to remove the arbitrator (Section 1037);
- by a court's decision to remove the arbitrator, if an arbitrator becomes *de jure* (e.g. legal incapacity) or *de facto* unable to perform his functions (Section 1038(1) sentence 2); or
- if the parties agree to terminate the arbitrator's mandate.

Immunity of arbitrators

Arbitrators are generally immune from liability for damages in their capacity as a decision-maker. They cannot be held liable if they render a decision that is legally incorrect, except for cases of intentional breach of duty (e.g. Section 45.1 DIS Rules 2018) or criminal offences. They enjoy more or less the same privilege as German state judges (by way of analogy of Section 839(2) BGB).

However, arbitrators are generally liable for breaches of their contract with the parties, in particular, in cases, where they:

- resign without good cause;
- fail to disclose circumstances which may lead to a challenge for lack of impartiality or independence; or
- unduly delay or even refuse to continue with the arbitration proceedings.

In their contract with the arbitrators or by reference to institutional rules, the parties can agree to restrict (e.g. Section 45.2 DIS Rules 2018) or exclude the arbitrator's liability (e.g. Article 40 ICC Rules). The validity of the restriction or exclusion is subject to the applicable law.

Interim relief

Can the parties apply with both courts and tribunals for interim relief?

Under the ZPO, the parties to an arbitration agreement are free to choose whether to seek interim relief with a court or an arbitral tribunal (Sections 1033, 1041). The parties can opt out of seeking interim relief with arbitral tribunals (Section 1041(1)). Whether the parties can also validly waive recourse to the courts is disputed among scholars and courts.

Before or during arbitration proceedings, a party can request a court to order interim relief (Section 1033), even if the place of arbitration is outside of Germany (Section 1025(2)) and if the court assumes international jurisdiction. In practice, German courts can order interim relief, subject to the circumstances and the fulfilment of certain requirements, *ex parte* and within 24 hours.

<u>What types of interim relief are available to parties?</u>

Courts may, for example, grant: (i) a pre-award attachment (Arrest) to secure a monetary claim; (ii) a preliminary injunction (*einstweilige Verfügung*) to secure any other claim; or (iii) a procedure to preserve evidence (*selbstständiges Beweisverfahren*).

Arbitral tribunals have a wider discretion than courts as regards the types of interim relief they can order. Contrary to a court, arbitral tribunals can only order interim measures against the parties to the arbitration agreement. Lacking coercive powers, arbitral tribunals cannot enforce interim measures if a party does not voluntarily comply with them. Upon request of a party, a court can enforce them (Section 1041(2)).

If the opposing party can prove that the interim measure – ordered by the court or an arbitral tribunal – was unjustified from the outset, the applicant is liable for damages (Sections 945, 1041(4)) resulting from the enforcement of such a measure.

Arbitration award

<u>Formal requirements for an arbitration award</u>

An award must:

- be in writing;
- be signed by the sole arbitrator or, in case of a three-member tribunal, by its majority;
- state the reasons upon which the arbitral tribunal has based its decision (unless the parties agree otherwise); and
- state the date of the award and the place of the arbitration (Section 1054).

A copy of the award signed by the arbitrators must be delivered to each party. A specific form of delivery is not required (Section 1054(4)).

<u>Is a time frame stipulated for the arbitration award?</u>

Unless agreed otherwise by the parties, the ZPO does not specify a time frame for rendering the award.

<u>Can an arbitral tribunal order costs for the parties? If yes, under what criteria?</u>

An arbitral tribunal has the power to allocate the costs of the arbitration at its discretion, unless the parties agree otherwise (Section 1057). By exercising such discretion, the arbitral tribunal must take into account all circumstances of the case, particularly its outcome. In practice, German arbitration practitioners usually follow the "costs follow the event" rule. Depending on the circumstances of the case, arbitral tribunals may also take into account e.g. "guerrilla tactics", or the outcome of jurisdictional objections or voluminous requests to produce.

<u>Can interest be included in the award and/or costs?</u>

An arbitral tribunal can grant interest in the award if a party has filed a respective claim. Otherwise, granting interest would qualify as an *ultra petita* ruling and constitute a ground for setting aside or refusing the enforcement of an award (Section 1059(2) No. 1(c) and Article V(1)(c) NYC).

Challenge of the arbitration award

On what grounds can an award be challenged?

According to Section 1059(2) (mirroring Article 34(2) ML), an award may be set aside only if:

1. the applicant shows sufficient cause that:
   (a) a party to the arbitration agreement was under some incapacity or the arbitration agreement is not valid; or
   (b) the opposing party was not given proper notice of the appointment of the arbitrator or of the arbitration proceedings or was otherwise unable to present its case; or
   (c) the arbitral tribunal has exceeded its authority; or
   (d) the composition of the arbitral tribunal or the arbitration proceedings was not in accordance with the ZPO or with an admissible agreement of the parties and this presumably affected the award; or
2. the court finds that:
   (a) the subject-matter lacks objective arbitrability under German law; or
   (b) recognition and enforcement of the award would violate public policy.

Section 1059(2) provides an exhaustive list of grounds on the basis of which an award can be set aside. The grounds in No. 1 have to be pleaded by the applicant ("[...] shows sufficient cause [...]"). The grounds in No. 2 are considered by the court *ex officio* ("[...] the court finds [...]"). A review of the merits by a court is not admissible (prohibition of the *révision au fond*).

The wording of Section 1059(2), "may be set aside", has to be read as "shall be set aside". A court does not have any discretionary powers: it has to set aside an award if a ground exists. An oral hearing is mandatory (Section 1063(1), first alternative).

Deviating from the ML (Article 34(4)), Section 1059(4) provides that a court will set aside the award and remit the case, in appropriate cases, to the arbitral tribunal. Further, Section 1059(5) stipulates that the arbitration agreement becomes operative again once the award has been set aside (except if the arbitration agreement is invalid).

Before arbitration proceedings are initiated, parties cannot validly waive setting-aside proceedings. After the award is issued or once a party becomes aware of a circumstance giving rise to invoke a ground listed in Section 1059(2) No. 1, a waiver to invoke this ground is valid. The grounds of No. 2 of Section 1059(2) (lack of objective arbitrability and violation of public policy) cannot be validly waived.

Is it possible to modify the arbitration award?

An application for the correction, interpretation or an additional award with the arbitral tribunal is admissible within one month after receipt of the award, unless agreed otherwise by the parties (Section 1058(1), (2)).

Recent examples of successful and unsuccessful challenges of arbitral awards

A recent order of the OLG München illustrates the general approach of courts to apply the grounds under Section 1059 in setting aside proceedings restrictively (OLG München, 9.11.2015, SchiedsVZ 2015, 303). There was reason to argue that the arbitral tribunal had incorrectly applied the applicable law. The OLG confirmed the prohibition of the *révision au fond* in post-award proceedings. It held that an award would only violate *ordre public* (Section 1059(2) No. 2(b)) if the violated provision is not only mandatory, but forms the basis of a functioning public or economic life. Further, the OLG held that the threshold of the violation of a party's right to be heard is high (Section 1059(2) No. 1(b), (d), No. 2(b)): if an arbitral tribunal has given a legal assessment of the merits of the claim, it can deviate from this assessment in the award. The right to be heard is only violated if the arbitral tribunal failed: (i) to inform the parties of the change of legal assessment; and (ii) to grant them the right to comment upon the amended legal assessment. The OLG also confirmed that arbitral tribunals do not have to address in a complete and exhaustive manner in the award every legal and factual argument submitted by the parties. Only if the reasons of the award are, in particular, self-contradictory, can an award be set aside for violation of Section 1054(2) (Section 1059(2) No. 1(d)).

Enforcement of the arbitration award

The application in enforcement proceedings is admissible if:

- it is in writing or put on record at the court registry (Section 1063(4)); and
- the award or a certified copy is annexed to the application (Section 1064(1)). The stricter admissibility requirements under Article IV NYC (e.g. original or duly certified copy of the arbitration agreement; translation of the award into official language of enforcement state) do not apply (Article VII(1) NYC). In practice, the applicant submits a translation of the award, or at least of its operative part.

A foreign award can be refused enforcement based on the reasons of Article V NYC.

<u>Can an arbitration award be enforced if it has been set aside at the seat of arbitration</u>?

An OLG has to refuse enforcement of an award which has been validly set aside (Article V(1)(e) NYC). If the European Convention applies, the application of Article V(1)(e) NYC is limited. Pursuant to Article IX(2) European Convention, a court can refuse enforcement only if the award has been set aside for reasons stated in Article IX(1)(a)-(d) European Convention (being identical to the reasons set out in Article V(1)(a)-(d) NYC). If an award has been set aside, e.g. for violation of public policy or lack of arbitrability at the place of arbitration, Article V(1)(e) NYC cannot be applied by the courts in Germany under the European Convention.

<u>Trends in enforcement</u>

The vast majority of foreign awards are enforced in Germany. In a recent decision, the BGH confirmed the distinction between the German *ordre public* national and international (BGH, 2.3.2017, NJOZ 2017, 802). The enforcement of foreign awards under the NYC is only subject to the German *ordre public* international, the standard of which is more lenient than the German *ordre public* national. Enforcement of a foreign award will only be refused if the arbitration proceedings have a serious defect affecting the basis of public and economic life.

Counsel and award debtors have to be aware of the "preclusion" case law in Germany: is an award debtor precluded from invoking grounds under Article V NYC in enforcement proceedings in Germany if he fails to invoke the same grounds in setting aside proceedings within the statutory time limits of the *lex loci arbitri*? The BGH had to decide on this question of preclusion only for the invalidity of arbitration agreements (Article V(1)(a) NYC). It held that an award debtor is not precluded from invoking the invalidity of an arbitration agreement in enforcement proceedings, even if he had not initiated setting-aside proceedings invoking the same ground (BGH, 16.12.2010, NJW 2011, 1290). As regards any grounds other than the invalidity of the arbitration agreement (e.g. violation of right to be heard, *ultra petita* decision, flawed constitution of arbitral tribunal (Article V(1) (b), (c), (d) NYC)), this question of preclusion has not yet been decided by the BGH. Although criticised by scholars and courts, the majority view of the OLGs[3] seems to be in favour of preclusion.

Investment arbitration

Germany is currently a party to more than 130 effective BITs, the ICSID Convention and the ECT.

Public debate in Germany has been fuelled by the ICSID arbitration pending between, *inter alia*, Vattenfall AB, a Swedish power company and Germany since 2012 (ICSID case No. ARB/12/12). Vattenfall AB made investments in a number of nuclear power plants in Germany. The ECT dispute arose from the 2011 amendment to Germany's Atomic Energy Law ("Amendment"). The Amendment stipulated that Germany's nuclear power plants are to be phased out by 2022. Vattenfall AB is claiming damages of more than €4 billion. The award is expected this year: The arbitral tribunal held a hearing on jurisdiction, merits and quantum[4] in October 2016. The latest publicly known development of the case is that the parties filed post-hearing briefs and cost submissions in 2017.

Further, the BGH made a referral for a preliminary ruling to the ECJ to decide in particular on the compatibility of ISDS mechanisms, such as arbitration clauses in Intra-EU BITs, with Articles 344, 267 and 18 TFEU (BGH, 3.3.2016, SchiedsVZ 2016, 328 (Achmea B.V./ Slovak Republic)). In September 2017, the Advocate General delivered its opinion in favour of compatibility. In March 2018, the ECJ issued its long-awaited decision. It declared that: (i) arbitral tribunals constituted under BITs do not qualify as courts for the purposes of Article 267 TFEU; and (ii) arbitration clauses in intra-EU BITs are incompatible with EU law as they have an adverse effect on the autonomy of EU law (ECJ, 6.3.2108, C-284/16).

* * *

Endnotes

1. Unless explicitly stated otherwise, any reference to sections are those of the ZPO.
2. As defined in Section 14 BGB.
3. OLGs: Regional higher courts.
4. Except for this hearing – which was made public via streaming on the ICSID website – the proceedings have been largely non-transparent.

Catrice Gayer
Tel: +49 211 975 59 136 / Email: catrice.gayer@hsf.com

Catrice Gayer regularly acts as counsel and arbitrator in international and national arbitration cases under the auspices of various institutional rules (ICC, DIS, SIAC, etc.) and *ad hoc*. The proceedings are governed by a variety of substantive and procedural rules. Her particular fields of industry are energy/infrastructure, IP and antitrust (including FRAND), commercial (agency, trade, distribution, licence), and corporate including M&A-related disputes. She also regularly acts as (co-)counsel in arbitration-related disputes before German courts and abroad. She has a particular expertise in Asia-related arbitrations. Her track record also includes the representation of national and foreign clients in civil and commercial disputes before the regional courts, share and asset deals, advising in compliance matters, and advising and drafting a broad range of supply, distribution, sale and corporate contracts.

Catrice has been recommended as a Rising Star (Commercial Arbitration) in *Expert Guides* and is ranked as Future Leader in Arbitration by *Who's Who Legal* (2018). She is an appointed member of the ICC Commission on Commercial Law and Practice. Catrice is a regional chair of the DIS40, a co-chair of the Young CEAC (Chinese European Arbitration Centre – below 45 group) and a member of the Executive Committee of AIJA. She is admitted to the bar in Germany and holds a *Maîtrise en Droit* (Paris XII) and a Postgraduate Laws Certificate (Queen Mary/UCL (London)). Catrice regularly speaks on international arbitration at conferences and publishes on international dispute resolution and corporate matters.

Thomas Weimann
Tel: +49 211 975 59 136 / Email: thomas.weimann@hsf.com

Thomas Weimann is co-head of Herbert Smith Freehills' Disputes practice in Germany. Before joining HSF, he was a partner at Clifford Chance for many years and head of that firm's Düsseldorf arbitration and litigation practice. Thomas enjoys a practice that spans a wide range of arbitration work, with a special focus on high-value construction-related disputes including plant construction, industrial engineering and civil construction projects and disputes (*inter alia* turn-key civil construction projects, power plants with a focus on turbines, sludge water plants, pulp mills, off-shore windfarms with a special focus on cable laying and converter platforms, chemical industry, subway projects, shopping malls and museums). He also sits as an arbitrator in proceedings under the auspices of the ICC, DIS, CIETAC and PCA and other renowned arbitral institutions. He has been counsel in more than 60 major construction arbitrations with a regional focus on Germany, the Arab region, the US and Russia. As President of the Chinese European Legal Association (CELA) and one of the founders of the Chinese-European Arbitration Centre (CEAC) seated in Hamburg, he has well developed links with China. Thomas speaks frequently at seminars and conferences, in particular in Greater China. Furthermore, he speaks at international conferences, *inter alia* the annual meeting of the International Bar Association and the St. Petersburg International Legal Forum.

Herbert Smith Freehills Germany LLP

Breite Straße 29-31, 40213 Düsseldorf, Germany
Tel: +49 211 975 59 136 / Fax: +49 211 975 59 099 / URL: www.herbertsmithfreehills.com

Hong Kong

James Yeung & Felda Yeung
Gall

Introduction

Arbitration in Hong Kong has thrived and Hong Kong is often the preferred seat in arbitration agreements, especially in cross-border deals with a connection to Hong Kong or the People's Republic of China ("**PRC**"). According to the 2015 International Arbitration Survey by Queen Mary University of London and White & Case, Hong Kong is ranked the third-most preferred and used seat worldwide, and the most favoured seat outside of Europe.

Arbitration in Hong Kong is governed by the Arbitration Ordinance ("**AO**") which is modelled on the UNCITRAL Model Law. Section 3 of the AO expressly provides that subject to the observance of safeguards that are necessary in the public interest, the parties to a dispute should be free to agree on how the dispute should be resolved; and that the Hong Kong Courts should interfere in the arbitration of a dispute only in very limited circumstances as expressly provided for in the AO.

Hong Kong Courts have consistently adopted a pro-arbitration and pro-enforcement stance and have emphasised in numerous judgments that they will only interfere in limited circumstances.

Hong Kong's pro-arbitration and pro-enforcement environment is attractive to commercial parties as it offers them certainty and confidentiality. The judge in charge of the Arbitration and Construction List summarised the relevant principles which are of importance when determining cases in relation to arbitration:

1) "*The primary aim of the court is to facilitate the arbitral process and to assist with enforcement of arbitral awards.*
2) *Under the Arbitration Ordinance ("Ordinance"), the court should interfere in the arbitration of the dispute only as expressly provided for in the Ordinance.*
3) *Subject to the observance of the safeguards that are necessary in the public interest, the parties to a dispute should be free to agree on how their dispute should be resolved.*
4) *Enforcement of arbitral awards should be "almost a matter of administrative procedure", and the courts should be "as mechanistic as possible"...*
5) *The courts are prepared to enforce awards except where complaints of substance can be made good. The party opposing enforcement has to show a real risk of prejudice and that its rights are shown to have been violated in a material way...*
6) *In dealing with applications to set aside an arbitral award, or to refuse enforcement of an award, whether on the ground of not having been given notice of the arbitral proceedings, inability to present one's case, or that the composition of the tribunal or*

the arbitral procedure was not in accordance with the parties' agreement, the court is concerned with the structural integrity of the arbitration proceedings. In this regard, the conduct complained of "must be serious, even egregious", before the court would find that there was an error sufficiently serious so as to have undermined due process...

7) *In considering whether or not to refuse the enforcement of the award, the court does not look into the merits or at the underlying transaction...*

8) *Failure to make prompt objection to the Tribunal or the supervisory court may constitute estoppel or want of bona fide...*

9) *Even if sufficient grounds are made out either to refuse enforcement or to set aside an arbitral award, the court has a residual discretion and may nevertheless enforce the award despite the proven existence of a valid ground...*

10) *The Court of Final Appeal clearly recognized...that parties to the arbitration have a duty of good faith, or to act bona fide.*[1]"

These principles, as summarised by Mimmie Chan J. in 2015, remain at the forefront of the Hong Kong Courts' mind.

Earlier this year, the Hong Kong Court again reinforced its favourable attitude towards arbitration by commenting that "*parties should be entitled to expect that the [Hong Kong] Court will enforce arbitration agreements and arbitral awards made pursuant thereto as a matter of course*",[2] in considering whether a costs dispute between a solicitors' firm and its client should be arbitrated.

Separately, in ***Lasmos Limited v Southwest Pacific Bauxite (HK) Limited***,[3] a service company alleged that a company failed to pay for services rendered under the agreement and sought to wind up the company on the basis the company should be deemed to be insolvent due to its failure to pay. The Companies Judge of the Hong Kong High Court held in January 2018 that if a company disputes the debt relied on by the petitioner and the contract under which the debt is alleged to arise contains an arbitration agreement that covers any dispute relating to the debt, and the company takes the steps required under the arbitration agreement and files evidence at Court to demonstrate this, then the winding-up petition should be dismissed, unless there are exceptional cases which justify a stay of the winding-up petition instead of an immediate dismissal.

Further, to ensure that the AO's objectives are respected, the Hong Kong Courts have the discretion to penalise a party's unsuccessful challenge to the validity of an arbitration agreement or an arbitral award with an order to pay the successful party's legal costs on an indemnity basis.

As Hong Kong continues to foster and develop arbitration, Hong Kong arbitral awards are also readily enforceable in multiple foreign jurisdictions as a Convention Award via the New York Convention.[4] There is also a mechanism to enforce Hong Kong arbitral awards in the PRC via the Arrangement Concerning Mutual Enforcement of Arbitral Awards.

Further, to maintain its international status in the arbitration sphere, Hong Kong has also recently enacted legislation to allow for third parties to fund arbitration in Hong Kong and clarify that disputes of intellectual property rights can be arbitrated.

Arbitration agreement

To minimise disputes in relation to the validity of the arbitration agreement when a dispute subsequently arises, parties should exercise caution in drafting the arbitration agreement.

Whilst an arbitration agreement can be either written or oral (as with any contract), an oral arbitration agreement does not attract any special protection under the AO, but is merely enforceable as a contract at common law. Under the AO, the arbitration agreement must be in writing and must specify that the parties agree to submit all or certain disputes to arbitration.

It is not necessary for the terms of the arbitration agreement to be included in the same document as the other contractual terms, but it is good practice to do so.

Further, whilst the AO provides for default mechanisms where the parties have no prior agreement on various procedural aspects, it is worthwhile to consider and specify the parties' agreement on the following matters when negotiating the arbitration clause:

1) the applicable substantive law;
2) the applicable procedural rules / administrative institution;
3) the seat of arbitration;
4) the number of arbitrators; and
5) the language to be used in the arbitration proceedings.

Arbitration procedure

Arbitration in Hong Kong may be *ad hoc* or administered by an institution.

Ad hoc arbitrations are arranged solely between the parties and the arbitrators. Parties may either adopt a specific set of arbitration rules or the rules drawn up by the parties themselves, whereas institutional arbitrations are governed by specific arbitration organisations.

Parties are at liberty to choose a particular set of arbitration rules applicable to their arbitration. The most commonly used institution in Hong Kong is the Hong Kong International Arbitration Centre ("**HKIAC**") and the most commonly used rules in Hong Kong are the HKIAC Administered Arbitration Rules (the "**HKIAC Rules**").

Generally, arbitration is commenced in Hong Kong when the claimant refers the dispute to arbitration. Under the HKIAC Rules, arbitration is deemed to be commenced once the HKIAC has received the Notice of Arbitration.

Once the arbitration procedure has commenced, the parties appoint a tribunal of arbitrators. Whilst parties are free to decide the number of arbitrators, typically a panel would consist of one or three arbitrators. Where a panel of three arbitrators is appointed, the applicant and the respondent would usually each appoint an arbitrator of their choice and the two appointed arbitrators would then jointly appoint the third arbitrator to comprise the panel. If the amount in dispute is not substantial, it is more cost-efficient to agree on appointing a sole arbitrator.

Once the sole arbitrator is appointed or the arbitral tribunal is constituted, it will first convene a preliminary meeting and issue directions to manage the case. Typical directions include the filing of pleadings, discovery of evidence, filing of factual and expert witnesses, and setting a timeline for the conduct of arbitration. It is also possible for an arbitration to be conducted on a 'papers' or 'document only' basis.

Arbitrators

In Hong Kong, parties often nominate and appoint senior members of the bar or retired judges as arbitrators. Additionally, all prospective arbitrators are required to sign a statement confirming his or her impartiality and independence. Accordingly, whilst parties often correspond amongst themselves on who would be the most appropriate candidate once a nomination has been made, challenges to the appointment of arbitrators are uncommon.

Under the AO, a challenge to an arbitrator can be made if circumstances exist that give rise to justifiable doubts as to their impartiality or independence, or if they do not possess the requisite qualifications agreed to by the parties. Under the HKIAC Rules, the grounds for challenge are wider, as a party may challenge an arbitrator under the same grounds as the AO, or if the arbitrator becomes *de jure* or *de facto* unable to perform his or her functions or for other reasons fails to act without delay.

Under the HKIAC Rules, such a challenge must be made within 15 days after the confirmation of that arbitrator, or within 15 days after a party becomes aware or ought reasonably to have become aware of the circumstances giving rise to a challenge. The HKIAC will determine any challenge of an arbitrator unless, upon receiving the challenge, the arbitrator withdraws or the other party agrees.

Interim relief

Under the AO, a tribunal generally has the power to grant interim measures similar to those granted by the Hong Kong Courts.

For example, a tribunal has the power to grant Mareva injunctions – which has the effect of freezing a party's assets – or an Anton Piller order, which allows for the physical collection of evidence from a party's premises. A tribunal can also require a party requesting interim measures to provide security in connection with that measure, which is similar to a Hong Kong Court's direction for fortification from a party seeking urgent injunctive relief.

The tribunal's power is derived from Sections 35 and 56 of the AO, but the parties can agree to 'opt-out' of such provisions in the arbitration agreement or subsequently.

However, even if the tribunal has the power to grant interim relief, it is important to consider whether it is more appropriate to apply to the Tribunal or to the Hong Kong Court (which also has jurisdiction to grant interim relief in aid of foreign proceedings under Section 45 of the AO) for the specific relief sought. One key factor to consider is whether interim relief is sought against a third party not subject to the arbitration agreement. If so, it may be beneficial to seek the assistance of the Hong Kong Court. Whilst a tribunal has jurisdiction to grant a Mareva injunction, local banks may act to comply with a Mareva injunction granted by a Hong Kong Court more swiftly.

Arbitration award

The tribunal may make an award at any time during the arbitration on different aspects of a dispute. If an interim measure is sought, the tribunal will usually give brief reasons for granting or dismissing the application.

The final award, which is given after the substantive hearing, is usually written in two parts.

The first part of the award typically sets out the arbitration agreement and identifies the gist of the dispute between the parties. It will name the tribunal, the hearings and record the pleadings filed and the orders and directions made. At the end, the award will spell out the orders made after hearing the parties' submission.

The second part of the award will explain the tribunal's reasoning, as Section 67 of the AO requires that the award include reasons unless otherwise agreed by the parties. If procedural challenges were raised, then the tribunal will set out its reasons as to why it decided it has jurisdiction to adjudicate the dispute. The tribunal will then go into its reasoning for its decision on the substantive dispute.

The benefit of dividing the award is that it enables parties to exhibit the first part of the award as evidence or public record while the confidentiality of the matter is reserved in the second part.

Challenge of the arbitration award

Under the AO, the adjudication of arbitration is final and there is a mechanism to convert an arbitral award into a judgment of the Hong Kong Court. This is a convenient measure that gives assurance to the successful party for prompt enforcement.

Save for very limited grounds of procedural irregularity or arbitrator's misconduct, there is a very low chance for appeal. Review based on merits is not allowed. In Hong Kong, parties may expressly agree in the arbitration agreement to the effect that an award may be appealed in certain limited circumstances, for instance if the arbitrator has made an error of law or displays apparent bias.

Enforcement of the arbitration award

An arbitral award can be enforced in Hong Kong once you obtain the leave of the Hong Kong Court and the judgment is entered in the terms of the award.

As an arbitration-friendly jurisdiction, the Hong Kong Courts hear and grant numerous applications for the recognition and enforcement of both domestic and international arbitral awards.

If uncontested, the application can be decided on the papers and, once leave has been obtained, the Court order is served on the defendant. The defendant will then have 14 days to apply to set aside the leave. If no such application is made, then the Hong Kong Court will issue a judgment in terms of the arbitral award. Thereafter, all methods of enforcement of a judgment, such as garnishing the debtor's bank account, become available to the judgment creditor.

If the application for leave to enforce an arbitral award is contested, then the defendant will have to satisfy a high threshold of proving to the Hong Kong Courts that the case falls within the limited grounds for refusal of enforcement. The defendant will need to prove that:

1) a party to the arbitration was under some incapacity;
2) the arbitration agreement was not valid;
3) it was not given proper notice of the appointment of the arbitrator or the arbitral proceedings or was otherwise unable to present its case;
4) the award deals with a difference not contemplated by or not falling within the terms of the submission to arbitration or contains decisions on matters beyond the scope of the submission to arbitration;
5) the composition of the arbitral authority or arbitral procedural was not in accordance with the agreement of the parties or the law of the country where the arbitration took place; or
6) the award has not yet become binding on the parties or has been set side or suspended by a competent authority of the country in which, or under the law of which, it was made.

Overall, the Hong Kong Courts have residual discretion to refuse to enforce a Convention Award if the award is in respect of a matter which is not capable of settlement by arbitration under the laws of Hong Kong or it would be contrary to public policy to enforce the award.

However, even where any of the grounds for refusal of enforcement has been proven, the Hong Kong Courts have a residual discretion to order enforcement.

The grounds for refusal of enforcement of non-Convention awards are mostly identical to the grounds relating to Convention Awards. In addition, the court can also refuse to enforce a non-Convention award for any other reason the court considers it just to do so.

* * *

Endnotes

1. *KB v S* [2015] HKEC 2042, paragraph 1.
2. *Fung Hing Chiu Cyril v Henry Wai & Co* (a firm) [2018] HKCFI 31, paragraph 57.
3. [2018] HKCFI 426.
4. Hong Kong is a signatory to the New York Convention via the PRC's accession.

James Yeung
Tel: +852 3405 7638 / Email: jamesyeung@gallhk.com

James Yeung is a Hong Kong qualified lawyer with over 14 years' post-qualification experience. James specialises in commercial dispute resolution and has handled numerous high-profile litigation, arbitration and mediation cases.

James regularly acts in contentious matters for major banking and financial institutions, listed companies, building managers, casinos and major corporations in Hong Kong and overseas. His experience includes handling shareholders' disputes, unfair prejudice claims, contractual disputes, professional negligence claims and fraud claims. With his construction law background, James also has considerable experience in handling construction disputes for major developers, main contractors and sub-contractors.

James completed his LL.B. and PCLL at the University of Hong Kong. He was admitted as a Solicitor in Hong Kong in 2002. James is fluent in English, Cantonese and Mandarin.

Felda Yeung
Tel: +852 3405 7674 / Email: feldayeung@gallhk.com

Felda joined the firm as a trainee solicitor in 2011 and was admitted as a Solicitor in Hong Kong in 2013.

Felda has experience in commercial and civil litigation, with a focus on arbitration, contractual disputes and fraud investigations. Recent arbitration related work includes enforcing foreign arbitration awards in Hong Kong and defending applications to set aside arbitration awards. Recent litigation work includes assisting in large-scale cross-border actions worth in excess of HK$1 billion at both the Court of Appeal and Court of Final Appeal stage and obtaining various injunctions and urgent interim relief both in support of Hong Kong proceedings and in aid of foreign proceedings.

Felda completed her LL.B. and PCLL at the University of Hong Kong. She also completed a LL.M. in Arbitration and Dispute Resolution at the University of Hong Kong and is a member of the Chartered Institute of Arbitrators.

Gall

3/F, Dina House, Ruttonjee Centre, 11 Duddell Street, Central, Hong Kong
Tel: +852 3405 7688 / URL: www.gallhk.com

India

Ganesh Chandru, Prashant Kumar & Palak Taneja
Lakshmikumaran & Sridharan

Introduction

The use of alternative dispute resolution ("**ADR**") mechanisms in India has its roots in ancient times when disputes were settled through several mechanisms including the resolution of commercial disputes by chambers.[1] The judiciary in India is overburdened because of the increase in the number of litigation cases that are filed, and also because of the long pendency of such cases. Therefore, ADR methods such as arbitration, mediation, conciliation and *Lok Adalats* (people's court) are all the more important in India for the speedy resolution of disputes.

The first legislative recognition of arbitration in modern India was the enactment of the [Indian] Arbitration Act, 1899 which was based on the English Arbitration Act of 1899. This was followed by the inclusion of arbitration-related provisions in the Code of Civil Procedure, 1908 and Arbitration (Protocol and Convention) Act, 1937 which gave effect to the Geneva Protocol on Arbitration Clauses 1923 and the Geneva Convention on the Execution of Foreign Arbitral Awards 1927 ("**Geneva Convention**").[2]

In 1940, the British-era government enacted a comprehensive and self-contained code, the [Indian] Arbitration Act. After India's independence in 1947, commercial activity increased considerably and arbitration started receiving more attention. On 10 June 1958, India became a signatory to the Convention on the Recognition and Enforcement of Foreign Arbitral Awards, 1958 ("**New York Convention**") and ratified it on 13 July 1960. To give effect to this Convention, India enacted the Foreign Awards (Recognition and Enforcement) Act, 1961. Only those foreign awards are enforceable that arise out of legal relationships, whether contractual or not, considered as commercial under the law in force in India. Further, India follows the reciprocity principle and limits the enforcement of arbitral awards to those made in other New York Convention and Geneva Convention countries.

The law on arbitration in India was substantially contained in three enactments, namely, the Arbitration Act, 1940, the Arbitration (Protocol and Convention) Act, 1937 and the Foreign Awards (Recognition and Enforcement) Act, 1961. The need to consolidate and reform the country's arbitration law further gained traction after the Model Law on International Commercial Arbitration was propounded by the United Nations Commission on International Trade Law (UNCITRAL) in 1985 ("**the Model Law**") and the introduction of economic reforms in India in 1991. In order to facilitate business, India adopted the Model Law in its entirety except for a few variations and enacted the Arbitration and Conciliation Act, 1996 ("**the Act**"), with the objective "*to consolidate and amend the law relating to domestic arbitration, international commercial arbitration and enforcement* *of foreign arbitral awards as also to define the law relating to conciliation...*"[3] It is a comprehensive piece of legislation that lays down the law on arbitration in India, and is divided into four parts: Part I on Arbitration seated in India; Part II on Enforcement of Foreign Awards; Part III on Conciliation; and Part IV contains Supplementary Provisions. There is only one legislation for arbitration in India, for both international and domestic arbitration.

Varied interpretation of the provisions of the Act led to a growing sense of dissatisfaction among the users of arbitration. Attempts to remedy most of these issues have been made by way of the Arbitration and Conciliation (Amendment) Act, 2015 ("**the Amendment Act**"). The Amendment Act has followed most of the recommendations of the Law Commission of India's 246th Report ("**Law Commission Report**") and also introduced certain new provisions which are unique to the Indian jurisdiction. As per the amended law, High Courts and the Supreme Court exercise exclusive jurisdiction in relation to international commercial arbitration.[4] Further, pursuant to the Commercial Courts, Commercial Divisions and Commercial Appellate Division of High Courts Act, 2015 ("**Commercial Courts Act**"), special commercial divisions have been set up in High Courts, and commercial courts have been set up in the District Courts, to hear and dispose arbitration matters involving commercial disputes[5] of a specified value.[6] 'Specified Value' means that the amount in dispute is above INR One Crore, i.e. INR 10 Million (about US$ 154,000). In order to bring more cases within the ambit of commercial courts, the Cabinet of the Central Government of India approved the Commercial Courts Act Amendment Bill on 7 March 2018, which has proposed that the 'specified value' be decreased from INR 10 Million to INR 300,000 (about US$ 4,600).

There are many arbitral institutions in India. Some of the popular ones are the Indian Council of Arbitration ("**ICA**"), International Centre for Alternative Dispute Resolution ("**ICADR**"), the Delhi International Arbitration Centre ("**DAC**"), Nani Palkhivala Arbitration Centre ("**NPAC**"), and the recently established Mumbai Centre for International Arbitration ("**MCIA**"). All these institutions have their own arbitral rules, panel of arbitrators, and offer venues for conducting arbitral hearings. Foreign arbitral institutions like Singapore International Arbitration Centre ("**SIAC**") work through their representative (marketing) offices in India. SIAC established its first overseas representative office in Mumbai, Maharashtra in the year 2013 and a second one in GIFT City, Gujarat, in 2017. However, all SIAC arbitrations are administered out of the Singapore office. The London Court of International Arbitration ("**LCIA**") established a subsidiary in India called LCIA-India in 2009. However, it closed down its operation in 2016.

The concept of institutional arbitration is still at a nascent stage in India. To keep up with the momentum to reform India's image as an international arbitration hub, a High-Level Committee headed by Retired Justice B.N. Srikrishna ("**Srikrishna Committee**") was constituted to propose recommendations for the institutionalisation of arbitration in India. The Committee submitted its report on 30 July 2017 and proposed significant reforms to incorporate international best practices and to bring Indian arbitration law in line with international standards. It also made recommendations for tweaks to be made to the amendments to the Act that came into force in October 2015. At present, the majority of the arbitrations in India are conducted on an *ad hoc* basis. Pursuant to the recommendations of the Srikrishna Committee, the Cabinet of the Central Government of India approved the Arbitration and Conciliation (Amendment) Bill, 2018 ("**Amendment Bill 2018**") on 7 March 2018 which provides for creation of an independent body called the "Arbitration Council of India" which will grade arbitral institutions and accredit arbitrators. The Amendment Bill 2018 also proposes some further amendments to the Act.

Arbitration agreement

The Act does not prescribe a particular format to draft an arbitration agreement. However, as per section 7 of the Act, a valid arbitration agreement must be in writing. The writing could be a document signed by the parties or an exchange of letters or other means of telecommunication that can be produced as a record of the agreement. Further, an arbitration agreement may be in the form of an arbitration clause in a contract or in the form of a separate agreement. The words used should disclose the intention and obligation of the parties to go to arbitration and not merely contemplate the possibility of going to arbitration.[7] Therefore, while drafting an arbitration clause, care must be taken to clearly express the parties' intention to arbitrate.

Section 7(5) of the Act provides that reference in a contract to a document containing an arbitration clause constitutes an arbitration agreement. In a recent judgment in ***Inox Wind Ltd. v. Thermocables Ltd.***, the Supreme Court of India clarified that "*though general reference to an earlier contract is not sufficient for incorporation of an arbitration clause in the later contract, a general reference to a standard form would be enough for incorporation of the arbitration clause*".[8]

Arbitrability

Section 2 (1)(f) of the Act defines international commercial arbitration, as follows:

"Section 2 (1)(f). 'international commercial arbitration' means an arbitration relating to disputes arising out of legal relationships, whether contractual or not, considered as commercial under the law in force in India..." (Emphasis added.)

The Supreme Court of India in ***A. Ayyasamy v. A. Paramasivam and Ors.***[9] ("***Ayyasamy***") noted that certain disputes like criminal offences of a public nature, disputes arising out of illegal agreements and disputes relating to status, such as divorce, cannot be referred to arbitration. The court also pointed out some of the categories of disputes that are generally treated as non-arbitrable:

(i) patent, trade marks and copyright;

(ii) anti-trust/competition laws;

(iii) insolvency/winding up;

(iv) bribery/corruption;

(v) fraud; and

(vi) criminal matters.

In terms of IP rights, the matter will not be arbitrable if the dispute arises as regards the grant of the right itself. However, for disputes arising out of commercial contracts involving such rights – for instance, disputes arising out of copyright licensing agreements are arbitrable. In other words, *inter partes* disputes are arbitrable.

Arbitrability of disputes where allegations of criminal offence and/or corruption are raised

It is a well-settled principle that **only** if a matter is commercial, is it arbitrable.

In India as well as in other countries, one of the objections which a reluctant Respondent tries to raise to thwart the arbitral process is to allege that there are elements of fraud and/or corruption which are connected to the subject matter of the arbitration, and therefore the matter is not arbitrable.

There are two relatively recent judgments of the Supreme Court of India which are very instructive on the issues involving allegations of fraud and/or corruption.

In case of foreign-seated arbitration, the Supreme Court in ***World Sport Group (Mauritius) Ltd. v. MSM Satellite (Singapore) Pte. Ltd.***[10] held that allegations of fraud do not affect the validity of the arbitration agreement and under section 45 of the Act, the court can refer the dispute to arbitration.

In case of domestic arbitration, the Supreme Court in ***Ayyasamy***[11] has held that matters that involve allegations of "serious fraud" would not be arbitrable, but matters that had "mere allegations" of fraud were arbitrable. Serious allegation of fraud would entail "extensive evidence", and the matter would generally be "complex in nature".

Joinder / Consolidation

The Act does not contain any provision for joinder of third parties and consolidation of arbitrations. However, court decisions in this regard are instructive.

The Supreme Court of India has analysed the issue of joinder of third parties in ***Chloro Controls (I) Pvt. Ltd. v. Severn Trent Water Purification Inc. & Ors.***[12] and held that the expression, 'person claiming through or under', as provided under section 45 of the Act, would mean and include within its ambit multiple and multi-party agreements. This enables even the non-signatory parties to some of the agreements to be made parties to the arbitration. The court further held that "*...In the cases of group companies or where various agreements constitute a composite transaction like mother agreement and all other agreements being ancillary to and for effective and complete implementations of the mother agreement, the court may have to make reference to arbitration even of the disputes existing between signatory or even non-signatory. However, the discretion of the court has to be exercised in exceptional, limiting, befitting and cases of necessity and very cautiously*".[13]

As regards Consolidation, the decision of the Supreme Court of India in ***Olympus Superstructures Pvt. Ltd v. Meena Vijay Khetan and Ors.***,[14] is very useful. It was held that, where there are disputes and differences in connection with the main agreement and also disputes in regard to "other matters", "*connected*" with the subject-matter of the main agreement, arbitration shall be governed by the general arbitration clause of the main agreement. The disputes under the main agreement and disputes connected therewith can be referred to the same arbitral tribunal.[15]

Therefore, in appropriate cases, Joinder of parties and Consolidations of arbitration are possible in India.

Competence-competence / Doctrine of separability

The principles of competence-competence and separability are statutorily recognised under section 16 of the Act. The arbitral tribunal is empowered to decide matters relating to the scope of its own authority and validity of the arbitration agreement. The Act recognises that arbitration clauses are separable from the main contract and an arbitration clause which forms part of a contract shall be treated as an agreement independent of the other terms of the contract.

As per section 16(5) of the Act, if the tribunal rejects a challenge to its jurisdiction, it shall continue with the arbitral proceedings and make an award. The parties can challenge such an award under section 34 of the Act only after the final award has been rendered.[16] However, if the tribunal accepts a challenge to its jurisdiction, the order is directly appealable to court under section 37(2)(a) of the Act.

Arbitration procedure

Commencement of arbitration

Section 21 of the Act provides that a party may invoke arbitration by sending a request for the dispute to be referred to arbitration. The arbitral proceedings commence on the date on which such a request is received by the opposite party.

Seat of arbitration

Pursuant to section 20 of the Act, parties are free to agree on the place of arbitration, failing which the place of arbitration shall be determined by the arbitral tribunal. As per section 20(3) of the Act, the tribunal may meet at any place as it considers appropriate for consultation, hearing etc., unless otherwise agreed by the parties.

In a recent Supreme Court decision in ***Indus Mobile Distribution Private Ltd. v. Datawind Innovations Private & Ors.***,[17] it was held that as the juridical seat of arbitration was Mumbai, the courts in Mumbai alone would have jurisdiction to the exclusion of all other courts as regards applications made to court in relation to arbitral proceedings (even if no cause of action arose in Mumbai). This reiterates the principle of "curial support" for arbitration matters.

In the absence of any clear provision in the Act, the uncertainty as to whether two Indian parties can choose a foreign seat for arbitration was answered in ***GMR Energy Limited v. Doosan Power Systems India Private Limited & Ors.***[18] ("***GMR Energy***"). The Delhi High Court endorsed the view that two Indian parties can opt for a foreign seat of arbitration. An arbitral award made in an arbitration seat outside India would be treated as a foreign award under Part-II of the Act (Enforcement of Foreign Awards) and not under Part-I of the Act (Arbitrations seated in India). The court relied on the decision of the Madhya Pradesh High Court in ***Sasan Power Ltd. v. North American Coal Corp. (India) (P) Ltd.***,[19] which also held that two Indian parties were free to arbitrate in a place outside India, and an award rendered pursuant thereto would be a foreign award. An appeal against the decision of the single judge in ***GMR Energy*** has been filed before a division bench of the Delhi High Court and is pending.

Rules on evidence

Section 19(1) of the Act provides that the Civil Procedure Code, 1908 or the Indian Evidence Act, 1872 are not binding on the arbitral tribunal and section 19(2) provides that parties are free to agree on the procedure to be followed for the proceedings. Failing such an agreement, the arbitral tribunal is empowered to conduct proceedings as it considers appropriate.[20] Section 19(4) of the Act empowers the arbitral tribunal to determine the admissibility, relevance, materiality and weight of any evidence. The Supreme Court of India in the case of ***Srei Infrastructure Finance Limited v. Tuff Drilling Private Limited***,[21] held that the arbitral tribunal may draw guidance from the fundamental principles underlying the Code of Civil Procedure or the Indian Evidence Act.

The tribunal is empowered to appoint expert(s) to report to it on specific issues.[22] Section 26(2) of the Act provides that, if a party requests or if the arbitral tribunal considers it necessary, the experts shall participate in the oral hearing where the parties can cross-examine the expert on his report.

As regards the IBA Rules on taking of Evidence in International Arbitration, there appears to be not that many instances in India where the parties have adopted the said Rules.

Confidentiality, privilege and disclosure

There is no provision in the Act at present that specifically provides for arbitration proceedings or evidence to be kept confidential. However, the Act provides for confidentiality for conciliation proceedings under section 75 of the Act. Parties are free to incorporate confidentiality clauses in their arbitration agreements or choose institutional rules that provide for confidentiality. The MCIA Rules 2017 under Rule 35 provides for confidentiality of all matters relating to the proceedings and the award. The deliberations of the tribunal shall also be confidential. Under Rule 35.4 of the MCIA Rules 2017, the arbitral tribunal is empowered to take appropriate measures, including issuing an order or award for sanctions or costs, if a party breaches confidentiality of the proceedings. The Srikrishna Committee has recommended that a new provision may be added in the Act providing for confidentiality of arbitral proceedings unless disclosure is required by legal duty, to protect or enforce a legal right, or to enforce or challenge an award before a court or judicial authority.[23] The Amendment Bill 2018 has proposed inclusion of new section 42A in the Act, which would provide that the arbitrator and arbitral institutions shall maintain confidentiality of all arbitral proceedings except the award.

The principle of "attorney-client privilege" is provided for under sections 126 and 129 of the Indian Evidence Act, 1872. While the Indian Evidence Act does not *per se* apply to arbitration proceedings in India, the fundamental principles underlying the Evidence Act may be used as a guide for arbitration proceedings.[24]

Pursuant to section 27 of the Act, the arbitral tribunal may seek the court's assistance in taking evidence which includes production of documents. The arbitrator has the general power to order discovery, inspection and production of documents.

Fast-track procedure

The Amended Act also provides for resolution of disputes by a fast-track procedure under section 29B of the Act if the parties so agree. By opting for this procedure, parties may decide not to have oral hearings. The award is to be made within six months from the date of constitution of tribunal, unless extended by six months by agreement of parties or extended by court upon an application made by a party.

Arbitrators

The parties to an arbitration are free to agree on a procedure for appointing the arbitrator(s). If the parties fail to appoint an arbitrator or the selection mechanism has failed:

(a) in case of domestic arbitration, an application for appointment can be made to the High Court; and

(b) in case of international commercial arbitration, the parties can directly approach the Supreme Court for the appointment of arbitrator(s).[25]

The amended section 12 of the Act provides that an arbitrator can only be challenged if: (a) circumstances exist which give rise to justifiable doubts as to his independence or impartiality; or (b) he does not possess the qualifications as agreed between the parties.

When a person is approached regarding his possible appointment as an arbitrator, he has to make a disclosure in writing in a form specified in the *Sixth Schedule* of the Act, which essentially mandates an arbitrator to make disclosures regarding potential Conflict of Interest as well as provide the circumstances which are likely to affect his ability to devote sufficient time to the arbitration, and to complete the arbitration within 12 months.

The Amendment Act has incorporated the *Fifth* and *Seventh Schedules* in the Act which have been drawn from the Orange and Red lists of the IBA Guidelines on Conflicts of Interest in International Arbitration.[26] The grounds stated in the *Fifth Schedule* act as a guide in determining whether any circumstances exist that give rise to justifiable doubts as to the arbitrator's independence or impartiality. Section 12(5) of the Act, in effect, provides that if any of the grounds mentioned in the *Seventh Schedule* are attracted, then a person shall be ineligible to be appointed as an arbitrator unless the parties expressly agree in writing to waive the applicability of the provision. In ***HRD Corporation (Marcus Oil and Chemical Division) v. GAIL (India) Limited (Formerly Gas Authority of India Ltd.)***,[27] the Supreme Court held that for grounds listed under the *Fifth schedule*, the arbitral tribunal is empowered to adjudicate on the challenge and its decision can only be challenged in a setting-aside petition after the award is made. However, in case of a challenge on the grounds mentioned under any of the categories listed in the *Seventh Schedule*, the arbitrator is ineligible to continue his duties and an application to terminate his mandate can be filed directly before the court, pursuant to section 14 (2) of the Act.

The Act does not have an express provision at present regarding immunity of arbitrators. However, the Srikrishna Committee has proposed the insertion of a provision (based on the Arbitration Act of the UK) to absolve arbitrators from liability in discharge of their duties.[28] The Amendment Bill 2018 has proposed inclusion of a new section 42B that would protect an arbitrator from being sued for any act or omission done in good faith during the course of the arbitration proceedings. As regards administrative assistance to the arbitral tribunal, the Act empowers the arbitrators to arrange for administrative assistance by a suitable institution or person with the consent of the parties.[29]

Interim relief

Under the Indian law, parties have the right to approach the courts under section 9 of the Act (or arbitral tribunal, under section 17 of the Act) for interim measures. Some of the interim measures available to the parties include:

(a) the preservation, interim custody or sale of any goods which are the subject-matter of the arbitration agreement;

(b) securing the amount in dispute in the arbitration;

(c) order for detention, preservation or inspection of any property or thing which is the subject-matter of the dispute in the arbitration;

(d) interim injunction or the appointment of receiver; and

(e) such other interim measure of protection as may appear to be just and convenient to the court or arbitral tribunal.

Further, the arbitral tribunal has the same power for making orders as the court has for the purpose of, and in relation to, any proceedings before it.

There have been significant amendments to sections 9 and 17 of the Act to make interim measures more effective. Section 9(2) of the Act provides that where parties have obtained a court order for a pre-arbitration interim measure, the arbitral proceedings must commence within 90 days of such order. Once the tribunal is constituted, the court shall not entertain any application for interim measure unless the court finds that the remedy provided under section 17 may be inefficacious.[30] Section 17(2) of the Act provides that the orders of the arbitral tribunal shall be enforceable in the same manner as an order of the court.[31]

Interim measures of protection from Indian courts for arbitrations seated outside India

In ***Bhatia International v. Bulk Trading S.A. and Anr*** ("***Bhatia International***"),[32] the courts interpreted section 2(2) of the Arbitration Act to mean that Part I of the Act applied to arbitrations held in India, and also to arbitrations conducted outside India, unless it was expressly or impliedly excluded. This led to parties using this judgment to make application for setting aside foreign awards under Part I of the Act (which contains section 34 – the set-aside provision).[33] This led to a lot of criticism of Indian arbitration in international legal circles. The Supreme Court of India in ***Bharat Aluminium v. Kaiser Aluminiun Technical Services*** ("***BALCO***"),[34] overruled ***Bhatia International*** and held that Part I of the Act will not be applicable to arbitrations seated outside India. However, this led to a situation where parties could not get interim relief from Indian courts against possible dissipation of assets where the seat of arbitration was outside India. To overcome this lacuna, section 2(2) of the Act has been amended in 2015 to clarify that provisions for interim measures provided under section 9, which falls under Part I of the Act, shall apply to international commercial arbitrations even if the seat of arbitration is outside India.

Anti-suit injunction

Section 8 of the Act provides that where an action in a matter which is the subject of an arbitration agreement is brought before a judicial authority, the courts must refer the parties to arbitration unless it finds that *prima facie* no valid agreement exists. Similarly, under section 45 of the Act, the court can refer the parties to arbitration where arbitration is seated outside India. The Supreme Court of India in ***Sasan Power Limited v. North American Coal Corporation India Private Limited,***[35] clarified that where a matter is brought before a court under section 45 of the Act, the court can only look into the question as to whether the arbitration agreement is "*null and void, inoperative or incapable of being performed but not the legality and validity of the substantive contract*".

Anti-arbitration injunction

There have been instances where the courts in India have granted injunctions in aid of domestic litigation but have been overturned by the Supreme Court of India.

In ***World Sport Group (Mauritius) Ltd v. MSM Satellite (Singapore) Pte Ltd,***[36] the Supreme Court set aside the anti-arbitration injunction granted by a Division Bench of the Bombay High Court and opined that the only bar to refer parties to foreign-seated arbitration is where the arbitration agreement was null and void, inoperative or incapable of being performed.

Security for costs

While there is a provision under sections 9 and 17 of the Act for securing the amount in dispute, there is no express provision under the Act for security for costs. However, it can fall within the ambit of sections 9 and 17 of the Act which allows the court or the arbitral tribunal, as appropriate, to make any interim measure in an arbitration as a court could make for the purpose of, and in relation to, any proceedings before it. Thus, the court or tribunal may grant security for costs in an arbitration. MCIA Rule 29(e) provides that the arbitral tribunal can order any party to provide security for legal or other costs in any manner it thinks fit. In India, applications for security for costs are quite rare.

Arbitration award

Section 31 of the Act, which provides for the form and content of an arbitral award, states that the award must be in writing and signed by all or majority of the arbitrators. The arbitral award shall state the reasons upon which it is based, unless the parties have agreed otherwise or if it is a consent award. The award shall state the date and place of arbitration.

As the majority of arbitrations in India are conducted on an *ad hoc* basis without any institutional oversight, there was a tendency for arbitration proceedings to be protracted for years, resulting in delay in the rendering of awards. This is one of the main reasons India was seen as a less preferred seat of arbitration. To rectify this problem, the Amendment Act has added section 29A to the Act, which provides that the award shall be made within a period of 12 months from the date the arbitral tribunal enters upon the reference. The parties may agree to an extension of not more than six months.[37] If the award is not made within a period of 12 months or the extended period, the mandate of the arbitrator(s) shall terminate unless the court has, on an application in writing made before it, extended the period for making the award, either prior to or after the expiry of the period of 12 or 18 months, as the case may be.

This strict timeline has made it practically difficult for parties involved in complex and document-intensive arbitration matters to complete the arbitration within 12/18 months. To this end, the Srikrishna Committee recommended that section 29A of the Act be amended to:

(a) limit its application to domestic arbitrations only, and not international commercial arbitrations;
(b) provide for a six-month period for the submission of pleadings;
(c) provide that the time limit for completion of arbitral proceedings starts to run after the six-month time period;
(d) provide for the continuation of the mandate of the arbitral tribunal during the pendency of an application to extend the time limit; and
(e) provide that the application is deemed granted if it is not disposed of within the period mentioned in section 29A (i.e. within 60 days).

The Amendment Bill 2018 has proposed an amendment to exclude international arbitrations from the purview of section 29A. Further, there is also a proposal that the period of 12 months to make an award (which would apply only to domestic arbitrations) should commence from the date of completion of pleadings by the parties.

Costs

The Act also allows the arbitral tribunal to order costs. The Amendment Act introduces a new section 31A to the Act which is based on the Law Commission's recommendation that "*The loser-pays rule logically follows, as a matter of law, from the very basis of deciding the underlying dispute in a particular manner; and as a matter of economic policy, provides economically efficient deterrence against frivolous conduct and furthers compliance with contractual obligations*."[38] The tribunal has the discretion to decide the amount of such costs and when such costs are to be payable. However, when ordering costs the tribunal may have regard to the conduct of parties; whether a party has succeeded partly in that case; frivolous counter-claims leading to delay; and reasonable offer to settle by one party.

Interest

Section 31(7)(a) of the Act provides that unless otherwise agreed by the parties, the arbitral tribunal may include in the award interest, at such rate as it deems reasonable on the whole or any part of the sum awarded, for the whole or any part of the period from the date when the cause of action arose until the date of the award.

As regards post-award interest, section 31(7)(b) of the Act provides that, unless the award otherwise directs, any sum directed to be paid in an arbitral award shall carry interest at a rate of 2% higher than the current rate of interest prevalent on the date of award, from the date of the award to the date of payment. "Current rate of Interest" means the highest of the maximum rates at which interest may be paid on different classes of deposits (other than those maintained in savings accounts or those maintained by charitable or religious institutions) by different classes of scheduled banks, in accordance with the directions given or issued to banking companies generally by the Reserve Bank of India ("RBI") under the Banking Regulation Act 1949.[39] For example, if the maximum rate of interest to be paid by any Scheduled Bank as directed by the RBI at any given period is say 7%, then the post-award interest would be 9% (i.e. 7% + 2%). Until the Amendment Act of 2015, the statute provided for a default rate of post-award interest of 18% *per annum*.

Challenge of the arbitration award

In India, there is no provision in the Act for appeal against an award. The only recourse for a party is to file an application to set aside the award on very limited grounds under section 34 of the Act.[40]

Section 34 of the Act provides that an arbitral award may be set aside by the court only if the party making the application furnishes proof that:

(i) the party was under some incapacity;

(ii) the arbitration agreement was not valid;

(iii) proper notice of the appointment of an arbitrator was not given or the party was unable to present its case;

(iv) the award fell outside the scope of the arbitration agreement;

(v) composition of the tribunal or the arbitral procedure was not in accordance with the agreement of the parties;

(vi) the subject matter of the dispute is not capable of settlement by arbitration; or

(vii) the award is in conflict with the public policy of India.

In the past, the ground of "public policy" was often used to set aside awards in India. An analysis of some of the cases where 'public policy' has been discussed by the Supreme Court of India is as follows:

In the case of ***Renusagar Power Electric Co v. General Electric Co***[41] ("***Renusagar***"), the Supreme Court held that the term "public policy" should be construed narrowly. It held that enforcement of a foreign award would be refused on the ground that it is contrary to public policy if it is contrary to fundamental policy of Indian law; the interests of India and justice or morality. In the case of ***Oil and Natural Gas Corporation v. Saw Pipes Ltd. ("Saw Pipes")***,[42] the issue was whether an award made in India could be set aside on the ground of "public policy" as the arbitral tribunal had incorrectly applied the law of liquidated damages. The Supreme Court added the ground of "patent illegality" under section 34 to challenge an arbitral award.

In the case of ***Bhatia International***,[43] the Supreme Court held that Part I of the Act would apply to arbitrations seated outside India, unless it was expressly or impliedly excluded. In ***Venture Global Engineering v. Satyam Computer Services Ltd***,[44] the ratio in ***Bhatia International*** was followed and the Supreme Court applied the expanded view of public policy and ruled that a foreign award can be set aside under the public policy exception in section 34(2)(b)(ii), which fell under Part I of of the Act.

In ***BALCO***,[45] the Supreme Court held that Part I would not be applicable to arbitral proceedings seated outside India, and overruled Bhatia International. This judgment only applied prospectively, i.e. to agreements executed on or after 6 September 2012 (the date of the judgment). However, the Supreme Court in BALCO did not distinguish the term "public policy" under section 34 and section 48 of the Act (which deals with foreign awards).

In ***ONGC Ltd v. Western Geco International Ltd*** ("***Western Geco***"),[46] the Supreme Court interpreted the term "public policy" in section 34 of the Act widely. The Court held that the term "fundamental policy of India", which is an ingredient in the interpretation of the term "public policy", included judicial approach, principles of natural justice and Wednesbury's principle of reasonableness.

In ***Associate Builders v. DDA***,[47] when applying the public policy test under section 34 of the Act, the Supreme Court held that the court "*does not act as a court of appeal and consequently errors of fact cannot be corrected. A possible view by the arbitrator on facts has necessarily to pass muster as the arbitrator is the ultimate master of the quantity and quality of evidence to be relied upon when he delivers his arbitral award. Thus an award based on little evidence or on evidence which does not measure up in quality to a trained legal mind would not be held to be invalid on this score*".

With respect to fundamental policy of Indian law, the court held that challenge would include factors such as: violations of foreign exchange legislation; disregarding orders and binding judgments of superior courts; and three principles followed in the ***Western Geco***[48] judgment. The court held that factors for an award to be construed as being against justice and morality would include: an award shocking the conscience of the court; and the tribunal awarding sums more than the parties' claim. The court also held that award would be patently illegal if the award was induced by fraud or corruption; the award contravenes the substantial law of India where the illegality goes to the root of the matter; the award contravenes the Act; and the tribunal failed to decide the dispute in accordance with the terms of the contract.

The amendment to section 34 has significantly restricted the scope for setting aside the award on the grounds of public policy. Explanation 1 to section 34(2)(b) clarifies that an award is in conflict with the public policy of India only if the award:

- was induced or affected by fraud or corruption or in violation of section 75 (confidentiality as regards conciliation) or section 81 (matters discussed in conciliation proceedings used as evidence in arbitral or judicial proceedings); or
- is in contravention with the fundamental policy of Indian law; or
- is in conflict with the most basic notions of morality and justice;[49] or
- in case of domestic arbitrations, the award may be set aside if it is vitiated by patent illegality on the face of the award. However, an award cannot be set aside merely on the ground of an erroneous application of the law.[50]

From the above analysis, it is clear that the Indian courts are taking a pro-arbitration approach. The courts are hesitant to set aside domestic awards and allow applications for resisting enforcement of foreign awards on mere allegations of violation of public policy. Moreover, the scope of public policy has been clarified and narrowed by the amendments.

Prior to the Amendment Act, a petition to set aside an award led to an automatic stay of the enforcement proceedings until the petition under section 34 was finally disposed of, virtually depriving the award creditor of the benefits of an award made in his favour. Section 36 has been amended in an attempt to rectify this anomaly. It provides that an application filed under section 34 to set aside the award shall not by itself render the award unenforceable.[51] The amendment requires the party to file a separate application for stay of the enforcement proceedings. While considering the application for grant of stay, the court can even order the award debtor to furnish security.[52]

<u>Can an award be modified?</u>

An award once made is final and binding. It cannot be modified save for correction, interpretation and additional award (on aspects missed out). Section 33 of the Act empowers the arbitral tribunal to correct any error in computation, any clerical or typographical error or any errors of a similar nature, either upon a request by a party, or on its initiative within 30 days of receipt of the award by the parties. The arbitral tribunal can also give an interpretation of a specific point or part of the award[53] or make an additional award[54] as to any claim presented in the arbitral proceedings, but omitted from the award.

Enforcement of the arbitration award

India is a signatory to both the New York Convention and Geneva Convention. Part II of the Act provides for enforcement of foreign awards under both conventions. Only those foreign awards that arise out of legal relationships, whether contractual or not, considered as commercial under the law in force in India, are enforceable. Further, India follows the reciprocity principle and limits the enforcement of arbitral awards to those made in other New York Convention and Geneva Convention countries. The awards that are recognised are those that have been made at a seat in a country notified by the Central Government of India under section 44 and section 53 of the Act, respectively.

Formal requirements

The party applying for the enforcement of a foreign award shall, at the time of the filing an application for enforcement, produce before the court the original award or a copy thereof, duly authenticated in the manner required by the law of the country in which it was made. The party also needs to produce the original agreement for arbitration or a duly certified copy thereof and such evidence as may be necessary to prove that the award is a foreign award.[55] In case the award or agreement to be produced is in a foreign language, the party seeking to enforce the award shall produce a translation in English certified as correct by diplomatic or consular agent of the country to which the party belongs, or certified as correct in such other manner as may be sufficient according to the law in force in India.[56]

Conditions for enforcement of a foreign award

Enforcement of a foreign award may be refused under section 48 of the Act on broadly similar grounds as provided in section 34 of the Act, except that an application to resist enforcement of a foreign award under section 48 cannot be made on the ground that the award was patently illegal and therefore against the public policy of India. Some important case laws in this regard are discussed below:

In the case of ***Shri Lal Mahal Limited v. Progetto Grano Spa***[57] ("***Shri Lal Mahal***"), the Supreme Court held that the wider meaning given to the expression "public policy" in the *Saw Pipes* case would not be applicable in the case of enforcement under section 48 of the Act. The court applied the decision of *Renusagar*, and held that the expression "public policy of India" must be given a narrow meaning. Therefore, an award cannot be refused enforcement under section 48 of the Act if it is "patently illegal".

In ***Cruz City 1 Mauritius Holdings v. Unitech Limited,***[58] the Delhi High Court held that the defence of public policy to resist enforcement of a foreign award, is extremely narrow and the same could not be equated to offending any particular provision or a statute. The expression "fundamental policy of law" must be interpreted in that perspective and must mean only the fundamental and substratal legislative policy and not a provision of any enactment.

In the case of ***NTT Docomo Inc v. Tata Sons Limited,***[59] the arbitral tribunal had ruled in favour of Docomo in a dispute arising out of a shareholder agreement. Docomo filed an application before the Delhi High Court for enforcement of the award. Tata Sons had initially resisted the enforcement, but subsequently withdrew all its objections in relation to the enforcement of the award. The Reserve Bank of India ("**RBI**") filed an intervention application on the ground that Shareholders' Agreement between Docomo and Tata Sons was violative of the Foreign Exchange Management Act ("**FEMA**") Regulations. It contended that inasmuch as it concluded that FEMA Regulations need not be looked into, the award was illegal and contrary to the public policy of India. The court held that the sum awarded by the arbitral tribunal was in the nature of damages and not price of the shares. It further held that there was nothing in the shareholders' agreement as interpreted by the award which was opposed to the public policy or fundamental policy of India. The court rejected the RBI's argument, held that the award was enforceable and also that there was nothing in the Consent Terms between the parties which could be said to be contrary to any provision of Indian law, much less opposed to public policy or void or voidable under the Indian Contract Act.

In ***Glencore International AG v. Dalmia Cement (Bharat) Limited***,[60] an application was filed by Glencore for enforcement of an arbitration award made by a tribunal constituted under the LCIA Rules. Dalmia Cement filed objections under section 48 of the Act, contending that the award was opposed to the public policy of India, as the arbitral tribunal had awarded damages in favour of Glencore, without Glencore establishing or furnishing any documentary proof of the loss suffered by it. The court noted that Dalmia Cement had full opportunity to contest the veracity and the evidentiary value of the documents produced by Glencore, and rejected Dalmia's objections under section 48 of the Act.

The issue of interpretation of "public policy" with respect to enforcement of foreign awards was recently dealt by the Delhi High Court in ***Daiichi Sankyo Company Ltd. v. Malvinder Mohan Singh and Ors***,[61] and the court ruled in favour of enforcement of the award. Taking a pro-arbitration approach, the court followed the ratio laid down by the Supreme Court in *Shri Lal Mahal* and held that the scope of "public policy" under section 48(2)(b) of the Act is narrow in comparison to section 34(2)(b)(ii) of the Act. "Fundamental Policy of Indian Law" does not mean provisions of the statute, but substratal principles on which Indian Law is founded. A special leave petition, filed before the Supreme Court of India seeking permission to appeal against the above decision of the Delhi High Court, was dismissed *in limine* by the Supreme Court. Therefore, the judgment of the Delhi High Court in favour of enforcement of the foreign award stands good.

<u>Can an arbitration award be enforced if it has been set aside at the courts of the seat of arbitration</u>?

Pursuant to section 48(1)(e) of the Act, at the request of the party against whom enforcement of a foreign award is invoked, the courts may refuse enforcement if the award has not yet become binding on the parties, or has been set aside or suspended by a competent authority of the country in which, or under the law of which, that award was made.[62] In other words, it is the discretion of the court to refuse enforcement if the award was set aside by a court at the seat of arbitration.

<u>Trends of enforcement in India – pro-arbitration or anti-arbitration</u>

As regards recent trends of enforcement in India, we can say that it is pro-arbitration. The amendments to the Act, including the provisions dealing with recourse against awards and enforcement, were made in the year 2015. A Presidential ordinance was promulgated on 23 October 2015 to amend the Act. Within two months the Amendment Act was passed by the Parliament, based on the ordinance and was made effective from 23 October 2015. A year thereafter, i.e. in January 2017, a high-level committee was constituted to look at the institutionalisation of the arbitration mechanism in India, *viz.*, the Srikrishna Committee. Within seven months of its constitution, the committee came up with its report, proposing among other things, tweaks to the amendments made to the Act, so as to remove practical problems faced by the users of arbitration in India. Pursuant to the recommendations of the Srikrishna Committee, the Cabinet of the Central Government of India approved the Amendment Bill 2018 on 7 March 2018. It is also pertinent to note from the judgments discussed under the headings, "Challenge of the arbitration award" and "Enforcement of the arbitration award", that the judiciary in India has been increasingly supportive of arbitration.

Investment arbitration

Bilateral Investment Treaties (BITs)

As of this date, India has signed 83 Bilateral Investment Treaties ("**BITs**"). However, in the year 2017, India gave notice to 58 countries terminating the BITs, and has suggested that they renegotiate the treaty based on the Model BIT that India came up with in 2016. The Model BIT has been criticised, as it is perceived to be in favour of the host state.

Multi-lateral Investment Treaties (MITs)

India is not a party to any of the major Multi-lateral investment treaties. Specifically, India is not a party to the ICSID Convention or even the Energy Charter Treaty. However, India has signed the India-ASEAN Comprehensive Economic Cooperation Agreement (India-ASEAN CECA). ASEAN (Association of South East Asian Nations) consists of Thailand, Indonesia, Vietnam, Philippines, Malaysia, Singapore, Myanmar, Cambodia, Laos and Brunei.

Recent investment arbitration cases against India

In recent years, about 23 investment arbitrations were commenced against India. Out of these cases, three investment arbitration awards were rendered against India, in: (i) ***White Industries v. Republic of India***; (ii) ***Devas v. India***; and (iii) ***Deutsche Telekom v. India***.

In ***White Industries v. Republic of India***,[63] an award was made against India. In this case, an ICC award in a commercial arbitration between White Industries and Coal India was sought to be enforced in India. As it was delayed for many years, White Industries initiated a BIT arbitration under the India-Australia BIT and an award was eventually rendered in its favour. The Union of India did not take any recourse against this award. We understand that the matter was settled and the payment was made pursuant to the award.

We understand that the awards made in ***Devas v. India*** and in ***Deutsche Telekom v. India*** have been challenged and are pending.

Treatment of investment arbitration awards by national courts

The manner in which the national courts in India treat investment arbitral awards has not been tested to date.

* * *

Endnotes

1. *See Bharat Aluminium v. Kaiser Aluminium* (2012) 9 SCC 552 at para 30.
2. *Ibid* at para 36.
3. Preamble to the Act.

4. Section 2(1)(e) of the Act and section 11 of the Act.
5. Section 2(1)(c) of the Commercial Courts Act defines a "commercial dispute" and covers the subject matters that would fall within its ambit.
6. Sections 2(1)(i) and 10 of the Commercial Courts Act.
7. *Jagdish Chander v. Ramesh Chander*, (2007) 5 SCC 719 at para 8.
8. 2018 SCC OnLine SC 3 at para 19.
9. (2016) 10 SCC 386 at para 14.
10. (2014) 11 SCC 639 at para 36.
11. (2016) 10 SCC 386 at paras 23 and 18.
12. (2013) 1 SCC 641 at para 165.1.
13. *Ibid* at para 165.2.
14. (1999) 5 SCC 651.
15. *Ibid* at para 30.
16. Section 16(6) of the Act.
17. (2017) 7 SCC 678 at paras 20 and 21.
18. (2017) SCC OnLine Del 11625 at paras 44 and 45.
19. (2015) SCC OnLine MP 7417 at paras 57 and 72.
20. Section 19(3) of the Act.
21. 2017 SCC OnLine SC 1210 at para 16.
22. Section 26(1) of the Act.
23. Srikrishna Committee Report at pages 71 and 72.
24. *Srei Infrastructure Finance Limited v. Tuff Drilling Private Limited*, 2017 SCC OnLine SC 1210 at para 16.
25. Section 11(6) of the Act.
26. Law Commission Report, page 30 at para 59.
27. 2017 SCC OnLine SC 1024 at para 13.
28. Srikrishna Committee Report at pages 70 and 71, para 12.
29. Section 6 of the Act.
30. Section 9(3) of the Act.
31. Section 17(2) of the Act.
32. (2002) 4 SCC 105 at para 32.
33. *See Venture Global Engineering v. Satyam Computer Services Ltd.*, (2008) 4 SCC 190.
34. (2012) 9 SCC 552 at paras 89, 195 and 196.
35. (2016) 10 SCC 813 at para 49.
36. (2014) 11 SCC 639 at paras 39 and 40.
37. Section 29A (3) of the Act.
38. Law Commission Report, page 34 at para 71.
39. Section 2 (b) of the Interest Act, 1978.
40. Section 34 (1) of the Act.
41. 1994 Supp (1) SCC 644 at para 66.
42. (2003) 5 SCC 705 at para 22.
43. (2002) 4 SCC 105 at para 32.
44. (2008) 4 SCC 190 at paras 37 and 47.
45. (2012) 9 SCC 552 at paras 89, 195 and 196.
46. (2014) 9 SCC 263 at paras 35, 38 and 39.
47. (2015) 3 SCC 49 at para 33.
48. 2014 (9) SCC 263 at paras 35, 38 and 39.
49. Explanation 1 to section 34(2) of the Act.

50. Section 34(2A) of the Act.
51. Section 36 (2) of the Act.
52. Section 36 (3) of the Act.
53. Section 33 (1) (b) of the Act.
54. Sections 33 (4) and (5) of the Act.
55. Section 47 (1) of the Act.
56. Section 47 (2) of the Act.
57. (2014) 2 SCC 433 at para 29.
58. 2017 SCC OnLine Del 7810 at para 97.
59. 2017 SCC OnLine Del 8078 at paras 51, 61 and 64.
60. 2017 SCC OnLine Del 8932 at para 38.
61. 2018 SCC OnLine Del 6869 at paras 61, 96 and 97.
62. Section 48 (1) (e) of the Act.
63. Award dated 30 November 2011.

Ganesh Chandru
Tel: +91 97171 18642 / Email: ganesh.chandru@lakshmisri.com

Ganesh Chandru is an Executive Partner at Lakshmikumaran & Sridharan ("L&S") and he heads the firm's International Arbitration Practice Group. He is admitted to practice in India, England & Wales and Singapore and is a Fellow of the Chartered Institute of Arbitrators, UK and the Singapore Institute of Arbitrators.

His practice encompasses advising and representing parties in international arbitration matters (under Rules of SIAC, ICC, LCIA, SCMA, UNCITRAL as well as *ad hoc*) and in arbitration matters seated in India that are conducted pursuant to the Arbitration and Conciliation Act, 1996. He also advises and represents parties in litigation matters before the courts. He sits as an arbitrator in international arbitrations and is a member of the Panel of Arbitrators of SIAC, Singapore Institute of Arbitrators and the Kuala Lumpur Regional Centre for Arbitration.

Prior to joining L&S in New Delhi in 2015, he spent more than 16 years in Singapore specialising in International Arbitration and Dispute Resolution. He worked with some top International law firms and Singapore law firms. Between 2002 and 2007, Ganesh was the Counsel & Assistant Registrar of the Singapore International Arbitration Centre. He supervised the administration of about 500 arbitrations during his five-year stint at SIAC, and also pioneered SIAC's initiatives in India. He has been recognised in the *Global Arbitration Review 100* (2009) as a "Significant" name and has been listed as one of the "Future Leaders" by *Who's Who Legal* and the *Global Arbitration Review* (GAR), London in the first edition of *Arbitration: Future Leaders 2017* as well as in *Who's Who Legal: Arbitration 2018.*

Prashant Kumar
Tel: +91 11 4129 9894 / Email: prashant.kumar@lakshmisri.com

Prashant Kumar is a Senior Associate in the International Arbitration Practice Group of Lakshmikumaran & Sridharan. Prashant obtained a Bachelor of Laws degree with first class honours from the Gujarat National Law University in May 2010. He has very good experience in arbitration and commercial matters and has appeared before the Supreme Court of India, and various High Courts and tribunals.

Palak Taneja
Tel: +91 11 4129 9954 / Email: palak.taneja@lakshmisri.com

Palak Taneja is an Associate in the International Arbitration Practice Group of Lakshmikumaran & Sridharan. She graduated from the Georgetown University Law Center, Washington, D.C. in May 2016 with a Master of Laws degree in International Business and Economic Law and completed a Certificate Course in International Arbitration and Dispute Resolution. She also interned with the International Chamber of Commerce in New York. Palak obtained a dual degree of Bachelor of Arts and Bachelor of Laws with first class honours from the University School of Law and Legal Studies, GGSIPU, New Delhi in July 2014.

Lakshmikumaran & Sridharan

5, Link Road, Jangpura Extension, New Delhi 110014, India
Tel: +91 11 4129 9800 / URL: www.lakshmisri.com

Ireland

Kevin Kelly & Heather Mahon
McCann FitzGerald

Introduction

"*The realisation, in the words of Lord Simon of Glaisdale…, that litigation, while certainly preferable to personal violence, is not in itself an intrinsically desirable activity, has encouraged the search for other methods of dispute resolution each of which has attracted it adherents and enthusiasts. One of the oldest and best established of these systems is that of arbitration.*"[1]

Legislation and the UNCITRAL Model Law

There has been a good history of arbitration being supported in Ireland. The Arbitration Act 1954 was passed "*to make further and better provision in respect of arbitrations*" and gave effect to the Geneva Convention of 1927 on the execution of foreign arbitral awards. The Arbitration Act 1980 gave effect to the New York Convention of 1958 on the recognition and enforcement of foreign arbitral awards and certain provisions of the Washington Convention of 1965 on the settlement of investment disputes. The Arbitration (International Commercial) Act, 1998 adopted the UNCITRAL Model Law for international commercial arbitration.

However, the 1954, 1980 and 1998 Acts have been repealed and the legislation which governs arbitration proceedings in Ireland now is the Arbitration Act 2010 (the "**2010 Act**") which applies to all arbitrations, both domestic and international. The law governing international arbitration is based on the UNCITRAL Model Law and the 2010 Act adopts the UNCITRAL Model Law, as amended on 7 July 2006.

The UNCITRAL Model Law is reproduced in its entirety as a schedule to the Act. Section 6 of the 2010 Act provides that, subject to the provisions of that Act, "*the Model Law shall have the force of law in the State*".

The 2010 Act (and, through it, the UNCITRAL Model Law) applies to all arbitrations commenced in Ireland on or after 8 June 2010. It restates that effect is given to the Geneva Convention and Protocol 1923, the New York Convention 1958 and the Washington Convention 1965.

Courts

There is no special national court for international or domestic arbitrations. Section 9 of the 2010 Act states that the High Court is the relevant court for the purposes of the Act.

Arbitration bodies

There are a number of arbitration bodies in Ireland. Arbitration Ireland (The Irish Arbitration Association) comprises members from bodies, firms and persons actively involved in the practice of international arbitration in Ireland. The Chartered Institute of Arbitrators also has an Irish branch. There are also industry-specific bodies which support arbitration, such as Engineers Ireland.

Arbitration agreements

In writing

The 2010 Act applies Option 1 of Article 7 of the UNCITRAL Model Law (the "**Model Law**") to the requirements of an arbitration agreement. An arbitration agreement is defined as "*[a]n agreement … to submit to arbitration … disputes which have arisen or which may arise … in respect of a defined legal relationship whether contractual or not*". The arbitration agreement must be in writing, whether in the form of an arbitration clause in a contract or in the form of a separate agreement. An agreement will be in writing if its content is recorded in any form, notwithstanding that the arbitration agreement or contract may have been concluded orally, by conduct or other means. "*In writing*" includes electronic data interchange, email, telegram, telex or telecopy. It may be in the exchange of the claim and the defence and it may be incorporated by reference.

Disputes excluded from the 2010 Act

Section 30 of the 2010 Act clarifies that the 2010 Act does not apply to:

(i) disputes regarding the terms or conditions of employment or the remuneration of employees;

(ii) arbitrations conducted under Section 70 of the Industrial Relations Act 1946; or

(iii) arbitrations conducted by a property arbitrator appointed under Section 2 of the Property Values (Arbitration and Appeals) Act 1960.

Consumer disputes, where the arbitration clauses are not individually negotiated and where the disputes are worth less than €5,000, are only arbitrable at the election of the consumer. A "*Consumer*" is a person acting outside his trade, business or profession.

Arbitrator's jurisdiction

An arbitrator is permitted to rule on the question of his or her own jurisdiction pursuant to Article 16(1) of the Model Law. This provides that the "*arbitral tribunal may rule on its own jurisdiction*", which includes any questions regarding the existence or validity of the arbitration agreement, thereby granting the arbitrator primary responsibility for deciding whether he or she has jurisdiction to decide the dispute. However, this power is not final as an appeal can be made to the High Court under Article 16(3), and there is no appeal allowable from the High Court's decision. An assertion that the tribunal does not have jurisdiction must be raised no later than the submission of the statement of defence, as per Article 8 of the Model Law.

In *Mayo County Council v Joe Reilly Plant Hire Limited*,[2] the High Court refused an application for a direction pursuant to Article 16(3) of the Model Law, and Order 56 Rule (1) (3) (f) of the Rules of the Superior Courts, that an arbitrator had no jurisdiction to adjudicate upon a claim made by the respondent against the applicant. The dispute arose in respect of the costs of works carried out by the respondent on behalf of the applicant. The contract between the parties contained an arbitration clause, which gave the arbitrator a broad power to hear a dispute of any kind, whether arising during or after the completion of the works or after the determination of the contract. The applicant did not dispute that there was a valid arbitration clause in the contract, but argued that the clause was no longer operative, as the respondent had accepted payment under the contract, and as such, there had been accord and satisfaction.

The court stated that the fact of accord and satisfaction was not a basis to challenge the arbitrator's jurisdiction (though it may instead constitute a defence to the claim made by the respondent in the arbitration). It was held that in circumstances where the existence of an arbitration clause is not in dispute, the courts will be very slow to interfere with the arbitrator's ruling on his own jurisdiction.

More recently, in *Achill Sheltered Housing Association CLG v Dooniver Plant Hire Ltd*,[3] the High Court held that a preliminary ruling by the arbitrator, that he had been validly appointed, came within the scope of Article 16(3). If an arbitrator was incorrect in determining that he had been validly appointed, he had no *locus standi* to decide a challenge to his jurisdiction, let alone to arbitrate a dispute between the parties.

Article 14 of the Model Law provides that if "*an arbitrator becomes de jure or de facto unable to perform his functions, or for other reasons fails to act without undue delay, his mandate terminates if he withdraws from his office or the parties agree upon termination*". The High Court may decide upon the termination of the mandate, but the decision of the High Court is not subject to appeal.

Validity of an arbitration agreement

The courts in this jurisdiction have long been supportive of the arbitral process and there is a line of recent authority which clearly establishes that Article 8 of the Model Law does not create a discretion to refer or not to refer matters to arbitration. If there is an arbitration clause and the dispute is within the scope of the arbitration agreement, and there is no finding that the agreement is null and void, inoperative or incapable of being performed, then a stay must be granted (*BAM Building Ltd v UCD Property Development Company Ltd*[4]). However, an element of judicial confusion persisted for a time as to the correct standard to be adopted in deciding whether to uphold an arbitration clause.

In the case of *The Lisheen Mine v Mullock & Sons (Shipbrokers) Ltd*,[5] the court considered the standard to be applied to this question. Previous cases had suggested quite a low threshold to be met by a party seeking to have proceedings referred to arbitration (*P Elliot & Co Ltd (In Receivership and In Liquidation) v FCC Elliot Construction Ltd*[6]). However, Cregan J held that the issue as to whether a valid arbitration agreement exists should be given "full judicial scrutiny", as opposed to being considered on a mere *prima facie* basis. He felt that the courts were the most appropriate venue in terms of efficiency and cost, given that the determination as to whether an arbitration agreement exists is a question of law.

This position has been followed in the case of *Sterimed Technologies International v Schivo Precision Ltd.*[7] McGovern J held that the onus is on the defendants to establish the existence of the arbitration agreement. If it discharges that burden, then the onus shifts to the plaintiffs to show that the arbitration agreement was null and void if the court proceedings are not to be stayed. The High Court stayed proceedings pending the outcome of the arbitration in Charlotte, North Carolina. Similarly, McGovern J stayed proceedings under Article 8(1) of the Model Law in *BAM Building Ltd v UCD Property Development Company Ltd*[8] on the basis that the dispute between the parties was the subject of an arbitration agreement.

In contrast, McGovern J refused to stay proceedings in *Kellys of Fantane Ltd v Bowen Construction Ltd*,[9] where he was satisfied that the parties had agreed that the discrete issue of the obligations arising out of a process of conciliation should be determined by the courts without any further conciliation or arbitration process.

Challenge to arbitrator

Article 12 of the Model Law provides that an arbitrator may be challenged if circumstances exist that give rise to justifiable doubts as to his impartiality, independence, or if he does not possess the qualifications agreed upon by the parties. The arbitrator's decision in respect of the challenge can itself be challenged by application to the High Court under Article 13 of the Model Law. The decision of the High Court is not subject to appeal.

Arbitration by agreement only

Irish law will only allow an arbitral tribunal to assume jurisdiction over individuals or entities where the parties so agree. Section 16 of the 2010 Act provides that an arbitrator may not direct that different proceedings be consolidated or heard at the same time without the agreement of the parties.

The High and Circuit Courts have power, under Section 32 of the 2010 Act, to adjourn court proceedings otherwise properly before the courts to facilitate arbitration if the relevant court thinks it appropriate to do so, provided the parties consent.

In the recent case of *Maguire v Motor Services Limited t/a MSL Park Motors & Anor*,[10] the two plaintiffs brought proceedings seeking damages from the defendants for a breach of contract in relation to the purchase of a new motor vehicle. There was a binding arbitration agreement between one plaintiff, the owner of the vehicle, and the motor dealer who had supplied it. Proceedings between them had been stayed to allow for arbitration. The issue was whether by virtue of this arbitration agreement the court should stay also proceedings between that plaintiff and the vehicle manufacturer and as between the second plaintiff and the vehicle manufacturer. Barrett J held that, while an arbitration agreement can apply to a non-party, they must meet a "sufficient connection" test, which was not met here. He held that the stay of the proceedings between the vehicle owner and the motor dealer was not appealable, but overruled the second stay, as the individual parties had not agreed between them that a dispute would go to arbitration. There was no reason why factually related but substantively different claims could not separately be adjudicated or arbitrated simultaneously without the need for further management by the court.

For arbitrations conducted in Ireland under the 2010 Act, Irish law governs the formation, validity and legality of arbitration agreements to the extent set out in that Act.

Arbitration procedure

Commencement of arbitration

Section 74 of the Statute of Limitations 1957 (as amended by the 2010 Act) sets out the manner in which arbitral proceedings are to be commenced. They are deemed to be commenced on the date on which the parties to an arbitration agreement provide as being the commencement date or, where no provision has been made by the parties as to the commencement, the date on which a written communication containing a request for the dispute to be referred to arbitration is received by the respondent. Section 74(2) makes provision for when a written communication is deemed to have been received. Article 21 of the Model Law provides that arbitral proceedings commence on the date on which a request for that dispute to be referred to arbitration is received by the respondent. The applicable limitation period will depend on the particular cause of action in law which is the subject matter of the dispute. The limitation period for contractual claims where the contract is under hand is six years from the date of the commencement or accrual of the cause of action, and 12 years where the contract is under seal, unless the parties have agreed a different limitation period (which they may do).

Procedural rules

Article 19 of the Model Law provides that the parties are entitled to set their own procedure and, failing agreement on that, it is for the arbitrator to conduct the arbitration in such manner as it considers appropriate. Chapter V of the Model Law sets out provisions regarding the conduct of arbitral proceedings covering such matters as equal treatment, determination of rules of procedure, place of arbitration, commencement, language, statements of claim and defence, hearings and written proceedings, default of a party, experts appointed by the tribunal and court assistance in taking evidence.

The parties will determine the procedure they wish to follow, particularly through the adoption in the arbitration agreement of specific institutional or trade association rules. However, if no rules are chosen and the parties cannot subsequently agree upon how the procedure is to be conducted, the arbitrator can set the procedure, which will generally be done at a procedural meeting between the parties and the tribunal, following which the tribunal will issue an order for directions. This meeting can be conducted in person or remotely, for example, by telephone. Sometimes, the parties can agree all of the procedures and provide an agreed note to the arbitrator. Article 24 of the Model Law provides that, subject to any contrary agreement by the parties, the tribunal shall decide whether to hold oral hearings, or whether the proceedings shall be conducted on the basis of documents and/or materials. If there is any question about conflicting evidence, an oral hearing is preferable so that witnesses can be examined and cross-examined.

Arbitrators are expected to treat both parties equally, with impartiality, and to give each side the opportunity to put forward their case. The maxims "*audi alteram partem*" and "*nemo index in causa sua*" ("*always hear both sides*" and "*no-one should be a judge in his own cause*" respectively) are basic principles of fair procedures which arbitrators should follow. Article 18 of the Model Law sets out that obligation in respect of fair procedures in express terms.

Oath or affirmation

Unless the parties agree otherwise, the tribunal has the power to direct that a party to an arbitration agreement or a witness be examined on oath or affirmation, and the tribunal can administer oaths for that purpose (Section 14 of the 2010 Act). Subject to the agreement of the parties, the tribunal may also: order consolidation of arbitral proceedings or concurrent hearing where the parties agree to the making of such an order (Section 16); award interest (Section 18(2)); order security for costs (Section 19); require specific performance of a contract (save in respect of land) (Section 20); and determine costs (Section 21(3)). The arbitrator is also expected to render a reasoned award in writing.

Privilege of documents

Documents will be exempt from production if they can be said to fall into a recognised category of privilege. The usual types of privilege in this context are legal professional privilege applying to documents prepared in contemplation of legal proceedings ("litigation privilege") and documents prepared for the purpose of giving or obtaining legal advice ("legal advice privilege"). Generally, communications between a party and its lawyers, whether external or in-house, will attract privilege if they are for the dominant purpose of receiving or requesting legal advice or relate to legal proceedings, whether in being or in contemplation. There is a limited exception in respect of in-house lawyers who cannot claim legal professional privilege protection when the company is under investigation by the European Commission in competition proceedings. Without-prejudice communications, which are used in the context of trying to reach settlement or narrowing issues in dispute, are exempt from production, subject to limited exceptions. They need not be stated to be "without prejudice" if their purpose is to reach a settlement; also, stating that they are "without prejudice" will not protect them if they are not truly aimed at the purpose of reaching a settlement. In general terms, privilege in documents may be waived by the party who prepared the document or the party for whom it was prepared, and care should be taken by clients and advisors not to waive privilege inadvertently.

Confidentiality

There is no express statutory provision in the 2010 Act that arbitration proceedings are to be confidential or that the parties are subject to an implied duty of confidentiality. However, in practice there is English authority (which is of persuasive effect in the Irish courts) to the effect that the existence and content of arbitration proceedings usually remain confidential. The implied duty of confidentiality was affirmed by the English Court of Appeal in *Ali Shipping Corp v Shipyard Trogir*.[11] This was the first case where confidentiality was considered by the Court of Appeal, which confirmed that a general duty of confidentiality was implied at law. It recognised that the boundaries of this duty had not yet been delineated, and recognised a number of exceptions to the duty, such as consent, court order, or leave of the court. In situations where preservation of the confidentiality of the arbitration is deemed crucial to both parties, it is advisable to explicitly detail the extent of the obligation in the arbitration clause.

Arbitrators

The essence of arbitration as a private means of resolving a dispute is that the parties may choose their arbitrator, and they can decide on whether to have one or more arbitrators. In the absence of agreement on appointment, or a default mechanism, the 2010 Act provides that the number of arbitrators shall be one. Given that agreement upon the identity of the arbitrator can be difficult to reach, especially when a dispute has arisen on some aspect of the substance of the agreement, it is prudent to include a mechanism for the appointment by an agreed nominating professional body, with provision that the parties will be bound by the choice made by such nominating professional body. There is no equivalent to the guides which are commonly used in international arbitration such as *Smit's Roster of International Arbitrators*, although members of the Chartered Institute of Arbitrators have their details displayed on the Institute's website.

If the parties' method for selecting an arbitrator does not produce a result, the High Court will, pursuant to Article 11 of the Model Law, appoint the arbitrator on application to it.

The High Court may intervene in the selection of an arbitrator where the parties cannot agree upon an arbitrator and have no default mechanism in their agreement for appointment, or where there is a challenge under Article 13 of the Model Law.

Bias and conflicts of interest

The arbitrator should not be biased and this is enshrined in Article 12 of the Model Law, which provides that where a person is approached in connection with appointment as an arbitrator, they are obliged to disclose any circumstances that are likely to give rise to justifiable doubts as to impartiality or independence. The duty to make such disclosure is on-going and an arbitrator is obliged to disclose any such circumstances throughout the proceedings.

Immunity

Section 22 of the 2010 Act provides that an arbitrator "shall not be liable in any proceedings for anything done or omitted in the discharge or purported discharge of his or her functions".

Such immunity also extends to any agent, employee, advisor or expert appointed by the arbitrator. This followed the old common law position from the case of *Redahan v Minister for Education and Science*[12] that arbitrators enjoy immunity from suit in negligence except in cases of bad faith.

Arbitral secretaries

There any no rules or requirements in Ireland as to the use of arbitral secretaries and their use is not common.

Interim relief

Preliminary relief and interim measures

An arbitrator in Ireland is permitted to award preliminary or interim relief, and need not seek the assistance of the High Court to do so.

Article 17 of the Model Law provides that, unless otherwise agreed by the parties, and upon the application of one of the parties, the arbitrator has the power to order such interim measures of protection as may be considered necessary and to make a preliminary order. The arbitrator can order a party to:

(a) maintain or restore the *status quo* pending the termination of the dispute;

(b) take action that would prevent, or refrain from taking action that is likely to cause, current or imminent harm or prejudice to the arbitral process itself;

(c) provide a means of preserving assets out of which a subsequent award may be satisfied; or

(d) preserve evidence that may be relevant and material to the resolution of the dispute.

The arbitrator does not need to seek the assistance of the court to make any of these orders. However, Article 9 of the Model Law, along with Section 10 of the 2010 Act, provide that, before or during arbitral proceedings, a party may itself also request from the High Court an interim measure of protection. However, unless otherwise agreed, the court may not rely on Article 9 of the Model Law to order security for costs or discovery of documents; those are matters to be addressed by the arbitrator.

Anti-suit injunction

There is no Irish case law on anti-suit injunctions in aid of arbitration. It would seem, however, that the position under EU law has recently changed. Anti-suit injunctions were prohibited by the Court of Justice of the European Union in *Paul Turner v Felix Fareed Ismail Grovit [2004] Case No C-159-02* and *Allianz SpA (formerly Riunione Adriatica di Sicurta SpA) and Generali Assiarazioni Generali SpA v West Tankers Inc [2009] C-159-07*, on the basis that they were inconsistent with the Brussels Convention and the principle of mutual trust between member courts. In the recent case of *Gazprom OAO v Lithuania*,[13] the Court of Justice of the European Union ruled that an anti-suit injunction issued by an arbitral tribunal to prevent court proceedings in breach of an arbitral agreement is enforceable in the EU and that such an injunction is not covered by the Brussels I Regulation. It was held that proceedings for the recognition and enforcement of an arbitral anti-suit award are covered by national and international law, such as the New York Convention and not by the Brussels I Regulation. The court did not overrule its previous position in respect of a court's jurisdiction to grant anti-suit injunctions, but rather it distinguished a court-issued injunction from one granted by an arbitral tribunal. As a result, some commentators have suggested that it is arguable that arbitral tribunals now have greater anti-suit powers than judges in

EU Member States' courts. The position adopted in the *West Tankers* case may now be open to question, because in the *Gazprom* case the Advocate General observed that the prohibition on anti-suit injunctions in *West Tankers* may now be untenable due to revisions in the Brussels I Regulation, which came into force in 2015 (Regulation 1215/2012).

Where Irish court proceedings are involved and an arbitration agreement exists, rather than seeking an anti-suit injunction, a party may bring an application under Article 8 of the Model Law effectively to stay any Irish court proceedings. Article 8 of the Model Law provides that "*a court before which an action is brought in a matter which is the subject of an arbitration agreement shall, if a party so requests not later than when submitting his first statement on the substance of the dispute, refer the parties to arbitration unless it finds that the agreement is null and void, inoperative or incapable of being performed*" (discussed above).

Security for costs

An order for security for costs can be a significant advantage to a party facing a claim in arbitration, and equally may become an obstacle for a claimant in bringing forward its claim. Pursuant to Section 10(2) of the 2010 Act, the High Court is not allowed to make any order for security for costs, unless the parties agree otherwise; rather an application is to be made to the arbitrator.

Section 19 of the 2010 Act provides that unless agreed otherwise by the parties, the arbitrator may order a party to provide security for the costs of the arbitration. However, qualifications with regard to the basis upon which such security might be ordered by the arbitrator are set out at Section 19(2) of that Act. In particular, the arbitrator may not order security solely because an individual is resident, domiciled or carrying on business outside of Ireland or, in respect of a corporate, it is established, managed or controlled outside of Ireland.

Arbitration award

Making an award

Article 31 of the Model Law provides that the award shall be in writing, be signed by the arbitrator (or, if there is more than one, the majority of the arbitrators) and also set out the reasons upon which it is based, unless the parties have agreed that no reasons are to be given. The award shall also state its date and the place of arbitration. Copies of the award as made are to be delivered to the parties.

If an award also deals with costs, the tribunal must also deal with the requirements set out in Section 21 of the 2010 Act. Usual practice for an arbitrator, in domestic arbitrations, is to obtain payment of any outstanding fees before making the award available to either party. This is usually achieved by writing to both parties to inform them that the award may be taken up upon the discharge of the outstanding fees and expenses. As both parties will usually be jointly and severally liable for the arbitrator's fees and expenses, if they cannot come to an agreement to split the fees as an interim approach, one or other party will typically pay the fees and expenses and then obtain the award. The question of costs (including who is ultimately liable for the arbitrator's fees and expenses), if not dealt with in the award, will be dealt with subsequently at either a hearing or by submissions or both, leading to an award on costs.

In a situation where the arbitrator delays unduly in making his or her award, it is possible for either party to apply to the High Court pursuant to Section 9(1) of the 2010 Act and Article 14 of the Model Law to terminate the mandate of the arbitrator for failure to render the arbitral award without undue delay.

Remedies

The law applicable to the dispute will dictate the remedies that may be sought in arbitration. Subject to that, an arbitrator may determine and award damages as an Irish court would and may order any of the common law and equitable remedies including specific performance of a contract, save that without the agreement of the parties, it may not award specific performance relating to a contract for the sale of land pursuant to Section 20 of the 2010 Act.

Interest

Section 18(1) of the 2010 Act states that the party to an arbitration agreement may agree on the arbitral tribunal's powers regarding the award of interest. Unless otherwise agreed, Section 18(2) permits the tribunal to award simple or compound interest from the dates agreed, at the rates and with the rests that it considers to be fair and reasonable. It can determine such interest to be payable on all or part of the award in respect of any period up to the date of the award, or on all amounts claimed in the arbitration and outstanding at the commencement of the arbitration but paid before the award in respect of any period up to the date of payment.

Fees and costs

Section 21(1) of the 2010 Act provides that, subject to an exception for consumers (Section 21(6) of the 2010 Act regarding unfair terms), the parties may make such provision with regard to the costs of the arbitration as they see fit. The parties may, therefore, agree in advance of any dispute as to how costs will be dealt with (for example, each side will bear its own costs).

If there is no agreement pursuant to Section 21(1), or if the consumer exception applies, the tribunal shall determine, by award, those costs as it sees fit. In making a determination as to costs, the tribunal is obliged to specify the grounds on which it acted, the items of recoverable costs, fees or expenses, as appropriate, and the amount referable to each, as well as by whom and to whom they shall be paid. The general principle in respect of costs for domestic arbitrations is that the costs are at the discretion of the arbitrator, who will exercise his/her discretion in the same manner as would a court, which is that costs usually "follow the event", and the loser pays unless there is some reason not to make such an order, such as the existence of an effective *Calderbank Offer* for an amount greater than the amount awarded by the arbitrator, or where the successful party grossly exaggerates its claim.[14]

Funding litigation

Irish law still retains a prohibition against maintenance and champerty, which generally preclude those with no legitimate interest in proceedings taking part in the proceedings or obtaining any benefit therefrom. This was most recently reaffirmed by the Supreme Court in *Persona Digital Telephony Ltd v Minister for Public Enterprise, Ireland.*[15] However, contingency fees are, subject to limits and rules on methods of calculation, permissible under Irish law. Success fees and fee arrangements involving payment contingent on success are permitted.

It is also of note that it has been recently held in *Greenclean Waste Management Limited v Leahy (No 2)*[16] that After the Event Legal Costs insurance does not fall foul of the prohibition against champerty and maintenance and is, therefore, legal. After the Event Legal Costs insurance is a type of insurance policy that provides cover for the legal costs incurred in bringing or defending litigation. The policy is purchased after a legal dispute has arisen and typically provides cover for a party's own outlay, and the liability to pay the other party's legal costs in the event that the other party obtains an award of costs against it. The facts of the case required the court to consider the effect such insurance has on an application for security for costs. It was found that the existence of After the Event Legal costs insurance could be taken into account in the course of an application for security for costs. The decision of the High Court was subsequently appealed by the defendant. Although the Court of Appeal allowed the appeal, it was satisfied that such a policy could be taken into account if there was a realistic probability that the policy would cover the costs of the defendant.

Challenge to an arbitration award

Challenges to an award

There is no appeal against an arbitral award under the 2010 Act. The exclusive recourse is an application to a court to set aside the award. However, there are limited grounds upon which such an application may be made. These grounds are set out at Article 34 of the Model Law as follows:

"(a) the party making the application furnishes proof that:

(i) the party to the Arbitration Agreement referred to in Article 7 was under some incapacity, or the said agreement is not valid under the law to which the parties have subjected it or, failing any indication thereon, under the law of this State;

(ii) the party making application was not given proper notice of the appointment of an arbitrator or of the arbitral proceedings or was otherwise unable to present his case;

(iii) the award deals with the dispute not contemplated by or not falling within the terms of the submission to arbitration, or contains decisions on matters beyond the scope of the submission to arbitration, provided that, if the decisions on matters submitted to arbitration can be separated from those not so submitted, only that part of the award which contains decisions on matters not submitted to arbitration may be set aside; or

(iv) the composition of the arbitral tribunal or the arbitral procedure was not in accordance with the agreement of the parties, unless such agreement was in conflict with the provision of this Law from which the parties cannot derogate, or failing such agreement, was not in accordance with this Law; or

(b) the court finds that:

(i) the subject matter is not capable of settlement by arbitration under the law of this State; or

(ii) the award is in conflict with the public policy of this State."

If satisfied that any of the above grounds are made out, the High Court can set aside the arbitral award. An application to set aside the award may not be made after three months from receipt by the applicant of the award. Alternatively, if there is a request under Article 33 of the Model Law to correct or interpret an award, or to issue an additional award, the applicant has three months from the date on which that request had been disposed of by the tribunal.

The Irish High Court recently, and for the first time, considered the meaning of 'arbitral award' for the purposes of Article 34. In *FBD Insurance Public Limited Company v Samwari Ltd*,[17] it was noted by the court that 'arbitral award' is not defined by the Model Law, nor is it defined by the 2010 Act. It was held that in order for the court to have jurisdiction under Article 34 to set aside a decision of an arbitral tribunal, the decision must be one that was made on the merits of the case and it must meet the formal requirements of Article 31. The court observed that this must include a partial award if it met these criteria, but that procedural rulings and orders made during the course of the arbitration are not amenable to challenge under Article 34.

Under Irish law, a party may no longer:

- state a case to the High Court on a question of law;
- ask the High Court to remit the award to the arbitrator;
- ask the High Court to remove the arbitrator for misconduct;
- ask the High Court to set aside the award for misconduct; or
- seek relief where the arbitrator is not impartial or where the dispute involves a question of fraud.

In summary, recourse for a disappointed party is, broadly speaking, confined to a complaint that:

- the particular party was unable to present its case; or
- the award is in conflict with public policy.

Enforcement of the arbitration award

Enforcement of an award

Ireland ratified the New York Convention on the Recognition and Enforcement of Foreign Arbitral Awards in 1981 and no reservations have been entered. The relevant legislation is now the 2010 Act.

Ireland has not signed and/or ratified any regional conventions concerning the recognition and enforcement of arbitral awards.

Approach of the national courts to recognition and enforcement

There is no divergence in the rules on the enforcement of domestic and non-domestic awards (Article 35 of the Model Law). Article 36 of the Model Law applies in relation to the grounds for refusing recognition or enforcement of an award.

The Irish courts have shown a supportive approach to the enforcement of arbitral awards. Hussey and Dunne on "*Arbitration Law*" observe that the vast majority of challenges to the award of an arbitrator are rejected, and the strong presumption in favour of upholding an arbitrator's award has been reiterated in a number of cases, including: *Keenan v Shield Insurance*[18] and *Limerick City Council v Uniform Construction Limited.*[19] This was most recently seen in *Hoban v Coughlan,*[20] where the court upheld an award made by an arbitrator where the applicant had been absent from the proceedings but had been given adequate opportunity to engage with the process.

Section 23(1) of the 2010 Act provides that an arbitral award shall be enforceable in the State either by action or by leave of the High Court, in the same manner as a judgment or order of that court with the same effect. The 2010 Act expressly excludes any possibility of an appeal in relation to the recognition and enforcement of an arbitral award.

In the case of *Yukos Capital Sarl v OAO Tomskneft VNK,*[21] the Irish High Court set aside an *ex parte* order granting the applicant leave to serve arbitration-related proceedings outside the jurisdiction and to dispense with the requirement for personal service of the proceedings. The High Court refused to assume jurisdiction over the respondent on the grounds that it was not appropriate to do so, having regard to the interests of both parties. There were a number of considerations as to why the High Court in that case refused to deal with an application for enforcement of an arbitral award. The parties, the arbitration, and the performance of the underlying contract had no connection with Ireland. Further, the party against whom enforcement was sought had no assets in Ireland. The High Court decided that there was no benefit to be gained by the applicant where enforcement proceedings were also under way in the French and Singapore courts.

In *Avobone NV v Aurelian Oil and Gas Ltd*,[22] the respondents sought the Irish High Court to decline jurisdiction in an enforcement action for an arbitral award granted by the International Chamber of Commerce in London in the jurisdiction of England and Wales, on the basis that the respondents had no assets within the jurisdiction. The court referred with approval to the judgment of Kelly J in *Yukos Capital*, where he noted that the presence of assets within the jurisdiction was not a pre-requisite for the granting of leave to serve out of the jurisdiction on an application to enforce an arbitral award.[23] McGovern J applied the "solid practical benefit test" enunciated by Mustill LJ in *Insurance Corporation of Ireland v Strombus International Insurance Co.* [1985] 2 Lloyd's Rep. 138 at 144, and found that the applicants had established that a solid practical benefit would ensue to them if they were to enforce the arbitral award in Ireland, as it could then apply to garnishee this debt from the Irish parent company.

Public policy

The leading Irish case on public policy in the context of enforcement of arbitral awards confirms that the public policy relevant to enforcement actions brought before the Irish courts is the public policy of Ireland, and not that of the seat of the arbitration or where the award has been rendered (*Broström Tankers AB v Factorias Volcano SA*).[24] In that case, which concerned an application to enforce a foreign arbitral award under the New York Convention (implemented by the Arbitration Act 1980, and now the 2010 Act), Kelly J enforced the award despite arguments that it was contrary to Irish public policy. The judge said (quoting from Cheshire and North's Private International Law), "*I am satisfied that I would be justified in refusing enforcement only if there was ... some element [of] illegality, or possibility that enforcement would be wholly offensive to the ordinary responsible and fully informed member of the public*". Kelly J made it clear that the Irish courts would take a restrictive approach to the concept of public policy in Article 34 of the Model Law, similar to that in other jurisdictions;

> "The case law and the textbook writers make it clear that the public policy defence to an enforcement application is one which is of a narrow scope. It extends only to a breach of the most basic notions of morality and justice. In this regard, I derive considerable assistance from the decision in *Parsons & Whitmore Overseas Co. Inc. v. Société Général de l'Industrie du Papier* 508 F. 2d 969 (2nd Cir, 1974) [a decision of Circuit Judge Joseph Smith]. In the course of his judgment, Judge Smith says this, and I quote: "Perhaps more probative, however, are the inferences to be drawn from the history of the convention as a whole. The general pro-enforcement bias informing the convention and explaining its supersession of the Geneva Convention points towards a narrow reading of the public policy defence. An expansive construction of this defence would vitiate the Convention's basic efforts to remove pre-existing obstacles to enforcement... We conclude, therefore, that the Convention's public policy defence should be construed narrowly. Enforcement of foreign arbitral awards may be denied on this basis only where enforcement would violate the forum state's most basic notions of morality and justice."[25]

This decision was mentioned with approval by McGovern J in *FBD Insurance Public Limited Company v Samwari Ltd.*[26]

Investment arbitration

Investor state arbitrations

Ireland signed the Washington (ICSID) Convention in 1966. Ireland ratified the Washington Convention in 1981. Ireland has only ever been a party to one Bilateral Investment Treaty (with the Czech Republic), which was terminated by consent on 1 December 2011.

The Arbitration Act 2010 applies to all arbitrations, including treaty arbitrations. Certain provisions of the Arbitration Act 2010 do not apply to proceedings under the ICSID Convention. These are set out in section 25 of that Act.

* * *

Endnotes

1. O'Donnell J in *Galway City Council v Samuel Kingston Construction Limited* [2010] IESC 18.
2. [2015] IEHC 544.
3. [2018] IEHC 6.
4. [2016] IEHC 582 at para 6.
5. [2015] IEHC 50.
6. [2012] IEHC 361.
7. [2017] IEHC 35.
8. [2016] IEHC 582.
9. [2017] IEHC 357.
10. [2017] IEHC 532.
11. [1999] 1 WLR 314 (CA (Civ Div)).
12. [2005] 3 I.R. 64.
13. Case C-536/13, 13 May 2015.
14. *Shelley-Morris v Bus Atha Cliath* [2003] 1 I.R. 232.
15. [2017] IESC 27.
16. [2014] IEHC 314.
17. [2016] IEHC 32.
18. [1988] I.R. 89.
19. [2007] 1 I.R. 30.
20. [2017] IEHC 301.
21. [2014] IEHC 115.
22. [2016] IEHC 636.
23. [2014] IEHC 115 at para 112.
24. [2004] IEHC 198.
25. [2004] IEHC 198 at para 28.
26. [2016] IEHC 32 at para 33.

Kevin Kelly
Tel: +353 1 607 1205 / Email: kevin.kelly@mccannfitzgerald.ie

Kevin leads the firm's Construction Group. He has aligned his extensive construction practice, which includes construction disputes, with a recognised expertise in all aspects of public procurement law/tendering. Kevin is a Fellow of the Chartered Institute of Arbitrators. He has considerable experience in leading the construction advice on large-scale building and infrastructure projects, and advising on the resolution of disputes associated with such projects including via court, arbitration, mediation, conciliation and independent expert, particularly with a view to avoiding or minimising conflict during the construction phase and seeking to have subsequent disputes resolved in an efficient and cost-effective manner.

Heather Mahon
Tel: +353 1 607 1206 / Email: heather.mahon@mccannfitzgerald.com

Heather holds a degree in Law and German and an M. Litt from Trinity College Dublin, and qualified as a barrister in 2000. She was in practice at the Bar from 2000–2006. Heather then took up a position with the Office of Parliamentary Counsel to the Government, with responsibility for legislative drafting. She later held a position in the senior management of the Law Reform Commission, with responsibility for a long-running legislation project in the Commission. She has lectured at third level in a number of areas and is a fluent German speaker. She is currently a senior associate with McCann FitzGerald.

McCann FitzGerald

Riverside One, Sir John Rogerson's Quay, Dublin 2, Ireland
Tel: +353 1 829 0000 / Fax: +353 1 829 0010 / URL: www.mccannfitzgerald.ie

Italy

Micael Montinari, Martina Lucenti & Filippo Frigerio
Portolano Cavallo

Introduction

The provisions regulating arbitration proceedings in Italy are located in the last chapter of the last book of the Italian Civil Procedure Code ("**CPC**"), specifically in Sections 806 to 840.

In addition, there are several special laws that regulate arbitration in specific sectors, e.g.: (a) Legislative Decree no. 5 of 2003, providing specific rules on arbitration agreements included in companies' bylaws; (b) Legislative Decree no. 50 of 2016, regulating arbitration proceedings in public contracts; and (c) Law no. 262 of 2005, concerning arbitration proceedings in financial markets.

Italy is a signatory party of the New York Convention, with no reservations. Its provisions were transferred into internal law by means of Law no. 62 of 1968.

Further, Italy is also a party to: (a) the European Convention on International Commercial Arbitration signed in Geneva in 1961; (b) the Convention on the Settlement of Investment Disputes Between States and Nationals of Other States signed in Washington in 1965; and (c) the United Nations Convention on Contracts for the International Sale of Goods signed in Vienna in 1980.

The CPC's provisions are applicable to both domestic and international arbitration, except when explicitly provided by the same CPC.

It should be highlighted that in Italy there are several institutions (mostly Chambers of Commerce) that have established Chambers of Arbitration. Most of them issue their own rules on arbitration.

The last report on ADR issued indicates that there are currently 143 Chambers of Arbitration in Italy, 66 of which were instituted by Chambers of Commerce.

Section 832 CPC recognises the relevance of such rules, stating that an arbitration agreement can refer to them. In case of contrast between the arbitration agreement and the Chamber of Arbitration's rules, the first shall prevail.

The most important institution is Milan's Chamber of Arbitration, which has issued very effective rules on arbitration which are translated into several languages and very flexible, so that they can be adapted to all kinds of arbitration proceedings.

The latter handled 134 arbitration proceedings in 2016 (last data available) and estimates an average duration of around one year (far below the average duration of civil proceedings, which is currently 840 days).

Arbitration agreement

Pursuant to Sections 807 and 808 CPC, the arbitration agreement shall be in writing and shall determine the boundaries of the controversy that the parties have devolved to arbitrators.

Section 806 of the CPC provides that the parties may refer any disputes to be heard by an arbitration tribunal except for:

- disputes involving inalienable rights; and
- disputes explicitly excluded by the law.

Italian law excludes the referral of employment matters to an arbitration, except when:

- the arbitration is established by the law; or
- provided in the appropriate collective employment agreements or contracts.

Pursuant to Section 817, par. 1 CPC, arbitrators have the exclusive competence to rule on their jurisdiction to award the dispute before them, under the terms of the arbitration agreement. Therefore, the Italian legislative system fully recognises the *Kompetenz-Kompetenz* principle.

Section 817, par. 2 CPC reinforces the above by stating that arbitrators have exclusive competence to rule on their jurisdiction even when the latter is challenged before a court, and where there are new reasons which appear only at a later stage.

It is important to note that a party who wishes to challenge the Arbitral Tribunal's jurisdiction must raise the question at the time of the first defensive act, i.e. the first defensive brief submitted or at the first hearing, following acceptance of the arbitrators. Failure to do so prevents the party challenging the award at a later stage, claiming that arbitrators did not have the jurisdiction to award the controversy. On the contrary, the appeal is always permitted when the dispute cannot be referred to arbitration on the basis of Section 806 CPC.

The same limitation for appeals applies if, at the time of the first defensive act, a party fails to challenge a counterparty's arguments that do not fall within the boundaries of the arbitration agreement.

Where the tribunal confirms its jurisdiction to decide on a matter and orders the prosecution of the proceedings, the arbitrators can issue a non-final award. The latter can be challenged before the Court of Appeals only along with a final award pursuant to Section 827, par. 2 CPC.

On the contrary, when arbitrators ascertain and declare they do not have the jurisdiction to rule on a dispute, they will issue a ruling in the form of an award.

Further, pursuant to Section 819-*ter* CPC, arbitrators' jurisdiction is not excluded by the fact that the same dispute is currently pending before a court.

The decision of a court on its jurisdiction is always appealable before the Supreme Court of Cassation by means of a special petition called "*regolamento di competenza*". The latter is aimed at securing a decision which will clearly state which is the competent body between the court or the Arbitral Tribunal to rule on the matter.

Filing of the *regolamento di competenza*'s petition under Section 819-*ter* CPC does not trigger the automatic suspension of the proceedings.

Reflecting the same timing required for raising jurisdictional objections before an arbitral tribunal, a party wishing to challenge the court's competence to rule on a matter must immediately raise the objection with the statement of defence ("*comparsa di risposta*"). Failure to raise the objection implies that the Arbitral Tribunal's competence is definitely excluded for that specific controversy.

As noted by several authors, the abovementioned provisions do not provide the means for resolving a dispute in cases where both the Arbitral Tribunal and the court confirm or deny their competence to decide the specific controversy.

Section 816-*quater* CPC dictates a series of rules applicable to so-called multi-party arbitrations, i.e. proceedings with more than two parties. The conditions according to which a multi-party arbitration proceedings can be started are two: (i) the arbitration agreement shall bind all the parties; and (ii) the Arbitral Tribunal shall be appointed, lacking an agreement between the parties, by a third party or each party shall appoint its own arbitrator or instruct a third party to appoint him.

If the conditions above are not both met and the presence of all the parties is required by the law (so-called mandatory joinder or "*litisconsorzio necessario*"), the arbitration proceedings cannot move forward and each party may start a dispute before the competent ordinary court.

Arbitrators

The party that wishes to start the arbitration proceedings shall, pursuant to an arbitration agreement that empowers the parties to appoint their own arbitrator, serve the other party (-ies) with a writ containing the invitation to appoint their own arbitrator(s) within 20 days. Failure to meet the deadline empowers the plaintiff to file a petition with the President of the competent court (where the arbitration has its seat) to appoint one or more arbitrators.

Absent such a determination of the arbitration agreement, the party who wishes to start an arbitration proceedings shall file a petition to the President of the competent court, i.e. the court of the place which is the arbitration's seat. The latter shall appoint the requested number of arbitrators.

The President of the court can refuse only when the arbitration agreement: (a) manifestly does not exist; or (b) manifestly provides for arbitration proceedings abroad (i.e. when the arbitration proceeding's seat is placed abroad).

In any case, Section 809 CPC requires an odd number of arbitrators.

In addition, the parties can provide for a third entity to appoint the arbitrators. Normally, arbitration agreements vest the power to appoint one or more arbitrators with Chambers of Arbitration, pursuant to their own rules.

Under Italian law, an arbitrator can be challenged for a number of reasons, specifically:

(a) if he/she does not have the qualifications explicitly agreed by the parties;

(b) if he/she, an entity, association, or company where he/she is a director has an interest in the controversy;

(c) if he/she or his/her spouse is: (i) a close relative up to the fourth degree of; or (ii) lives with; or (iii) regularly enjoys a close relationship with one of the parties, an authorised representative of one party or one of the attorneys;

(d) if he/she or his/her spouse has pending proceedings with or a severe hostility with one of the parties, an authorised representative of one party or of one of the attorneys;

(e) if he/she is bound to one of the parties, or to a company controlled by it, or to a subject that controls the party or to a company placed under joint control, by a working relationship of any kind or by other patrimonial or associative relationship capable of reducing his/her independence, or if he/she is a legal guardian of one of the parties; or

(f) if he/she was a consultant, an assistant or the counsel of one of the parties in a previous phase of the dispute or was a witness in it.

The party who appointed an arbitrator can challenge him/her only if the reason that impedes his/her appointment becomes known only at a later stage.

The challenging of an arbitrator does not prevent the prosecution of the arbitration proceedings, unless so ordered by the Arbitral Tribunal. However, if the arbitrator is discharged, the activities carried out by him/her or with his/her cooperation are ineffective.

In addition to the above, Chambers of Arbitration tend also to take into account additional grounds that compromise the independence of arbitrators, e.g. the IBA Guidelines on Conflicts of Interest in International Arbitration.

Under Section 813-*ter* CPC, an arbitrator is personally liable towards the parties when:

(a) fraudulently or with gross negligence, he/she omits or delays his/her activity and for this reason he/she is discharged and replaced, or when he/she unjustifiably renounces his/her office; or

(b) fraudulently or with gross negligence, he/she omits or impedes the issuance of the award within the deadline established by the law.

Arbitration procedure

By the time decided by the Arbitral Tribunal, the parties shall appear at the first hearing. The rules of the arbitration proceedings can be freely decided by the parties. Absent an agreement, the rules (including seat and language) are determined by the Arbitral Tribunal.

Arbitrators are bound by the duty to ensure respect to the due process rules, granting the parties equal and reasonable opportunities to defend themselves.

With respect to the evidential phase, the parties or the Arbitral Tribunal may delegate specific acts to one or more arbitrators.

Witnesses can be heard also in places different from the seat of arbitration, such as the place where the arbitrator is located, or at the witness's home or office. The Tribunal may also authorise written witness testimony.

If a witness refuses to appear before the Arbitral Tribunal, and the arbitrators deem it appropriate, they can request the President of the court where the arbitration has its seat to order the witness' appearance.

Further, the Arbitral Tribunal may appoint one or more technical experts (entities can also be appointed) to assist the arbitrators in some specific technical matters.

The arbitrators are also empowered to request a public administrative body to provide written information regarding an act or a document of the latter that the arbitrators deem appropriate to examine.

Notably, each Chamber of Arbitration generally provides for its own rules of procedure and on the taking of evidence, which sometimes are similar to the general rules under the CPC. Arbitral Tribunals can also choose to follow the IBA Rules on the Taking of Evidence in International Arbitration.

Interim relief

Section 818 CPC prevents Arbitral Tribunals issuing interim remedies (either provisional or conservative measures), unless otherwise provided by the law.

The applicant shall apply to the competent court for interim relief in support of arbitration under the general rules of the CPC. As a result, courts will generally have jurisdiction to grant interim measures.

Section 669-*quinquies* CPC states that when there is an arbitration proceeding ongoing or there is an arbitration agreement in place, the court to which the party may apply to obtain an interim measure is the one that would have jurisdiction for the merits, absent the arbitration agreement.

Under general civil procedural laws, the remedies available on an interim basis are:

(a) judicial seizure, aimed at securing goods whose ownership is being challenged;

(b) cautionary seizure, aimed at securing assets when the alleged creditor fears that the debtor could dispose of them so that the guarantee on the credit might be lost;

(c) reporting of new works, or of potential damages in order to avoid damages taking place as a consequence of new work being started or of other goods placing the claimant's property or possessions in danger;

(d) preliminary investigation proceedings, aimed at securing evidence to be later used in a proceeding, when there is the risk that such evidence may be lost; or

(e) in all other cases, the court can issue any kind of measure it deems most appropriate for reasons of urgency (Section 700 CPC) when:
   - the application is likely to be successful on the merits (so-called, *fumus boni iuris*); and
   - there is danger in any delay (so-called, *periculum in mora*).

Given the above, Arbitral Tribunals are not vested with the power to issue interim remedies, therefore they do not have the power either to enforce them or to otherwise ensure their effectiveness.

By the contrary, there is only one provision under Italian law, relating to the arbitration of certain company disputes, that empowers arbitrators to issue an interim measure.

Article 35 of Legislative Decree no. 5 of 2003 states that companies' articles of association may authorise shareholders to determine, by way of arbitration, the validity of the company's resolutions.

Where an arbitration proceeding is started for such a purpose, article 35, par. 5, (D. Lgs. no. 5 of 2003) empowers the Arbitral Tribunal appointed pursuant to the arbitration agreement to provisionally suspend the enforceability of a company's resolutions while their validity is challenged. The order issued by the Arbitral Tribunal cannot be otherwise challenged.

Commentators generally exclude analogic interpretations of such a provision. Therefore, its scope cannot be extended beyond the strict limits of the Legislative Decree where the piece of law is placed.

From a more general standpoint, the same article provides that until the Arbitral Tribunal is established, the court which would be competent to determine the controversy absent the arbitration agreement retains the interim general power to suspend the enforceability of the company's resolution.

Arbitration award

Pursuant to Section 820, par. 2 CPC, if the parties have not determined the deadline for the arbitrators to issue the final award, the latter shall be rendered within 240 days from the acceptance of the appointment. Such term can be extended upon the agreement of the parties or, upon the request of one party, by the President of the Tribunal, who shall give the chance to the other parties to rebut.

Section 820, par. 4 CPC states that the term is extended by 180 days, absent a different determination by the parties, in case: (a) preliminary activities are required; (b) the Tribunal appoints an expert; (c) the Tribunal issues a partial or interim award; or (d) one or more arbitrators are replaced.

Chambers of Arbitration tend to further specify these deadlines, and provide for mechanisms of control aimed at making sure the duration of the arbitral proceedings is kept as reasonable as possible.

The Arbitral Tribunal shall decide pursuant to the law, unless the parties declare that the arbitrators may decide on an equitable basis.

The award is rendered by the Arbitral Tribunal and signed by the arbitrators. The signature of the majority of arbitrators is sufficient only if the award is accompanied by a declaration that all arbitrators participated in the deliberation, but not all of them wanted to or could sign it.

Pursuant to Section 824-*bis* CPC, the award has the exact same effectiveness as a court's ruling.

With the award, the Arbitral Tribunal directs also which party shall fully or partially bear the costs of the proceedings, and the legal fees and expenses of the winning side. Chambers of Arbitration generally publicise the costs of arbitration proceedings, so that the parties can easily predict what will be the final costs they might have to bear.

Challenge of the arbitration award

Section 829 CPC states that a party can challenge the award only upon the following grounds:

1. if the arbitration agreement is invalid, provided that such an objection was raised in the first submission after the arbitrators' acceptance of the appointment;
2. if the arbitrators were not appointed pursuant to Sections 809-815 and/or Section 832, provided that such an objection was raised during the proceedings;
3. if the award was rendered by a person who could not be appointed as an arbitrator, as set forth under Section 812 CPC;
4. if the award includes provisions that fall beyond the scope of the arbitration agreement, only if such an objection was raised during the arbitration proceedings;
5. if the award does not include the reasoning, the decision, and/or the signature of the arbitrators (within the limits analysed above);
6. if the award was rendered after the expiration of the timeframe provided by the law or by the arbitration agreement, only in case the appealing party – before the deliberation of the award – served the others and the arbitrators a declaration through which he/she intended to take advantage of this ground;
7. if the formalities required by the parties have not been respected, only in case such formalities were provided under express sanction of nullity and the latter was not otherwise healed;
8. if the award contradicts a previous award or a judicial decision between the parties not any longer appealable (i.e. *res judicata*), only if such award or decision was lodged during the arbitration proceedings;

9. if the Arbitral Tribunal failed to comply with the due process rules;
10. if the award does not decide on the merits of the proceedings when the merits should have been decided;
11. if the award contains contradictory provisions; or
12. if the award has not awarded on some claims and/or objections, pursuant to and within the boundaries of the arbitration agreement.

Notably, a party cannot challenge the award for a reason of nullity if: (i) he/she caused it; (ii) he/she waived it; or (iii) he/she did not immediately raise on the next defensive occasion the objection of a violation of a proceedings' rule.

Generally, the award cannot be challenged on the basis of errors of law, except when such ground is expressly provided in the arbitration agreement or is expressly provided by the law (e.g., in labour law controversies).

Nonetheless, it is always possible to challenge the award if it is in contrast with the public order.

In addition, the award can also be challenged with two other mechanisms: (i) revocation of the award; and (ii) opposition of a third party to the award.

The revocation proceeding is an extraordinary method of challenging the award provided by Section 395 CPC. It can be triggered only when there are serious vices that affect it, namely: fraud of a party; forgery; discovery of unknown documents; or if there is an award affected by a fraud of the arbitrator(s).

In addition, third parties can oppose the award and request it to be declared null if the award endangers their rights and they have not been in a position to take part in the arbitration proceedings. The proceeding is regulated by Section 404 CPC.

Material errors or omissions that do not impact the merits of the decision can be amended using the award-correction proceedings, pursuant to Section 826 CPC.

Within one year from the issuance of the award, each party can request the Arbitral Tribunal to amend the award in case: (i) there are material or calculation errors; or (ii) the award lacks the indication of the name of the arbitrator(s), the arbitration's seat or the parties' names. The Tribunal shall proceed within 60 days from the request, having heard the parties. If the Tribunal does not provide, the same request may be filed with the competent court (i.e. the court of the place which is the arbitration's seat).

Enforcement of the arbitration award

In accordance with Section 825 CPC, to enforce a domestic award the interested party shall lodge with the law clerk of the court in the area where the arbitration took place:

(a) the original or a certified copy of the award; and

(b) the original or a certified copy of the document including the arbitration clause.

Once the court ascertains the formal validity of the award, it will declare the enforceability of the award with a decree. The parties are informed by the law clerk of the lodging of the award.

The most evident difference between the enforcement of domestic and international awards is that Italian arbitral awards already have, from the date of their last signature, the same effect as a ruling of the judicial authority, and can be appealed – notwithstanding the filing with the court – to obtain enforceability.

The analysis carried out by the court is merely formal. Indeed, the court cannot consider the merits of the arbitral award differently from what happens in relation to international arbitral awards.

An interested party may file an appeal ("*reclamo*") against a decree, denying or upholding enforceability. The parties will be summoned and the court decides the controversy with an order issued in chambers.

Pursuant to Section 839 CPC, a party that wishes to enforce an international arbitral award in Italy must file a petition with the President of the Court of Appeals for the area in which the counterparty resides. If the counterparty is not located in Italy, the competent court is the Court of Appeals of Rome.

Along with the petition, and in accordance with article IV of the New York Convention, the petitioner shall lodge:

(a) an original copy of the award;

(b) the original or a certified copy of the document including the arbitration clause, or an equivalent document; and

(c) the certified Italian translations of these documents.

During this phase of the proceedings, the other party will not be summoned.

Having ascertained that the award is formally valid, the President of the Court of Appeals will declare the enforceability of the international award in a decree with a brief reasoning.

If the President's decree denies enforceability for merely formal reasons (such as that there is no Italian translation), the petitioner may file the petition again.

Enforceability of the award will be denied by the President on the merits, if: (i) under Italian law the arbitrators do not have jurisdiction to decide the dispute; or (ii) the award contains provisions contrary to public order.

In relation to disputes excluded under Italian law, in accordance with the second requirement, public order is ascertained in relation to domestic sources of law, such as the Italian Constitution, principles of criminal law and European law.

Commentators have noted that such proceedings should also be admissible in order to obtain enforceability for partial and non-final arbitral awards.

In addition, under article VIII of the Geneva Convention of 1961, an award is admissible even without the reasoning.

In contrast to the above, if the President's decree denies enforceability on the merits or if it upholds the petition and declares the award enforceable, the interested party may file an opposition brief with the Court of Appeals.

The opposition must be filed within 30 days from:

(a) the communication of the decree that denies enforceability; or

(b) the serving of the decree that declares the enforceability.

The proceedings are governed by the provisions of the ordinary proceedings.

Pursuant to Section 840, par. 3 CPC, which almost perfectly mirrors article V of the New York Convention, should the Court of Appeals ascertain that one or more of the following circumstances exist, the enforceability of the award will be denied if:

(a) the parties were under some incapacity;

(b) the arbitration agreement is invalid under the applicable law or, failing any indication thereon, under the law of the country where the award was made;

(c) the party against whom the award is invoked was not given proper notice of the appointment of the arbitrator or of the arbitration proceedings;

(d) the unsuccessful party was unable to present its case;

(e) the award falls outside the submission to arbitration, or it contains decisions on matters beyond the scope of the submission to arbitration. Decisions on matters falling within the submission that can be separated from those not within the submission may be recognised and enforced;

(f) there was an incorrect composition of the arbitral authority;

(g) the arbitral procedure was not in accordance with the arbitration agreement or, where there is no agreement, in accordance with the law of the country where the arbitration took place; or

(h) the award has not yet become binding on the parties, or has been set aside or suspended by a competent authority of the country in which, or under the law of which, that award was made.

In relation to the final circumstance above, the Court of Appeals has the power to suspend the proceedings pending a judgment on the annulment or suspension requested to the foreign authority that issued the award. Upon the request of the petitioner, the court can suspend the proceedings and order the counterparty to provide adequate warranties. The provision of warranties is entirely at the discretion of the court.

In addition to the *ex parte* proceedings mentioned above, the enforceability may be denied if, under Italian law, the dispute cannot be devolved to arbitrators or if the award contains provisions which are contrary to public order.

The statutory limitation for enforcing an award is 10 years.

The final ruling of the Court of Appeals can eventually be appealed to the Supreme Court of Cassation only for violations of laws pursuant to Section 360 CPC.

Micael Montinari
Tel: +39 06/69 6661 / Email: mmontinari@portolano.it
Micael Montinari focuses on litigation; his clients include retail chains, fashion houses and brands, media/digital players. He heads the dispute resolution team (which is ranked by *The Legal 500* and *Chambers & Partners* since respectively 2006 and 2009). His experience includes a broad range of matters, including commercial and business and intellectual property disputes as well as arbitration, often with a significant cross-border element. He is also ranked by *Chambers Global* for Dispute Resolution (both Europe and Global), and was recognised as a *Client Choice International* Awards 2017 winner in the Litigation Practice area. Micael has almost 19 years of experience in all forms of commercial and corporate litigation (contractual disputes, corporate-related matters, unfair competition, passing-off, advertising issues, etc.), interim and injunctive proceedings, proceedings before the competition and consumers' authority and other Italian agencies (Communications Authority, Data Protection authority, etc.), arbitration proceedings (including *ad hoc* and managed arbitration) serving as counsel and arbitrator, and mediation.

Martina Lucenti
Tel: +39 06/69 6661 / Email: mlucenti@portolano.it
Martina joined Portolano Cavallo in 2017. She focuses on domestic and international litigation and arbitration. Martina assists Italian and foreign clients in commercial and corporate disputes, post-M&A litigation, directors' and officers' liability suits, liability of financial and insurance intermediaries and insolvency litigation. She has also assisted companies in civil actions for vicarious liability brought before criminal courts. Martina acted as sole arbitrator and co-arbitrator in proceedings administered by the Milan Chamber of Arbitration. She is also a member of ArbitralWomen. In 2005, she obtained a Diploma in English Commercial Law from the College of Law of London. In 2008, she qualified as Solicitor of the Senior Courts of England and Wales (non-practising). Martina graduated *summa cum laude* from the Università Cattolica del Sacro Cuore in Milan in 2000. She was admitted to the Italian Bar in 2003.

Filippo Frigerio
Tel: +39 06/69 6661 / Email: ffrigerio@portolano.it
Filippo Frigerio joined Portolano Cavallo in 2015, under the terms of an intern work agreement secured through Bocconi University, becoming later in the year, upon earning his Law degree from the Luigi Bocconi Commercial University, one of the firm's attorneys-at-law. While completing his university studies, Filippo attended courses at the Law School of the University of Minnesota, Minneapolis, USA, for a period of five months.

Filippo lends his expertise to both Italian and foreign clients in matters of disputes and arbitration on civil and commercial matters, as well as of new technologies, digital media, and Italian and European legislation concerning the protection of personal data. Furthermore, he provides legal assistance to operators in the broad life sciences field.

Portolano Cavallo

via Rasella 155, 00187 Rome / Piazza Borromeo 12, 20123 Milan, Italy
Tel: +39 06/69 6661 / Fax: +39 06/6966 6544 / URL: www.portolano.it

Kosovo

Dr. Christian W. Konrad, Konrad & Partners
& Virtyt Ibrahimaga

Introduction

Kosovo is the youngest state on the European continent. It declared its independence on 17 February 2008 and has since then been officially recognised by more than half of the UN Member States, including 23 out of 28 European Union countries. The government of Kosovo continuously strives for further diplomatic recognition and membership in international organisations. Kosovo is currently in the process of European integration. Through the Stabilisation and Association Agreement with the EU, the country is working towards the harmonisation of its laws and regulations with EU standards.

In September 2008, the Law on Arbitration of Kosovo (Law No. 02/L-75) (**Law on Arbitration**), which is based on the UNCITRAL Model Law, came into effect. This law is considered to satisfy the formal and substantive requirements of a modern arbitration law, its provisions having *lex specialis* character in relation to the Law on Contested Procedure with regard to arbitration procedure.[1] The Law on Arbitration regulates domestic and international arbitration and sets forth the procedures for enforcing domestic (Article 38) and foreign (Article 39) arbitral awards. The Law on Foreign Investment (Law No. 04/L-220), enacted in 2014, further favours the use of arbitration in international relationships. With the adoption of international standards, Kosovo has the necessary framework to promote itself as an arbitration-friendly jurisdiction.

Since 2011, arbitration services have been available within the Kosovo Chamber of Commerce at the Kosovo Permanent Tribunal of Arbitration and within the American Chamber of Commerce in Kosovo (**AmCham**) at the Alternative Dispute Resolution Center. In June 2011, the Chamber of Commerce introduced the Kosovo Arbitration Rules (**Kosovo Arbitration Rules**), based on the UNCITRAL Arbitration Rules (as revised in 2010). The Kosovo Arbitration Rules are also applied by the Alternative Dispute Resolution Center at AmCham.

Due to divergent positions on its statehood, the Republic of Kosovo is not yet eligible to become a contracting state to the New York Convention on the Recognition and Enforcement of Foreign Arbitral Awards (**New York Convention**). Nonetheless, Kosovo's courts recognise foreign arbitral awards (Law on Arbitration Article 39.1). The documents to be filed before the Kosovo courts when applying for the recognition and enforcement of an international award (Law on Arbitration Article 39.3) are similar to those to be filed under the corresponding provision of the New York Convention (Article IV). In addition, the Law on Arbitration substantially reflects the grounds for refusal of recognition and enforcement under Article V of the New York Convention (Law on Arbitration, Articles 39.4–39.5).

Furthermore – again, in spite of Kosovo not being a contracting state to the New York Convention – the Foreign Investment Law expressly stipulates that international arbitral awards "shall be enforceable in accordance with the New York Convention, regardless as to whether or not that convention is otherwise binding on Kosovo" (Foreign Investment Law, Article 16.4). There are therefore express provisions for international awards to be recognised and enforced in accordance with the New York Convention in Kosovo.

Arbitration agreement

An arbitration agreement can either be signed as a separate agreement attached to the main contract, or may be included as an arbitration clause within the contract. In either case, the consent of the parties to arbitrate disputes must be in writing and clearly state the parties' intention to settle contractual disputes through arbitration. The Law on Arbitration states that the conclusion of an arbitration agreement by letter, telegraph, fax, email or any other electronic form is considered to fulfil the requirement of a written form. For consumer contracts, the agreement is only deemed to be validly concluded when all parties personally sign the document containing the arbitration clause, including via electronic signature (Article 6).

Under Article 5 of the Law on Arbitration, all disputes are arbitrable as long as the relief sought has a "civil-judicial and economic-judicial" character. Public law disputes, criminal law cases and family matters, are not arbitrable.

Disputes arising from consumer contracts are arbitrable. The Law on Consumer Protection recognises expressly the arbitration courts as forums for settling consumer-related disputes,[2] and it does not set any restrictions on the conclusion of an arbitration agreement prior to the arising of the dispute. However, in order to protect the weaker party, provisions which oblige the consumer to submit the disputes exclusively to arbitration are considered as unfair contract conditions and therefore void. According to Article 50 (1) of the Law on Consumer Protection, "unfair" is a contractual condition which has not been individually negotiated by the parties and which, contrary to good faith, creates a significant imbalance in the rights and obligations of the parties under the contract, to the detriment of the consumer. The condition is considered as individually not negotiated when it has been drafted in advance and the consumer has therefore not been able to influence the content of the condition, particularly in the context of a pre-formulated standard contract.

Labour law disputes are considered as non-arbitrable within the current legal framework in Kosovo.[3] The Law on Labour expressly provides for mediation in its provisions and not the possibility of arbitration for settling labour law disputes.[4]

The Law on Arbitration accepts the *competence-competence* doctrine (Article 14, Law on Arbitration). This principle vests an arbitral tribunal with the right to decide whether it has jurisdiction over the dispute presented before it, and whether the arbitration agreement is valid. The *competence-competence* principle is also provided under Article 24 of the Kosovo Arbitration Rules.

The validity of an arbitration agreement may not be challenged on the grounds of invalidity of the underlying contract. The separability principle is set forth in Article 14.1 of the Law on Arbitration, which provides that an arbitral tribunal should decide on the validity of an arbitration agreement and that "*for that purpose, an arbitration clause, which forms part of a contract, shall be treated as an agreement independent of the terms of the contract*".

Arbitration procedure

Under Article 18 of the Law on Arbitration, unless otherwise agreed by the parties, the arbitration proceedings commence on the date the Respondent receives the Request for Arbitration. The Respondent is deemed to have received the Request for Arbitration on the day that it is delivered physically to it or deemed to have been received if it is delivered at its habitual residence, place of business or mailing address of the addressee (Article 4, Law on Arbitration).

The Law on Arbitration follows the Model Law's guarantees of two fundamental arbitration principles: equal treatment of the parties; and the opportunity to present one's case (Article 16.1). The parties to an arbitration are free to determine the procedural rules applicable to the dispute. The Law on Arbitration provides that in the absence of an agreement by the parties on the procedural rules, the arbitral tribunal shall determine the applicable rules.

The hearing of the case does not necessarily have to take place at the place of arbitration. The place of arbitration is agreed upon by the parties or, in the absence of an agreement, is established by the arbitral tribunal, taking into consideration the circumstances of the case and the convenience of the parties and the arbitral tribunal. Unless otherwise agreed, the arbitration proceedings are not public (Law on Arbitration, Article 21.1), and the arbitrator and other participants must keep all information confidential.

The parties may agree the language of the proceedings, failing which this is determined by the arbitral tribunal. The language applies to all written and oral submissions. The arbitral tribunal may order prompt translation of all relevant documents into the language or languages to which the parties have agreed (Law on Arbitration, Article 19). Similar provisions are included in Article 19 of the Kosovo Arbitration Rules.

The Law on Arbitration stipulates that each party shall have the burden of proving the facts relied upon to support its claim or defence. The arbitral tribunal has the discretion to decide what evidence is relevant and admissible, and to exclude evidence it deems to be irrelevant (Article 23.2). Courts may assist the arbitral tribunal or a party (with the approval of the arbitral tribunal) in the taking of evidence, or to perform judicial acts which the arbitral tribunal is not authorised to carry out (Law on Arbitration, Article 28).

The arbitral tribunal may require the parties to produce documents, exhibits or other evidence within such a period as the arbitral tribunal deems appropriate (Law on Arbitration, Article 23.4).

Evidence of witnesses may be presented in the form of testimonies or written statements signed by a witness, provided that the witness is made available at the hearing, if their examination is requested. The details of each witness (name, address, etc.) shall be communicated to the other party at least 15 days before the hearing (Law on Arbitration, Article 24).

Apart from witness testimonies and evidence presented by the parties, the arbitral tribunal may appoint one or more experts to produce a written report on specific issues to be determined by the arbitral tribunal. The arbitral tribunal may ask the parties to provide to the expert all documents that the expert might need in order to prepare an expert opinion. After the delivery of a written expert report, the parties and/or the arbitral tribunal (where necessary) may request that the expert appear at a hearing to be cross-examined. "At this hearing", the parties have the right to submit their own expert reports (Law on Arbitration, Article 25).

Arbitrators

Under the Law on Arbitration, the parties are free to determine the number of arbitrators (provided that the panel is composed of an uneven number of arbitrators) and to choose any selection method for appointing the arbitrator or arbitrators. In the event of no consensus on the selection method or number of arbitrators,[5] the arbitral tribunal shall consist of a panel of three arbitrators. The Law on Arbitration follows the Model Law's default rules and provides that each party shall appoint one arbitrator, and these two arbitrators shall appoint the chair. If any appointments are not made within the required time period (30 days), the Kosovo courts will, upon request of one of the parties, make a default appointment (Law on Arbitration, Article 9.4).

Article 5 of the Kosovo Arbitration Rules regulates the issue in a slightly different manner. It provides that "*if the parties have not previously agreed, the appointing authority shall decide whether the case shall be referred to a sole arbitrator or to a three-member arbitral tribunal, taking into account all relevant circumstances*".

The Law on Arbitration does not establish any restrictions regarding the citizenship of arbitrators. It establishes the general requirements for arbitrators, i.e. an arbitrator shall be impartial and independent of the parties. The arbitrator does not have to be a qualified lawyer. The parties may, however, require an arbitrator to have certain skills or qualifications.

Before accepting an appointment, a prospective arbitrator must disclose any circumstances that might raise justifiable doubts regarding the arbitrators' impartiality or independence. Even after the appointment, an arbitrator is obliged to disclose any such circumstances as soon as they arise (Law on Arbitration, Article 10.1).

Non-disclosure of the above-mentioned circumstances may give rise to a challenge of an arbitrator by the parties. Arbitrators may be challenged only if there are circumstances that give rise to justifiable doubts as to the arbitrators' impartiality or independence, or if the arbitrator does not have the qualifications required by the parties (Law on Arbitration, Article 10.2).

Article 11 of the Law on Arbitration allows the parties to freely designate the procedure for challenging arbitrators. Absent such agreement, Article 11.2 provides that "*the party which intends to challenge an arbitrator shall within fifteen days after the appointment of an arbitrator, or after circumstances listed in article 10, par.2, became known to that party, send notice of its challenge to the other party and the other members of the tribunal*". In case the other party does not agree to the resignation of the respective arbitrator, or the arbitrator under challenge does not resign, the tribunal shall decide on the challenge. If the challenge is not successful, a dissatisfied party may initiate court proceedings within 15 days of receipt of the rejection decision, in order to have the question of an arbitrator's challenge decided by the state court. While such a request is pending, the arbitral tribunal, including the challenged arbitrator, may continue the arbitral proceedings and render an award (Law on Arbitration, Article 11.4). Similar provisions are contained in the Kosovo Arbitration Rules (Articles 12-14).

Furthermore, the arbitrator's mandate terminates if the arbitrator becomes *de jure* or *de facto* unable to perform his or her function or, for other reasons, fails to act without undue delay. In such a case, if the arbitrator does not resign or if the parties do not agree on the termination of the arbitrator's mandate, the law allows the state court to render the final decision. The court can make that decision upon the request of any party or member of the tribunal. No appeal is allowed against a court's decision on this matter (Law on Arbitration, Article 12).

The Arbitration Law does not contain any provisions concerning the liability of arbitrators. Article 16 of the Kosovo Arbitration Rules provides that, save for intentional wrongdoing, the parties waive, to the fullest extent permitted under the applicable law, any claim against the arbitrators, the appointing authority, the Permanent Tribunal and any person appointed by the arbitral tribunal based on any act or omission in connection with the arbitration.

Interim relief

Regardless of the wording of the arbitration agreement or the commencement of arbitration proceedings, according to the Law on Arbitration, each party is entitled to request interim measures from state courts and the state court is further empowered to grant the requested measure if the party proves that it may suffer immediate or irreparable damage or loss if such a measure is not taken (Article 8).

Article 15.1 of the Law on Arbitration provides that an arbitral tribunal may issue interim measures if requested by a party. The arbitral tribunal has to be provided with credible evidence that, in the event such a preliminary order is not issued, the party requesting it will suffer immediate or irreparable injury, loss or damage. The arbitral tribunal may order any interim measure against the other party that it deems appropriate and may order any party to provide "appropriate security". A court may order the enforcement of an interim measure issued by an arbitral tribunal unless a party has already requested a court to enforce an interim measure on the same matter (Law on Arbitration, Articles 8 and 15.2).

Interim measures issued by an arbitral tribunal based in Kosovo become effective after having been declared enforceable by the court. The competent court for such declaration is the Basic Court in Pristina – Department for Commercial Matters, the only competent court for commercial matters for the whole of Kosovo.

The Law on Arbitration does not provide an exhaustive list of admissible types of interim measures that may be granted by the arbitral tribunal. Kosovo Arbitration Rules provide for interim measures that take into account the preservation of property and evidence, i.e. under Article 27(2), a party may apply: (i) for an order to preserve the other party's property; (ii) for an order to preserve evidence that may be relevant and material to the resolution of the dispute; and (iii) require the other party to take or refrain from taking certain actions that are likely to cause current or imminent harm or prejudice the arbitral process itself. The arbitration rules do not have a *numerus clausus* character, i.e. if the rules of the arbitral tribunal had been applied, the arbitral tribunal would have been able to order such interim measures, but would not have been limited to the above-mentioned measures, since the interim measures fall within the scope of the Law on Contested Procedure (Article 296).[6]

If a preliminary order issued by an arbitral tribunal proves to be unjustified, the party in whose favour the interim measure was issued is obliged to compensate the party against which the order was issued and enforced. The arbitral tribunal also has the power to decide on the justification of the preliminary order and matters related to the compensation of damages referred to above (Law on Arbitration, Article 15.3).

Arbitration award

An arbitration award is final and may not be appealed against. The Law on Arbitration does not provide for any specific timeframe within which the arbitration award shall be rendered. With regard to the decision-making, form and correction of an award, the Law on Arbitration largely follows the Model Law standards. The award must be in writing, shall include the reasons on which it is based unless the parties have agreed otherwise, signed by the majority of arbitrators, provided that the award states the reasons for the absence of a signature, and shall contain the place and date on which the award was rendered. The Law on Arbitration does not address the issue of dissenting opinions, namely whether the arbitral tribunal is to issue the dissenting opinion of an arbitrator.

The Law on Arbitration contains provisions on settlement of disputes. According to Article 32, the parties may settle their dispute at any time during the proceedings, as long as the award has not been rendered. In such a case, the parties are to inform the arbitral tribunal about the settlement and may request to convert their settlement agreement into an award, unless the settlement is in violation of public policy (*ordre public*). The law ensures that the resulting award has the same force and effect as any other arbitral award on the merits of the case.

In its award, the arbitral tribunal shall determine the costs of the arbitration and, unless the parties have otherwise agreed, decide which parties are to bear these costs, and in what proportion. Pursuant to Article 34.1 of the Law on Arbitration, the costs of the arbitration include the fees of the arbitral tribunal, the arbitrator's costs, counsel's fees, and expenses and representatives of the parties (claimed during the proceedings and to the extent that the arbitral tribunal finds them reasonable), travel and other witness expenses (as approved by the arbitral tribunal), and fees and expenses of the court when acting as the appointing authority of arbitrators. Unless otherwise agreed by the parties, costs are borne by the unsuccessful party (Law on Arbitration, Article 34.3). The Law on Arbitration does not contain any provisions on whether the parties are entitled to recover interest.

Challenge of the arbitration award

Vesting the parties with an unlimited right to appeal an award would take away one of the main advantages of arbitration – its ability to deliver fast and cost-effective dispute resolution. Consistent with this interest, the law provides only limited grounds for the annulment of an award.

An award may be annulled if the contesting party resisting proves that (Law on Arbitration, Article 36.2):

(a) a party to the arbitration agreement did not have the capacity to act;

(b) the arbitration agreement is not valid under the law determined as applicable by the parties or the arbitral tribunal or, in the absence of such determination, under the law applicable in Kosovo;

(c) the applicant was not given proper notice of the appointment of an arbitrator or of the arbitral proceedings or was otherwise unable to present his case;

(d) the award deals with an issue not contemplated by or not falling within the terms of the submission to arbitration, or it contains decisions on matters beyond the scope of the submission to arbitration, provided that, if the decisions on matters submitted to arbitration can be separated from those not so submitted, that part of the award which contains decisions on matters submitted to arbitration may be recognised and enforced;

(e) the composition of the arbitral tribunal or the arbitral procedure was not in accordance with the provisions of [the Law on Arbitration] or a valid arbitration agreement, under the condition that such defect had an impact on the arbitral award; or

if the court finds that:

(a) arbitration is prohibited by law; or

(b) the enforcement of the award leads to a result which is in conflict with public policy.

The timeframe for requesting a court to set aside an arbitral award can be stipulated by the parties in their arbitration agreement. In the absence of an agreement on this issue, the request for setting aside shall be brought within ninety (90) days from the day on which the Claimant in the annulment proceedings receives the award. Once the request is submitted, the court may, where appropriate, set aside the award and resubmit the case to the arbitral tribunal to resume the arbitral proceedings or to take such other action as, in the arbitral tribunal's opinion, will eliminate the grounds for setting aside. According to Article 37 of the Law on Arbitration, the decisions of the court shall have the form of a court order. Prior to the issuance of a court order regarding the challenge of an award, the court shall hear all parties.

Enforcement of the arbitration award

The Law on Arbitration sets forth the legal requirements for the enforcement of domestic arbitral awards and recognition and enforcement of foreign arbitral awards (awards made outside Kosovo). Its Article 38.1 provides that "*an arbitral award made by an arbitral tribunal in Kosovo shall be enforced when declared enforceable by the Court*". A request to declare an arbitral award enforceable shall be accompanied by the arbitral award or a certified copy thereof. However, a request shall be rejected if the court determines that one or more grounds for setting aside an award are satisfied (Law on Arbitration, Article 38.2).

Arbitral awards rendered outside Kosovo are subject to recognition and enforcement. In order to have an arbitral award enforced, the requesting party shall file with the Basic Court in Pristina – Department for Commercial Matters an application, accompanied by the authenticated original award, or a certified copy thereof, and an original arbitration agreement or its duly certified copies. When the arbitral award or arbitration agreement is written in a foreign language, the party shall supply a duly certified translation of the abovementioned documents into an official language of Kosovo (Albanian or Serbian).

Grounds for refusing the enforcement and recognition of an award

Although the Law on Arbitration does not expressly refer to the New York Convention, the provisions dealing with recognition and enforcement (Law on Arbitration, Article 39) mirror the correlating provisions under Article V of the New York Convention. Similar to the New York Convention, refusal of recognition or enforcement may be raised by a party or by the court.

A party may raise the following grounds for refusal (Law on Arbitration, Article 39.4):

(a) lack of capacity of the parties to conclude an arbitration agreement;

(b) invalidity of the arbitration agreement under the applicable law;

(c) lack of a fair opportunity to be heard during arbitral proceedings;

(d) the award deals with matters not covered by the submission to arbitration;

(e) the composition of the arbitral tribunal or the conduct of the arbitral proceedings was not in accordance with the applicable law;[7] or

(f) the final award has not yet become binding on the parties, or has been set aside or suspended by a competent authority.

Recognition and enforcement of an award "may" be refused by a court based on any one or more of the above grounds.

Recognition and enforcement of an award, however, "shall" be refused by a court if it finds that the subject matter of the dispute is not capable of settlement by arbitration under the laws of Kosovo, or the recognition or enforcement of the award would be contrary to the public policy (*ordre public*) of Kosovo (Law on Arbitration, Article 39.5).

Investment arbitration

In 2009, Kosovo joined the International Center for Dispute Resolution. The government has signed investment agreements providing for investor-state arbitration with Albania, Austria, Belgium, Luxembourg, Macedonia, Turkey, Switzerland and the United Arab Emirates.

Placing economic growth as its first priority, Kosovo has undertaken numerous economic and legal reforms in order to make the country more attractive to foreign investors. In 2011, the government took substantive steps to open Kosovo to foreign investment through the enactment of the Public Private Partnership (PPP) Law, which is harmonised with European Council regulations and EU *Acquis Communitaire*.

The Law on Strategic Investments in the Republic of Kosovo (Law No. 05/L-079), which came into force in February 2017, supplements the legal and regulatory framework for investments by providing investors in strategic economic sectors with several opportunities and thus increasing Kosovo's competitiveness in attracting foreign investments.

The Law on Foreign Investment, enacted in 2014, incorporates international standards on investment protection, including fair and equitable treatment, full and constant protection, security and the transfer of rights. In the absence of an agreement on the settlement of disputes between a foreign investor and the state, the Law on Foreign Investment allows foreign investors to require that investment disputes are settled through domestic or international arbitration, with the procedural rules as chosen by the foreign investor. The Foreign Investment Law stipulates that investors may utilise the following alternative dispute resolution mechanisms:

(a) the ICSID Convention, if both the foreign investor's country of citizenship and Kosovo are parties to the said Convention at the time of the request for arbitration;
(b) the ICSID Additional Facility Rules, if the jurisdictional requirements for personal immunities *per* Article 25 of the ICSID Convention are not fulfilled at the time of the request for arbitration;
(c) the United Nations Commission on International Trade Law (UNCITRAL) Rules. In this case, the appointing authority referred to therein will be the Secretary General of ICSID; or
(d) the International Chamber of Commerce Rules.

Pursuant to Article 2 of the Law on Foreign Investments, the minimum capital amount that has to be contributed by a foreign investor, directly or indirectly, to a business organisation established in Kosovo in order to be considered as a foreign investment organisation, is 10%.

Kosovo is currently facing two investment treaty claims. The first case, *Axos Capital Ltd. v. Republic of Kosovo* (ICSID Case No. ARB/15/22), concerns the privatisation of Kosovo's telecom company, PTK. In 2013, Axos, as a part of the consortium, won a tender to buy 75% of PTK's shares. At the end of 2013, however, the government of Kosovo terminated the transaction. As the claim is based on Germany's bilateral investment treaty with Yugoslavia, it might provide some clarity as to whether investors may invoke any of Serbia's investment protection agreements signed prior to Kosovo's declaration of independence. The second investment claim, *Mabco Construction SA v. Republic of Kosovo* (ICSID Case

No. ARB/17/25), was filed in July 2017 by a Swiss construction company. The claim is based on Kosovo's bilateral investment treaty with Switzerland and concerns the acquisition of shares in a tourism venture. Both cases are pending.

* * *

Endnotes

1. Law No. 04/L-118 on Amending and Supplementing the Law No.03/L-006 on Contested Procedure, Article 26.
2. Law No. 04/L-21 on Consumer Protection, Article 1 (1.18).
3. Iset Morina, "Arbitration and arbitration procedure", 2015, Prishtina, p.171.
4. Law No. 03/L-212 on Labour of Kosovo, Article 81.
5. The consensus should be reached within 15 days after the receipt of the notice of arbitration by the Respondent (Law on Arbitration, Article 9.3).
6. Iset Morina, "Arbitration and arbitration procedure", 2015, Prishtina, p.238.
7. Article 39.4(d) of the Law on Arbitration omits the wording of Article V(1)(d) of the New York Convention that "The composition of the arbitral authority or the arbitral procedure was not in accordance with the agreement of the parties, or, failing such agreement, was not in accordance with the law of the country where the arbitration took place" (emphasis added), being "a distinction which is of no material significance." (A. Gojani; "Recognition and Enforcement of Kosovo-made Arbitral Awards in New York Convention Countries: A Comparative Study", *Journal of Alternative Dispute Resolution in Kosovo*, Vol. 2, June 2016, p.72.)

Dr. Christian W. Konrad
Tel: +43 1 512 95 00 / Email: c.konrad@konrad-partners.com

Dr. Christian W. Konrad is the founding partner of Konrad & Partners, an international law firm offering comprehensive legal services in the area of dispute resolution, with a particular focus on international commercial and investment arbitration. He has represented international organisations and businesses in a broad range of arbitration and litigation disputes. The disputes involved long-term energy contracts, complex construction contracts, concession agreements, entitlement to natural resources, immunity from jurisdiction, infrastructure projects, as well as mergers and acquisitions. He regularly advises clients on the protection of their investments and on the enforcement of arbitral awards and court judgments. Dr. Konrad frequently acts as arbitrator, is a fellow of the Chartered Institute of Arbitrators and a member of the panels of various arbitration institutions worldwide. Dr Konrad serves as Vice-President of the Kosovo Permanent Tribunal of Arbitration.

Virtyt Ibrahimaga LL.M.
Tel: +381 38 227 358 / Email: virtyt.ibrahimaga@lawfirm-iot.com

Mr. Virtyt Ibrahimaga is the President of the Kosovo Permanent Tribunal of Arbitration in Kosovo. He is a lawyer educated in Germany and has represented local and international companies in domestic and international litigation and arbitrations concerning telecommunications contracts, concession agreements, entitlements to natural resources, immunity from jurisdiction, distribution and agency contracts, as well as property matters. Virtyt regularly advises clients on the protection of their investments and on the enforcement of arbitral awards and court judgements, and has served as co-arbitrator and as chairman of the Arbitral Tribunal in domestic arbitration proceedings.

Konrad & Partners

Rotenturmstrasse 13, 1010 Vienna, Austria
Tel: +43 1 512 95 00 / Fax: +43 1 512 95 00 95 / URL: www.konrad-partners.com

Lithuania

Paulius Docka
PRIMUS attorneys at law

Introduction

The Law on Commercial Arbitration was introduced in 1996. A new version was adopted in 2012. Since the adoption of the essential legislation, arbitration has started gaining popularity in Lithuania.

Lithuanian courts make no distinction between international commercial arbitration and local commercial arbitration. At the same time, Lithuanian courts tend to follow international pro-arbitration trends, thereby allowing business to benefit from a truly liberal approach to arbitration which is developing in international commercial arbitration.

Lithuanian arbitration regulation is based on UNCITRAL Model Law. In 2012, the Law on Commercial Arbitration of the Republic of Lithuania (the LCA), which is based on the 1985 UNCITRAL Model Law on International Commercial Arbitration (UNCITRAL Model Law), was amended to match the changes adopted by the General Assembly in 2006.

The LCA explicitly states that it shall be interpreted and its definitions shall be subsidiarily governed by the UNCITRAL Model Law. Therefore Lithuanian courts in their case law often refer to the UNCITRAL Model Law, stating that "logical, systematic and functional relationships" between the LCA and UNCITRAL Model Law, and historical background of adoption of the LCA, allow it to be interpreted by subsidiary application of UNCITRAL Model Law.

Moreover, Lithuania has ratified the ICSID Convention, the Energy Charter Treaty and the Convention on Conciliation and Arbitration within the Commission on Security and Cooperation in Europe of 1992.

Lithuania has been a member of the New York Convention since 1996. Local courts strictly adhere to this international treaty. Lithuania has made a reciprocity reservation by allowing recognition and enforcement of an arbitral award in the territory of Lithuania, if such arbitral award was made in a state which is a party to the New York Convention.

There is a strong willingness in Lithuania to create an attractive forum for business to resolve its disputes outside the courtroom. It stimulates legislators and courts to take a liberal, enforcement-oriented approach to arbitration, based on internationally accepted standards and principles of commercial arbitration.

Arbitration agreement

Arbitration agreements may be concluded by tacit understanding or in writing, regarding existing or future disputes.

The Supreme Court of Lithuania confirmed that arbitration is generally recognised as an alternative method of dispute resolution equal to legal proceedings organised in the national courts (*L.B. v. State Property Fund*, 2014). This alternative jurisdiction is rooted in parties' free will and agreement to transfer the specific dispute to arbitration.

An arbitration agreement is considered valid if the parties sign a document which includes an arbitration clause, or else exchange documents (including electronic documents) which confirm that they agree on arbitration, or the parties exchange claim and response in which both parties confirm that they agree on arbitration, or if there are other circumstances which prove that parties agree on arbitration.

Agreement to arbitrate the dispute not only gives the parties the right to refer to arbitration, but also waives their right to refer the dispute to any state court. According to the Supreme Court of Lithuania, the principle of *pacta sunt servanda* applies to the arbitration agreement (*L.B. v. State Property Fund*, 2014). Therefore the validity and capability of execution of the arbitration agreement shall be established separately from the main agreement. The doctrine of arbitration agreement separability that was established in the case law of Lithuanian courts long ago (ex. *Marketing Service v. Nemunas AB*, 2001), is constantly applied in practice today.

The LCA provides for application of the *competence-competence* principle in Lithuania, meaning that if the arbitral tribunal is constituted, it is the only competent body to decide on the validity of the arbitration agreement. According to the LCA, courts are allowed to declare the arbitration agreement null and void before the dispute is referred to arbitration. Once the arbitration proceedings are initiated, Lithuanian courts strictly follow the doctrine of competence-competence and refuse to accept claims related to the validity of the arbitration agreement, or shall not consider the claim related to that matter if such claim was already admitted (*Tarptautinė statybos korporacija, UAB v. ALSTOM Power Sweden Aktienbolag AB*, 2012).

According to Article 12 of the LCA, all disputes may be settled by arbitration except disputes arising from constitutional, family and administrative matters; also disputes connected with patents, trademarks and service marks may not be submitted to arbitration. Disputes arising out of employment or consumer contracts may be referred to arbitration only if the arbitration agreement is concluded after the dispute arises.

Moreover, after recent amendments the LCA provides that initiating bankruptcy proceedings against a party to the arbitration agreement shall have no impact on the arbitration proceedings or the validity of the arbitration agreement.

Disregarding the general pro-arbitration approach, the Supreme Court of Lithuania has in several cases concluded that disputes arising out of the investigation of a legal person's activities, and disputes regarding procurement contract price changes, cannot be referred to arbitration. The Supreme Court of Lithuania has explained that the doctrine of *numerus clausus* applies to disputes that cannot be referred to arbitration, and such disputes have to be provided by law (*WTE Wassertechnik GmbH and Požeminiai darbai AB v. Environmental Projects Management Agency* under the Ministry of Environment of the Republic of Lithuania and *Kauno vandenys* AB, 2011).

At the same time, the Supreme Court of Lithuania tends to evaluate each case individually and, in cases of purely commercial dispute, tends to allow arbitration even in cases arising out of procurement contracts. The list of non-arbitrable disputes still remains very short and sustainable.

In 2012, the Supreme Court of Lithuania referred to the European Court of Justice a question for a preliminary ruling on whether the courts may refuse to recognise an arbitral anti-suit injunction on the ground that it would restrict its "right to determine itself whether it has jurisdiction to hear the case under the rules on jurisdiction in the Brussels I Regulation".

In May 2015 (C-536/13) the Grand Chamber of the ECJ provided an answer to the Supreme Court of Lithuania. The ECJ had already ruled in the earlier case of *Gasser v. MISAT* (C-116/02), and even more clearly in *Turner v. Grovit* (C-159/02), that anti-suit injunctions between the state courts of different Member States are incompatible with European law and thus inadmissible. ECJ reconfirmed its case lase developed in *Allianz and Generali v. West* Tankers (C-185/07) and justified the finding of incompatibility with European law by referring to a general principle that every court seized itself determines whether it has jurisdiction to resolve the dispute before. The ECJ ruled that Regulation No 44/2001 was intended to prevent only conflicts of jurisdiction between courts of the EU Member States and not conflicts between a court and an arbitral tribunal, and the "Brussels I" Regulation expressly excludes arbitration from the scope of that regulation.

Arbitration procedure

The arbitral procedure is started on the day the secretariat of VCAA receives the claim or the request for arbitration in compliance with the requirements of VCCA, unless it has been agreed otherwise between the parties.

Hearing of the case can take place outside the seat of arbitration and there are no limiting provisions either in the LCA or VCCA rules. Moreover, parties are free to use any language of arbitration, although it should be noted that VCCA administers arbitration only in English, Russian and Lithuanian.

The general rule is that the parties to arbitration are free to agree on arbitration procedure. In the absence of party agreement, the LCA gives the tribunal the power to conduct the arbitration in the manner it considers appropriate. The tribunal's discretion is only limited by general principles requiring fair treatment, equal procedural rights, autonomy, economy and cooperation. The LCA provides that the arbitral tribunal, in deciding cases, should apply the principles of *ex aequo et bono* or *amiable compositeur* only if the parties have expressly authorised it to do so.

The LCA provides that arbitral proceedings are confidential. Furthermore, VCCA rules provide that, unless the parties agree otherwise, an arbitral tribunal should hear a case in closed proceedings. However, it should be emphasised that if the award is challenged, the review procedures in national courts shall not be confidential. The court, upon the request of the interested party, may declare the case material non-public to protect confidential information and commercial secrets.

Moreover, on 1 July 2017, recent amendments of the LCA came into power. The said amendments ensure more confidentiality for arbitration proceedings even when the state courts are involved. The state courts shall ensure confidentiality and restricted assets (even to the finished cases); if the state court is involved in assistance for taking evidence, imposition of injunction measures or challenging an arbitration award, the said cases shall be considered as confidential by default.

There are no specific provisions on disclosure or discovery in arbitration within the LCA or VCCA rules. However, arbitrators and the parties are guided by the general rule that the arbitral tribunal may order any of the parties to submit relevant evidence. Also the IBA Rules on Taking Evidence in International Arbitration are not obligatory under VCCA rules or the LCA. However, arbitrators and the parties often refer to these rules. It has to be admitted that the continental approach to the taking of evidence, rather than what applies in common law countries, is adopted in Lithuania. Thus, production orders are limited to specific identifiable documents.

Courts may assist the arbitral tribunal or a party in taking evidence. The arbitrators and parties are allowed to participate in the procedure of taking evidence in court by giving explanations, asking questions or exercising other rights necessary for the collection of evidence.

The rules of VCCA allow the arbitral tribunal to order expertise to determine certain circumstances, or in cases where issues pertaining to the applicable foreign law have to be clarified. There are no more special regulations regarding expert evidence, however IBA Rules on the Taking of Evidence in International Arbitration are commonly applied in practice.

Arbitrators

Any natural person with full legal capacity may be appointed as an arbitrator, irrespective of his or her nationality, unless otherwise agreed by the parties. The parties are free to agree on a procedure for appointing arbitrators.

According to Article 14 of the LCA, if there is no prior agreement and if the arbitration consists of three arbitrators, each party selects one arbitrator, and the two of them appoint the third one. If the arbitration has a sole arbitrator, and if the parties cannot agree on the appointment, an arbitrator is appointed by the head of the permanent arbitral institution upon the request of any of the parties. The same rule also applies if one party does not appoint an arbitrator (or two arbitrators do not appoint the third one) within 20 days from the date the respective party had to appoint an arbitrator.

The courts have very limited powers to intervene in the appointment of arbitrators. Basically the law provides only one case where the court may intervene in the selection of arbitrators, and only in *ad hoc* proceedings.

The court may intervene in the selection of arbitrators in case of *ad hoc* proceedings, provided that a party fails to appoint an arbitrator, or in case two arbitrators appointed by the parties fail to appoint the chairman of the tribunal; an arbitrator/chairman of the tribunal is then appointed by Vilnius regional court within 20 days from the date the respective party had to appoint an arbitrator.

Article 14 of the LCA does not establish any specific restrictions on acting as an arbitrator. Anyone who has full legal capacity may serve as an arbitrator in Lithuania.

The law establishes general requirements for arbitrators, i.e. an arbitrator shall be impartial, independent and competent.

Arbitrators may be challenged only if there are circumstances that give rise to justifiable doubts as to his or her impartiality or independence, or if he or she does not possess the qualifications agreed to by the parties. The IBA Guidelines on Conflicts of Interest in International Arbitration are not mandatory under VCCA rules and the LCA. However, arbitrators and the VCCA secretariat frequently address these guidelines. The procedure of verification of independence and impartiality is diligently managed by the secretariat of VCCA, and the secretariat reviews the arbitrator's declaration in detail. It must be emphasised that not a single award has been set aside for this reason in Lithuania.

In the current landmark case by the Court of Appeal of Lithuania, the court formed case law requiring the highest standard of independence for arbitrators, and applied IBA Guidelines on Conflicts of Interest in International Arbitration. In the abovementioned case, regarding the recognition and enforcement of the interim measures award made by an *ad hoc* arbitration tribunal in Estonia, the Court of Appeal of Lithuania emphasised that, despite a party's right to freely choose the arbitrator on its side, the arbitrator has to be impartial and independent. After evaluating relations between the claimant and arbitrator appointed on the claimant's side, the nature of the relationship, its duration and the time passed after, the Court of Appeal of Lithuania established that it qualified for the Non-Waivable Red List of the IBA Guidelines on Conflicts of Interest in International Arbitration. Thus, the Court of Appeal of Lithuania stated that the third arbitrator appointed, who was unlawfully appointed on the side of the party to the proceeding, shall also be considered to have been appointed unlawfully. Having this in mind, the Court of Appeal of Lithuania refused to recognise and enforce the award on interim measures made by an *ad hoc* arbitration tribunal in Estonia, on the grounds of Article V (1) (d) and Article 5 (2) (b) of the New York Convention.

Lithuanian courts also have powers in *ad hoc* arbitration. If a party fails to appoint an arbitrator, the Vilnius County Court of the Republic of Lithuania shall appoint an arbitrator. The same procedure shall be involved if the parties fail to nominate a solo arbitrator. The involvement of Vilnius County Court ensures the fast and transparent nomination of arbitrators in both cases, as the judge usually issues the ruling in less than 20 days after the deadline for the abovementioned actions passes.

Under the rules of the VCCA, except for cases where such disclaimer is not allowed under the applicable law, neither arbitrators, the VCCA, the chair, nor the secretariat or employees of the VCCA are liable to any persons for any actions or mistakes in arbitration proceedings.

Moreover, the current case law of the Supreme Court of Lithuania (1 September 2016, case No. e3K-3-387-421/2016) establishes that the independence requirements might be applicable not only to arbitrators but also the arbitration institution itself. This case law is especially relevant when dealing with newly found arbitration institutions.

The arbitrator's mandate terminates when the arbitrator resigns or the parties agree upon the removal of the arbitrator from office. Under VCCA rules, the arbitrator is obliged to resign from office in case an arbitrator becomes *de jure* or *de facto* unable to perform the arbitrator's functions or delays performing these functions without any valid reasons.

Interim relief

The arbitral tribunal may, at the request of a party and upon informing other parties, rule on interim measures, which have the aim of ensuring that a party's request or relief will be enforced or that the evidence of the case will be preserved. However, the parties may agree otherwise and not to grant the tribunal such rights.

The LCA grants the parties to the arbitration proceedings a right to request the following interim measures: 1) prohibition of engagement by the party in certain transactions or taking of certain actions; 2) obligation of the party to keep safe assets related to arbitral proceedings, provide a monetary deposit or a bank or insurance guarantee; and 3) obligation of the party to preserve evidence that may be significant in arbitral proceedings.

For such interim measures to be enforced a party has to prove that: 1) claims are likely to be founded (however, the determination of such likelihood does not affect the power of the arbitral tribunal to subsequently give a different arbitral award or order in arbitral proceedings); 2) the failure to take the measures can substantially preclude the enforcement of the arbitral award or render it impossible; and 3) interim measures are cost-effective and proportionate to the goal sought.

An emergency arbitrator, who can order urgent interim measures, may be appointed under Article 35 of VCCA rules. An order made by an emergency arbitrator can be modified later by the arbitral tribunal.

Under Article 27 of the LCA, a party is entitled to request Vilnius Regional Court to take interim measures or require evidence before the commencement of arbitral proceedings or the constitution of an arbitral tribunal. At the same time, the refusal of the court to take interim measures or preserve evidence does not preclude a party from requesting an arbitral tribunal to apply interim measures or preserve evidence during arbitral proceedings.

Courts may assist the arbitral tribunal or a party in taking evidence. Evidence is collected at court, *mutatis mutandis* applying the provisions of the Code of Civil Procedure of the Republic of Lithuania (e.g. the appropriate court may be instructed to carry out certain procedural actions (question parties, third parties and witnesses, inspect location, etc.)).

Arbitration award

The major formal requirement for an arbitral award is that it must be made in writing and signed by arbitrators or an arbitrator. An award of the arbitral tribunal must be in writing and signed by a majority of the arbitrators, with the other arbitrators indicating their reasons for not signing.

In cases where the arbitrator or arbitrators disagree with the majority, they shall have the right to state their dissenting opinion in writing, which shall be enclosed with the arbitral award.

The LCA does not provide any specific timeframe within which the arbitration award shall be rendered. Part 6 of Article 8 of the LCA establishes a general principle that arbitral proceedings shall conform to the principles of autonomy of the parties, competition, cost-efficiency, cooperation and rapidity. Therefore some permanent arbitration institutions in their arbitration rules establish more detailed regulation. The arbitral award must state the reasons upon which it is based, unless the parties have agreed otherwise.

For example, VCCA rules provide that a final arbitration award shall be made as soon as possible after the main hearing, but not later than 30 days following the last main hearing. In exceptional cases, the Arbitration Rules of VCCA allow the chair of VCCA to extend at his/her own discretion the term for making an award for another period of up to 30 days, or longer provided the parties consent thereto. Before signing any arbitral award, the arbitral tribunal is obliged to submit it in draft form to VCCA (the secretariat) which, in no more than 10 days, shall assess the compliance of the arbitral award with the requirements of form (in this case, the legitimacy and validity of the award is not assessed).

Costs are usually awarded from the losing party upon advance request from the winning party, unless otherwise agreed in the arbitration agreement. Although the award of interest is allowed and interest is usually awarded together with the claimed amounts, it is important to emphasise that, according to the case law of Lithuanian courts, awarding punitive interest is contrary to the public order of the Republic of Lithuania and therefore is prohibited.

Challenge of the arbitration award

It has already been mentioned above that Lithuanian judges are pro-arbitration and very conservative in dealing with award-challenging issues. The Lithuanian courts system has established that all award challenges go directly to the Court of Appeal of Lithuania, and this ensures that the limited number of senior judges having academic degrees are involved in the procedure of review of the awards.

According to Article 50 of the LCA, challenge of the award has to be heard within 90 days after filing claim on annulment. However, depending on the workload of the Court of Appeals of Lithuania, the procedure of challenge of the arbitration award may take three to six months. The ruling of the Court of Appeals is subject to appeal to the Supreme Court of Lithuania.

Coherent and consistent case law of the Lithuanian courts confirms that the appeal of arbitration awards in the Republic of Lithuania is not possible. When a court receives a claim regarding a matter subject to an arbitration agreement, the court shall refuse to accept the claim (*Valbis UAB v. Schenker UAB*, 2011). Moreover, you can be almost 100% sure that the court will refuse to review the arbitral award on the issues of proper evaluation of factual background and application of laws (*Ballsbridge Advisory Ltd v. M. Ž., O. B. and V. S.*, 2014).

Of course, the law provides traditional grounds for challenging arbitral awards. It is possible to challenge an award on strict grounds established by law. Para 3 of Article 50 of the LCA allows the Court of Appeal of Lithuania to set aside an arbitral award where the appellant party provides evidence that:

1. one party to an arbitration agreement, according to applicable laws, was legally incapable or the arbitration agreement is not valid according to laws applicable according to the agreement of the parties or, in the absence of an agreement of the parties on law governing the arbitration agreement, according to the laws of the state in which the arbitral award was made;
2. the party in respect of which the arbitral award is intended to be invoked has not been duly notified of the appointment of an arbitrator or arbitral proceedings or has not been otherwise enabled to give his explanations;
3. the arbitral award has been made in relation to a dispute or part thereof which has not been submitted to arbitration. Where part of the dispute which has been submitted to arbitration may be distinguished, the part of the arbitral award that resolves matters submitted to arbitration may be recognised and enforced;
4. the composition of an arbitral tribunal or arbitral proceedings does not conform to the agreement of the parties and/or the imperative provisions of this Law;
5. the dispute may not be submitted to arbitration according to the laws of the Republic of Lithuania; or
6. the arbitral award is in conflict with the public policy of the Republic of Lithuania.

One of the most recent successful challenges of arbitral decisions was made in the case *Giraitės vandenys UAB v. Grundolita* UAB, 2014. In this case the Court of Appeals of Lithuania held invalid a partial award made by the arbitral tribunal of the permanent arbitration institution, Vilnius international and the national commercial arbitration court. In a partial award, the arbitral tribunal ruled on its competence to hear the dispute. The dispute arose from the fact that the parties to the arbitration clause had not agreed directly which permanent arbitration institution or *ad hoc* arbitration was entitled to resolve the dispute. The Court of Appeals of Lithuania, after analysing the arbitral clause from the agreement, decided that the intentions of the parties were to resolve any dispute in the International Court of Arbitration of the International Chamber of Commerce. Thus, the Court of Appeals of Lithuania declared null and void a partial decision of Vilnius international and national commercial arbitration court regarding its competence to hear a dispute.

Nor should you be worried about the courts' interpretation of public policy in challenging awards. Lithuanian courts have already ruled a number of times that public policy is to be understood as international public policy, the fundamental principles of due process and mandatory rules of substantive law embedding generally accepted principles of law (*Farmak AB v. Baltijos farmacijos centras* UAB, 2013).

Award-challenging proceedings do not freeze enforcement proceedings. However, after accepting an application to set aside an arbitral award, the Court of Appeals of Lithuania may suspend the enforcement of the award at the request of a party.

Enforcement of the arbitration award

Lithuanian courts recognise the presumption of validity of an arbitration decision established both in UNCITRAL Model Law, as well as in the New York Convention.

According to the LCA, the party willing to recognise and enforce the arbitration award shall provide to the Court of Appeal of Lithuania an application, accompanied by the original copy of an arbitral award requested to be recognised and enforced, and of an original arbitration agreement or its duly certified copies. When the arbitral award or arbitration agreement is made in a foreign language, the applying party shall supply a duly certified translation of the abovementioned documents in the Lithuanian language.

The LCA does not provide any specific grounds for refusal to recognise or enforce the arbitral award, and refers to the provisions of the New York Convention. Thus, it shall refuse to recognise or enforce foreign arbitral awards only under the grounds of Article V of the New York Convention.

Lithuanian courts strictly follow international practice in the application of Part 1 and Part 2 of Article V of the New York Convention, refusing to consider the grounds stipulated in Part 1 of Article V of the Convention unless a party makes a request to consider one or several grounds to refuse recognition and enforcement of the foreign arbitral award. Part 1 of the Article V of the New York Convention is applied by Lithuanian courts *ex officio*.

On 15 June 2017, the Supreme Court of Lithuania issued a landmark ruling, which states that foreign arbitration awards are subject for recognition and enforcement in Lithuania without any statutory limitation (*Suraleb INC. vs. Minsk Tractor Plant*, 2017). Despite the fact of five years' statutory limitation applicable for local arbitration awards, in case of foreign arbitral award countdown of five years, the statutory limitation period shall start from the day the foreign award is recognised in Lithuania. Moreover, the same case involved issues of recognition of U.S. court decision on recognition and enforcement of the above-mentioned award in the U.S. and award of additional penalties. The Supreme Court of Lithuania ruled that the part of the U.S. court regarding recognition of an award in the U.S. is not enforceable under the general rule *exequatur sur exequatur ne vaut*; however, the second part, i.e. award of additional interest, is subject to recognition in Lithuania.

Requests concerning recognition of foreign arbitral awards are heard by the Court of Appeals of Lithuania and written proceedings are applied. Rulings of the Court of Appeals of Lithuania on recognition and enforcement of a foreign arbitral award may be appealed to the Supreme Court of Lithuania within one month. Thus the same system as in the case of challenging of arbitral awards applies in this case. Involvement of the highest-tier courts ensures very modern, consistent and pro-arbitration case law in Lithuania.

Investment arbitration

Lithuania signed and ratified the Washington Convention on the Settlement of Investment Disputes Between States and Nationals of Other States (ICSID, 1965). It came into force in Lithuania on 5 August 1992. Lithuania is a party to the Energy Charter Treaty (which entered into force in Lithuania on 13 December 1998). Moreover, Lithuania is a party to more than 50 Bilateral Investment Treaties (BITs) or other multi-party investment treaties.

The Supreme Court has developed theory that the defence of state immunity should be allowed only in disputes governed by public law; while in disputes governed by private law, such defence should not be allowed.

Most Lithuanian BITs provide a right of recourse to ICSID. Most of the treaties also allow investors to pursue an arbitration claim through an *ad hoc* tribunal applying the rules contained within the Washington Convention, an *ad hoc* tribunal constituted in accordance with the UNCITRAL rules; and/or any other tribunal acting in accordance with any other arbitration rules may be mutually agreed by the parties. Numerous BITs refer to the use of a commercial arbitral institution, e.g. ICC arbitration in Paris or SCC Stockholm arbitration.

Paulius Docka, FCIArb
Tel: +370 5 248 7337 / Email: Paulius.Docka@primus.legal

Paulius Docka is an attorney at law with more than 17 years of experience. He graduated from Vilnius University Faculty of Law and the University of Leicester, UK.

Mr. Docka started his career at the Ministry of Justice of the Republic of Lithuania. He continued his professional carrier at an Ernst & Young affiliated law firm and in 2005 established a law firm, which currently bears the name PRIMUS and is one of the largest pan-Baltic law firms.

He is a member of the ICC Institute of World Business Law, a Fellow of the Chartered Institute of Arbitrators, a member of the International Arbitration Institute, a member of the Russian Arbitration Association and Silicon Valley Arbitration & Mediation Center. Mr. Docka is also a member of ICC Central and Eastern European Arbitration Group (CEEAG).

Paulius Docka is recommended arbitrator by Vienna International Arbitral Center, Kuala Lumpur Regional Centre for Arbitration, Vilnius Court of Commercial Arbitration and EHF Court of Arbitration.

Mr. Docka was nominated as a highly recommended dispute resolution lawyer by *Chambers and Partners*, and as a leading aviation lawyer by *Who's Who Legal: Aviation Finance* and *Aviation Contentious*.

He mainly focuses on arbitration and aviation transactions.

PRIMUS attorneys at law

7 Konstitucijos Ave., Vilnius, Lithuania
Tel: +370 5 248 7337 / URL: www.primus.legal

Macedonia

Kristina Kragujevska
Konrad & Partners

Introduction

The demand for a transparent, time-efficient and cost-effective forum for dispute resolution has grown stronger with the steady increase of foreign investments in South-Eastern Europe. This has resulted in legislation being passed in Macedonia that allows parties to custom-tailor their arbitration proceedings using internationally recognised standards and instruments.

To bring Macedonian arbitration law in line with international standards, the commission for drafting the 2006 Law on International Commercial Arbitration (**LICA**) decided to adopt the original text and structure of the 1985 UNCITRAL Model Law (**1985 ML**) to the greatest extent possible. LICA applies exclusively to international commercial arbitration where the place of arbitration is in Macedonia. The legal framework under which domestic entities can bring their disputes to arbitration is provided for in Chapter 30 of the Law on Civil Procedure (**LCP**).

A major revision of LICA is planned to be published by the end of 2018. It is not yet disclosed by the working group whether the revision will result in an arbitration law applicable both to international and domestic arbitration. In any case, the revision will incorporate the 2006 amendments of the 1985 ML.

The main arbitration institution in Macedonia – the Permanent Court of Arbitration – has the authority to administer both domestic and international disputes. In 2011, consistent with its intention to incorporate the well-established international practices, the Court altered its structure with the adoption of the new Rulebook of the Court (the **Rulebook**). These changes led to immediate results, especially with regard to the shortening of the proceedings.

Macedonia is a party to the 1958 New York Convention on the Recognition and Enforcement of Foreign Arbitral Awards (**New York Convention**). Macedonia, as then part of Yugoslavia, acceded to the New York Convention on 26 February 1982. In September 2009, the Macedonian government notified the UN Secretary General of its decision to withdraw the reciprocity reservation; no other reservations have been made. Macedonia is also a party to the 1961 European Convention on International Commercial Arbitration and the 1965 Washington Convention on the Settlement of Investment Disputes between States and Nationals of Other States (**ICSID**).

Arbitration agreement

The agreement to arbitrate under LICA can be concluded in the form of a contractual clause in a contract or as a separate contract. Regardless of the choice, the will of the parties to have their dispute finally resolved through arbitration has to be expressed in writing. The written form requirement is fulfilled if the clause is contained in: (i) a document signed by the parties; or (ii) an exchange of letters, telex, telegrams or other means of communication which will provide a record of the agreement. Any defect of the written form requirement is cured by an exchange of statements of claim and defence in which the existence of an agreement is alleged by one party and not denied by the other. Any reference to a contract, including reference to general terms and conditions, which contains an arbitration clause, constitutes an arbitration agreement, but only if the written form is met and the reference is such as to make that clause part of the contract (Art.7 LICA).

In addition to the writing requirement, an arbitration agreement has to refer to a defined legal relationship, whether contractual or not (Art.2.6 LICA). Naturally, such a relationship can only be established on the assumption that the prerequisites for subjective arbitrability are met, i.e. the parties to the agreement to arbitrate had legal capacity to enter into such a contract.

With regard to objective arbitrability, LICA stipulates that any dispute for which an exclusive jurisdiction of a court in Macedonia is not provided can be submitted to arbitration. With this, and in line with the Model Law, the term "commercial" is given a wide interpretation as to cover all relationships of a commercial nature. If a claim is filed with a court for the same dispute and between the same parties, the court shall reject the claim, unless it finds that the arbitration agreement is null and void, or incapable of being performed.

The principle of competence-competence is incorporated under Art.16 LICA. The arbitral tribunal may rule on its own jurisdiction, and rule thereby on any objections with respect to the existence and validity of the arbitration agreement. The principle of separability is also recognised, providing that an arbitration clause which is part of a main contract will be treated as an agreement independent of the other terms of the contract. LICA does not deviate from the original text of the 1985 ML with regard to these principles, and further provides that the decision of the arbitral tribunal that the contract is null and void does not entail *ispo jure* the invalidity of the arbitration clause.

Arbitration procedure

The arbitration proceedings, unless otherwise agreed by the parties, commence on the date on which the request for the dispute to be referred to arbitration is received by the respondent (Art.21 LICA). LICA further provides for the possibility for the parties, or the arbitral tribunal, to state the facts supporting the claim, the points of issue and the relief or remedy sought within a determined period of time.

The Rulebook provides a detailed list on the information that has to be contained in the statement of claim, such as a detailed description of the parties, the arbitration agreement, the statement of facts and the request for relief, the name(s) of the arbitrators, determination of the value of the dispute, and all the evidence that is considered to be relevant (Art.42 Rulebook).

The place of arbitration, if not otherwise chosen by the parties, shall be Skopje. The arbitral tribunal may, if such decision is considered appropriate, meet at another place.

The parties are free to determine the rules of the procedure. In the absence of such agreement, the arbitral tribunal will conduct the procedure in such manner as it deems appropriate (Art.19 LICA).

Further, the parties are free to agree on the procedure for taking of evidence. Therefore, the parties may also agree on the IBA Rules on the Taking of Evidence. In the absence of any such agreement, the arbitral tribunal has wide discretion regarding the conduct of the evidentiary proceedings, subject to the mandatory provision of the law such as equal treatment of the parties, the right to be heard, public policy, etc. This discretion entitles the arbitral tribunal to determine the admissibility, relevance and weight of any evidence. Although there are no special provisions in LICA regarding the hearing of witnesses, both written statements and oral hearings, including cross-examinations, are possible.

The arbitral tribunal is authorised to request the parties disclose certain documents. If the party does not comply with a request of the arbitral tribunal, the arbitral tribunal can request assistance from the competent court in Macedonia (Art.27 LICA).

The arbitral tribunal may also appoint experts. Furthermore, the tribunal may request from the parties to provide the expert with all relevant information or to produce or provide access to any relevant documents, goods or other property for his/her inspection. If a party and an expert (either appointed by one of the parties or the arbitral tribunal) disagree on the relevance of the requested information and documents, the opposing party can request a decision in relation to the issue. Upon submission of the expert report, the parties can request the expert to attend an oral hearing to be cross-examined on the findings of his/her expert report (Art.52 Rulebook).

Subject to any agreement to the contrary, the arbitral tribunal can decide to hold an oral hearing or to conduct the proceedings without a hearing, solely based on the documents and other materials. In case of an oral hearing, the parties must be given advance notice. All statements, documents and other information submitted to the arbitral tribunal by one of the parties must also be delivered to the other party in due time.

LICA provides for confidential proceedings, such that unless otherwise agreed by the parties, the arbitration procedure is not open to the public.

Arbitrators

Consistent with the 1985 ML, LICA allows the parties to determine the number of arbitrators and does not require an odd number of arbitrators to be selected. If the parties cannot reach an agreement, then as a default rule the arbitral tribunal will consist of three arbitrators (Art.10 LICA). Parties are free to agree on a procedure for the appointment of the arbitrators. Failing such agreement, each party will appoint one arbitrator, and the two arbitrators thus designated will appoint the President of the arbitral tribunal.

The Rulebook provides for a slightly narrowed choice and gives the parties the right to decide whether the dispute shall be settled by a sole arbitrator or an arbitral tribunal composed of three arbitrators. Subject to any provision to the contrary, the Rulebook specifies the threshold of €30,000 in dispute as the upper limit, above which an arbitral tribunal of three arbitrators will be appointed. In this case, each party will appoint one arbitrator and the President of the Court will appoint the President of the arbitral tribunal (Art.28 Rulebook).

The President of the arbitral tribunal is always chosen from the list of arbitrators provided by the Court. Such limitation is not set for the parties – they are free to nominate an arbitrator not enrolled in the list (Art.30 Rulebook).

Generally, any natural person having full legal capacity can be appointed as an arbitrator. This implies that an arbitrator does not have to be a qualified lawyer, although the parties can agree on certain (professional) qualifications required for being appointed as an arbitrator.

Prior to his/her appointment, any arbitrator must disclose any circumstances which might raise doubts as to her/his impartiality or independence. The challenge of an arbitrator on the basis of his/her impartiality has to indicate any potential link to the parties, direct or indirect financial income or potential possession of confidential information in relation to the dispute, or any other information that might affect the impartiality of the arbitrator. In case the respective arbitrator does not resign, or the other party does not agree to the exemption, the decision regarding the exemption will be made by the arbitral tribunal, respectively, by the President of the Court. The right to challenge is also given to the party who nominated the arbitrator, but only for reasons that were not disclosed at the time of the appointment and discovered thereafter (Art.35 Rulebook).

The mandate of the arbitrator will be terminated if, due to legal or factual reasons he/she becomes unable to perform his/her function, or for other reasons fails to perform without undue delay, the respective arbitrator resigns, or the parties agree on the termination. If the parties cannot agree on the termination of the arbitrator's mandate, each party may request the President of the Court to decide on the termination of the mandate of the arbitrator (Art.37 Rulebook).

In case of termination of the mandate, a substitute arbitrator will be appointed under the same requirements that were applicable for the appointment of the arbitrator being replaced. In case an arbitrator has been replaced, unless otherwise agreed by the parties, the hearing has to be repeated. The repetition of the hearing is mandatory in case the procedure was conducted by a sole arbitrator (Art.39 Rulebook).

Interim relief

The arbitral tribunal may, at the request of a party, order interim measures against the other party which the arbitral tribunal considers necessary in respect of the subject matter of the dispute. The arbitral tribunal may also request the party to provide appropriate security in connection with the interim measure (Art.17 LICA).

Under Macedonian arbitration law, it is possible to apply both to domestic courts and to the arbitral tribunal for the issuance of an interim measure either before or during the arbitral proceedings. However, considering the arbitral tribunal's lack of enforcement powers, in case the party does not comply with the interim measure ordered by the arbitral tribunal, the party upon whose proposal the measure was issued may address the competent court for legal assistance. Taking into consideration that there are no special courts for arbitration matters in Macedonia, legal assistance, if such is required, is provided by the Basic Courts (Art.17(2) LICA; Art.56(2) Rulebook).

Both the LICA (in relation to international arbitration) and the LCP (in relation to domestic arbitration) provide that the Court shall immediately reject any claim that is filed before the Basic Court for the same dispute and between the same parties for which an arbitration agreement has been concluded. Accordingly, anti-arbitration injunctions are not stipulated under Macedonian law.

Arbitration award

The arbitration award shall be in writing, and shall be signed by the sole arbitrator, the arbitrators, or respectively by the majority of the arbitrators. In the latter case, the arbitral award has to state the reason for any omitted signatures. If majority cannot be reached, the chairing arbitrator shall have a deciding vote.

The award shall state the reasons upon which it is based, unless the parties agreed otherwise.

The award shall state the date on which it was made and the place of arbitration. The award shall be deemed to have been rendered on that day and at that place (Art.31 LICA).

Neither LICA nor the Rulebook prescribe a time limit for the rendering of the award. The Arbitration statistics for the year 2015 show that the average timeframe in which the proceedings are finalised, including the rendering of the arbitral award, was from four to twelve months.

A copy of the signed award is to be delivered to each party. Within 30 days of receipt of the award, a party can request the arbitral tribunal to correct any errors in computation, any typographical errors or errors of a similar nature in the award, or the arbitral tribunal can be requested to provide an additional interpretation of a specific part of the award. In case the request is considered to be justified, the arbitral tribunal will provide the correction or the interpretation. The interpretation shall be considered to be part of the original award (Art.33 LICA).

In addition, each party can request an additional award to be rendered with regard to issues that the arbitral tribunal failed to address in the original award. The additional award has to be rendered within 60 days of receipt of the request, provided that the same was justified (Art.33 LICA).

The arbitral tribunal shall allocate the costs of the proceedings, taking into account the outcome of the dispute. If the claim was successful only in part, the tribunal shall allocate the costs on a *pro rata* basis. The parties may, however, depart from this general rule, and allow for the tribunal to allocate the costs in a manner it deems fit (Art.7 Rules on Costs).

Challenge of the arbitration award

A claim for annulment shall be filed with the competent Basic Court, and must be based on at least one of the limited grounds for setting aside the award:

- a party in the procedure was incapable of concluding the arbitration agreement or to be a party to the arbitration agreement;
- a valid arbitration agreement does not exist under the applicable law to the agreement;
- the party has not been duly informed about the appointment of the arbitrators or the initiation of the arbitration proceedings or was otherwise unable to present its case;
- the arbitral award deals with a dispute not covered by the arbitral agreement, or contains decisions on issues beyond the scope of the arbitration agreement. If the default concerns only a part of the award that can be separated, only that part of the arbitral award shall be set aside;
- the composition of the arbitral tribunal or the arbitration procedure were not in accordance with the arbitration agreement, unless such agreement was in conflict with a provision of LICA from which the parties cannot derogate;
- the subject matter of the dispute cannot be settled by way of arbitration; or
- the arbitral award is in conflict with the public policy.

The claim for annulment can be filed within three months from the day of receipt of the award. LICA provides the possibility for the Court to postpone the commencement of the procedure for annulment and to provide the arbitral tribunal with additional time to correct the defects that could lead to the setting-aside of the award. However, so far there is no recorded case in which an arbitral award has been annulled in Macedonia.

Enforcement of the arbitration award

An arbitral award (in conformity with the provisions of LICA) has the effect of a final judgment and can be enforced.

Any award enacted outside of the Republic of Macedonia is considered a foreign arbitral award, and will thus be recognised and enforced in accordance with the New York Convention.

The procedure for recognition of a foreign arbitral award is conducted before the Basic Court where the opposing party has its seat of business. The procedure is initiated with an application for recognition of a foreign arbitral award. In accordance with the formal requirements of the New York Convention, the application shall be filed with originals, or certified copies of the arbitration award and the arbitration agreement.

Investment arbitration

There are 38 bilateral investment treaties in force in Macedonia, with an additional two in process of ratification. Macedonia is a party to the ICSID Convention. The Convention provides for arbitration in case of a dispute between the state and a foreign investor.

To date, Macedonia has been involved in four investor-state disputes:

- In 2007, the Greek company Hellenic Petroleum brought proceedings against the Republic of Macedonia before the International Chamber of Commerce (ICC), and succeeded on the grounds of violation of a contract for the sale of the oil refinery OKTA.
- In 2009, the electricity provider EVN AG brought proceedings against the Republic of Macedonia under the ICSID Rules of Arbitration. In 2011, upon the request of both parties, the arbitral tribunal issued an award on agreed terms pursuant to Rule 43(2) of the ICSID Rules of Arbitration, incorporating the settlement reached by the parties.
- In 2009, the Swiss confectionary affiliate Swisslion brought proceedings against the Republic of Macedonia before ICSID. In its decision of July 2012, the arbitral tribunal decided that the Republic of Macedonia breached its obligations under public international law by failing to accord fair and equitable treatment to the Claimant's investment. However, all other claims of the Claimant were dismissed and the Respondent was ordered to pay €350,000.00 of the Claimant's legal costs and expenses.
- In 2015, Guardian Fiduciary Trust, Ltd. brought proceedings against Macedonia before ICSID. The arbitral tribunal dismissed the Claimant's claim due to lack of jurisdiction, and ordered the Claimant to pay the costs of the proceedings.

Kristina Kragujevska
Tel: +389 230 65 441 / Email: k.kragujevska@konrad-partners.com
Kristina Kragujevska is an Associated Attorney at Konrad & Partners. She represents and advises clients on a variety of commercial and corporate transactions and disputes, with a particular focus on the protection of foreign investment. She is a member of the Macedonian Bar Association.

Konrad & Partners

Bulevar Kiro Gligorov 4, 1000 Skopje, Republic of Macedonia
Tel: +389 230 65 441 / Fax: +389 230 65 441 / URL: www.konrad-partners.com

Malaysia

Khong Aik Gan, Joon Liang Foo & Lim Bee San
Gan Partnership

Introduction

The Malaysian Arbitration Act 1952 ("**the 1952 Act**") was incorporated in one of Malaysia's states, Sarawak, as early as 18 June 1952, and this act was subsequently incorporated in other states of Malaysia on 1 November 1972. Meanwhile, the Convention on the Recognition and Enforcement of Foreign Arbitral Awards Act 1985 ("**the 1985 Act**") was enacted to give effect to the provisions of the Convention on the Recognition and Enforcement of Foreign Arbitral Awards, passed at New York on 10 June 1958 ("**the New York Convention**").

The 1952 Act and the 1985 Act formed the earliest legislative framework in Malaysia for laws relating to arbitration. In 2005, both these acts were replaced by the Arbitration Act 2005 ("**the Act**") which, amongst others, sought to reform the law relating to domestic arbitration, provide for international arbitration, and the recognition and enforcement of awards. It seeks to promote international consistency of arbitral regimes based on the model law adopted by the United Nations Commission on International Trade Law on 21 June 1985.

The Act came into force on 15 March 2006, is modelled on the UNCITRAL Model Law 1985 on International Commercial Arbitration 1985 and is similar to the New Zealand Arbitration Act 1969.[1] It applies to both domestic and international arbitrations conducted in Malaysia and varies only with regard to certain aspects of the Act such as enforcement. The 1952 Act is still applicable but only in relation to arbitral proceedings commenced before 15 March 2006.[2]

With effect from year 2006, the Act is the principal source of law and regulation relating to international and domestic arbitration. Section 30(1) of the Act allows parties to a domestic arbitration to determine the substantive law applicable and in the absence of agreement, the substantive laws of Malaysia shall apply.

An international arbitration is defined in the Act as an arbitration where one of the parties to the arbitration agreement, the seat of arbitration, the subject matter of the dispute or a substantial portion of the commercial obligations of the parties lie in a state outside Malaysia. An Pinternational arbitration could also arise where parties expressly agree that the arbitration relates to more than one state. On the other hand, a domestic arbitration is defined as any arbitration that is not an international arbitration.

In relation to international arbitration, the arbitral tribunal shall determine the dispute according to the laws agreed upon by the parties as applicable to the substance of the dispute, failing which the dispute shall be decided based on the law determined by the rules on the conflict of law based on Section 30(4) of the Act.

In 2011, the Arbitration (Amendment) Bill 2010[3] was passed to promote and encourage arbitration. Among others, the amendments passed in this bill limit court intervention and to discourage the use of inherent powers, and that no reference on a question of law is allowed unless the question of law substantially affects the rights of one or more of the parties. After the amendment, the grounds allowed under Section 10 of the Act for the court to refuse an application to stay a court proceeding for the existence of an arbitration agreement has also been reduced to just one ground, i.e. that if the arbitration agreement is null and void, inoperative or incapable of being performed.

Malaysia is a signatory to the New York Convention starting from 5 November 1985. Therefore, an arbitral award from Malaysia is enforceable in more than 148 countries which are contracting states to the New York Convention.[4] As for foreign awards where seats of arbitration are from these 148 countries, Section 38 of the Act allows such foreign awards to be recognised and enforced in Malaysia, including an award made in international arbitration with a seat in Malaysia.

Apart from the New York Convention, Malaysia is also a signatory to the Comprehensive Investment Treaty between members of the Association of Southeast Asia Nations[5] (ASEAN), as well as a party to the Convention on the Settlement of Investment Disputes between States and Nationals of Other States 1965 (ICSID Convention).[6]

The main arbitral institution in Malaysia that both carries out the administration function and provides a venue for commercial arbitrations is the Kuala Lumpur Regional Centre for Arbitration (KLRCA) established in 1978. KLRCA was recently renamed the Asian International Arbitration Centre ("AIAC"), on 28 February 2018, pursuant to the Arbitration (Amendment Act) 2018.[7]

Effective from 9 March 2018, AIAC will use the AIAC Arbitration Rules 2018 as its latest arbitration rules. The contents of the AIAC Arbitration Rules 2018 are the same as the KLRCA Rules (as revised in 2017), and both the rules adopt the UNCITRAL Arbitration Rules as revised in 2013, with some modifications. Similarly, other existing rules such as the KLRCA i-Arbitration Rules and the KLRCA Fast Track Arbitration Rules, which were introduced to cater for the growing demands of the global business community, will be renamed accordingly, "AIAC i-Arbitration Rules 2018" and "AIAC Fast Track Arbitration Rules" in year 2018. The i-Arbitration Rules regulate arbitration of disputes arising from commercial transactions premised on Islamic principles, whereas the Fast Track Arbitration Rules are designed for parties who wish to obtain an award in the fastest way with minimal costs.[8]

Apart from the AIAC, arbitrations are also administered by a number of other professional institutions such as the Association of Architects of Malaysia and the Institute of Engineers Malaysia for disputes arising from the standard forms of contract provided by these institutions.

Arbitration agreement

Section 9 of the Act provides a statutory definition and form of an arbitration agreement. An "arbitration agreement" is defined as an agreement by the parties to submit to arbitration all or certain disputes which have arisen or which may arise between them in respect of a defined legal relationship, whether contractual or not. Provided that it is in writing, an arbitration agreement may:

(a) be an arbitration clause in an agreement signed by both parties;

(b) be in the form of a separate agreement signed by both parties;

(c) be an exchange of communication which provides a record of the agreement;

(d) arise from pleadings exchanged between parties where the existence of an arbitration agreement is alleged by one party and is not denied by the other; or

(e) be a reference in an agreement to a document containing an arbitration clause.

The Federal Court of Malaysia, in the case of ***Ajwa For Food Industries Co (Migop), Egypt v. Pacific Inter-Link Sdn Bhd,***[9] had referred and relied on two English cases of *Baker v. Yorkshire Fire and Life Assurance Company* [1892] 1 QB 144, where it was held that it is not necessary in all cases for the written agreement referring the matter to arbitration to be signed by both parties; and *Morgan v. (W) Harrison Ltd* [1907] 2 Ch 137 at p.104, where the court held that an arbitration agreement may be deduced from correspondence between the parties.

Another example is the case of ***Sebor (Sarawak) Marketing & Services Sdn Bhd v. SA Shee (Sarawak) Sdn Bhd,***[10] where the Malaysian Court held that written agreement for arbitration can be deduced from the minutes recording the agreement and the written acceptance by the arbitrator of his appointment.

Clearly for an arbitration agreement to come under the purview of Malaysian laws, it may come in various forms, and could even exist in exchange of correspondence, as long as the intention of the parties could be shown to be bound by such agreement.

Most civil disputes (as opposed to criminal matters) are arbitrable in Malaysia under the Act, so long as the parties have agreed to submit to arbitration under an arbitration agreement. Under Section 4 of the Act, there is no requirement that the dispute be commercial in nature or arise out of a contractual relationship. However, an arbitration agreement which is contrary to public policy will not be arbitrable, in which case the public policy must be considered in a Malaysian context.

Being consistent with the principle of privity of contract, an arbitration agreement does not bind a non-party or strangers to the agreement. Despite this, a party to an arbitration agreement is able to assign its rights under the agreement to a third party, by which the third party (who then becomes the assignee) is bound.

In line with the modern arbitral practice, the doctrine of severability/separability and the concept of *Kompetenz-Kompetenz* is well recognised under Section 18 of the Act, which provides power for an arbitral tribunal to rule on its own jurisdiction, including on any objection with respect to the existence or validity of the arbitration agreement. This is consistent with Article 16 of Model Law.

Meanwhile, Section 18(2) of the Act provides that an arbitration clause which forms part of an agreement shall be treated as an agreement independent of the other terms of the agreement, and a decision by the arbitral tribunal that the agreement is null and void shall not *ipso jure* entail the invalidity of the arbitration clause.

Therefore, it is very clear from the Act that an arbitration clause can still be considered valid even if the rest of the contract in which it is included is determined to be invalid and the arbitral tribunal is empowered under Section 18(1) of the Act to make such ruling.

Given that an arbitration agreement is a contract, the grounds on which a contract can be avoided are equally applicable to a party to an arbitration agreement who intends to challenge the said arbitration agreement.

Under the Malaysian Contracts Act 1950, a contract may be avoided where it is entered without free consent, for example, when it is entered by coercion, undue influence, fraud, misrepresentation or mistake. Thus, when any of these is proven, such an arbitration agreement would become void.

Rights to arbitrate disputes failing within a valid arbitration agreement can be waived by both parties by initiating proceedings in court and taking steps in such proceedings. However, if a party initiates a court proceeding and the other party objects to the same on the ground that there is a valid arbitration agreement, the latter party may apply to stay the court proceeding and refer the disputes to arbitration, and Section 10(1) of the Act provides that it is compulsory for the court to stay the court proceeding in the presence of a valid arbitration agreement. This shows the pro-arbitration stance intended by the parliament under the Act.

Arbitration procedure

Unless parties otherwise agree in their arbitration agreement, arbitral proceedings commence on the date on which a request is issued by one party to the other for the dispute to be referred to arbitration. Pursuant to Section 23 of the Act, the request is to be in writing. Other than this, there are no formal requirements under the Act for making the request. Some institutional rules, if adopted by the parties, may require specific matters to be stated in the request for arbitration.

An example of this is Rule 2 of the KLRCA/AIAC Arbitration Rules, requiring the submission of a copy of the notice of arbitration to the director of the KLRCA/AIAC, together with a copy of the arbitration agreement, confirmation of service of the notice of arbitration on all other parties, and payment of a registration fee.

Parties are also free to reach consensus on the procedures of the arbitration pursuant to Section 21 of the Act. In the absence of such agreement, the Act allows the appointed arbitrator to make directions for the rules and procedures to be followed. In international arbitration, it is not uncommon for parties to adopt memorial-style directions to be adopted, with parties following the sequence of submitting their pleadings, witness statements, documents and experts' reports.

On the issues of evidence law for arbitration, the Malaysian Evidence Act 1950, which sets out strict rules of evidence, is inapplicable to arbitration proceedings.[11] In practice, some evidential requirements are agreed by parties in which rules of evidence in common law are applied.

While the International Bar Association Rules on the Taking of Evidence in International Arbitration (IBA Rules on Evidence) are not incorporated into the Act, it is not uncommon for experienced arbitrators in Malaysia, when dealing with domestic and international arbitrations, to take guidance from and include the IBA Rules in their procedural orders.

Under the Act, there is no specific requirement or prohibition of expert evidence. As such, whether or not evidence of experts is to be taken is dependent on the nature of the dispute, and thus the necessity of expert evidence. In accordance with Section 28 of the Act, the arbitral tribunal may appoint an expert to assist it, unless otherwise agreed by the parties.

In certain jurisdictions, the duty of confidentiality of arbitral proceedings and information is codified into their legislation, e.g. Section 14A and 14B of the New Zealand Arbitration Act 1996. There is no such similar provision under the Act, but it is common practice for parties to expressly have a confidentiality clause in their arbitration agreement so that all matters relating to the arbitral proceedings shall be treated as and kept confidential.

Rule 16 of the KLRCA/AIAC Arbitration Rules 2017 does provide that the arbitral tribunal, the parties, all experts, all witnesses and the KLRCA/AIAC shall keep confidential all matters relating to the arbitral proceedings including any award, except for the purposes of enforcement or challenge of an award, or to adhere to any legal duty to disclose.

Exceptions to the general rule of confidentiality are that when parties subsequently agree to the contrary to waive the confidentiality requirement, or where a court makes an order granting permission to disregard the confidentiality obligation. Confidentiality is also not available with respect to documents in the public domain.

Each document filed in the courts and read out in open court is a public document. As such, the confidentiality of the arbitral proceedings may be lost in the event that the award is challenged and the arbitration documents are produced in the High Court. For comparison, Sections 22 and 23 of the Singaporean International Arbitration Act provide on application of the parties, that court proceedings under this Act may be heard otherwise than in open court and that parties may apply to restrict publication of information in this proceeding. However, there is no such corresponding provision under the Act.

There is no relevant statutory governing provision in respect of matters to which the duty of confidentiality extends, as to whether it covers the existence of the arbitration, pleadings, documents produced, the hearing and/or the award; it depends on any confidentiality agreement entered into by the parties.

Arbitrators

The Act promotes parties' autonomy, according to which parties are free to determine the number of arbitrators of their own volition. In the absence of agreement, the Act provides that there shall be three arbitrators in an international arbitration, and one arbitrator in a domestic arbitration (Section 12).

Section 13 of the Act further provides that parties have freedom to determine the procedure for appointing the arbitrator or the presiding arbitrator. Otherwise, the Act provides procedures on the same, which generally cover three circumstances which may possibly arise, i.e. (i) if there is no agreement between the parties on the appointment procedure in their arbitration agreement, (ii) if there is disagreement between the parties, or (iii) if they refuse to exercise the right to appoint a member of the arbitral tribunal. In any of these situations, parties may request the Director of KLRCA/AIAC to appoint the arbitrator, who must do so within 30 days, failing which the parties may apply to the High Court for such appointment.

An arbitrator owes a statutory duty to disclose any circumstances likely to give rise to justifiable doubts as to his impartiality or independence under Section 14(1) of the Act. The circumstances which can raise an issue as to impartiality, among others, are that the arbitrator is engaged in a personal, business or professional relationship with one party to a dispute, or that he has an interest in the outcome of the dispute.

As such, the issue as to the impartiality or independence of an arbitrator is one of the grounds to challenge an arbitrator. To bring such a challenge, parties must be able to show justifiable doubts as to the impartiality or independence of the arbitrator.

Apart from this, an arbitrator may be challenged if he does not possess the necessary qualifications agreed to by the parties, as provided under Section 14(3) of the Act.

In practice, the application of the IBA Guidelines on Conflicts of Interest, which require all arbitrators to be free of bias, has been pervasive in Malaysia. There are specific declaration forms given by both Pertubuhan Arkitek Malaysia (PAM), which is the Malaysian Institute of Architects, and the KLRCA/AIAC which must be signed by every arbitrator before confirmation of their appointment. In Malaysia, experienced arbitrators who deal with domestic and international arbitrations are well aware of the said guidelines.

Interim relief

The Act confers power on the arbitral tribunal to order interim relief respecting the subject matter of the dispute, and the order is only addressable to the parties to the arbitration agreement. This power is enshrined in the Act under Section 19: "[U]nless otherwise agreed by the parties, a party may apply to the arbitral tribunal for any of the following orders: (a) security for costs; (b) discovery of documents and interrogatories; (c) giving of evidence by affidavit; and (d) the preservation, interim custody or sale of any property which is the subject matter of the dispute." Section 19(2) also provides that the arbitral tribunal may require any party to provide appropriate security in connection with the measures that are ordered. In the absence of parties' agreement or adoption of rules of arbitration in the arbitration agreement in relation to the procedures for applying interim reliefs, it is at the discretion of the arbitral tribunal to determine such procedures. The arbitral tribunal will apply the common law tests when determining whether or not to grant a particular interim relief that is sought by the parties, and the interim measure will be granted in the form of an interim award which attracts the application of provisions (Sections 38 and 39) under the Act relating to the recognition and enforcement of an award.

Pursuant to Section 11 of the Act, a party may apply to the High Court for any interim measure before or during arbitral proceedings for similar interim relief and in addition, amongst others, appointment of a receiver and security for the amount in dispute. Parties cannot contract the statutory right to seek interim reliefs from the High Court under Section 11 of the Act out of their arbitration agreement.

Despite that the High Court may grant interim reliefs in support of arbitrations in an international arbitration regardless of whether the seat of arbitration is in Malaysia, the High Court should be mindful of Sections 8 and 10 of the Act which set a limitation on court intervention. Section 8 expressly provides that "no court shall intervene in matters governed by this Act, except where so provided in this Act". Meanwhile, the use of the word "shall" in Section 10 renders it mandatory for the court to grant a stay of court proceedings unless the arbitration agreement is null and void, inoperative or incapable of being performed.

An arbitrator has the power equivalent to that of a judge in court after the constitution of the arbitral tribunal. However, parties should first make an application to the arbitral tribunal unless such an interim order is to bind third parties or is to be enforced effectively where it cannot be done by the interim order made by the arbitrator.[12]

The parliament's intention of this is demonstrated in Section 11(2) of the Act, which provides that: "[W]here a party applies to the High Court for any interim measure and an arbitral tribunal has already ruled on any matter which is relevant to the application, the High Court shall treat any findings of fact made in the course of such ruling by the arbitral tribunal as conclusive for the purposes of the application." This corresponds to the rationale that the arbitrator is in a better position to make an expeditious and informed decision on the interim relief sought, given that the arbitrator has already had all facts and possibly documents presented before him in the pending arbitration. In cases of *ex parte* and urgent applications, parties should be allowed to apply to the courts for such interim relief, as such similar application to the arbitrator may prevent the necessary element of surprise, or result in delay.

It is a matter of discretion whether or not an arbitral tribunal is to make an award for security for costs. It may depend on whether there is evidence of a real risk that the respondent would not be able to recover the costs incurred from the claimant, and the likely effect of awarding such security for costs on stifling a genuine claim of the party against whom the security is sought.

Arbitration award

The requirements for an arbitration award are provided under Section 33 of the Act which provides that an award shall be made in writing and be signed by the arbitrator(s). In arbitral proceedings with more than one arbitrator, the signatures of the majority of all members of the arbitral tribunal shall be sufficient, provided that the reason for any omitted signature is stated (Section 33(2)).

Additionally, an award shall state the reasons upon which it is based, unless the parties have agreed otherwise or the award is an award on agreed terms. An award shall also state its date and the seat of arbitration. Unless otherwise agreed by the parties, an award has to be a reasoned award whereby it should set out the facts, the explanation of the arbitral tribunal's findings, and how the arbitral tribunal reached its conclusion. This is to enable the parties to comprehend the award and understand why certain points were decisive.

Nothing in the Act requires the award to be rendered within a specific time frame. Section 46 of the Act gives the High Court power to grant an extension to any limitation of time in the arbitration agreement for an award be issued. This intervention by the court can, nonetheless, be excluded by the agreement of the parties. Under Rule 11 of the KLRCA/AIAC Arbitration Rules, the default period for rendering of final award is limited to three months from the date of final submissions, extendable by consent of parties and consultation of the Director of the KLRCA.

Article 12 of the Fast Track Arbitration Rules even provides that for a document-only arbitration, the arbitral tribunal shall publish the final award no later than 90 days from the commencement of the arbitration. With regard to an arbitration with a substantive oral hearing, the arbitral tribunal shall publish the final award expeditiously and no later than 160 days from the commencement of the arbitration, extendable by agreement.

As for costs, in the absence of agreement, Section 44 of the Act vests in arbitral tribunals the discretion to award costs. The principles for awarding costs are derived from the common law, and the arbitral tribunal may refer to existing Malaysian case laws and the relevant provision in the Rules of Court 2012, where appropriate. The general rule is that costs follow the event, wherein the unsuccessful party will bear the costs. In any event, if parties wish not to follow the general rule, they should state the reasons for doing so. Articles 40 to 42 of the UNCITRAL Rules, adopted in the KLRCA/AIAC rules, provide jurisdiction on determination and allocation of costs.

In practice, the arbitral tribunal may take into account, amongst others, the following factors in considering the quantum of cost to be awarded:[13]

- the complexity of the matter;
- the requirement of skill, specialised knowledge and responsibility, and the expenditure of time and labour, by the solicitor or counsel;
- the value of the subject matter in dispute; and
- whether there are other solicitors or counsel who get paid for the work done, and so the amount of work required has been reduced.

Unless otherwise agreed by the parties, Section 33(6) of the Act provides that the arbitral tribunal may award interest on any sum of money ordered and determine the rate of interest, where the tribunal is allowed to make reference to the interest rates that may be awarded by the Malaysian courts. However, there is no provision in the Act that expressly allows pre-award interest to be awarded, hence leaving this issue open to argument. In such instance, parties may make an express agreement to grant jurisdiction to the arbitral tribunal to award pre-award interest.

Challenge of the arbitration award

An arbitral award is final and binding against the parties to an arbitration agreement and those parties cannot appeal the award under the Act.[14] However, where the seat of the arbitration is in Malaysia, the parties may apply to have the award set aside by the High Court. It appears that such right to set aside the award cannot be excluded by the parties.

An application to set aside an award must be made within three months of receipt of the award under Section 37 of the Act. Parties may apply to set aside an award based on the grounds and circumstances set out in Section 37 which include but are not limited to the following:

- the award is in conflict with the public policy of Malaysia;
- the making of the award was induced or affected by fraud or corruption; or
- a breach of the rules of justice occurred.

Nonetheless, an application to set aside an award does not automatically stay the enforcement of the award, and parties have to make an application to stay such enforcement.

Despite not having a right to appeal, parties may refer questions of law arising out of an award to the High Court, which fundamentally affect the rights of one or more of the parties, for a decision under Section 42 of the Act. In determining a question of law, the High Court has the power to affirm, vary, set aside or remit the award to the arbitral tribunal for reconsideration of the relevant question/issue.

However, it is to be noted that parties may waive such rights to appeal to the High Court, as evidenced in rule 1(c) of the KLRCA/AIAC Rules, which says that where the seat of arbitration is Malaysia, Section 41, Section 42, Section 43 and Section 46 of the Malaysian Arbitration Act 2005 (Amended 2011) shall not apply.

Section 35 of the Act provides for correction and interpretation of an award or additional award. In any event, if the arbitral tribunal considers the request made to be justified, it shall make the correction or give the interpretation within 30 days of receipt of the request, and such interpretation shall form the award. Also, the arbitral tribunal may correct any error of the type referred to in part (a) above-mentioned on its own initiative within 30 days of the date of the award.

In furtherance to that, unless otherwise agreed by the parties, a party may, within 30 days of receipt of the award and upon notice to the other party, request the arbitral tribunal to make an additional award as to claims presented in the arbitral proceedings but omitted from the award. Should the arbitral tribunal consider the request justified, it shall make the additional award within 60 days from receipt of such request.

In any event, the arbitral may extend the period of time within which it shall make a correction, interpretation or an additional award, when it thinks necessary.

Enforcement of the arbitration award

Generally, an arbitration award is enforceable by making an application under Section 38 of the Act to recognise such award. As mentioned earlier, a foreign arbitration award can be enforced in Malaysia, subject to and in accordance with Section 38 of the Act.

To enforce an arbitration award, registration of the award as a judgment of the High Court is required. An application for enforcement is made *ex parte* and is usually ordered as of right, whereupon the arbitration agreement and a duly certified copy of the award (with a translation into English if it is neither in the national language nor the English language) are produced. The order for registration of the award is to be served on the respondent, who has 14 days to make an application to set aside the registration. Pending the disposal of the application to set aside the registration, the enforcement of the award will be stayed.

Registration or enforcement of an award may be refused based on the grounds set out in Section 39 of the Act. None of the grounds concern the merits of the arbitration award. This simply shows that the Malaysia courts, when determining whether an award ought to be registered, will not sit on appeal over the correctness of the award. However, if the merits of the award may be challenged under the laws of the country which issued the award and on which basis the award is set aside; such an award is not capable of registration in Malaysia.

Recent authorities in Malaysia have suggested that the Malaysian courts are maintaining friendly attitudes towards arbitration and are therefore more inclined to recognising and enforcing arbitration awards. This is demonstrated in a Federal Court decision in ***Government of India v. Cairn Energy India Pty Ltd & Anor***.[15]

Investment arbitration

Malaysia is a signatory to a number of bilateral investment treaties. Thus far, Malaysia has entered into 71 bilateral investment treaties (BITs), starting with its first BIT signed with the Netherlands on 15 June 1971,[16] and the most recent BIT signed with Syrian Arab Republic on 7 January 2009.[17]

* * *

Endnotes

1. Sundra Rajoo, WSW Davidson, *The Arbitration Act 2005*, Introduction, Sweet & Maxwell Asia, 2007 (page 2).
2. Section 51(2) of the Act.
3. The Malaysian Parliament's website at http://www.parlimen.gov.my/files/billindex/pdf/2010/DR422010E.pdf.
4. New York Convention Arbitration's website at http://www.newyorkconvention.org/countries.
5. Nuclear Threat Initiative's website at http://www.nti.org/learn/treaties-and-regimes/association-southeast-asian-nations asean/.
6. International Centre for Settlement of Investment Disputes's website at https://icsid.worldbank.org/en/Documents/icsiddocs/List%20of%20Contracting%20States%20and%20Other%20Signatories%20of%20the%20Convention%20-%20Latest.pdf.
7. The Kuala Lumpur Regional Centre's website at https://klrca.org/ and the Asian International Arbitration Centre's website at http://www.aiac.world.
8. The Kuala Lumpur Regional Centre's website at https://klrca.org/Arbitration-Fast-Track-Arbitration for existing rules and visit http://www.aiac.world/Arbitration-Fast-Track-Arbitration for new rules applicable in year 2018.
9. [2013] 7 CLJ 18.
10. [2000] 1 LNS 15; [2000] 6 MLJ 1 at 7.
11. Section 2 of the Malaysian Evidence Act 1950.
12. *Lady Muriel (Owners) v. Transorient Shipping Ltd* (The Lady Muriel) [1995] 2 HKC 320.

13. Order 59 Rule 16 of the Rules of Court 2012.
14. Section 36 of the Act.
15. [2011] 6 MLJ 441.
16. The United Nations Conference on Trade and Development's website at http://investmentpolicyhub.unctad.org/IIA/CountryBits/127.
17. *Ibid.*

Khong Aik Gan
Tel: +603 7931 7060 / Email: khongaik@ganlaw.my

Khong Aik is a litigation and dispute resolution partner at Gan Partnership with more than 20 years of practice experience. He has an extensive dispute resolution & litigation practice experience focusing on corporate and commercial disputes including property disputes involving joint venture agreement, development work and acquisition of land.

In 2010/2011 issue of the *Asia Pacific Legal 500*, Khong Aik was described as an 'experienced litigation lawyer' who has a 'depth of knowledge' and 'trouble shooting skills' that are complemented by a 'meticulous and thorough approach'.

The 2017 publication of the *Legal 500 Asia Pacific* described Khong Aik as 'very competent and commercial in his approach'. Khong Aik is a Mediator with the Malaysian Mediation Centre and Adjunct Professor to the Shi Liang College of Law, University of Changzhou, Jiangsu, China.

Joon Liang Foo
Tel: +603 7931 7060 / Email: joonliang@ganlaw.my

Joon Liang started his practice in 2000 in dispute resolution in one of the largest law firms in Malaysia where he practised some eight years, and has extensive experience in complex arbitrations and litigation, including in securities and construction disputes.

He has advised a wide range of clients including amongst others, the state government, Ministry of Works, insurers, foreign contractors, and government-linked companies, across a broad spectrum of litigation matters in court and in arbitration, with his main focus being construction and securities transaction disputes.

Joon Liang is a Fellow of the Chartered Institute of Arbitrators, United Kingdom, and committee member of the Malaysian Branch of the Chartered Institute of Arbitrators. He also sits on the panel of arbitrators and adjudicators of the Kuala Lumpur Regional Centre of Arbitration.

Lim Bee San
Tel: +603 7931 7060 / Email: beesan@ganlaw.my

Bee San, a graduate from University of Malaya with Bachelor of Laws (Hons), was called to the Malaysian Bar in 2012. Bee San has since started her legal practice under the guidance of Gan Khong Aik in Gan Partnership.

Bee San gained her experience as a young litigator by handling one of the banking portfolios for the firm on her own and assisting Khong Aik in numerous significant and highly complex matters in the Malaysian courts and arbitration, where the cases involved land disputes, civil claims based on breach of contracts and/or tortious conducts, insurance and defamation. At the same time, Bee San provides corporate advisory services in negotiation and drafting of commercial agreements.

Gan Partnership

D-32-02 Menara SUEZCAP 1, KL Gateway, No. 2 Jalan Kerinchi, Gerbang Kerinchi Lestari,
59200 Kuala Lumpur, Malaysia
Tel: +603 7931 7060 / Fax: +603 7931 8063 / URL: www.ganlaw.my

Malta

Denia Ellul
Fenech Farrugia Fiott Legal

Introduction

Being strategically located in the centre of the Mediterranean Sea between Europe and Northern Africa, coupled with the fact that Malta places English as one of the official languages of the island, our jurisdiction offers an attractive seat for the out-of-court settlement of international disputes, with high professional standards in the legal fields. The use of arbitration as a method of alternative dispute resolution has gained momentum over the past years, especially in the fields of commerce, insurance and the maritime sector.

Arbitration in Malta is governed through Chapter 387 of the Laws of Malta (the "Act", "Arbitration Act"), which operates as the *lex arbitri* providing for the basic framework for arbitration procedures having their seat in Malta. The Act and the Arbitration Rules established by virtue of Legal Notice 387.01, provide a number of default rules of procedure which are applicable to different forms of arbitration.

The law regulating arbitration in Malta is split into two separate branches under the same Act. Part IV of the Arbitration Act governs the conduct of arbitration in the domestic arena, which include disputes having at their core any claim or controversy arising from or relating to an agreement concluded between the parties to the dispute, the breach, invalidity, termination or failure to comply therewith. The subsequent section of the Act, Part V, provides the legal framework which regulates international commercial arbitration involving disputes which in some way transcend national boundaries. In an attempt to create a harmonised level-playing field across the board, the Arbitration Act also incorporates into Maltese law a number of international conventions within its legislative framework, such as the UNCITRAL Model Law on International Commercial Arbitration (1985) (the "Model Law") and the New York Convention on the Recognition and Enforcement of Foreign Arbitral Awards, amongst others.

The Act establishes the Malta Arbitration Centre (the "MAC"), a body corporate having a distinct legal personality, constituted in line with the purposes and functions of the Act, which started its operations in the year 2000. The MAC supports arbitration proceedings in terms of premises, facilities, staff and panels of arbitrators. The functions of the MAC *inter alia* include the promotion of Malta as a seat for international arbitration and the provision of the required facilities for the conduct of arbitration, and to advise the Maltese Government on any matter related to the field of Arbitration.

The latest autonomous and independent body set up in the field of arbitration in Malta is the Office of the Arbiter for Financial Services, established by virtue of Act XVI of the Laws of Malta, and came into force in April of 2016. This body is intended to mediate, investigate and adjudicate complaints submitted by both national and foreign natural persons, and micro-enterprises, against financial service providers. Complaints may be lodged against entities licensed by the Malta Financial Services Authority, whether still holding a licence or otherwise, which include banks, financial institutions, insurance companies and/or brokers, investment services providers, trustees and pension providers. The Arbiter for Financial Services renders a binding award, with any compensation payable by the financial service provider capped at €250,000 together with any additional costs and interests. The Arbiter offers an efficient avenue for legal recourse in respect of relatively minor claims and disputes in the field of financial services.

Arbitration agreement

Like most other jurisdictions, Maltese law regards the arbitration agreement as the cornerstone of arbitral proceedings. The Act adopts the definition enshrined under Article 7 of the Model Law in establishing the meaning and form of an arbitration agreement under the laws of Malta. Thus, subject to certain provisions set out under the Act, an arbitration agreement is defined as "an agreement by the parties to submit to arbitration all or certain disputes which have arisen or which may arise between them in respect of a defined legal relationship, whether contractual or not". Since the parties to arbitration proceedings waive their right at law to launch proceedings before national courts, the Model Law further requires that the agreement to submit a dispute to arbitration is recorded in writing. The Model Law further provides for a list of written instruments which would constitute a valid agreement in terms of form, including an exchange of statements of claim and defence whereby the existence of an agreement is alleged by one party and not denied by the other.

The commencement of arbitration proceedings may be launched based on two types of agreements, either:

- on the basis of an arbitration clause incorporated within the principal agreement entered into by and between the parties to the dispute which records their consent to settle any future disputes by way of arbitration; or
- the parties may enter into a separate submission agreement, regulating the terms of the arbitration after the dispute has already arisen.

The principle of separability *vis-à-vis* the validity of underlying agreement from the arbitration clause contained therein, is a principle established in the Model Law as transposed in the laws of Malta. The notion that the arbitration clause constitutes a separate and independent agreement which survives the termination of the principal contract, has also been judicially accepted. Furthermore, the arbitral tribunal upholds the principle of competence-competence, whereby it is vested with the authority to rule on the existence of its own jurisdiction, including any objections raised with respect to the validity of the arbitration. The arbitral tribunal may bifurcate the proceedings when a plea regarding its jurisdiction is raised, whereby it may either render its ruling as a preliminary question in the initial stages of the proceedings, or alternatively incorporate its decision in an award on the merits.

Arbitration procedure

Arbitral proceedings commence on the same date on which a request for the settlement of a dispute through arbitration is received by the respondent. It is commonplace that proceedings are conducted in private, and therefore it has the potential of remaining confidential. Where an appeal from the award rendered is sought, the result must preserve the confidentiality of the arbitration, disclosing solely those facts which are strictly essential for the enforcement of the judgment.

The place of the seat of arbitration is generally stipulated by the parties to the dispute. In the absence of such determination, the Arbitral Tribunal shall determine the seat, taking into account the subject matter of the case at hand together with considering the convenience of the parties from a logistical perspective. Nevertheless, owing to the flexibility of the arbitration procedure, it is possible that the tribunal meets at any other place, other than its seat, for several purposes, such as the hearing of witnesses, experts or the parties themselves, or the inspection of evidence brought forward during the proceedings.

Save any provision stipulating otherwise in the arbitration agreement, the arbitral tribunal is empowered to appoint one or more experts, where the tribunal does not have the relevant expertise. Alternatively, it may request the parties to submit expert evidence to the tribunal. The Model Law allows for the cross-examination of the expert's contemporaneous documents or his oral report. In addition, while the intervention of domestic courts is limited during arbitration proceedings, an arbitral tribunal, or any party with the approval of the arbitral tribunal, may request the court's assistance in taking evidence, in accordance with the rules set out under the Code of Organisation and Civil Procedure, Chapter 12 of the Laws of Malta.

Arbitrators

Under Maltese law, there is no permanent body of arbitrators readily available to hear the case at hand. Nevertheless, the MAC may from time to time draw up specific panels of arbitrators both for domestic arbitration and for international commercial arbitration. To date, the MAC has drawn up a variety of arbitration panels constituted for specific subject-matters of the dispute at hand, such as the Banking, Finance, Accounting and Taxation Panel, the Medical Panel, the Maritime Panel, the Building Construction Panel, the Industrial Legislation Panel and the Insurance Panel.

The Model Law grants a substantial amount of discretion to the parties when appointing the panel of arbitrators, in terms of number, nationality and procedure of appointment which testifies to freedom given to the parties to dictate the process. Subject to what otherwise may be agreed by the parties, the number of arbitrators presiding over the arbitration proceedings shall be three. Furthermore, no person shall be prohibited from acting as an arbitrator by reason of his or her nationality. With regards to the manner to be followed for the appointment of the arbitrators, the parties are also free to establish a specific procedure. In the absence of such parameters set by the parties, each party is to elect one arbitrator and, in turn, the two arbitrators appoint a third arbitrator to complete the panel. Where the parties opt for a single arbitrator and cannot reach a consensus as to who shall fill that role, our domestic courts shall make the appointment in their stead. It should be noted that the MAC holds a register of individuals who are deemed to be fit and proper arbitrators, by reason of their experience and knowledge in the field.

In light of the heavy involvement of the parties in the framework of the proceedings, the independence and impartiality of the arbitrators is fundamental for the production of a lawful award. Thus, an arbitrator may be challenged if circumstances exist that question his or her independence and impartiality. An additional ground upon which an arbitrator may be challenged, is due to the lack of qualities agreed to by the parties. The parties retain the autonomy to determine the procedure for challenging an arbitrator. Failing agreement, a party intending to challenge an arbitrator presiding over an international arbitration dispute having its seat in Malta, is bound to follow the procedure outlined in the Model Law. In such case, a party may challenge an arbitrator within 15 days after becoming aware of the members constituting the panel or the circumstances giving rise to justifiable grounds for challenge, by delivering a written statement to the arbitral tribunal. Where the challenged arbitrator does not accede to the challenge or where the other party opposes the said challenge, the matter is settled by the arbitral tribunal itself.

Interim relief

In cases of extreme urgency, domestic courts have the power to issue interim measures in support of the arbitral process. Subject to any provisions contained in the arbitration agreement, any party to the dispute may request the court in Malta to issue a precautionary action any time after the commencement of the arbitral proceedings, for the purpose or maintaining the *status quo*, protecting assets or evidence pending the outcome of the arbitral proceedings. The precautionary acts which can be issued are limited to those enlisted under the Code of Organisation and Civil Procedure, Chapter 12 of the Laws of Malta which include: (a) a warrant of description whereby the party against whom the caution is taken is ordered not to move particular goods from a specific location; (b) a warrant of seizure which allows for the confiscation of goods; (c) a warrant of seizure of a commercial going concern; (d) a garnishee order which allows for the seizure of funds and other movable goods belonging or due to the party against whom the action is taken and which are in the possession of third parties; (e) a warrant of impediment of departure; (f) a warrant of arrest of sea vessels located in Maltese territorial waters; (g) a warrant of arrest of aircraft found in Malta; and (h) a warrant of prohibitory injunction which restrains the performance of a particular action.

Any precautionary act issued by way of interim relief by the domestic courts shall remain in force until it expires or until such time that the arbitral award is rendered. Furthermore, such precautionary acts shall be rescinded should the party against whom the action is taken provide a form of security or deposit deemed sufficient in the eyes of the law as to protect the rights claimed in the act.

Arbitration award

Similarly to the arbitration agreement, the Model Law sets out the requirements for a final and binding award constituting a *res judicata*, subject to a challenge or procedures relating to the correction and interpretation of the award. A valid arbitration award ought to be in writing, stating the date and place of the arbitration and bearing the signature of the arbitrator or arbitrators constituting the panel. Where multiple arbitrators form the panel, the signatures of the majority of the arbitrators shall suffice.

Awards rendered by an arbitral tribunal may, unless otherwise agreed to by the parties, include monetary compensation including debt due under contract or compensation for damages, punitive damages, injunctions and declaratory relief, rectification, restitution and adaptation of contracts. Furthermore, the tribunal is empowered to establish the costs and interests, when the award is rendered.

Unless otherwise agreed to by the parties, costs are borne by the losing party. Nevertheless, the arbitral tribunal retains the discretion to apportion the costs between the parties in a different manner. Costs would generally include the fees of the arbitral tribunal, travel and other expenses incurred by the tribunal, fees incurred in relation to the engagement of experts, costs for legal representation and assistance of the successful party, if these costs were claimed during the proceedings and approved by the arbitral tribunal, and any fees payable to an arbitration institution. In apportioning costs, the arbitral tribunal considers a number of factors, such as whether the claimants' claim was fully or partially upheld, or whether the settlement of the dispute necessitated a ruling on a complex point of law. The infrastructure of arbitration in Malta strives at safeguarding efficient and cost-effective proceedings. Thus, it is commonplace that the party hindering an expeditious process is penalised for causing delay and this may be reflected in the costs' orders.

Challenge of the arbitration award

A party who is dissatisfied with the outcome after an award is rendered, may either attack the unfavourable award at its core by challenging its validity before the national courts of the seat of the arbitration, or alternatively, attempt to block enforcement and recognition in the country where this is sought, by setting it aside (subsequent para).

An award rendered upon the conclusion of international commercial arbitration in Malta may be appealed before the Court of Appeal on any point arising out of a valid and final award. The Court of Appeal shall only proceed with hearing the case if it is satisfied that: determining the point of law in question will undermine or uphold the rights of one or more parties; the point of law raised is one which was raised before the arbitral tribunal or was otherwise relied on for the final ruling; the award of the arbitral tribunal on the point of law is *prima facie* open to justifiable doubts and the nature of the appeal does not seem dilatory or vexatious. In situations where such criteria are not met, it is likely that the Court of Appeal would dismiss the case. The appeal is to be filed within a 15-day period, which starts running from the day that the applicant was notified about the award.

The Court of Appeal in Malta would be expected to set aside an award pursuant only to the grounds exhaustively set out in the Act, which transposes article 34 of the Model Law for this purpose. The award shall be set aside if the court is satisfied that: (a) one of the parties to the arbitration agreement was under some incapacity or incapability to conclude the agreement, or there is a lack of a valid agreement in general; or (b) the aggrieved party was not given sufficient and proper notice of the appointment of the arbitral tribunal or was not in a position to present his case; or (c) the award deals with matters not covered by the arbitration clause or submission agreement, or falls outside the scope of that initially submitted; or (d) the composition of the arbitral tribunal or the procedure followed was in breach of mandatory provisions or the Act; or (e) the subject matter of the dispute was not capable of settlement by arbitration under the laws of Malta; and/or (f) the award is in conflict with the public policy in Malta.

Enforcement of the arbitration award

As in most other jurisdictions, an arbitral tribunal constituted under the laws of Malta is *functus officio*, for its mandate terminates once an award is rendered and has no further role to play in its enforcement and recognition. For the purposes of enforcement and recognition of international awards, the Act transposes the New York Convention on the Recognition and Enforcement of Foreign Arbitral Awards, the Geneva Protocol on Arbitration Clauses and the Geneva Convention on the Execution of Foreign Arbitral Awards. These provide for the legal force and effect of a foreign award within the Maltese territory, together with the grounds upon which the same enforcement and recognition being sought may be refused by the local courts.

Foreign awards may be registered with the MAC which would, in turn, render them enforceable in the same manner as if they were rendered domestically, thus constituting an executive title under Maltese Law and having the same legal effect as a judgment pronounced by the Maltese Courts, constituting a *res judicata*.

Investment arbitration

To date, Malta has signed 25 Bilateral Investment Treaties, 20 of which are currently in force and two have been terminated. Malta is also a party to several multilateral investment treaties, such as the Energy Charter Treaty which was first signed in 1991, and the Convention on the Settlement of Investment Disputes between States and Nationals of other States.

While Malta is a party to several Bilateral Investment Treaties, Treaties with Investment Provisions and Investment-Related Instruments; to date, no arbitration proceedings have been launched by investors against the State of Malta. Nevertheless, there were two cases, *Belegging-Maatschappij "Far East" v. Austria* and *OperaFund v. Spain*, both initiated in 2015, where Malta was the home state of the investor to the claim.

Denia Ellul
Tel: +356 254 96400 / Email: dellul@fff-legal.com

Dr. Denia Ellul joined Fenech Farrugia Fiott Legal as an Associate Lawyer in 2017. She attended the University of Malta, and successfully completed a Bachelor of Laws degree, followed by a Doctor of Laws degree in 2014. Following her graduation from the University of Malta, Denia commenced her employment with a local law firm which helped her gain the necessary knowledge in various fields of law, including corporate law, commercial law, cross-border tax planning and financial-legal matters. In 2016, Denia furthered her legal studies at the University of Amsterdam in the Netherlands, where she read a Masters degree in International Trade and Investment. She successfully submitted and defended her thesis entitled, "The Rule of Law in Post-Award Remedies: A Critical Analysis of the Annulment Procedure under ICSID".

In view of her experience, Denia's main practice areas include corporate and trusts law, financial services, regulated entities and alternative dispute resolution.

Fenech Farrugia Fiott Legal

Ewropa Business Centre, Level 3 – Suite 702, Dun Karm Street, Birkirkara, BKR 9034, Malta
Tel: +356 254 96400 / URL: www.fff-legal.com/

Mexico

Adrián Magallanes & Montserrat Manzano
Von Wobeser y Sierra, S.C.

Introduction: an insight into arbitration in Mexico

Over the past three decades, arbitration has been an alternative dispute resolution ("ADR") mechanism increasingly used in Mexico to settle commercial and investment disputes.

The Fourth Title, "Commercial Arbitration", Fifth Book "Commercial Trials" of the Mexican Code of Commerce ("the Commerce Code") was enacted in 1993.

This special chapter is applicable at a Federal level, and mirrors the 1985 UNCITRAL Model Law on International Commercial Arbitration ("Model Law") and its 2006 amendment, which was incorporated into the Commerce Code in 2011 with minor modifications, regarding:

(i) The number of arbitrators in case there is no agreement between the parties in this respect; the Model Law establishes that in the event there is no agreement between the parties in this respect, the number of arbitrators shall be three, while the Commerce Code requires one.

(ii) Interim relief requests: under the Commerce Code, the power of national courts to grant interim measures is explicitly recognised. A special procedure is regulated for granting interim measures.

(iii) The form of the arbitration agreement which, under the Commerce Code, shall always be in writing.

This is basically Mexico's legal framework governing both domestic and international commercial arbitration, together with international treaties to which Mexico is party, and any other legal provisions which may establish a different arbitration procedure or the non-arbitrable nature of certain disputes, when the seat of arbitration is Mexico.

Considering the increasing use of ADR mechanisms in Mexico for resolving domestic and international disputes, the Federal Executive government, together with several research institutes and academics, are currently working on a bill proposing a national ADR law, which aims to establish a *common platform* for conducting disputes under an ADR mechanism, including arbitration (*e.g.* minimum standard of principles governing ADR proceedings).

The Mexican legal system does not have specialised courts dealing only with arbitration; thus, if the intervention of a national court is required, the case will be referred to a competent court, selected randomly by an electronic system.

Since 1971, Mexico has been party to the New York Convention of 1958 ("NY Convention"), currently the most important international treaty regarding the recognition and enforcement of foreign arbitral awards. Mexico has no reservations to the application of this convention.

With respect to investment arbitration, Mexico has recently signed the Convention on the Settlement of Investment Disputes between States and Nationals of Other States ("ICSID Convention"), which is currently in the process of ratification.

In addition, Mexico is party to the Inter-American Convention on International Commercial Arbitration (the "Panama Convention") ratified in 1977, and party to the Inter-American Convention on Extraterritorial Validity of Foreign Judgments and Arbitral Awards ("Montevideo Convention") ratified in 1987.

Regarding the institutions and/or rules used in arbitration proceedings in Mexico, the most commonly used institutions and/or rules are, for domestic proceedings, the Arbitration Centre of the Mexico City Chamber of Commerce (CANACO), the Arbitration Centre of Mexico (CAM) and the Construction Arbitration Centre (CAIC), and for both domestic and international proceedings, the International Court of Arbitration of the International Chamber of Commerce (ICC).

The arbitration rules of these institutions are all available in Spanish and English.

Arbitration agreement

Formalities

Under Article 1423 of the Commerce Code, an arbitration agreement must necessarily be in writing and included in a document signed by the parties. Also, an arbitration agreement may be validly executed:

(i) through an exchange of letters, telex, telegram, fax or any other means of electronic communication that properly records the existence of the agreement;

(ii) by reference to a document containing an arbitration agreement, as long as such agreement is in writing and from the reference it can be concluded that such clause is indeed part of the agreement; or

(iii) through an exchange of a written communication and a written answer in which the agreement is affirmed by one party without being denied by the other.

These formalities are consistent with Option I of Article 7 of the Model Law and Article II of the NY Convention.

Enforcement of arbitration agreements

Mexico is generally considered an "arbitration-friendly" jurisdiction, since its constant and general approach enshrines the principle of "non-intervention" (Article 1421, Commerce Code), whose purpose is to make arbitration agreements effective and to fulfil the intention of the parties when executing them.

Considering this, if court proceedings have been initiated in violation of an arbitration agreement and enforcement of the said agreement is required, the judge must, according to Article 1424 of the Commerce Code and at the request of one party, refer them to arbitration, unless it finds that the arbitration agreement is null and void, inoperative or incapable of being performed.

Article 1464 of said Code provides that such request shall be made in the first written motion on the merits of the dispute submitted by the requesting party.

Under Mexican law, an arbitration agreement will no longer be enforceable if, for example:

(i) one of the parties did not have legal capacity during the execution of the agreement (Article 1798 of the Mexican Federal Civil Code);

(ii) consent to the agreement was granted by mistake or under duress (Article 1812 of the Mexican Federal Civil Code); or

(iii) the subject matter of the agreement is not arbitrable.

Additionally, the following reasons have been considered by national courts as grounds for refusing enforcement of such agreement under Article 1424 of the Commerce Code: (i) withdrawal from the agreement to arbitrate by both parties; and (ii) death of one or more arbitrators specifically chosen by the parties in the contract, with no possibility of substituting them.

Despite the commencement of proceedings before national courts and observing the *kompetenz-kompetenz* principle, in order to avoid dilatory tactics, arbitration may still be initiated or continued, and an award can be issued while the decision of the national court regarding the validity of the arbitration agreement is pending.

According to Article 1432 of the Commerce Code, if the tribunal decides on jurisdiction before ruling on the merits, any party may request a final decision by a national court, within 30 days of the notification of such decision. This decision is not subject to appeal.

When assessing the validity of the arbitration agreement under Mexican law, consideration needs to be given to the separability principle (Article 1432, Commerce Code) by both national courts and arbitral tribunals. According to said principle, any arbitration agreement included in a contract shall be considered as a separate, independent agreement, and thus, a ruling stating that a contract is null and void does not entail the invalidity of the arbitration clause.

<u>Arbitrability of disputes</u>

According to different provisions of Mexican law, there are certain matters that are not arbitrable, such as disputes arising from:

(i) land and water resources located within national territory and resources within the exclusive economic zone, or resources related to any of the sovereign rights regarding such zone;

(ii) acts of authority or acts related to the internal regime of the state and of federal entities;

(iii) internal regimes of Mexican embassies and consulates and their official proceedings (Article 568 of the Federal Code of Civil Procedure);

(iv) disputes related to the administrative termination of contracts executed by the National Hydrocarbons Commission (Articles 20 and 21 of the Hydrocarbons Law);

(v) disputes regarding the lawfulness of administrative rescissions or the early termination of contracts executed between public entities and private parties (Law of Acquisitions, Leases, and Services of the Public Sector, Article 80 and the Law of Public Sector and Related Services, Article 98);

(vi) personal and commercial bankruptcy proceedings (Article 1 of the Bankruptcy Law);

(vii) criminal liability (Article 1 of the National Code of Criminal Procedure);

(viii) issues related to family law and civil status (these must be decided by national courts (Article 52 of the Superior Court of the Federal District Organisational Act);

(ix) tax matters (Article 1 of the Administrative Federal Court Organisational Law);

(x) labour disputes (Article 123, Section XXXI of the Mexican Constitution);

(xi) agrarian disputes (Article 27, Section XIX of the Mexican Constitution); or

(xii) under Article 27 of the Industrial Property Law, only disputes affecting private rights exclusively can be subject to arbitration. If they concern the public interest, they are not arbitrable.

Joinder/Consolidation of third parties

There is no specific provision on joinder or consolidation of third parties in the Commerce Code specifically regarding arbitration proceedings; this will depend mainly on the arbitration rules chosen by the parties (institutional or *ad hoc)* and the additions or modifications to these that they may agree to.

It is worth mentioning that according to Mexican Law there are several cases where non-signatories of an arbitration agreement may be bound by it, such as:

(i) assignment of rights;

(ii) succession;

(iii) merger of companies; and

(iv) acquisition of shares of simplified stock companies.

Arbitration procedure

Commencing proceedings

Pursuant to Article 1437 of the Commerce Code and unless otherwise agreed by the parties, arbitration proceedings are deemed to be initiated on the date the respondent receives the request for arbitration.

Similarly, national institutions administering arbitration proceedings consider the date on which the request for arbitration is received by the institution as the date of commencement of the proceedings (see CANACO Arbitration Rules, Article 3(2) and CAM Arbitration Rules, Article 6(2)).

Can hearings take place outside of the seat of arbitration?

As established in Article 1436 of the Commerce Code, irrespective of the seat of arbitration and unless otherwise agreed by the parties, the tribunal can hold hearings in any other place as it deems appropriate.

The arbitration rules of some national institutions have similar provisions (see CAM Arbitration Rules, Article 20(2)).

Rules on evidence

Article 1439 of the Commerce Code provides that the parties shall – within the scheduled calendar – express all the facts on which their claim is based, disputed points, their respective initial submissions and provide the tribunal with all the documents and evidence they deem necessary to support their case; yet, no specific provisions regarding the types of evidence to be admitted, rules governing the taking of evidence, disclosure issues, etc., are found in the Commerce Code.

As a general principle, applying not only to the taking of evidence but to the entire proceeding, the right of each party to be heard and present its case, as well as the principle of equal treatment of the parties during the proceedings, must be observed by the arbitral tribunal at all times.

As a common practice, in Mexico both arbitrators and parties tend to apply the IBA Rules on the Taking of Evidence in International Arbitration. However, to the extent that the parties do not agree on the applicability of any specific rule, the tribunal may determine the procedure, first according to the agreement between the parties on that specific matter or, failing such agreement, at its own discretion.

Rules on privilege and disclosure

Mexican legislation does not have specific or mandatory provisions regarding privileged documents or disclosure of evidence; nevertheless, according to Article 1435 of the Commerce Code, the parties are free to agree on any rules of procedure to be followed by the arbitral tribunal, which includes rules for evidentiary purposes.

Failing agreement between the parties on these matters, the arbitral tribunal may conduct the procedure at its own discretion, subject to the provisions of the Commerce Code dealing specifically with arbitration. This discretionary power allows the tribunal to, for example, order the production of documents as it deems necessary; if the party required to produce certain documents refuses or fails without a valid reason to do so, the tribunal may draw adverse inferences from such failure or refusal.

Rules on expert evidence

There are no specific rules under Mexican Law regarding witness statements or expert reports. Under Article 1435 of the Commerce Code, the parties are free to agree on the rules applying to the taking of evidence, and thus to witness statements and expert reports. In the absence of such agreement, the tribunal will have the power to conduct the proceedings as it deems appropriate and to decide on matters related to their admissibility and evidentiary value.

Usually, in proceedings seated in Mexico, witness statements and expert reports are delivered by way of a written statement; later, during the hearing, these witnesses and/or experts are subject to direct examination by the party who offered their testimony and/or report, cross-examined by the opposing party, and may also be questioned by the tribunal. There is no official requirement for the witnesses' statements or experts' reports to be sworn in, but they are made aware by the tribunal of their general duty to tell the truth.

As to experts appointed by the tribunal, Article 1442 of the Commerce Code empowers the tribunal to appoint one or more experts to report to it on specific issues.

Confidentiality

The Commerce Code is silent as to the confidentiality of arbitration proceedings. However, Article 1435 of the Commerce Code gives the parties broad discretion to agree on the confidentiality of the proceedings and/or of any documentation presented by the parties to the tribunal during the proceedings.

If no agreement is reached between the parties and the tribunal has not made any statement or order with regard to the confidentiality of the proceedings and/or documentation, there is nothing that imposes upon the parties the duty of keeping these confidential.

In practice, parties lean towards agreeing on such confidentiality matters either by tailor-made rules to apply to the arbitration proceedings or by *default*, when selecting an institution to administer the proceedings pursuant to its rules of arbitration.

Under Article 5 of CANACO's arbitration rules and Article 5 of Appendix 1 of CAM's arbitration rules, arbitration proceedings are confidential save an express agreement of the parties to the contrary.

In addition, Mexican law upholds the general principle that prevents attorneys from revealing information received from their clients in the exercise of their legal profession. Failure to observe such duty amounts to a criminal offence and is subject to tort liability.

Arbitrators

Appointment of arbitrators

According to Article 1427(II) of the Commerce Code, the parties are free to agree on the number and method of selection of the arbitrators, either by specifically determining such rules or by subjecting themselves to the rules of an institution. Failing such agreement, the proceedings shall be conducted by a single arbitrator (Article 1426, Commerce Code).

Under said article, the Commerce Code provides a standard procedure for selection of arbitrators: in case of a single arbitrator, if the parties cannot reach an agreement, a judge will appoint, at the request of any party, the person who shall act as single arbitrator. When facing proceedings with three arbitrators, each party shall appoint one, and the two appointed arbitrators shall select the third; if any party fails to appoint an arbitrator within 30 days from receiving the request of the other party to do so, or the two already appointed arbitrators fail to agree on the appointment of the third within 30 days after the appointment of the second arbitrator, the third arbitrator shall be appointed by a national judge. The decision of the judge in both cases is final and thus subject to no appeal.

Mexican law provides that any person with legal capacity – except for judges, their secretaries and members of the Council of the Federal Judiciary, according to Article 101 of the Mexican Constitution – may act as arbitrator, provided there are no special requirements agreed by the parties that arbitrators must meet.

In this regard, the Commerce Code provides that, unless otherwise agreed between the parties, no person shall be precluded by reason of his/her nationality from acting as an arbitrator.

Additionally, Article 1428 of the aforementioned Code imposes a duty upon any person who has been designated as a candidate for appointment as arbitrator or who has already been appointed as such, to inform the parties of all possible circumstances that may give rise to doubts as to his/her impartiality or independence and which may constitute grounds for challenge.

Challenge of arbitrators

Challenges to arbitrators can only be based on circumstances that raise doubts as to their impartiality or independence, or on the lack of a quality they must have according to the arbitration agreement (Article 1428, Commerce Code).

Pursuant to Article 1429 of the Commerce Code, the parties may determine the procedure to challenge arbitrators but, in the absence of such agreement, the Commerce Code establishes that any party who wishes to challenge the appointment of a person as arbitrator must send to the tribunal, within 15 days from its constitution or from the date on which the party attains knowledge of the existence of the circumstances on which the challenge is based, a letter explaining the reasons believed to justify such challenge.

The arbitral tribunal must rule on the issue. If a challenge is unsuccessful, the petitioner may file before a judge a request for review of the matter, which is subject to no appeal.

Even if the decision is pending before the judge, the arbitral tribunal, including the arbitrator being challenged, may continue with the proceeding and issue an award (Article 1429, Commerce Code).

IBA Guidelines on conflict of interest

There are no legal provisions regarding the ethical duties of arbitrators in matters related to conflict of interest; however, arbitrators and parties tend to agree on the use of the IBA Guidelines on Conflicts of Interest in International Arbitration.

Terminating an arbitrator's mandate

The common reasons for an arbitrator's mandate to be terminated are:

- Rendering of the award (Article 1449, Commerce Code).
- Claimant withdrawing its claim (Article 1449, Commerce Code).
- By agreement between the parties to terminate the proceeding (Article 1449, Commerce Code).
- An arbitrator withdraws from its mandate.
- By decision of the arbitral tribunal or national court in a challenge procedure (Article 1429, Commerce Code).

Immunity of arbitrators

According to Article 1480 of the Commerce Code, arbitrators and arbitral tribunals may be held liable – together with the requesting party – for any damages arising from the granting of interim measures. No other similar provisions are found in the Commerce Code regarding the rest of the proceeding.

Secretaries to the arbitral tribunal

The Commerce Code and arbitration rules of CANACO, CAM and the ICC do not contain express provisions regarding the possibility of the tribunal designating a person as administrative secretary to assist during the arbitration proceeding; however, it is common practice in international arbitrations for tribunals seated in Mexico do so, following agreement of the parties in this respect.

In arbitration proceedings seated in Mexico, the administrative secretaries act upon the tribunal's instructions and always under its supervision and thus the tribunal is responsible for administrative secretaries' conduct. Their role is understood to be circumscribed to organisational and administrative tasks (see Note to Parties and Arbitral Tribunals on the Conduct of the Arbitration under the ICC Rules of 2017).

Interim relief

Types available and application procedure

Under the Commerce Code (Article 1425) parties may request from a court an interim measure of protection – before or during the arbitral proceedings.

Similarly, Article 1433 of said Code provides that the arbitral tribunal may, at the request of either party, order the necessary provisional remedies required to protect the subject matter under dispute.

The Commerce Code does not incorporate provisions that define the types of interim measures that an arbitral tribunal may grant. Accordingly, arbitral tribunals and courts are allowed complete discretion to grant any kind of preliminary and interim measures of protection and relief (Articles 1433 and 1478, Commerce Code).

Additionally, Article 1479 of the Commerce Code provides that all interim measures ordered by an arbitral tribunal shall be recognised as binding, and, unless otherwise determined by the tribunal, such interim measures shall be enforceable upon request to the courts.

The court to which enforcement of a tribunal-ordered interim measure is requested according to Article 1480 of the Commerce Code may refuse enforcement if – among other things: the court considers such refusal to be based on one or more of the grounds set forth in Article 1462, Section I (a), (b), (c) or (d) and Section II of the Commerce Code, which are the same grounds for refusing enforcement of an arbitral award; if the tribunal's order regarding a provision of security was not complied with; or if the interim measure has been terminated or suspended, either by the tribunal or by a national court in which the arbitration procedure is being heard.

According to Mexican law provisions and precedents regarding interim relief in procedures other than arbitration, two main circumstances are required to justify the granting of interim relief: the likelihood of success of the requesting party on the merits (*fumus boni iuris*); and the urgency to grant the relief sought (*periculum in mora*) (see also Article 17(A)(1) of the Model Law).

Anti-suit injunctions

Mexican law does not expressly regulate the power of national courts to order anti-suit injunctions aiming to prevent a party from initiating or continuing proceedings before a court (whether national or international).

Security costs

Pursuant to Article 1433 of the Commerce Code, unless otherwise agreed by the parties, the arbitral tribunal is entitled to order, at the request of either party, the interim measures it deems necessary to preserve the subject matter of the dispute. Accordingly, the tribunal may freely decide to request the presentation of a guarantee or security in an amount sufficient to cover any damages arising from the enforcement of the interim measure.

Arbitration award

Formal requirements of awards

Article 1448 of the Commerce Code establishes the formal requirements for an award to be valid under Mexican law in arbitration proceedings seated in Mexico. These are:

- The award must be in writing.
- The award shall be signed by the arbitrators (if there is more than one arbitrator, the signature of the majority shall suffice).
- Unless otherwise agreed by the parties or in case the award is by consent and rendered in the terms agreed by the parties (Article 1447, Commerce Code), the award shall be reasoned.
- The award must set forth the date on which it was rendered and indicate the seat of arbitration.

Once the award is rendered, the tribunal shall give notice to the parties by delivering a copy of it, signed by the arbitrators.

Time frame

There is no specific time frame under Mexican law for a tribunal to render its award. Thus, such time limit will depend on the applicable arbitration rules.

Awarding costs

There are no limitations in the Commerce Code for a tribunal to allocate remedies allowed by law as it deems appropriate. Thus, provided the parties have included a request in this respect as part of their claims, the tribunal is entitled to award interest (simple or compound) according to the rate agreed by the parties and in case there is no agreement in this respect, at the annual legal rate of 6% (Article 362, Commerce Code).

Challenge of the arbitration award

Appeal and grounds for challenge of an award

Under Mexican law, arbitral awards are considered final and are subject to no appeal. Nevertheless, according to Article 1457 of the Commerce Code, awards may be challenged and set aside under a few restrictive grounds enumerated in said article, which are the same as those provided by Article V of the NY Convention.

In this respect, the interested party must prove that:

- One of the parties to the arbitration agreement did not have legal capacity, or that the agreement was not valid under the law the parties have subjected it to, or, failing such agreement, under Mexican law.
- The party was not given proper notice of the appointment of an arbitrator or of the arbitral proceedings, or was unable to defend its rights.
- The award deals with issues not included or falling outside of the scope of the arbitration agreement.
- The composition of the arbitral tribunal or the arbitral procedure was not in accordance with the agreement between the parties, unless such agreement was contrary to mandatory provisions of the Fourth Title of the Commerce Code.

Or the court must determine that:

- The subject matter of the dispute is not arbitrable under Mexican law.
- The award is contrary to public policy.

The request for setting aside an award must be filed within a period of three months from the date on which notice of the award is given to the parties, and the challenge proceeding may take up to one year.

There are no ordinary remedies against the decision of the national court in this regard, and thus it is final and cannot be appealed, but it can be challenged through an *amparo* proceeding (a constitutional remedy intended to protect constitutional rights which allows the challenge of any act of authority or law provision considered unconstitutional). However, under no circumstances may either the first instance court or the *amparo* court review the merits of the award.

Modification of awards

Pursuant to Articles 1450 and 1451 of the Commerce Code, either party may – unless a different time period was agreed by them and with prior notice to the other party – request the tribunal to:

- Correct an error of calculation, copying, typographical or of a similar nature in the award.
- If the parties so agree, give an interpretation upon an issue or upon a specific part of the award.
- Render an additional award regarding any claim sought in the proceedings but omitted in the final award.

Enforcement of the arbitration award

Conventions regarding the enforcement of awards; requirements for enforcement

Under the NY Convention and Article 1461 of the Commerce Code, awards shall be deemed to be binding in Mexico regardless of the country in which they are issued and, upon written request made to the judge by the interested party, they shall be enforced.

The party seeking enforcement shall provide the national judge, together with its request for enforcement, the original or a certified copy of both the arbitration agreement and the award; these documents must be apostilled (legalised) and accompanied by a translation into Spanish if the original language is a different one.

After the request has been filed, the judge shall grant the party against which the enforcement of the award is sought, a 15-day period to file an answer and present evidence. Upon the expiration of this time period, and regardless of whether the parties have offered any evidence, the judge shall summon the parties to appear to a pleading hearing within the next three days.

The grounds for denial of enforcement of an award under Article 1462 of the Commerce Code mirror the grounds established in Article V of the NY Convention. These are:

- One of the parties to the arbitration agreement did not have legal capacity, or the agreement was not valid under the law the parties have subjected it to, or, failing such agreement, under Mexican law.
- The party was not given proper notice of the appointment of an arbitrator or of the arbitral proceedings, or was somehow unable to present its case.
- The award deals with issues not contemplated in or falling outside of the scope of the arbitration agreement.
- The composition of the arbitral tribunal or the arbitral procedure was not in accordance with the agreement between the parties or, absent such agreement, was contrary to the law of the seat of arbitration.
- The award is either not yet binding on the parties or was set aside by a court at the seat of arbitration.
- The subject matter of the dispute is not arbitrable under Mexican law.
- The award is contrary to public policy.

Enforcement of awards set aside at the seat

Article 1462 of the Commerce Code governs the recognition and enforcement of awards. The wording of this article states that such recognition and enforcement of awards *may* be denied if one or more of the grounds are found to exist; thus, its wording is rather permissive and gives judges discretion as to whether to enforce an award which was set aside in the seat of arbitration.

Trends of enforcement – pro-arbitration or anti-arbitration?

Over the past decade, there has been a growing tendency among Mexican courts to favour enforcement of foreign arbitral awards. Currently arbitration, and ADR mechanisms in general, are being more broadly used, to the point that, recently, the Mexican Constitution was amended to include, in Article 17, a reference to ADR mechanisms. Mexican Federal courts have issued legal precedents declaring the right to access ADR mechanism to be a fundamental right recognised by the Mexican Constitution.

Investment arbitration

Bilateral investment treaties (BITs)

According to the United Nations Conference on Trade and Development (last consulted on March 22, 2018, 19:30hrs; available at http://investmentpolicyhub.unctad.org/IIA/CountryBits/136), Mexico has 35 BITs, of which 30 are in force.

Multilateral investment treaties (MITs)

Until recently, Mexico was not party to the ICSID Convention; however, on January 11, 2018, representatives of the Mexican government signed this Convention. Its ratification date and its subsequent entry into force are still pending.

Before the signing of the ICSID Convention, Mexico's common practice was to include a dispute resolution clause providing for arbitration, pursuant to the additional facility rules of ICSID in most of its international treaties with an investment chapter (such as NAFTA).

Additionally, Mexico is party to over 16 international treaties with investment provisions, such as: the Comprehensive and Progressive Agreement for Trans-Pacific Partnership (CPTPP); the Mexico-Northern Triangle Free Trade Agreement (El Salvador, Guatemala and Honduras); the Montevideo Treaty (Argentina, Bolivia, Brazil, Chile, Colombia, Ecuador, Mexico, Paraguay, Peru, Uruguay and Venezuela); and the Mexico-European Free Trade Association. (See United Nations Conference on Trade and Development: http://investmentpolicyhub.unctad.org/IIA/CountryOtherIias/136#iiaInnerMenu).

Recent investment arbitration cases

Over the years, Mexico has participated in dozens of investment arbitrations as respondent State. Many of them have been settled before a final award is rendered, while others have been decided by a final award.

Adrián Magallanes
Tel: +52 55 5258 1018 / Email: amagallanes@vwys.com.mx
Adrián is partner of Von Wobeser y Sierra and a member of the firm since 2002. He has acted as counsel in *ad hoc* and institutional arbitrations (ICC, LCIA, ICSID-AAA, ICDR, UNCITRAL, CAM, CANACO) in the commercial, infrastructure, energy, oil and gas and investor-state sectors. He also frequently acts as arbitrator. Adrián regularly appears before Mexican courts in various types of litigation proceedings, particularly in commercial and administrative law-related disputes. His experience also includes several class action cases, transnational litigations and constitutional law trials (amparos). He is Chair of the Arbitration Commission of the Mexican Bar Association, and a professor of International Litigation at the Escuela Libre de Derecho. He is admitted to practice in Mexico and New York, and has working experience in Washington, D.C. and Beijing.

Montserrat Manzano
Tel: +52 55 5258 1018 / Email: mmanzano@vwys.com.mx
Montserrat is Partner of the Arbitration Practice of Von Wobeser y Sierra. She has 14 years of experience as an attorney and has participated in more than 50 arbitrations as arbitrator, secretary, arbitral tribunal assistant or counsel, in arbitrations conducted under the rules of the ICC, AAA, UNCITRAL, PCA, ICSID, complementary mechanism of ICSID and CAM. She has solid experience in dispute resolution related to administrative law and government contracting. She has participated in both commercial and investment arbitrations, in various sectors, including the following: energy, construction, port, shipping, chemical, involving both Mexican and foreign law. She is member of Arbitral Women and actively involved in diversity initiatives.

Von Wobeser y Sierra, S.C.

Paseo de los Tamarindos 60, piso 4, col. Bosques de las Lomas, Mexico City, P.C. 05120, Mexico
Tel: +52 55 5258 1000 / Fax: +52 55 5258 1098 / +52 55 5258 1099 / URL: www.vonwobeserysierra.com

Norway

Erlend Haaskjold
Arntzen de Besche Advokatfirma AS

Introduction

Arbitration is the preferred method of dispute resolution in commercial matters. In Norway, the majority of commercial disputes of any importance are resolved by arbitration, not by litigation in the ordinary courts. There may be a number of possible explanations for this. In arbitration, the parties are free to elect the arbitrators of their choice. An arbitration panel established by mutual agreement may be tailored so as to secure the required expertise for the particular dispute. As there is normally no right to appeal an arbitral award, the parties will have a binding decision after one hearing. Finally, the parties normally retain control over the arbitration process; this flexibility is normally not available within the ordinary court system.

A particular feature of arbitration in Norway is the extensive use of *ad hoc* arbitration. Whereas institutional arbitration is widely used in Denmark and Sweden, there is no generally recognised arbitration institute in Norway. Arbitration *ad hoc* provides the parties with the necessary dynamics to resolve a commercial dispute as quickly and correctly as possible. The parties are at liberty to appoint the arbitrators of their choice, and to agree on a binding time frame for the case preparation. Specific rules for the proceedings may be established if this is required. The Norwegian legislation is generally regarded as "arbitration friendly". The courts will normally assist with the services usually rendered by an arbitration institute, such as the appointment of arbitrators and legal service of documents.

A large proportion of the arbitrations in Norway are international. Norwegian arbitrators are, due to their neutrality, in high demand. The similarity of the law in Denmark, Norway, and Sweden has created a common Scandinavian market for arbitration. Thus, it is not uncommon for a Norwegian arbitrator to sit in a case in Sweden, or for a Danish arbitrator to take appointment in Norway. Scandinavian law is often described as a hybrid between the typical common law and civil law jurisdictions. In international commercial disputes, Scandinavian law is therefore often regarded as a convenient compromise, both for choice of law and for seat of arbitration. The international flavour of commercial arbitration is increasing.

The Norwegian Arbitration Act 2004 provides the legal framework for arbitration in Norway. The Act applies equally to national and international arbitrations. As only a few of the rules are mandatory, the parties retain autonomy over the dispute resolution process. The Arbitration Act is to a large extent based on the UNCITRAL Model Law. There are few significant differences between the Arbitration Act and the Model Law. One important difference is, however, that the Norwegian Arbitration Act does not require that arbitration agreements are entered into in writing.

Norway is a signatory to the New York Convention. The Convention was ratified in 1961. There are no reservations to the general obligations of the Convention, and its provisions are incorporated in the Norwegian Arbitration Act of 2004.

Arbitration agreement

An agreement to arbitrate may be made in nearly any commercial matter. The agreement may concern a dispute that has already arisen, or the parties may agree that all potential disputes in a particular relationship, typically a contract, shall be resolved by arbitration. Today, most commercial contracts contain an arbitration clause. There are no formal requirements to such agreements, and even an oral agreement to arbitrate is enforceable in principle. However, the importance normally attached to an agreement to arbitrate, will inevitably lead the courts to look for clear evidence that an arbitration agreement has, in fact, been entered into. In consumer disputes, arbitration agreements may only be entered into after the dispute has arisen.

An arbitration agreement may be drafted in different ways. At the initial stage of arbitral proceedings, it is not uncommon that the parties disagree as to the extent of the arbitration agreement they have entered into. Much effort is therefore made to ensure that an arbitration clause in a commercial contract is properly drafted so as to correspond to the common intention of the parties at the time of entry into of the contract. In the event that a contract with an arbitration clause is later supplemented with an addendum or an amending agreement, it is assumed that the arbitration clause in the original agreement will also apply to any dispute arising under the subsequent agreement.

When the parties agree to refer to arbitration a dispute that has already arisen, the arbitration agreement will often take the form of "terms of reference". In order to save time and costs, the parties may agree on some basic facts that the arbitration tribunal can use as a factual background for the award.

The Arbitration Act is based on the principle of separability. When a contract contains an arbitration clause, the agreement to arbitrate is treated as an agreement separate and distinct from the contract of which it is a part. It is fully possible that the arbitration agreement is governed by a different choice of law than the main contract. More importantly, the termination or invalidity of the main contract does not necessarily affect the arbitration agreement.

The arbitration agreement will normally contain the parties' express choice of the law applicable to the substance. The law thus chosen shall be applied by the arbitral tribunal. Accordingly, the Arbitration Act states that the arbitral tribunal shall apply the rules of law that have been chosen by the parties as applicable to the merits. A reference in the arbitration agreement to the law or legal system of a country shall, unless otherwise indicated, be construed as a reference to the substantive law of that country and not to its rules on choice of law. If the parties have not chosen a law in the arbitration agreement, the arbitral tribunal shall apply the rules of law as designated by applying Norwegian choice of law rules. The arbitral tribunal shall only decide a case on the basis of fairness if the parties have expressly authorised it to do so.

A dispute is considered non-arbitrable if the subject matter is not capable of being settled by agreement between the parties. A dispute is also likely non-arbitrable in cases where a third party's consent is required, and in some aspects as far as it concerns rights *in rem*. Furthermore, a claim is non-arbitrable if the relief sought may only be granted by a state authority or the courts. Such cases include declaration of bankruptcy, taxation, the existence and validity of patents, certain competition law disputes such as imposition of fines, ordering a company to cease and desist activities harmful to competition, and granting clearance for acquisitions of businesses.

Arbitration procedure

The arbitration process is normally initiated by the issuance of a "notice to arbitrate". This is a formal letter from one of the parties to the other where particulars of the dispute are given, and a request to resolve the dispute by arbitration is made. A particular point to note is that such notice will prevent prescription of a claim.

As most arbitrations in Norway are *ad hoc*, the parties will then agree on a panel of arbitrators. Normally, the panel will consist of three arbitrators, and it is not uncommon that the parties reach agreement on all the arbitrators. The advantage of such procedure is that the arbitration tribunal will have the necessary expertise. Alternatively, each of the parties may nominate one arbitrator, who then appoint the third arbitrator together. Once the arbitration panel has been established, the chair will invite to a case management conference. The purpose is to fix a date for the main hearing and to agree on a time frame and format of the written submissions. The parties will also agree on the presentation of evidence and witnesses.

In smaller disputes, the parties may agree to appoint a sole arbitrator. As there is no requirement for an oral hearing, the arbitration award may be given on the basis of the case documents.

Arbitrators

The Arbitration Act requires that the arbitrators be impartial and independent of the parties, and qualified for the appointment. As most arbitration tribunals are established by the agreement of the parties, it is relatively rare to see disputes as to the suitability of a particular arbitrator. In commercial disputes, counsel will normally conduct extensive scrutiny of potential candidates in order to avoid complications at the enforcement stage. However, the Arbitration Act empowers the ordinary courts to decide on objections made against an arbitrator appointed in accordance with the prescribed procedure. Appointment of an arbitrator may only be challenged on specific grounds. Such grounds may be that there is serious doubt as to the arbitrator's impartiality or independence, or that the arbitrator does not have the qualifications agreed between the parties. As a main rule, the panel will consist of three arbitrators. It is not uncommon that the parties reach agreement on all the arbitrators. The advantage of such procedure is that the arbitration tribunal will have the necessary expertise for the dispute. Alternatively, each of the parties may nominate one arbitrator, who then together appoint the third arbitrator. Alternatively, the parties may agree on a neutral body to make a default appointment.

The courts may not intervene in the selection of arbitrators. However, if the arbitral panel cannot be constituted in accordance with the arbitration agreement, each of the parties may request that the local courts appoint the missing arbitrator(s). The appointment made by the court is final and cannot be appealed.

There is no provision to the effect that arbitrators are immune from liability. There is a general consensus that an action based upon error in fact or in law, will not succeed. However, there may be basis for a claim against an arbitrator in the event of serious misconduct or breach of the criminal law, such as corruption. There have been no such cases in Norway.

Interim relief

Unless otherwise agreed between the parties, an arbitral tribunal has the power to order the parties to undertake certain measures, such as preserving assets or the production of evidence. An order to this effect, however, is not enforceable. Failure to comply with an order made by the tribunal, may influence the assessment of the evidence. The parties may ask the ordinary courts to issue an order for interim relief. Such court order will be enforceable.

The arbitral tribunal may request the ordinary courts to take depositions from witnesses and make an order for the production of documentary evidence. The arbitrators have the right to attend the court hearing when the witnesses are examined, and they may ask questions.

Arbitration award

The arbitration award shall be in writing and signed by all the arbitrators. The Arbitration Act contains a provision (which is rarely used) to the effect that the majority of the tribunal may sign, provided that the reason for all arbitrators not signing is stated in the judgment. The place and date of the award must be given. There is no fixed time limit for the award. However, most arbitrators avoid delay. If time is of the essence, a separate agreement may be made as to time limits for the award. According to the Arbitration Act, a signed copy of the arbitration award shall be filed with the local court and kept in the court's archive. Non-compliance with this provision does not make the award unenforceable.

The law does not impose any limits on the available remedies. In principle, an arbitration tribunal has the same power as the ordinary courts. The most common remedy in commercial disputes is damages in the event of breach. However, the arbitration tribunal may also grant the remedy of specific performance, which will be enforced by the relevant authorities on the basis of the arbitration award. The only limit to the power of the arbitration tribunal is interim measures.

The arbitration tribunal is empowered to make such cost order as it deems just. Although the rules of cost in the Civil Procedure Act are not directly applicable in arbitration, these rules may nevertheless exert some influence on the cost award. In essence, the winning party is entitled to have his cost paid by the other party. However, exemption from the cost liability may be made if there has been doubt about the result, or if there is some other justification for each of the parties paying their own costs and expenses.

Challenge of the arbitration award

An arbitration award is final and binding. There is no right of appeal. It is, of course, possible for the parties to agree on a right to appeal, but this is rarely seen in practice.

An arbitration award may be challenged on the grounds of procedural impropriety. Such challenge must be made within three months of receipt of the arbitration award. The most frequent grounds for challenging an award are that a party has not been given notice of the arbitration, that the award falls outside the scope of the arbitration agreement, or that there has been a violation of the basic principles of due process. It is very rare that a claim for the setting-aside of an arbitration award succeeds.

A claim that an arbitration award is invalid must be made in the form of a lawsuit before the courts, and the lawsuit must be filed within three months from the day the party received the arbitral award.

The parties may not waive the right to challenge an award by agreement before the dispute has arisen. The statutory provisions on the right of challenge to an award are therefore mandatory. It is generally assumed that waiver would violate the basic principles of justice and fairness, and that the statutory grounds for the setting-aside of an award are minimum rights in a democratic society. The Norwegian act does not adopt the view that waiver of the right to challenge may be based on the principle of party autonomy.

Enforcement of the arbitration award

Norway ratified the New York Convention on the Recognition and Enforcement of Foreign Arbitral Awards in 1961. The Convention has since been in effect, and its provisions are now incorporated into the 2004 Arbitration Act.

An arbitral award shall be recognised and enforceable, irrespective of the country in which it was made. Recognition and enforcement of an award requires that an original or certified copy of the award is made available. In addition, if the award has not been rendered in Norwegian, Swedish, Danish or English, the party shall also provide a certified translation. Documentary proof of the arbitration agreement or other basis for arbitration may also be requested.

Investment arbitration

Norway is currently party to 15 bilateral investment treaties (BITs) and 29 treaties with investment provisions (TIPs). Norway signed the ICSID Convention in 1966, the Energy Charter Treaty in 1995, and the International Energy Charter in 2015. So far, there has been no investment arbitration case against Norway.

Erlend Haaskjold
Tel: +47 23 89 46 08 / Email: erh@adeb.no
Erlend Haaskjold is a leading arbitration practitioner in Norway. He is Partner in the Litigation and Dispute Resolution Group at Arntzen de Besche law firm in Oslo. He is admitted to the Supreme Court of Norway and has presented a great number of cases before all instances of regular courts. He has extensive experience as an arbitrator in national and international disputes. He lectures commercial law at the Law Faculty at the University of Oslo.

Arntzen de Besche Advokatfirma AS

P.O. Box 2734 Solli, 0204 Oslo, Norway
Tel: +47 23 89 40 00 / Fax: +47 23 89 40 01 / URL: www.adeb.no

Portugal

Nuno Albuquerque, Luís Paulo Silva & Maria Amélia Mesquita
N-Advogados & CM Advogados

Introduction

Nowadays, arbitration as a dispute resolution method has become a true success in Portugal, and has been increasingly used in both international and domestic disputes involving both private and public law.

The Portuguese Arbitration Law (PAL) is regulated in the Annex to Law no. 63/2011, of December, which is based on the Model-Law on International Commercial Arbitration, UNCITRAL/UNCITRAL of 1985, remodelled in 2006, which entered into force in March 2012.

This arbitration law aimed to introduce a more modern arbitration regime and promote Portugal as a seat for international arbitration and also tried to reconcile – whenever it saw usefulness in this – the solutions already tested in the application of Law no. 31/86, with the guidelines and inspirations in several national laws regulating arbitration that have been approved in the last 15 years in other countries.

PAL is characterised by the following fundamental points:

- as stated in the UNCITRAL Model Law, PAL respects the autonomy of the arbitration process;
- as advocated by UNCITRAL, for the formal validity of the arbitration agreement, it is required to give greater flexibility to compliance with the written form requirement;
- PAL also confers jurisdiction on state courts to rule on the competence of arbitral tribunals only where the arbitration agreement is manifestly null and void, inoperative or incapable of being performed.

Portugal also joined the New York Convention on the Recognition and Enforcement of Foreign Arbitral Awards of 1958 ("CNI 1958") on 16 January 1995. However, it is in force in the Portuguese legal system with an express reservation of reciprocity (but not with the commercial reserve), and applies only in relation to arbitration decisions rendered in states that are also party to this Convention. The grounds for the refusal of recognition and for the annulment of arbitral awards are, in the Portuguese law, broadly in line with the grounds for refusal of recognition laid down in CNI 1958.

Regarding the international arbitration legal regime, it is regulated in Chapter IX of PAL. According to the 49th Article, international arbitration is a private and voluntary means of resolving a dispute, with a contractual nature or not, the interests of international trade being at stake.

Thus, PAL states in Article 49 no. 2, which is applicable to international arbitration, the same internal rules, *mutatis mutandis*.

PAL also integrates the general arbitration regime and must be applied to all arbitral proceedings, including the necessary arbitration and certain special arbitrations, unless a special law expressly determines otherwise. Only those special laws may punctually or generically derogate from the application of PAL or establish a procedural regime different from that provided for therein.

The most prominent commercial arbitration institution in Portugal is the Arbitration Centre of the Portuguese Chamber of Commerce and Industry, whose rules entered into force in March 2014 and reflect both the changes introduced by PAL and international best practice. The Centre may act as an appointing authority if agreed between the parties in the arbitration agreement.

There are no international arbitration bodies based in Portugal, although the ICC has a national committee in Portugal, which assists the court in the appointment of Portuguese arbitrations.

Arbitration agreement

The first chapter of PAL is dedicated to the arbitration agreement.

Any litigation concerning patrimonial interests may be submitted by the parties, through an arbitration agreement, to the decision of arbitrators, unless the same litigation is subject exclusively to the courts of the State (e.g. criminal and insolvency disputes) or to compulsory arbitration (e.g. certain labour disputes, and disputes regarding the introduction of generic drugs in the market), according to Article 1, no. 3 of PAL.

As determined by Article 1, the arbitration agreement may have as its subject matter a present dispute, even if it concerns a State court (arbitration agreement), or any litigation arising out of a contractual or non-contractual legal relationship (arbitration clause).

The State and other public law bodies can also celebrate arbitration conventions if such agreements have the object of private law disputes, and since they are authorised by law.

Those agreements must, in order to be valid and effective, comply with several requirements. In fact, the arbitration agreement must be in written form, and this requirement is fulfilled when it appears in a document signed by the parties, an exchange of letters, telegrams, fax or other means of communication.

It is considered that the arbitration agreement meets the requirement in written form when it appears in electronic, magnetic, optical, or other type of support, offering the same guarantees of reliability, intelligibility and conservation.

Also referred to as an arbitration agreement is the reference made to a contract containing an arbitration clause, provided that such contract complies with the written form and the remission is made in such a way as to make that clause an integral part, thereof, of the contractual clauses.

One of the principal requirements of the arbitration agreement is determination of the subject-matter of the dispute and specification of the legal relationship underlying the disputes from which they may emerge.

In fact, the arbitration clause shall include a detailed statement of the dispute in order to ensure that no matter submitted to arbitration is excluded, since the arbitral court may only know of the issues contained therein.

According to Article 3 of PAL, any arbitration clause that does not fulfil the requirements stated in Articles 1 and 2 of PAL is void.

Article 4 of the PAL, for its part, provides the conditions on which the arbitration agreement may be modified, revoked or terminated:

- *Modification*: it may be modified by the parties until the acceptance of the first arbitrator, or with the agreement of all the arbitrators, until the delivery of the arbitral award.
- *Revocation*: it can be revoked until the delivery of the arbitration award.
- *Expiry*: the death or extinction of the parties does not terminate the arbitration agreement nor extinguish the arbitration.

Regarding the competence of the arbitral tribunal, Article 18 says that this tribunal may decide on its own jurisdiction, even if for that purpose, it becomes necessary to assess the existence, validity or effectiveness of the arbitration agreement – see Article 18/1 of PAL.

This legal provision gives the letter of the law to the fundamental principle of arbitration, the principle of competence-competence: that the arbitral tribunal has full competence to solve all questions raised in the arbitral proceedings relating to it, whether of a substantive nature relating to the merits of the case, or of a procedural nature. The principle of competence-jurisdiction enshrines the autonomy of the arbitral tribunal in relation to the jurisdiction of the state courts.

Arbitration procedure

Parties are free to agree on the procedural rules, including with respect to the commencement of the arbitration (e.g. by adopting institutional rules that provide for a different procedure).

According to Article 33 of PAL, the arbitration procedure begins when the defendant receives the submission request of that dispute – this will happen if nothing is stipulated in the Agreement of the parties. Usually, the arbitration dispute request is known as "notice to arbitration". The law does not provide for the minimum contents of that request.

This will happen even before the constitution of the arbitral tribunal, outside the jurisdiction of that court. Within the time limits determined by arbitral tribunal or stipulated by the parties, the claimant submits his petition, expressing his request and the facts on which it is based. On the other hand, the defendant presents his complaint, explaining his position in relation to the plaintiff's petition.

With the application and the objection, the claimant and defendant, respectively, may join documents which they deem relevant, and mention in the written pieces other documents or other evidence that may emerge.

The arbitral tribunal may admit, or not, any means of proof, and it has the power to deliberate the value of the evidence.

The defendant may file a counterclaim if the object is covered by the arbitration agreement.

Even though PAL is silent on this exact point, the truth is that the arbitration notification should contain the following elements:

- the parties' names;
- summary description of the dispute;
- clear formulation of the intention to submit the dispute to arbitration;
- arbitration agreement identification;
- number of arbitrators to be constituted by the arbitral tribunal;
- identification of the arbitrator that the Claimant intends to intervene as sole arbitrator – if that has been specified;

- identification of the referee of the appointing party; and
- place of arbitration.

Regarding the place of arbitration, the Portuguese Arbitration Law also gives wide discretion to the parties, according to Article 31. In the absence of the parties' agreement, the arbitral tribunal sets the location taking into account the circumstances of the case and the convenience of the parties. The arbitral tribunal also can – if the parties do not agree anything to the contrary – gather in a location that it deems convenient.

With respect to the disclosure in the arbitral process, the Portuguese jurisdiction also considers the IBA's guidelines (also known as "soft law"), which will support the legal loopholes between the different jurisdictions and the way the courts operate. Those orientations provide to the arbitrators a relative strength to admit, or not, the means of evidence, and its suitability to each case.

Such guideline is also stated in the second part of Article 19, no. 2 of the UNCITRAL Model Law – and, by its influence, Article 30, no. 4 of PAL which, however, as was clear from the preparatory work, should be considered non-imperative.

In relation to the other matters regulated in this article, the hierarchy of norms is the following:

- contractual freedom of the parties;
- fundamental principles of the process and other mandatory rules established by law; and
- the arbitral powers of the arbitral tribunal in matters of procedure.

The Portuguese Legislator took into consideration, in the preparation of PAL, the guidelines of all major international arbitration institutions, for their efficiency, flexibility, antiquity and neutrality to all parties involved in resolving a dispute under its auspices.

The Portuguese Arbitration Law also took into consideration the combination of the best civil law features and the equity of the common law system, in its several legal provisions, for example, in the case of third parties' intervention, stated in Article 36 of PAL.

Arbitrators have a legal duty to be independent and impartial and are also subject to the rules of suspicion and impediment that apply to judges.

Furthermore, the arbitration procedure is confidential and that duty shall also apply to all the arbitrators, parties and the arbitration institutions involved, according to Article 30 no. 5 of PAL. This duty shall also apply at all pre-procedural stages, in the course of the proceedings and after the proceedings have been completed, and shall relate to the whole content of the arbitration proceedings.

Arbitrators

The parties are free to choose the number of arbitrators, through the arbitration agreement or subsequent written document signed by the parties, according to Article 10 no. 1 of PAL.

Nevertheless, if the arbitration tribunal is to be constituted by a single arbitrator and there is no agreement between the parties on such designation, such arbitrator is appointed by the state court at the request of either party – Article 10 no. 2 of PAL. Should the arbitral tribunal be composed of three or more arbitrators, each party chooses an equal number of arbitrators and those arbitrators choose the presiding arbitrator – Article 10 no. 3 of PAL. No-one may be forced to act as arbitrator until the full acceptance of that nomination.

In accordance with Article 12 of PAL, if the arbitrator accepts the nomination, only the excuse based on a supervening case that prevents the arbitrator to perform such function, is legitimate.

Each appointed arbitrator shall, within 15 days of the notification of his designation, declare in writing the acceptance of the charge to the party appointing him (unless otherwise agreed by the parties). If, within this period, nothing is declared, the non-acceptance of the order by the arbitrator shall be understood.

Anyone who is invited to serve as an arbitrator must disclose all circumstances that may give rise to doubts as to his impartiality and independence – Article 13 of PAL.

It should also be pointed out that if an arbitrator who has accepted the charge, unjustifiably excuses himself from the exercise of his function, he is liable for damages caused – Article 12 no. 6 of PAL.

This last question also converges with the matter of the immunity of judges. The Portuguese Arbitration Law opted for the express provision of the two cases which may incur arbitrator's liability, namely:

- Article 12 no. 6: "The arbitrator who accepted the charge, unjustifiably excused himself from the performance of his duties, shall be liable for damages caused."
- Article 43 no. 4: "Arbitrators who unjustifiably prevent the decision from being delivered within the prescribed period shall be liable for the damages caused."

At first sight, it is believed that the mere arbitrator's fault may be enough. However, as a general rule, the responsibility of the arbitrators is only the result of particularly serious situations, and fraud is often required. Usually, however, it is the rules of the institutionalised arbitration centres themselves that serve as a reference to cases of immunity of arbitrators.

Non-Portuguese nationals can, and indeed do, act as arbitrators in arbitrations seated in Portugal or where hearings are held in Portugal. There are no specific immigration or other requirements.

Interim relief

Interim relief and preliminary orders are regulated in Chapter IV of the Portuguese Arbitration Law. Article 20 determines that the arbitral tribunal has the legal power to issue interim measures, at the request of one of the parties and hearing the opposing party. The interim measures are temporary measures, decreed by sentence through which the arbitral tribunal instructs or orders one party to:

(a) maintain the current situation, or restore the *ex ante* situation, while the dispute has not finished;

(b) not to perform such acts that may cause prejudice to the arbitral process;

(c) ensure the preservation of assets or rights concerning the arbitral award; or

(d) preserve evidence which may be relevant to the outcome of the dispute.

In the arbitral process we don't have specific precautionary measures, which are thus all unnamed.

Indeed, the Portuguese Arbitration Law precautionary measures coincide with those foreseen for Portuguese civil proceedings, between Articles 362 to 409 of the Portuguese Code of Civil Procedure, such as the enrolment of assets. But these are not exhaustive because, in arbitration, what matters is to resolve the conflict as soon as possible and in the most effective manner, irrespective of the scope and nature of the measure.

An interim measure required under the Article 20 of the PAL can only be decreed if:

- there is a serious likelihood of the existence of the right claimed by the applicant and he can show sufficiently founded fear of his injury; and
- the damage resulting to the defendant from the order does not considerably exceed the damage that the applicant intends to avoid.

Still in this matter, there are two concrete situations that need to be distinguished: the decree of the injunction; and the execution of it.

In fact, the arbitral tribunal may order the precautionary measures required and timely to the good outcome of the litigation. However, certainly, due to lack of coercive powers of the arbitral tribunal, it cannot ensure the execution of the decreed measures. Thus, the injunction can be decreed by the arbitral tribunal and be enforced through recourse to the state court in accordance with Articles 27 and 28 of PAL.

Despite the fact that the arbitral procedure is strictly based on the principle of adversarial proceedings, the truth is that reality doesn't apply to the interim measures under penalty of losing its useful effect. To solve this issue PAL, inspired by the UNCITRAL Model Law in its 2006 version, in Article 17-B, solved the problem with the "preliminary orders", foreseen and regulated in Article 22 of PAL.

These measures, the specific regime of which is provided for in Article 23 of PAL, allow the arbitral tribunal to take a decision on the conduct to be taken by one party, at the request of the other, without hearing the requested party.

While both interim measures and preliminary orders are binding upon the parties, only the first may be enforced by state courts.

Anti-suit injunctions are expressly forbidden by Article 5(4) of the PAL.

Arbitration award

The arbitrators judge the dispute under the law, unless the parties agree that they shall decide *ex aequo et bono* or as *amiable compositeur* (Article 39).

In an arbitral proceeding with more than one arbitrator, any decision of the arbitral tribunal shall be taken by a majority of its members, excepting the cases in which is not possible to form a majority, in which case the decision is taken by the president of the court – Article 40 no.1.

The requirements regarding the sentence are foreseen in Article 42 of the PAL, these being quite important because the non-fulfilment of the requirements may lead to nullity of the sentence.

<u>Form of decision</u>

The sentence should be reduced to writing and signed by the arbitrator or arbitrators.

<u>Content of award</u>

- The award must mention the date on which it was given and the place of arbitration (determined in accordance with Article 31 of PAL).
- The award must state the reasons upon which it is based, unless the parties agree to waive the reasoning or if the parties have reached an understanding – Article 41 of PAL.
- The award must include in the judgment the apportionment by the parties of the costs directly resulting from the arbitration proceedings.

The awards must be pronounced within the term of 12 months since the acceptance of the last arbitrator. However, these deadlines can be freely extended by mutual agreement, or by court decision, once or twice, always for consecutive periods of 12 months, well-founded. Nevertheless, the parties can object to deadline extension.

The arbitral awards are always notified to the parties and a copy is always signed and sent to the parties by the arbitrator or arbitrators, producing the award's effect on the date of its notification, and it shall take effect immediately on the notification date.

Challenge of the arbitration award

There is no specialist arbitration court for voluntary arbitration in Portugal. State courts, in particular Courts of Appeal – which are the default courts for assistance and control under PAL – are familiar with the law and practice of international arbitration, generally applying PAL in a predictable and consistent manner.

As a rule, arbitral awards will only be subject to appeal if expressly foreseen by the parties; hence, the grounds on which an award may be appealed against before state courts will vary according to party specification. In international arbitrations seated in Portugal, appeal will only be possible to another arbitral tribunal if the parties so have agreed and regulated its terms.

<u>Correction and clarification of the award</u>

Within 30 days of receiving notice of the award, any party may ask the arbitral tribunal to make an additional award concerning parts of the claim or claims submitted in the arbitral proceedings but omitted from the award. Any additional award must be rendered within 30 days of the request. (Article 45 no.5.)

<u>Challenge of the award</u>

According to Article 46 of the PAL, the challenge of an arbitration award may only take the form of an annulment request. The challenge of the award must be submitted to the competent state court accompanied by the following elements:

- certified copy of the arbitral award; and
- translation of the award delivered in a foreign language (if applicable) to Portuguese.

The Portuguese Arbitration Law, like the New York Convention, sets narrow grounds to set aside the award. Indeed, the arbitral award can only be annulled by the competent state court if:

A) the party making the request demonstrates that:
   I. one party to the arbitration agreement was affected by incapacity, or that the agreement is not valid under the law to which the parties have subjected it or even the terms of this law;
   II. some of the fundamental principles referred in the Article 30 (1) were infringed and it had a decisive influence on the resolution of the dispute;
   III. the composition of the arbitral tribunal or the arbitration proceedings were not in accordance with the agreement of the parties, unless this agreement conflicts with a provision of this law from which the parties cannot derogate or, in the absence of such an agreement, which has not complied with this law and, in any case, that this disagreement had a decisive influence on the resolution of the dispute;
   IV. the judgment has been given on a dispute not covered by the arbitration agreement or contains decisions that go beyond the arbitration agreement;

V. the arbitral tribunal ordered a higher amount or a different object of the request, knew of issues that it shouldn't take a decision on, or did not decide on questions that it had to consider;

VI. the judgment was rendered in violation of the requirements established in Article 42, nos. 1 and 3; or

VII. the judgment was notified to the parties after the maximum deadline for the effect fixed in accordance with Article 43; or

B) the court finds that:

I. the subject-matter of the dispute cannot be settled by arbitration under Portuguese law; or

II. the content of the award offends the principles of the international public order of the Portuguese State.

The annulment request may be filed only within 60 days of the date on which the party seeking such annulment has received the notification of the judgment or, if an application has been made in accordance with Article 45, from the date on which the arbitral tribunal rendered a decision on that request.

In the process of annulment of an arbitration award or in other circumstances, with the exception of an appeal, the state court may not know the merits of the matter decided by the arbitral tribunal, and such questions must be referred to another arbitral tribunal for consideration – Article 46, no. 9 of PAL.

Enforcement of the arbitration award

There is no specific trend of Portuguese courts regarding the enforcement of arbitral awards. But Portuguese courts are fairly knowledgeable of the matter and quite prone to enforce awards.

Portuguese courts will reject recognition and enforcement of awards that have been set aside or suspended by the courts of the country in which the award was rendered or under the law of such country.

National awards

According to Article 46 of the Portuguese Arbitration Law, it is possible to execute the sentence if the part that requests the execution of the award to the competent state court provides, with the enforcement request, the following documents:

- the original of the judgment or a certified copy thereof; and
- translation of the award into Portuguese, if it is written in a foreign language.

In the case of a generic award of condemnation, their settlement is made in accordance with paragraph 6 of Article 716 of the Portuguese Code of Civil Procedure. This liquidation may also be requested from the arbitral tribunal according to paragraph 5 of Article 45, in which case the arbitral tribunal, hearing the other party, and producing evidence, makes a complementary decision, judging equally within the limits proved.

It should be noted that an arbitral award, even if it has been the subject of an application for the annulment of a judgment, may be enforced. However, the challenging party may request that the challenge have suspensive effect on the execution provided, for that purpose, it offers a bond within the period set by the court. In this case, the provisions of Article 733 of the Portuguese Code of Civil Procedure apply.

International awards

As established in the New York Convention on the Recognition and Enforcement of Foreign Arbitral Awards, Portugal recognises and enforces arbitration awards handed down in other Contracting States under the rules laid down in national law.

Investment arbitration

Portugal is party to several bilateral and multilateral treaties regarding the recognition and enforcement of arbitral awards. The most important bilateral treaties include those between Portugal and Portuguese-speaking countries, such as Angola, Cape Verde, Guinea-Bissau, Mozambique and Sao Tome and Principe. As for multilateral treaties, Portugal is a party to the Geneva Convention on the Execution of Foreign Arbitral Awards, the Washington Convention on the Settlement of Investment Disputes between States and Nationals of other States, and the Inter-American Convention on International Commercial Arbitration.

Despite that the legal arbitration framework is relatively recent in Portugal, it is curious that between 1851 and 1930, a number of disputes were recorded in a book by Francisco Castro Caldas, dating from 1935, in which Portugal was a part, 13 of which were international investment arbitrations, and where one of the parties was the State. These arbitrations were related, namely, to compensate British and American "loyal subjects" for the termination of the concession of the railroad of *Lourenço Marques* to the border of the Transvaal, and for its appropriation by the Portuguese Kingdom.

In the last 20 years, Portugal has ratified a vast set of Investment Protection Treaties ("TIPs"), which are integrators of arbitration clauses, and with a broad protection of investment.

The ICSID Convention

The Convention for the Resolution of Disputes stands among the various instruments that over the past decades have focused on investment arbitration, relating to investments between States and Nationals of other States, held in Washington, DC, in 1965, which established the International Center for the Settlement of Investment Disputes ("ICSID"), of which Portugal has been a member since 1984.

Treaty of the Energy Charter

The Energy Charter Treaty, also signed in Lisbon in 1994, is another multilateral treaty that covers rules about the resolution of disputes occurring specifically in the energy sector.

In fact, from the late 1960s onwards, several States began to enunciate a program of bilateral treaties for the promotion and protection of investment ("Bilateral Investment Treaties" or "TBI"), mechanisms of the Washington Convention. In recent decades, Portugal has been following, along with other countries of the European Union, ratifying and signing bilateral agreements and treaties.

However, nowadays, investment arbitration has been expanding in Portugal, counting on the diligent performance of companies that are already aware of this reality and are starting to adopt investment arbitration as a mean of settling disputes.

Third-party funding

No regulation on third-party funding of arbitration exists in Portugal. Given the high costs of some commercial claims and the need for small and medium-sized Portuguese companies to finance the pursuit of their claims, coupled with the increase in international arbitration and the steady economic growth in size and complexity of commercial transactions in Portugal, it is expected that third-party funding will feature increasingly in commercial and international disputes in Portugal.

Given the fact that there is no regulation on third-party funding, it would seem prudent for arbitration agreements to include certain provisions to provide more certainty in potential claims, and in particular: (1) the obligation to disclose the existence of funding agreements in the event of disputes, and the content to be disclosed; and (2) acknowledgment by the parties that, as a security measure to avoid a potential annulment of the award or refusal of its recognition and enforcement under the 1958 New York Convention, the funder's eventual uplift should not comprise any recovery of costs or indemnity due to the prevailing party in the arbitration or litigation.

Nuno Albuquerque
Tel: +253 609 310/330 / Email: nunoalbuquerque@nadv.pt
Born on July 19, 1964, in Angola. Nuno has a law degree, University of Coimbra (1988). Nuno is inscribed in Portugal's bar association, as a lawyer, since 1990; in Angola's Bar association, since 2008; in Paris' Bar association, since 2014. He is an insolvency administrator, inscribed in the official list since 1995. Nuno is the executive director of CAAL – Angolan Arbitration Centre for Litigation, since 2012. He is a certified mediator – public and private mediation ICFML, Catholic University, Oporto, 2014. Arbitrator for CAAD – Administrative Arbitration Centre; for TAD – Sports Arbitral Court (where he is also Vice-President) since 2015; for the Arbitration Centre for Property and Real Estate, since 2016. Nuno is the founding partner of "N-Advogados & CM Advogados".

Luís Paulo Silva
Tel: +351 609 310/330 / Email: luispaulosilva@nadv.pt
Born on September 29, 1983, in Guimarães, Portugal. Luís has a law degree, University of Minho (2006). Luís is inscribed in Portugal's Bar association, as a lawyer, since 2008. He is a postgraduate in Tax Law, Corporate Law, Judiciary Law and Arbitration. Luís is a member of the Spanish Club of Arbitration, since 2012. Presently, he is a lawyer at "N-Advogados & CM Advogados".

Maria Amélia Mesquita
Tel: +351 253 609 310/330 / Email: ameliamesquita@nadv.pt
Born on November 4, 1986, in Braga, Portugal. Amélia has a law degree, University of Minho (2010) and a Masters in Judiciary Law, University of Minho (2013). Amélia is inscribed in Portugal's Bar association, as a lawyer, since 2014. She is a certified mediator – public and private mediation ICFML, Catholic University, Oporto, 2016 and she has also been legally qualified to give professional training, since 2010. Amélia has also been a member of the Spanish Club of Arbitration, since 2013 and a ICC YAF member, since 2015. Presently, she is a lawyer at "N-Advogados & CM Advogados". Since 2017, she is also post-graduate on Fashion Law, by the Portuguese Catholic University.

N-Advogados & CM Advogados
Rua Bernardo Sequeira, n.º 78, 1st floor, 4715-671 Braga, Portugal
Tel: +351 253 609 310/330 / Fax: +351 253 609 311 / URL: www.nadv.pt

Romania

Adrian Iordache & Raluca Danes
Iordache Partners

Introduction

Legal provisions. Starting from 2013, the main body of law applicable to arbitration in Romania is set out in Book IV "*On Arbitration*" (hereinafter *"Domestic arbitration provisions"*) and in Book VII, "*On International Arbitration and the Effects of Foreign Arbitral Awards*", of the Civil Procedure Code (hereinafter, "*International arbitration provisions*").

UNCITRAL Model Law. Although the Civil Procedure Code is not based on UNCITRAL Model Law, it does accord with its principles.

International treaties. Romania ratified the New York Convention on 21.07.1961, reserving the right to apply the convention only to: (i) disputes arising from contractual or non-contractual relationships which are considered commercial under Romanian law; and (ii) recognition and enforcement of arbitral awards made in the territory of another contracting State.

Romania has also ratified through Decree No. 281/1963 the European Convention on International Commercial Arbitration (Geneva) and, through Decree No. 62/1975, the Washington Convention on the Settlement of Investment Disputes between States and Nationals of Other States.

Provisions regarding recognition and enforcement of arbitration awards are also included in bilateral treaties concerning legal assistance in civil and commercial matters. Such treaties have been concluded by Romania with Macedonia (ratified through Law No. 356/2004), Algeria (ratified through Decree no 418/1979), Cuba (ratified through Decree No. 67/1981), etc.

Domestic arbitration vs international arbitration. Romanian Civil Procedure Code includes a distinction between domestic arbitration and international arbitration.

However, the differences in treatment are not substantial. The principal difference is that in international arbitration, procedural time-limits are extended in recognition of the possible extra-jurisdictional complexities of international disputes.

However, to classify a dispute as "international", the law requires a foreign element. International arbitration provisions stipulate that an arbitration is international if it arises out of a private law relationship with a foreign element and such provisions govern any international arbitration seated in Romania, provided that at least one of the parties has its domicile/residence or offices outside Romania. The parties can exclude the applicability of the international arbitration provisions only in writing.

Arbitration bodies in Romania. Romanian law also recognises the jurisdiction of permanent arbitration bodies. In Romania, arbitration institutions are usually attached to the regional Chambers of Commerce or to bilateral (international) Chambers of Commerce.

A recent prominent project of such nature is the *Bucharest International Arbitration Court* (BIAC) organised under the aegis of the American Chamber of Commerce in Romania with the cooperation of some of the major national and international law firms in the market (www.bucharestarbitration.org).

The oldest arbitration body in Bucharest is the Court of International Commercial Arbitration attached to the Chamber of Commerce and Industry of Romania (http://arbitration.ccir.ro/). Starting January 1, 2018, the Court of International Commercial Arbitration attached to the Chamber of Commerce and Industry of Romania, adopted new Rules of Arbitration. The new rules are meant to shorten the length and costs of the arbitration procedure.

National courts. The parties or arbitral tribunals can resort to court assistance – at "Tribunal" level – in matters such as the taking of evidence and the enforcement of Interim Relief. Furthermore, as arbitration awards may be challenged before the Courts of Appeal which have exclusive jurisdiction to hear annulment actions and (where annulment is granted and where retrial is not appropriate) to seize the matter and judge on merits.

Arbitration agreement

Written form. Pursuant to Romanian provisions on international arbitration, the arbitration agreements require *written form* (document, wire, telex, fax, email, etc.) *that can provide text evidence* of agreement for validity purposes.

Validity. The arbitration agreement is deemed valid in Romania if it meets the formation conditions according to any of the following laws: (i) the law chosen by the parties – *lex voluntatis*; (ii) the law governing the dispute – *lex causae*; (iii) the law of the agreement that comprises the arbitration clause – *lex contractus*; or (iv) Romanian law.

Moreover, any arbitration agreement governed by Romanian law has to abide by the Romanian Civil Code, which states that agreements are valid if the following conditions are met: the parties have legal capacity to conclude the agreement; the consent of the parties is free from any coercion or undue influence; and the subject matter and the *causa* of the agreement are in accordance with the applicable law.

Autonomy. The validity of the arbitration agreement may not be challenged on the grounds of invalidity of the contract containing it, as the international arbitration provisions expressly stipulate the separability principle.

Principle of competence-competence. As regards both international arbitration and domestic arbitration, the principle of competence-competence applies, and arbitral tribunals rule on their own jurisdiction. Moreover, arbitral tribunals will decide on competence even if identical disputes are pending before the courts or other arbitral tribunals, except if the arbitral tribunal considers it necessary to stay the proceedings.

Relevant provisions also stipulate that parties must plead jurisdiction matters before any pleading on the merits. However, in international arbitration disputes, tribunals may decide to rule on jurisdiction matters together with the final award on merits.

Arbitrability of disputes. International arbitration provisions stipulate that all disputes are arbitrable as long as: (i) the relief sought has a pecuniary character (i.e. it is expressed in money); (ii) it concerns rights that parties can freely dispose of; and (iii) the jurisdiction of such dispute is not exclusive to a State Court according to the law governing the seat of arbitration.

Under the international arbitration provisions, if a State or a State undertaking is involved in a dispute, such State cannot invoke its own incapacity to stand in arbitration or the lack of arbitrability of the dispute, on the ground of its own laws.

Consolidation and joinder of third parties. Where the Arbitration Agreement is silent in respect of third party joinders or consolidation, third parties are entitled to participate in arbitration proceedings only with their agreement and the agreement of all parties (except for parties that only support the defence of one of the parties).

Arbitration procedure

Arbitration rules. International arbitration provisions stipulate that parties to an *ad hoc* arbitration can set out their own arbitration rules, or they can refer to a pre-existing set of rules (of an arbitration institution, or those set out by a procedural law).

If parties fail to do so, the arbitral tribunal shall determine the arbitration rules, using either their own set of rules, or a pre-existing set of rules.

However, in both institutional and *ad hoc* arbitration, as a matter of public order, the arbitral tribunal must observe due process principles such as equality of treatment of the parties, respecting their right to defence and the principle of hearing both parties on all issues in dispute.

Commencing an arbitration. To initiate an arbitration, one must submit the request for arbitration to the arbitral tribunal (for *ad hoc* arbitration) or to the secretariat of the court of arbitration (for institutional proceedings). In case of *ad hoc* arbitration, usually parties follow the provisions of the arbitration agreement regarding the appointment of the arbitral tribunal.

Hearings. Hearings are to be held at the indicated place of arbitration, which can differ from the seat of arbitration. The place of arbitration is agreed upon by the parties or, in the absence of such indication, established by the arbitral tribunal. There are no legal restrictions in this regard.

Language. Under international arbitration provisions, parties can choose the language of the procedure. Should the parties fail to choose, the language shall be that of the contract giving rise to the dispute, or a widely spoken language to be decided by the arbitral tribunal.

Administration of evidence. Generally, all evidence is ordered and taken by the arbitral tribunal. However, if the intervention of a court is required to such end (e.g. to apply sanctions on witnesses or experts), the arbitral tribunal or the parties (with the arbitral tribunal's agreement) may request the assistance of the State Court which rules in accordance with the State law.

Unless the parties have agreed otherwise in the arbitration agreement, the provisions regarding the taking of evidence for domestic arbitration also apply for international arbitration. For example, the parties can agree on the applicability of IBA Rules on the Taking of Evidence in International Commercial Arbitration; the only limit in this matter is public order. In this matter, the Rules of Arbitration of Bucharest International Arbitration Court expressly specify that the Arbitral Tribunal may refer to internationally recognised procedural principles or practices or other codified procedures such as the applicable International Bar Association's Rules on the Taking of Evidence in International Commercial Arbitration.

Nevertheless, in case of institutional arbitration, specific rules can apply, rules which can differ from the above-specified provisions.

Under domestic arbitration provisions, parties should submit the evidence in *limine litis* (at the start of the procedure). Accepted evidence are written documents, witnesses, expert reports, local research, and the cross-examination of the other party, under the condition that such evidence is useful for the arbitral tribunal to grant the award.

Disclosure and privilege. Full disclosure is not customary in domestic procedural law and default rules on international arbitration are silent on the matter. However, parties can seek and plead that tribunals order disclosure of specific documents showing relevance, and arbitral tribunals can seek support from local courts in enforcing such orders.

With regard to limits to disclosure, the arbitration provisions are silent, but the provision regulating State litigations provides certain limits, such as regarding: documents that refer to personal or private matters; documents that could break one's obligation to professional secrecy; or documents that could expose a person to criminal charges.

Civil Procedure Code is silent on the existence and treatment of issues of privilege. However, the common body of the law and precedent of the European Convention of Human Rights protects legal privilege as part of the right to defence and can be invoked accordingly.

Arbitrators

Appointment. Rules for the appointment of arbitrators are common to domestic and international arbitration.

In general, unless otherwise regulated by the arbitration clause or the rules of the relevant arbitration institution, parties are free to appoint the arbitrators of their choosing.

Where the parties disagree with regard to appointment of a sole arbitrator, or of the presiding arbitrator, or if a party fails to make an appointment, the parties can request the court (at "Tribunal" level) with territorial jurisdiction to appoint the arbitrator/presiding arbitrator. The court decides within 10 days, and such decision is not subject to appeal.

Rules of arbitration of the Bucharest International Arbitration Court provide that the arbitral tribunal shall consist of one or three arbitrators in accordance with the choice of the parties. Where parties fail to choose, then the Governing Board shall appoint the arbitrator (the party appointed arbitrator / the sole arbitrator / the chairman) from the BIAC's then current list of arbitrators.

Challenging the appointment of an arbitrator. Similar to the challenge to sitting judges in regular courts, the parties can challenge an arbitrator, within 10 days from the date when such party became aware of the arbitrator's appointment or, as the case may be, from the occurrence of the ground for challenge. The challenge is settled by the tribunal within 10 days, and the decision is not subject to appeal.

Institutional rules on this may differ: for example, Rules of Arbitration of the Bucharest International Arbitration Court provide that parties can submit a challenge, whether for an alleged lack of impartiality or independence, or otherwise within 15 days from receipt by that party of the notification of the appointment or confirmation of the arbitrator / from the date when the party making the challenge was informed of the facts and circumstances on which the challenge is based, and the Governing Board shall decide on the admissibility and, at the same time, if necessary, on the merits of a challenge.

IBA Guidelines on conflict of interest are not adopted as such by Romanian law, unless expressly provided in the arbitration agreement or the institutional arbitration rules (for instance, the current edition of the Rules of Arbitration of the Bucharest International Arbitration Court – www.bucharestarbitration.org – incorporate the IBA Guidelines by reference).

Immunity of arbitrators. Arbitrators are not expressly granted immunity with regard to the award, but they can only be held liable if: (i) they resign after accepting the appointment;

(ii) they fail to attend the hearings or present their decision within the deadline provided in the arbitration agreement or the law; (iii) they fail to observe the confidential nature of the arbitral proceedings; or (iv) they breach their duties with bad faith or gross negligence.

Secretaries to the arbitral tribunal. Arbitration provisions set out in the Civil Procedure Code are silent on this matter, but usually this issue is regulated by the applicable rules of the arbitration, especially in institutional arbitration. Rules of Arbitration of the Bucharest International Arbitration Court provide that the Arbitral Tribunal may appoint a secretary or clerk. In *ad hoc* proceedings, the matter is decided by agreement among the parties and arbitral tribunal.

Interim relief

As per international arbitration provisions, unless otherwise stated in the arbitration agreement, the arbitral tribunal, upon request, can order interim or conservatory relief.

In case the measures ordered by the arbitral tribunal are wilfully not observed, the enforcement of such measures can be ordered by the court, which shall rule in accordance with the State law.

Arbitration award

Formal requirements for an arbitration award are set up in the Domestic Arbitration Provisions of the Civil Procedure Code, which also apply to international arbitration.

An arbitral award must be in a written form and, must include: (i) the members of the tribunal; (ii) the place and date of the award; (iii) the names of the parties and their identification data; (iv) a reference to the arbitration agreement; (v) the subject of the dispute and the summary of arguments presented by each party; (vi) the factual and legal grounds of the award; (vii) the decision; (viii) the signatures of all arbitrators and, if applicable, the signature of the arbitral assistant.

In the case of dissenting opinion, the dissenting arbitrator drafts and signs his own opinion, which is attached to the majority award.

Nevertheless, if the arbitration is institutional, specific rules of such institution may add other requirements.

In international arbitration proceedings, an arbitral award must be delivered within 12 months from the constitution of the arbitral tribunal.

Costs. Where the parties fail to agree on the running costs of arbitration, the rules on international arbitration provide that each party shall bear the fees and expenses of its appointed arbitrator or, if the dispute is referred to a single arbitrator, they shall equally split the costs. In institutional arbitration, this is subject to variation by the rules of an arbitration.

On the question of costs awards, unless otherwise agreed or provided by institutional arbitration rules, the general rule applies, in that the unsuccessful party bears the costs of the other party to the extent of the award on merits.

Interest. The arbitral tribunal may award interest, on request, if the substantive law allows it. Currently, under Romanian substantive law, if the interest rate is not contractually agreed, the interest rate is 6% per annum for agreements including a foreign element or expressed in foreign currency.

Challenge of the arbitration award

Grounds for challenging the award. Once served to the parties, the arbitration award can be challenged within one month to the Court of Appeal, on the following grounds:

(a) the dispute was not arbitrable;

(b) the arbitral tribunal decided the dispute in the absence of an arbitration agreement or on the basis of a void or inoperative agreement;

(c) the arbitral tribunal was not constituted according to the arbitration agreement;

(d) the party challenging the award was absent on the hearing on the merits and the summoning procedure was not legally fulfilled;

(e) the decision was rendered after the expiry of the agreed time limit although termination had been invoked by one of the parties and there was no party agreement for the continuation of the arbitration;

(f) the arbitral tribunal decided on matters not requested, or awarded more than was requested;

(g) the decision did not include the reasons, did not state the date and place where it was rendered, or was not signed by the arbitrators;

(h) the arbitral award is in violation of public policy, good morals or mandatory provisions of the law; or

(i) after the award was rendered, the Constitutional Court rendered its decision on the unconstitutionality objection raised in the arbitration, declaring unconstitutional the law or piece of legislation or provision thereof which formed the subject of the objection. (In this situation, the time limit for challenging the award is three (3) months from the publication of the Constitutional Court decision in the Romanian Official Journal.)

With some exceptions, the national courts tend to keep the arbitral awards in place. For example, in 2017 all the set-aside proceedings were dismissed.

The most common ground for the challenge of the arbitration agreement is the violation of the public order, good morals or mandatory provisions of the law.

If the award is set aside, the Court can remand the award to the arbitral tribunal if: (i) at least one party requested it; or (ii) the award was annulled for the following grounds:

(a) the arbitral tribunal was not constituted according to the arbitration agreement;

(b) the party challenging the award was absent on the hearing on the merits and the summoning procedure was not legally fulfilled;

(c) the arbitral tribunal decided on matters not requested or awarded more than was requested;

(d) the decision did not include the reasons, did not state the date and place where it was rendered, or was not signed by the arbitrators;

(e) the arbitral award is in violation of public policy, good morals or mandatory provisions of the law; or

(f) the Constitutional Court rendered its decision on the unconstitutionality objection raised in that arbitration.

If the parties do not request the case to be remanded, the court shall retain jurisdiction and settle the case on the merits, within the limitations of the arbitration agreement.

Enforcement of the arbitration award

Domestic and national awards. Domestic arbitral awards are directly enforceable, just as the national court decisions are. Foreign arbitral awards must first be granted recognition and enforcement by the Romanian courts; thereafter they also require vesting regular writ of execution.

The Civil Procedure Code applies mainly to the recognition and enforcement of international arbitral awards that do not fall under the international conventions [New York, (1958), Geneva, (1961)] or by bilateral agreements.

Foreign arbitral awards can be recognised and enforced in Romania, under the Civil Procedure Code, by Romanian State Courts, if the following two conditions are met: (i) the dispute is arbitrable in Romania; and (ii) the award is in accordance with Romanian private international law public order.

The request for recognition and enforcement of an arbitral award shall be submitted to the Tribunal and shall enclose the award and the arbitration agreement.

Recognition and enforcement of the foreign award may be refused, in the event that the party against whom the award is being recognised and enforced proves any of the following:

(a) the parties lacked capacity to conclude the arbitration agreement in accordance with the provisions applicable to each party, as determined by the law of the State where the award was rendered;

(b) the arbitration agreement was void in accordance with the law governing such agreement as per the parties' choice or, absent such choice, in accordance with the law of the State where the award was rendered;

(c) the party against which the award is invoked was not duly informed on the appointment of arbitrators or on the arbitral procedure, or was prevented from using all its defences in the arbitration;

(d) the constitution of the arbitral tribunal or the arbitral procedure was not in accordance with the parties' agreement or, absent such agreement, with the law of the place of arbitration;

(e) the award resolves a dispute that exceeds the arbitration agreement. Nevertheless, if certain elements of the award are in accordance with such arbitration agreement and such aspects can be separated from the remaining aspects, the award can be partially recognised; or

(f) the arbitral award has not become binding for the parties, or was set aside or suspended by a competent authority of the State where it was rendered or in accordance with the law of such State.

In ruling over the recognition and enforcement of the foreign awards, Romanian courts cannot proceed to analysing the merits of the dispute.

Should a request for setting aside the award or a request for suspending the award have been filed to the competent authority of the State where such award was rendered, the Romanian court can stay the recognition and enforcement proceedings. To this end, the party seeking enforcement and recognition of the award may request the court to order the other party to deposit a certain bail.

Investment arbitration

Bilateral Investment Treaties. Romania ratified over 80 BITs (a comprehensive list can be found on the Romanian Ministry of Foreign Affairs website (http://www.mae.ro/en)).

Most BITs provide that the investor may choose to submit the dispute for settlement to: (i) ICSID; (ii) an *ad hoc* tribunal established either according to the parties' mutual agreement (if allowed and if the parties reach an agreement); or (iii) an *ad hoc* arbitral tribunal established by UNCITRAL arbitration rules.

Currently, there are five ICSID pending cases involving Romania, based on a Canada BIT, a Netherlands BIT, a Sweden BIT, a Switzerland BIT and an Italy BIT.

In respect of BITs, European Parliament and European Council adopted Regulation (EU) No. 1219/2012 establishing transitional arrangements for bilateral investment agreements between Member States and third countries, which addresses the status of the bilateral investment agreements of the EU Member States under EU law, and establishes the terms, conditions and procedures under which the EU Member States are authorised to amend or conclude bilateral investment agreements. BITs concluded with non-EU countries that have been signed prior to December 2009 will remain in force until they are replaced by new treaties between the EU itself and the relevant third countries. The BITs signed after December 2009 will be subject to review by the EU Commission.

On March 17, 2017, Romania adopted Law No. 18/2017 regarding the termination of the BITs concluded between Romania and other EU Member States. Most of the BITS contain sunset clauses with terms of 10 years, or 15 years or 20 years starting from termination.

Energy Charter Treaty. Romania ratified the Energy Charter Treaty in 1994 and International Energy Charter in 2015. Currently ICSID case No. ABR/14/28/2014 is based upon the Energy Charter Treaty arbitration agreement and the Switzerland BIT.

Treatment of investment arbitration awards by Romania. The Romanian State did not voluntarily comply with the first award against Romania rendered by ICSID. The annulment proceedings filed by Romania were rejected on February 26, 2016, but to date, the State has not observed the award, as EU Commission Decision No. 2015/1470 of March 30, 2015 concluded that the compensation awarded by ICSID amounts to incompatible State aid.

Adrian Iordache
Tel: +40 740 880 908 / Email: adrian@iordache.partners
Adrian Iordache is a leading business lawyer with wide experience in international contracting, air law and international arbitration. Educated in the UK, Canada and France and practising in Bucharest, Romania, he is a Solicitor (England and Wales) and a member of the D.C. Bar as well as admitted to practice in NY State and Bucharest. He is a member of the Chartered Institute of Arbitrators, London (MCIArb), New York State Bar Association and a Listed Arbitrator of the BIAC – Bucharest International Arbitration Court.

Raluca Danes
Tel: +40 741 345 796 / Email: raluca@iordache.partners
Raluca Danes is a young lawyer with experience in litigation, contract law and arbitration. Currently following the International Arbitration LL.M. program at Bucharest University, she has been admitted to practice at the Bucharest Bar since 2013.

Iordache Partners

Mosilor 21 St, floor 4, District 3, Bucharest, Romania
Tel: +40 374 069 069 / Fax: +40 374 676 767 / URL: www.iordache.partners.com

Russia

Sergey Kovalev, Sergey Kislov & Artem Antonov
Kovalev Tugushi and partners

Introduction

Generally, international commercial arbitration is regulated by the Law of the Russian Federation dated July, 7, 1993 No. 5338-1 "On International Commercial Arbitration" (the Law on ICA). Procedural rules on the enforcement of arbitral awards and challenges to them are provided by Commercial (*Arbitrazh*) Procedural Code which makes references to international treaties – for example, the 1958 New York Convention on Recognition and Enforcement of Foreign Arbitral Awards.

That Law on ICA is based on the provisions of the UNCITRAL Model Law on International Commercial Arbitration 1985. Thus generally, most of the rules regarding the arbitration agreement, arbitration procedure and arbitral award comply with UNCITRAL Model Law, except for a few issues especially adopted in 2006 and later. For instance, the competence of an arbitral tribunal to grant interim measures is stipulated in current legislation but tribunal orders are not enforceable under the procedure.

In 2015, amendments to the Law on ICA in Russia affected both domestic arbitration and international commercial arbitration. The new Federal Law of 29 December, 2015 "On Arbitration (*treteyskiy* proceedings) in the Russian Federation" came into force September, 1, 2016 (the New Law). The New Law predominantly regulates domestic arbitration (both institutional and *ad hoc* arbitration) but some provisions are applicable to international arbitration:

a) registration of arbitration institutions by the Russian Ministry of Justice (with a preliminary recommendation of the Council on modernisation of arbitration proceedings under the auspices of the Ministry of Justice (the Council)), establishing strict rules for launching and functioning of arbitration institutions;
b) an obligation to deposit arbitral awards and to store case materials in arbitration institutions (for *ad hoc* arbitration – in an arbitration institution specified in an arbitration agreement or a clause, or in the commercial court at the place of the enforcement of an award);
c) compulsory enforcement of an arbitral award, if the arbitral award provides for any changes in state or other registers (including shareholders' register); and
d) arbitrability of corporate disputes, but the arbitration proceedings may be conducted only under the auspices of an arbitration institution, in accordance with the special rules on corporate dispute resolution – the rules have to be approved, published and deposited in the register.

Launching arbitration institutions in Russia and arranging their everyday work is getting harder due to unnecessary complications regarding access to Alternative Dispute Resolution

(ADR). Initially it was predetermined by the need to avoid the use of domestic arbitration institutions with fraudulent purposes and reduce the activity of in-house "*treteyskiy*" arbitration institutions. This new approach also applies to international arbitration seated in Russia:

- International arbitration institutions have to be approved by a recommendation of the Council and registered by the Russian Government.
- Rules on international commercial arbitration, on corporate or other disputes, and on expedited arbitration, must be approved, published and deposited in accordance with the rules of the Ministry of Justice.
- Foreign arbitration institutions have to be well-known and recognised worldwide to be registered.

One of the key amendments is the broadening of the scope of "international arbitration" under Russian law. Previously, arbitration was deemed to be international if a dispute arose out of foreign trade relations or other international relations, or concerned a foreign party or a Russian company with foreign investments. Recently the scope has been extended: a dispute is now considered to be international if it arises out of foreign trade relations or other international relations, concerns a foreign party or a Russian company with foreign investments, a foreign company with Russian investments, or if obligations are to performed abroad or closely connected to a foreign state.

The Council has registered only two domestic arbitration institutions in the last two years given the total amount of 14 applications (including one dismissed application by a foreign arbitration institution). Two other arbitration institutions are entitled to administer arbitration in accordance with the federal law, without special registration: the International Commercial Arbitration Court at the Russian Federation Chamber of Commerce and Industry; and the Maritime Arbitration Commission at the Chamber of Commerce and Industry of the Russian Federation.

There are several benefits of arbitration compared to litigation in Russia:

- Arbitration provides a higher level of professionalism and the people who resolve the disputes are more qualified to do so. Judges in state courts, especially the district courts, do not generally have sufficient qualifications and knowledge to resolve cross-border disputes due to the high caseload of straightforward cases, although judges in commercial (*arbitrazh*) courts can generally deal with complicated cases with a foreign element.
- Arbitration, unlike litigation, provides confidentiality and privacy. In commercial courts in Russia, judgments and hearings are made public, with the final judgment containing all information about the dispute, including sums, names and contents of documents, although courts of general jurisdiction do not provide full publicity about a dispute.

Arbitration in Russia does, however, have a few significant drawbacks:

- Arbitration in Russia generally takes more time than litigation. The average length of court proceedings in commercial courts is about six months; while the usual situation at the International Commercial Arbitration Court (ICAC) is that arbitration takes about 10 or 12 months, Russian parties to arbitration rarely execute the award voluntarily. Generally, it can take up to six months to enforce an arbitral award in Russia.
- Arbitration is much more expensive than litigation. The state can charge a court fee of up to US$3,000 to consider a dispute in the commercial court, in contrast with the typically higher costs of arbitration.

Recent reform of Russian arbitration law is deemed to be quite controversial because it is providing some arbitration-friendly steps, while arbitration institutions' activity in Russia is becoming more strictly regulated.

Arbitration agreement

An agreement is required to be in writing. An agreement can be concluded in written form by:

- Exchange of letters, messages on teletype, telegraph or other electronic means so long as it provides the identity of the other party.
- Exchange of procedural documents, if one party states the existence of the agreement, and the other party does not protest.
- Reference to another document, if the nature of the reference makes the arbitration agreement part of the main agreement, including the rules of on-exchange trading, for example, tenders for concluding contracts of sale of goods, securities, foreign currency repurchase agreements, and sale of financial derivatives.

The Law on ICA provides another way to conclude an arbitration agreement in written form. This includes a clause on resolving disputes in the articles of incorporation of a legal entity, by means of arbitration.

Separate arbitration agreement

An arbitration agreement can be concluded either as a clause in the main contract or as a separate arbitration agreement. The clause in the main contract is considered to be independent from the rest of the contract. This means that a clause in the main contract is sufficient for an arbitration agreement to exist.

A reference to another document which contains the arbitration agreement is enforceable and qualifies as a written form of arbitration agreement (see above, Substantive/formal requirements). A reference to the rules of an arbitration institute is considered to be an arbitration agreement; however, in that case the clause referring to the institute is considered to be a clause of the main contract.

As for the common approach, an arbitration agreement is not affected if the main contract is found to be invalid.

Parties are now entitled to conclude an arbitration agreement to resolve corporate disputes but the clause has to be included in the chapter of a legal entity. (Shareholders of joint stock companies who number more than 1,000, or shareholders of public joint stock companies, cannot enter into arbitration agreements.)

Arbitration procedure

Russian law does not stipulate any mandatory procedural rules for arbitration proceedings. Arbitration must be confidential and hearings held in camera if agreed by parties. In general, the rules on arbitral procedure are unified with UNCITRAL Model Law on International Commercial Arbitration.

Russian law does not provide default rules on arbitration, except that:

- If the respondent does not present any response or evidence to a claim, the arbitral tribunal may still continue proceedings. This does not mean, however, that the respondent is taken to have accepted these claims. The arbitration agreement can alter the application of this rule.

- The inappropriate conduct of the parties in arbitration proceedings is a ground for refusal to enforce. In that case, it is important to determine the applicable law.

Other rules on arbitration procedure (the commencement, language of arbitration, hearings, presenting evidence) comply with provisions of UNCITRAL Model Law on International Commercial Arbitration and respect the autonomy of parties to arbitration and arbitral tribunal to determine the procedure.

The rules applicable to the court proceedings are not applicable to private dispute resolution, such as arbitration. The HCCH Convention on the Service Abroad of Judicial and Extrajudicial Documents in Civil and Commercial Matters 1965 is not applicable to the service of Russian parties, as concluded by the Supreme Court of Russian Federation in its Ruling on 5 November 2015 in the case No. A08-4781/2014. The issue of appropriate service by the arbitral tribunal depends on the applicable procedural rules, including arbitration rules and the law of the seat of arbitration.

The New Law and further amendments introduce new rules on state courts' powers in support of arbitration. For instance, an arbitral tribunal with a seat of arbitration in Russia, or a party to arbitration with the preliminary consent of an arbitral tribunal, may apply to a competent state court for assistance in obtaining evidence.

The state court assists in obtaining written, material evidence or other documents. The request has to be submitted to the state court at the place where the evidence is located. The court conducts hearings to consider the request for obtaining evidence. The court will dismiss the request of an arbitral tribunal or a party to arbitration if: (1) the requested evidence does not comply with requirements for the evidence in accordance with the Russian procedural rules; (2) rights and interests of third parties may be involved; (3) a dispute being considered by an arbitral tribunal is not arbitrable; and (4) the requested information involves state secrets or any other secret information of third parties.

Arbitrators

The Law on ICA provides general rules on the impartiality and independence of arbitrators. Only reasonable doubts as to an arbitrator's impartiality and/or its independence may lead to impartiality or independence being challenged. Russian legislation does not explain what circumstances may constitute such reasonable doubts or what the requirements are. Additional requirements to an arbitrator's candidacy may be agreed by parties to the arbitration agreement.

Recent amendments introduce several requirements for a sole arbitrator (or at least one arbitrator out of three):

- An arbitrator must have higher education.
- An arbitrator must be aged 25 or older.
- An arbitrator cannot be a natural person who does not have full legal capacity or is under custody or guardianship.
- An arbitrator cannot hold a post as a judge, advocate or other professional, where a conflict of interest would arise.
- An arbitrator cannot be appointed if the person's profession does not allow them to act as an arbitrator. For example, according to Article 3 of the Law on the Status of Judges in the Russian Federation, a judge cannot be an arbitrator (save retired judges).
- An arbitrator cannot be appointed if their capacity as a judge, prosecutor, attorney, notary, etc. has been terminated due to an offence incompatible with their profession.

Parties are free to choose the number of arbitrators and the appointment procedure.

The only requirement is that the number has to be odd. If parties fail to agree on the number of arbitrators, the number is three. The competent state court may assist if any party or a third person ignores its obligations on appointment under an arbitration agreement.

In proceedings with three arbitrators, both parties appoint one of the arbitrators and the appointed arbitrators appoint the third one. If within 30 days of their appointment the appointed arbitrators have not appointed the final arbitrator, a state court appoints the third arbitrator upon the party's request.

The same rule applies to the sole arbitrator if parties fail to agree on the candidacy.

The arbitrator will be dismissed if the arbitrator recuses him or herself, or the parties agree to cease the arbitrator's mandate. If the parties do not agree, the dispute is resolved by the competent court.

There are two main grounds for challenging an arbitrator:

- The existence of any facts that cause doubts concerning the impartiality and independence of the arbitrator.
- Failing to comply with requirements set by the federal law or parties' agreement.

Interim relief

There are two options in order to obtain interim relief in the Russian Federation, either via state courts or arbitrations.

As a rule of thumb, interim measures issued by foreign courts or arbitral tribunals are not enforceable in Russia because they do not meet the criteria of finality and are not 'awards on the subject matter of the case', as required by clause 26 of Information Letter No. 78 of the Presidium of the Supreme Arbitrazh Court, dated 7 July 2004, and clause 33 of the Ruling of the Plenary session of the Supreme Arbitrazh Court of the Russian Federation No. 55 rendered on 12 October 2006.

In *AB Living Design (Sweden) v Sokos Hotels St. Petersburg* (Russian Federation) (ruling of the Presidium of the Supreme Arbitrazh Court of the Russian Federation, No 6447/10, 5 October 2010) the Supreme Arbitrazh Court confirmed that since an interim award issued by the arbitration tribunal is of preliminary character and can be subsequently amended by the tribunal, it cannot be enforced via the New York Convention.

The court also expressed the concern that awards on interim measures are rendered in summary fashion and without proper and in-depth examination of the available evidence.

The Law on ICA confers its jurisdiction on international arbitration tribunals located in the territory of Russia, i.e. with a Russian 'seat', apart from arts 8–9 and 35–36, which apply irrespective of the seat of the arbitration. Clauses of the Law on ICA dedicated to interim measures, namely 9 and 17, mirror the provisions of the Model Law. Article 9 is of special relevance since it gives parties to the arbitration the power to seek interim measures in support of international commercial arbitration from the *arbitrazh* court.

Specifically, according to art 9 of the Law on ICA, it is not incompatible with an arbitration agreement for a party to request from a court, before or during arbitral proceedings, an interim measure of protection and for a court to grant such measure.

Meanwhile, art 90(3) of the APC provides that 'the *arbitrazh* court at the location of the arbitration tribunal or at the location or residence of the debtor or the debtor's property may grant interim measures upon the motion of a party in arbitral proceedings'.

Citing art 90(3) in *AB Living Design* (Sweden), the Supreme Arbitration Court clarified that refusal to enforce interim measures issued in arbitration does not in itself preclude a party from applying for interim measures from the state courts.

Therefore the parties are able to use interim measures issued directly by Russian *arbitrazh* courts to leverage their advantage in ongoing international commercial arbitration.

The principles laid down in *Edimax Limited (Cyprus) v S.P. Chigirinsky (Russian Federation)* (No. A40-19/09-0T-13) are of particular interest here.

After failing to recover losses suffered from an unperformed contractual obligation via personal guarantee, issued by the defendant for the benefit of his company, Edimax simultaneously filed a suit with LCIA for damages and the Moscow Arbitrazh Court for a freezing order on the defendant's assets in support of ongoing arbitration.

The Moscow Arbitrazh Court (first instance) took a formalistic approach and dismissed the suit, reasoning that art 90 APC does not expressly provide for the right of the *arbitrazh* court to issue interim measures in support of international commercial arbitration. Edimax managed to overturn the decision in its favour in the appellate court (Arbitrazh Appeal Court). Then the defendant's wife, arguing that the court of appeal lacked jurisdiction to hear the case because Mr Chigirinsky had issued a guarantee in his personal capacity, successfully annulled the appeal court's decision.

In the hearing before the Supreme Arbitrazh Court of the Russian Federation, Edimax maintained that the courts had incorrectly applied the law. That final appeal was successful and the case was once again directed at the cassation court, which upheld the freezing order.

Although the primary legal issues discussed by the Supreme Arbitrazh Court concerned the possibility of conferring jurisdiction of the *arbitrazh* court on the individual after a divorce, the important collateral conclusion was that it is possible to protect assets located in Russia during international commercial arbitration by obtaining interim measures directly from Russian state courts. In such a case, general rules governing interim measures in domestic litigation should be applied.

Wrapping up the abovementioned, interim measures obtained via arbitration is not enforceable in Russia, and, unfortunately, abiding by them is a rare occasion for Russian parties. Interim measures issued by a state court in support of arbitration are effective, but generally speaking, Russian courts are reluctant to order any interim relief.

Arbitration award

Article 31 of the Law on ICA mostly replicates the one in the Model law and therefore provides similar requirements, stating that an award has to be made in writing, and be signed either by the sole arbitrator or by all three arbitrators, or the majority of the arbitrators if the reason for any omitted signature is stated in the award.

The award shall state the reasons upon which it is based, arbitration fee and costs as well as the method of distributing them between the parties. The award shall state its date and the place. The award shall be deemed to have been made at that place. After the award is made, a copy signed by the arbitrators shall be delivered to each party.

Article 33 of the Model law on "Correction and interpretation of award; additional award" is literally incorporated in the Law of ICA with one addition: a state court that is considering challenging the award may adjourn the case to provide arbitration time to correct, interpret or render an additional award in order to eliminate grounds for challenging the original award.

Challenge of the arbitration award

A party to arbitration is entitled to file the application challenging the arbitral award within three months from when the party obtained the arbitral award.

The current legislation provides that a party to arbitration has the right to apply to a state competent court in the seat of arbitration for challenging the final arbitral award. This is an exclusive right of the parties to arbitration.

Parties are entitled to waive the right to challenge the arbitral award. The parties may agree in an arbitration agreement or a clause that the arbitral award is final and no party has the right to challenge the arbitral award. Any objections may be heard in enforcement proceedings.

The parties may change the jurisdiction for challenging the awards in the arbitration agreement to the court that is local to one of the parties.

The non-parties to arbitration are entitled to challenge an arbitral award which concerns their rights.

The Law on ICA provides exclusive grounds for challenging international arbitral awards seated in Russia:

- A party to an arbitration agreement was incapable: that is, a party was lacking legal capacity at the time when the arbitral proceedings took place, or the arbitration agreement is invalid according to the applicable rules.
- A party to the arbitration was not duly served or notified of the arbitration, including the time and place of the hearings, or has not been given the possibility to present its reasonable objections.
- The arbitral award rendered over the dispute is not covered by the arbitration agreement or exceeds the scope of arbitration agreement. If the part which is not covered by the agreement can be separated from the rest of the award, only that part would be invalid. This provision is to prevent arbitral awards being given without jurisdiction.
- The arbitral tribunal or the arbitration procedure did not comply with the arbitration agreement or with federal law.
- The dispute resolved by the arbitral award is not subject to arbitration under federal law.
- The arbitral award contradicts the public policy of the Russian Federation.

The two last grounds for challenging may be applied by the court without a party's request. The other grounds have to be stated and proved by a party challenging an arbitral award.

An application to challenge an arbitral award must be submitted within three months from the moment it was delivered to the party.

A state court must not revise an arbitral award on its merits or in any other way review the factual circumstances.

A court order for the annulment (setting aside) of an arbitral award or the denial of an application for the annulment (setting aside) cannot be revised by the commercial court of appeal and can only be appealed in the cassation appeal.

The competent court may stay the setting-aside proceedings by a motion of one of the parties and remit the award to a tribunal for eliminating grounds for annulment (setting aside) of the award (save non-arbitrability and public policy).

Enforcement of the arbitration award

The Russian Federation is one of the contracting states to the New York Convention. The Union of Soviet Socialist Republics, as the predecessor to the Russian Federation, signed the New York Convention on 29 December 1958, which was ratified in August 1960 and came into force on 22 November 1960.

A foreign arbitral award may be enforced on the territory of the Russian Federation if an application on its enforcement is filed within three years from the moment that such a foreign arbitral award came into force.

Foreign arbitral awards are enforceable in Russia if they meet certain requirements (please see below). For example, an award will not be enforceable if it includes punitive damages, because awarding such damages contradicts the public policy of the Russian Federation.

The local commercial court has to consider an application for the recognition and enforcement of the foreign arbitral award within one month from the date of its filing. However, in practice the enforcement proceedings at the court of first instance take about four to six months because of high volumes of caseloads in the commercial courts and potential adjournments.

If an arbitral award is declaratory and the international treaties of Russia stipulate the recognition of such awards, it has to be recognised in Russia without a further enforcement procedure.

The procedure for the enforcement of an arbitration award is the same for awards made both in the jurisdiction of the Russian Federation and for foreign arbitration awards.

The application for the enforcement of the award has to be filed to the competent state court of the subject of the Russian Federation at the:

- debtor's place of stay or residence; or
- location of the debtor's property, if the debtor's place of stay or residence is unknown.

The parties are entitled to change court jurisdiction – an application for enforcement on the parties' agreement may be submitted to the competent court in the seat of arbitration, or to a competent court which is local to the winning party.

An award cannot be enforced if:

- The arbitral award has not yet become binding on the parties.
- The party against whom an arbitral award was issued has not been timely and properly notified.
- The arbitral award over the dispute is not covered by the arbitration agreement or exceeds the scope of the arbitration agreement. If the part which is not covered by the agreement can be separated from the rest of the award, only that part would be invalid.
- The arbitral tribunal or procedure do not comply with the parties' agreement or applicable law in the seat of arbitration.
- The dispute is not arbitrable under the Russian legislation.
- The enforcement of the arbitral award would contradict the public policy of the Russian Federation.

Investment arbitration

Russia does not have a law that governs investment treaty arbitration. Any investment arbitration with its seat within Russia's territory would be conducted in accordance with the Law on International Commercial Arbitration, 7 July 1993 (as amended).

Russia signed the Washington Convention on 16 June 1992 but has not ratified it and Russia does not take advantage of its right to arbitrate disputes under the Washington Convention.

The Energy Charter Treaty was signed by the Russian Federation and provisionally applied until 18 October 2009, but it is not currently effective for the state (see Yukos case).

As for the regional conventions, Russia is a party to the Moscow Convention on Protection of the Rights of the Investor dated 28 March 1997. The Convention is applicable for investment disputes between the following CIS states: Armenia, Belarus, Republic of Moldova, Tajikistan, Kazakhstan and Kyrgyzstan. The Convention stipulates obligations of host states towards foreign investors and provides for a dispute-resolution mechanism (art 11): state courts, the Economic Court of the Commonwealth of Independent States (the Economic Court), other international courts and international arbitration institutions. On 23 September 2014, the Economic Court ordered that the provisions of art. 11 were not an arbitration agreement for the purposes of investment disputes' resolution under the Convention and the right to refer a dispute to a particular international court shall be stipulated in national legislation, agreed by parties or anchored in a separate treaty between them. This approach reduces the Convention's attractiveness for foreign investors.

Russia is a party to numerous bilateral treaties (BITs). Almost all Russian BITs in force provide for a fair and equitable treatment clause.

BITs that were concluded in the 1990s stipulate arbitration under the Rules of the Arbitration Institute at the Stockholm Chamber of Commerce (SCC) or *ad hoc* arbitration under the UNCITRAL Rules as dispute-resolution tools.

BITs of 2000s envisaged arbitration under the ICSID Convention or the ICSID Additional Facility Rules, or *ad hoc* arbitration under the UNCITRAL Rules. A number of BITs only provide for *ad hoc* arbitration, with no rules stipulated.

Many Russian BITs also stipulate a competent court of arbitration of the Contracting Party and competent state courts as forums for dispute resolution.

The Russian government issued a resolution of 30 September 2016 No. 992 "On conclusion of international treaties on investment promotion and protection" (not yet effective), which are deemed to be guidelines for negotiating BITs. The guidelines set up the contents of future BITs and dispute resolution tools. As for the guidelines, both institutional and *ad hoc* arbitration are possible, and institutional rules are not specified.

Currently the Russian Federation negotiates investment treaties with states where Russian investors have significant commercial interests.

Sergey Kovalev, Managing Partner, Attorney-at-law, Ph.D.
Tel: +7 916 651 45 21 / Email: s.kovalev@ktaplaw.ru

Sergey is a recognised practitioner with vast experience in the areas of bankruptcy and distressed assets recovery in Russia, and 23 years of dispute resolution experience.
From 2011 to 2017, Sergey successfully headed a dispute resolution department at Egorov Puginkiy Afanasiev and partners Law Offices, managing a team of 60 lawyers.
Sergey has advised on over 1,000 successful litigation and arbitration cases.
He has participated in foreign litigations and was involved in preparing and holding legal positions for arbitration institutions and foreign courts including: ICAC, the High Court of Justice in England, LCIA, CAS, civil and criminal Swiss courts, and the Dutch Courts.
Sergey is widely recognised by many legal rankings: *Best Lawyer, Who's Who Legal, Chambers* (Band 4, dispute resolution, Russia).

Sergey Kislov, Partner, Attorney-at-law
Tel: +7 965 375 59 11 / Email: s.kislov@ktaplaw.ru

Sergey Kislov is a distinguished practitioner in the area of insurance and corporate litigations, complex bankruptcy proceedings and disputes with state authorities, with 14 years of dispute resolution experience.
His extensive experience is based on his efficient approach and methods, while providing a complex defence of his clients' interests both before commercial courts, courts of common jurisdiction and non-judicial procedures.
He has represented major corporations from Russia, the USA, Germany, China, France, Sweden, Brazil, Portugal, South and North Korea. Many of these were large, complex projects that benefited from his approach and experience.
Sergey is an attorney-at-law, an arbitrator of the Independent Arbitration Chamber, and an arbitrator of the Russian Arbitration Association.

Artem Antonov, Senior Associate, Attorney-at-law
Tel: +7 965 385 86 57 / Email: a.antonov@ktaplaw.ru

Artem Antonov is a Senior Associate of Kovalev, Tugushi & Partners practicing commercial and insolvency litigation as well as international commercial arbitration.
He has a wide range of experience in gaining control over bankruptcy procedures, maintaining litigations against unlawful creditors, restoration of corporate control and recovering of stripped assets. Artem provides full scale legal support of commercial arbitration disputes and litigations on recognition and enforcement of foreign judicial acts or arbitral awards and also obtaining interim measures before national courts in support of foreign proceedings.

Kovalev Tugushi and partners

Ruzheyniy Lane 3, 119121 Moscow
Tel: +7 495 902 72 72 / URL: www.ktaplaw.ru

Singapore

Kelvin Poon & Daryl Sim
Rajah & Tann Singapore LLP

Introduction

New York Convention

Singapore acceded to the New York Convention on the Recognition and Enforcement of Foreign Arbitral Awards ("**New York Convention**") on 21 August 1986, with reservation that the New York Convention will only apply to the recognition and enforcement of awards which are made in the territory of another contracting State. On 19 November 1986, the New York Convention entered into force.

Arbitration legislation

Arbitration in Singapore is primarily governed by two laws: the Arbitration Act (Cap. 10) ("**AA**"), which governs domestic arbitrations; and the International Arbitration Act (Cap. 143A) ("**IAA**"), which primarily governs international arbitrations.

Generally, Part II of IAA, which governs International Commercial Arbitrations, will only apply to arbitrations that are an "international arbitration". Arbitrations will be considered international if:[1]

(a) at least one of the parties to the arbitration agreement, at the time of the conclusion of the agreement, has its place of business in any State other than Singapore;

(b) one of the following places is situated outside the State in which the parties have their place of business:

  (i) the seat of the arbitration agreement;

  (ii) any place where a substantial part of the obligations is to be performed or the place with which the subject matter of the dispute is most closely connected; or

  (iii) the parties expressly agree that the subject matter of the arbitration agreement relates to more than one country;

(c) the seat of the arbitration if determined in, or pursuant to, the arbitration agreement is situated outside the State in which the parties have their place of business; or

(d) any place where a substantial part of the obligations of the commercial relationship is to be performed.

In addition to the above, Part II of the IAA will also apply to arbitrations where the parties have agreed in writing that the IAA shall apply.[2]

On the other hand, the AA applies to arbitrations where the seat of arbitration is Singapore and where Part II of the IAA does not apply to that arbitration.[3]

The IAA has essentially incorporated the UNCITRAL Model law ("**Model Law**"), with some modifications. Such modifications include, but are not limited to:

(a) the default number of arbitrators shall be one[4] (the default number is three under the Model Law);

(b) in an arbitration with three arbitrators, the third arbitrator shall be appointed by agreement of the parties[5] (the third arbitrator is appointed by the two party-nominated arbitrators under the Model Law);

(c) the inclusion of additional grounds for setting aside an award;[6] and

(d) the replacement of the Model Law provisions on the recognition and enforcement of foreign arbitral awards.

In addition, the IAA provides for the recognition and enforcement of foreign arbitral awards which are made in the territory of another New York Convention contracting State.

The primary difference in approach between the AA and the IAA is the level of judicial supervision over the arbitration. For example, the AA permits an appeal to the Singapore Court on a question of law arising out of the award made in a domestic arbitration[7] (though such avenue of appeal may be excluded by agreement of the parties[8]) whereas no such avenue of appeal is available for international arbitrations under the IAA.

Arbitration body

The principal arbitration body for Singapore is the Singapore International Arbitration Centre ("**SIAC**"). The SIAC Rules (6th Edition, 1 August 2016) ("**SIAC Rules**") are the primary rules of arbitration at the SIAC. In addition, the following rules may be used at the SIAC:

(a) the Investment Arbitration Rules of the SIAC (1st Edition, 1 January 2017), used for international investment arbitrations;

(b) the UNCITRAL Arbitration Rules (2010), primarily used for *ad hoc* arbitrations; and

(c) the SIAC SGX-DT Arbitration Rules (1st Edition, 1 July 2005) and the SIAC SGX-DC Arbitration Rules (1st Edition, 27 March 2016), used for disputes arising from derivative trading and derivative clearing, respectively.

In addition to administering the aforementioned rules, the IAA has also:

(a) appointed the President of the SIAC as one of the statutory authorities for the appointment of arbitrators under the IAA;[9] and

(b) appointed the Registrar of the SIAC as the statutory authority for taxation of costs.[10]

Arbitration agreement

Requirements of an arbitration agreement

Under the IAA, an "arbitration agreement" is an agreement by the parties to submit to arbitration disputes which have arisen or may arise between them in respect of a legal relationship.[11]

An arbitration agreement may be in the form of a clause in a contract or in the form of a separate agreement. An arbitration agreement must be in writing and may include electronic communications.[12]

Where the arbitration agreement does not expressly provide the governing law of the arbitration agreement, the implied choice of law for the arbitration agreement is likely to be the same as the expressly chosen law of the substantive contract.[13]

Arbitrable disputes

Generally, all disputes are arbitrable unless it would be contrary to public policy.[14] The Singapore Courts have held that there will ordinarily be a presumption of arbitrability, provided the dispute falls within the scope of the arbitration agreement.[15] This presumption (of arbitrability) may be rebutted if it can be shown that:

(a) the Singapore Parliament intended to preclude a particular type of dispute from being arbitrated, such intention being evidenced by either the text or the legislative history of the statute in question; or

(b) it would be contrary to the public policy considerations involved in that type of dispute to permit it to be resolved by arbitration.[16]

As such, disputes concerning the liquidation of an insolvent company[17] and claims which arise upon insolvency[18] are not arbitrable.

Joinder and consolidation of third parties

Parties who are not parties to the arbitration agreement are not permitted to be joined in an arbitration unless all parties to that arbitration agreement consent to the joinder.[19]

Where parties have adopted the SIAC Rules, such rules permit the consolidation or joinder of third parties under certain circumstances.

Rule 7 of the SIAC Rules provides that a party or non-party to the arbitration may file an application with the Registrar of the SIAC (for joinders prior to the constitution of the arbitral tribunal) or the arbitral tribunal (for joinders after the constitution of the arbitral tribunal) for one or more additional parties to be joined as a claimant or a respondent in an arbitration, provided that any of the following criteria are satisfied:

(a) the additional party is *prima facie* bound by the arbitration agreement; or

(b) all parties, including the additional party to be joined, consent to the joinder.

The SIAC Court will then, after considering the views of all parties (including the additional party to be joined) and the circumstances of the case, decide whether or not to grant the joinder.

Rule 8.1 of the SIAC Rules provides that, prior to the constitution of any arbitral tribunal, a party may file an application with the Registrar of the SIAC to consolidate two or more arbitrations pending under the SIAC Rules provided that any of the following criteria are satisfied:

(a) all parties have agreed to the consolidation;

(b) all the claims in the arbitrations are made under the same arbitration agreement; or

(c) the arbitration agreements are compatible, and: (i) the disputes arise out of the same legal relationship(s); (ii) the disputes arise out of contracts consisting of a principal contract and its ancillary contract(s); or (iii) the disputes arise out of the same transaction or series of transactions.

Generally, where consolidation is sought for arbitrations that have already constituted a arbitral tribunal, the same arbitral tribunal must be constituted in each arbitration. Thus, Rule 8.7 provides that, after the constitution of any arbitral tribunal, a party may file an application with the arbitral tribunal to consolidate two or more arbitrations pending under the SIAC Rules provided that any of the following criteria are satisfied:

(a) all parties have agreed to the consolidation;

(b) all the claims in the arbitrations are made under the same arbitration agreement, and the same arbitral tribunal has been constituted in each of the arbitrations, or no arbitral tribunal has been constituted in the other arbitration(s); or

(c) the arbitration agreements are compatible, the same arbitral tribunal has been constituted in each of the arbitrations, or no arbitral tribunal has been constituted in the other arbitration(s), and: (i) the disputes arise out of the same legal relationship(s);

(ii) the disputes arise out of contracts consisting of a principal contract and its ancillary contract(s); or (iii) the disputes arise out of the same transaction or series of transactions.

The SIAC Court (for consolidations prior to the constitution of a arbitral tribunal) and the arbitral tribunal (for consolidations after the constitution of a arbitral tribunal) will, after considering the views of all parties and the circumstances of the case, decide whether or not to grant the consolidation.

Competence of arbitral tribunal to rule on its jurisdiction

The arbitral tribunal may rule on its own jurisdiction, including on any objections as to the existence or validity of the arbitration agreement (doctrine of *kompetenz-kompetenz*).[20] In addition, an arbitration clause which forms part of a contract shall be treated as a separate and independent agreement from the other terms of the contract (doctrine of separability). As such, a decision by the arbitral tribunal that a contract is null and void will not necessarily lead to the invalidity of the arbitration agreement.

If a party objects to the arbitral tribunal's jurisdiction, it must raise this objection no later than the submission of the statement of defence. However, the arbitral tribunal may admit an objection to jurisdiction outside this time if it considers the delay justified.[21]

A party may appeal the arbitral tribunal's ruling on jurisdiction to the Singapore High Court.[22] Such appeal may be made regardless of whether the arbitral tribunal had ruled that it had or did not have jurisdiction.[23] The appeal must be made within 30 days after having received notice of the arbitral tribunal's ruling on jurisdiction.[24] However, this avenue of appeal is not open to a party if the arbitral tribunal's preliminary ruling on jurisdiction touches upon the merits of the dispute.[25]

If the arbitral tribunal's preliminary ruling on jurisdiction does touch upon the merits of the dispute, a party may apply to the Singapore Court to set aside the award on the grounds set out in Article 34(2) of the Model Law, as added to by Section 24 of the IAA. Such grounds include the setting aside of the award on the basis that the arbitral tribunal has no jurisdiction for lack of a valid arbitration agreement.[26]

Arbitration procedure

Commencement of arbitration

Unless otherwise agreed by the parties, the arbitral proceedings commence on the date on which a request for the dispute to be referred to arbitration is received by the respondent.[27]

Where parties have adopted the SIAC Rules, Rule 3 of the SIAC Rules provides that the arbitration is commenced when a claimant files a Notice of Arbitration with the Registrar of the SIAC, which shall include:

(a) a demand that the dispute be referred to arbitration;

(b) the names, addresses, telephone numbers, facsimile numbers and electronic mail addresses, if known, of the parties to the arbitration and their representatives, if any;

(c) a reference to the arbitration agreement invoked and a copy of the arbitration agreement;

(d) a reference to the contract or other instrument (e.g. investment treaty) out of or in relation to which the dispute arises and, where possible, a copy of the contract or other instrument;

(e) a brief statement describing the nature and circumstances of the dispute, specifying the relief claimed and, where possible, an initial quantification of the claim amount;

(f) a statement of any matters which the parties have previously agreed as to the conduct of the arbitration or with respect to which the Claimant wishes to make a proposal;

(g) a proposal for the number of arbitrators, if not specified in the arbitration agreement;

(h) unless otherwise agreed by the parties, the nomination of an arbitrator if the arbitration agreement provides for three arbitrators, or a proposal for a sole arbitrator if the arbitration agreement provides for a sole arbitrator;

(i) any comment as to the applicable rules of law;

(j) any comment as to the language of the arbitration; and

(k) payment of the requisite filing fee under these Rules.

Rules of evidence

The arbitral tribunal has the power to determine the admissibility, relevance, materiality and weight of any evidence.[28] This is similarly reflected in Rule 19 of the SIAC Rules.

The arbitral tribunal is also empowered by the IAA to make orders or give directions to any party for, among other things: (a) the giving of evidence by affidavit; and (b) the preservation and interim custody of any evidence.[29] This is similarly reflected in Rule 27 of the SIAC Rules.

Nevertheless, from our past experience, as a matter of practice, arbitral tribunals typically use the IBA Rules on the Taking of Evidence in International Arbitration as a guideline. However, there is no mandatory requirement to adopt the IBA Rules.

Confidentiality

The IAA does not provide specifically for confidentiality in arbitration. Nevertheless, the Singapore Courts have held that the obligation of confidentiality is to be implied in arbitration proceedings,[30] the scope of which is to be determined in the context of each case and the nature of the information or documents at issue.[31]

Where parties have adopted the SIAC Rules, Rule 39 of the SIAC Rules expressly provides that, generally, arbitral proceedings are to be kept confidential, unless otherwise agreed by the parties. However, Rule 39.2 of the SIAC Rules provides that disclosure may be made to a third party in the following circumstances:

(a) for the purpose of making an application to any competent court of any State to enforce or challenge the Award;

(b) pursuant to the order of, or a subpoena issued by, a court of competent jurisdiction;

(c) for the purpose of pursuing or enforcing a legal right or claim;

(d) in compliance with the provisions of the laws of any State which are binding on the party making the disclosure or the request or requirement of any regulatory body or other authority;

(e) pursuant to an order by the arbitral tribunal on application by a party with proper notice to the other parties; or

(f) for the purpose of an application for joinder or consolidation under the SIAC Rules.

Emergency arbitration

The IAA recognises emergency arbitrations by defining "arbitral tribunal" to include emergency arbitrators. As such, emergency arbitrators are treated no differently to other arbitral tribunals, are provided with the same powers as other arbitral tribunals and may, with leave of the Singapore High Court, have their awards enforced in the same manner as a judgment or order to the same effect.[32]

Where parties have adopted the SIAC Rules, such parties may seek emergency interim relief by applying to the Registrar of the SIAC.[33] If the President of the SIAC determines that such application should be accepted, the President shall appoint an emergency arbitrator.[34] The emergency arbitrator shall have the power to order or award any interim relief and shall make his/her interim order or award within 14 days from the date of his/her appointment.[35] The emergency arbitrator shall have no power to act once the arbitral tribunal is constituted and such arbitral tribunal: (i) may reconsider, modify or vacate any interim order or Award issued by the emergency arbitrator; and (ii) is not bound by the reasons given by the emergency arbitrator.[36]

Arbitrators

Appointment of arbitrators

Unless otherwise agreed by the parties, the default number of arbitrators to be appointed is one.[37] In an arbitration with three arbitrators, unless otherwise agreed by the parties, each party shall appoint one arbitrator and the parties shall, by agreement, appoint the third arbitrator.[38] However, where parties have adopted the SIAC Rules and unless otherwise agreed by the parties, the third arbitrator shall be appointed by the President of the SIAC.[39]

Challenging the appointment of an arbitrator

An arbitrator may be challenged only if circumstances exist that give rise to justifiable doubts as to his impartiality or independence, or if he does not possess qualifications agreed to by the parties. A party may challenge an arbitrator appointed by him, or in whose appointment he has participated, only for reasons of which he becomes aware after the appointment has been made.[40] This is similarly reflected in Rule 14 of the SIAC Rules.

The Singapore Courts have held that bias may be manifested in three forms:[41]

(a) actual bias;

(b) imputed bias, which arises where an arbitrator may be said to be acting in his/her own cause (e.g. where he/she has a pecuniary or proprietary interest in the case); and

(c) apparent bias, which arises when a reasonable and fair-minded person with knowledge of all the relevant facts would entertain a reasonable suspicion that the circumstances might result in the arbitral proceedings being affected by apparent bias if the arbitrator was not removed.

Termination of arbitrator's mandate

Generally, the mandate of the arbitral tribunal terminates with the termination of the arbitral proceedings.[42] Notwithstanding this general rule, the arbitrator is still permitted to:

(a) correct the award, either when requested to do so by a party within 30 days of the receipt of the award by such party,[43] or of its own initiative within 30 days of the date of the award;[44]

(b) if so agreed by the parties, interpret the award when requested to do so by a party within 30 days of receipt of the award by such party;[45]

(c) unless otherwise agreed by the parties, make an additional award as to claims presented in the arbitral proceedings but which were omitted from the award;[46] and

(d) where a court suspends the setting-aside proceedings in order to give the arbitral tribunal an opportunity to resume the arbitral proceedings or to take such other action as, in the arbitral tribunal's opinion, will eliminate the grounds for setting aside.[47]

Immunity of arbitrators

An arbitrator shall not be liable for negligence in respect of anything done or omitted to be done in the capacity of arbitrator or for any mistake in law, fact or procedure made in the course of arbitral proceedings or in the making of an arbitral award.[48]

Interim relief

Interim powers

The arbitral tribunal is empowered to make orders or give directions to any party for an interim injunction or any other interim measure.[49] Unless otherwise agreed by the parties, the arbitral tribunal may also make any interim measures of protection it considers necessary in respect of the subject matter of the dispute. This includes directing a party to provide appropriate security in connection with such measure.[50] The broad powers granted to the arbitral tribunal by the IAA are also mirrored in the SIAC Rules.[51]

Where the arbitral tribunal has not yet been constituted, it is not incompatible with the IAA for a party to apply to the Singapore Court for an interim measure of protection and for the Singapore Court to grant such measure. However, the power of the Singapore Court to order an interim measure only applies where an arbitral tribunal (including an emergency arbitrator[52]), institution or other person vested by the parties with such power has no power or is unable for the time being to act effectively.[53] Moreover, an order by the Singapore Court for an interim measure shall cease to have effect if the arbitral tribunal makes an order which expressly relates to the whole or part of the court-ordered interim measure.[54]

Stay of proceedings

If a party institutes proceedings against another party in respect of a matter that is the subject of an arbitration agreement between the parties, the other party may apply to the Singapore Court to stay the proceedings. The Singapore Court shall make an order to stay proceedings unless it is satisfied that the arbitration agreement is null and void, inoperative or incapable of being performed.[55]

In determining whether there is a valid and operative arbitration agreement, the Singapore Court will only conduct a *prima facie* review.[56] If the Singapore Court is satisfied that, *prima facie*, there is a valid and operative arbitration agreement, the Singapore Court will stay the proceedings in favour of arbitration.

Arbitration award

An arbitral award must:[57]

(a) be in writing and signed by the arbitrator or arbitrators;[58]

(b) state the reasons upon which it is based, unless the parties have agreed that no reasons are to be given or if the award is issued pursuant to a settlement; and

(c) state the date of the award and the place (seat) of arbitration.

Where parties have adopted the SIAC Rules, the arbitral tribunal shall submit the draft award to the Registrar of the SIAC within 45 days from the date on which the arbitral tribunal declares the proceedings closed.[59]

Award on costs

Unless otherwise agreed by the parties, an arbitral tribunal may award costs. In addition, unless the award states otherwise, an arbitral award may be taxable by the Registrar of the SIAC.[60]

Unless otherwise agreed by the parties, an arbitral tribunal may award simple or compound interest (at such rate as the arbitral tribunal considers appropriate), for any period ending not later than the date of payment, on the whole or any part of any sum awarded in the arbitral proceedings.[61]

There is no express requirement for an arbitral tribunal to award costs to the successful party (i.e. costs following the event). In addition, there is no public policy of Singapore to ensure that costs are assessed on the basis of any particular principle, including the proportionality principle.[62] Nevertheless, from our past experience, arbitral tribunals typically award costs to the successful party.

Challenge of the arbitration award

Setting aside of award

An award may be set aside on the following grounds:[63]

(a) a party to the arbitration agreement was under some incapacity or the arbitration agreement is not valid;

(b) the party making the application was not given proper notice of the appointment of the arbitrator or of the arbitral proceedings or was otherwise unable to present its case;

(c) the award deals with a dispute that does not fall within the terms of the arbitration agreement or contains decisions on matters beyond the scope of submission to arbitration;[64]

(d) the composition of the arbitral tribunal or the arbitral procedure was not in accordance with the agreement of the parties;

(e) the subject matter of the dispute is not capable of settlement by arbitration; or

(f) the award is in conflict with the public policy of Singapore.

In addition, the main body of the IAA provides that an award may also be set aside on the following grounds:[65]

(a) the making of the award was affected by fraud or corruption; or

(b) there is a breach of natural justice in connection with the making of the award.

A party challenging an award must file an application with the Singapore High Court within three months from the receipt of the award.

Singapore is generally regarded as 'pro-arbitration'. It is generally well established under Singapore arbitration jurisprudence that the Singapore Court's power to set aside awards must and should only be exercised charily.[66]

In keeping with the above principle:

(a) a high threshold must be crossed before the Singapore Court will set aside an award for breach of natural justice on account of a procedural breach. Such breach cannot be of a trifling nature and must be serious enough to justify the Singapore Court's discretion to set aside the award;[67] and

(b) there is a presumption of arbitrability so long as the dispute falls within the scope of an arbitration agreement (see above).[68]

In addition, the Singapore Court may, where appropriate and requested to do so by a party, suspend the setting-aside proceedings and remit the matter back to the original arbitral tribunal to resume the arbitral proceedings or to take such action that, in the arbitral tribunal's opinion, will eliminate the grounds for setting aside.[69] The court's power to remit matters back to the original arbitral tribunal is an *alternative* to setting aside the award. Therefore, the court will not have the power to remit the matter back to the original tribunal if the award has already been set aside.[70]

Modification of award

Within 30 days of receipt of the award (or such other period as agreed upon by the parties), a party may request the arbitral tribunal to:

(a) correct in the award any errors in computation, any clerical or typical errors or errors of a similar nature; or

(b) provide an interpretation of a specific part of the award.

If the arbitral tribunal considers the request justified, it shall make the correction or give the interpretation within 30 days of receipt of the request.[71] An arbitral tribunal may also correct any errors in computation, any clerical or typical errors or errors of a similar nature of its own initiative within 30 days of the date of the award.[72]

Enforcement of the arbitration award

Awards made in Singapore

An award made in Singapore may, by leave of the Singapore High Court, be enforced in the same manner as a judgment or order to the same effect. Where such leave is given, the judgment may be entered in terms of the award.[73]

In addition, given that Singapore is a party to the New York Convention, an award made in Singapore may also be enforced in other New York Convention States, subject to the applicable arbitration laws of that State.

Foreign awards

An award made in a New York Convention State other than Singapore ("**Foreign Award**") may, by leave of the Singapore High Court, be enforced in the same manner as a judgment or order to the same effect. Where such leave is given, the judgment may be entered in terms of the award.[74]

A party seeking to enforce a Foreign Award must produce to the Singapore Court:[75]

(a) the duly authenticated original award or a duly certified copy of such award;

(b) the original arbitration agreement under which the Foreign Award purports to have been made under or a duly certified copy of such agreement; and

(c) if the Foreign Award or arbitration agreement is in a foreign language, a translation of it in the English language, duly certified in English as a correct translation.

The Singapore Courts may refuse enforcement of a Foreign Award if the party against whom enforcement is sought proves any one of the following grounds:[76]

(a) the party to the arbitration agreement was, under the law applicable to such party, under some incapacity at the time the arbitration agreement was made;

(b) the arbitration agreement is not valid;

(c) the party making the application was not given proper notice of the appointment of the arbitrator or of the arbitral proceedings or was otherwise unable to present its case;

(d) the award deals with a dispute that does not fall within the terms of the arbitration agreement or contains decisions on matters beyond the scope of the submission to arbitration;[77]

(e) the composition of the arbitral tribunal or the arbitral procedure was not in accordance with the agreement of the parties; or

(f) the Foreign Award has not yet become binding on the parties or has been set aside by a competent authority of the State in which the award was made.

The Singapore Courts may also refuse enforcement of a Foreign Award, without the application of a party, on the following grounds:

(a) the subject matter of the Foreign Award is not capable of settlement by arbitration under the law of Singapore; or

(b) the enforcement of the Foreign Award would be contrary to the public policy of Singapore.

An award made in a State that is not a signatory to the New York Convention may also be enforced in Singapore in the same manner as a judgment to that effect with leave of the Singapore High Court.[78]

As stated above, Singapore is generally regarded as 'pro-arbitration' and typically recognises and enforces Foreign Awards. The Singapore Courts will typically employ a mechanistic approach to the enforcement process of Foreign Awards and will only refuse enforcement if the grounds provided in the IAA are established.[79]

Investment arbitration

Singapore ratified the International Convention for the Settlement of Investment Disputes ("**ICSID**") between States and Nationals of Other States ("**ICSID Convention**") on 14 October 1968. The ICSID Convention was made effective in Singapore, via the Arbitration (International Investment Disputes) Act on 13 November 1968. To date, there have been no claims made against Singapore under the ICSID Convention.

Singapore is also a party to over 40 bilateral investment treaties, around 20 free trade agreements and numerous multilateral investment treaties. In particular, Singapore is a party to the ASEAN Comprehensive Investment Agreement ("**Comprehensive Investment Agreement**"), a multilateral investment treaty between all ASEAN States.[80] Generally, under the Comprehensive Investment Agreement, a disputing investor may submit a claim under the ICSID Convention and the ICSID Rules of Procedure for Arbitration Proceedings provided that both the disputing Member State and the non-disputing Member State are parties to the ICSID Convention.

Third-party funding

Third-party funding of arbitration proceedings is governed by the Civil Law Act (Cap. 43) ("**CLA**"), the Civil Law (Third-Party Funding) Regulations 2017 ("**CLR**") and the Legal Profession (Professional Conduct) Rules 2015 ("**LPR**").

Generally, third-party funding of a "prescribed dispute resolution proceeding" by a "qualifying Third-Party Funder" is permitted in Singapore.[81]

Under the CLR, a "prescribed dispute resolution proceeding" includes the following:[82]

(a) international arbitration proceedings (as defined by the IAA, see above);

(b) court proceedings arising from or in connection with international arbitration proceedings;

(c) mediation proceedings arising from or in connection with international arbitration proceedings;

(d) applications for a stay of proceedings under the IAA or applications for the enforcement of an arbitration agreement; and

(e) proceedings for or in connection with the enforcement of an award under the IAA.

Third-party funding may only be provided by a "qualifying Third-Party Funder". Among other things, a "qualifying Third-Party Funder" must meet the following criteria:

(a) that the Third-Party Funder carries on the principal business of funding costs for dispute-resolution proceedings; and

(b) has a paid-up share capital of not less than S$5 million or the equivalent amount in foreign currency; or not less than S$5 million or the equivalent amount in foreign currency managed assets.

Where a Third-Party Funder is funding the costs of the proceeding, certain disclosure requirements are imposed by the LPR. Among other things, a legal practitioner must disclose to the court or tribunal (as applicable) and to every other party to the proceedings:[83]

(a) the existence of any third-party funding contract relating to the costs of such proceedings; and

(b) the identity and address of the Third-Party Funder involved in such funding.

In addition, various restrictions are imposed on legal practitioners with respect to Third-Party Funders. For example, the LPR prohibits a legal practitioner from holding any share or ownership in, or receiving any commission, fee or share of proceeds from, Third-Party Funders:[84]

(a) which the legal practitioner or law practice has introduced or referred to a client of the legal practitioner or law practice; or

(b) which has a third-party funding contract with a client of the legal practitioner or law practice.

* * *

Endnotes

1. Section 5(2) of the IAA.
2. Section 5(1) of the IAA.
3. Section 3 of the AA.
4. Section 9 of the IAA.
5. Section 9A of the IAA.
6. Section 24 of the IAA.
7. Section 49(1) of the AA.
8. Section 49(2) of the AA.
9. Section 8(2) of the IAA.
10. Section 21 of the IAA.
11. Section 2A(1) of the IAA.
12. Section 2A(3)-(4) of the IAA.
13. *BCY v BCZ* [2016] SGHC 249, [49].
14. Section 11(1) of the IAA.
15. *Tomolugen Holdings Ltd and another v Silica Investors Ltd* and other appeals [2015] SGCA 57, [76].
16. *Tomolugen Holdings Ltd and another v Silica Investors Ltd* and other appeals [2015] SGCA 57, [76].
17. *Tomolugen Holdings Ltd and another v Silica Investors Ltd* and other appeals [2015] SGCA 57, [77].
18. *Larson Oil and Gas Pte Ltd v Petropod Ltd* (in official liquidation in the Cayman

Islands and in compulsory liquidation in Singapore) [2011] 3 SLR 414, [45].
19. *PT First Media TBK v Astro Nusantara International BV & others* [2013] SGCA 47.
20. Article 16(1) of the Model Law, First Schedule of the IAA.
21. Article 16(2) of the Model Law, First Schedule of the IAA.
22. Article 16(3) of the Model Law, as modified by Section 10 of the IAA.
23. Section 10(3) of the IAA.
24. Pursuant to Section 10(4) of the IAA, a party may appeal the decision of the Singapore High Court only with leave of the Singapore High Court.
25. *AQZ v ARA* [2015] SGHC 49.
26. *AQZ v ARA* [2015] SGHC 49, [72].
27. Article 21 of the Model Law, First Schedule of the IAA.
28. Article 19 of the Model Law, First Schedule of the IAA.
29. Section 12(1) of the IAA.
30. *International Coal Pte Ltd v Kristle Trading Ltd* [2009] 1 SLR(R) 945.
31. *AAY and others v AAZ* [2011] 1 SLR 1093; [2009] SGHC 142, [54].
32. Section 2(1) of the IAA.
33. Paragraph 1, Schedule 1 of the SIAC Rules.
34. Paragraph 3, Schedule 1 of the SIAC Rules.
35. Paragraph 8-9, Schedule 1 of the SIAC Rules.
36. Paragraph 10, Schedule 1 of the SIAC Rules.
37. Section 9 of the IAA.
38. Section 9A of the IAA.
39. Rule 11 of the SIAC Rules.
40. Article 12 of the Model Law, First Schedule of the IAA.
41. *PT Central Investindo v Franciscus Wongso and others* and another matter [2014] SGHC 190, [15]–[18].
42. Article 32(3) of the Model Law, First Schedule of the IAA.
43. Article 33(1)(a) of the Model Law, First Schedule of the IAA.
44. Article 33(2) of the Model Law, First Schedule of the IAA.
45. Article 33(1)(b) of the Model Law, First Schedule of the IAA.
46. Article 33(3) of the Model Law, First Schedule of the IAA.
47. Article 34(4) of the Model Law, First Schedule of the IAA.
48. Section 25 of the IAA.
49. Section 12(1) of the IAA.
50. Article 17 of the Model Law, First Schedule of the IAA.
51. Rule 30 of the SIAC Rules.
52. Under the IAA, the definition of "arbitral tribunal" includes emergency arbitrators.
53. Section 12A(6) of the IAA.
54. Section 12A(7) of the IAA.
55. Section 6 of the IAA.
56. *Tomolugen Holdings Ltd and another v Silica Investors Ltd* and other appeals [2015] SGCA 57, [63].
57. Article 31 of the Model Law, First Schedule of the IAA.

58. Where the arbitration has more than one arbitrator, the signature of the majority of arbitrations shall suffice, provided that the reason for the omitted signature(s) is stated (Article 31(1) of the Model Law, First Schedule of the IAA).
59. Rule 32.3 of the SIAC Rules.
60. Section 21(1) of the IAA.
61. Section 20(1) of the IAA. See also Section 12(5) of the IAA.
62. *VV and another v VW* [2008] 2 SLR® 929, [31].
63. Article 34(2)(a) of the Model Law, First Schedule of the IAA.
64. If the decision on matters submitted to arbitration can be separated from those not so submitted, only that part of the award which contains decisions on matters not submitted to arbitration may be set aside (Article 31(2)(a)(iii) of the Model Law, First Schedule of the IAA).
65. Section 24 of the IAA.
66. *TMM Division Maritima SA de CV v Pacific Richfield Marine Pte Ltd* [2013] 4 SLR 972, [1].
67. *Prometheus Marine Pte Ltd v King, Ann Rita* and other matters [2017] SGHC 36, [86].
68. *Tomolugen Holdings Ltd and another v Silica Investors Ltd* and other appeals [2015] SGCA 57, [76].
69. Article 34(4) of the Model Law, First Schedule of the IAA.
70. *AKN and another v ALC and others* and other appeals [2015] SGCA 63.
71. Article 33(1) of the Model Law, First Schedule of the IAA.
72. Article 33(2) of the Model Law, First Schedule of the IAA.
73. Section 19 of the IAA.
74. Section 29 of the IAA.
75. Section 29 of the IAA.
76. Section 31(2) of the IAA.
77. When the Foreign Award contains decisions on matters not submitted to arbitration but those decisions can be separated from decisions on matters submitted to arbitration, the award may be enforced to the extent that it contains decisions on matters so submitted (Section 31(3) of the IAA).
78. Section 46 of the AA.
79. *Aloe Vera of America, Inc v Asianic Food (S) Pte Ltd and another* [2006] 3 SLR(R) 174, [46].
80. Brunei Darussalam, the Kingdom of Cambodia, the Republic of Indonesia, the Lao People's Democratic Republic, Malaysia, the Union of Myanmar, the Republic of the Philippines, the Republic of Singapore, the Kingdom of Thailand and the Socialist Republic of Vietnam.
81. Pursuant to Section 5B(2) of the CLA, "[a] contract under which a qualifying Third-Party Funder provides funds to any party for the purpose of funding all or part of the costs of that party in prescribed dispute resolution proceedings is not contrary to public policy or otherwise illegal by reason that it is a contract for maintenance or champerty".
82. Rule 3 of the CLR.
83. Rule 49A of the LPR.
84. Rule 49B of the LPR.

Kelvin Poon
Tel: +65 6232 0403 / Email: kelvin.poon@rajahtann.com
Kelvin Poon is an equity partner with the firm's international arbitration practice. Kelvin regularly acts in major construction, corporate and commercial disputes for private and public listed companies, major international corporations, and financial institutions. Kelvin has represented clients in numerous institutional and *ad hoc* arbitrations involving ICC, JCAA, LCIA, SIAC and UNCITRAL rules. He also regularly appears in the High Court and the Court of Appeal in Singapore. Kelvin is a Fellow of the Chartered Institute of Arbitrators.

Daryl Sim
Tel: +65 6232 0356 / Email: daryl.sim@rajahtann.com
Daryl Sim is a senior associate (foreign lawyer) with the firm's international arbitration and construction practice. He graduated from Monash University with a Bachelor of Laws (with Honours) and a Bachelor of Behavioural Neuroscience. Daryl has experience in a wide variety of dispute resolution matters, including investor-state disputes, international and domestic arbitrations and foreign litigation. In addition, Daryl has extensive experience advising multinational corporations on both contentious and non-contentious matters in Myanmar.

Rajah & Tann Singapore LLP

9 Battery Road, #25-01, Singapore 049910
Tel: +65 6535 3600 / Fax: +65 6225 9630 / URL: www.rajahtannasia.com

Spain

Luis Cordón Procter, Sheila Muñoz Muñoz & Diana del Moral Bernal
Cases & Lacambra

Introduction

The law on arbitration

The Spanish Arbitration Act 60/2003 of 23 December 2003 (SAA), as stated in the Preamble, is based on the model law, as well as in the subsequent works from the United Nations Commission for International Trade Law (UNCITRAL), to incorporate technical progress, and to answer the new needs of arbitral practice, especially regarding the requirements of the arbitral convention and the adoption of interim measures.

The Model Law is more readily comprehensible for international traders, accustomed to flexible rules that are readily adaptable to the particularities of specific cases arising in a wide diversity of scenarios. The success of this Model Law is the result of an exhaustive exercise in comparative law, which is why the SAA does not really respond to the traditional canons of Spanish law but facilitates its application by actors working out of economic areas where Spain maintains active and growing commercial relations.

New York Convention

The New York Convention on Recognition and Enforcement of Arbitral Awards was signed by Spain on 29 April 1977. Spain adhered from such date without making any reservation to this Convention, and applies it to the enforcement of arbitral awards made in non-Member States.

The New York Convention has been adopted by many States. Some of them apply this Convention *erga omnes*, which means from the rest of the world, without limiting its applicability to arbitrations connected to other Member States. Due to this *erga omnes* effect, this Convention becomes the general rule for such Member States.

Other treaties on recognition and enforcement of arbitration awards

Spain has signed the European Convention on International Commercial Arbitration of 21 April 1961, ratified by Spain on 5 March 1975, as well as the Geneva Convention of 1961 on International Commercial Arbitration.

Is there a different arbitration law for international arbitration?

There is not a different arbitration law for international arbitration in Spain. The Spanish arbitration system follows a monistic approach instead of a dualistic approach; therefore, instead of having different rules for international and domestic arbitration, Spain has only one arbitration act for both. The SAA applies in general to domestic and international arbitration conducted on Spanish soil.

Under the SAA, an arbitration is considered international when, according to article 3:

- at the time when the arbitration agreement is concluded, the parties are domiciled in different States;
- the following places are located outside the State in which the parties are domiciled: (a) the place of the arbitration as determined in the arbitral agreement; (b) the place where the obligations deriving from the discussed legal relationship are to be performed; or (c) the place to which the subject matter of such dispute is most closely related; or
- the interests of international trade could be affected by the legal relationship from which the dispute arises.

In addition to the aforementioned, under the SAA the regulation of international arbitration may be inspired by some of the provisions laid down in treaties ratified by Spain or in laws with special provisions on arbitration.

Overview of arbitration bodies and any foreign arbitration institutions

In contrast with other European States, Spain has several arbitral institutions. The main internal bodies providing arbitration services in Spain are the:

- Madrid Court of Arbitration (*Corte de Arbitraje de Madrid*).
- Civil and Trade Court of Arbitration (*Corte Civil y Mercantil de Arbitraje* – CIMA).
- Spanish Court of Arbitration (*Corte Española de Arbitraje*).
- Arbitral Tribunal of Barcelona (*Tribunal Arbitral de Barcelona*).

For international arbitrations, it is worth noting that the International Chamber of Commerce is headquartered in Barcelona (ICC).

The proliferation of different arbitral bodies in Spain during the last few years is starting to be seen as a problem by stakeholders, which is why in December 2017 an agreement between the Madrid Court of Arbitration, CIMA and the Spanish Court of Arbitration was signed in order to unify such three arbitral bodies in one. The implementation of this strategy aims to increase the attractiveness of Spain as an arbitration forum. Additionally, these three signing arbitral institutions are currently considering the possibility of unifying with other Spanish arbitral bodies in the near future.

Are there any special national courts for international arbitration?

There are no special national courts to hold international arbitration proceedings in Spain. Nevertheless, international arbitration bodies such as the International Chamber of Commerce (ICC), the Stockholm Chamber of Commerce (SCC), or the International Center for the Settlement of Investment Disputes (ICSID), usually rent out offices for local arbitration bodies in order to hold oral hearings.

Notwithstanding the aforementioned, some national courts have powers regarding international arbitration. For example, the Civil and Criminal Section of the Autonomous Supreme Court of the region of domicile of the party against whom the recognition is applied, and the First Instance Courts, are entitled to recognise and enforce international arbitration awards according to article 8.6 of the SAA.

Arbitration agreement

Arbitration agreement and the drafting of arbitration clauses

According to article 9.1 of the SAA, the arbitration agreement may adopt the form of either a separate agreement or an arbitration clause in a broader contract, and must express the parties' willingness to submit to arbitration all or certain disputes arising between them in respect of a given legal relationship, whether contractual or otherwise.

In order for an arbitration agreement to be considered valid under the SAA provisions, it is necessary for this agreement to be made in writing, in a document signed by the parties or an exchange of letters, telegrams, telexes, faxes or other telecommunication methods that ensure a record of the agreement is kept (article 9.3 SAA).

If the arbitration agreement is contained in an adhesion contract, its validity and interpretation will be governed by the specific rules applicable to such contracts (article 9.2 SAA).

Regarding international arbitrations, article 9.6 of the SAA specifically provides that for an arbitration agreement to be reputed valid and the dispute arbitrable, it must comply with the requirements of the rules of law chosen by the parties to govern the agreement, or by the applicable substantive law, or by Spanish law.

What disputes are arbitrable?

In Spain, matters within the free disposition of the parties are considered arbitrable; which means matters in which the autonomy-of-the-parties principle allows them to choose a different dispute resolution method, out of the jurisdictional authorities of their respective States, submitting their dispute to the decision of an individual offering the guarantee of objectivity and impartiality. Article 2 of the SAA expressly states that disputes on matters considered by law to involve free choice are apt for settlement by arbitration. This assertion reveals that the real legal basis of the arbitration institution lodges in the free autonomy of the parties regarding disposable matters.

By contrast, all matters excluded from the free disposition of the parties – such as criminal matters – are considered non-arbitrable. The former Spanish Arbitration Act 36/1988, of 5 December 1988, listed in article 2 the disputes considered to be non-arbitrable:

- those matters in which a final judicial resolution has been issued, except for aspects related to their enforcement;
- matters inseparably united to other matters excluded from the free choice of the parties;
- matters in which the law requires the intervention of the Public Prosecution in representation of those without capacity or representation to act in trial; and
- labour arbitrations.

Although the Spanish Arbitration Act 36/1988 was abolished by the SAA, the aforementioned exclusions are still considered to be applicable.

The Spanish judicial system also allows, under certain circumstances, the removal from jurisdiction of some ongoing matters to the benefit of, on the one hand, the diminution of the terms (arbitration proceedings are usually associated with shorter terms than jurisdiction proceedings) and, on the other hand, the principle of speciality of the arbitrator.

Joinder/consolidation of third parties

The SAA does not contain any specific provision on joinder or consolidation of a third party and does not provide for a regulatory framework for consolidation of arbitral proceedings either.

However, most Spanish arbitral institutions have regulated this issue in their own regulations. By way of example, the ICC Code on Arbitration made on 1 January 2012 (recently modified on 1 March 2017), on efficiency and a more affordable arbitration model, introduces a change to the previous system by which arbitrators or the arbitral institution are now entitled to decide directly about any type of judicial objection, as well as any question related to joinder or consolidation of several claims in a sole process (in article 6(3)).

Principles of competence-competence and separability

The principle of competence-competence is expressly recognised in article 22 of the SAA, which clearly states that arbitrators may rule on their own jurisdiction, including any pleas with respect to the existence or validity of the arbitration agreement, or any others whose acceptance would prevent consideration of the merits of the case. Their decision may only be challenged by means of an application to set aside the final or a separate award on jurisdiction.

Under the SAA, the principle of competence-competence includes the separability principle in the sense that the validity of the arbitral agreement established as a clause of a contract does not depend on the validity of the contract itself, the arbitrator having competence to judge and declare the validity of the arbitral agreement even if the contract is declared null.

Arbitration procedure

Starting arbitration proceedings

Unless otherwise agreed by the parties, arbitration will commence on the date on which a request to submit the dispute to arbitration is received by the respondent, as stated in article 27 of the SAA, meeting the requirements established in the arbitration agreement.

The specific requirements needed by such request, in order for it to be valid and to allow the arbitration proceedings to commence, are specified in each arbitration institution's internal rules. By way of example, the ICC rules contain in article 4 an exhaustive list of the formalities and the information that the request of arbitration must contain.

Hearings outside the seat of arbitration

Under article 26 of the SAA, the parties can freely determine the place of the arbitration. Failing such agreement, it will be determined by the arbitrators, taking into consideration the circumstances of the case and the convenience of the parties. Arbitrators may, unless otherwise agreed by the parties, meet at any place they deem appropriate for hearing witnesses, experts or the parties, inspecting goods or documents, or examining persons.

Rules on evidence

At the beginning, the parties are free to choose the applicable rules on evidence, subject in any case to the requirements of the institution through which the arbitration will take place as well as observing the principles of equality, review and rebuttal. The SAA only regulates this matter in article 30 by which, subject to any contrary agreement by the parties, the arbitrators will decide whether to hold oral hearings for the presentation of statements or evidence and the issuance of conclusions, or whether the proceedings will be conducted in writing only. Unless the parties have agreed that no hearings will be held, they will be announced by the arbitrators at an appropriate stage of the proceedings, if so requested by a party.

Additionally, IBA rules on evidence, of 29 May 2010, can be taken into consideration by arbitrators by way of an inspiration guide (not compulsory), especially regarding international arbitration.

Rules regarding privilege and disclosure

There are no rules or laws providing for an arbitrator's privilege or immunity. Nevertheless, article 21.1 of the SAA establishes an arbitrator's liability for damages in case of improper performance of their duties based on bad faith, temerity or wilful misconduct.

With regard to the disclosure rules, according to article 24.2 of the SAA the arbitrators, the parties and the arbitral institutions are bound to honour the confidentiality of the information received on the occasion of arbitration according to the confidentiality principle. This principle is one of the main advantages of the arbitration system and one of the reasons for its success, since it allows the parties to protect their public reputation. However, occasionally courts may require arbitrators or arbitral institutions to disclose part of the information or documentation provided during arbitral proceedings if the substantive matter is linked to the merits of a judicial dispute and disclosure is absolutely necessary to resolve it.

IBA Rules on the taking of evidence in international arbitration

As explained above, the IBA rules on evidence are generally followed in international arbitrations which take place in Spain. However, arbitrators are not obliged to follow the IBA provisions, as they are not considered as positive law. The nature of the IBA rules on evidence in Spain is merely indicative, not binding. Our courts have specifically declared that Spanish arbitrators are only subject to the SAA and the specific regulations of each arbitral institution.

Rules regarding expert evidence

Article 32 of the SAA empowers arbitrators to appoint, unless otherwise agreed by the parties, one or more experts at their own initiative or at the request of a party. If the parties have no objections to it, after delivering their reports, experts appointed by the arbitral tribunal shall participate in the hearing.

Within this framework, since the SAA does not provide any stipulation regarding the treatment and timing of expert evidence, it is common to apply within arbitral proceedings by analogy the general provisions contained in our Procedural Law for judicial proceedings (Act 1/2000, of 7 January 2000), by which expert reports must be submitted by the parties at least five days prior to the hearing taking place.

New LCIA and IBA guidelines

Currently, there are no guidelines for taking the new LCI and IBA guidelines into consideration beyond the consideration of their principles as mere inspirations for international arbitrations held in Spain. These rules are still not considered as positive law in our country.

Confidentiality of arbitration proceedings

According to article 24.2 of the SAA, the arbitrators, the parties and the arbitral institutions are bound to honour the confidentiality of the information received on the occasion of arbitration.

The confidentiality principle is one of the main advantages of the arbitration system, since it allows the reputation of the parties to be publicly protected. This principle is one of the reasons that drive most investors, traders and companies to choose arbitration. It affects the information and documentation regarding the substance of dispute as well as any type of document and evidence connected to the arbitration proceedings (awards, submissions, etc.).

Arbitrators

Appointment of arbitrators

Under article 15 of the SAA, in arbitration not to be decided *ex aequo et bono* and conducted by a single arbitrator, such person will be required to be an attorney if acting as such, unless otherwise agreed by the parties. When arbitration is conducted by three or more arbitrators, at least one must be an attorney.

Additionally, the parties are free to agree on a procedure for appointing the arbitrator or arbitrators, providing the principle of equality is honoured. Failing such agreement, the SAA establishes some rules for the appointment of an arbitrator:

- In an arbitration with a sole arbitrator, he will be appointed by the court at the request of a party.
- In an arbitration with three arbitrators, each party will appoint one arbitrator, and the two arbitrators thus appointed will appoint the third arbitrator, who will preside the proceedings. If a party fails to appoint the arbitrator within 30 days of receipt of a request to do so from the other party, or if the two arbitrators fail to agree on the third arbitrator within 30 days of the latest acceptance, the appointment will be made by the court at the request of a party. Where more than one claimant or respondent is involved, the latter will appoint one arbitrator and the former another. If claimants or respondents cannot agree on the appointment, all arbitrators will be appointed by the court at the request of a party.
- Where more than one claimant or respondent is involved, the latter will appoint one arbitrator, and the former another. If claimants or respondents cannot agree on the appointment, all arbitrators will be appointed by the court at the request of a party.
- In an arbitration with more than three arbitrators, they will be appointed by the court at the request of a party.

If arbitrators cannot be appointed under the procedure agreed to by the parties, any party may apply to the competent court to appoint the arbitrators or, as appropriate, to adopt the necessary measures therefor. When arbitrators have to be appointed by the court, it will draw up a list of three names for each arbitrator to be appointed. Where a sole or a third arbitrator is to be appointed, the court will also have regard to the advisability of appointing an arbitrator of a nationality other than those of the parties and, as appropriate, of those of the arbitrators already appointed, in light of the circumstances prevailing. The arbitrators are subsequently appointed by lot.

Moreover, it is common for each specific arbitral institution to demand additional requirements of arbitrators in order to compose the list of eligible arbitrators. The secrecy of some arbitral institutions in preparing and giving access to the lists of eligible arbitrators has been highly criticised.

<u>Challenging an arbitrator</u>

An arbitrator may be challenged only in the event of justifiable doubts affecting his impartiality or independence arising, or if he does not possess the qualifications agreed to by the parties. A party may challenge an arbitrator appointed by him, or in whose appointment he has participated, only for reasons of which he/she becomes aware after the appointment was made, as provided in article 17.3 of the SAA.

The procedure under which the challenge of an arbitrator shall take place is established in article 18 of the SAA. The parties may agree on a procedure for challenging arbitrators but failing such agreement, a party who intends to challenge an arbitrator must state the grounds for the challenge within 15 days after becoming aware of the acceptance, or of any circumstances that may give rise to justified doubts about the arbitrator's impartiality or independence.

Unless the challenged arbitrator withdraws from his office or the other party agrees to the challenge, the arbitrators will decide on the challenge. If the challenge under any of the precedent procedures is not successful, the challenging party may submit the challenge as grounds for objecting to the award.

Are the IBA Guidelines on conflict of interest taken into account in your jurisdiction?

As happens with respect to the IBA rules on evidence, the IBA rules on conflict of interest are taken into consideration only as a guide or inspiration in order to make sure the impartiality principle reigns during the arbitration proceedings. Nevertheless, as previously explained, such rules are not positive law in Spain, which is why they are not compulsory for arbitrators, who are only obliged to follow the SAA previsions and the specific regulations of each arbitral institution in this matter. This indicative character has been declared, among others, by the Appeal Court of Madrid, in the ruling nº 506/2011 of 30 June 2011, and by the Supreme Court of Justice of Madrid, in the ruling nº 92/2017 of 23 March 2017. It is notable that the Supreme Court of Justice has specifically declared that these IBA rules are balanced upon the issuing of rulings about arbitrators' conflicts of interest.

Terminating an arbitrator's mandate

As stated in article 38 of the SAA, an arbitrator's mandate is terminated when the arbitral proceedings terminate, if it is either with a final award, or if: (i) the claimant withdraws his claim, unless the respondent takes exception thereto and the arbitrators acknowledge a legitimate interest on his part in obtaining a final settlement of the dispute; ii) the parties mutually agree on the termination of the proceedings; or iii) the arbitrators find that continuation of the proceedings is unnecessary or impossible.

There are other exceptional reasons why an arbitrator's mandate may expire before the termination of the arbitral proceedings based on grounds of abstention and/or challenge affecting their impartiality and/or independence, as well as on the failure or impossibility of the arbitrator to act. As stated in article 17 of the SAA, an arbitrator should abstain or, on the contrary, be challenged by the parties only if circumstances that give rise to justifiable doubts regarding his impartiality or independence arise, or when the eligible arbitration is not qualified according to the qualification requirements agreed by the parties. According to article 18 of the SAA, the parties are free to agree on a procedure for the challenging of arbitrators; failing such agreement, article 18.2 of the SAA provides for the procedure to follow. In connection to the failure or impossibility of the arbitrator to act, article 19 shall be considered.

Immunity of arbitrators

As previously indicated, arbitrators are not afforded immunity from suit. They are subject to very high standards of liability, which is why they can be held responsible for damages and prejudices caused when acting in bad faith, temerity or wilful misconduct, as determined in article 21.1 of the SAA. Arbitrators or arbitral institutions acting on their behalf are bound to take liability insurance or equivalent security for the amount established in the specific arbitral institution rules. It is not unknown in Spain for this liability to be demanded in court if the parties challenge the arbitrator before an ordinary jurisdiction.

Secretaries to the Arbitral Tribunal

There are no specific provisions contained in the SAA restricting the activities of Secretaries to the Arbitral Tribunal. Thus, this matter is directly regulated by each arbitral institution, who are entitled to freely define the duties, competences and working tasks of this administrative organism. By way of example, the ICC rules provide an open list of the Secretary of the Court's powers: to receive the claims; to confirm the numbers of arbitrators and their identification; to issue certified copies of the arbitration awards; to request the payment of the provision of funds of the arbitration proceedings; to prepare notes and other type of documents to the parties, arbitrators or whosoever's information, etc.

Interim relief

Types of interim relief available

Article 23 of the SAA establishes that arbitrators are allowed to grant any interim measures deemed necessary in connection with the object of the dispute, at the request of a party and without prejudice to any contrary agreement signed by the parties. In such cases, the arbitrators may require the claimant to furnish sufficient security.

In connection with such interim reliefs, it is common that arbitrators apply the different types of measures listed in article 727 of the Spanish Procedural Law by analogy (Act 1/2000 of 7 January 2000). Some of those are: preventive seizure of goods; judicial intervention or administration of productive goods; goods depository, etc.

Judicial intervention is usually needed in order to enforce interim measures adopted within arbitral proceedings.

Can the parties apply to both courts and tribunals for such interim relief?

Effectively, parties may apply to either courts or arbitral tribunals in order to be granted any interim measure.

With regard to the interim reliefs adopted by arbitral tribunals, the SAA provides that those interim measures must be connected to the subject matter of the dispute, being enforceable before any court. Regardless of the form adopted by arbitral decisions on interim measures, the rules on setting aside and enforcement of the awards will apply to them.

In addition, the arbitration agreement does not prevent the parties, prior to or during the arbitral proceedings, from applying to a court for interim measures, or the court from granting such measures. Article 8.3, in connection with article 11.3 of the SAA, allows such possibility.

Can and do national courts order anti-suit injunctions in aid of international arbitration?

The response to this question is found in article 722 (first paragraph) of the Spanish Procedural Law (Act 1/2000, of 7 January 2000), which regulates the injunctions in arbitration proceedings and foreign litigation, determining that whoever may prove to be a party of an arbitration agreement may seek injunctions from the court prior to the arbitration proceedings. Whoever may prove to be a party in a pending arbitration proceedings in Spain may also seek them; or, as appropriate, whoever may have sought the court's certification referred to in article 15 of the SAA (arbitrator's judicial appointment); and/or in the event of institutional arbitration, whoever may have duly filed an application to the relevant institution according to their regulations.

Can and do national courts order anti-arbitration injunctions in aid of domestic litigation?

According to the second paragraph of article 722 of the Spanish Procedural Law, whoever can prove to be party to any jurisdictional or arbitration proceedings being conducted in a foreign country may seek injunctions from a Spanish court, except in cases where the main matter at issue should solely lie within the competence of Spanish courts.

The foregoing means that anti-arbitration injunctions in aid of domestic litigation cannot be requested if it is proven that the sole competence of a specific matter corresponds to the Spanish courts.

Security for costs

As indicated above, article 23 of the SAA establishes that arbitrators may, at the request of the parties, adopt any interim measures deemed necessary in connection with the object of the dispute, requiring the claimant to furnish sufficient security.

Arbitration award

Formal requirements

According to article 37 of the SAA, an arbitration award must fulfil the following formal requirements in order to be valid and enforceable:

- It has to be issued within six months of the date of submission of the statement of defence or of the expiration of the deadline therefor, unless otherwise agreed by the parties.
- It has to be issued in writing and signed by the arbitrators. Arbitrators may specify the sense of their votes.
- It has to argue the grounds upon which it is based, unless the award is issued as a way of termination by mutual agreement of the parties.
- It must express the date and the place of arbitration.
- It has to contain a decision regarding the costs of the arbitration, subject to the agreement of the parties.
- It has to be expressly notified to the parties on arbitration, according to the form and within the time frame agreed by them or, failing that, by delivering a signed copy of the award to each party.

Time frame

Under article 37.2 of the SAA, subject to any contrary agreement of the parties, the arbitrators must deliver the award within six months of the date of submission of the statement of defence or, failing that, of the deadline for its submission. Unless otherwise agreed by the parties, this term may be extended by the arbitrators for a period of no longer than two months under a duly justified ground. Additionally, the failure to deliver the award on time will not affect its validity, unless otherwise agreed by the parties.

Costs

An arbitral tribunal may order costs for the parties. This issue is regulated in article 37.6 of the SAA, which establishes that the award shall express, subject to agreement of the parties, the arbitrators' decision on arbitration costs, which shall include the arbitrator's fees and expenses and, as appropriate, the fees and expenses of the parties' defence or representatives, the cost of the service rendered by the institution conducting the arbitration, and all other expenses incurred in the arbitral proceedings. The arbitral award usually includes an itemisation of the expenses and costs.

Under the SAA provisions, the possibility of claiming interest on arbitration costs is not expressly regulated. Interests can be included in the final award, but only regarding the principal amount claimed in the proceedings.

Challenge of the arbitration award

Appeal of an arbitration award

As a general rule, an award may not be appealed to ordinary jurisdiction in Spain. As established in article 43 of the SAA, an arbitral award constitutes *res judicata*, which means that there is no other action against it except for those seeking to set it aside or, as appropriate, the object of a request of review under provisions on final sentences established in our Procedural Law (Act 1/2000, of 7 January 2000).

Grounds for challenge

The SAA provides in article 41 a restricted list of grounds under which an award may be challenged. All such reasons must be demonstrated, in any case, by the applicant party:

- the arbitration agreement does not exist or is not valid;
- the applicant party has not properly received notice of the appointment of an arbitrator and/or of the arbitral proceedings, or otherwise has not been able to present his case;
- when the arbitrators decide about questions not subject to their jurisdiction;
- when the arbitrators have not observed the agreement of the parties regarding their appointment and/or the arbitral proceeding, unless such agreement does not respect any imperative provision of the SAA or, failing such agreement, arbitrators have proceeded against the SAA;
- when the arbitrators decide about non-arbitrable matters; or
- if the award violates the public order.

Despite such grounds being thought to be a strict list by the Spanish legislator, since the arbitration proceedings were originally configured under the SAA as a sole instance proceeding, a tendency to abuse the utilisation of some of these reasons is observable (especially the public order umbrella, which can be used to provide cover to challenge an arbitration award, which could transform the nature and essence of the proceedings into a second instance one).

<u>Modification of an arbitration award</u>

Under article 39 of the SAA, the parties are entitled to apply for the correction, rectification or re-interpretation of the award, and/or for the issuance of an additional award within 10 days of its notification, unless another time has been agreed by the parties. These modifications of the award are allowed in the following cases:

- Correction of the award if any errors in computation, clerical, typographical or similar errors are identified.
- Interpretation of a specific point or part of the award, when this point or part is not considered sufficiently clear.
- Additional award, if a party observes that the award has not decided about any submitted request or claim.
- Rectification of part of the award, in case of partial overextension regarding non-arbitrable matters or questions not submitted to the decision of the arbitrators.

<u>Recent examples of successful and unsuccessful challenges of arbitral awards</u>

Even if the number of successful challenges of an arbitral award in Spain cannot be considered relevant, a new trend is recently perceptible: the growing interest of some tribunals (Supreme Justice Court of Madrid, by way of example) to control the reasoning of arbitral awards based on the application of the control-of-public-order test (article 41.1.f) of the SAA). The application of this test is currently allowing ordinary courts to challenge some arbitration awards. However, this test could open a dangerous window, since it may put Spanish arbitration proceedings at risk (if the validity of the awards is frequently challenged), causing what is known as the international arbitration 'escape'.

It has been additionally observed that some arbitral awards have been successfully challenged based on the bad faith intervention of some arbitrators, by resolving the dispute without the third arbitrator opinion (in case of arbitral tribunals composed of three arbitrators).

Enforcement of the arbitration award

The enforcement of international awards is regulated in article 46 of the SAA, which refers to the application of the Convention on Recognition and Enforcement of Arbitral Awards made in New York on 29 April 1977.

In order to enforce international and domestic arbitration awards, the formal requirements needed in Spain are established in our Procedural Law (article 523 of Act 1/2000, of 7 January 2000) by reference to the Spanish legal system on recognition and enforcement of international rulings.

Can an arbitration award be enforced if it has been set aside at the courts of the seat of arbitration?

Article 45 of the SAA establishes that awards in Spain are enforceable even when an action has been brought to set them aside. Nevertheless, in that case, the concerned party may apply to the competent court for suspension of the enforcement, if it provides security for the value of the sentence plus any damages that may stem from delayed enforcement. The court, upon receipt of the application for suspension, will hear the executant and will deliver a decision on the security to be furnished. The Clerk of the Court will raise the suspension and will order the continuation of the enforcement upon confirmation of dismissal of the action for setting aside the award.

Trends of enforcement – pro-arbitration or anti-arbitration?

Spain is considered a pro-arbitration State. This is evidenced by article 517.2.2º of the Spanish Procedural Law (Act 1/2000, of 7 January 2000), by which arbitral awards are considered as enforcement titles (together with other titles as judicial rulings), which is why they can be automatically enforceable before the ordinary courts.

Investment arbitration

Spain has signed more than 88 bilateral investment treaties (BITs). The last BIT signed was between Spain and Haiti in 2012 and is not yet in force. Spain is also a member of a large number of multilateral treaties. Regarding investment treaties, Spain has been a signatory to the ICSID Convention since 21 March 1994, and the Energy Charter Treaty since 17 December 1994.

Spain has around 30 arbitration proceedings open in different arbitral tribunals for reform of the electricity sector, and the cuts to renewable energies carried out by the Spanish Government between 2010 and 2013. Recently Spain has lost two arbitrations (one sentencing Spain to pay €53 million plus costs of proceedings plus 1.5% interest, and another one sentencing Spain to pay €128 million plus interest) and won another two.

The treatment of investment arbitration awards by our national courts is exactly the same as the enforcement of a court ruling or an award not related to investment. Our Spanish Procedural Law (Act 1/2000, of 7 January 2000) states in its article 517 that arbitration awards shall involve enforcement.

Spain has challenged the €128 million award for considering whether there may be a conflict of interest with one of the arbitrators for being part of the arbitral tribunal in another case concerning the same issue. Spain has also challenged recognition sought by the winning party, demanding the annulment of the admission.

Luis Cordón Procter
Tel: +34 93 611 92 32 / Email: luis.cordon@caseslacambra.com

Luis Cordon is the partner who leads the Litigation and Arbitration practice at Cases & Lacambra. He has extensive experience in arbitration, as he regularly acts as an arbitrator and as counsel in arbitral proceedings, both domestic and international, in trading, specialised banking and investment cases.

Luis Cordon has been nominated to act as an arbitrator before the Madrid Court of Arbitration (*Corte de Arbitraje de Madrid*), Spanish Court of Arbitration (*Corte Española de Arbitraje*) and the Barcelona Arbitration Tribunal (*Tribunal Arbitral de Barcelona*), with several awards rendered since 2014. He has also represented his clients in international arbitration cases before ICC, SCC, ICSID and UNCITRAL, among others.

He is a regular lecturer of Barcelona Bar Association and associate professor of international law at ISDE (*Instituto Superior de Derecho y Economía*). He is a member of the International Bar Association Arbitration Committee and the Spanish Club of Arbitration (CEA), where he is currently a member of the drafting sub-committee for Good Governance and Organisation of Arbitral Institutions. He also collaborates in relevant publications, economic journals and specialist magazines, having recently contributed to the *Spain Arbitration Review* publication with the article, "the responsibility of arbitrators and the truncated tribunals", and also in the preparation of the *Legal Encyclopaedia of the Spanish Arbitration*.

Luis Cordón has been recognised by the 2017 edition of *Leaders League* as highly recommended Lawyer in International Arbitration and Commercial Litigation. Before joining Cases & Lacambra, Luis Cordón developed his career in the litigation department of PwC, based in the Barcelona office. Previously, he was a lawyer in the litigation area of Deloitte.

Sheila Muñoz Muñoz
Tel: +34 93 611 92 32 / Email: sheila.munoz@caseslacambra.com

Sheila Muñoz Muñoz is a senior associate at Cases & Lacambra, in the Litigation and Arbitration practice. She has extensive experience in litigation and arbitration, focused on credit institutions. Before joining Cases & Lacambra, Sheila worked in the law department of Banco Bilbao Vizcaya Argentaria (BBVA) in Madrid. Before that she was in the litigation department of Cuatrecasas Gonçalves Pereira, in its Barcelona office.

Diana del Moral Bernal
Tel: +34 93 611 92 32 / Email: diana.moral@caseslacambra.com

Diana del Moral is an associate at Cases & Lacambra in the Litigation and Arbitration practice. She has experience in litigation and arbitration, focused on banking law as well as corporate and commercial dispute resolution. Before joining Cases & Lacambra, Diana was a member of the Corporate and Civil Law Department of Garrigues, based in Granada. Diana del Moral has various publications on international trade and law, "The boom of the International Trade: Expanding the arbitration" being notable, published in issue 43 of the magazine *La Gaceta Jurídica de la Empresa Andaluza*, in September 2013.

Cases & Lacambra

Paseo de la Castellana, 8 28046, Madrid / Av. Pau Casals, 22, 08017, Barcelona, Spain
Tel: +34 91 061 24 50 / Fax: +34 93 512 61 24 / URL: www.caseslacambra.com

Sweden

Pontus Scherp & Fredrik Norburg
Norburg & Scherp Advokatbyrå AB

Introduction

Sweden has established itself as one of the most favoured places for the resolution of international disputes through arbitration. Sweden has a long history of being perceived internationally as an arbitration-friendly, neutral and reliable jurisdiction which has attracted parties from all over the world to resolve their disputes by arbitration in Sweden or using Swedish arbitrators. Arbitration has for a long time also been the preferred dispute resolution method for commercial disputes in Sweden. A large number of Swedish commercial contracts include an arbitration clause. As a result, many Swedish lawyers have a sound knowledge of arbitration law and Swedish courts are experienced in handling challenge proceedings and other arbitration-related matters.

The Arbitration Institute of the Stockholm Chamber of Commerce (the SCC) has had an important role in this development and is one of the main reasons why many international contracts include an arbitration clause designating Sweden as the seat of arbitration. The SCC is an internationally renowned arbitration institute with approximately 200 new cases filed per year, which makes it one of the leading arbitration institutions in the world. Approximately half of the cases handled by the SCC are international. The SCC also plays a leading role as an administrator of investor-state disputes and has a caseload second only to ICSID.

The SCC is committed to conform with the latest developments in international arbitration. A set of revised rules for arbitrations and expedited arbitrations entered into force on 1 January 2017, in time for the SCC's 100-year anniversary. The purpose of the revision of the rules was to make arbitration in Sweden even more attractive to both international and domestic parties by improving the efficiency of the proceedings even further. Some of the key changes in the 2017 SCC Rules are presented in the sections below, for example, new provisions on joinder, consolidation, multiple contract arbitration, administrative secretary and so-called summary procedure.

Another important factor behind Sweden's position as a popular arbitration seat is the modern and flexible arbitration law of Sweden, which is built on the fundamental principle of party autonomy. The Swedish Arbitration Act is the main law governing arbitration in Sweden. The Arbitration Act allows the parties to tailor-fit their dispute resolution to suit the needs of commercial parties, and there are only a few mandatory rules which are there to ensure due process. The Arbitration Act also offers accessibility to independent and arbitration-friendly courts, which are widely regarded as swift and effective. Lawyers familiar with the UNCITRAL Model Law will find few surprises in the Arbitration Act since it follows the Model Law in substance, with only minor deviations. The act is applicable to both domestic and international arbitration. Sweden has signed and ratified the New

York Convention without any reservations. Sweden is also a member of the Energy Charter Treaty (the ECT) and the ICSID Convention.

Efforts are made in order for Swedish arbitration law to stay in line with the best practices of international arbitration. In 2015, a committee of prominent legal experts issued a report, proposing certain revisions of the Arbitration Act for the purpose of making arbitration in Sweden even more attractive to both Swedish and international parties. The suggested revisions include allowing English language in challenge proceedings before ordinary courts, and specific rules to facilitate multi-party arbitrations. More details of some of the proposed amendments are mentioned below. A government bill has not yet been issued, but is expected during 2018.

Arbitration agreement

Lawyers familiar with the UNIDROIT principles will find that Swedish contract law shares many of its traits. The cornerstones are the principles of party autonomy and *pacta sunt servanda* and, as in the UNIDROIT principles, it is the common intention of the parties that determines the content of an agreement. This also applies to arbitration agreements governed by Swedish law. Unless otherwise agreed, Swedish law governs the arbitration agreement if the agreed seat of the arbitration is Sweden.

An arbitration agreement is defined in the Arbitration Act as an agreement between two or more parties to refer disputes arising from an identified legal relationship to resolution by one or more arbitrators. The Act thereby stipulates three cumulative requirements that must be fulfilled in order for an arbitration agreement to be valid and enforceable:

(i) an agreement between the parties to refer the dispute to arbitration;

(ii) identification of a legal relationship; and

(iii) an unambiguous reference to arbitration.

Contrary to many other arbitration laws, there is no mandatory requirement that an arbitration agreement must be in writing under Swedish law. This is in line with Swedish contract law, which is based on the formation of an agreement by an offer which is accepted. Oral agreements and implied consent, e.g. declaratory conduct, are sufficient for a party to be bound by an arbitration agreement. However, in order to avoid evidentiary problems, most arbitration agreements are in writing. Having no required form allows arbitrators and courts to be flexible when determining if an arbitration agreement has been concluded.

The requirement of identification of a legal relationship excludes the possibility for parties to enter into an arbitration agreement that covers all future disputes in general. The identification of the legal relationship can be explicit or implicit and as such need not necessarily be set out in the arbitration agreement. Typically, the legal relationship consists of a commercial contract or an existing dispute.

In order for an arbitration agreement to be valid, there must be a reference to arbitration. However, this does not prevent parties from entering multi-tier clauses, e.g. that they shall pursue other forms of dispute resolution procedure (e.g. negotiation or mediation) before resorting to arbitration.

An arbitration agreement is valid and enforceable as long as the three prerequisites are met. The parties are free to agree on further issues in their arbitration agreement, but the Arbitration Act provides provisions to determine any lack of agreement between the parties concerning aspects such as language of the proceedings, governing law or number of arbitrators.

The scope of the parties' contractual agreement to arbitrate is not only limited by the prerequisites for a valid arbitration agreement, but also by the concept of arbitrability. The arbitrability of a dispute is determined by both Swedish law and the applicable law to the arbitration agreement. All disputes concerning matters which the parties are free to settle by way of agreement are arbitrable under Swedish law. Arbitrability is, therefore, rarely an issue in commercial arbitration in Sweden, since parties are generally entitled to settle commercial disputes by way of agreement.

The arbitral tribunal is authorised to rule on its own jurisdiction under the principle of competence-competence. A competent court has, however, the final say on whether or not the arbitral tribunal has jurisdiction to decide the dispute. An action may be brought before court both before and after the initiation of the arbitral proceedings, although the court action does not prevent the arbitration from continuing pending the final outcome of the court proceedings.

To determine whether an issue is covered by an arbitration agreement, a method named doctrine of assertion is applied. The doctrine provides that a circumstance asserted by a claimant shall be assumed to exist for the purpose of determining jurisdiction under an arbitration agreement. Thus, if a claimant asserts e.g. that its claim is based on a specific contract, or the breach thereof, the arbitrators shall assume that this is correct when determining whether the claim falls under the arbitration clause contained in such contract. Once the issue of jurisdiction is determined, the circumstances thus asserted will be adjudicated on the merits.

The doctrine of separability is also applied in Sweden. Thus, the validity of the arbitration agreement shall be determined independently, and invalidity of the main contract does not automatically affect the jurisdiction of the tribunal under the arbitration agreement.

A fundamental principle in Swedish arbitration law is that a party must consent to be bound by an arbitration agreement. Therefore, third party intervention and joinder require the consent of all original parties. Consent does not have to be recorded in writing and can, as such, be found impliedly or by declaratory conduct. The same limits apply to consolidation of multiple arbitrations between two parties. Unless the parties consent, it is required that all relevant arbitration agreements allow for consolidation of the disputes. There are no explicit rules of this in the Arbitration Act. However, the committee tasked with reviewing the Arbitration Act concluded that consolidation can often save costs and simplify proceedings, and has therefore proposed an explicit provision in the Act stating that consolidation is possible if the parties consent and the arbitrations involve the same arbitrators, provided that the arbitrators deem it advantageous for the arbitral proceedings. Furthermore, the 2017 SCC Rules now contain provisions allowing joinder of additional parties (Article 13) and consolidation of arbitrations (Article 15). Under a new Article 14 of the SCC Rules, a party may under certain circumstances also bring claims under multiple contracts in the same arbitration.

In conclusion, Swedish law and the new SCC Rules respect the parties' agreement to arbitrate and facilitate the common intention of the parties' agreement: to have an effective, expeditious resolution of the dispute.

Arbitration procedure

The fundamental principle of party autonomy is respected under Swedish law and an arbitration seated in Sweden can therefore be arranged to fit the parties' needs and expectations. The Arbitration Act contains few mandatory rules concerning the conduct of the arbitration procedure, and those that exist serve to protect the principles of equal treatment and due process. The overall aim of the Arbitration Act is to facilitate an arbitration procedure suited to the needs of the parties that is impartial, practical and fast.

The procedure used by Swedish arbitrators is typically in line with best practices for the conduct of international arbitration and the use of international "soft law" rules and guidelines, such as the IBA Rules on the Taking of Evidence, is widespread. The procedure is therefore predictable and normally in line with the expectations of parties, legal counsel and fellow arbitrators from other jurisdictions.

The arbitral procedure, including its commencement, is primarily determined by the parties' agreement (including agreed institutional rules). Failing such agreement, the Arbitration Act generally leaves it to the arbitral tribunal to decide the conduct of the proceedings. Provisions are in place to expedite the procedure when the parties have not specifically agreed to regulate the arbitration procedure by, for example, choosing institutional rules. In practice, institutional rules are applied in most arbitration proceedings seated in Sweden.

Unless otherwise agreed by the parties, arbitration is formally commenced by the filing of a request for arbitration. The following information must be included in a request for arbitration for an arbitral proceeding to be deemed initiated:

(i) an express and unconditional request for arbitration;

(ii) a statement of the issue which is covered by the arbitration agreement and which is to be resolved by the arbitrators; and

(iii) a statement of the party's choice of arbitrator where the party is required to appoint an arbitrator.

A party has an absolute right under Swedish law to a hearing prior to the tribunal's determination of an issue on the merits. However, the parties may agree to exclude that right and it is only absolute in the regard that it may not be denied by the arbitral tribunal. If the tribunal denies a hearing, despite the request from a party, it may be considered a violation of due process. A subsequent challenge proceeding could thereby potentially set aside the award. If the parties have not chosen a venue for the hearing, it is for the arbitral tribunal to decide. Nothing prevents a hearing from being held in a different country than at the seat.

An innovation in the 2017 SCC Rules is Article 39 which introduces a "summary procedure". In cases where, e.g., a party has made allegations that are manifestly unsustainable, or when an award could not be rendered in favour of a party as a matter of law even assuming alleged facts are true, the tribunal may, upon request of a party, decide issues of fact or law by summary procedure.

The parties are free to agree on rules of evidence. Failing such an agreement, it is a general rule that arbitration is adversarial and, therefore, it is for the parties to invoke and present the evidence they wish to rely on. The parties are free to present any and all evidence, in whatever form, that they wish to rely on. Evidence may only be refused by the arbitrators in cases where the arbitrators either find that the evidence is manifestly irrelevant, or if refusal is justified having regard to the time at which the evidence is submitted.

Arbitrators may, upon request by a party, order the other party to produce evidence, including documents and objects. The parties are free to agree on the procedure for the production of documents and other evidentiary issues. Failing such agreement, the arbitrators may decide these issues at their discretion. In international arbitration, arbitrators seated in Sweden are commonly guided by the IBA Rules on the Taking of Evidence in Commercial

Arbitration in this regard. The IBA Rules are familiar to Swedish counsel and arbitrators also in the sense that the approach to document production in the IBA Rules is similar to the approach in domestic court proceedings.

Production orders issued by arbitrators are not enforceable in Sweden, although in practice many parties agree to follow such orders and other procedural decisions issued by the arbitrators during the arbitration. However, Swedish courts are authorised to assist the arbitration process in the taking of evidence. Thus, upon request by a party and after approval of the arbitrators, a party may file a document request with a district court, and this court may order production of documents held by the other party or a third party.

Court assistance can also be obtained when a party would like to examine a witness under oath. Under Swedish law, arbitrators cannot administer oaths, and a witness is not obliged by law, as before a court, to appear and give testimony before an arbitration tribunal. Decisions on the production of documents and witness testimony rendered by a district court under these provisions are enforceable. It should be noted that the same court assistance may also be sought if the arbitration is seated outside Sweden, e.g. in case the documents requested or the witness to be examined are located in Sweden.

Arbitration proceedings in Sweden are private unless otherwise agreed between the parties. Moreover, the arbitrators must adhere to the principle of confidentiality when they perform their duties. The SCC and other arbitration institutions are also bound by the provisions on confidentiality to the extent set out in their respective arbitration rules. As regards the parties, they are not bound by a duty of confidentiality unless this has been agreed between the parties. Witnesses and experts are bound by a duty of confidentiality to the extent this has been agreed with them or if this follows from professional rules.

The Arbitration Act does not contain any provision concerning which substantive law to apply in a dispute, but the choice agreed between the parties should be followed in accordance with the principle of party autonomy. The committee tasked with reviewing the Arbitration Act has also proposed an express provision to this effect. It is proposed that if the parties have not agreed on an applicable law, the arbitrators are to decide on which law to be applied, taking particular account of which law the dispute is most closely connected to. This should be regarded as a codification of current practice.

Arbitrators

An objective of the Arbitration Act is to expedite arbitration proceedings with impartial and independent arbitrators and prevent any obstructing behaviour from a party or a selected arbitrator. In order to do this, the competent courts are authorised to make swift and final decisions on the challenge of an arbitrator, as well as appointing arbitrators when a party is passive.

There are no mandatory requirements in the Arbitration Act with regard to the composition and appointment of the arbitral tribunal other than that the arbitrators must be impartial and have legal capacity. If the number of arbitrators is not specified in the arbitration agreement, the default rule under the Act provides for three arbitrators. The previous SCC Rules also had a default rule of three arbitrators. This has changed in the 2017 SCC Rules. Under Article 16 of the new SCC Rules, the Board shall decide whether the Arbitral Tribunal shall consist of a sole arbitrator or three arbitrators, having regard to the complexity of the case, the amount in dispute and any other relevant circumstances.

Secretaries to an arbitral tribunal are frequently appointed. Article 24 of the new SCC Rules governs the appointment and tasks of an administrative secretary. The provision provides that the parties must approve the appointment and that the arbitral tribunal shall consult the parties regarding the tasks of the administrative secretary.

With respect to multi-party arbitration, Article 17(5) of the 2017 SCC Rules prescribes a procedure for appointment of arbitrators for when there are multiple claimants or respondents. The procedure implies that if the parties on either side have not been able to jointly appoint an arbitrator, the SCC shall appoint the entire arbitral tribunal. The commission has proposed that a similar provision should be included in the Arbitration Act, with the difference that the district court shall appoint all arbitrators.

The test for impartiality and independence is based on objective grounds. It does not have to be concluded that the arbitrator is actually partial. The decisive factor is instead whether or not the arbitrator may appear partial. Hence, the relevant test is whether there is any circumstance that may diminish confidence in the arbitrator's impartiality. The IBA Guidelines for Conflict of Interest in International Arbitration, and also other international rules and guidelines, have been referred to by the Swedish Supreme Court in its assessment of the impartiality of an arbitrator. This confirms the development of Swedish arbitration law to be closely linked to the developing best practices in international arbitration.

Under the Arbitration Act, assistance by a district court to appoint an arbitrator is available in the following situations:

(i) if the respondent fails to appoint an arbitrator within 30 days after receipt of request for arbitration;

(ii) if the two party-appointed arbitrators fail to appoint a third within 30 days after the second arbitrator's appointment;

(iii) if the parties have agreed that they shall appoint an arbitrator jointly and the parties fail to agree on an arbitrator within 30 days from the date of the notification of one party with regard to the question of such joint appointment; or

(iv) if the parties have agreed that a third party shall appoint an arbitrator and this party fails to appoint one within 30 days after the third party was requested to undertake the appointment.

The competent district court generally handles the application for the appointment of an arbitrator swiftly, by a single judge and without an oral hearing. The final decision of the district court to appoint or remove an arbitrator may not be appealed.

A party may request that an arbitrator is removed if the arbitrator is partial, or lacks independence, as well as if the arbitrator delays the proceedings. If the parties have not agreed on a different procedure, the challenge is to be tried by the arbitral tribunal including the challenged arbitrator. Under the Arbitration Act, the parties may agree that an arbitration institute shall determine challenges against an arbitrator, and institutional rules often contain procedures in this regard. Under the SCC Rules, for instance, the SCC Board may release an arbitrator if challenged by a party.

If the tribunal (or institute) decides to remove the challenged arbitrator, the decision is final and cannot be appealed. However, if the challenge is denied by the tribunal, a party may request within 30 days from the date of the arbitral tribunal's decision that the challenge is tried by a district court. The district court's decision to remove an arbitrator is final, but if the challenge is denied by the district court, the decision may be appealed to the appellate court within 30 days.

A party who wishes to remove an arbitrator must make such request within 15 days from the date of becoming aware of the appointment and the circumstances giving rise to the challenge. If the party fails to make such a request within 15 days, the right to challenge is deemed forfeited.

The arbitral tribunal is to receive reasonable compensation for its work and expenses. Even though the tribunal or the arbitration institute sets the fees, the parties may bring an action before the competent court to have the fees reviewed and possibly reduced. The Supreme Court has interpreted the right to appeal the fees to include also the fees that may be set by an arbitration institute. It should, however, be noted that with respect to fees determined by an arbitration institute, this right to review of the fees in reality probably should be regarded as a formal right rather than a substantive one. The court would most likely find that the parties are bound by their agreement to let an arbitration institute decide the fees. Nonetheless, the committee that has reviewed the Arbitration Act, has proposed an exception from the right to appeal the fees in certain cases where the fee was set by an arbitration institute.

The arbitral tribunal or the arbitration institute may and normally does require the parties to provide security for the arbitrators', and, when applicable, the arbitration institute's fees and expenses. If a party refuses to pay its part of the advance on costs, and the other party therefore pays the advance for both parties, it has been held by the Supreme Court that a specific agreement is needed between the parties for the arbitral tribunal to be able to order a separate award on the non-paying party's portion of the advance on costs. The SCC Rules include a provision that aims to provide such authorisation for the tribunal.

Interim relief

The arbitral tribunal and the courts have concurrent jurisdiction to order interim measures, unless the parties agree otherwise. Thus, the parties have the choice of selecting the forum that best suits their particular needs.

Swedish courts are authorised to grant a number of different interim measures before or during the arbitral proceedings including, for example, prohibitive measures to restrain a party from carrying out certain actions, positive measures to require a party to take certain action, and measures aimed at ensuring the future enforcement of the final award.

The courts have a wide discretion to grant enforceable orders for interim relief. The courts are also authorised to order *ex parte* measures as well as to impose interim measures on third parties. The parties are not prevented from seeking interim measures from a court by having already applied for, or even been granted, an interim measure by the arbitral tribunal.

The arbitral tribunal is afforded extensive powers to order interim measures. These powers include the authority of the arbitral tribunal to order a party to secure evidence or to undertake certain actions to secure the claim which is to be adjudicated in the dispute. It is for the arbitral tribunal to decide when the granting of interim measures is justifiable. The Arbitration Act essentially allows the arbitral tribunal to grant the same kinds of interim measures as the UNCITRAL Model Law, including ordering a party to:

(i) maintain or restore the status quo pending determination of the dispute;

(ii) take action that would prevent, or refrain from taking action that is likely to cause, current or imminent harm or prejudice to the arbitral process itself;

(iii) provide a means of preserving assets out of which a subsequent award may be satisfied; or

(iv) preserve evidence that may be relevant and material to the resolution of the dispute.

As in many other jurisdictions, an order issued by an arbitral tribunal is not enforceable in Sweden. In practice, however, many parties comply with such orders, and a party's failure to comply may affect the outcome of the arbitration. Tribunals are not empowered to order interim measures against third parties. The committee reviewing the Arbitration Act has proposed that arbitral tribunals should be able to order a security measure through a special award, if this is allowed by the arbitration agreement. Such special awards would then become enforceable.

The courts and the arbitral tribunal normally require the requesting party to provide security for any loss which may be suffered by the other party as a result of the interim measure.

The SCC Rules contain a possibility to appoint an emergency arbitrator that is authorised to try and grant a request for interim relief prior to the constitution of an arbitral tribunal. The SCC shall seek to appoint such emergency arbitrator within 24 hours from the request, and a decision must be rendered by the emergency arbitrator within five days of the referral of the request to the arbitrator.

Arbitration award

Swedish law contains few formal and material requirements regarding the award. The few that exist are in place in order to ensure the enforceability of the award by providing certain minimum requirements. Unless otherwise agreed by the parties, the prerequisites for the content of the award are the following:

(i) the arbitral tribunal must apply and base its award on the applicable law or rules of law, i.e. not decide the dispute *ex aequo et bono*, or as *amiable compositeur* unless agreed upon by the parties;

(ii) the arbitral tribunal must limit its determination to the parties' respective request for relief;

(iii) the arbitral tribunal cannot base its award on facts other than those presented by the parties; and

(iv) the arbitral tribunal must consider all claims submitted to it.

Furthermore, clear instructions to the parties as to how to appeal the award must be included in an award whereby the tribunal has concluded the proceedings without ruling on the merits. Furthermore, the award must contain instructions to the parties on how to appeal the decision regarding the compensation to the arbitrators, which may be done by application to the district court within three months from the date the party received the award. Deviations from any of these requirements may make the final award challengeable and mean it could eventually be set aside. Such award may also be difficult to enforce.

The statutory minimum requirements as to the form of the award are the following:

(i) the award must be made in writing;

(ii) the award must be signed by the arbitrators;

(iii) the award must state the seat of arbitration; and

(iv) the award must state the date upon which the award is made.

If the award does not fulfil the requirements of being in writing and signed by the arbitrators, it may still be rectified by amendment in order to avoid invalidity of the award. The fact that the award does not contain information about the seat or the date it was made does not automatically lead to invalidity of the award.

There are no formal requirements for the deliberations and the tribunal may organise the deliberations as it sees fit. Every arbitrator has a right to take part in the resolution of the dispute and be given an equal opportunity to influence the award. This right is, however, not unlimited and if two arbitrators are in agreement on the outcome, the third arbitrator cannot prolong the deliberations by demanding continued discussions in order to persuade the others. The majority of the arbitrators may decide an issue if an arbitrator fails to participate in the deliberations without a valid excuse. A dissenting arbitrator is entitled to attach a dissenting opinion to the award.

The arbitral tribunal may not render a default award. Thus, even if a party fails to take part in the proceedings, the award must be based on an adjudication of the merits of the case including all arguments and evidence filed with the arbitral tribunal. Such an award has the same validity as any other award.

The parties are allowed to request that the tribunal records a settlement agreement in a consent award, which is then enforceable and recognisable under the New York Convention. It also renders the dispute *res judicata*.

The tribunal may in the final award order a party to compensate the other party for legal costs incurred in the arbitration together with interest. The Arbitration Act does not contain any provisions on how the legal costs should be distributed. However, as a general rule, the costs are distributed in accordance with the principle that costs follow the event, i.e. that the losing party will be ordered to compensate the winning party's reasonable legal costs. Under the new SCC Rules, when apportioning the costs of the arbitration, regard may also be taken to each party's contribution to the efficiency and expeditiousness of the arbitration and any other relevant circumstances.

The parties are free to agree on any time limits with respect to the rendering of the award. If the parties have not done so, there are no specific time limits under the Arbitration Act. The default time limit for rendering the award under the SCC Rules is six months from the date upon which the case was referred to the arbitral tribunal but, upon request from the arbitral tribunal, this time limit may be extended by the SCC. According to recent statistics, for the majority of cases administered under the SCC Rules the award has been rendered within 6-12 months.

Challenge of the arbitration award

A Swedish arbitral award is final and binding as of the day it is rendered and cannot be appealed on the merits. The award may only be challenged on certain, narrowly defined formal and procedural grounds. Swedish arbitration law adheres to the principle of the finality of the awards and the parties are considered to have waived their right to challenge the award on the merits. Furthermore, there are only very rare cases where the ruling of the competent court on the challenge may be appealed to a higher court, which requires a leave to appeal from the court of appeal.

There is currently a distinction in the Arbitration Act between an action to declare an award invalid *ab initio* and an action to set aside the award. The grounds for invalidity are limited to the protection of the public interest and the rights of third parties. Such actions do not have to be initiated within a certain time period. The grounds for setting an award aside are designed to protect the interests and individual rights of the parties participating in the arbitration. These challenges must be commenced within three months from the date the award was received by the party challenging the award. Furthermore, a specific ground may be deemed to have been forfeited by a party if the party does not make an objection to any procedural irregularity during the arbitration procedure.

This distinction between grounds for invalidity and grounds for setting aside could, however, soon be history. The committee reviewing the Arbitration Act has proposed that the invalidity rules be repealed. Instead, the public policy rule that is currently one of the grounds for invalidity would become a new ground for setting aside an award. This would mean that a challenge on public policy grounds must be initiated within three months.

The committee has also proposed that court proceedings where an award is challenged may be conducted in the English language, if this is requested by one of the parties and the opposite party agrees to it. In practice, large parts of the challenge proceedings are already today conducted in English, among other things in the sense that documents need not be translated into Swedish.

International parties choosing Sweden as their seat have the opportunity to enter into an agreement in which they waive in advance their right to challenge an award on grounds for setting aside an award, but the grounds for invalidity of awards cannot be waived beforehand. The Arbitration Act allows the tribunal to correct, amend and interpret the award after it has been rendered. This possibility exists in order to avoid unnecessary and costly involvement of courts.

In practice, it is very rare for an award to be set aside or declared invalid.

Enforcement of the arbitration award

The Convention on the Recognition and Enforcement of Foreign Arbitral Awards of 1958 (the New York Convention) has been in effect in Sweden since it was ratified without reservations in 1972. The provisions of the Convention have since then been incorporated in the Arbitration Act.

Swedish courts generally have an arbitration-friendly approach, and the provisions of the New York Convention are only seen as minimum requirements. Therefore, an award may be recognised even though it would not be recognised by courts in another contracting state.

The limited grounds for refusal, the burden of proof of the challenging party, and the general pro-enforcement attitude of the courts, have resulted in very few cases where enforcement has been refused.

Investment arbitration

Stockholm is one of the leading fora for investment treaty arbitration. About 120 of the bilateral investment treaties (BITs) entered into between states provide that the disputes between the investor and the host states are to be resolved by arbitration under the auspices of the SCC Rules. The 2017 SCC Rules include a set of new provisions on investment treaty disputes, supplementing the SCC ordinary Arbitration Rules. Furthermore, the ECT designates arbitration under the SCC Rules as one of the dispute-resolution methods available to foreign investors protected by the ECT.

Pontus Scherp
Tel: +46 8 661 20 80 / Email: pontus.scherp@norburgscherp.se

Pontus Scherp is an experienced arbitration and litigation lawyer based in Stockholm, Sweden and one of two founding partners of Norburg & Scherp Advokatbyrå, a specialist firm for arbitration and litigation founded in 2013. Pontus Scherp acts as counsel and as an arbitrator in international and domestic arbitration and he represents clients before Swedish courts. He was recently included in Arbitration Future Leaders 2017 and Litigation by *Who's Who Legal* and *Global Arbitration Review*, who identify him as one of the foremost arbitration experts in Sweden. He is also recommended for dispute resolution by *Chambers and Partners*, *The Legal 500*, *Euromoney's Expert Guides* and *Leaders League*. He is a Fellow of the Chartered Institute of Arbitrators (FCIArb).

Fredrik Norburg
Tel: +46 8 658 20 80 / Email: fredrik.norburg@norburgscherp.se

Fredrik Norburg is an experienced arbitration and litigation lawyer based in Stockholm, Sweden and one of two founding partners of Norburg & Scherp Advokatbyrå, a specialist firm for arbitration and litigation founded in 2013. Fredrik Norburg has worked as a dispute-resolution specialist at other firms since 1999. In 2003 he founded Young Arbitrators Sweden (YAS) at the SCC Institute, and in 2004-2012 he was the secretary of the Swedish Arbitration Association (SAA). Fredrik Norburg acts as counsel in Swedish and international arbitration under, e.g. the SCC Rules, the UNCITRAL Rules and the ICC Rules, and in commercial litigation before Swedish courts of all instances. He is also regularly appointed as an arbitrator in Swedish and international arbitration. Fredrik Norburg is recognised in *Chambers & Partners*, *The Legal 500*, and *Expert Guides*.

Norburg & Scherp Advokatbyrå AB

Birger Jarlsgatan 15, SE-111 45 Stockholm, Sweden
Tel: +46 8 420 035 00 / Fax: +46 8 501 215 91 / URL: www.norburgscherp.se

Switzerland

Catherine Anne Kunz, Angela Casey & Courtney Furner
LALIVE

Introduction

Switzerland has a long-standing reputation as one of the preferred venues for international arbitration, whether in *ad hoc* proceedings or in proceedings administered under the rules of the leading arbitration institutions. Several factors account for this reputation, including Switzerland's political neutrality, developed infrastructure, qualified arbitration practitioners and a very arbitration-friendly legal framework.

In Switzerland, international arbitrations are governed by Chapter 12 (Articles 176-194) of the Swiss Private International Law Act ("**PILA**"), a modern and liberal arbitration law which has been in force since 1989. Although Switzerland's arbitration law is not based on the UNCITRAL Model Law, there are no major differences between the two sets of rules, but Chapter 12 PILA is much shorter. With its concise 18 articles, Chapter 12 PILA provides a streamlined set of essential provisions, which ensure the proper constitution and functioning of the arbitral tribunal and guarantee the respect of the parties' fundamental procedural rights, while giving the parties all the necessary flexibility to tailor the arbitration proceedings according to their needs.

Switzerland is currently in the process of modernising and further improving the user-friendliness of its arbitration law by revising Chapter 12 PILA. The proposed revision is limited and will not bring about fundamental changes to Switzerland's international arbitration law. Indeed, the aim of the revision is essentially to preserve and enhance the most attractive features of Chapter 12 PILA, as well as to enact the key developments of the Swiss Federal Supreme Court's jurisprudence on international arbitration.

In Switzerland, domestic arbitration is governed by Part 3 of the Swiss Code of Civil Procedure ("**SCCP**"), which applies to arbitrations seated in Switzerland where, at the time of the conclusion of the arbitration agreement, all parties had their domicile, seat or habitual place of residence in Switzerland. However, parties to a domestic arbitration may choose to apply Chapter 12 PILA, but must express this choice in writing.

While many arbitrations in Switzerland are *ad hoc*, *i.e.* not governed by a specific set of arbitration rules, parties frequently choose to apply the arbitration rules of a specialised institution. The most frequently used arbitration rules in Switzerland are:

- the Rules of Arbitration of the ICC International Court of Arbitration (**ICC Rules**);
- the Swiss Rules of International Arbitration (**Swiss Rules**), a uniform set of arbitration rules issued by the Swiss Chambers' Arbitration Institution; and
- the Code of Sports-related Arbitration applicable before the Court of Arbitration for Sport (**CAS/TAS Rules**).

In addition to the Court of Arbitration for Sport, Switzerland hosts many other international organisations or dispute-settlement institutions, such as the United Nations, the World Trade Organization, the World Intellectual Property Organization, the International Air Transport Association, the International Olympic Committee (IOC) and major international sports organisations such as FIFA and UEFA.

Arbitration agreement

Swiss arbitration law provides that any dispute with an economic interest may be subject to arbitration (Article 177 PILA). This broad definition of arbitrability opens arbitration in Switzerland to a wide range of commercial disputes.

The cornerstone of arbitral proceedings in Switzerland is the existence of a valid arbitration agreement. The arbitration agreement must be made in writing to be formally valid (Article 178(1) PILA). The signature of the parties is not required.

As regards substantive validity, an arbitration agreement must comply with either the law chosen by the parties to govern the arbitration agreement, the law governing the object of the dispute, in particular the law applicable to the principal contract, or Swiss law (Article 178(2) PILA). This alternative test reflects Switzerland's pro-arbitration approach: it enables tribunals to uphold an arbitration agreement that would be invalid under the law chosen by the parties or the law applicable to the principal contract, provided that it at least satisfies the requirements of Swiss law. Under Swiss law, what is decisive is the intent of the parties to subject their dispute to arbitration.

Swiss law recognises the doctrine of separability, pursuant to which the invalidity of the principal contract does not automatically render the arbitration agreement it contains unenforceable (Article 178(3) PILA). Applying the separability doctrine, the Swiss Supreme Court recently upheld an arbitration clause contained in a draft contract which was ultimately never signed.[1]

Swiss law is based on the principle of privity of contract by which an arbitration clause is binding and has legal effect only on the parties that have originally agreed to it. Case law has, however, recognised certain exceptions to this rule. In particular, the Swiss Supreme Court has held that the arbitration agreement may be extended to a third party in cases where the third party participated in the negotiations or performance of the contract, thereby demonstrating a willingness to be bound by the arbitration agreement.

Arbitration procedure

The arbitration commences when one of the parties seizes the arbitrator(s) designated in the arbitration agreement or, in the absence of such a designation, when one of the parties initiates the procedure for the constitution of the arbitral tribunal (Article 181 PILA). Chapter 12 PILA does not contain any rules on the constitution of the arbitral tribunal and refers to the agreement of the parties (Article 179 (1)). The parties may seek the assistance of the state courts at the seat of the arbitration in the absence of such agreement.

The parties are free to decide on the procedural rules applicable to the arbitral proceedings either directly or by reference to an existing set of arbitration rules or other procedural rules of their choice. If the parties do not agree on the procedure, it will be determined by the arbitral tribunal. Irrespective of the procedural rules chosen by the parties, the arbitral tribunal must ensure equal treatment of the parties, and their right to be heard in adversarial proceedings (Article 182(3) PILA).

The arbitral tribunal is competent to decide on its own jurisdiction (competence-competence principle), even if proceedings concerning the same subject-matter and between the same parties are already pending before a state court, unless there are serious reasons to stay the arbitration (Article 186(1) and (1*bis*) PILA). Any objection to the arbitral tribunal's jurisdiction must be raised prior to any defence on the merits (Article 186(2) PILA). Similarly, a party which considers that its procedural rights have been violated must raise an objection immediately; a failure to do so entails the forfeiture of the right to complain of that violation at a later stage.

Swiss arbitration law does not address the confidentiality of the arbitral proceedings. In practice, confidentiality undertakings are often included in the applicable procedural rules or in the institutional rules chosen by the parties (*e.g.* Article 43 of the Swiss Rules). In Switzerland, exceptions to confidentiality undertakings apply if disclosure is required by a legal duty, to protect or pursue a legal right or to enforce or challenge an award in legal proceedings before a judicial authority.

Swiss arbitration law does not contain specific rules on the taking of evidence, disclosure or discovery. Nor does it contain specific rules of privilege. The arbitral tribunal determines the applicable rules for the taking, as well as the admissibility, relevance and materiality, of evidence. In so doing, the arbitral tribunal must have due regard to any agreements reached by the parties. In practice, arbitral tribunals will often be guided by the IBA Rules on the Taking of Evidence in International Arbitration.

If coercive assistance is required in the taking of evidence, the arbitral tribunal, or a party with the arbitral tribunal's consent, may request such assistance from the court at the seat of the arbitration (Article 184(2) PILA).

Any person may be a fact or expert witness in a Swiss-seated arbitration. The applicable arbitral procedure determines who, when, where, in what form and by whom a witness may be heard and examined (Article 182 PILA). It is common for arbitral tribunals seated in Switzerland to require parties to submit a written witness statement for each of their fact witnesses, in line with Article 4 of the IBA Rules on the Taking of Evidence in International Arbitration. These witness statements may take the form of a sworn affidavit made under oath, although signed declarations are more often used in practice. There are no mandatory rules on oath or affirmation, but the arbitral tribunal may seek guidance from Article 8(4) of the IBA Rules on Evidence in International Arbitration. Providing false testimony to an arbitral tribunal seated in Switzerland may entail criminal sanctions as when made before state courts (Article 309 Swiss Criminal Code).

While parties regularly appoint their experts, arbitral tribunals sitting in Switzerland retain the discretion to appoint their own experts. There is no requirement that experts be selected from a particular list. According to the case law of the Swiss Supreme Court, tribunal-appointed experts must be independent and impartial; conversely, party-appointed experts are not expected to be impartial. It is for the arbitral tribunal to assess the probative value of both forms of evidence. Swiss-seated arbitral tribunals occasionally use witness conferencing.

The use of tribunal secretaries is common, especially in complex cases. The main rule concerning the use of a tribunal secretary is the requirement that he or she be independent and impartial in the same way as the arbitrators themselves. According to the Swiss Supreme Court, the tasks of the tribunal secretary may include drafting of certain parts of the award, provided this is done under the control of the arbitral tribunal and in accordance with its instructions.[2]

Arbitrators

Pursuant to the principle of party autonomy, the parties enjoy freedom in the selection, removal and replacement of arbitrators (Article 179 PILA).

In the absence of an agreement, the parties may apply to the state court at the seat of the arbitration to appoint, remove or replace arbitrators (Article 179(2) PILA). The state court will appoint the arbitral tribunal unless a summary examination of the case reveals that there is no valid arbitration agreement between the parties (Article 179(3) PILA).

Generally, the parties are free to agree on the number of arbitrators (Article 179(1) PILA); the default position under Swiss law is for three arbitrators to be appointed.

In Switzerland, anyone may serve as an arbitrator. The only non-waivable requirement imposed by law on an arbitrator sitting in an arbitration in Switzerland is that he or she be independent and impartial (Article 180(1)(c) PILA). Aside from the requirements of independence and impartiality, the parties are free to agree on additional qualifications.

The Swiss state court at the seat of the arbitration enjoys wide discretion in the appointment of arbitrators at the request of a party, subject only to the requirements that appointees have to be independent and impartial (Article 180(1)(c) PILA) and meet any specific requirements contained in the arbitration agreement (Article 180(1)(a) PILA). There is no set list of arbitrators from which arbitrators are selected by state courts, unless the parties agree otherwise. Some institutional rules provide that the arbitrators must be selected from a list maintained by the institution (*e.g.* for disputes submitted to the Court of Arbitration for Sport). The Swiss Chambers (which administer the Swiss Rules) do not maintain any list of arbitrators.

Chapter 12 PILA is silent on the specific requirements for the disclosure of conflicts in the case of international arbitration proceedings. The Swiss Rules Provide that an arbitrator must remain impartial and independent of the parties at all times and must disclose all relevant facts which might give rise to justifiable doubts about his or her independence and impartiality (Article 9 Swiss Rules). This approach embodies the transnational principle of disclosure in international arbitration set out in General Standard 7 of the IBA Guidelines on Conflicts of Interest in International Arbitration. The Swiss Supreme Court has held on several occasions that the IBA Guidelines on Conflicts of Interest in International Arbitration are a valuable tool when determining questions of conflict of interest, and is likely to influence the practice of both institutions and state courts in Switzerland.[3]

An arbitrator may be challenged on the following grounds:

- circumstances exist that give rise to justifiable doubts as to his or her independence (Article 180(1)(c) PILA);
- the arbitrator does not meet a requirement agreed upon by the parties (Article 180(1)(a) PILA); or
- there exists a ground for challenge under the institutional rules agreed by the parties (Article 180(1)(b) PILA).

Once the arbitral tribunal has been constituted, a party may only challenge an arbitrator whom it nominated or in whose appointment it participated based on information discovered after the appointment (Article 180(2) PILA). The arbitral tribunal and the other party must be informed immediately of the grounds for the challenge.

The parties are otherwise free to agree on the procedure for challenging an arbitrator, including on possible time limits for the challenge. If the parties have not agreed on the procedure for challenging an arbitrator (including by reference to institutional rules), either party may apply to the competent Swiss state courts at the seat of the arbitration for a decision on the challenge. The decision of the state courts on the challenge of an arbitrator is final (Article 180(3) PILA).

Interim relief

Unless otherwise agreed by the parties, the arbitral tribunal may, at the request of either party, order interim measures. The arbitral tribunal has a wide discretion as to the type and content of those measures (Article 183(1) PILA). Those measures may include anti-suit injunctions to enjoin a party from starting or pursuing litigation in breach of the arbitration agreement, and anti-enforcement injunctions to prevent a party from enforcing another award or judgment.

The power of the arbitral tribunal to order interim measures is not unlimited, in that the arbitral tribunal lacks the power to enforce its orders on interim measures (Article 183(2) PILA). The arbitral tribunal may request the assistance of state courts if a party does not comply voluntarily with the order for interim measures. Assistance of the state courts may also be sought if interim measures are required against a third party.

As long as the arbitral tribunal is not (yet) constituted and there is no other private instance empowered to grant interim relief, the parties may request state courts in Switzerland to order interim relief. The prevailing view in Switzerland is that, unless otherwise agreed by the parties, the jurisdiction of the arbitral tribunal to order interim measures in an international arbitration is not exclusive but is concurrent with that of state courts. In other words, the party requesting interim relief may – even after the arbitral tribunal is constituted – freely choose whether to apply for such measures before state courts *or* the arbitral tribunal. The state courts will, however, apply their own rules to the admissibility and availability of interim measures.

Arbitration award

Article 189(1) PILA provides that the arbitral award shall be rendered according to the procedure and in the form agreed upon by the parties. In the absence of such agreement, Article 189(2) PILA provides that the award shall be rendered by a majority or, in the absence of such majority, by the chairperson alone.

The award must be in writing, set forth the reasons on which it is based, and be dated and signed. The arbitral tribunal may grant damages, relief for specific performance as well as interim and declaratory relief.

Chapter 12 of the PILA is silent on the admissibility of dissenting opinions. The Swiss Supreme Court has ruled that, where the parties have not agreed to the contrary, the majority of the arbitral tribunal may decide upon whether and how to communicate a dissenting opinion to the parties. A dissenting opinion does not form part of the award itself, but it may be annexed to the award or delivered to the parties separately.

Swiss arbitration law does not set a time limit within which the arbitral tribunal must render its award. However, if the parties and the arbitrator have agreed on a specific time limit for the rendering of the award, this agreement is binding on the parties and the arbitrator. The failure of an arbitrator to render the award within the agreed timeframe may give rise to a ground for challenge.

The arbitral tribunal will also render a decision on the costs of the arbitration and their allocation (even if Swiss arbitration law contains no specific provision to that effect). The items which are part of the arbitration costs and the allocation of the costs between the parties are to be determined in accordance with the parties' agreement (directly or by reference to any agreed arbitration rules). Absent an agreement between the parties, these issues will be determined by the arbitral tribunal, which enjoys a broad discretion in this respect.

Challenge of the arbitration award

International arbitral awards, whether final, partial or interim, may be set aside pursuant to Article 190 PILA. The setting-aside proceedings are directly brought before the Swiss Federal Supreme Court (Article 191 PILA), Switzerland's highest court. This remedy is not an appeal, as the Swiss Supreme Court does not review the factual findings of the arbitral tribunal. For the setting-aside application to be admissible, the applicant must have standing to challenge the award (Article 76 Supreme Court Act) by having either:

- participated, or been precluded from participating, in the arbitration; or
- been directly affected by the award and having an interest worthy of protection.

The limited grounds upon which an international arbitral award may be set aside in Switzerland are the following (Article 190(2) PILA):

- the arbitral tribunal was irregularly constituted;
- there is a wrong decision on jurisdiction;
- the arbitral tribunal ruled beyond the claims submitted to it, or failed to decide on the claims;
- there is a violation of the right to be heard, or of the principle of equal treatment of the parties; or
- the award is incompatible with public policy.

Interim awards can be challenged only on the grounds of the irregular constitution of the arbitral tribunal and a wrong decision on jurisdiction (Articles 190(2)(a) and (b) PILA).

A full application to set aside the award must be filed within 30 days of the notification of the award (Article 100(1) Supreme Court Act). This time limit cannot be extended. The Swiss Supreme Court typically renders its decision on the setting-aside application within six to eight months. Parties are only exceptionally granted a second exchange of submissions or the right to present oral arguments. The setting-aside application must be filed in one of the official Swiss languages (*i.e.* French, German or Italian; Article 42 Supreme Court Act).

There is no automatic stay of enforcement of an arbitral award pending the decision on the setting-aside application (Article 103(1) Supreme Court Act), but a stay of enforcement may be granted in exceptional cases. The party requesting the stay must demonstrate that:

- the immediate enforcement of the award exposes that party to serious and irreparable harm in its legitimate interests; and
- the challenge itself has a very strong *prima facie* chance of success.

If the Swiss Supreme Court sets aside an international arbitral award, it may only annul the challenged award and remand the case to the same arbitral tribunal for the rendering of a new award (so-called "cassatory" nature of the action for annulment; Article 77 Supreme Court Act), but does not issue its own decision on the merits.

The threshold for the setting-aside of an award rendered in Switzerland is extremely high, as confirmed by the low number of cases which have resulted in the complete or partial setting-aside of the award.[4]

If neither party has its domicile, place of habitual residence, or place of business in

Switzerland, it may, by an express declaration in the arbitration agreement or in a subsequent written agreement, explicitly waive the right to challenge the award (in whole or in part) (Article 192 PILA). The Swiss Supreme Court has held that this waiver is not applicable in sports arbitration.

Parties also have the possibility to seek a revision of an arbitral award in certain exceptional circumstances. Revision is an extraordinary means of correcting an award, which is final and binding and is only rarely granted. The grounds for revision of an arbitral award are limited and include in particular the following (Article 123 Supreme Court Act):

- the outcome of the award has been influenced by a criminal offence; or
- a party has subsequently discovered material facts or decisive evidence on which it was unable to rely in the arbitration proceedings.

Enforcement of the arbitration award

An arbitral award rendered by an international arbitral tribunal seated in Switzerland is final and binding and has the same legal effect as a final decision by a state court. As a result, it is automatically enforceable throughout Switzerland.

The recognition and enforcement of a foreign arbitral award in Switzerland is governed by the New York Convention on Recognition and Enforcement of Foreign Arbitral Awards of 1958 (Article 194 PILA). A party applying for recognition or enforcement of a foreign award in Switzerland must include with its application the original or a copy of the arbitral award and arbitration agreement, together with any translations into the official language of the place at which enforcement is sought (French, German or Italian) (Article IV of the New York Convention). In practice, Swiss courts take a liberal, pragmatic and pro-enforcement approach to the New York Convention and will only insist upon strict compliance with the form requirements regarding authentication and certification if the authenticity of the documents submitted with the application is disputed. Swiss state courts will usually not insist upon compliance with the translation requirement if the documents are in English.

Once Swiss state courts are satisfied that the requirements of Article IV of the New York Convention are met, recognition and enforcement will only be denied upon one of the limited grounds listed in Article V of the New York Convention. These grounds can be summarised as follows:

- party incapacity or invalidity of the arbitration agreement (Article V(1)(a));
- no proper notice of the appointment of the arbitrator or the proceedings or a party is otherwise unable to present its case (Article V(1)(b));
- the award of the arbitral tribunal is on matters beyond or outside of the scope of the arbitration (Article V(1)(c));
- irregular composition of the arbitral tribunal or procedure contrary to the parties' agreement or, in the absence of such agreement, of the laws applicable at the seat of the arbitration (Article V(1)(d));
- the award is not binding pursuant to the laws applicable at the seat of the arbitration or set-aside at the seat (Article V(1)(e));
- non-arbitrability of the dispute (Article V(2)(a)); or
- the award is contrary to the public policy of the country in which its recognition or enforcement is sought (Article V(2)(b)).

In Switzerland, the threshold for successfully resisting recognition and enforcement of a foreign arbitral award on the basis of Article V of the New York Convention is extremely high and will only be met in exceptional circumstances.

Investment arbitration

Switzerland has been a party to the Washington Convention for the Settlement of Investment Disputes Between States and Nationals of Other States since 1968, and to the Energy Charter Treaty since 1998. Having signed 127 BITs with other countries, of which 113 are currently in force, Switzerland has one of the largest bilateral investment protection treaty (BIT) networks in the world.

A Swiss seat is frequently chosen for investment-treaty arbitration outside of the ICSID annulment procedure and consequently such disputes are increasingly subject to setting-aside procedures before the Swiss Supreme Court. Most recently, the Swiss Supreme Court has, for example, dismissed an application to set aside an interim award on jurisdiction rendered in an Energy Charter Treaty arbitration opposing Yukos Capital to the Russian Federation, on the basis that the latter's challenge was premature as the interim award only addressed three out of a total of five jurisdictional issues.[5]

* * *

Endnotes

1. Decision of the Swiss Supreme Court 142 III 239 (4A_84/2015), 18 February 2016.
2. Decision of the Swiss Supreme Court 4A_709/2014, 21 May 2015, para. 3.3.2.
3. Decision of the Swiss Supreme Court 142 III 521 (4A_386/2015), 7 September 2016, para. 3.1.2.
4. See F. Dasser, P. Wójtowicz, *Challenges of Swiss Arbitral Awards* – Updated and Extended Statistical Data as of 2015, in ASA Bull. 2/2016, p. 280, p. 282.
5. Decision of the Swiss Supreme Court, 143 III 462 (4A_98/2017) dated 20 July 2017.

Catherine Anne Kunz
Tel: +41 58 105 2000 / Email: ckunz@lalive.ch

Catherine Anne Kunz is Counsel at LALIVE in the international arbitration team. She is dual-qualified in Switzerland and in England and Wales (solicitor). Catherine has acted as counsel and as arbitrator in numerous international arbitration proceedings, in particular in the energy, telecommunications and construction sectors, governed by a variety of procedural and substantive laws including Swiss, English, Spanish and Russian law. Catherine is recognised by leading publications as one of the future leaders in the field of international arbitration (*Who's Who Legal: Arbitration* – Future Leaders 2017 and 2018).

Angela Casey
Tel: +41 58 105 2000 / Email: acasey@lalive.ch

Angela Casey joined LALIVE in 2017. Her main area of practice is international arbitration, both commercial and investor-state, involving a variety of sectors. Before joining LALIVE, Angela completed her legal training with Pestalozzi Attorneys at Law in Zurich and Geneva, and at the Civil Court of the Canton Basel-Stadt. She was also an intern in the international arbitration group of Wilmer Cutler Pickering Hale and Dorr LLP in London. Angela studied law at the Universities of Basel and Zurich (Bachelor 2011, Master 2012). From 2012 to 2014, she worked as a research and teaching assistant at the University of Basel, where she obtained her Ph.D. in 2015. Her doctoral thesis, which explores the topic of employment law disputes in arbitration, was published in 2016.

Courtney Furner
Tel: +41 58 105 2000 / Email: cfurner@lalive.ch

Courtney Furner joined LALIVE in 2017. Her main areas of practice are international commercial and investment arbitration and public international law. Before joining LALIVE, Courtney worked as Associate to the Honourable Justice Robert Mazza of the Supreme Court of Western Australia, Court of Appeal (2015–2016) and in the dispute resolution team of Norton Rose Fulbright (2010–2014) in Australia. She has also tutored on civil procedure at the University of Western Australia (2015) and interned at the United Nations International Criminal Tribunal for the former Yugoslavia (2008). Courtney holds a Bachelor of Laws and a Bachelor of Arts from the University of Western Australia (2012) and an LL.M. in International Dispute Settlement (MIDS) from Geneva Law School and the Graduate Institute of International and Development Studies (MIDS-Young ICCA Scholar and Valedictorian, 2016–2017).

LALIVE

Rue de la Mairie 35, Geneva, Switzerland
Tel: +41 58 105 2000 / Fax: +41 58 105 2060 / URL: www.lalive.ch/en/index.php

Turkey

Prof. Av. Esra Bicen
EB LEGAL

Introduction

In Turkey, international arbitration is governed by International Arbitration Law ("Law No. 4686" or "MTK"), which has been effective since 5 July 2001. MTK is based on the language of the UNCITRAL Model Law on International Commercial Arbitration ("UNCITRAL Model Law"). In addition, the following national laws are applicable to international commercial arbitration in certain procedural aspects:

- Law on Principles to be respected when Applying to Arbitration regarding Disputes arising from Public Service Concession Agreements (Law No. 4501) effective since 22 January 2000;
- Civil Procedure Law (Law No. 6100) effective since 1 October 2011;
- Law on Private International Law and Procedural Law (Law No. 5718 or "PILA") effective since 4 December 2007; and
- 1958 New York Convention on the Recognition and Enforcement of Foreign Arbitral Awards ("NY Convention") effective since 30 September 1992. In ratifying the NY Convention, Turkey declared that "The State will apply the Convention only to recognition and enforcement of awards made in the territory of a Contracting State," and that "This State will apply the Convention only to differences arising out of legal relationships, whether contractual or not, that are considered commercial under national law."

In addition to the above national laws, Turkey concluded bilateral investment treaties on mutual judicial assistance and ratified multilateral investment conventions, the Convention on Settlement of Investment Disputes between States and Nationals of Other States ("ICSID Convention"), the Energy Charter Treaty ("ECT") and the Energy Charter Protocol on Energy Efficiency and related Environmental Aspects (See section, ***Investment arbitration***, below).

Turkey has a strong institutional framework administering national and international commercial arbitration. Until recently, the most commonly used commercial arbitration centres were: (i) Istanbul Chamber of Commerce Arbitration and Mediation Centre ("ITOTAM"); and (ii) Turkish Union of Chambers and Exchanges Arbitration Council ("TOBB Arbitration Council"). As of 1 January 2015, pursuant to the Law on Istanbul Arbitration Centre (Law No. 6570), Istanbul Arbitration Centre ("ISTAC") has been added to these institutions. International Chamber of Commerce Turkey National Committee has been the sole foreign institution administered under TOBB since 1950.

Effective as of 20 December 2017, the Regulation on Public Procurement Construction

Works made the choice of ISTAC a requirement for procurement contracts involving domestic parties, and made it optional to choose either ISTAC or MTK for procurement contracts involving foreign residents. Regulation also made choice of the Turkish language, and İstanbul or Ankara as the place of arbitration, requirements for domestic procurement contracts. Parties to public procurement contracts involving foreign residents may freely choose the language of arbitration and applicable law on the merits, but would be required to choose Istanbul or Ankara as the place of arbitration and the competent national court concerning civil procedural aspects of the dispute would be the civil court of first instance (*asliye hukuk mahkemesi*) located at the city of the contracting public agency.

While MTK is based on UNCITRAL Model Law, ISTAC and other national arbitration centre rules are heavily influenced by the ICC Arbitration Rules ("ICC Rules") including 2017 ICC Expedited Rules and ICC Emergency Arbitrator Rules. Given that ISTAC has been promoted by the Turkish government to gain popularity over other national arbitration centres going forward, the following responses will focus on the ISTAC Rules and MTK.

Arbitration agreement

Under MTK and ISTAC Rules, the constituent elements of an arbitration agreement consist of (i) a binding commitment to arbitration by the parties, (ii) on an arbitrable matter, which is (iii) recorded in writing. An arbitration agreement may be executed in the form of a signed agreement or an arbitration clause (as an integral part of an agreement or by incorporation by reference) as well as in the form of an oral agreement recorded in an electronic exchange of communication between the parties. In multiple contracts, as long as the arbitration agreements are compatible, and the disputes arise from the same legal relationship, such disputes may be settled in a single arbitration.

Under Turkish law, the following disputes cannot be made the subject of arbitration:

- Disputes involving rights over immovable property.
- Intellectual property disputes.
- Disputes related to bankruptcy, insolvency and liquidation.
- Tax and customs disputes.
- Antitrust and unfair competition disputes.
- Labour disputes.
- Disputes related to administrative law, except for concession contracts.

An arbitration agreement is valid if it is valid under the law chosen by the parties or in the absence of such choice, under Turkish law as the law of the seat of arbitration. In addition, both MTK and ISTAC Rules recognise the principles of competence-competence and separability. The arbitration agreement is considered autonomous and shall be treated independently from the underlying agreement. Consequently, a decision rendering the main contract null and void shall not, *ipso facto*, affect the validity of the arbitration agreement.

Arbitration procedure

ISTAC arbitral proceedings start with submission of the request for arbitration and deposit of the registration fee to the Secretariat of ISTAC ("Secretariat"). Unless agreed otherwise, the seat of arbitration shall be Istanbul. ISTAC Rules allow that hearings may take place in any place other than the seat of arbitration.

Arbitral proceedings shall be governed by the ISTAC Rules. In case the ISTAC Rules are silent, the rules agreed by the parties shall apply. If there is no such agreement, a sole arbitrator or the arbitral tribunal may designate the applicable rules to the arbitral proceedings. In cases of taking evidence, this may include IBA Rules on the Taking of Evidence and Turkish professional rules of conduct for attorneys concerning privileges and rules on disclosure of information and documents under the Turkish Civil Procedure Law.

Under MTK, parties to an arbitration may freely choose the applicable law or rules to the procedure. In the absence of such preference by the parties, the arbitrator or the arbitral tribunal shall apply MTK provisions and if MTK is silent, the respective provisions of the Turkish Civil Procedure Law. At its discretion, the arbitral tribunal may decide to hear expert witnesses. MTK also allows party-appointed witnesses. Tribunals may seek judicial assistance from civil courts of first instance concerning matters of taking evidence. Civil courts of first instance shall apply evidence rules of the Turkish Civil Procedure Law.

Unless otherwise agreed by parties, ISTAC arbitration is confidential. Evidence and pleadings can be kept confidential based on the agreement of the parties in the arbitration agreement or in the terms of reference and in MTK proceedings in the assignment certificate (*görev belgesi*).

Arbitrators

Both MTK and ISTAC Rules follow UNCITRAL Model Law's principles applicable to arbitrators. Party autonomy in constituting the arbitral tribunal, deciding upon the number of arbitrators, and prohibition of discrimination based on nationality, are common provisions adopted from UNCITRAL Model Law. The parties may choose the arbitrators directly or in case there is disagreement, may delegate to an appointing authority; i.e. under MTK to the civil courts of first instance and under ISTAC Rules, the International Board of Arbitration.

Under MTK, the scope of review by the civil court of first instance is broader than that of the International Board of Arbitration. The court, in particular, is authorised to review applications for appointment and objections to arbitral jurisdiction, disclosures and challenges to the impartiality of arbitrators.

Both MTK and ISTAC Rules impose upon the arbitrator a mandatory duty to disclose circumstances which would give rise to justifiable doubts as to his or her impartiality or independence before and throughout the arbitral proceedings.

Under MTK, parties may freely agree on the procedure to challenge an arbitrator. If no such agreement exists, the default procedure provided in MTK shall apply. The challenging party notifies the other party with a written statement including reasons for the challenge, and if there is no agreement or withdrawal, it may seek court intervention. Challenge to the entire or majority of the members of a tribunal shall be made to the court. The time limit to raise a challenge is 30 days.

When an arbitrator fails to perform his duties or there is impossibility to act, his mandate may be terminated by voluntary withdrawal, agreement by parties or by court intervention. Termination of the mandate of an arbitrator does not end the arbitral proceedings but a substitute arbitrator is appointed to replace him. In the event of termination of the mandate of the entire or majority of the members of a tribunal, the arbitral proceedings ends. If an arbitrator fails to perform his duties for no justifiable reason, he shall be liable to indemnify the parties for any losses caused.

ISTAC Rules set a default mechanism for challenging arbitrators. The challenge request shall be made to the Secretariat by submitting a reasoned statement. The time limit for raising a challenge is 30 days. In case there is no agreement or withdrawal, the International Board of Arbitration will decide on the challenge request. If the challenge is accepted, or an arbitrator becomes unable *de facto* or *de jure* to perform his duties, the Board may decide to terminate the arbitrator's mandate. Termination does not lead to the end of the arbitral proceedings, but the terminated arbitrator shall be replaced. If an arbitrator is replaced after the closing of the proceedings, the Board may decide that the remaining arbitrators can terminate the arbitral proceedings without substituting the terminated arbitrator.

The decisions on appointment, challenge and replacement of arbitrators rendered by the appointing authorities shall be final.

Interim relief

MTK and ISTAC Rules accept the power of the arbitral tribunal to order interim measures besides the courts, both before and during the arbitral proceedings. However, the arbitral tribunal cannot order a preliminary injunction or a preliminary attachment order (i.e. seizing of assets) that is enforceable by national execution offices, and interim measures that relate to third parties would require involvement of national courts.

Prior to the arbitrators taking duty, a party may apply directly to the Secretariat to obtain interim legal protection pursuant to the ISTAC Emergency Arbitrator Rules. The arbitral tribunal may order a party to put up appropriate security. If a party does not comply with the decision of the arbitral tribunal, the party that is seeking the interim measure may apply to national courts to issue an interim measure under the Turkish Civil Procedure Law and Execution and Bankruptcy Law. Requesting an interim measure from the court will not waive the arbitration agreement or affect the powers of the arbitral tribunal. Although in theory, courts may assist the arbitration process by ordering injunctions, no such precedent is publicly available.

Arbitration award

Provisions of MTK and ISTAC Rules as to form and contents of the arbitral award are similar. The award shall be reasoned and state the names of parties and arbitrators, the decision and its date and the seat of arbitration. The arbitral tribunal may render partial awards. The final award shall be made in writing, signed and notified to the parties.

Parties, within 30 days from notification of the award, may request a correction of computational and clerical errors or an interpretation of the award from the court or, in case of ISTAC arbitration, from the Secretariat.

Parties may also seek an additional award from the arbitral tribunal concerning matters omitted from the award. The arbitral tribunal renders the additional award within 60 days from receipt of such request. Decisions concerning the correction and interpretation of awards shall become an integral part of the final award. Issuance of the final award terminates the mandate of the arbitral tribunal and ends the arbitration proceedings.

The award shall fix the costs of arbitration, and legal and expert fees and expenses. The arbitral tribunal may fix an advance payment on costs, taking into consideration the facts, the nature of the dispute and the length of the arbitration. Upon request, the arbitral tribunal may decide to separate the advance on costs and shall render the final allocation of costs in its final award. Failure to remit an advance on costs may result in suspension of arbitral proceedings. Unless one of the parties decides to substitute payment of the non-performing party within 30 days (15 days in ISTAC arbitration), the arbitral tribunal terminates the arbitration proceedings.

Challenge of the arbitration award

The issue to set aside the arbitral award and applicable standards therefor are regulated under MTK. Application to set aside an arbitral award is not considered an appeal proceeding in which the correction of the decision on merits is reviewed. The request for setting aside or annulment of an award is made before the competent civil court of first instance within 30 days from notice of the award (or from notice of the decision correcting or interpreting the award).

MTK provides the following grounds for challenging an arbitral award:

- Grounds to be considered on the court's own motion:
  - the subject matter of arbitration is not capable of settlement by arbitration under Turkish law; or
  - the award is in conflict with Turkish public policy.
- Grounds to be proven by the challenging party:
  - incapacity of a party or invalidity of the arbitration agreement under applicable law or failing an indication thereon, under Turkish law;
  - the party making the application was not given proper notice of the appointment of an arbitrator or of the appeal proceedings, or was otherwise unable to present his case;
  - the award exceeds the term of the submission of award;
  - irregularity in the arbitral procedure or composition of the tribunal;
  - violation of the equal treatment principle; or
  - the award deals with a dispute not contemplated by or not falling within the terms of the submission to arbitration, or contains decisions beyond the scope of the submission to arbitration.

Parties are allowed to partially or wholly waive the right to request annulment. Turkish-resident parties can waive the right only when the award is rendered. Foreign residents can waive it in advance. The decision of annulment is subject to appeal before the Turkish Court of Appeal (*Yargitay*) but a higher level of judicial review (*karar duzeltme*) is not available. Grounds for appeal are limited to the grounds for annulment. Request for annulment is not very common in Turkish practice and therefore, Turkish courts would only set aside an arbitral award if the defect leading to annulment is clear and evident.

Enforcement of the arbitration award

Between 1927 and 1982, recognition and enforcement of arbitral awards were subject to Turkish Procedural Code and the Turkish Court of Appeal made no distinctions between domestic and foreign awards. From 1982 onwards, enactment of Turkish Private

International Law and Procedural Law established the principles for recognition and enforcement of foreign arbitral awards in Turkey (PILA Law No. 2675: Articles 43 through 45). Turkey ratified the New York Convention on the Recognition and Enforcement of Foreign Arbitral Awards, which entered into force as of 30 September 1992. PILA Law No. 2675 was replaced with PILA Law No. 5718, effective from 12 December 2007. PILA 5718 basically incorporated the text of the NY Convention.

The 1982 Constitution of the Republic of Turkey and PILA 5718 have provisions giving priority to international treaties over national laws. Turkey has concluded bilateral treaties on judicial assistance, some involving provisions for enforcement of foreign arbitral awards. Turkey also ratified multilateral investment conventions, i.e. the ICSID Convention and Energy Charter Treaty and Energy Charter Protocol, which have their own regimes for enforcement of foreign arbitral awards.

The NY Convention is the most important instrument in the recognition and enforcement of foreign arbitral awards and since PILA gives priority to international treaties, it is applied as the first resort. Hence, the PILA provisions on enforcement are rarely used. The NY Convention is applied in Turkey if the award is made in a contracting state. The NY Convention does not provide rules applicable to enforcement proceedings, but in Article III refers to the rules of procedure of the enforcing state. Therefore, procedural rules under PILA 5718 shall apply to enforcements under the NY Convention.

Under PILA 5718, request for enforcement is made to the civil court of first instance agreed by the parties; if no such agreement exists, to the court of domicile of the party against whom the enforcement is sought; if there is no domicile, to the court of the place against whom enforcement is sought has its ordinary residence; in the absence of ordinary residence, to the court of place where properties that can be seized are located. The request shall include original arbitration agreement or clause, and a final, binding and certified copy of the arbitral award together with a certified Turkish translation. Enforcement proceedings are considered expedited proceedings, although a hearing must be set. Enforcement cases can be heard during judicial holiday and the decision of the civil court of first instance shall be subject to appellate review.

Turkish courts may refuse enforcement request based on Article V of the NY Convention (which are also incorporated into Article 62 of PILA 5718) as follows:

- Grounds to be considered upon court's own motion:
  - the subject matter of the difference is not capable of settlement by arbitration under Turkish law; or
  - the award would be contrary to Turkish public policy.
- Grounds to be proven by the challenging party:
  - incapacity of a party or invalidity of arbitration agreement under applicable law or failing an indication thereon, under Turkish law;
  - the party making the application was not given proper notice of the appointment of arbitrator or of the appeal proceedings, or was otherwise unable to present their case;
  - the composition of the arbitral authority or arbitral procedure was not in accordance with the agreement of the parties, or failing such agreement, was not in accordance with the law of the country where the arbitration took place;
  - the award deals with a dispute not contemplated by or not falling within the terms of the submission to arbitration, or contains decisions beyond the scope of the submission to arbitration; or

- the award has not yet become binding on the parties or has been set aside or suspended by a competent authority of the country in which, or under the law of which, that award was made.

The Turkish Court of Appeal has a pro-arbitration stand in its consistent decisions on upholding enforcement of foreign arbitral awards over the last two decades.

Concerning preliminary issues of partial enforcement and *revision au fond*, the Court of Appeal shares the common view that: (i) the enforcing court has discretion to grant partial enforcement if the enforceable part of the award is distinguishable and quantifiable for the purpose of enforcement (Yargitay 19th Civil Chamber, E.2003/7270, K. 2003/12888, T.18.12.2003); and that (ii) the court before which the enforcement is sought cannot review the merits of the case by rejecting the allegation of violation of the right to assert defences (Yargitay 19th Civil Chamber, E.2000/7171, K. 2000/7602, T.09.11.2000).

Concerning grounds for refusal of enforcement, the Court of Appeal again has made significant improvements by changing its older precedents, especially with respect to violations of Turkish public policy.

In its infamous 1976 *Keban Dam* decision (Yargitay 15th Civil Chamber, E.1617, K. 1052, T.10.03.1976), the Turkish Court of Appeal found the application of ICC Rules of Arbitration and submission of statement of claim to the ICC Secretariat to be a side-stepping of Turkish Procedural Law and considered certification of the award by the ICC Court of Arbitration to be a violation of the Turkish public policy. The Court of Appeal later changed this view and decided that certification of the awards by the ICC Court of Arbitration pursuant to the ICC Rules did not violate Turkish public policy, and that such provision of the ICC Rules did not infringe the independence of the arbitrators (Yargitay 15th Civil Chamber, E.2383, K. 3667, T.10.07.1991).

Similarly, in its highly criticised 1996 *Soma Power Plant* decision (Yargitay 15th Civil Chamber K. 1996/627, T.01.02.1996 and General Assembly of Civil Chambers, E.1999/15235, K. 1999/273, T.05.05.1999), the Court of Appeal interpreted parties' choice of "Turkish laws in force" in the agreement to cover both laws applicable to the substance of the dispute and to the arbitration proceedings, i.e. Turkish procedural law, whereas both the arbitral tribunal and Swiss Federal Court interpreted the scope of choice of law to cover Turkish substantive laws only, in the absence of an open reference to the Turkish procedural laws. The Turkish Court of Appeal upheld the decision of the lower court refusing enforcement, on the ground that the award infringed upon parties' choice of law applicable to the arbitration, which it considered a violation of Turkish public policy.

Turkish Court of Appeal, in a later decision (Yargitay 11th Civil Chamber E.2000/3992, K. 2000/4704, T.26.05.2000) changed its view on the scope of choice-of-law clauses and upheld the enforcement of the foreign arbitral award, stating that parties' reference to apply ICC arbitration and conciliation rules, and the absence of any specific reference to Turkish procedural laws in the governing law clause, would imply that the parties had mutually agreed to apply the procedural laws of the foreign competent authority.

In addition to the affirmative trend on the judicial side, the Turkish government incentivised enforcement lawsuits by waiving the court fees formerly applied to the certification of domestic arbitral awards and enforcement of foreign arbitral awards pursuant to Article 36 of the General Communique No. 77 on Judicial Fees Law, effective 4 October 2016.

Investment arbitration

Enforcement of ICSID arbitral awards and Energy Charter Treaty awards is subject to special regimes promulgated under such treaties. The ICSID Convention provides that each party must abide by and comply with the terms of the award. Unless an ICSID award is annulled or the enforcement is stayed, contracting states are bound to enforce an ICSID award. The Energy Charter Treaty provides that arbitral awards, including interest, shall be final and binding upon the parties. The Energy Charter Treaty requires contracting states to recognise and enforce the awards as if they were a final decision of their domestic courts. Self-executing force of ICSID and Energy Charter Treaty awards does not at all interfere with the issue of sovereign immunity from execution at the enforcement stage.

Turkey has been a party to numerous investment treaty arbitration cases under the ICSID Convention and the Energy Charter Treaty. In case of an unfavourable decision, given that sovereign immunity protection applies to property allocated to public services, Turkey accepts the award without need to resort to the enforcement mechanism, and immediately pays the investors upon notification of the award.

A summary of the ICSID arbitration decisions involving Turkey is provided below:

The first ICSID arbitration case was initiated by Motorola Credit Corporation Inc. against Turkey on 21 November 2005. The case was later settled between the parties, ending the ICSID arbitration.

A second ICSID arbitration case was brought against Turkey on 22 March 2002 by an American investor, PSEG Global Inc., in relation to the Konya-Ilgin power plant concession contract. Turkey's jurisdictional objection, alleging no investment had actually been made by the Claimant, was dismissed. Turkey was ordered to pay PSEG Global Inc. an amount of US$ 9,061,480 in damages together with interest, and an amount of US$ 4,602,750 to cover arbitration costs and expenses. Turkey paid these sums to the Claimant without having to go through an enforcement procedure.

Turkey has been successful in other ICSID arbitrations brought against it under the Energy Charter Treaty and bilateral investment treaties signed between Claimants' states and Turkey, concerning disputes under power generation and distribution concession contracts, namely the cases brought by: (i) the Cypriot Libananco Holdings Co. dated 19 April 2006; (ii) the Polish Europe Cement Investment and Trade S.A. dated 6 March 2007; (iii) the Polish Cementownia "Nowa Huta" S.A. dated 15 April 2008; and (iv) the Dutch Alapli Elektrik B.V. dated 16 July 2008.

The arbitral tribunals hearing the first three of these cases dismissed each one based on lack of jurisdiction under the BITs, and the Energy Charter Treaty due to the Claimants' failure to prove ownership or control of the investment in accordance with the respective provisions of the BITs and the Energy Charter Treaty at the time of alleged expropriation by Turkey. It was also noted in the arbitral awards that these independent proceedings were in fact brought in parallel by the claimants, each of which had an affiliation with the Turkish resident Uzan Group who, in bad faith, allegedly restructured their shareholdings in the Cukurova Elektrik A.S. and Kepez Elektrik Turk A.S. after being in dispute with Turkey concerning purported expropriation of CEAS and KEPEZ with the aim of obtaining damages under the investment shield of the Energy Charter Treaty and ICSID Convention. The arbitration cases were dismissed in the above order on 2 September 2011, 13 August 2009 and 17 September 2009, respectively.

The dispute in ICSID arbitration brought by Alapli Elektrik B.V. against Turkey concerned a concession contract to develop, finance, construct, own, operate and transfer a combined power plant in Turkey. The concession contract was signed by the first project company in October 1998. In April 1999, Alapli Elektrik B.V. was established as a subsidiary of one of the project sponsors, and in March 2000 acquired the shares of a second project company. The second project company was then assigned the rights of the first project company in the concession contract and the assignment was approved by the Turkish Ministry in November 2000. In 2000, Turkey implemented a series of legislative changes to concession contracts, such as converting their administrative law nature to private law, eliminating Treasury Guarantees and bringing certain restrictions to energy sales agreements. Claimant sought relief, alleging that these legislative changes led to a loss of its investment and violated provisions of the Turkey-Netherlands BIT and the Energy Charter Treaty.

On 16 July 2012, the arbitral tribunal dismissed all Alapli Elektrik's claims for lack of jurisdiction under the Netherlands-Turkey BIT and the Energy Charter Treaty, based on the findings that the: (i) Dutch company acquired its investment with the sole purpose of manufacturing international jurisdiction at a time when the project was in delay under the concession contract commitments; and (ii) the facts that were at the root of the dispute (i.e. that the new Law No. 4501 would involve negotiating a new contract and renegotiating the tariff and other terms) were already known to the sponsors of the project. In conclusion, the arbitral tribunal decided that the investment was not a *bona fide* investment, as it was performed at a time when the facts of the dispute were already known and that a dispute was already a high probability; therefore, the tribunal had no jurisdiction over the investment as it could not benefit from the international protection granted by the ICSID/BIT/ECT mechanism.

Prof. Av. Esra Bicen
Tel: +90 212 283 0053 / Email: ebicen@eblegal.net

Professor Bicen has 20 years of experience as a litigation and transaction lawyer in Turkey and in the United States. Her practice, lectures and publications focus on corporate, commercial (gaming, fintech, healthcare) and financial compliance, ISDA, EPC, procurement contracts and international arbitration.

From 1997 to 2000, she practised with a leading Istanbul law firm specialising in international investments, cross-border financings, public tenders and dispute resolution. From 2003 to 2007, she practised complex litigation with a leading American law firm. Between 2008 and 2011, she served as a General Counsel responsible for Ernst & Young Central and Southeast Europe area, and headed EY's investment consulting firm in Turkey.

In 2011, she was appointed as a part-time faculty member at John F. Kennedy University School of Law while continuing her law practice with a tier-one Istanbul law firm. Since 2015, she has maintained her law practice EB LEGAL in Istanbul and Silicon Valley and continues to teach at John F. Kennedy University School of Law on contract law and international arbitration. Professor Bicen is a member of the New York State and Istanbul Bars.

EB LEGAL

Nisbetiye On Residence 44, Nisbetiye Cad. No. 10, Levent, 34340 Istanbul, Turkey
Tel: +90 212 283 0053 / Fax: +90 212 283 0057 / URL: www.eblegal.net

UAE

Thanos Karvelis & Maria Palmou
Galadari Advocates & Legal Consultants

Introduction

Arbitration in the UAE is governed by the provisions of the UAE Civil Procedure Code (CPC, Federal Law No. 11 of 1992 as amended) that are specific to arbitration, namely Articles 203–218, 235–238 (what is known as the Arbitration Chapter). UAE is a civil law jurisdiction, therefore the CPC draws from the civil law tradition. The Arbitration Chapter applies in arbitrations seated in any of the seven Emirates that comprise UAE (Abu Dhabi, Dubai, Sharjah, Ajman, Umm al Quwain, Ras al Khaimah and Fujeirah).

However, the Arbitration Chapter will not apply where the seat of arbitration is Dubai International Financial Centre (DIFC). DIFC, a free zone within the Emirate of Dubai, is a common law jurisdiction empowered by federal legislation to enact autonomously its own regulatory and legal framework for all civil and commercial matters and has its own independent courts. The DIFC has its own arbitration law, DIFC Arbitration Law No. 1 of 2008, based upon the UNCITRAL Model Law on International Commercial Arbitration (unlike the Arbitration Chapter), which will apply in arbitrations seated therein. Parties may freely provide for the DIFC as the seat of the arbitration irrespective of whether there is any connection of the parties or the matter in dispute with DIFC.

Similarly, the Arbitration Chapter will not apply in arbitrations seated in Abu Dhabi Global Market (ADGM), a free zone within the Emirate of Abu Dhabi, which is also an autonomous common law jurisdiction with its own laws and courts, including an arbitration-specific legal framework (Arbitration Regulations 2015).

The Arbitration Chapter will be the main focus of this chapter.

UAE law recognises the right of the contracting parties to agree on the rules that will apply in the arbitration proceedings save for certain mandatory provisions (Article 212 CPC). In most arbitrations in the UAE contracting parties adopt institutional arbitration rules, including rules issued by well recognised international bodies such as the ICC International Court of Arbitration, or the LCIA, or, less often, the UNCITRAL Arbitration Rules. In parallel, there is a significant, and increasing, number of arbitration institutions based in the UAE. A by no means exhaustive list includes the following:

- *Dubai International Arbitration Centre (DIAC)*

  DIAC is currently one of the busiest arbitration centres in the Gulf region. The rules in force are the 2007 Arbitration Rules. The default language of arbitration is English. DIAC has recently issued new Arbitration Rules; however, the new rules are not yet effective at the time of writing (March 2018).

- *The Abu Dhabi Commercial, Conciliation and Arbitration Centre (ADCCAC)*

  ADCCAC was the first centre in the GCC to solve national and international commercial disputes. ADCCAC is often the preferred venue for the resolution of disputes by Abu Dhabi-based parties. The rules in force are the 2013 Procedural Regulations of Arbitration. Notably, the default language of the arbitration proceedings is Arabic, unless the parties agree otherwise.
- *DIFC–LCIA*

  DIFC–LCIA was established in 2008 in association with the London Court of International Arbitration (LCIA). DIFC–LCIA administers arbitrations under the DIFC–LCIA Arbitration Rules 2016 largely modelled on the LCIA Arbitration Rules. The DIFC–LCIA Arbitration Centre is independent of the DIFC Courts. The popularity of DIFC–LCIA is on the rise.
- *Sharjah International Commercial Arbitration Centre (Takheem) (SICAC)*

  SICAC is based in the Emirate of Sharjah and was established in 2009 under the auspices of the Sharjah Chamber of Commerce and Industry. SICAC administers arbitrations under its own Arbitration Rules.
- *Ras Al Khaimah Centre of Reconciliation and Commercial Arbitration (RAKCRCA)*

  RAKCRCA is based in the Emirate of Ras Al Khaimah and was established in 2008. RAKCRCA forms part of the Ras Al Khaimah Chamber of Commerce and Industry. RAKCRCA has issued its own arbitration rules (Articles of Association of the RAKCRCA).
- *Emirates Maritime Arbitration Centre (EMAC)*

  Based in DIFC, EMAC was recently established by the Dubai Government and aims to provide specialised maritime arbitration services. EMAC supervises mediation and arbitration processes in accordance with the EMAC Arbitration Rules effective as of June 2016. EMAC Arbitration Rules provide for a hybrid form of *ad hoc* arbitration, with some case management.
- *Islamic Centre for Reconciliation and Arbitration (IICRA)*

  IICRA is a non-profit independent organisation active since 2007, facilitating the resolution of Islamic finance and banking disputes under Islamic *Shari'a*. IICRA supervises arbitrations under its own set of rules.

Parties may combine any rules of their choosing with any seat within the UAE. Such selection will in turn determine the applicable arbitration law and curial courts. However, the selection of DIFC or ADGM as the seat must be explicit. For example, if the arbitration clause simply refers to "Dubai" as the seat, then "onshore Dubai" will be the seat (and thus the Arbitration Chapter applicable), not DIFC.

Under UAE law, there is no sovereign immunity as such and government entities may freely agree to arbitration as a means of dispute resolution. However, no claim may be brought against government entities without first obtaining consent from the Ruler's Court, a process that aims primarily to promote amicable settlement. In any event, an arbitral award (or court judgment) may not be enforced by means of seizing or attaching public property (Article 247 CPC and other legislation specific to some Emirates).

The UAE is a party to the New York Convention on the Recognition and Enforcement of Foreign Arbitral Awards (1958) without any reservations (Federal Decree No. 43 of 2006). The New York Convention entered into force in the UAE on 19 November 2006.

Other multilateral conventions relating to the recognition and enforcement of arbitral awards, to which UAE is a party, include the following:

- The Riyadh Convention on Judicial Cooperation between States of the Arab League (1983). The Riyadh Convention entered into force in 1999.
- The GCC Convention for the Execution of Judgments, Delegations and Judicial Notifications (1987). The GCC Convention entered into force in 1995.
- The ICSID Convention (1965) ratified by the UAE in 1982.

In addition, UAE is a party to numerous relevant bilateral treaties.

Arbitration agreement

Article 203 CPC provides the substantive and formal requirements for a valid arbitration agreement.

In particular, the agreement to subject disputes to arbitration may be included in the original contract, usually in the form of an arbitration clause or, less frequently, in the form of a separate document, or entered into subsequently, for example in the form of terms of reference (Article 203(1) CPC). The arbitration agreement may also be incorporated by reference, as in a charter party. It may include all or only some of the disputes arising under the relevant contract. The wording of the arbitration agreement must be clear and undisputable.

Notably, execution of terms of reference is not mandatory under the Arbitration Chapter but is very often the (best) practice (although certain local arbitration rules specifically require the execution of such terms, for example Article 36 paragraph 4 of the ADCCAC Procedural Regulations of Arbitration).

The arbitration agreement must be in writing (Article 203(2) CPC). This will usually mean the requirement to actually sign the relevant page containing the arbitration clause. However, it is accepted that the arbitration agreement may be entered into by means of exchange of correspondence.

Importantly, the person signing the arbitration agreement is required to have special authority (Article 203(4) CPC). Such special authority may be presumed for legal representatives of corporate entities, for example managers of limited liability companies established under the UAE Commercial Companies Law.

The subject matter of the dispute must be specified in the arbitration agreement (Article 203(3) CPC). It is generally accepted that both contractual claims and claims in tort relating to a contractual relationship may be subjected to arbitration.

However, arbitration is not permissible where the subject matter of the dispute is not capable of being reconciled or where the parties may not dispose of the disputed right (Article 203(4) CPC). Generally, matters that may not be arbitrated include criminal matters, bankruptcy, matters of public policy (for example, disputes relating to the registration of real estate transactions), labour disputes, and disputes arising from registered commercial agency and distribution agreements.

Although the CPC does not expressly provide for the doctrine of separability, this doctrine is recognised by the UAE courts. In addition, arbitration rules of local institutes do explicitly provide for the separability of the arbitration clause from the main contract (for example, Article 6.1 of the DIAC Arbitration Rules).

Similarly, *kompetenz-kompetenz* is also recognised by prevailing case law. Again, local arbitration rules do include explicit provisions to this effect (for example, Article 6.2 of DIAC Arbitration Rules).

While a valid arbitration agreement, irrespective of the seat of the arbitration, prohibits a contracting party to bring action before UAE courts, if the other party fails to object at the first hearing, then the arbitration agreement is deemed waived and the courts will be competent to hear the dispute (Article 203(5) CPC).

Arbitration procedure

Where institutional rules apply, the arbitration will commence in accordance with the relevant provisions, usually with the filing of a request for arbitration to the arbitration institution. In *ad hoc* arbitration, the arbitration will commence by means of a notice of arbitration sent by the claimant to the respondent. The notice will usually include the claimant's proposal for the appointment of arbitrator(s) or a proposed process for such appointment (for example, appointment by an arbitration institution – without, however, applying necessarily the respective arbitration rules in the arbitration).

Failure of a party to participate in the arbitral proceedings does not prevent the progress of the proceedings and the issuance of the arbitral award (Article 208(2) CPC).

Contracting parties may agree the applicable procedural rules freely without being bound by the procedural requirements of the CPC (for example, with regard to rules of evidence) save for those procedural provisions set out in the Arbitration Chapter (Article 212(1) CPC).

Such mandatory provisions include the right to a fair trial (Article 212(1) CPC), the impartiality and independence of the arbitrator(s) (Article 207(4) CPC), the requirement for an uneven number of arbitrators (Article 206 CPC), or the examination of witnesses of facts and witnesses of expertise under oath (Article 211 CPC).

The choice of procedural rules is usually made by reference to rules of an arbitration institution. Local institutional rules include provisions regarding evidence and generally give wide powers to the tribunal to decide on the rules of evidence to be applied (for example, Article 27.2 of the DIAC Arbitration Rules). In *ad hoc* arbitrations, if the parties are unable to agree on the procedural rules, the same will be decided by the arbitrator (Article 212(1) CPC). It is not uncommon for the IBA Rules on the Taking of Evidence to form part of the rules of evidence applicable to the proceedings.

That said, it should be noted that UAE is a civil law jurisdiction, therefore disclosure requirements in litigation before courts are generally very limited. Among others, a litigant is generally not obliged to disclose detrimental information. While contracting parties are free to choose their own process, and therefore agree to more extensive disclosures, parties based in the UAE, and generally parties more familiar with civil law doctrines and practices, are rather reluctant to accept wider disclosure requirements.

In addition, the principle of "without prejudice" is not readily recognised by the UAE legal system. Consequently, documents marked as such, usually correspondence relating to settlement proposals and negotiations, may be produced and will be admitted by the arbitral tribunal, unless the parties expressly agree to treat such correspondence as confidential and not disclose it in the arbitration.

Unless otherwise agreed by the parties or provided for in the adopted arbitration rules, the arbitral tribunal is required to call the first hearing within 30 days from acceptance of its appointment (Article 208(1) CPC). In practice, this will be a preliminary hearing for the arbitrator to set out, in consultation with the parties, the detailed process of the arbitration.

There is no provision in the Arbitration Chapter requiring that a hearing on the merits of the dispute takes place and the arbitration may be conducted on a documents-only basis. That said, it is generally expected that written testimonies of factual and expert witnesses are subject to cross-examination at a main hearing. Local arbitration rules include specific provisions to this effect (for example, Article 29.4 of the DIAC Arbitration Rules). Hearings may be conducted by means of a teleconference (this is particularly common for the first, preliminary hearing) and/or may be held at a venue outside the seat of the arbitration convenient for the parties and/or the tribunal.

Under the Arbitration Chapter, the courts may intervene in the arbitration upon referral by the arbitral tribunal to penalise witnesses who fail to appear or are reluctant to answer questions, and to order the production of documents in the possession of third parties that are necessary to render an award or appoint judicial experts. In such a case, the arbitral proceedings must be suspended until the issuance of the court judgment (Article 209(2) CPC). Moreover, the same provision of the Arbitration Chapter requires the suspension of the arbitration proceedings if a preliminary issue arises that falls outside the jurisdiction of the arbitrator, if a document produced in the arbitration is challenged as forged, or another issue of criminal nature arises, in all cases until issuance of the judgment of the competent court.

Notably, neither the DIFC Arbitration Law nor the ADGC Arbitration Regulations contain similar provisions. In addition, Article 27.4 of the ADCCAC Procedural Regulations of Arbitration stipulates that the tribunal has the discretion to continue the arbitration if it considers that a decision on such preliminary issue or criminal matter is not required for the adjudication of the dispute at hand.

The confidentiality of the arbitration proceedings is recognised in the UAE despite the lack of express legislative provisions. Local institutional rules do include provisions to this effect.

Arbitrators

The parties are free to agree the appointment of arbitrator(s) whom they consider suitable, usually by reference to the appointment provisions of the arbitration rules that the parties have adopted (for example, Articles 8–11 of the DIAC Arbitration Rules, Articles 5–8 of the DIFC–LCIA Arbitration Rules). In *ad hoc* arbitrations, if the parties fail to agree, the arbitrator(s) will be appointed by the court upon application of one of the parties (Article 204(1) CPC). The decision of the court cannot be appealed (Article 204(2) CPC).

The arbitrator must not be a minor, legally incapacitated, under guardianship, deprived of his civil rights following criminal conviction, or bankrupt (Article 206(1) CPC). There are no restrictions regarding nationality, gender or faith. Some arbitration rules of local institutions do provide that the sole arbitrator or the chairman of the tribunal may not be of the same nationality as any party unless agreed otherwise (for example, Article 10 of DIAC Arbitration Rules, Article 6 of the DIFC–LCIA Arbitration Rules).

The Arbitration Chapter does not include any provision with regard to the default number of arbitrators, other than that the number must be uneven (Article 206(2) CPC). On the other hand, arbitration rules of local institutions do provide that the default position is sole arbitrator (for example, Article 8.2 of DIAC Arbitration Rules, Article 5.8 of the DIFC–LCIA Arbitration Rules).

The arbitrator(s) must accept their appointment in writing (Article 207(1) CPC). If they then resign without good reason, they may be liable to pay compensation (Article 207(2) CPC).

Arbitrators cannot be dismissed, except with the agreement of all parties. Nevertheless, at a party's request, the court can remove an arbitrator if it is proven that the arbitrator deliberately acted negligently (Article 207(3) CPC).

Furthermore, an arbitrator may be recused by the court at a party's request on the same grounds as those applicable for the recusal of a court judge, essentially circumstances compromising his integrity (Article 207(4) CPC). The application for challenge must be filed within five days from either the appointment of the arbitrator or the date on which the cause of disqualification occurs or becomes known. The court judgment is subject to appeal. It should be noted that the grounds for disqualification of an arbitrator are interpreted by the UAE courts narrowly (for example, an arbitrator will not be disqualified simply on the basis that he works for the same law firm as the counsel of one of the parties).

However, where the parties have agreed to apply institutional arbitration rules, any challenge against the arbitrator will be governed by such rules to the exclusion of the courts (for example, Articles 13 and 14 of the DIAC Arbitration Rules, Articles 10 and 11 of the DIFC–LCIA Arbitration Rules, Articles 11 and 12 of the ADCCAC Procedural Regulations of Arbitration).

Interim relief

UAE courts are empowered to grant interim measures before or after the commencement of arbitration proceedings, including in support of actions for the enforcement of arbitral awards (Article 22 CPC). Any agreement of the parties contracting out the power of the courts is void (Article 24 CPC). An application for interim measures before the courts does not constitute in itself a waiver of the arbitration clause. The power of UAE courts to render interim measures is irrespective of whether the arbitration is domestic (seated in the UAE) or foreign (seated outside UAE). The range of interim remedies available to the courts is wide. As confirmed by the relevant case law, such remedies may include attachment orders over immovable or movable assets in the UAE for the claimant to secure his claim or enforce an arbitral award in his favour, for example: deposits with banks or shares (Article 252 *et seq*. CPC); movable assets held, or payments due to the defendant by third parties (Article 257 *et seq*. CPC); arrest of vessels; orders preventing liquidation of bank guarantees issued in favour of the defendant (which are treated as attachments of the relevant instrument); imposition of a travel ban on an award debtor who refuses to comply (Article 329 CPC) or even detention of the same (Article 324 CPC); injunctions to preserve evidence; and orders for the production of documents in possession of third parties (Article 209(2) CPC).

Attachment orders, arguably the most common form of interim remedies sought, are granted *ex parte*. Where the attachment order is sought prior to the commencement of the arbitration, the claimant must commence arbitration proceedings within eight days, otherwise the order is deemed void (Articles 255(2), 261(2) CPC). The successful claimant may be required to provide appropriate security (and this is often done).

While there are no provisions in the UAE law that would give ground to the issuance of an "anti-suit injunction" of other (mainly common law) jurisdictions, the right of the defendant in an action before courts to object to the jurisdiction of the courts on the basis of the existence of an arbitration agreement (whether the arbitration proceedings are ongoing or not), as long as such defence is made in the first hearing of the action as provided by Article 203(5), has a similar, albeit limited, effect.

As for the powers of the arbitral tribunal to grant interim relief or order conservatory measures, there are no specific provisions in UAE law. However, local arbitration rules include detailed provisions to this effect (for example, Article 31 of the DIAC Arbitration Rules, Article 25 of the DIFC–LCIA Arbitration Rules, Article 25 of the ADCCAC Procedural Regulations of Arbitration).

In this context, the tribunal can issue any provisional orders, or take other interim or conservatory measures it considers necessary. Indicatively, the tribunal is empowered to take measures relating to the conservation, storage, sale or disposal of documents or goods which form part of the subject matter of the dispute (such as an order for deposit with a third party or an order for the sale of perishable goods); order a party to provide security for the amount in dispute or for arbitration costs (including legal fees); or in general, order on a provisional basis any relief which the tribunal would have power to grant in a final award. The tribunal may grant such interim relief, subject to appropriate security provided by the applicant. In practice, arbitral tribunals often grant interim relief.

It should be noted that the Arbitration Chapter lacks specific provisions for the recognition and enforcement of interim measures issued by arbitral tribunals by means of an application to UAE courts – similar, for example, to Article 17H of the UNCITRAL Model Law, Article 24(2) the DIFC Arbitration Law, or Section 28 of the ADGM Arbitration Regulations. However, a successful applicant may rely on the wide wording of Article 22 CPC and apply to the UAE courts for a judgment in support of the arbitration proceedings.

Arbitration award

Under the Arbitration Chapter, the arbitration award must be issued in the UAE, otherwise it will be treated as a foreign arbitral award (Article 212(4) CPC). The award must be in writing, issued by majority, record any dissenting opinion, comprise a copy of the arbitration agreement, a summary of the parties' cases and the evidence produced, the reasoning, state the place and date of issuance, bear the signatures of all arbitrators (both its reasoning and dispositive parts) and, if an arbitrator refuses to sign, a statement to this effect (Article 212(5) CPC). The award is deemed issued on the date it is signed by all arbitrators (Article 212(7) CPC) and must be delivered to the parties within five days thereafter (Article 213(3) CPC).

The parties are free to agree the language of the award, which will be usually the language of the arbitration. In the absence of such agreement, the award must be written in Arabic (Article 212(6) CPC). However, an official Arabic translation will be required for recognition and enforcement purposes.

The above formal requirements are reflected to a great extent in local institutional arbitration rules (for example, Article 37 of the DIAC Arbitration Rules, Article 26 of the DIFC–LCIA Arbitration Rules, Article 25 of the ADCCAC Procedural Regulations of Arbitration).

The award must be rendered within six months from the date of the first hearing (Article 210(1) CPC), unless the parties agree otherwise explicitly or implicitly, or grant the arbitrator the power to extend that period, or, in rarer cases, the court extends it upon application of one of the parties (Article 210(2) CPC).

Awards may be interim as well as final and may also be by consent of the parties. The tribunal may award all forms of relief including damages (including loss of profit or opportunity), specific performance, and interim measures.

UAE law formally recognises payment of interest, and courts routinely enforce awards of interest. Tribunals will usually award interest at a rate of 9% per annum (although it is not unknown for tribunals to award interest at a rate as much as 12% in relation to commercial debts or as a punishment to recalcitrant parties). The parties are also free to stipulate an agreed rate of interest. Notably, an arbitral tribunal may award compound interest if so agreed by the parties, unlike courts that will only award simple interest.

With regard to costs, under the Arbitration Chapter the arbitrators may award their own fees and expenses and the costs of the arbitration against the losing party subject to amendments by the courts (Article 218 CPC). However, the meaning of arbitration costs is interpreted restrictively, and it is generally accepted that they do not include legal fees (but include fees and expenses of tribunal-appointed experts), unless the arbitration agreement, including the applicable institutional rules or the terms of reference if any, clearly empower the tribunal to award full costs.

In this context, rather recent case law interpreted the wording of DIAC Arbitration Rules (Article 37.10 and Article 2.1 of the Appendix – Costs of Arbitration thereof) as not to include legal costs within the meaning of the arbitration costs. Similar limitations to the power of the tribunal may apply on the face of the wording of Article 28 paragraphs 7 and 9 of the ADCCAC Procedural Regulations of Arbitration. On the other hand, Article 28.3 of the DIFC−LCIA Arbitration Rules expressly provides the power of the tribunal to award reasonable legal costs and expenses incurred by a party.

Generally, costs are allocated on the basis of the parties' relative success in the arbitration or in accordance with the principle that costs follow the event. An award on costs may be made after the issuance of the award on the merits of the dispute.

The award becomes *res judicata* with regard to its subject matter upon its issuance.

Enforcement and challenge of the arbitration award

Domestic awards

Under UAE law, an arbitration award is not subject to appeal on its merits (Article 217(1) CPC). However, enforcement of the award is subject to ratification by the courts (Article 215(1) CPC). In parallel, the losing party may apply to the courts for the nullification of the award (Article 216(1) CPC). There is no time limit for the ratification or annulment of an award.

The ratification process commences with a filing of an ordinary court action before the competent court of first instance. The award will not be reviewed on its merits, as confirmed by the constant jurisprudence of the UAE courts. The court will only ascertain that the arbitration was conducted in accordance with the requirements of the Arbitration Chapter, that the award meets the respective requirements with regard to its form and content, and that enforcement of the award will not violate public policy.

Once ratified, the award will be presented to the court of execution and will be enforced as any court judgment (Article 215(2) CPC).

Challenge of the award by the losing party is allowed only on the grounds set out in Article 216(1) CPC, essentially for defects of the arbitration agreement or procedural irregularities, i.e. without review of the award on its merits (although it is not uncommon for award debtors to resist enforcement on grounds having to do with the substance of the award). In particular, the award may be nullified only if:

- it is issued without or on the basis of an invalid or expired arbitration agreement (Article 216(1)(a) CPC), for example an arbitration agreement that is not in writing (Article 203(2) CPC);
- the tribunal exceeds its jurisdiction (Article 216(1)(a) CPC);

- the tribunal is not properly appointed (Article 216(1)(b) CPC);
- the arbitrator does not fulfil the requirements of the law, i.e. impartiality and independency (Article 207(4)CPC) as well as lack of the incapacitating instances of Article 206(1) (Article 216(1)(b) CPC);
- the award is issued by some of the arbitrators only (Article 216(1)(b) CPC);
- the subject matter of the dispute is not defined in the arbitration agreement (Article 216(1)(b) CPC);
- the person who concluded the arbitration lacked capacity (Article 216(1)(b) CPC);
- the award does not meet the requirements with regard to form and content (Article 216(1)(c) CPC), for example failure by the arbitrator to include the arbitration agreement in the award or to sign both the reasoning and the dispositive parts of the award (Article 212(5) CPC); or
- in case of other procedural defects having an effect on the award (Article 216(1)(b) CPC), for example, failure to provide to the losing party a fair opportunity to present its case (Article 212(1) CPC), failure to examine witnesses on oath (Article 211CPC), issuance of the award out of time without a valid extension (Article 210(1) and (2) CPC).

Public order is not specifically listed within the exhaustive list of grounds of Article 216 (1) CPC for the nullification of arbitration awards, although it may be argued that it is at least implied within the wording of Article 216(1)(c) CPC ("if there is a nullity in the award or a nullity of the proceedings having an effect on the award"). In any event, the UAE courts routinely include public order within the grounds preventing ratification, or allowing nullification, of arbitration awards and consider potential violations of the public order *ex officio*.

The definition of public order is found in Article 3 of the Law of Civil Transactions (UAE Federal Law No. 5 of 1985 as amended, the Civil Code) and is deemed to include matters relating to personal status such as marriage, inheritance and lineage, matters related to systems of government, freedom of trade, circulation of wealth, rules of individual ownership and the other rules and foundation upon which society is based, in such a manner as not to conflict with the definitive provisions and the fundamental principles of the Islamic *Shari'a*.

In practice, UAE courts tend to invoke violations of the public order in case of procedural irregularities, such as improper signing of the award (Article 212(5) CPC), even number of arbitrators (Article 206(2) CPC), lack of impartiality and independence of an arbitrator (Article 207(4) CPC), and whether the subject matter of a particular dispute may be referred to arbitration (Article 203(4) CPC).

The losing party may challenge an arbitration award in defence of an application for the ratification of the award by the successful party (Article 216(1) CPC). However, the UAE courts have confirmed that an application for the nullification of the award may be made prior to the commencement of the ratification proceedings. A waiver of the right to challenge is void if made prior to the issuance of the award (Article 216(2) CPC).

The judgment of the court for the ratification or annulment of an arbitration award is subject to appeal before the court of appeal and then before the court of cassation (Article 217(2) CPC). In practice, ratification/annulment proceedings may take between six months to more than one year.

Foreign awards

Enforcement of foreign arbitration awards is subject to essentially the same conditions applicable for the enforcement of foreign court judgments (Articles 235, 236 CPC).

However, by virtue of Article 238 CPC, provisions of multilateral and bilateral international treaties to which UAE is a party relating to the enforcement of foreign arbitration awards (and court judgments) supersede the provisions of the Arbitration Chapter.

As explained above, the New York Convention on the Recognition and Enforcement of Foreign Arbitral Awards (1958) has been incorporated in the UAE legal system since 2006. Therefore, enforcement of foreign arbitration awards is subject to the conditions set out in the New York Convention, including the grounds for the refusal of enforcement of Article V of the New York Convention (unless enforcement under another available bilateral or multilateral is more favourable, Article VII(1) of the New York Convention).

While there have been cases in the past where the UAE courts did not apply the New York Convention within the strict terms of its provisions (refusing, for example, enforcement of an international award for breach of procedural requirements of the Arbitration Chapter, such as the examination of witnesses under oath), in the past decade or so the UAE courts have consistently enforced international arbitration awards under the terms of the New York Convention, in compliance with its terms (albeit with some occasional setbacks). In this context, the courts have repeatedly confirmed that the procedural requirements of the Arbitration Chapter apply to domestic arbitration awards, while the requirements of the New York Convention apply to the enforcement of international arbitration awards.

For completeness, in the rare instances where the New York Convention (or some other multilateral or bilateral treaty) would not apply, the conditions of Articles 235 and 236 CPC for the enforcement of foreign arbitration awards are the following:

- reciprocity (Article 235(1) CPC);
- the UAE courts did not have jurisdiction to try the dispute (Article 235(2)(a) CPC);
- the arbitration tribunal had jurisdiction at the seat of the arbitration (Article 235(2)(b) CPC);
- the parties to arbitration were properly notified and represented (Article 235(2)(c) CPC);
- the arbitration award has acquired the force of *res judicata* in accordance with the law of the seat of the arbitration (Article 235(2)(d) CPC);
- the award does not conflict with a judgment of the UAE courts and does not conflict with *bonos mores* or public order of the UAE (Article 235(2)(e) CPC); or
- the subject matter of the dispute is arbitrable under the laws of the UAE and is capable of enforcement under the laws of the seat of the arbitration (Article 236 CPC).

Thanos Karvelis
Tel: +971 4377 8100 / Email: thanos.karvelis@galadarilaw.com

Thanos Karvelis leads the international arbitration and the construction practice of GALC, a leading law firm based in Dubai, UAE.

Thanos serves regularly as lead counsel in international commercial and construction arbitrations in Europe and the Middle East, both *ad hoc* and before many arbitration institutions (ICC, LCIA, DIAC, ADCCAC, DIFC-LCIA etc.). He is also listed with DIAC as a qualified Arbitrator.

He has over 20 years of experience in international construction projects as well as a strong track record in multi-billion cross-border corporate transactions in a wide range of industries.

He is the author of several publications in the fields of arbitration law and construction law.

Thanos holds an MSc in Business.

Maria Palmou
Tel: +971 4377 8100 / Email: maria@galadarilaw.com

Maria joined Galadari Advocates and Legal Consultants in 2015 as a Senior Associate. Based in Dubai, she focuses on commercial and dispute resolution work within the Arbitration, Corporate and Construction teams.

With degrees in both Law and Business, Maria's education and prior work experience enables her to have a deep understanding of financial and commercial principles. She has a wide range of experience across the corporate, commercial and construction sectors, with both front-end and dispute-resolution capabilities.

Her extensive involvement in arbitration and court litigation processes, as well as her experience in mergers & acquisitions and privatisation, commercial contracts and agreements, enables Maria to offer clients a comprehensive skill set.

Galadari Advocates & Legal Consultants

P.O. Box 7992, Dubai, United Arab Emirates
Tel: +971 4377 8100 / Fax: +971 4393 7755 / URL: www.galadarilaw.com

USA

Chris Paparella, Malik Havalic & Elizabeth Zhou
Hughes Hubbard & Reed LLP

Introduction

Despite its size and complex dual federal and state legal system, the United States is a favourable forum for international arbitration. The country's federal and state arbitration statutes and decisional law reflect a strong public policy in favour of arbitration, especially international arbitration. Nowhere is this pro-arbitration policy more clearly expressed than in the Federal Arbitration Act (the "FAA") and the cases decided under the act, which together govern international arbitration in the United States. The FAA has three chapters. The first chapter of the FAA governs cases involving interstate or foreign commerce. The second chapter implements the New York Convention, which the United States signed in 1958.[1] The third chapter of the FAA implements the Panama Convention, which the United States signed in 1978.[2]

The FAA governs the scope of arbitration agreements and requires courts to enforce the agreements according to their terms.[3] Taking into account the dual nature of the U.S. legal system, the FAA overrides or "pre-empts" state laws that conflict with federal arbitration law or undermine its policies. State law generally governs substantive issues, such as the interpretation of an arbitration agreement and its terms. In this regard, U.S. courts will ordinarily honour the parties' contractual choice of law, whether that of a U.S. state or another country.

New York, Florida, and Texas are particularly popular venues for international arbitration. The American Arbitration Association ("AAA") and its international division, the International Center for Dispute Resolution ("ICDR"), are both sited in New York but operate nationally and, in the case of the ICDR, internationally. They administer all types of domestic and international commercial disputes. The International Chamber of Commerce ("ICC") has a New York office with counsel and staff that administer North America-based ICC arbitrations. A number of other organisations, including JAMS and CPR, also administer international arbitrations in the United States.

Some states have created organisations to facilitate the administration of arbitration proceedings. For example, the New York International Arbitration Center was established in 2012 to provide access to information on arbitrating in New York and coordinate access to hearing locations. In Manhattan, the New York state court system has assigned a senior judge in its Commercial Division, the Hon. Charles E. Ramos, to hear court cases concerning international arbitration to ensure efficient and consistent adjudication.[4] In public remarks, Justice Ramos has emphasised his intent to apply the pro-arbitration policy set out in the FAA and federal case law, and his decisions since being appointed reflect the pro-arbitration public policy of the FAA and New York state law.

Arbitration agreements

The FAA's primary focus is to regulate how U.S. courts interact with arbitration proceedings.[5] Unlike arbitration laws in some other countries, the FAA does not contain extensive regulations on the necessary components and formalities of arbitration agreements. Instead, subject to the country's pro-arbitration policy, arbitration agreements in the United States are treated like other commercial contracts: courts look to generally applicable principles of contract law to interpret and give effect to arbitration agreements.[6] But both U.S. federal and state courts have developed a body of jurisprudence regarding the scope of arbitration agreements and the division of authority between arbitrators and courts.

Arbitrability

In determining whether a particular dispute is arbitrable, U.S. courts analyse the language of the relevant arbitration provision. Often, arbitration clauses will provide for the arbitration of all disputes "aris[ing] out of" or "relat[ing] to" the contract.[7] Where an agreement uses this type of language, U.S. courts will construe the arbitration provision "as broadly as possible" to allow for arbitration.[8]

Although U.S. courts favour arbitration and seek to read arbitration provisions broadly, parties are free to narrow the scope of arbitrable matters through a carefully crafted arbitration agreement. For instance, in *World Rentals and Sales, LCC v. Volvo Const. Equip. Rents, Inc.*, the court held that disputes involving a company's affiliates were not arbitrable because the arbitration agreement expressly excluded affiliates from the agreement to arbitrate.[9] The courts will also honour narrow arbitration agreements where parties have sought to ensure that only certain types of issues are arbitrable, such as by enumerating or specifying the issues that are subject to arbitration under their agreement.[10]

One area of frequent debate is whether arbitrability is to be decided by the courts or the arbitrators. U.S. federal courts have held that arbitrability is for the arbitrators to decide if the parties' arbitration agreement is broad enough to grant the arbitrators this power.[11] Typically, this question is answered by the arbitration rules referred to in the arbitration clause, because such rules are deemed to be part of the parties' arbitration agreement. For example, both the ICC and the AAA's International Dispute Resolution Procedures ("ICDR Rules") grant the arbitrators jurisdiction to decide arbitrability. The intermediate U.S. federal appellate courts (which are called the circuit courts) are split over the extent to which federal courts should scrutinize the delegation of arbitrability issues to the arbitrators. Most circuit courts have applied the Supreme Court's instruction to defer to arbitrators on questions of arbitrability when there is "clear and unmistakable evidence" that the parties delegated such questions to the arbitrators.[12] This can occur when, for example, the parties incorporate in their arbitration agreement arbitration rules that provide the arbitrators will decide jurisdiction. However, the Fifth, Sixth, and Federal Circuits have adopted a second layer of scrutiny whereby a court still conducts a "spot-check" of the arbitration agreement to determine whether the assertion of arbitrability is "wholly groundless," even if the parties expressed an intent to leave such questions to the arbitrators.[13] Most recently, the Tenth and Eleventh Circuits have expressly rejected this approach, which increases the likelihood that circuit courts which have not taken up the issue will ultimately decide against deeper judicial scrutiny and reject the "wholly groundless" exception.[14]

When it comes to class action arbitrations, the courts take another view, and will typically favour "judicial resolutions of class arbitrability".[15] The courts often must distinguish between whether a party has agreed to arbitrate anything at all (typically a question for the courts) and whether a party has agreed to arbitrate the particular dispute involved (a question for the arbitrators, assuming the parties have granted the arbitrators this jurisdiction). This distinction can be blurred when a non-party to an arbitration agreement seeks to arbitrate with a party to an arbitration agreement. The Federal Court of Appeals for the Second Circuit has held that the arbitrators can be granted jurisdiction to decide this question, because the question is whether the signatory has agreed to arbitrate with this particular non-party.[16] Although the Fifth Circuit has agreed with the Second Circuit on this issue,[17] the Federal Court of Appeals for the Ninth Circuit has declined to compel arbitration where the non-party relied solely on conclusory allegations of an agency relationship.[18]

Joinder

U.S. courts, as opposed to arbitrators, typically decide whether a non-party to an arbitration agreement may be compelled to participate in arbitration or whether a non-party to an arbitration agreement may compel someone who has signed an arbitration agreement to arbitrate with the non-party. The Supreme Court has held that "traditional principles of state law allow a contract to be enforced by or against non-parties to the contract through assumption, piercing the corporate veil, alter ego, incorporation by reference, third-party beneficiary theories, waiver and estoppel".[19] General principles of joinder and the consolidation of third parties apply. If the non-party demonstrates through its conduct that it is "assuming the obligation to arbitrate", the non-party can be compelled to arbitrate.[20] Additionally, if the non-party "knowingly seeks the benefits of the contract containing the arbitration clause", the non-party can be estopped from avoiding arbitration.[21]

The same principles apply where a non-party seeks to compel arbitration with a party to an arbitration agreement. For example, in New York, a signatory to an arbitration agreement was bound to arbitrate with a non-party because of the "close relationship between the entities".[22] Courts also recognize principles of estoppel as a basis to arbitrate with non-signatories. This is usually in instances where a non-signatory defendant seeks to compel arbitration with a signatory after the signatory sues the non-signatory in court. Even in such circumstances, however, the courts in recent decisions have applied the estoppel doctrine narrowly, and have required that the signatory's claims rely or otherwise depend on the written agreement containing the arbitration clause.[23] As noted above, the jurisdiction to decide whether a signatory must arbitrate with a non-signatory has been found to lie with the arbitrators rather than the court if the signatory agreed to arbitrate under arbitration rules that contain a broad grant of jurisdiction to the arbitrators.

Another instance in which the joinder of non-parties to an arbitration agreement arises involves corporations that have subsidiaries or affiliated entities. In these instances, courts have applied traditional concepts of corporate law and determined that where a company which has entered into an arbitration agreement exercises complete control over a subsidiary and uses that control to commit wrongdoing, the parent corporation may be compelled to arbitrate in a dispute related to its subsidiary.[24] Additionally, a corporation which is a non-signatory to an arbitration agreement may be able to compel arbitration where its subsidiary is a signatory to the agreement.[25] Similarly, a parent corporation may be required to arbitrate based on an arbitration agreement with a subsidiary.[26]

Separability

Courts in the United States have developed a body of law concerning the separability (or severability) of arbitration clauses contained in contractual agreements. Applying the doctrine of separability, U.S. courts will typically preserve the parties' agreement to arbitrate even where there is a challenge to the validity of the underlying contract containing the arbitration clause. This situation can arise, for example, where a party claims to have been fraudulently induced to sign the contract or argues for other reasons that it was null and void from inception,[27] or where a clause or obligation in that contract is unenforceable or invalid by operation of law.[28] Where, however, a second contract entirely invalidates an earlier contract that had an arbitration clause, a court has declined to enforce the superseded agreement to arbitrate.[29]

Arbitration procedure

The FAA does not contain extensive rules concerning arbitration procedure. Accordingly, in the United States, the contracting parties are free to choose the mechanisms and procedures in their arbitration agreement.[30]

Typically, contracting parties agree to arbitrate under a particular set of arbitration rules administered by a designated arbitration institution, e.g., the ICC or AAA. Each arbitration institution has its own unique set of arbitral procedures.[31]

The AAA administers arbitrations and has different sets of rules that govern various types of disputes, including its ICDR Rules for international cases.[32] Additionally, the AAA has rules governing preliminary hearings and scheduling, selection of arbitrators, evidence, designation of the locale where the arbitration will be held, filing deadlines for written submissions, and fees. The ICC also has an extensive set of procedural rules, which were most recently amended in January of 2012.[33] These rules govern the joinder of parties, interim relief, hearings, and other case management techniques, which give the arbitrator(s) broad authority over the timing and nature of submissions of written and oral evidence. Other organisations like JAMS and CPR have their own unique rules and procedures.

Significantly, some U.S. states have adopted default arbitration procedures. These procedures apply where the arbitration agreement is otherwise silent regarding procedures, rules, or administration. Arizona, California, and Texas are among the states that have adopted default arbitration rules.[34]

Arbitrators

In the U.S., the parties to an arbitration can determine the number of arbitrators that will decide their dispute and how the arbitrators are selected. Typically the parties regulate this either in their arbitration clause or by selecting a set of rules or an administrative body.[35] For example, the AAA's ICDR Rules provide for the appointment of one arbitrator where the parties have not specified the number of arbitrators in their agreement, unless the AAA administrator "determines in its discretion that three arbitrators are appropriate because of the large size, complexity or other circumstances of the case".[36] Alternatively, the parties may agree that arbitrators will be selected by an arbitration institution or court.

Where the arbitration agreement does not contain provisions governing the selection of arbitrators, FAA section 5 provides for the courts to "appoint an arbitrator or arbitrators or umpire, as the case may require, who shall act under the said agreement with the same force and effect as if he or they had been specifically named therein [...]".[37] Further, even where an arbitration agreement contains an arbitrator-selection provision, courts will step in to select an arbitrator where the arbitrator-selection provision itself is "fundamentally unfair".[38] Similarly, if an arbitrator exhibits bias during the arbitration proceedings, a party to the arbitration may challenge the award in a post-arbitration court proceeding.[39]

Interim relief

The FAA is silent on the issue of interim relief. However, parties which have agreed to an arbitration in the U.S. may seek an injunction from a U.S. state or federal court. Some U.S. states have statutes that specifically address interim relief in aid of arbitration. For example, New York state's procedural law permits parties to seek an injunction and other provisional relief in aid of an arbitration where "the award to which the applicant may be entitled may be rendered ineffectual", if interim relief is not granted.[40]

Texas and Florida have also adopted laws concerning interim relief in aid of arbitration, enabling parties to get an injunction in relation to arbitration proceedings.[41]

If the parties have opted to arbitrate under the rules of an arbitration institution, the institution's interim relief procedures govern. The ICDR Rules leave the parties free to seek interim relief from the courts in appropriate cases.[42] In the ICC, a special emergency arbitrator may be appointed to matters requiring urgent attention.[43] The arbitrator may order "any interim or conservatory measure it deems appropriate".[44] Under the ICC Rules Article 29(2), parties must abide by all orders issued by an emergency arbitrator. Similarly, the ICDR adopted emergency arbitral relief procedures pursuant to Article 6 of its International Dispute Resolution Procedures.[45] Article 6 provides for the appointment of an emergency arbitrator to rule on applications for interim relief. It should be noted that in the case of judicial injunctions, the courts have an array of mechanisms, including contempt of court, to compel enforcement. By contrast, there are questions as to how to enforce an injunction issued by an arbitrator.

Arbitration award

The FAA does not require an arbitration award to take a particular form. A number of states, including New York, Texas, and Florida, require that the award must be in writing and signed by the arbitrators.[46] Florida and Texas require a reasoned decision, unless the parties agree otherwise.[47] This is similar to the requirements imposed on arbitrators by the ICC and ICDR Rules.[48] In general, however, parties can agree to the form any award must take. In New York, for example, the courts have vacated an award where the arbitrators failed to draft the award in the agreed-upon form.[49]

The FAA and state laws do not generally impose limitations or constraints on the types of relief the arbitrators are permitted to award, provided the award does not violate public policy. The parties themselves may, however, circumscribe the relief available in their agreement to arbitrate. For example, the parties can limit the types of damages the arbitrators can award. Limitations on the ability to award punitive or consequential damages are common and generally enforceable. Equally, the parties can agree that the arbitrators cannot award legal fees to the prevailing party. If the parties do not specifically agree on the types of relief available, an arbitrator can grant any form of relief that is rationally related to the purpose of the original agreement, taking into account the applicable laws.[50] Arbitrators may also award pre- and post-award interest, in accordance with the rules of the arbitration and the applicable state or federal laws.[51]

Unlike the rule that prevails in many other jurisdictions, in the U.S. legal system, parties to a lawsuit are generally required to bear their respective legal fees regardless of who wins.[52] This contrasts with the practice in international arbitration, where arbitrators are typically free to award attorneys' fees and arbitration costs to the winning party. The FAA is silent as to fee and cost allocation, but courts interpreting the FAA have held that it does not prohibit an award of fees and costs.[53] State arbitration laws in New York, Florida, and

Texas do not explicitly preclude arbitrators from awarding fees and costs.[54] The courts in these states have been willing to allow arbitrators to award attorneys' fees and costs, particularly if the parties' agreement provides for such recovery or if the parties have otherwise demonstrated the intent to do so, such as when both parties request costs and fees in their pleadings[55] or if the arbitral rules chosen by the parties permit their recovery.[56]

Challenge of the arbitration award

Because of the strong federal policy favouring arbitration, it is difficult to succeed in challenging an arbitration award in the United States. Public policy and judicial precedent impose severe limits on the courts' ability to review arbitration awards, and parties cannot agree to expand the scope of that review.[57]

A party which seeks to challenge an international arbitration award in a U.S. court must file a proceeding within three months after the award is filed or delivered.[58] The court must have both personal jurisdiction over the parties and subject matter jurisdiction over the case. Personal jurisdiction is acquired if the responding party[59] is located in the jurisdiction where the court sits or has agreed to arbitrate in the jurisdiction.[60] If the responding party is located outside the state, the challenging party must establish personal jurisdiction through the activities and contacts of the responding party in the forum state. The guidelines for doing so will be found in the applicable state and federal laws on personal jurisdiction.[61]

Because the FAA does not confer original federal court subject matter jurisdiction for an action to vacate an award governed by the New York or Panama Conventions (as opposed to actions to enforce arbitration agreements or confirm awards), a party that seeks to vacate an award in federal court must establish an independent basis for federal court subject matter jurisdiction.[62] The two sources of federal subject matter jurisdiction are 28 U.S.C. § 1331 and 28 U.S.C. § 1332, which respectively grant federal courts the power to hear cases "arising under" federal laws or involving complete diversity among the parties.[63] Some courts have held that 9 U.S.C. § 205 provides a basis for federal jurisdiction.[64] As a practical matter, such cases are generally heard in federal court because the typical response to an application to vacate is an application by the respondent to confirm the award. The federal courts do have original jurisdiction over an application to confirm, and hence over the related application to vacate.

Section 11 of the FAA provides the grounds upon which a court can modify an arbitration award. These grounds are:

1. Where there was an evident material miscalculation of figures or an evident material mistake in the description of any person, thing, or property referred to in the award.
2. Where the arbitrators have awarded upon a matter not submitted to them, unless it is a matter not affecting the merits of the decision upon the matter submitted.
3. Where the award is imperfect in matter of form not affecting the merits of the controversy.

A party which seeks to vacate an award in its entirety faces serious obstacles. Section 10 of the FAA strictly limits the grounds upon which a court may vacate an award. Those grounds are:[65]

1. where the award was procured by corruption, fraud, or undue means;
2. where there was evident partiality or corruption in the arbitrators;
3. where the arbitrators were guilty of misconduct in refusing to postpone the hearing upon sufficient cause shown, or in refusing to hear evidence pertinent and material to

the controversy, or of any other misbehaviour by which the rights of any party have been prejudiced; or

4. where the arbitrators exceeded their powers, or so imperfectly executed them that a mutual, final, and definite award upon the subject matter submitted was not made.[66]

With respect to corruption, fraud or undue means a party must "(1) establish the existence of the alleged fraud or undue means by clear and convincing evidence, (2) demonstrate due diligence in attempting to discover the fraud before entry of the award, and (3) demonstrate that the fraud was material to the arbitrators' decision".[67] Courts have generally held that the party must provide evidence of intentional malfeasance by the other party to successfully vacate an award on the grounds of corruption, fraud, or undue means.[68]

Courts have vacated awards for partiality or corruption where a "reasonable person would have to conclude that an arbitrator was partial to one party to the arbitration".[69] There is no requirement to prove actual bias; partiality can "be inferred from objective facts inconsistent with impartiality".[70] For example, an arbitrator's failure to disclose certain relationships or interests may suggest bias, but non-material or insubstantial relationships will not satisfy the evident partiality standard.[71]

An arbitration award can be vacated for arbitrator misconduct where a court finds that an arbitrator was guilty of misconduct that compromises the "fundamental fairness" of the arbitral proceeding.[72] Examples of misconduct rising to this level include when an arbitrator has refused "to hear evidence pertinent and material to the controversy",[73] or held the proceeding during a time one party specified he was unavailable,[74] or refused to grant an adjournment to accommodate the schedule of a key witness.[75] *Vacatur* on this ground is only permitted when "the arbitrator's exclusion of evidence prejudices one of the parties".[76]

Vacatur of an award because the arbitrators exceeded their powers[77] is perhaps the most difficult of the four grounds because courts have "consistently accorded the narrowest of readings" to this provision of the FAA.[78] The U.S. Supreme Court has held that exceeding powers occurs "only when [an] arbitrator strays from interpretation and application of the agreement and effectively dispense[s] his own brand of industrial justice [...]".[79] Thus, a court will not analyse the correctness of the arbitrator's decision on a particular issue; the court is limited to determining the scope of the arbitrator's powers.[80]

In addition to the FAA's four grounds for *vacatur*, some U.S. courts have held that an arbitration award can be vacated if it is in "manifest disregard" of the law. In the 2008 case *Hall St. Associates*, however, the U.S. Supreme Court held that FAA section 10(a) provides the exclusive grounds for vacating an arbitration award.[81] After *Hall St. Associates*, there is still some debate in the federal courts as to the continuing viability of the manifest disregard doctrine. Some courts have reasoned that manifest disregard constitutes exceeding the arbitrators' authority and thus remains a viable ground to set aside an award. Regardless, successful *vacatur* on this ground is, in practice, extraordinarily difficult to obtain. An appeals court recently described manifest disregard as a "last resort" doctrine.[82] A party seeking to vacate an arbitration award for manifest disregard must show: (1) that the law that was allegedly ignored was clear; (2) that the arbitrators did in fact err in their application of the law; and (3) that the arbitrators knew of the law's existence and its applicability to the issues before them.[83] Since the birth of the manifest disregard doctrine in 1960, the authors are aware of only one international arbitration award that has been partially vacated on this ground. It should be noted that the decision vacating the award was issued by a New York state court and is currently on appeal.[84]

Overall, the courts in the United States have demonstrated hostility to challenges to awards and may even sanction the challenging party in an appropriate case.[85]

Enforcement of the arbitration award

U.S. courts play an active role in enforcing international arbitration awards. The courts regularly and consistently issue judgments confirming such awards. Following the arbitrator's issuance of an award, a party can file a motion or petition to confirm the award in federal[86] or state court.[87] The petition to confirm must include the arbitration agreement and the award. The party seeking confirmation can also support the petition with any necessary affidavits, briefs, or other documents. A party must move to confirm an award within three years from the entry of the award.[88] Once a judgment confirming the award has been issued, the winning party can enforce that judgment using the various enforcement procedures available in every state. These procedures include freezing assets of the judgment debtor, if a monetary award is involved.

To confirm an award, a court must have personal or quasi *in rem* jurisdiction over the parties.[89] In addition to jurisdiction over the parties, the court must also have subject matter jurisdiction to enforce an award. The U.S. federal courts have original subject matter jurisdiction over proceedings to confirm international arbitration awards pursuant to the FAA. This means a proceeding to confirm an international award can be brought in federal court or, if it is brought in state court, the respondent can remove the case to federal court.[90]

Provided the jurisdictional requirements are met, once a party properly submits a motion to confirm an award, a party which resists enforcement has the burden of proving it has a defence to enforcement.[91] Confirmation of an award is generally a summary process unless the opposing party resists confirmation of an award and proves that one of the seven defences provided by the FAA applies. These defences are:

1. the parties to the agreement […] were […] under some incapacity, or the agreement is not valid under the law;
2. the party against whom the award is invoked was not given proper notice of the appointment of the arbitrator or of the arbitration proceedings;
3. the award deals with a difference not contemplated by or not falling within the terms of the submission to arbitration, or it contains decisions on matters beyond the scope of the submission to arbitrate;
4. the composition of the arbitral authority or the arbitral procedure was not in accordance with the agreement of the parties;
5. the award has not yet become binding on the parties, or has been set aside or suspended by a competent authority of the country in which, or under the law of which, that award was made;
6. the subject matter of the difference is not capable of settlement by arbitration; or
7. the recognition or enforcement of the award would be contrary to the public policy of the country in which enforcement or recognition is sought.[92]

A party that opposes the confirmation of an award rendered outside the United States is restricted to the seven grounds detailed above, and its burden is a heavy one.[93] Where an award is rendered inside the U.S., the domestic provisions of the FAA apply.[94] A party that opposes the confirmation of an award rendered inside the U.S. can thus seek to vacate or modify the award under FAA sections 10 and 11, as discussed above. Recently, the Court of Appeals for the Second Circuit has gone so far as to confirm an award despite it having been set aside in the seat of arbitration, Mexico.[95] The Second Circuit's decision discussed the competing principles of comity owed to a foreign court's ruling and that of a U.S. court's discretion to confirm arbitral awards. The court ultimately ruled in favour of a U.S. court's discretion based largely on exceptional circumstances, *i.e.* Mexico's introduction of retroactive legislation that barred claimants from recovery.

Because of the public policy favouring arbitration, particularly international arbitration,[96] U.S. courts "must confirm an award unless it is vacated, modified, or corrected".[97]

Investment arbitration

As a signatory to the Convention on the Settlement of Investment Disputes Between States and Nationals of Other States, the United States is a member of the International Centre for Settlement of Investment Disputes ("ICSID").[98] The United States is also a leading signatory of the North American Free Trade Agreement ("NAFTA") and is committed to "protect[ing] cross-border investors and facilitat[ing] the settlement of investment disputes".[99] The United States enjoys observer status to the Energy Charter Conference, but is not a signatory to the Energy Charter Treaty.[100]

Finally, the United States is a party to dozens of bilateral investment treaties ("BITs") and multi-party investment treaties ("MITs"). Each BIT is structured on the basis of a standard model, which is periodically updated by the U.S. Department of State and the Office of the United States Trade Representative ("USTR"). The current version was completed in 2012.[101] A full list of each BIT currently in effect is maintained by the Department of State.[102]

Acknowledgments

The authors gratefully acknowledge the assistance of associates Sigrid Jernudd, Ashley R. Hodges and Lauren Morris with this article.

* * *

Endnotes

1. Convention on the Recognition and Enforcement of Foreign Arbitral Awards of 1958, 21 U.S.T. 2517, 330 U.N.T.S. 38, June 10, 1958.
2. Inter-American Convention on International Commercial Arbitration of 1975, OAS/SER. A20 (SEPEF), 14 I.L.M. 336 (1975), January 30, 1975.
3. *Rent-A-Ctr., W., Inc. v. Jackson*, 130 S. Ct. 2772, 2776 (2010).
4. For statutory reasons explained below, most legal actions concerning international arbitration are heard in the federal, not state, courts.
5. 9 U.S.C. § 1.
6. *Rent-A-Ctr., W., Inc. v. Jackson*, 130 S. Ct. 2772, 2776 (2010).
7. *WorldCrisa Corp. v. Armstrong*, 129 F.3d 71, 75 (2d Cir. 1997); *Genesco, Inc. v. T. Kakiuchi & Co., Ltd.*, 815 F.2d 840, 848 (2d Cir. 1987) (requiring arbitration where the arbitration clause contained "relating to" language); *Sedco v. Petroleos Mexicanos Mexican Nat'l Oil*, 767 F.2d 1140, 1145 (5th Cir.1985) (requiring arbitration where "arising out of" language was used).
8. *Collins & Aikman Prods. Co. v. Building Sys., Inc.*, 58 F.3d 16, 19 (2d Cir.1995).
9. *World Rentals and Sales, LLC v. Volvo Const. Equip. Rents, Inc.*, 517 F.3d 1240, 1246 (11th Cir. 2008).

10. *See, e.g.*, *Negrin v. Kalina*, 2010 WL 2816809, at *5-6 (S.D.N.Y. July 15, 2010) (finding that where an arbitration clause limited covered disputes to disputes over profit distributions or non-compliance with bylaws, claims for breach of fiduciary duty, unjust enrichment, tortious interference with contract, fraud, and conversion were not covered by the arbitration clause and thus could be litigated in court); *In re TFT-LCD (Flat Panel) Antitrust Litig.*, 2013 WL 3784938, at *3 (N.D. Cal. Jul. 18, 2013) (finding that where an arbitration clause limited covered disputes to disputes concerning "the terms of this Agreement," antitrust claims related to price determination were not covered by the Agreement's arbitration clause, even where the agreement stated that prices would be set forth in one party's pricing guidelines).
11. *See, e.g.*, *Contec Corp. v. Remote Solution Co.*, 398 F.3d 205, 208 (2d Cir. 2005) (holding that where parties adopt rules that empower the arbitrators to decide arbitrability, "the incorporation serves as clear and unmistakable evidence of the parties' intent to delegate such issues to an arbitrator").
12. *AT&T Techs., Inc. v. Commc'ns Workers of Am.*, 475 U.S. 643, 649, 106 S.Ct. 1415, 89 L.Ed.2d 648 (1986) ("[T]he question of arbitrability ... is undeniably an issue for judicial determination. Unless the parties clearly and unmistakably provide otherwise, the question of whether the parties agreed to arbitrate is to be decided by the court, not the arbitrator."). *See also Jones v. Waffle H., Inc.*, 866 F.3d 1257, 1268 (11th Cir. 2017) (listing circuit courts adopting the Supreme Court's holding).
13. *Douglas v. Regions Bank*, 757 F.3d 460, 462 (5th Cir. 2014); *Turi v. Main Street Adoption Services, LLP*, 633 F.3d 496, 511 (6th Cir. 2011); *Qualcomm Inc. v. Nokia Corp.*, 466 F.3d 1366, 1371 (Fed. Cir. 2006).
14. *Jones v. Waffle H., Inc.*, 866 F.3d 1257, 1269 (11th Cir. 2017) (listing circuit courts adopting the Supreme Court's holding); *Belnap v. Iasis Healthcare*, 844 F.3d 1272, 1286 (10th Cir. 2017); *see also see, e.g.*, *Simmons v. Hankey*, 2017 WL 424850, at *5 (C.D. Cal. Jan. 30, 2017) (citing Tenth Circuit in rejecting "wholly groundless" exception).
15. *See Chesapeake Appalachia, LLC v. Scout Petroleum, LLC*, 809 F.3d 746, 758 (3d Cir. 2016), *cert. denied*, 137 S. Ct. 40 (2016); *Catamaran Corp. v. Towncrest Pharmacy*, 864 F.3d 966, 973 (8th Cir. 2017). *But see Wells Fargo Advisors, LLC v. Sappington*, -- F.3d --, 2018 WL 1177230, at *5 (2d Cir. Mar. 7, 2018) (declining to require more explicit language to delegate the question of class arbitrability to an arbitrator).
16. *See Contec Corp. v. Remote Solution, Co.*, 398 F.3d 205, 211 (2d Cir. 2005) (considering the relationship between the parties and the arbitration clause at issue); *see also Ross v. Am. Express Co.*, 547 F.3d 137, 144 (2d Cir. 2008) (noting that signatories failing to avoid arbitration against a non-party generally "had some sort of *corporate* relationship to the signature party").
17. *Brittania-U Nigeria, Ltd. v. Chevron USA, Inc.*, 866 F.3d 709, 715 (5th Cir. 2017).
18. *See Mohamed v. Uber Techs., Inc.*, 848 F.3d 1201, 1214 (9th Cir. 2016).
19. *Arthur Andersen LLP v. Carlisle*, 556 U.S. 624, 631 (2009).
20. *Thomson-CSF, S.A. v. Am. Arbitration Ass'n*, 64 F.3d 773, 777 (2d Cir. 1995).
21. *Everett v. Paul Davis Restoration*, 771 F.3d 380, 383 (11th Cir. 2014) (internal quotations omitted).
22. *Thomson-CSF, S.A. v. Am. Arb. Ass'n*, 64 F.3d 773, 779 (2d Cir. 1995).
23. *Waymo LLC v. Uber Technologies, Inc.*, 870 F.3d 1342, 1347 (Fed. Cir. 2017); *White v. Sunoco, Inc.*, 870 F.3d 257 (3d Cir. 2017); *In re Henson*, 869 F.3d 1052 (9th Cir. 2017) (all rejecting application of the estoppel doctrine against a signatory where the signatory's claims against a non-signatory were insufficiently related to the agreement

containing an arbitration clause).

24. *See Variable Annuity Life Ins. Co. (VALIC) v. Dull*, 2009 WL 3064750, at *4 (S.D. Fla. Sept. 22, 2009).
25. *Barton Enterprises, Inc., v. Cardinal Health, Inc.*, 2010 WL 2132744, at *4 (E.D. Mo. May 27, 2010).
26. *Apple Inc. v. BYD Co. Ltd.*, 2016 WL 1212638, at *8 (N.D. Cal. Mar. 2, 2016).
27. *Buckeye Check Cashing, Inc. v. Cardegna*, 546 U.S. 440, 445 (2006) (holding that "an arbitration provision is severable from the remainder of the contract").
28. *Beletsis v. Credit Suisse First Boston, Corp.*, 2002 WL 2031610, at *6 (S.D.N.Y. Sept. 4, 2002).
29. *Casa del Caffe Vergnano S.P.A. v. ItalFlavors, LLC*, 816 F.3d 1208, 1214 (9th Cir. 2016).
30. Dept. of Commerce, *International Arbitration, Ad Hoc Arbitration* (Mar. 2005) (stating that parties engaging in *ad hoc* arbitration may choose the rules under which their arbitration will be carried out).
31. Except when using arbitration rules, such as the UNCITRAL Rules, that are not associated with an arbitral institution, parties should agree to use the rules of the organisation they designate to administer the case.
32. *See* American Arbitration Association, *ICDR, International Dispute Resolution Procedures* (Jun. 1, 2009) ("ICDR Rules").
33. ICC Rules of Arbitration (Jan. 1, 2012) ("ICC Rules").
34. *See, e.g.*, Ariz. Rev. Stat. §§ 12-1501-1518 (2015); Tex. Civ. Prac. & Rem §§ 171.041-171.055 (2014); Cal. Code. Civ. Proc. §§ 1280-1284.3 (2014).
35. The parties are well-advised not to stipulate a particular arbitrator in their clause. Doing so can create problems of enforceability if the arbitrator is unavailable or unwilling to hear the case when the dispute arises. The parties should also agree that the case will be decided by an uneven number of arbitrators so as to avoid deadlock.
36. *See, e.g.*, ICDR Rules Art. 5.
37. FAA §5: 9 USC § 5 (2012).
38. *Nishimura v. Gentry Homes, Ltd.*, 338 P.3d 524, 534-35 (Haw. 2014) (finding an arbitration-selection provision fundamentally unfair where one party exercised exclusive control over the pool of potential arbitrators from which the arbitrator would be selected).
39. *Id.* at 532; *Doctor's Assocs., Inc. v. Stuart*, 85 F.3d 975, 981 (2d Cir. 1996) (finding that where the defendants challenged the selected arbitrator based on bias, the defendants would not be able to present credible evidence of bias where the case had not yet gone to arbitration).
40. NY CPLR § 7502(c); *see, e.g.*, *Rockwood Pigments NA, Inc. v. Elementis Chromium LP*, 2 N.Y.S.3d 94, 96-97 (N.Y. App. Div. 2015) (finding relief appropriate).
41. Tex. Civ. Prac. & Rem. Code § 172.175 (2013); Fla. Stat. § 684.0028 (2014).
42. *See, e.g.*, ICDR Rules Art. 6 (6).
43. ICC Rules, Art. 29. ICC Rules Art. 29 and Appendix V, however, require that the parties "opt out" of their emergency procedures.
44. ICC Rules Art. 28.1.
45. ICDR Rules Art. 37.
46. NY CPLR § 7507; Fla. Stat. Ann. § 684.0042; Tex. Civ. Prac. & Rem. Code Ann. § 172.141.

47. Fla. Stat. Ann. § 684.0042; Tex. Civ. Prac. & Rem. Code Ann. § 172.141.
48. *See* ICC Rules Art. 31; *see also* ICDR Rules Art. 30.
49. *Cat Charter, LLC v. Schurtenberger*, 646 F.3d 836, 843 (11th Cir. 2011) ("An arbitrator may also exceed her authority by failing to provide an award in the form required by an arbitration agreement."); *Am. Centennial Ins. Co. v. Global Int'l Reinsurance Co., Ltd.*, 2012 WL 2821936 (S.D.N.Y. July 9, 2012) (same).
50. *See Am. Laser Vision v. The Laser Vision Inst., L.L.C.*, 487 F.3d 255, 258–59 (5th Cir. 2007), *abrogated on other grounds by Hall Street Assocs., L.L.C. v. Mattel, Inc.*, 552 U.S. 576 (2008); *Executone Info. Sys., Inc. v. Davis*, 26 F.3d 1314, 1320 (5th Cir. 1994); *Anderman/Smith Operating Co. v. Tennessee Gas Pipeline Co.*, 918 F.2d 1215, 1219 (5th Cir. 1990) ("[A]rbitrators have traditionally enjoyed broad leeway to fashion remedies.").
51. Tex. Civ. Prac. & Redm. Code § 172.144 (permitting an award of interest); AAA Commercial Rules Art. R-43(d)(i) (permitting an award of interest).
52. The parties are free to agree to a different rule in their contract. Moreover, certain statutes provide for an award of legal fees to the prevailing party for claims based on the statute.
53. *Painewebber, Inc. v. Bybyk*, 81 F.3d 1193, 1202 (2d Cir. 1996); *Turnberry Assocs. v. Serv. Station Aid, Inc.*, 651 So. 2d 1173, 1175 (Fla. 1995) ("Absent a clear directive from the legislature, we see no reason why the parties may not also voluntarily agree to allow the collateral issue of attorney's fees to be decided in the same forum as the main dispute."); *see also Stone & Webster, Inc. v. Triplefine Int'l Corp.*, 118 F. App'x 546, 550 (2d Cir. 2004); *IBK Enters., Inc. v. One Key, LLC*, 19 Misc.3d 1131(A), at *5 (Sup. Ct. N.Y. County May 13, 2008), *aff'd*, 70 A.D.3d 948 (N.Y. App. Div. 2010); *Cassedy v. Merrill Lynch, Pierce, Fenner & Smith, Inc.*, 751 So. 2d 143, 145, 149 (Fla. 1st DCA 2000) (emphasis added).
54. *Kamakazi Music Corp. v. Robbins Music Corp.*, 684 F.2d 228, 231 (2d Cir. 1982); Fla. Stat. Ann. § 682.11 ("Unless otherwise provided in the agreement or provision for arbitration, the arbitrators' and umpire's expenses and fees, together with other expenses, not including counsel fees, incurred in the conduct of the arbitration, shall be paid as provided in the award."); Tex. Civ. Prac. & Rem. Code Ann. § 172.145(b). The Fifth Circuit has held that this statute authorises an arbitrator to award costs and legal fees in an international arbitration seated in Texas. *Saipem America v. Wellington Underwriting Agencies Ltd.*, 335 F. App'x 377, 381 (5th Cir. 2009).
55. *See, e.g.*, *Synergy Gas Co. v. Sasso*, 853 F.2d 59, 64 (2d Cir. 1988).
56. *Shaw Grp., Inc. v. Triplefine Int'l Corp.*, 2003 WL 22077332, at *2 (S.D.N.Y. Sept. 8, 2003), *aff'd*, 322 F.3d 115 (2d Cir. 2003) (confirming an arbitrator's award of attorneys' fees because the contract provided for arbitration under the ICC Rules, which authorised award legal of fees to the prevailing party); *IBK Enters., Inc. v. One Key, LLC*, 19 Misc.3d 1131(A), at *5 (Sup. Ct. N.Y. County May 13, 2008) (declining to vacate an award where the parties had incorporated the American Arbitration Association's Construction Arbitration Rules ("AAA Construction Rules") into their contract, and such rules expressly empowered the arbitrator to awarded attorneys' fees); *aff'd*, 70 A.D.3d 948 (N.Y. App. Div. 2010); *Cassedy v. Merrill Lynch, Pierce, Fenner & Smith, Inc.*, 751 So. 2d 143, 145, 149 (Fla. 1st DCA 2000) (directing trial court to reinstate an arbitrator's award of attorneys' fees on the grounds that the arbitrator was authorised to award such fees by virtue of the parties' NASD submission agreement – which committed to arbitration "the present matter in controversy, as set forth in the attached statement of claim, answers *and all related counterclaims and/or third party claims which may be asserted*") (emphasis added).

57. *Hall Street Assocs., L.L.C. v. Mattel, Inc.*, 552 U.S. 576, 578 (2008); *Scandinavian Reinsurance Co. Ltd. v. Saint Paul Fire & Marine Ins. Co.*, 668 F.3d 60, 71 (2d Cir. 2012).
58. FAA § 13.
59. The moving party cannot predicate jurisdiction on its own presence in the state.
60. *See Ins. Corp. of Ireland, Ltd. v. Compagnie des Bauxites de Guinee*, 456 U.S. 694, 704 (1982) (noting that "lower federal courts have found such consent [to personal jurisdiction] implicit in agreements to arbitrate"); *Reed & Martin, Inc. v. Westinghouse Electric Corp.*, 439 F.2d 1268, 1276-77 (2d Cir.1971); *Harch Hyperbarics, Inc. v. Martinucci*, 2010 WL 3398884, at *5 (E.D. La. Aug. 20, 2010).
61. *See generally* Charles A. Wright & Arthur R. Miller, *Federal Practice and Procedure: Civil* § 1069 (3d ed. 2010).
62. *Int'l Ship. Co., S.A. v. Hydra Offshore, Inc.*, 875 F.2d 388, 391 n.5 (2d Cir. 1989) (affirming the district court's holding that a motion to vacate a Convention award did not have subject matter jurisdiction); *Yusuf Ahmed Alghanim & Sons, W.L.L. v. Toys "R" Us, Inc.*, 126 F.3d 15, 23 (2d Cir. 1997); *Banco De Santander Central Hispano, S.A. v. Consalvi Int'l Inc.*, 425 F. Supp. 2d 421, 425 n.2 (S.D.N.Y. 2006) (collecting cases showing that district courts do not have original jurisdiction over motions to vacate arbitral awards under the New York Convention); *see also Baltin v. Alaron Trading Corp.*, 128 F.3d 1466, 1469 (11th Cir. 1997) ("FAA sections 10 and 11, which allow courts to vacate, modify, or correct arbitration awards, do not confer federal subject matter jurisdiction."); *Smith v. Rush Retail Ctrs., Inc.*, 360 F.3d 504, 506 (5th Cir. 2004) (FAA section 10 does not confer federal subject matter jurisdiction); *see, e.g.*, *Ingaseosas Int'l Co. v. Aconcagua Investing Ltd.*, 2011 WL 500042, at *3-4 (S.D. Fla. Feb. 10, 2011) (dismissing motion to vacate arbitration award after finding court had not been granted subject matter jurisdiction under the New York Convention), *aff'd*, 479 F. App'x 955 (11th Cir. 2012).
63. 28 U.S.C. § 1331; 28 U.S.C. § 1332. The Supreme Court's decision in *Vaden v. Discover Bank* enables parties seeking to compel arbitration under section 4 of the FAA to "look through" the petition and establish subject matter jurisdiction if the underlying dispute implicates federal law. 556 U.S. 49 (2009). However, a circuit split has emerged as to the permissibility of a "look through" under FAA sections 9 and 10 in confirmation and vacatur proceedings. *Compare Doscher v. Sea Port Group Securities, LLC*, 832 F.3d 372, 388 (2d Cir. 2016) (applying *Vaden* to permit court to "look through" to the underlying subject matter of the dispute to establish federal question jurisdiction on a petition to vacate under section 10) *with Goldman v. Citigroup Glob. Mkts. Inc.*, 834 F.3d 242, 255 (3d Cir. 2016) (rejecting "look through" for Section 10 motions to vacate); *see also Ortiz-Espinosa v. BBVA Securities of Puerto Rico, Inc.*, 852 F.3d 36, 45 (1st Cir. 2017) (discussing circuit split and siding with Second Circuit to apply "look through" approach to Sections 9 and 10).
64. *Reid v. Doe Run Resources Corp.*, 701 F.3d 840, 843-44 (8th Cir. 2012); *Infuturia Global Ltd. v. Sequus Pharmaceuticals, Inc.*, 631 F.3d 1133, 1138 (9th Cir. 2011); *Besier v. Weyler*, 284 F.3d 665, 669 (5th Cir. 2002). *But see Albaniabeg Ambient Sh.p.k. v. Enel S.p.A.*, 169 F. Supp. 3d 523, 528 (S.D.N.Y. 2016).
65. *Hall St. Assocs., L.L.C. v. Mattel, Inc.*, 552 U.S. 576, 578 (2008).
66. FAA § 10(a)(1)-(4).
67. *Houston Gen. Ins. Co. v. Certain Underwriters at Lloyd's London*, 2003 WL 22480058, at *1 (S.D.N.Y. Oct. 31, 2003) (citation omitted).
68. *Bauer v. Carty & Co., Inc.*, 246 F. App'x 375, 378 (6th Cir. 2007); *Natl. Cas. Co. v. First State Ins. Grp.*, 430 F.3d 492, 499 (1st Cir. 2005); *PaineWebber Group,*

Inc. v. Zinsmeter Trusts P'ship, 187 F.3d 988, 991 (8th Cir. 1999) ("[O]ther circuits have uniformly construed the term undue means as requiring proof of intentional misconduct.").

69. *Morelite Const. Corp. v. New York City Dist. Council Carpenters Ben. Funds*, 748 F.2d 79, 84 (2d Cir. 1984).
70. *Scandinavian Reinsurance Co. Ltd. v. Saint Paul Fire & Marine Ins. Co.*, 668 F.3d 60, 72 (2d Cir. 2012).
71. *Id. See also Peoples Security Life Ins. Co. v. Monumental Life Ins. Co.*, 991 F.2d 141, 146 (4th Cir. 1993); *Health Services Management Corp. v. Hughes*, 975 F.2d 1253, 1264 (7th Cir. 1992).
72. *Tempo Shain Corp. v. Bertek, Inc.*, 120 F.3d 16, 20 (2d Cir. 1997); *Hoteles Condado Beach v. Union De Tronquistas Local 901*, 763 F.2d 34, 39 (1st Cir. 1985) (an arbitrator "must give each of the parties to the dispute an adequate opportunity to present its evidence and argument").
73. FAA § 10(a)(3); *Fairchild v. Alcoa, Inc.*, 510 F. Supp. 2d 280, 287 (S.D.N.Y. 2007) ("That provision applies to cases where an arbitrator, to the prejudice of one of the parties, rejects consideration of relevant evidence essential to the adjudication of a fundamental issue in dispute, and the party would otherwise be deprived of sufficient opportunity to present proof of a claim or defense.").
74. *Tube & Steel Corp. of Am. v. Chicago Carbon Steel Prods.*, 319 F. Supp. 1302, 1304 (S.D.N.Y. 1970).
75. *Tempo Shain Corp. v. Bertek, Inc.*, 120 F.3d 16, 20 (2d Cir. 1997).
76. *Rai v. Barclays Capital, Inc.*, 739 F. Supp. 2d 364, 372 (S.D.N.Y. 2010), *aff'd*, 456 F. App'x 8 (2d Cir. 2011).
77. FAA § 10(a)(4).
78. *Westerbeke Corp. v. Daihatsu Motor Co., Ltd.*, 304 F.3d 200, 220 (2d Cir. 2002) (citation omitted).
79. *Stolt–Nielsen S.A. v. AnimalFeeds Int'l Corp.*, 559 U.S. 662, 671 (2010).
80. *Westerbeke Corp. v. Daihatsu Motor Co., Ltd.*, 304 F.3d 200, 220 (2d Cir.2002) (citation omitted).
81. *Hall St. Assocs., L.L.C. v. Mattel, Inc.*, 552 U.S. 576, 578 (2008).
82. *Sotheby's Int'l Realty Inc. v. Relocation Grp. LLC*, 588 Fed. Appx. 64, 65 (2d Cir. 2015) (internal citation omitted).
83. *Id.* at 65-66.
84. *Daesang Corp. v. Nutrasweet Co.*, 55 Misc.3d 1218(A), *5 (N.Y. Sup. Ct. 2017) (ordering partial vacatur on basis of manifest disregard and remanding back to Tribunal for redetermination) (appeal pending); *See also The "Manifest Disregard of Law" Doctrine and International Arbitration in New York,* Report by the Committee on International Commercial Disputes of the New York City Bar Association (August 2012) at 6.
85. *DigiTelCom, Ltd. v. Tele2 Sverige AB*, 2012 WL 3065345, at *7-8 (S.D.N.Y. July 25, 2012) (issuing sanctions against law firm and requiring reimbursement of attorneys' fees for frivolous motion to vacate arbitral award); *Ingram v. Glast, Phillips & Murray*, 196 F. App'x 232, 233 (5th Cir. 2006) (upholding sanctions of attorneys' fees, costs, and expenses against attorneys for their bad-faith conduct, which included the pursuit of post-arbitration litigation "knowing that it was a 'complete sham'"); *B.L. Harbert Int'l, LLC v. Hercules Steel Co.*, 441 F.3d 905, 914 (11th Cir. 2006), *abrogated on other grounds by Frazier v. Citifinancial Corp., LLC*, 604 F.3d 1313 (11th Cir. 2010)

(expressing future intention to issue sanctions for frivolous petitions to vacate arbitral award).

86. FAA § 6.
87. NY CPLR § 7510.
88. FAA § 207.
89. *See Sonera Holding B.V. v. Çukurova Holdings A.Ş.*, 750 F.3d 221, 223 (2d Cir. 2014); *First Inv. Corp. of Marshall Islands v. Fujian Mawei Shipbuilding, Ltd.*, 703 F.3d 742, 750-51 (5th Cir. 2012); *Frontera Resources Azerbaijan Corp. v. State Oil Company of the Azerbaijan Republic,* 582 F.3d 393, 397 (2d Cir. 2009); *S & Davis Int'l, Inc. v. Republic of Yemen*, 218 F.3d 1292, 1303–05 (11th Cir. 2000).
90. FAA § 207 (incorporated by FAA § 302 so as to apply to Panama Convention awards).
91. *Encyclopaedia Universalis S.A. v. Encyclopaedia Britannica, Inc.*, 403 F.3d 85, 90 (2d Cir. 2005).
92. New York Convention Art. V; *Yusuf Ahmed Alghanim & Sons v. Toys "R" Us, Inc.*, 126 F.3d 15, 19 (2d Cir. 1997).
93. *Gulf Petro Trading Co., Inc. v. Nigerian Nat. Petroleum Corp.*, 512 F.3d 742, 747 (5th Cir. 2008).
94. *Commercial Risk Reinsurance Co. Ltd. v. Security Ins. Co. of Hartford*, 526 F. Supp. 2d 424, 427 (S.D.N.Y. 2007) ("However, because the arbitration occurred in the United States, the Award as to the Commercial Risk Bermuda company is also governed by the FAA provisions applicable to domestic arbitration awards.") (citing *Zeiler v. Deitsc*, 500 F.3d 157, 164 (2d Cir. 2007)).
95. *Corporación Mexicana De Mantenimiento Integral v. Pemex-Exploración Y Producción*, 832 F.3d 92 (2d Cir. 2016).
96. *Deloitte Noraudit A/S v. Deloitte Haskins & Sells*, U.S., 9 F.3d 1060, 1063 (2d Cir. 1993) (citing *Mitsubishi Motors Corp. v. Soler Chrysler-Plymouth, Inc.*, 473 U.S. 614, 629-631 (1985)); *see, e.g.*, *Crescendo Maritime Co. v. Bank of Commc'ns Co.*, 2016 WL 750351, at *10 (S.D.N.Y. Feb. 22, 2016) (confirming foreign arbitral award).
97. *Hall Street Assocs., L.L.C. v. Mattel, Inc.*, 552 U.S. 576, 577 (2008) (internal citations and quotations omitted).
98. See ICSID, Database of ICSID Member States, available at: https://icsid.worldbank.org/apps/ICSIDWEB/about/Pages/Database-of-Member-States.aspx?tab=UtoZ&rdo=BOTH.
99. See U.S. Department of State, NAFTA Investor-State Arbitrations, available at: http://www.state.gov/s/l/c3439.htm.
100. See Energy Charter Conference, Members and Observers, available at: http://www.energycharter.org/who-we-are/members-observers/.
101. Available at: http://www.state.gov/e/eb/ifd/bit/index.htm.
102. Available at: http://www.state.gov/e/eb/ifd/bit/117402.htm.

Chris Paparella
Tel: +1 212 837 6000 / Email: chris.paparella@hugheshubbard.com
Christopher Paparella is a partner at Hughes Hubbard & Reed in New York. He concentrates on international arbitration and financial services litigation. He has represented clients in international and domestic arbitrations in New York, London, Mexico City, Paris, Amsterdam and elsewhere. Mr. Paparella has developed particular familiarity and skill in the energy and process industries, and has represented participants in offshore and onshore oil and gas production facilities, as well as a variety of downstream process plants and other facilities. He has also represented financial institution clients in federal and state court litigation and arbitration involving mortgage-backed securities, securities fraud, lender liability and foreign exchange transactions. Mr. Paparella has been ranked by *Chambers USA, Chambers Global* and *The Legal 500* as one of the leading international arbitration lawyers in the United States.

Malik Havalic
Tel: +1 212 837 6000 / Email: malik.havalic@hugheshubbard.com
Malik Havalic is a senior associate in Hughes Hubbard's New York office. He has worked on complex commercial and investor-state disputes. He has been engaged in AAA/ICDR, ICSID, ICC, PCJ, JAMS, and *ad hoc* arbitrations. Mr. Havalic has experience with the oil and gas, aerospace and defense, life science, pharmaceuticals, financial services, and news media industries, among others.

Elizabeth Zhou
Tel: +1 212 837 6000 / Email: elizabeth.zhou@hugheshubbard.com
Elizabeth Zhou is an associate in Hughes Hubbard's New York office and has worked on arbitration matters under the ICSID and UNCITRAL rules.

Hughes Hubbard & Reed LLP

One Battery Park Plaza; New York, New York 10004, USA
Tel: +1 212 837 6000 / Fax: +1 212 422 4726 / URL: www.hugheshubbard.com

NOTES